DID THE MILLENNIUM DEVELOPMENT GOALS WORK?

Meeting future challenges with past lessons

Edited by Hany Besada, Leah McMillan Polonenko
and Manmohan Agarwal

First published in Great Britain in 2017 by

Policy Press
University of Bristol
1-9 Old Park Hill
Bristol
BS2 8BB
UK
t: +44 (0)117 954 5940
pp-info@bristol.ac.uk
www.policypress.co.uk

North America office:
Policy Press
c/o The University of Chicago Press
1427 East 60th Street
Chicago, IL 60637, USA
t: +1 773 702 7700
f: +1 773-702-9756
sales@press.uchicago.edu
www.press.uchicago.edu

British Library Cataloguing in Publication Data
A catalogue record for this book is available from the British Library

Library of Congress Cataloging-in-Publication Data
A catalog record for this book has been requested

ISBN 978-1-4473-3570-2 hardcover
ISBN 978-1-4473-3572-6 ePub
ISBN 978-1-4473-3573-3 Mobi
ISBN 978-1-4473-3571-9 ePdf

The rights of Hany Besada, Leah McMillan Polonenko and Manmohan Agarwal to be identified as editors of this work has been asserted by them in accordance with the Copyright, Designs and Patents Act 1988.

Cover design by Hayes Design
Front cover image: Globe of the World © studiocasper/ istockphoto
Printed and bound in Great Britain by CPI Group (UK) Ltd, Croydon, CR0 4YY
Policy Press uses environmentally responsible print partners

Contents

Contents

List of figures, tables and boxes

Figures

Tables

Boxes

List of abbreviations

AAOIFI	Accounting and Auditing Organization for Islamic Financial Institutions
ACP	Albanian Communist Party
ADER	average daily energy requirement
ALMP	active labour market programme
AMDC	African Mineral Development Centre
ATS	alternative trading system
AUM	assets under management
AWID	Association for Women's Rights in Development
BEAM	Basic Education Assistance Module
BL	Better Life
BPFA	Beijing Platform for Action
BRICS	Brazil, Russia, India, China and South Africa
BRT	Bus Rapid Transit
BWPI	Brooks World Poverty Institute
CAPMAS	Central Agency for Public Mobilization and Statistics
CCT	conditional cash transfer
CDB	China Development Bank
CEDAW	Convention on the Elimination of All Forms of Discrimination against Women
CELADA	Coalition for Equitable Land Acquisitions and Development in Africa
CEPAL	Economic Commission for Latin America and the Caribbean
CERD	Committee on the Elimination of Racial Discrimination
CGAP	Consultative Group to Assist the Poor
ChCC	Chile Crece Contigo
CH-Ethiopia	Christian Horizons-Ethiopia
CH-Global	Christian Horizons-Global
CHI	Children's Homes International
CIGI	Centre for International Governance Innovation
COPE	In Care of the People
CPPC	Centre for Public Policy Cooperation
CPRC	Chronic Poverty Research Centre
CRC	UN Convention on the Rights of the Child
CRPD	Convention on the Rights of the Persons with Disabilities

CSO	civil society organisation
CSW	UN Commission on the Status of Women
CUI	Center for Understanding Islam
DFRRI	Directorate for Food, Road and Rural Infrastructure
DIIS	Danish Institute for International Studies
DRG	debt relief gain
EAP	East Asia and Pacific
ECD	early childhood development
ECOSOC	United Nations Department for Economic and Social Affairs
ECOWAS	Economic Community of West African States
EDU	Ethiopian Democratic Union
EFA	Education for All
EFCC	Economic and Financial Crimes Commission
EME	emerging market economy
EPL	employment protection legislation
EPLF	Eritrean People's Liberation Front
EPRDF	Ethiopian People's Revolutionary Democratic Front
EPRP	Ethiopian People's Revolutionary Party
ERD	Emergency Relief Desk
ERF	Economic Research Forum
FAO	Food and Agriculture Organization
FAS	Femmes Africa Solidarité
FCUBE	free compulsory basic education
FDI	foreign direct investment
FDRE	Federal Democratic Republic of Ethiopia
FEI	food energy intake
FGN	Federal Government of Nigeria
FJP	Freedom and Justice Party
FOS	Federal Office of Statistics
FPI	foreign portfolio investment
G7	Group of Seven (Canada, France, Germany, Italy, Japan, UK, US)
g7+	not to be confused with G7
G30	Group of Thirty
GAD	Gender and Development
GCC	Gulf Cooperation Council
GDP	gross domestic product
GEMAP	Governance and Economic Management Assistance Programme

GNI	gross national income
GoE	Government of Ethiopia
GPRSP	Ghana Poverty Reduction Strategy paper
HDI	Human Development Index
HDR	Human Development Report
HIPC	heavily indebted poor country
HLP	High-Level Panel
HOI	Human Opportunity Index
HSIU	Haile Selassie I University
IBSA	India, Brazil and South Africa
IBSA-HS	IBSA Human Settlements Group
ICD	International Cooperation for Development
ICEIDA	Icelandic International Development Agency
ICPC	Independent Corrupt Practices Commission
ICPD	International Conference on Population and Development
ICT	information and communication technologies
IDG	International Development Goal
IDPS	International Dialogue on Peacebuilding and Statebuilding
IDS	Institute of Development Studies
IFAD	International Fund for Agriculture Development
IFPRI	International Food Policy Research Institute
ILO	International Labour Organization
IMF	International Monetary Fund
IPJ	Joan Kroc Institute of Peace and Justice
IPOs	initial public offerings
IPRS	Interim Poverty Reduction Strategy
IREWOC	International Research on the Exploitation of Working Children
ISE	Institute for State Effectiveness
ISRIC	World Soil Information
IT	information technology
ITUC	International Trade Union Confederation
IUCN	International Union for Conservation of Nature
IZA	Institute for the Study of Labor (Bonn)
LAC	Latin America
LDC	least developed country
LEEDS	Local Economic Empowerment and Development Strategy
LGBTI	lesbian, gay, bisexual, transgender and intersex
LULUCF	land use, land-use change and forestry

MAGEBT	Mahber Gesgesti Behere Tigray (Progressive Tigray People's Movement)
MDB	multilateral development bank
MDGs	Millennium Development Goals
M&E	monitoring and evaluation
MENA	Middle East and North Africa
MGI	McKinsey Global Institute
MIFFs	middle-income fragile and failed states
MLLT	Marxist–Leninist League of Tigray
MoE	Ministry of Education
MSMES	micro, small and medium scale enterprises
NAC	National Advisory Council
NAME	North Africa and Middle East countries
NAME 1	the oil and natural gas exporting countries: Libya, Algeria, Saudi Arabia and Kuwait
NAME 2	all the NAME countries not in NAME 1
NAPEP	National Poverty Eradication Programme
NBS	National Bureau of Statistics
NEEDS	National Economic Empowerment and Development Strategy
NEET	not in education, employment or training
NEP	New Economic Policy
NER	Net Enrolment Ratio
NGOs	non-governmental organisation
NITEL	Nigerian Telecommunication Limited
NLC	National Literacy Campaign
NPC	Nigerian National Planning Commission
NPSIA	Norman Paterson School of International Affairs
NREGA	National Rural Employment Guarantee Act
NSI	North–South Institute
ODA	overseas development assistance
ODAC	Open Democracy Advice Centre
ODI	Overseas Development Institute
OECD	Organisation for Economic Co-operation and Development
OECD DAC	OECD Development Assistance Committee
OSSAP-MDGs	Office of the Senior Special Assistant to the President on the MDGs
PDP	People's Democratic Party
PE	private equity
POA	Platform of Action
PPP	public–private partnership

PRSP	Poverty Reduction Strategy Paper
REST	Relief Association of Tigray
RTI	right to information
SA	South Asia
SAIIA	South African Institute of International Affairs
SAP	Structural Adjustment Programming
SDG	Sustainable Development Goal
SDSN	Sustainable Development Solutions Network
SEEDS	State Economic Empowerment and Development Strategy
SIS	State Information Service
SME	small and medium-sized enterprises
SNE	special needs education
SOAS	School of Oriental and African Studies
SOE	state-owned enterprises
SPARC	State Partnership for Accountability and Capability
SSA	sub-Saharan Africa
SWAP	sector wide approach programme
SWF	sovereign wealth funds
SWTS	School-to-Work Transition Surveys
TGE	Transitional Government of Ethiopia
TNO	Tigrayan National Organization
TPLF	Tigrayan People's Liberation Front
TUSA	Tigrayan University Students' Association
TVTC	Technical and Vocational Training Centre
UBE	Universal Basic Education
UDSSC	urban, decentralised, South–South cooperation
UNCSD	United Nations Conference on Sustainable Development
UNCTAD	United Nations Conference on Trade and Development
UN DESA	United Nations Department of Economic and Social Affairs
UNDP	United Nations Development Programme
UNECA	United Nations Economic Commission for Africa
UNEP	United Nations Environment Programme
UNESCAP	United Nations Economic and Social Commission for Asia and the Pacific
UNESCO	United Nations Educational, Scientific and Cultural Organization
UNFPA	United Nations Population Fund
UNHCR	United Nations High Commissioner for Refugees

UN-Habitat	United Nations Human Settlements Programme
UNICEF	United Nations International Children's Emergency Fund
UNIFEM	United Nations Development Fund for Women
UNPO	Unrepresented Nations and People Organization
UNSDSN	United Nations Sustainable Development Solutions Network
UNU-WIDER	United Nations University World Institute for Development Economics Research
UNZ	United Nations Zimbabwe
UPE	universal primary education
WBGDG	World Bank Gender and Development Group
WFP	World Food Programme
WHO	World Health Organization
WID	Women in Development

Notes on contributors

Adebusuyi Isaac Adeniran holds a PhD in Development Sociology. He is presently a Senior Lecturer/Researcher at Obafemi Awolowo University, Ile-Ife, Nigeria and a Visiting Researcher at The Harriet Tubman Institute for Research on Global Migrations of African Peoples, York University, Canada and The Nordic African Institute, Uppsala University, Canada. He is a recipient of the International Sociological Association (ISA) doctoral scholarship (2011), Africa Initiative (AI) doctoral research grant (2011) and CODESRIA's Comparative Research Network (CRN) grant (2012). He has published widely in renowned local and international outlets. Among his recent publications are 'Engendering an endogenous framework for socio-economic development in the Economic Community of West African States (ECOWAS) sub-region' (*Critical Sociology* 40, 2 (March), 2014) and *Regional Economic Communities: Exploring the Process of Socio-economic Integration in Africa* (co-edited book with Lanre O. Olutayo) (CODESRIA, 2014). He specialises in Economic Community of West African States (ECOWAS) and international development, Chinese–African relations, transnationalism, migration, integration and identity studies.

Manmohan Agarwal is the Reserve Bank of India Chair Professor at the Centre for Development Studies at Thiruvananthapuram, Kerala, India. Earlier he had retired as a Professor from Jawaharlal Nehru University, New Delhi, India where he taught for almost 30 years. Subsequently, he was a senior fellow at the Centre for International Governance Innovation (CIGI) at Waterloo Canada where he worked on issues of the world economy including the G20 and South–South cooperation. He is also Senior Fellow at Research and Information Systems for Developing Countries, New Delhi and an adjunct senior fellow with the Institute of Chinese Studies. He has also worked for a number of years at the World Bank and the International Monetary Fund. His research has been mainly in the area of international economics and development economics. More recently he has been working on the role of current account imbalances in generating the 2008 crisis, the impact of the crisis on developing countries, the G20 and macro coordination and the role of developing countries in the G20. In the area of development economics apart from South–South cooperation he is working on MDGs and also the aid architecture including Southern development cooperation.

Laura Agosta is a development professional with ten years' experience in design, management and research for governance, civil society strengthening and state modernisation. She held managerial and consulting positions for projects at multilateral agencies, public and private sector, and international civil society organisations in Latin America, South Asia, Eastern Europe, Africa. Laura Agosta specialises in access to information, media and civil society development, and institutional performance management. Laura holds a Master of Public Administration degree from Columbia University, 2012.

Saleh Ahmed is currently pursuing Graduate Interdisciplinary Doctoral Program in Arid Lands Resource Sciences (with a minor in Global Change) at the University of Arizona (USA). He is also working as a Graduate Research Associate with the Joint University of Arizona & Columbia University International Research and Application programme (irapclimate.org). Saleh is interested in climate impacts on rural livelihoods in low-income communities in the Global South. For his doctoral dissertation, Saleh is focusing on differential impacts of climate change among various population groups and their access to climate services for improved adaptation decision-making. Previously, he worked and conducted research based on both academia and international development agencies on issues related to climate-resilient local development.

Olabanji Akinola holds a PhD in Political Science and International Development Studies from the University of Guelph, Ontario, Canada. He holds a MA in International Studies (Political Science) from the Graduate Institute of International and Development Studies, Geneva, Switzerland, and a MA in Political Science (International Development Studies) from the University of Guelph. His research interests revolve around politics, development, governance, and social policy in Africa, and some of his publications have appeared as journal articles, policy briefs and book chapters.

Ragui Assaad is Professor at the Humphrey School of Public Affairs at the University of Minnesota, where he chairs the Global Policy area and co-chairs the Master of Development Practice programme. He has been a Research Fellow of the Economic Research Forum (ERF) since 1994 and currently serves as its thematic leader for Labor and Human Resource Development and as a member of its board of trustees. He is also a research fellow of the Institute for the Study of Labor (IZA) in Bonn, Germany. His current research focuses on education and labor markets in the Arab World.

Armando Barrientos is Professor of Poverty and Social Justice at the Global Development Institute at the University of Manchester in the UK. His research focuses on the linkages existing between welfare programmes and labour markets in developing countries, and on policies addressing poverty and population ageing. Recent books include *Social Protection for the Poor and Poorest* (2008, edited with D Hulme, Palgrave); *Just Give Money to the Poor* (2010, with J Hanlon and D Hulme, Kumarian Press); *Demographics, Employment and Old Age Security: Emerging Trends and Challenges in South Asia* (2010, edited with Moneer Alam, MacMillan), and *Social Assistance in Developing Countries* (2013, Cambridge University Press).

Hany Besada is Deputy Executive Director, Diamond Development Initiative (DDI) and Research Professor at the Institute of African Studies, Carleton University. He is also Non-Resident Senior Research Fellow with the UN University Institute for Natural Resources in Africa, United Nations. He is a Senior Fellow with the Centre on Governance at the University of Ottawa. Until very recently he was Regional Advisor, African Mineral Development Centre (AMDC) at the United Nations Economic Commission for Africa (UNECA). Prior to that he was Theme Leader: Governance of Natural Resources at the North–South Institute (NSI) in Ottawa, Canada and Research Specialist on the United Nations High-Level Panel Secretariat – Post 2015 Development Agenda, United Nations Development Program (UNDP) in New York. Professor Besada worked as Program Leader and Senior Researcher at the Centre for International Governance Innovation (CIGI) in Waterloo, Canada where he oversaw the Health and Social Governance Program. Before moving to Canada, he was the Principal Researcher: Business in Africa at the South African Institute of International Affairs (SAIIA) in Johannesburg, South Africa. Professor Besada has worked as Policy Advisor for the South African Ministry of Local and Provisional Government, Amnesty International, United Nations Associations, the Joan Kroc Institute of Peace and Justice (IPJ) and the Office of US Senator Dianne Feinstein. He has consulted for the United Nations University Institute for Water, Environment and Health; United Nations Office for Sustainable Development; United States International Development Agency; African Capacity Building Foundation; and the Government of Sierra Leone.

Sarah Bradshaw is Professor of Gender and Sustainable Development in the School of Law at Middlesex University, London. She has published numerous articles around gendered experiences of poverty and poverty alleviation, women's movements and gendered rights. In 2013 she published her third book *Gender, Development and Disasters* (Edward Elgar).

Kathryn Anne Brunton is an assistant researcher for the Centre on Governance whose work focuses on land governance, food security and human rights. She currently serves on the Board of Directors for the Coalition for Equitable Land Acquisitions and Development in Africa (CELADA) and has most recently worked with the Canadian federal government and UNESCO's International Institute for Educational Planning. She holds a Bachelor of Commerce from the University of British Columbia and a Masters of Arts in Globalization and International Development from the University of Ottawa.

Joshua Castellino is Professor of Law and Dean of the School of Law at Middlesex University, London, and Adjunct Professor of Law at the Irish Centre for Human Rights, Galway, Ireland. He has authored seven books in international law and human rights law, on self-determination, title to territory and indigenous people's rights, besides many articles on a range of these and other legal sub-topics.

Cristina D'Alessandro is a Senior Fellow at the Centre on Governance of the University of Ottawa (Canada) and a Research Fellow at the Research Centre PRODIG (Université Paris 1 Panthéon Sorbonnne, CNRS), Paris, France and a Professor at the Paris School of International Affairs (Sciences-Po, Paris, France). Previously she served as a Knowledge Expert at the African Capacity Building Foundation in Harare (Zimbabwe) and as a Professor at the University Lumière Lyon 2. She holds a number of board positions: Advisory Board Member for the Qatar National Priority Research Program NPRP 6-1272-5-160 'Governance of Natural Resources in Africa'; member of the International Advisory Board of the *Canadian Journal of Development Studies*; member of the editorial board of the journals *L'Espace politique* and the *African Geographical Review*; member of the Scientific Board of the journal *EspacesTemps.net*. Dr D'Alessandro holds: an Habilitation from l'Université Bordeaux Montaigne (France); a post-doctorate from the West Virginia University (West Virginia, USA); a Masters and a PhD in development geography from the University François-Rabelais de Tours (France); and a bachelor of geography from the University of L'Aquila (Italy). She is well published in French, English and Italian with a series of books and papers. As an international scholar with experience in three continents (Africa, Europe, America), she also serves as an advisor and expert for international organisations and institutions. Her teaching, research and publication activity focuses on: urban planning, management and transformation; natural resource and environmental governance; political, economic and territorial governance; institutional capacity building; and leadership.

Bineta Diop is the Founder and President of Femmes Africa Solidarité (FAS), an international NGO that seeks to foster, strengthen and promote the leadership role of women in conflict prevention, management and resolution in Africa. Mme Diop was named one of the 100 most influential people in the world by *Time Magazine* in 2011. In 2014 she was appointed by the Chairperson of the African Union Commission as Special Envoy on Women, Peace and Security.

Nancy Elbassiouny is currently a Senior Research Officer at Faculty of Islamic Studies, Hamad bin Khalifa University, in Doha Qatar. Prior to joining QFIS, Nancy worked for several years for the Saudi Arabian Cultural Mission in Washington DC and for several NGOs throughout the world, ranging from Pakistan, Egypt, Morocco and the United States. She also served as the director of the Center for Understanding Islam (CUI) located in the US. She also has experience working in the diplomatic field and has experience in conflict resolution. Nancy has done extensive public speaking and has lectured at several American universities on the topic of Islam, Muslims and specifically on the topic of gender equity. Nancy earned a Master's Degree in Diplomacy and International Relations from Seton Hall University in South Orange, New Jersey, USA and she specialised in Global Negotiation and Conflict Resolution. She also earned her Bachelor's degree in Political Science from Fairleigh Dickinson University in Madison, New Jersey, USA.

Badye Essid is a Director of quantitative analysis and model approval, within the AMF Québec's provincial regulator. Essid has over seven years' experience in model development and Financial regulation. He leads a quantitative team in charge of overseeing Banks models compliance to Basel rules. From 2010 to June 2012, he worked as an Economist at the Centre for International Governance Innovation CIGI (an independent, nonpartisan economics think tank). CIGI's interdisciplinary work includes collaboration with policy-makers and business experts around the world. He holds a PhD in Applied Financial Economics from HEC Montreal. The focus of his thesis was on the impact of the monetary policy on stock and bond markets. He has successfully published many papers in prestigious academic journals.

Jeff Grischow is Associate Professor of History at Wilfrid Laurier University in Waterloo, Ontario, Canada. Dr Grischow teaches and researches in the areas of Global History, African History and Comparative Development Studies. His monograph, *Shaping Tradition: Civil Society, Community and Development in Colonial Northern Ghana, 1899–1957* (Brill, 2006), challenges the invocation of civil society as a tool for building community in the name of development. Related publications include articles on tsetse control in Northern Ghana and social capital in Ghana's Eastern Region. More recently Dr Grischow has published in the area of African disability history, and he is contributing to the forthcoming *Oxford Handbook of Disability History*.

Craig Hanson is the Global Director of Food, Forests & Water at World Resources Institute. In this role, he guides programmatic strategy, catalyses projects and ensures a focus on results, financial development and strong staff capacity. Craig has co-developed a number of leading initiatives, including Global Forest Watch, the Global Restoration Initiative, the Forest Legality Alliance, the Food Loss and Waste Protocol, Champions 12.3, and the Better Buying Lab. He is a co-author of the current World Resources Report, *Creating a Sustainable Food Future* (World Resources Institute, 2013–17) and lead author on publications such as *The Restoration Diagnostic* (World Resources Institute, 2015) and the *Corporate Ecosystem Services Review* (World Resources Institute, 2012).

Sarah Hoesch is a law graduate candidate from Ruprecht Karls University of Heidelberg, Germany. She has conducted research in various areas connected to Human Rights, for example, the conflict between free trade and human rights, and refugee rights. In that regard, she participated in a law clinic called ProBono Heidelberg providing assistance to refugees going through the complex and frightening legal process of asylum seeking. She was previously affiliated with Open Democracy Advice Centre (ODAC), a South Africa based organisation, promoting transparency in the public sector and aiming to improve Human Rights by providing a platform for citizens and other organisations to access information. During her work there and among other projects, she organised a conference on housing needs and was the production coordinator of a documentary on Blikkisdorp, a South African temporary relocation area outside of Cape Town.

Deborah Levison is a Professor at the Humphrey School of Public Affairs at the University of Minnesota. An economist and demographer, her research focuses on labour force work and chores of children and adolescents, mainly in the Global South, as well as interactions between work and educational outcomes. She is an investigator on the IPUMS-International project, which is dedicated to collecting, preserving, and distributing population census and related data from around the world to researchers, absolutely free.

Clare Lockhart is Director of ISE (the Institute for State Effectiveness), an organisation set up to promote the accountability of the state to its citizens. Clare is the co-author of *Fixing Failed States* (with Ashraf Ghani, OUP, 2008) and a number of publications on governance, economics and citizenship. She has worked in Europe, Asia, Africa and the Americas. She is a barrister and Member of the Bar of England and Wales. She has served on a number of task forces related to conflict prevention and post-conflict development, and currently serves on the board of the Alliance for Peacebuilding, the Asia Foundation, SOLA (The School of Leadership Afghanistan) and the Women's Regional Network.

Jason McFarlane holds a BA in International Development and Globalization from the University of Ottawa and an MA in Infrastructure Protection and International Security from the Norman Paterson School of International Affairs (NPSIA) at Carleton University. Notably, he holds NPSIA's William Barton Award in Arms Control and Disarmament for a paper he wrote investigating the cases of the Democratic People's Republic of Korea and the Islamic Republic of Iran to demonstrate the shortcomings of nuclear governance arrangements. He has worked as a research assistant on a variety of research projects related to the governance of natural resources in developing countries – through the North–South Institute and the University of Ottawa's Centre on Governance. He currently is employed in the Canadian public service.

Leah McMillan Polonenko is a Project Evaluator and Researcher with over a decade of experience in international development. She holds a PhD in Global Governance, specialising in Global Justice and

Human Rights. Dr Polonenko has worked on a variety of projects related to governance, human rights, and education in Canada and throughout Sub-Saharan Africa. Currently she is Project Coordinator for the Kenyan Portfolio of Edu-Vision 2020, an NGO that supports teachers through integrative and adaptive Internet-free digital tools. She is also an experiential education expert and has led university students on internship placements around the world. Most recently, she established an internship programme that brings students on a three-month intensive placement in Malawi. Dr Polonenko held the post of Assistant Professor of International Development for 4 years before entering the world of consulting; she continues to lecture at various universities. She is a fellow at the Tschepo Institute for Contemporary African Studies. Visit www.leahpolonenko.com for more information. Dr Polonenko lives in Abu Dhabi with her husband.

Sofia Samper is currently Consultant Junior Program Officer – Health Unit at the Aga Khan Foundation, Pakistan, where she is contributing to projects on maternal and child health as well as strengthening health systems in Central Asia. Previously, Sofia held the position of Researcher/Curator of contemporary international issues at the Canadian Museum for Human Rights, where she was involved in developing inaugural museum content. She has spent a term as intern with UN Women in the occupied Palestinian territories contributing to the Millennium Development Goals culture and development programme, focusing on women's social and economic rights. Sofia's areas of interest in include health, gender, and human rights, with a focus on social, economic and cultural rights. She has contributed to several publications, and completed an MA in Development Studies at the University of Sussex Institute of Development Studies as well as a BA in History and Literature from McGill University.

Alireza Saniei-Pour is an economist, affiliated with the Canadian ministry of environment and climate change. He is a postgraduate from University of Cape Town, South Africa and an alumni of the University of Ottawa, Canada. He is active in the fields of environmental and natural resource economics, pertaining to both emerging and developed countries. Additionally, he has expertise in the field of financial and social development. He was previously affiliated with Labour Research Services, a South African based not-for-profit consultancy; conducting research on the socio-economic impact of South African multination corporations' activities in the sub-saharan region in respect to labour and environmental standards. He is also a former member of the Economic Society of South Africa.

Mohammed Sayeed Showkath is a Research Associate of Water Desalination and Reuse in the Qatar Energy and Environment Research Institute. His research interests include Water Security, Conservation and Demand Management, Environmental Policy, Climate Politics, Low Carbon Economy. He obtained his BA degree in Mechanical Engineering, Anna University, 2007. He has a special interest in interfacing science and policy, developing a macro approach of environment, energy and water in the long-term planning.

Andrew Sheng is Distinguished Fellow of Asia Global Institute, The University of Hong Kong. He is Chief Adviser to China Banking Regulatory Commission, a Board Member of Khazanah Nasional Berhad and a member of the international advisory councils of China Investment Corporation, China Development Bank, China Securities Regulatory Commission, Securities and Exchange Board of India and Bank Indonesia Institute. Previously, he was a Chairman of the Securities and Futures Commission of Hong Kong and a central banker with Hong Kong Monetary Authority and Bank Negara Malaysia. He writes regularly on international finance and monetary economics, financial regulation and global governance for Project Syndicate, AsiaNewsNet and leading economic magazines and newspapers in China and Asia. His latest book is *Shadow Banking in China: An Opportunity for Financial Reform*, with Ng Chow Soon (2016, John Wiley).

M Evren Tok has received his MA and PhD from Carleton University, Ottawa, ON. Canada. His MA was in Political Economy and PhD was a collaborative degree in Public Policy and Political Economy. Dr Tok has been acting as the Co-LPI in the NPRP grant # NPRP 6-1272-5 − 160 and PI in NPRP 6-459-5 − 050 and his grants look into various corporate social responsibility practices globally and study entrepreneurship, ethics and values nexus. More recently, Dr Tok received an award by QNRF to organise a conference, CWSP10-C-0309-16001, entitled Public Policy, Entrepreneurship and Education Nexus (February, 2017) and is expected to produce preliminary findings for this and further research grant applications in the same topic. Dr Tok's most recent publication in collaboration with Prof Leslie Pal and Lolwah Al Khater is an edited volume looking into the policy making dynamics in Qatar and this book is the first and only academic study bringing together Qatari perspectives by Qatari scholars in Qatar.

Sam Vincent is a PhD candidate in the Department of International Development at the London School of Economics, and conducts research for the Security in Transition programme at the Civil Society and Human Security research unit. He also serves as a Research Associate at the Institute for State Effectiveness. Sam holds a degree in Social and Political Sciences and a Masters Degree in International Relations, both from Cambridge University.

Acknowledgements

This book is a compilation of insightful contributions from various passionate development practitioners and academics who were asked to devote their time and energy to this edited volume over the years. The idea behind the book was borne out of the United Nations Secretary General Panel Secretariat on the Post-2015 Development Agenda and the work that went into the drafting of the High-Level Panel Report in 2013. A special word of thanks goes to Dr Homi Kharas who was at the time the Lead Author and Executive Secretary of the Secretariat supporting the High-Level Panel, which was co-chaired by President Sirleaf of Liberia, President Yudhoyono of Indonesia and Prime Minister Cameron of the UK. The editors would also like to acknowledge and thank the entire Secretariat for their incredible support.

This volume would not have been possible without the tireless efforts, sacrifice and determination of Kathryn Anne Brunton, the book's project manager. The editors would like to thank Kathryn for all her research and editing, which was critical to the success of the book. Her strategic insights, valuable ideas and incredible inquisitiveness encouraged us to delve deeper into the literature around the MDGs and the SDGs processes. The editors would also like to thank Alireza Saniei-Pour for his research assistance and editing work.

Foreword

The year 2015 was meant to be one of change in the UN system (Puplampu, Hanson, Shaw, 2017). Instead, the inauguration of a populist era symbolised by the Trump Presidency's unilateralism and Prime Minister May's Brexit ambitions served to complicate any notion of 'Sustainable Development Goals', despite the courageous initial SDG 2016. Conversely, after a decade-and-a-half of the BRIC(S), global development has achieved its own momentum, symbolised by what Jan Nederveen Pieterse characterises as the shift from a North-South global axis to a South-East one.

This timely collection, by eminent analysts on important cases, goes well beyond the SDGs to present an overview of development in an unexpectedly 'post-multilateral' world (Warner, Shaw, 2017). Happily, its mix of established and rising scholars from the global South as well as the endangered North transcends the divide between academy and policy, university and think tank. It presents a universe of very global challenges, which contemporary competitive nationalisms cannot begin to address.

Given exponential global inequalities, the legacy of the era of MDGs needs to be superseded by more than the SDGs. This is particularly apparent given the undeniable nature of climate change, thus another landmark from 2015 – the Paris Climate Accord & Climate Alliance of COP21 – will need more attention than ever; hence the growing recognition of the increasingly central water-energy-food (WEF) nexus. A range of 'development' issues, which cannot be overlooked or postponed, will also need attention. These include the pressures of migration, the impact of a burgeoning global middle class, non-communicable diseases (NCDs), the ubiquity of illegal networks characterised by transnational organised crime (TOC), the proliferation of non-traditional security (NTS) threats and the irreversibility of religious fundamentalisms, many exacerbated by global medias.

Such an extensive, unanticipated development agenda post-2015 cannot begin to be addressed by traditional analyses or policies. This timely volume points to ways to transcend the SDGs and the MDGs to advance sustainable development. I have recently been honoured to serve as the foundation director of a new PhD on Global Governance and Human Security at the University of Massachusetts Boston; this offers novel ways to respond to such global challenges. Such imperative curriculum reform and related networks of innovation will need to become widespread if SDGs are to be identified, let alone addressed, in a post–multilateral era (Shaw, 2017). This original collection advances such an imperative, yet demanding, roadmap.

Timothy M Shaw
University of Massachusetts Boston
July 2017

References

Puplampu, K, Hanson, K, Shaw, TM (eds), 2017, *From MDGs to SDGs: Rethinking African development*, Abingdon: Routledge

Shaw, TM (2017) Transnational Africa(s): Ali Mazrui & culture, diaspora & religion,' in K Njogu and S Adem (eds) *Perspectives on culture & globalisation: The intellectual legacy of Ali A Mazrui*, Nairobi: Twaweza, 37–63

Warner, J, Shaw, TM (eds) (2017) *African foreign policies and international institutions*, New York: Palgrave Macmillan

ONE

Introduction: meeting future challenges with past lessons

Leah McMillan Polonenko and Hany Besada

The discipline of history is predicated on the belief that we need to look to the past to learn for our future. The famous words of George Santayana, 'Those who cannot learn from history are condemned to repeat it', speaks truth to the idea that unless lessons are learned, they risk being repeated (Santayana, 1905). All too often, disciplines outside of history forget the importance of this concept. In the discipline and practice of international development, forward-thinking agendas have too often forgotten the importance of exploration into the past. But in looking into the past, we can learn important lessons – some never again to duplicate, and some that can be the basis of important best practices. It is imperative not only to avoid duplication of past mistakes, but also to repeat lessons and experiences from the past that can enrich future development goals. This is the uniqueness of this book. At a time when scholars and practitioners are focusing on the 'post-2015 agenda', investigating future opportunities for the development agenda following the Millennium Development Goals (MDGs), we are asking: what happened before 2015? What lessons must we learn from the design and implementation of the MDGs? What worked? What did not? We contend that by looking into the recent past, we can make a more robust post-2015 agenda that builds upon the momentum set by the MDGs, but learns from both its mistakes and its victories. The MDGs emerged from the Millennium Summit of the United Nations in 2000, following the adoption of the United Nations Millennium Declaration which sought to ensure that there were overarching goals to be achieved within a set time period. Indeed, they were 'world's time-bound and quantified targets for addressing poverty in its many dimensions – income poverty, hunger, disease, lack of adequate shelter, and exclusion – while promoting gender equality, education and environmental sustainability. They [were] also basic human rights – the rights of each person on the planet to health, education, shelter and security' (UN, 2006). The emergence of the MDGs was the first time that we saw such a large global initiative using the monitoring concept of objectives, indicators and timelines as an integral component of the strategy. Organisations and states were not simply focused on *what* needed to change, but *by when*. To this end, the MDGs exemplified the spirit of the human rights-based approach to development – linking matters of human development with the need for universal equality. Indeed, quantitative measurements like *universal* primary education (Goal 2) and *halving* the proportion of people in extreme poverty (Goal 1) showed a shift in international development toward the need for concrete examples of change to the human condition. In the MDGs, indicators, and the length of time it takes to reach them, matter. For example, although the majority of African countries boasted enrolment rates higher than 90 per cent at the primary level of schooling, organisations and governments continued to strive toward 100 per cent – the goal not being achieved if *universal* primary education was not fulfilled. There was never a time in history where organisations and states were so focused on similar development concepts and initiatives. Even though past decades of development have been analysed to take a very particular theoretical framework (that is, 1950s modernisation theory, 1980s Structural Adjustment Programming (SAPs)), the MDGs was the first truly global initiative that included all realms of development policy makers and practitioners for its implementation – civil society, the public sector, private organisations, global organisations, bilateral donors, regional bodies and governments.

Globalisation and the MDGs

The fact that the MDGs garnered such global influence should come as no surprise given the time period in which it was conceptualised. Throughout the 1990s, development theory and practice was shifting to reflect two major shifts in history. One was the new phenomenon 'globalisation' which, after the fall of the Berlin Wall and with it the end to the cold war, clearly was reshaping the way the world operated and the way in which actors interacted. The second shift was a very evident backlash to previous development initiatives. Coming out of the 1980s and the backlash the SAPs invoked, many in the donor community, including NGOs, international organisations, civil society and governments, were searching for innovative ways for improving humanitarian assistance. The World Bank responded to such backlash by constructing the Poverty Reduction Strategy Papers (PRSP) as a more country-driven effort, given the obvious need for improvements to adjustment programming. The PRSPs are 'country-driven', 'results-oriented', 'comprehensive', 'partnership-oriented', and 'based on a long-term perspective' (IMF, 2014). With a more partnership-oriented policy in mind, the World Bank and IMF were major players in the deliberation and delivering of the MDGs. The IMF explained the PRSPs as 'provid[ing] the crucial link between national public actions, donor support, and the development outcomes needed to meet the United Nations' Millennium Development Goals' (IMF, 2014).

Globalisation ushered in the concept of global norms and a global civil society, as predicted by Keane (Keane, 2003). Indeed, the world was shifting from a Westphalian system to one where non-state actors were rivalling states in importance. The MDGs were unique in that they enabled all actors to participate in their implementation. Although the NGO community had been heavily involved in development execution in the past, the fact that the vast majority of development actors, including governments, NGOs and international donors, were working towards the same goals, the MDGs, was unprecedented. To be sure, there were similar measures in place before, but the fact that the MDGs bear very specific measurements confirms that all actors were closely aligned in their deliverables. For example, MDG 1 – eradicate extreme poverty and hunger – was achieved by reaching three indicators: halve, between 1990 and 2015, the proportion of people whose income is less than $1.25 a day; achieve full and productive employment and decent work for all, including women and young people; and halve, between 1990 and 2015, the proportion of people who suffer from hunger. The third MDG – promote gender equality and empower women – was determined by its indicator: eliminate gender disparity in primary and secondary education, preferably by 2005, and in all levels of education no later than 2015.

Criticisms of the MDGs

While for the most part the MDGs have been observed to serve the development and human rights communities well, there are four main criticisms of the MDGs. Two of these criticisms focus predominantly on the indicator approach to the MDGs. First, these indicators involved quantitative measurements. For example, MDG 2 – achieve universal primary education – did not consider the quality of learning, rather the number of children in the classroom. Critics argue that this does not capture the entire picture of education (McMillan, 2011). The other criticism was that the indicators might not be capturing a holistic understanding of the goal. Goal 3, for instance, aspires for gender equality, yet girls in the classroom is the only measurement.

This fails to capture a wide range of other measurements, including women in politics, salaries by gender, and so forth.

Others argue that the MDGs do not bring appropriate recognition to local needs and contexts. The MDGs depict globalisation at its finest – yet these overtly global policies are criticised as being too broadly oriented to be appropriate for local contexts. For example, globally-mandated goals and targets do not consider previously-set national baselines, nor do they enable countries to create their own tailor-made objectives that may be better suited for the local context (AbouZahr and Boerma, 2010). For example, it may be better for country X to focus on quality of education rather than enrolment numbers. The complete lack of devotion to Goal 8 – developing a global partnership for development, has likewise been heavily criticised for rendering western nations void of responsibility to fulfill the MDGs (Fehling et al, 2013).

Also, the MDGs bring global attention to certain issues, while overlooking others. Goal 6 – combat HIV/AIDS, malaria, and other diseases – has received the most criticism in terms of Goals. There are three targets for this Goal, two of which are specific to HIV/AIDS. Target 6.C – have halted by 2015 and begun to reverse the incidence of malaria and other diseases – focuses very specifically in its wording on malaria. Indeed, the wording of this Goal, and the subsequent indicators, have created an unprecedented focus on HIV/AIDS and malaria. Of course, these diseases are real and do need attention. The critique is that research, development and care for other diseases have received limited funding because they are not specifically mentioned in the Goals. Indeed, non-communicable diseases, mental health and disabilities – all major issues in every area of the globe – are completely ignored in the MDGs (Fehling et al, 2013; Magrath, 2009; Wolbring, 2011). Goal 2 – universal primary education – ignores secondary and tertiary education, and appeals to a western, formalised system of schooling (Mekonen, 2010; Tarabini, 2010). Although the Education for All policy, coming out of the 2000 Dakar World Conference on Education, shifted the focus to include all levels of schooling, the MDGs themselves remain focused solely on the primary level.

Finally, the MDGs have been criticised for their continued obsession with full attainment of set targets. This has seen countries at times focus on populations that are near goal attainment, rather than the absolute poorest of citizens. The goals have become the outcomes, shifting focus from perhaps other areas of equal importance. Indeed, the focus on the end goal, rather than progress, warrants criticism.

Globalisation and the MDGs

While the MDGs were in many ways simplistic in their measurements, however, one could argue that it was this simplicity that enabled so many actors to work together towards these common goals. To be sure, the MDGs comprised an overarching agenda followed by the vast majority of governments, non-state actors and other practitioners working in the arena of international development, including the human rights community. Funding proposals articulated the MDGs with which they were aligned, governments use MDG statistics in their documentation, and the World Bank and UN System created development agendas in countries that focused on MDG achievement. To say that the MDGs have been central to the last 15 years of development practice is an understatement. The defining feature of post-2000 international development policy and practice is the MDGs. World Vision puts it quite aptly in stating, 'the Millennium Development Goals…form a blueprint agreed to by all the world's countries and leading development institutions' (World Vision, 2015).

The fact that the majority of donors and government recipients aligned their strategies with the MDGs follows the features of a system predicated on globalisation. The idea of all actors complying with one set of key objectives supports the global social policy theory that the world is viewing its challenges, and steps for their obliteration, as holistic (Deacon, 2007). The success of the initial writing of the MDGs and the hastiness of donor support, seems appropriate given that in the years following the MDGs, both the Paris Declaration for Aid Effectiveness and the Accra Agenda for Action were conceptualised. In drafting these documents, donors agreed to work together more closely, further aligning their development strategies and expectations. Indeed, the period in which the MDGs were written showcases the globe working together closely toward common goals. As this volume will demonstrate, working towards a global agenda for development has both positive and negative outcomes – both lessons from which the post-2015 agenda can draw.

The way forward

On 30 May 2013, the High-Level Panel of Eminent Persons on the Post-2015 Development Agenda released *A new global partnership: Eradicate poverty and transform economies through sustainable development*, a report which sets out a universal agenda to eradicate extreme poverty in all its forms by 2030 and deliver on the promise of sustainable development (UN, 2013a). This followed months of work by the High-Level Panel, which was tasked in July 2012 by the United Nations (UN) secretary general to act as counsel for the formation of a new global agenda beyond the 2015 target date for the MDGs (UN, 2013b).

The Post-2015 Development Agenda will need developed and developing countries to accept their proper share of responsibility in accordance with their resources and capabilities as driven by five fundamental shifts. These will be: 1) The eradication of extreme poverty in all forms, 2) Inequality and inclusive economy transformation, 3) Peace and good governance, 4) Forging a new global partnership, and 5) The future of sustainable development given environmental, climate change obstacles (UN 2013c). Such five fundamental principles would transform our static understanding of development challenges into a dynamic model for action. Such five fundamental principles would transform our static understanding of development challenges into a dynamic model for action. Many of the chapters within this book address these fundamental opportunities.

The post-2015 development agenda: establishing new norms

Now that the MDGs have ended, responsibility for the Post-2015 Development Agenda is being shared among a comprehensive group: national governments, local authorities, international institutions, business, civil society organisations, foundations, other philanthropists and social impact investors, scientists and academics, and, of course, citizens (UN, 2013d). In fact, shaping popular opinion in support of the MDGs and Post-2015 Development Agenda is a critical component for which every stakeholder is responsible. Over time, popular opinion and general consensus of a particular topic can and should develop into an international norm. Before discussing specific shifts and recommendations, the following section speaks to the important cooperation changes that must be implemented for the future success of a development agenda moving forward.

At the forefront, establishing the post-2015 development goals as strong international norms was an important part of achieving their outcome. Such goals needed to be measurable for society to observe how well these international norms are being met. It is for this reason that the UN High-Level Panel recommended the development of measurable indicators used to observe progress for a limited number of high-priority goals with a clear time-frame and target (UN, 2013e). It even recommended a consortium of UN agencies to consolidate multiple reports of the various goals into a central, yearly review of how the agenda is being implemented (UN, 2013f). Without UN leadership in this regard, the agenda risked losing momentum and compromising the potential for resolve. Thus, the UN took extensive action on the elaboration of an agreement to follow the quickly elapsing MDGs. A series of targets were established to follow the expiration of the MDGs, as the High-Level Panel deemed this to be of utmost importance for the credibility of the UN within the international community. The Sustainable Development Goals (SDGs) are the result of these UN discussions. They articulate seventeen key goals that the international community is to achieve by 2030. They expand the MDGs to be more inclusive of climate change and to create more critical targets (for example, 'zero poverty' rather than 'half poverty' as the MDGs proposed).

The rise of the data revolution is sure to improve the quality and quantity of development data available to the multiple stakeholders. As mentioned previously, this meant established targets and indicators needed to be measurable on a variety of scales. In order for the global framework for development to be embedded in national plans, targets needed to be locally owned. Ownership of these targets at the local level was essential in establishing targets, goals and indicators that are tangible and context specific, recognising the culture, realities and perceptions of local communities.

At the local level, two important elements to successfully implementing local ownership of targets and increasing measurability of goals can be identified. First, it will be necessary to strengthen the reliability of existing indicators. Facilitating the collection and the quality of already existing data will set a base line for measuring future data as well as establish and increase the level of trust between groups. Second, an environment that will enable and favour Community Based Organisations (CBOs) for increased collaboration and interest-based solutions will be necessary for data to be measurable.

At the national level, in order to favour collection of data and ensuring that targets and indicators are locally owned, significant investment in telecommunications infrastructure as well as verification systems will be necessary. Reaching a broader audience by increasing the dialogue on public policy as well as creating more inclusive policies and building trust between different actors will play an important role making development data more measurable. Moreover, it will be important that indicators and data not only be measurable and representative of local realities, but also integrated in the decision-making process to reinforce accountability.

On the international scale, increased collaboration will be of importance in establishing a structure and norms for tackling extreme poverty and emphasising sustainable development practices. An international agreement on a single agenda and a profound recognition of all the stakeholders has been essential in forging a global partnership for data and increasing measurability.

As 2015 has now drawn to a close, this publication seeks to add research for the important question – *what happens after 2015?* Too often the development community has not adequately looked to the past, instead focusing on the future, setting ourselves up to make the same mistakes again. We can do better. We will do better. Representing a diverse range of perspectives, positions and locations, this publication presents a number insightful dialogues from a variety of leading scholars and practitioners from various backgrounds and regional representations to better understand how the MDGs helped or hindered certain regions, countries, and areas. Indeed, by learning from the past, we can make better policy decisions for the future.

The purpose and plan for the book

Given the current environment, there is a compelling need to undergo a broad-ranging analysis and to take stock of the progress, challenges and lessons emanating from the Millennium Development Goal project. The time has come to critically examine the effectiveness and impact of the MDGs in transforming the narrative around poverty and its many dimensions through multilateral organisations, emphasising what worked and what needs to change in the context of the Post-2015 Development Agenda.

Did the MDGs Work: Meeting Future Challenges with Past Lessons addresses the changing nature of poverty and inequality and the role of state but increasingly non-state actors, particularly philanthropists, private sector agents, civil society groups in shaping the debate around accountability, progress, inclusiveness. This collection was to a certain degree inspired by a process led by the UN Secretary General's High-Level Panel Secretariat on the Post-2015 Development Agenda that helped lead to the drafting of the High-Level Panel Report and accompanying background papers in May 2013. These background papers helped inform some of the thinking around the High-Level Panel Report. Members of the High-Level Panel Secretariat as well as many leading thinkers, practitioners and development scholars from around the world, wrote a number of these background papers.

This book is divided into four sections. Part One, 'Global challenges', discusses global challenges that hindered the attainment of the MDGs. These important lessons can help in shaping the implementation of the post-2015 agenda and the global response to this strategy. In Chapter Two, 'Antipoverty transfers and zero extreme poverty targets', Armando Barrientos examines the particular plight of impoverished individuals and explores the notion of 'transfers' for improving their livelihoods. In Chapter Three, 'Fragile and conflict-affected situations and the post-2015 development agenda', Clare Lockhart and Sam Vincent reflect on MDG attainment in fragile countries, highlighting the need for recognition of the peculiarities in these areas. McMillan Polonenko's Chapter Four, 'The impact of the global financial crisis on Millennium Development Goal attainment in Africa' examines the challenges to MDG achievement accelerated by the global financial crisis, providing important lessons for future financing of global initiatives. In Chapter Five, 'Resource geographies in urban spaces: insights from developing countries in the post-2015 era', Cristina D'Alessandro investigates integrated urban resource management, flows, governance, and hubs in developing countries given the Sustainable Development Goals (SDGs) have brought an increased attention to urban natural resources and sustainable development worldwide.

Part Two, 'Minority groups', discusses the challenges faced by specific minority groups in society. Although the MDGs did well to attempt inclusion, these chapters reflect on the realities of the MDGs to specific people groups. This provides lessons for future global strategies, notably the post-2015 agenda. In Chapter Six, 'The Millennium Development Goals, disability rights and special needs education in Ethiopia: a case study of the Oromiya region', Jeff Grischow explores the plight of disabled children in Ethiopia and the importance of inclusive education in global development agenda. Ragui Assaad and Deborah Levison's Chapter Seven, 'Facing the global challenge of youth employment', examines the specific circumstance of youth as a minority, reflecting on the need to consider their plight in the global economy more overtly. Chapter Eight by Sarah Bradshaw with Joshua Castellino and Bineta Diop, 'Women's role in economic development: overcoming the constraints', identifies the challenges faced by women and explores the possibilities for improving economic development frameworks for this gender-specific group. Chapter Nine by Sarah Hoesch and Alireza Saniei-Pour, 'Marginalised minorities in conflict: women and Millennium Development Goals', reflects on the legal, political, economic and ideological problems not addressed in the MDGs that undermine women's empowerment and gender equality.

Part Three of our volume, 'Micro challenges' highlights the local development consequences in a global strategy. While the MDGs framed a global agenda for action, it was in many cases too broad to work with the complexities of local realities. The chapters in this section return the reader to specific contexts of development, overarchingly showing that the post-2015 agenda needs to recognise peculiarities of each region, country and locality. In Chapter Ten, 'Ideas from early childhood development approaches to contribute to Millennium Development Goals' achievements in Latin America', Laura Agosta explains the challenges to children in Latin America and their reactions to the MDGs. Agosta considers varying approaches to tackle these unique issues. In Chapter Eleven, Adebusuyi Adeniran explores the challenges facing Nigeria in, 'Exploring the National Economic Empowerment and Development Strategy (NEEDS) as a micro-Millennium Development Goals' framework in Nigeria'. He specifically examines the concept of 'micro' and what it means in this particular country context. Chapter Twelve, 'Developmental crises affecting the United Nations' Millennium Development Goal achievements in Bangladesh: a critical perspective' by Saleh Ahmed, examines the specific development challenges that were faced by Bangladesh during MDG implementation, and how the country attempted to overcome these specialities. Chapter Thirteen by Olabanji Akinola, 'Between progress, stasis and reversals: an analysis of the Millennium Development Goals in Nigeria', examines important lessons for MDG achievement from Nigeria. Again, this highlights the Nigerian experience of facing micro issues at the state level while implementing the globally-crafted MDGs. Manmohan Agarwal and Badye Essid's Chapter Fourteen, 'North Africa and Middle East: economic performance and social progress' analyses the economic and social outcomes of the MDGs in the MENA region, providing important lessons for both present and future development in this area.

Finally, Part Four, 'Looking forward', provides concrete strategies for improving the post-2015 agenda based on lessons learned during the time of the MDGs. It also highlights key global challenges that need to be more acutely articulated in the post-2015 policy framework. In 'United Nations Millennium Development Goals (UN MDGs) and the Arab Spring: shedding light on the preludes?', Chapter Fifteen, written by M Evren Tok, Nancy Elbassiouny, Sofia Samper and Mohammed Sayeed Showkath, examines the Arab Spring and questions how to improve the post-2015 agenda through the lens of this movement.

In Chapter Sixteen, 'Food security, inclusive growth, sustainability and the sustainable development agenda', Craig Hanson with contributions from Tim Searchinger, Richard Waite, Betsy Otto, Brian Lipinski, Kelly Levin examines each of these key concepts and asks for a more articulated role of these central challenges in the post-2015 agenda. Finally, in Chapter Seventeen, Andrew Sheng's 'Outlook for global development finance: excess or shortage?' predicts the financing of the post-2015 agenda, questioning whether we have an excess or shortage of available resources for their implementation.

References

AbouZahr, C, Boerma, T, 2010, Five years to go and counting: Progress towards the Millennium Development Goals, *Bulletin of the World Health Organization* 88, 5, 324

Deacon, B, 2007, *Global social policy and governance*, Thousand Oaks, CA: Sage Publications

Fehling, M, Nelson, BD, Venkatapuram, S, 2013, Limitations of the Millennium Development Goals: a literature review, *Global Public Health* 8, 10, 1109–22

IMF (International Monetary Fund), 2014, Factsheet: Poverty reduction strategy papers, www.imf.org/external/np/exr/facts/prsp.htm

Keane, J, 2003, *Global civil society?* Cambridge: Cambridge University Press

Langford, M, 2010, A poverty of rights: Six ways to fix the MDGs, Ids Bulletin-Institute of Development Studies 41, 1, 83–91, doi: 10.1111/j.1759 5436.2010.00108.x

McMillan, L, 2011, *The impact of global education policy: Missing out on the 'local' in Southeastern Africa*, Dissertation, Waterloo: Wilfrid Laurier University

Magrath, I. 2009, Please redress the balance of millennium development goals, *British Medical Journal* 338, b2770, doi:10.1136/bmj.b2770

Mekonen, Y, 2010, An 'After 2015' agenda for Africa: Development from a human perspective, Addis Ababa: The African Child Policy forum (ACPf)

Santayana, G, 1905, *Reason in common sense*, New York: Charles Scribner's Sons

Tarabini, A, 2010, Education and poverty in the global development agenda: Emergence, evolution and consolidation, *International Journal of Educational Development* 30, 204–212, doi:10.1016/j.ijedudev.2009.04.009

UN (United Nations), 2006, *United Nations Millennium Development Project*, www.unmillenniumproject.org/reports/fullreport.htm

UN (United Nations), 2013a, *A new global partnership: Eradicate poverty and transform economies through sustainable development*, High-Level Panel of eminent persons on the Post-2015 Development Agenda 2013, https://www.un.org/sg/sites/www.un.org.sg/files/files/HLP_P2015_Report.pdf

UN (United Nations), 2013b, *High-Level Panel of eminent persons on the Post-2015 Development Agenda 2013*, under 'Letter from the co-chairs', www.un.org/sg/management/hlppost2015.shtml

UN (United Nations), 2013c, *High-Level Panel of eminent persons on the Post-2015 Development Agenda 2013*, under 'Executive summary', www.un.org/sg/management/hlppost2015.shtml

UN (United Nations), 2013d, *High-Level Panel of eminent persons on the Post-2015 Development Agenda 2013*, under 'Five transformative shifts', see more at www.saisreview.org/2014/10/16/shared-responsibility-and-joint accountability-advancing-the-post-2015-development-agenda/#sthash.oFEExwFM.ACGJKyvs.dpuf

UN (United Nations), 2013e, *High-Level Panel of eminent persons on the Post-2015 Development Agenda 2013*, under 'The shape of the post-2015 agenda', see more at www.saisreview.org/2014/10/16/shared-responsibility-and-joint accountability-advancing-the-post-2015-development agenda/#sthash.oFEExwFM.ACGJKyvs.dpuf

UN (United Nations), 2013f, High-Level Panel of eminent persons on the Post-2015 Development Agenda 2013, under 'Implementing the post-2015 agenda', see more at www.saisreview.org/2014/10/16/shared-responsibility-and-joint accountability-advancing-the-post-2015-development agenda/#sthash.oFEExwFM.ACGJKyvs.dpuf

UN (United Nations), 2014, *We can end poverty: Millennium Development Goals and beyond 2015*, www.un.org/millenniumgoals.

Wolbring G, 2011, People with disabilities and social determinants of health discourses, *Canadian Journal of Public Health* [*Revue Canadienne De Sante Publique*] 102, 317–19

World Vision, 2015, *Millennium Development Goals*, www.worldvision.org/content.nsf/6d1210430917461d8825735a007e2f2b/g8-goals

Part One
Global challenges

TWO

Antipoverty transfers and zero extreme poverty targets

Armando Barrientos

Introduction

Perhaps the most significant change in antipoverty policy in developing countries has been the growth of large-scale programmes providing direct transfers in cash and in kind to families and individuals facing poverty and vulnerability, with the objective of facilitating their escape from poverty. The spread of antipoverty transfer programmes since the turn of the century has been astounding. Our estimates suggest that by 2010 between 750 million and 1 billion people in developing countries lived in households receiving antipoverty transfers (Barrientos et al, 2010). This chapter examines the growth of antipoverty transfer programmes in low and middle income countries, and assesses their potential contribution to reducing poverty and eradicating extreme poverty.

The rapid growth of antipoverty transfer programmes has taken many in the international development community by surprise (Hanlon et al, 2010). Practice has sprinted ahead of the conceptual frameworks needed to study and assess them. As a consequence, there is some uncertainty around the orientation and scope of antipoverty transfers, especially in international policy debates. Some brief comments on approach and terminology will be helpful.

From an institutional perspective, antipoverty transfers are one of the components of social protection. Social protection includes *social insurance* which consists of schemes financed by contributions from workers and employers aimed at addressing life course and work contingencies; *social assistance* which includes tax-financed programmes addressing poverty; and *employment programmes*, whether 'active', facilitating employment and training, or 'passive', concerned with the protection of workers' rights.

In a developing country context, stakeholders sometimes conflate humanitarian and emergency assistance with social or public assistance.

The notion of safety nets, as employed by Bretton Woods institutions for example, makes no distinction between short-term emergency assistance and social or public assistance (Weigand et al, 2008). Humanitarian and emergency assistance has an important role to play in addressing the effects of disasters and conflict. But the recent expansion of social protection in the South is focused on establishing and developing longer-term institutions needed to eradicate poverty and deprivation.

The growth of social protection programmes has been swift in middle income countries, which is of great importance given the fact that a majority of poor people in the world lives in middle income countries. Progress has been slower in low income countries. To an extent, this is explained by acute constraints in financial resources and implementation capacity in these countries. Political factors are significant too. Limited democratisation and the absence of political competition can make elites unresponsive to the needs of their citizens. In aid-dependent countries, elites are able to 'export' poverty reduction to donors, which becomes a task for aid agencies. Successful antipoverty programmes require good technical analysis but also political support.

Democratisation and enhanced fiscal space in low and middle income countries, especially with recent economic growth in Africa, could become the drivers for the expansion of social protection. The role of democratisation in the development of social policy and related institutions is well documented (see Haggard and Kaufman, 2008; Huber and Stephens, 2012). Enhanced fiscal space in developing countries is explained by improvements in revenue collection capacity, especially corporate taxation linked to natural resources. Revenues from natural resource exploitation and from the spread of VAT have facilitated the financial conditions for the growth of antipoverty transfer programmes. In some cases, antipoverty transfer programmes have been established and justified as a means to share the gains from natural resource exploitation (Moss, 2011). The sources of financing also generate some challenges for low and middle country governments, especially relating to the sustainability of antipoverty transfer programmes and to the legitimacy of the emerging institutions.

Generalising from the experience of developing countries which have introduced and supported large-scale antipoverty transfer programmes, several factors can be found to generate political consensus behind the expansion of social assistance. They include: (i) strengthened social contracts – embedding shared solidarity values – as in South Africa or Brazil; (ii) the role of fiscal pacts around natural resource revenues and consumption taxes, which is the primary revenue source for governments in the South as in Bolivia or Argentina; (iii) awareness by policy makers and the mass public regarding the effectiveness of antipoverty transfers, especially through the findings from independent impact evaluations such as those in Mexico; (iv) broadly shared concerns regarding the adverse effects from structural transformation, as in India, Mexico or China. Political support for the expansion of social protection is often found to be associated with a renewed commitment to the gradual realisation of rights and social citizenship, and the pursuit of equity.

The diversity in social assistance programmes in the South and the specificity of the political processes and outcomes supporting them confirms the primacy of national policy and political processes in the emergence of social protection in each country.[1]

Current trends suggest that global poverty is no longer foremost an issue of poor countries but rather of people in poverty in low and middle income countries. The majority of people in extreme poverty today live in middle income countries (Sumner, 2010). However, as the global projections show, over time the global population in extreme poverty is likely to concentrate in sub-Saharan Africa. Sustaining recent trends in global poverty reduction into the future will require sustaining growth *and* ensuring that the distribution of the gains from growth favours disadvantaged groups. Driving global extreme poverty to zero, will involve paying special attention to policies facilitating the social and economic inclusion of groups in extreme poverty. It will require addressing the barriers preventing these groups from making full use of economic opportunities. This chapter assess the potential contribution of antipoverty transfer programmes to achieving these goals.

The rest of the chapter is divided into three sections. The second section makes the link between antipoverty transfers, inclusion of disadvantaged groups, and human development. This is central to permanent exit from poverty. The third section reviews the outcomes of existing antipoverty transfer programmes. The fourth section draws out the main policy lessons. A final section discusses the role of international aid and concludes.

Antipoverty transfers, inclusion, and human development

In developed countries, welfare states have been successful in integrating the provision of basic services, such as health and education, with social protection institutions. For the majority of countries in the North, social insurance and basic service provision are the largest components of welfare states and social assistance can be a relatively small and residual component (Adema, 2006).[2]

In developing countries, social insurance schemes and employment programmes are restricted in coverage (ILO, 2010). Even in Latin America and the Caribbean, where social insurance schemes can be traced back to the early twentieth century, coverage is restricted to workers in formal employment – around one half of the labour force. In Asia and Africa, a minority of workers are in formal employment and therefore social insurance is residual. The recent expansion of social protection in the South has concentrated on antipoverty transfers, the social assistance component (Fiszbein et al, 2014).

The political and economic conditions within which antipoverty transfers have emerged in developing countries in the last decade have encouraged a focus on self-standing flagship programmes, as opposed to integrated institutions. The reasons behind a programme approach are complex and often country specific. They include fiscal constraints, political opposition, knowledge gaps, the time window of international aid, and the hubris of silver bullets in international development policy. As a result, the focus of international discussions is largely on flagship programmes such as Mexico's *Progresa/Oportunidades*, Brazil's *Bolsa Escola/Familia*, South Africa's *Child Support Grant*, Ethiopia's *Productive Safety Net Programme*, India's *National Rural Employment Guarantee Scheme* to name a few.

In the pioneer countries, a shift in policy and practice from flagship programmes to stable and, more or less permanent, institutions is underway. In many Latin American countries, for example, ministries of social development combine and coordinate public policy on poverty and vulnerability (Cecchini and Martínez, 2011). Further institutionalisation of social assistance is a welcomed development and will determine the future shape of social protection in the South. It makes sense to approach antipoverty transfer programmes as embryonic social protection institutions, as opposed to short-term development projects.

In just a decade, social protection has become widely accepted in developing countries as an essential component of an inclusive development strategy. Growth delivers economic opportunity and basic services support productive capacity, but without social assistance they are unlikely to reach the poorest.

It is important to avoid a minimalist and residual poverty orientation in international development policy. The US$1.25 a day poverty line focuses primarily on physical subsistence in low income countries.[3]

Wellbeing thresholds help identify the worst off but are not endowed with unique standing. Extreme poverty can be represented, by the US$1.25 a day, but it is not reducible to it. It is also important to focus on poverty measures that take account of differences in wellbeing among disadvantaged groups.

People are not poor, they are in poverty. A significant proportion of those in poverty are in persistent poverty – around 40 per cent as a rough rule of thumb (CPRC, 2005). The proportion of people experiencing poverty within a year is significantly larger than those observed to be in poverty at a point in time. An implication is that the share of the population which is the focus of effective antipoverty policies is bound to be much larger than the poverty headcount rate as measured at one point in time.[4]

In high income countries, tax-transfer systems shape the distribution of income. Through progressive taxation and transfers, welfare states reduce the inequality in income generated by market processes to the benefit of the less advantaged.[5] In addition, universal provision of basic services such as education, health and housing aim to reduce disparities in access to these services. In low and middle income countries, on the other hand, tax and transfers systems can be neutral or even regressive in their effects (for Latin America see Lustig et al, 2013), and disparities in access to basic services, and in their quality, ensure the persistence in disparities in opportunity to the detriment of disadvantaged groups (see De Barros et al, 2009).

In the context of sustaining poverty reduction trends into the future, reducing disadvantage is hugely significant, perhaps more significant than focusing on changes in population-wide inequality measures, important as they are. Ensuring that growth is pro-poor, that tax-transfer systems are progressive, and that disadvantage groups have fair access to basic services are all essential components of a strategy to poverty eradication.

When the focus is on the population in extreme poverty, acute deficits in access to basic services create the conditions for persistent poverty and deprivation, lead to poverty traps, and disconnectedness and disengagement with growth and political processes. Recent studies have developed a Human Opportunity Index to draw attention to the distribution of access to basic services across population types sharing similar circumstances, in order to throw light on the role of disparities in opportunity (Brunori et al, 2013; Molinas Vega, 2012). Box 2.1 provides a description of the Human Opportunity Index approach and some estimates for education across countries in Africa and Latin America. The inclusion of groups in extreme poverty in redistribution of income and consumption and improved access to basic services will help maximise the poverty reduction effect of economic growth.

Sustainable exit from poverty requires the economic, social and political inclusion of people in poverty and extreme poverty. In policy terms, this implies the inclusion of disadvantaged groups in employment, fiscal redistribution, and preferential access to basic services. Antipoverty transfer programmes have demonstrated considerable effectiveness in reaching disadvantaged groups and facilitating inclusion.

Box 2.1: Human Opportunity Index

The Human Opportunity Index (HOI) measures coverage of basic services adjusted for disparities across population types with similar circumstances (typically groups partitioned according to education of parents, rural–urban location, and so on) (Molinas Vega et al, 2012; Barros et al, 2009). The index is intended to provide a measure of disparities in opportunity. The share of the population with access to services is adjusted by an index of dissimilarity which computes normalised and population weighted deviation from the mean across the population types. The index takes account of the fact that both the average coverage and its distribution are important in assessing opportunity. The Index varies between 0 and 100.

Brunori et al (2013) collected computed HOIs for countries in Latin America and Africa. Figure 2.1 shows the values for the HOI in education. Disparities in access to education explain, for example, why Brazil ranks lower than Paraguay, or Jamaica ranks higher than Chile. Brunori et al (2013) note that the HOI is closely correlated with gross national income (GNI) per capita and even more strongly correlated with the Human Development Index (HDI) for these countries.

Design and implementation

Antipoverty transfer programmes show considerable diversity in low and middle income countries. The design, scope and objectives of antipoverty transfer programmes reflect, to a large extent, local learning about what works in poverty reduction, economic development, institutional capacities and political processes and priorities. The expansion of antipoverty transfers in developing countries is largely driven by national politics and policy making (see among others,

Figure 2.1: Human Opportunity Index for education

Simple average of HOI for school attendance of 10-14 year olds and HOI for children finishing primary school on time

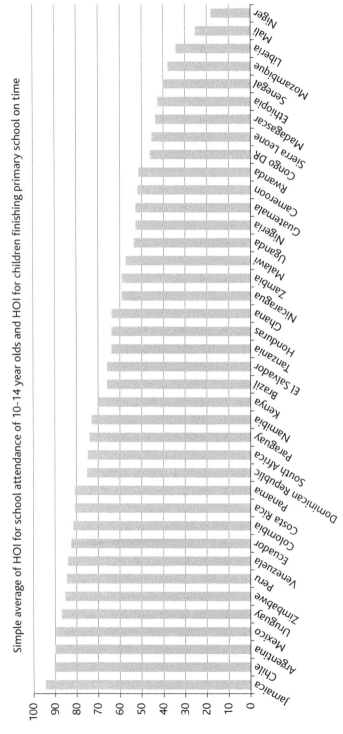

Data source: Brunori et al (2013)

Barrientos, 2013; Borges Sugiyam, 2011; Fiszbein and Schady, 2009; Grosh et al, 2008; Holzmann et al, 2009b).

Mexico's 1997 *Progresa/Oportunidades* developed out of a concern with the impact of agricultural liberalisation on intergenerational poverty persistence in rural areas. Its design, including transfers to families with children conditional on school attendance and primary healthcare utilisation, was a reaction to ineffective food subsidies (Levy, 2006). India's 2005 *National Rural Employment Guarantee Scheme*, providing 100 days employment on demand to unemployed heads of household, is a response to persistent poverty in rural areas designed around existing state level employment guarantees (Khera, 2011). South Africa's 1998 *Child Support Grant* extended social assistance to children in poor households, and was influenced by the perceived effectiveness of old age transfers (Lund, 2008). China's 1999 *Minimum Living Standards Scheme* was initially set up to provide assistance to older and disabled urban residents in poverty, but was swiftly extended to support growing numbers of unemployed workers from recently liberalised state owned enterprises (Chen and Barrientos, 2006).

The wider diversity in programme design calls for taxonomy (Barrientos, 2013).[6] Antipoverty transfer programmes include *pure transfers* for households or individuals in poverty, such as social pensions or child and family allowances; *transfers combined with asset accumulation*, like human development conditional cash transfers (CCTs), employment guarantees and asset protection transfers; and *integrated antipoverty transfers*, such as BRAC's *Challenging the Frontiers of Poverty Reduction: Targeting the Ultra-Poor* or Chile's *Ingreso Etico Familiar.*[7] Integrated anti-poverty transfer programmes combine several interventions and pay explicit attention to social and economic inclusion. These three ideal types are grounded on distinct perspectives on poverty: poverty as income or consumption deficits; poverty as consumption and productive asset deficits; and poverty as multidimensional and the outcome of social and economic exclusion. Figure 2.2 shows the rise on the number of programme starts globally. It shows growth in all three categories, but principally in programmes combining transfers with asset accumulation (human development CCTs and employment guarantees) and pure income or categorical transfers.

Scale and scope

New forms of social assistance in developing countries without exception target poor and poorest households. In most cases, this

Antipoverty transfers and zero extreme poverty targets

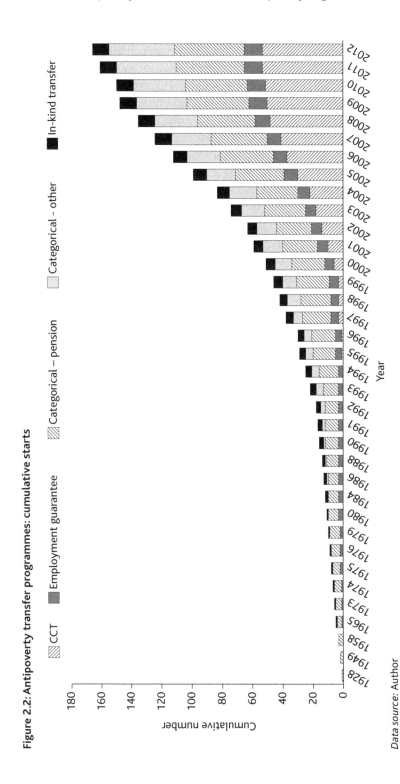

Figure 2.2: Antipoverty transfer programmes: cumulative starts

Data source: Author

involves a mix of selection strategies. *Progresa/Oportunidades* used geographic targeting to identify communities in rural Mexico with the highest levels of marginalisation, then a proxy means test to rank households on several deficit indicators, and finally community validation (Skoufias, 2005). This was closely replicated in Honduras' *PRAF II* programme, except that poverty incidence in marginalised communities was so high that it made more sense to select out the non-poor than to select in the poor, an affluence test. In Brazil, social assistance transfers such as *Bolsa Familia* and the *Benefício de Prestação Continuada*, the selection mix involves a comparison of per capita household income with the national poverty line, plus in the latter case a minimum age requirement of 65 years, the latter being an example of categorical selection. India's *National Rural Employment Guarantee* relies on self-selection by participants with earnings below the market rate or unemployed. Individuals who are unemployed and have a work card can request that work is assigned to them by the local authority. Assessments of selection effectiveness suggest that they broadly are effective in reaching their target population. Selection effectiveness improves with the size of the programme. Broad targeting works better than narrow targeting. And a combination of selection strategies works better than reliance on a single selection method (Coady, 2004). Increasingly, selection techniques rank households from poorest to moderately poor, with eligibility thresholds dependent on financial and policy parameters.

New forms of social assistance incorporate and operationalise a multidimensional understanding of poverty, and particularly extreme poverty. New forms of social assistance are increasingly designed as integrated interventions based around income transfers. *Progresa*, for example, combined income transfers with interventions on nutrition, schooling and health and, when scaled up to *Oportunidades*, it incorporated additional services included training, job search, youth inclusion, saving instruments and micro-enterprise development. This widening of the scope of the programmes follows on from the recognition that overcoming poverty requires integrated support on a number of dimensions, especially in a context in which basic services and insurance programmes exclude large numbers of poor and poorest households. Chile's *Chile Solidario* (*Ingreso Etico Familiar* since 2012) had the widest scope, focusing on seven dimensions of welfare and on 53 minimum thresholds (Barrientos, 2010). Income transfers are unlikely to be sufficient on their own to pull poor households out of poverty, even assuming their level could be raised significantly.

Conditions

Some social assistance programmes attach conditions to the continuation of transfer payments. Public works and employment guarantee programmes, Ethiopia's *Productive Safety Net Programme* for example, attach work conditions to participation in the programme, in part as a means to ensure self-selection among potential participants and also in order to improve community infrastructure. Latin American human development conditional transfer programmes aim to reduce the intergenerational persistence of poverty by supporting investment in health and schooling. Mexico's *Progresa/Oportunidades*, for example, requires that school-age children are enrolled and attend for at least 85 per cent of the time; that all household members visit primary healthcare centres, and that mothers attend nutrition training sessions. Failure to comply with these conditions can result in the suspension of transfers. More broadly, these programmes have adopted co-responsibilities which spell out the responsibilities and standards of performance of the programme agency on the one hand and the conditions applied on participant households on the other. These are formally established at the time households join the programme.

Issues relating to these conditions have been discussed extensively in the literature. First, there is a concern that conditions might in fact penalise households least able to comply with the conditions. Second, there is a concern that the effectiveness of conditions has not been fully established, with the implication that conditions might in fact be unnecessary or even counterproductive. Furthermore, even where conditions can be shown to be effective, it would be necessary to establish that the gains from conditions outstrip the additional administration and implementation costs. Third, there is a concern that compliance of the conditions falls primarily on mothers, with no form of compensation available. Fourth, and in view of the experience of developed countries with welfare reform, there is a concern that conditions might not be required for programme effectiveness but instead to secure political support from taxpayers.

In Latin America, the first concern, that conditions penalise those least able to comply with the conditions, has led some programmes to use non-compliance of conditions as a means to trigger further support for the participant households. This is the case in Brazil's *Bolsa Familia*. More broadly a distinction has been drawn between programmes with 'soft' and 'hard' conditions, which depends on the way in which programmes deal with non-compliance.

There is very little hard evidence on the *separate* effectiveness of conditions, but there is evidence that programmes with conditions achieve their objectives (Fiszbein and Schady, 2009).[8] Consequently, researchers have looked into the details of programme implementation to identify whether 'natural experiments' could throw light on this issue. The extension of the *Bono de Desarrollo Humano* in Ecuador, a human development transfer programme, is interesting because the programme was advertised, to beneficiary households and the general public, as including conditions on schooling and health but in practice the government was not in a position to implement the conditions. A study compared information on schooling responses from households who understood that there was a relevant condition in the programme and households reporting having no knowledge of conditions. It finds that the belief that conditions were part of the programme did influence positively their schooling decisions (Schady and Araujo, 2008). The initial introduction of Mexico's *Progresa/Oportunidades* seems to provide another 'natural experiment'. Compliance with schooling conditions is monitored through a form which beneficiaries take to school to be filled in, but for administrative reasons a group of beneficiaries were not issued with the forms. A study compares the schooling responses of beneficiary households without forms or knowledge of conditions, and other groups of beneficiary households. It finds that knowledge of conditions seems to have influenced schooling decisions at the secondary school level (de Brauw and Hoddinott, 2011). The studies suggest conditions may matter, but it is hard to generalise from these highly specific settings. At any rate, the effects are likely to be small, for example in Mexico school enrolment rates in primary education were above 90 per cent before the introduction of *Progresa/Oportunidades* so that the effect of conditions could at best bind on the 10 per cent of children not enrolled at school. A point often missed in policy discussions is that it is the marginal, not the average, effect of conditions that indicates their effectiveness.

Some researchers have pointed out that in many human development programmes mothers are the direct recipient of the transfer and the person primarily responsible for compliance with the conditions (Molyneux, 2006). In general, concerns over the extent of compliance costs must be taken on board by programme designers. It is also the case that conditions might enforce some degree of coordination between programme managers and other Ministries, health and education for example, which could strengthen implementation effectiveness (Cecchini and Madariaga, 2011).

Time windows and exit strategies

Another important feature of new social assistance relates to the time window for interventions. This raises some interesting issues at a more fundamental level. Limited time windows reflect a concern to avoid dependency. It is a feature of new social assistance programmes that they identify some 'graduation' process for beneficiary households. Most programmes include a regular review of eligibility at regular intervals, for example, every three years. Eligibility conditions also provide 'graduation' milestones such as children growing beyond school age or the death of pension beneficiaries.

Most of the programmes above aim to protect the poor from the harm done by persistent poverty; but they also aim to strengthen their productive capacity through facilitating investment in schooling, health and nutrition; and to strengthen their agency. The optimal time windows might well be different for each of these different functions. The protection role would be best performed by permanent institutions that come into play whenever households fall into poverty. The promotion role would be most effectively performed at specific points, for example, school-age children, expectant mothers. It is hard to envisage a time window for empowerment, though in practice it would be most effectively done with a mix of time-specific interventions and rights. Time windows reflect in part that one or other of these functions is dominant. Time windows are also one of the design features aimed at building credibility around social assistance programmes.

In developing countries, the design of time windows and 'graduation' mechanisms should take into account the nature, quality and coordination of the institutions charged with delivering public programmes. Graduation from a programme in a context in which supplementary programmes ensure 'propulsion' away from poverty for beneficiary 'graduates' will be very different to graduation in a context where the end of income transfer dumps beneficiary households straight back into precarious livelihoods. In the latter, graduation is problematic. Without appropriate consideration being given to follow-up interventions helping graduating households avoid falling back into poverty, the success of social assistance programmes will be limited.

Outcomes

The gains from improving our knowledge of what works in reducing and preventing poverty are large, and a strong focus on evaluation and research is a feature of recent social assistance in developing countries. The strength of evaluation processes associated with Mexico's *Progresa/Oportunidades*, for example, has become a 'gold standard' for antipoverty programmes elsewhere. In the case of Mexico, the attention paid to evaluation was required for the political sustainability of the programme. Securing reliable information on programme outcomes also contributes to improvements in programme design and implementation.

What is the impact of social assistance programmes? The quality of impact evaluation is not uniform across programmes. In many cases complete and comprehensive impact evaluations are not yet available. However, the findings to date suggest that programmes have had some success in achieving their objectives. Human development income transfer programmes in Latin America, for example, have had a measure of success in facilitating improvements in school enrolment, health prevention and nutrition levels (Fiszbein and Schady, 2009).

There is vast literature assessing the impact of social assistance in developing countries, here the focus will be on impacts on poverty, consumption and productive capacity.

Surprisingly, there is limited evidence on the impact of social assistance on poverty rates. Transfer levels are, as a rule, a fraction of the poverty line and therefore not expected to pull programme participants above the poverty line by themselves. Poverty rates are influenced by a range of factors in addition to social assistance. The common practice is to compare poverty rates among participant households including transfers and excluding transfers, but this approach ignores potential behavioural responses to the transfer among these households. Behavioural responses could reduce the impact of transfers, if they crowd out private transfers for example; or they can also enhance their impact if they lead to a reallocation of household productive resources (Barrientos, 2012).

Difference in difference impact evaluations can provide fairly precise estimates of the poverty reduction effectiveness of antipoverty transfers. Estimates of the poverty reduction impact of Mexico's *Progresa/Oportunidades* provide a very accurate impact assessment. This is because the programme was implemented among households in one set of locations in 1997. In another set of locations, households did not join the programme until two years later, in 1999. This enabled researchers to compare poverty among 'treatment' and 'control' groups of households. Using the fiftieth percentile of household consumption as a poverty line, Skoufias (2005) finds that *Progresa/Oportunidades* had a limited impact on the headcount poverty rate, with 11.7 per cent fewer individuals in poverty among the 'treatment' group; but a stronger impact on the poverty gap. Among households joining the programme in 1997, the poverty gap was more than one third smaller compared to households in the 'control' group. It also reduced the poverty gap squared by just over 45 per cent, which suggests that *Progresa/Oportunidades* had a stronger impact among the poorest beneficiaries.

The most direct impact of transfers is on household consumption. With few exceptions, impact evaluation studies observe a rise in household consumption following the receipt of transfers by households in poverty. Figure 2.3 draws from impact evaluation difference-in-difference estimates of change in household consumption in human development conditional transfer programmes. For most programmes, the observed rise in consumption is in line with the size of the transfer relative to household consumption. This could be interpreted to mean that the bulk of the transfer was consumed by beneficiary households. It is interesting to speculate on households' use of the difference between the additional consumption and the level of the transfer. Several explanations are relevant, including private

Figure 2.3: Difference in difference estimates of household consumption gains (change in total household consumption of treatment group minus change in consumption of control group)

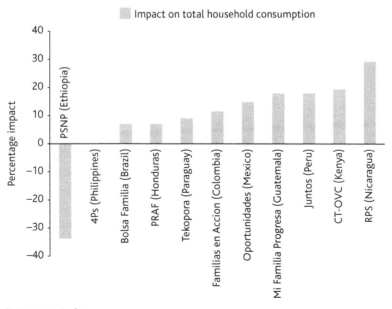

Data source: Author

transfers to relatives, neighbours or faith and community organisations, payments to officials, saving and investment, to name a few.

The impact of transfers on consumption reported in Figure 2.3 reflects fairly accurately the findings from studies of other programmes and regions.[9]

Studies focusing on the distribution of consumption find a more than proportionate growth in food consumption (Rubalcava et al, 2002).[10] Households receiving support from *Bono de Desarrollo Humano* in Ecuador had a 25 per cent increase in food expenditure, which was linked to improvements in nutritional status (Ponce and Bedi, 2010). In Colombia, a substantial increase in intake of protein-rich foods and vegetables was reported as a result of participation in *Familias en Acción* (Attanasio et al, 2004).

In addition to improving household consumption in the short run, most transfer programmes aim to reduce household poverty in the longer run. At its simplest, this is based on the proposition that improvements in current consumption have medium-run effects on human development, with implications for productivity. Addressing child nutrition, for example, is likely to improve child welfare, but also to facilitate learning. Increasingly, transfer programmes combine a concern with strengthening current consumption with facilitating investment in households' productive capacity. Asset-based programmes focus directly on enhancing the protection and accumulation of physical or financial assets. These in turn are expected to improve household productive capacity in the medium and longer run. The same applies to human development-focused programmes, which aim to improve the health status of household members and especially the schooling of children. To the extent that improvements in households' productive capacity are essential to sustainable and permanent exit from poverty, antipoverty transfer programmes can have an impact on the probability of poverty in the future.

There is strong evidence on the capacity of social assistance programmes to generate improvements in the schooling and health status of households in extreme poverty. The evidence base is stronger for programmes with explicit human development objectives, human development CCT programmes in particular (Fiszbein and Schady, 2009), but improvements in health status and schooling can be observed for categorical transfer programmes (Case and Wilson, 2000; Duflo, 2000; Barrientos, 2008). Social assistance transfer programmes have the capacity to lock in investment in the productive capacity of children in particular, with the potential to generate longer term escape from poverty. Figure 2.4 shows the impact of participation in selected

Figure 2.4: Impact on child labour and the value of transfers

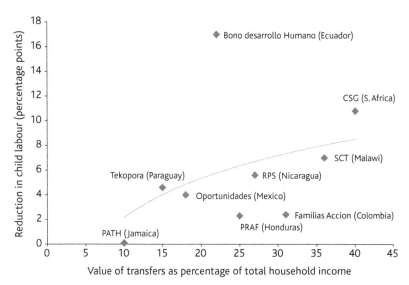

Data source: Author

social assistance programmes on child labour. The figure indicates an association between the size of the impact on child labour and the size of the transfer. As expected, larger transfers, as a proportion of household income/consumption, have stronger effects on child labour.

The capacity of social transfers to help lift credit constraints is likely to vary across programmes, target groups and environments. These effects are stronger among rural households with deficits in complementary 'productive' assets (for example, inputs, labour), and where credit constraints are directly targeted, as just discussed for the case of Bangladesh. Such integrated approaches to poverty alleviation are expected to maximise the benefits of social transfers through asset protection and enhancing households' self-employment generation capacity.

Arroyo Ortiz et al (2008) analyse the impacts of *Progresa/Oportunidades* on household consumption and investment. They find that households with long-term exposure to treatment enjoyed higher food consumption than those with a shorter period of treatment (see Figure 2.5). Furthermore, they find that households who joined the programme in 1998 showed gains in land, livestock and productive assets of around 4 per cent compared to households joining in 2003.

There is still more work to be done to identify with greater precision the impact of social assistance programmes in other developing countries. The knowledge gaps are largest in low income countries.

Figure 2.5: Longer-term impact on food consumption

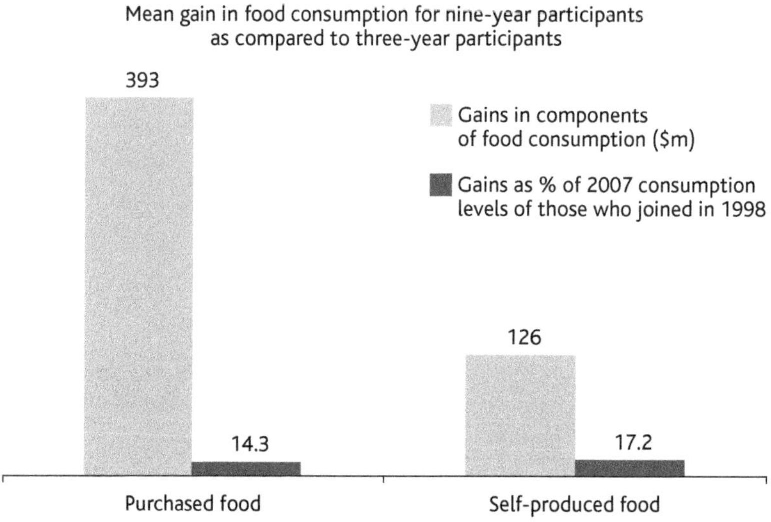

Mean gain in food consumption for nine-year participants
as compared to three-year participants

393

Gains in components
of food consumption ($m)

Gains as % of 2007 consumption
levels of those who joined in 1998

126

14.3   17.2

Purchased food   Self-produced food

Data source: Arroyo Ortiz et al (2008)

Research on the medium and longer term impact of antipoverty programmes is at a very early stage. With these provisos firmly in mind, the findings to date suggest that well-designed and well-implemented social assistance programmes can make an important contribution to the reduction of global poverty.

The role of technology

Social assistance transfer programmes increasingly integrate new technology in their implementation. In particular, biometric recognition, integrated multi-access information systems, electronic payment systems and mobile communications offer significant opportunities to improve service delivery and cost effectiveness. There are some concerns too, especially with regards to the extent to which technology reinforces exclusion and with defining the appropriate trade-offs with programme intermediation.

The use of technology in programme implementation creates opportunities from improvements in delivery. Biometric recognition is used in South Africa to deliver transfers in locations where financial outlets are not available. This ensures the full spatial coverage of the population in a secure way, but with significant costs (Gelb and Decker, 2011). Integrated multi-access information systems are in place in many Latin American countries, enabling fast and decentralised updating of information and monitoring of programme implementation. In addition to improvements in the operation of programmes, shared platforms across public agencies and services make available significant economies of scale. Effective information systems also enable a more dynamic response by public agencies to changes in beneficiary circumstances (Bassett et al, 2010). Potential exclusion of vulnerable groups lacking web access or competencies is an issue. Electronic payments systems and telephony have proved extremely effective in sub-Saharan Africa, especially in reducing the scope for corruption compared to alternative cascading financial transfers (Smith et al, 2010). There are also indications that improved privacy may lead to changes in the way that transfers are deployed by recipients.

A primary concern with the use of technology in the delivery of social assistance relates to potential trade-offs with intermediation. Social assistance programmes have a need for effective intermediation between programme agencies and participants. The design of integrated antipoverty programmes, for example, takes explicit account of intermediation as a tool to address social exclusion. A mapping of public programmes addressing poverty in Chile in the early 2000s found 143 programmes, and led programme designers to conclude that improving poverty reduction necessitated overcoming the barriers preventing groups in poverty from accessing these programmes. *Chile Solidario,* introduced in 2004, paid special attention to intermediation, with social workers tasked to bridge the gap between participant households and the range of public interventions. Large-scale human development transfer programmes in Latin America, like *Bolsa Familia* and *Progresa/Oportunidades* have incorporated intermediation to support households with additional needs. The important lesson flowing from these programmes is that technology will be most effective if it is deployed in support of intermediation functions, rather than as a substitute for it. Technology can secure significant improvements in the productivity of programme agencies and social workers.

Main lessons from the growth of antipoverty transfers

What are the main lessons learned so far from the experience of social assistance programmes in developing countries? The variety of social assistance programmes in developing countries and their rapid growth suggest caution in generalising from current experience. With this proviso, the main lessons can be summarised follows in the next paragraph.

Direct transfers to households in poverty are feasible for low and middle income countries and provide an effective policy instrument to address poverty, and extreme poverty. Large-scale antipoverty transfer programmes have developed faster in middle income countries. In the pioneer countries, antipoverty transfer programmes are coalescing into integrated social assistance showing growing institutionalisation. In low income countries, progress has been slower with a proliferation of pilot programmes. In aid-dependent countries, pilot transfer programmes often reflect limited national government ownership and concerns with sustainability. Progress in low income countries to date demonstrates that antipoverty transfers can be successfully adapted and implemented (Garcia and Moore, 2012). Policy reversals can be explained largely by shifts in political support (Maluccio, 2009; Moore, 2008). Social assistance has proved effective in reducing poverty but, as transfer levels are a fraction of the poverty line, the impact is stronger on the poverty gaps of groups in poverty and especially on the poverty gaps of the poorest.

Combining income transfers with human development objectives magnifies the impact of transfers in cash on households' productive capacity. The diversity of antipoverty programme design has encouraged considerable research and policy discussion on specific design features, especially on the role of cash and in-kind transfers, the effectiveness of conditions, and entry and exit strategies. Perhaps the main lesson from this discussion is that the diversity in programme objectives suggests a 'one size fits all' strategy would be inappropriate.[11] However, programmes with explicit human development objectives are likely to be more effective in addressing poverty persistence.

Well-designed and well-implemented social assistance can maximise the poverty reduction effects of relatively small budgetary allocations. Budgetary allocations to support large-scale antipoverty programmes are relatively small. An assessment of expenditure on antipoverty transfer programmes in high, low and middle income countries finds that for the majority of countries, social assistance absorbs between 0.5 and 1.5 per cent of gross domestic product. Many low income countries spend less than 0.5 per cent. A small number of high and low income countries spend more than 2 per cent of GDP mainly due to the primary role of social assistance in their social protection systems (Australia, New Zealand, South Africa for example); or the substantial flows of international aid supporting poverty reduction in low income countries (Ethiopia, Malawi, for example) (Barrientos, 2013).

Well designed and implemented antipoverty transfer programmes can lead to improvements in service provision for groups in poverty. This applies especially to human development conditional transfer programmes which explicitly link the transfer to the utilisation of basic services. They can generate synergies and horizontal integration in service provision; partly as a consequence of increased demand but also from the coordinated activities of public agencies. In large federal countries, antipoverty programmes have been shown to generate improvements in vertical integration of the government poverty reduction effort. In low income countries, on the other hand, where the implementation of antipoverty programmes is managed by parallel agencies (for profits and not for profits) improvements in service provision are harder to achieve.

Antipoverty transfers have (largely benign) political feedback effects. Research on this issue is yet to produce full and comprehensive results, but the weight of findings to date suggests that antipoverty transfer programmes can facilitate improved inclusion of disadvantaged groups. For the programmes studied, largely in Latin America and south Asia, participation in antipoverty transfer programmes is associated with higher voter registration and participation. In some countries concerns over whether programmes encourage clientelistic practices have been raised, but the design of the programmes, with rules-based participation and well publicised entitlements and regulations, reduces the incidence of these practices. Large-scale social assistance programmes can help extend citizenship to previously excluded groups, and support pro-poor policies.

What works? The following five factors have a strong influence on the effectiveness of antipoverty transfer programmes.

Human development focus

Effective social assistance programmes support sustainable and permanent exit from poverty. Inescapably, this requires paying close attention to strengthening the productive capacity of households in poverty and extreme poverty. Their most important asset is their capacity to work and therefore programmes that improve their productivity in the medium and longer term have a greater chance of success. This is the most innovative dimension of CCTs in Latin America, to link transfers to improvements in nutrition, schooling and health of participant households. By contrast, employment guarantee programmes such as India's National Rural Employment Guarantee or Ethiopia's Productive Safety Net Programme (PSNP) lack explicit human development objectives. It is feasible for programmes lacking explicit human development objectives to have human development impacts, but these can be maximised if programmes pay explicit attention to them.

Political embeddedness

To be sustainable, antipoverty transfer programmes require political support, which is more likely to be forthcoming in conditions where programmes enjoy a broader consensus. Arguably, the most important restriction on the scale up of antipoverty transfers in sub-Saharan Africa is associated with their weak political embeddedness, itself associated with aid dependence. Political support is a condition for effective antipoverty transfer programmes, but also an outcome of effective programmes.

Capacity

The effectiveness of antipoverty programmes depends to an important extent on the capacity of public agencies to formulate, design and implement programmes. Among the key requirements are: information systems, financial distribution systems, and monitoring and evaluation processes. Birth registration, for example, is essential to the implementation of child focused antipoverty transfer programmes. To an extent, capacity is directly associated with the level of economic development, hence the faster progress in middle income countries. There is a role for international aid to support the development of these competences in low income countries and to facilitate South–South technology and knowledge diffusion.

Scale and selection

Effectiveness in the selection of beneficiaries is important to the success of antipoverty programmes. Broad targeting works better than narrow targeting. While narrow targeting is technically feasible in most circumstances, errors in selection can undermine support for the programme. Low income countries generally show lower income or consumption inequality, and therefore selection is likely to be more costly and prone to errors. In middle income countries, selection issues are associated with fluid labour markets and precarious employment. Population groups just above the poverty line, but vulnerable to fall below it, can be large. The population estimated to be in poverty or extreme poverty at one point in time is a fraction of the population which experiences poverty over a longer period. Broad targeting works better in reaching these groups.

Exit strategies

Antipoverty programmes normally have well specified entry criteria, but lack clarity on exit strategies for participants. In some programme exit strategies are demographic (children leaving schools, pensioners dying) and in most programmes there are regular reviews of entry conditions. Research and policy on exit conditions and on pathways out of participation in antipoverty programmes is urgent. Linking antipoverty programmes with active labour market policies emerging in middle income countries provides a fertile ground for innovation. Links to productive employment as the key exit strategy are important. Ideally, antipoverty programmes can be scaled down as poverty reduces, and again exit criteria are essential to programme effectiveness.

Conclusions: antipoverty transfer programmes and zero goals

Antipoverty transfer programmes have supported progress towards achieving several of the Millennium Development Goals (MDGs), and they will continue to have a central role in the Post–2015 Development Agenda. Projections of poverty trends into the medium term, reviewed in the first section of this chapter, underline the need to sustain poverty reduction trends in middle income countries and the need to address the potential concentration of extreme poverty in low income countries and sub-Saharan Africa in particular. The coverage of antipoverty transfer programmes is expected to continue to grow in the next decades, particularly in low income countries. The consolidation and institutionalisation of social assistance in middle income countries is also likely to continue.

Antipoverty transfer programmes will prove essential in eradicating extreme poverty, and in maintaining this achievement.

A key contribution of antipoverty transfers will be to raise human development among groups in poverty and extreme poverty. Human development oriented transfers are explicitly aimed at facilitating household investment in the productive capacity of children in extreme poverty, in addition to improvements in household consumption and nutrition. Categorical transfer programmes, like social pensions, also show an impact on schooling and health status of children and other household members. This applies to middle income countries as well as to low income countries.

Integrated antipoverty transfer programmes are grounded on a multidimensional understanding of poverty and target intervention along several dimensions of wellbeing. *Challenging the Frontiers of Poverty Reduction: Targeting the Ultra-Poor* by Bangladesh Rural Action Committee (BRAC) combines interventions on health, nutrition, consumption, asset management and asset accumulation. Chile's *Chile Solidario* targeted interventions on seven dimensions: health, education, income, employment, registration, housing and intra-household relations.

Human development objectives also have implications for reducing disparities in access to services and opportunity in developing countries. Through extending access to, and utilisation of, basic services among disadvantaged groups, antipoverty transfer programmes can enhance opportunity. In the context of the HDI discussed in the first section, antipoverty transfer programmes can improve both the average coverage of basic services as well as reduce disparities in access. Improvements in the productive capacity of groups in poverty, and especially children, will contribute to drive down poverty and to sustain poverty reduction achievements.

Economic growth, progressive tax-transfer systems, and the provision of quality basic services are principal factors responsible for poverty reduction, but without antipoverty transfer programmes these factors may not extend to the poorest. In combination with growth and basic services, well-designed and well-implemented antipoverty transfer programmes have proved effective in improving outcomes for groups in extreme poverty and persistent poverty.

The evolution of antipoverty transfer programmes, particularly in middle income countries, shows a trend towards combining an expanded set of interventions and adding direct intermediation for the poorest households (Cecchini and Madariaga, 2011). This has implications for the emergence of stable institutions charged with poverty reduction, and for horizontal and vertical coordination of public agencies in addressing poverty and, by extension, progress towards zero goals. The emergence of ministries of social development tasked with addressing poverty in several middle income countries in Latin America and elsewhere, provides an institutional basis capable of driving down extreme poverty to zero and maintaining it there.

What is the role of international aid?

Antipoverty transfers have spread in most middle income countries, but progress in low income countries has been slower. While it is important to sustain poverty reduction trends in middle income countries, international aid has an important role in supporting poverty reduction in low income countries. In the latter, the slow progress in the emergence of large-scale antipoverty transfer programmes is due in large part to significant deficits in financial resources as well as design and implementation capacity. Political resistance is also an important factor in aid dependent countries.

There is an important supportive role for the Post-2015 Development Agenda to play here, but it is essential to identify appropriate contexts and potential boundaries.

International assistance has an important role in supporting low income countries seeking to introduce or scale up antipoverty transfer, especially through (i) facilitating the development of design and implementation capacity; by (ii) assisting low income countries overcome the set-up costs of these programmes, which can be large; and (iii) through helping countries to strengthen domestic revenue collection.

International organisations have longstanding experience and expertise in strengthening the capacity of public agencies in developing countries but, to date, strengthening capacity in antipoverty transfer programme design and delivery has not been a priority. Support for capacity development has focused on specialist areas, like monitoring and evaluation, of particular interest to donors. There are few examples of capacity building in social assistance delivery, especially training of welfare officers. Capacity building assistance schemes, such as SWAPs (sector wide approach programmes), have proved effective in improving service delivery in health and education. Similar schemes are also likely to prove effective in enhancing capacity in social assistance. Support for South–South cooperation in capacity building would be particularly effective in this context, and there are several successful examples available.[12]

The initial set-up costs associated with effective antipoverty transfer programmes can be significant. Antipoverty transfer programmes need comprehensive registration, financial infrastructure capable of supporting movements of cash safely and free from corruption, information systems supporting programme delivery as well as monitoring and evaluation. These require a very significant investment in capacity. International assistance can be very effective in financing this investment and also has a role in facilitating South–South policy and technology diffusion and research. Knowledge of what works in poverty eradication is a global public good.

The role of international aid in financing antipoverty transfers in developing countries beyond the short term is, however, limited. An important criticism of the way in which the MDGs have worked out as a policy influencing agenda, suggests that over time they became entrapped within the global UN agencies and their stakeholders. Antipoverty transfer programmes are best formulated and designed at the national level, through national political and policy processes. The most important, and successful, breakthroughs in antipoverty transfer programmes and poverty reduction in general, have been in countries that have introduced and scaled them up as part of national strategies – countries such as China, India and Brazil. There are important lessons for the role of international organisations in supporting antipoverty transfer programmes here. In the medium term antipoverty transfers must be financed domestically, this is essential to their sustainability and legitimacy. In the short term, supporting low and middle income countries to enhance their revenue collection capacity is crucial to ensuring the medium-term sustainability of these programmes. Sustained economic growth in low and middle income countries should provide the fiscal space needed to finance antipoverty transfer programmes in the medium term, especially in sub-Saharan Africa.

Acknowledgements

I am grateful to Alma Kudebayeva and Juan Miguel Villa for excellent research assistance.

Notes

[1]　There is a role for policy diffusion, but it is more likely to be domestic as opposed to cross-national. See Borges Sugiyama (2008; 2011).

[2]　The 2008 financial crisis in high income countries has renewed interest to the role of social assistance, see for example, Bitler and Hoynes, 2010.

[3]　Poverty reduction targets are best grounded on a prioritarian perspective on the value of assisting the worst off. A priority view attaches greater, social or ethical, value to improving the lives of disadvantaged groups. This is different from a sufficiency view which argues that there is a, social or ethical, value in people having enough wellbeing, for example. A sufficiency view attaches no value to improvements in the lives of those above this threshold. More importantly, it attaches no value to improvements in the lives of disadvantaged groups which fail to ensure they cross the minimum threshold or poverty line. A single focus on the poverty headcount rate is consistent with the sufficiency view, and shares its limitations.

[4]　For an application to Brazil's Bolsa Família, see Soares, 2010.

[5] The redistributive effects of welfare states can be overstated by studies based on cross-section data, as redistribution estimates, commonly the difference between the Gini of market income and the Gini of post transfer income, fail to distinguish between life course redistribution from redistribution from the rich to the poor. For a longitudinal study of redistribution in Sweden see Bengsston et al, 2012.

[6] For a functional classification of antipoverty transfers see Grosh et al, 2008.

[7] Better known internationally as *Chile Solidario*, the programme it replaced in 2012.

[8] Short-term experiments with conditions suggest that they can be effective in this context (see Baird et al, 2011).

[9] Several studies find a positive correlation between transfers and a rise in household consumption (see Arroyo Ortiz et al, 2008; Case and Deaton, 2003; Hoddinott and Skoufias, 2004; Maluccio, 2005; Skoufias et al, 2008; Case and Deaton, 1998). Studies for the extension of *Oportunidades* in urban areas, however, did not find a positive impact on consumption (see Angelucci and Attanasio, 2009).

[10] Fiszbein and Schady (2009) suggest that transfers might have the potential to shift the Engel curve among beneficiaries.

[11] A more promising avenue for assessing programmes' design features is to focus on the consistency existing between programme objectives and design features, as opposed to a one-sided focus on the latter.

[12] See the South–South cooperation programme on social protection supported by the UNDP and the Government of Brazil at http://south-south.ipc-undp.org/.

References

Adema, W, 2006, Social assistance policy development and the provision of a decent level of income in selected OECD countries, *OECD Social, Employment and Migration Working Paper* 38, August, Paris: OECD Department for Employment, Labour and Social Affairs

Angelucci, M, Attanasio, O, 2009, Oportunidades: Program effect on consumption, low participation, and methodological issues, *Economic Development and Cultural Change* 57, 479–506

Arroyo Ortiz, JP, Ordaz Diaz, JL, Li Ng, JJ, Zaragoza López, ML, 2008, *A diez años de intervención en zonals rurales*, Report, December, Evaluación Externa Del Programa Oportunidades 2008, México City: SEDESOL

Attanasio, O, Meghir, C, Vera-Hernandez, M, 2004, *Baseline report on the evaluation of* Familias en Acción (IFS Reports), London: Institute for Fiscal Studies

Baird, S, Mcintosh, C, Özler, B, 2011, Cash or condition? Evidence from a cash experiment, *Quarterly Journal of Economics* 126, 1709–53

Barrientos, A, 2008, Cash transfers for older people reduce poverty and inequality, in AJ Bebbington, AA Dani, A De Haan, M Walton (eds) *Institutional pathways to equity: Addressing inequality traps*, Washington, DC: World Bank

Barrientos, A, 2010, Protecting capabilities, eradicating extreme poverty: Chile Solidario and the future of social protection, *Journal of Human Development and Capabilities* 11, 579–97

Barrientos, A, 2012, Social transfers and growth. What do we know? What do we need to find out?, *World Development* 40, 11–20

Barrientos, A, 2013, *Social assistance in developing countries*, Cambridge: Cambridge University Press

Barrientos, A, Niño-Zarazúa, M, Maitrot, M, 2010, *Social assistance in developing countries Database Version 5*, Report, Manchester: Brooks World Poverty Institute, http://papers.ssrn.com/sol3/papers.cfm?abstract_id=1672090

Bassett, L, Mariano Blanco, G, Silva Villalobos, V, 2010, Management information systems for CCTS and social protection systems in Latin America: A tool for improved program management and evidence-based decision-making, Note, October, Washington, DC: World Bank

Bengsston, N, Holmlund, B, Walderstrom, D, 2012, Lifetime versus annual tax progressivity: Sweden 1968–2009, *IZA Discussion Paper* 6641, June, Bonn: IZA

Bitler, M, Hoynes, H, 2010, The state of the safety net in the post-welfare reform era, *NBER Working Paper* 16504, Cambridge, MA: NBER

Borges Sugiyama, N, 2008, Ideology and networks: The politics of social policy diffussion in Brazil, *Latin American Research Review* 43, 82–108

Borges Sugiyama, N, 2011, The difussion of conditional cash transfer programs in the Americas, *Global Social Policy* 11, 250–78

Brunori, P, Ferreira, FHG, Peragine, V, 2013, Inequality of opportunity, income inequality and economic mobility, *Policy Research Working Paper* 6304, January, Washington, DC: World Bank

Case, A, Deaton, A, 1998, Large scale transfers to the elderly in South Africa, *Economic Journal* 108, 1330–61

Case, A, Deaton, A, 2003, Consumption, health, gender and poverty, *Working Paper* 3020, April, Washington, DC: World Bank

Case, A, Wilson, F, 2000, Health and well-being in South Africa: Evidence from the Langeberg Survey, *Mimeo*, Princeton, NJ: Princeton University

Cecchini, S, Madariaga, A, 2011, *La trayectoria de los programas de transferencia con corresponsabilidad (PCT) en América Latina y el Caribe*, Report, April, Santiago: CEPAL

Cecchini, S, Martínez, R, 2011, *Protección social inclusiva en América Latina: Una mirada integral, un enfoque de derechos,* Santiago: CEPAL

Chen, J, Barrientos, A, 2006, Extending social assistance in China: Lessons from the Minimum Living Standards Scheme, *Chronic Poverty Research Centre (CPRC) Working Paper* 67, Manchester: CPRC

Coady, D, Grosh, M, Hoddinott, J, 2004, *Targeting of transfers in developing countries: Review of lessons and experience*, Washington, DC: World Bank

CPRC (Chronic Poverty Research Centre), 2005, *The Chronic Poverty Report 2004–05,* Manchester: CPRC

De Barros, RP, Ferreira, FHG, Molinas Vega, JR, Saavedra-Chanduvi, J, 2009, *Measuring equality of opportunities in Latin America and the Caribbean*, Washington, DC: World Bank

De Brauw, A, Hoddinott, J, 2011, Must conditional cash transfers programs be conditioned to be effective? The impact of conditioning transfers on school enrollment In Mexico, *Journal of Development Economics* 96, 359–70

Duflo, E, 2000, Grandmothers and granddaughters: Old age pension and intra-household allocation in South Africa, *Working Paper* 8061, December, Cambridge, MA: National Bureau Of Economic Research

Fiszbein, A, Schady, N, 2009, *Conditional cash transfers: Reducing present and future poverty*, Washington, DC: World Bank

Fiszbein, A, Kanbur, R, Yemstov, R, 2014, Social protection and poverty reduction: Global patterns and some targets, *World Development* 61, 167–77

Garcia, M, Moore, CMT, 2012, *The cash dividend: The rise of cash transfer programs in sub-Saharan Africa*, Washington, DC: World Bank

Gelb, A, Decker, C, 2011, Cash at your fingertips: Biometric Technology for transfers in resource-rich countries, *Working Paper* 253, June, Washington, DC: Center for Global Development

Grosh, M, Del Ninno, C, Tesliuc, E, Ouerghi, A, 2008, *For protection and promotion: The design and implementation of effective safety nets,* Washington, DC: World Bank

Haggard, S, Kaufman, RR, 2008, *Development, democracy and welfare states: Latin America, Asia and Eastern Europe*, Princeton, NJ: Princeton University Press

Hanlon, J, Barrientos, A, Hulme, D, 2010, *Just give money to the poor: The development revolution from the Global South*, West Hartford, CT: Kumarian Press

Hoddinott, J, Skoufias, E, 2004, The impact of PROGRESA on food consumption, *Economic Development and Cultural Change* 53, 37–61

Holzmann, R, Robalino, D, Takayama, N, 2009a, *Closing the coverage gap: The role of social pensions and other retirement income transfers*, Washington, DC: World Bank

Holzmann, R, Robalino, DA, Takayama, N, 2009b, *The role of social pensions and other retirement income transfers: Closing the coverage gap*, Washington, DC: World Bank

Huber, E, Stephens, JD, 2012, *Democracy and the left in Latin America: Social policy and inequality in Latin America*, Chicago, IL: University Of Chicago Press

ILO (International Labour Organization), 2010, *World Social Security Survey 2010/11*, Geneva: ILO

Khera, R (ed), 2011, *The battle for employment guarantee*, Delhi: Oxford University Press

Levy, S, 2006, *Progress against poverty: Sustaining Mexico's Progresa-Oportunidades Program*, Washington, DC: Brookings Institution Press

Lund, F, 2008, *Changing social policy: The child support grant in South Africa*, Cape Town: HSRC Press

Lustig, N, Pessino, C, Scott, J, 2013, The impact of taxes and social spending on inequality and poverty in Argentina, Bolivia, Brazil, Mexico, Peru and Uruguay, *CEQ Working Paper* 13, April, Tulane: Tulane University

Maluccio, JA, 2005, Coping with the 'Coffee Crisis' in Central America: The role of the Nicaraguan Red de Protección Social, *Food Consumption and Nutrition Division Discussion Paper* 188, February, Washington, DC: IFPRI

Maluccio, JA, 2009, Household targeting in practice: The Nicaraguan Red de Protección Social, *Journal of International Development* 21, 1–23

Molinas Vega, JR, Barros, RPD, Saavedra, J, Giugale, M, 2012, *Do our children have a chance? A human opportunity report for Latin America and the Caribbean*, Washington, DC: World Bank

Molyneux, M, 2006, Mothers at the service of the new poverty agenda: Progresa/Oportunidades, Mexico's conditional transfer programme, *Social Policy and Administration* 40, 425–49

Moore, C, 2008, Assessing Honduras' CCT programme PRAF, Programa de Asignación Familiar: Expected and unexpected realities, *Country Study* 15, April, Brazil: International Poverty Centre

Moss, T, 2011, Oil to cash: Fighting the resource curse through cash transfers, *Working Paper* 237, January, Washington, DC: Center For Global Development

Ponce, J, Bedi, AS, 2010, The impact of a cash transfer program on cognitive achievement: The Bono de Desarrollo Humano of Ecuador, *Economics Of Education Review* 29, 116–25

Rubalcava, L, Teruel, G, Thomas, D, 2002, Welfare design, women's empowerment and income pooling, Mimeo, April, Mexico City: Centro de Investigación y Docencia Económicas (CIDE)

Schady, N, Araujo, MC, 2008, Cash transfers, conditions, and school enrollment in Ecuador, *Economía* 8, 43–70

Skoufias, E, 2005, *Progresa and its impacts on the welfare of rural households in Mexico*, Washington, DC: International Food Policy Research Institute

Skoufias, E, Unar, M, González-Cossío, T, 2008, The impacts of cash and in-kind transfers on consumption and labour supply: Experimental evidence from rural Mexico, *Policy Research Working Paper WPS* 4778, November, Washington, DC: World Bank

Smith, G, Macauslan, I, Butters, S, Trommé, M, 2010, *New technologies in cash transfer programmes and humanitarian assistance*, Report, Oxford: The Cash Learning Partnership (CaLP)

Soares, SSD, 2010, Targeting and coverage of the Bolsa Família Programme: what is the meaning of eleven million families?, *One Pager* 117, Brazil: International Policy Centre for Inclusive Growth (IPC-IG)

Sumner, A, 2010, Global poverty and the new bottom billion: What if three-quaters of the world's poor live in middle-income countries?, *Working Paper* 349, November, Brighton: Institute Of Development Studies (IDS)

Weigand, C, Grosh, M, 2008, Levels and patterns of safety net spending in developing and transition countries, *SP Discussion Paper* 0817, June, Washington, DC: World Bank

THREE

Fragile and conflict-affected situations and the post-2015 development agenda

Clare Lockhart and Sam Vincent

Introduction

The High-Level Panel on the Post-2015 Development Agenda set the goal of ending extreme poverty by 2030 as the key task for the widely-anticipated successor set of development goals, now adopted as the Sustainable Development Goals. While acknowledging the daunting range of issues with which framers of the post-2015 agenda were confronted, this chapter focuses on the challenge of ending extreme poverty in fragile and conflict-affected situations by 2030. To address this question, we present our argument as follows. First, we describe the background context in which fragility and conflict exist, and then discuss the current state of lessons learned and policy agreement and divergence regarding international approaches to peace and security. In the third section, we emphasise the critical role of institutions – understood as the formal and informal rules of the game – both as constraints and as foundations to development, and then in the fourth section offer some recommendations on what key elements are needed in laying institutional foundations. In the fifth section, we make some suggestions about the 'how to' and suggest how responsibilities for implementing the goals might be assigned in practice. In the final section of the chapter we reflect on the impact of the Millennium Development Goals (MDGs) in fragile and conflict-affected situations and consider the implications of current understandings of conflict and fragility for the new generation of development objectives.

The changing context

The changing global composition of poverty and extreme poverty

Where poverty had been concentrated predominantly in the poorest countries during the MDG period 2000–14, there is agreement among development analysts that the geographical composition of global poverty has been undergoing significant change as a number of countries have graduated to middle-income status (Sumner, 2012; Kharas and Rogerson, 2012; Chandy and Gertz, 2011). There is, however, some debate within the development community as to whether the majority of the world's poor in 2015–30 will reside in middle-income or low-income countries. While the total number of people living in extreme poverty has fallen dramatically in recent years, it is estimated that for the first time in history the majority of the world's poor will soon fall within fragile and conflict-affected states (Kharas and Rogerson, 2012, 7; Chandy and Gertz, 2011, 10). Adding further nuance to this picture, some of these fragile and conflict-affected states will be regions within middle-income countries such as Iraq, Pakistan and Nigeria.[1] Indeed, it is suggested that while a decade ago most fragile states were low-income countries, today close to half are middle-income countries (OECD, 2013a). Meanwhile, the concentration of poverty is projected to shift from Asia to Africa.

Extreme poverty will therefore not be eradicated unless fragile and conflict-affected states (of both low- and middle-income status) and their international partners manage to devise workable, durable solutions to the profound challenges they face. The shifting geographies of poverty and fragility are nicely summarised by Gertz and Chandy (2011) as shown in Table 3.1.

Not only is the pattern of poverty changing, the reality and perception of the gap between rich and poor is widening, with growing middle classes emerging in many countries, and a super-wealthy elite now a feature of most societies, including the poorest (Sumner, 2012). The perception and reality of this gap can clearly

Table 3.1: Share of world's poor by country category (%)

	2005		2010	
	Low-income countries	Middle-income countries	Low-income countries	Middle-income countries
Fragile	19.6	0.9	23.7	17.1
Stable	53.9	25.6	10.4	48.8

Source: Gertz and Chandy, 2011

affect stability, as seen by protest movements around the world in recent years, from Occupy to the Arab Spring.

Where the population structure will age in middle-income countries, high birth rates will mean low-income fragile states remain youthful. In most fragile states the 15–34 age group makes up over one third of the population, a percentage that is expected to remain constant (OECD, 2013b, 99). It is further suggested that the 'youth bulge' in such countries may exacerbate the risk of fragility and conflict (Cincotta et al, 2003). In this context, education, skills and employment will be major challenges. Urbanisation of these populations similarly looks set to continue, posing profound rural and urban challenges. The rapid rise in innovation and use of technology brings new possibilities and threats.

Urbanisation is also a significant trend. According to the UN, the world population is expected to grow by 1 billion people within the next 12 years, with the global population projected to reach 9.6 billion in 2050 (ECOSOC, 2012a, xv).[2] Over the same period, the number of people living in cities will grow by 2.6 billion, from 3.6 billion in 2011 to 6.3 billion by 2050 (ECOSOC, 2011a, 1).[3] Consequently, the world rural population will actually begin to fall. By 2020 half the population of Asia will be urban, and by 2035, half the population of Africa will have followed suit (ECOSOC 2011a, 1).[4] The majority of this urbanisation will take place in developing countries, and by 2050 64 per cent of the population of the developing world will be urban (ECOSOC 2011a, 2). Trajectories of urbanisation in fragile states can be projected as in Table 3.2.

Environmental degradation, particularly in relation to climate change, is likely to place additional pressures upon the poorest in fragile states, and suggests a range of challenges in the context of rapid urbanisation, widespread slum-dwelling and the vulnerabilities that this entails.

The role of aid is changing, too. Remittances, significant and growing foundation funding, the emergence of new bilateral donors, South–South cooperation and increasing private investment in low-income countries, especially in the natural resources sector, all have

Table 3.2: Trajectories of urbanisation in fragile states (% of population)

Urbanisation	2000	2015	2050
Fragile states	33	38	56
Global average	46	54	67

Source: ISE research based on ECOSOC demographic data and OECD list of 43 fragile states (excl. Kosovo)

major implications. Aid is no longer the single biggest financial flow, even to the fragile states, but is increasingly overshadowed not only by private capital flows to many countries, but capital flight out of the countries. As recognised by the 2011 *Busan Partnership for Effective Development Co-operation*, there is a need to widen the debate beyond aid effectiveness (important though this remains) to the 'challenges of effective development', encompassing South–South and triangular cooperation and recognition of the 'central role of the private sector' (OECD, 2011a).

Trade and investment as drivers of inclusive economic growth will be required to provide jobs and livelihoods at scale, and underwrite the revenue base for the services required to tackle poverty. Fragile and conflict-affected states are often considered as poor and with dim prospects for future prosperity.[5] Yet, more than three quarters of the countries listed as 'fragile or failed' contain significant mineral or energy deposits, indicating significant potential for revenue generation but also serious challenges for natural resource governance and the 'resource curse' (Lockhart, 2012). Many of the countries that are termed as fragile or post-conflict by international organisations and development agencies are also termed 'frontier markets' by investors. The deep challenges of insecurity, extreme poverty, marginalisation and exclusion should not be brushed aside, but country context should be read through the lens of its potential and opportunities as well as its risks.

The contemporary nature of war and conflict

The nature and character of violent conflict has also changed. While the number of civil wars has declined significantly since peaking in the 1990s, for every casualty from a recognised war there are now nine casualties of organised crime and intra-state conflicts (UNDP, 2013b). At the same time, the character of violence has undergone a shift, so that '21st-century violence does not fit the 20th-century mould' (World Bank, 2011, 2). Contemporary conflict is characterised by the blurring of boundaries between forms of violence, combatants and civilians, motivations for fighting, and the lack of clear front lines or battlefields. Similarly, a declaration of peace is unlikely to mean an abrupt end to violence. Where wars may contain significant pockets of tranquillity, 'post-conflict' environments can be characterised by significant violent activity, often triggered by elections.

Second, there has been recognition that the categorisation of countries as 'fragile' or 'conflict-affected' risks obscuring the great cross-context diversity. There has been recognition that conflict and fragility can be driven by a variety of disparate factors that can interact differently in different settings, including: failure of economic growth; lack of inclusive growth; inability to perform state functions; exclusionary practices by the state; arbitrary governance; external difficulties.[6] There have been various efforts to distinguish between different types of fragility. Clearly, South Sudan does not face the same challenges as Syria. Different typologies attempt to disaggregate situations of conflict and fragility in different ways. For example, conflict and fragility could be categorised according to the source of the conflict: institutional disintegration at the centre (as in Nepal) could be distinguished from countries in which separatist movements have arisen within multi-ethnic states (as in Yugoslavia and Ethiopia), countries suffering persistent conflict (Democratic Republic of Congo, Somalia), state repression to quell dissident movements (El Salvador, Guatemala, Sudan). Exhaustive typologies are difficult to achieve since the conflict and fragility are seldom mono-causal. Sub-dividing fragility in this way may be helpful provided that it is recognised that all countries are unique. New states such as East Timor, South Sudan and Kosovo might be distinguished from authoritarian states in transition, or countries in endemic conflict, but these new states all face distinctive challenges. In order to evaluate each unique context, the World Bank recommends assessing the type of violence, the particular combination of international and external stresses, institutional challenges, the stakeholders that will need to be engaged, and the transition opportunities available (World Bank, 2011, 248–50). The factors affecting fragility, and the balance between them, change over time. Finally, it is important to distinguish between factors that can produce fragility or conflict and factors that can sustain existing conflict. This multidimensionality implies the need for a multidimensional approach encompassing and grasping the linkages between development, politics, security and justice, among others (Brinkman, 2013).

The debate on addressing extreme poverty in fragile and conflict-affected settings

Since the agreement on the MDGs in 2000, the challenges of violent conflict and fragility have come to the centre of development concerns. Recognition of the linkages between peace, security, governance and development is not new but has grown from the debates of the 1990s on 'linking' relief and development, as well as growing on-the-ground experience of coordination between multilateral and bilateral aid agencies, NGOs and military actors. Among many other major international reports, *Preventing deadly conflict* (Carnegie Commission on Preventing Deadly Conflict, 1998) and *A more secure world: Our shared responsibility* (UN, 2004), had recognised the pre-eminence of establishing peace and security in order for development processes to take root, the importance of wellbeing and socio-economic progress in order to establish and maintain peace, and the fundamental importance of capable states in both keeping the peace and underwriting development.

Although the Millennium Declaration itself contained no specific goal on reducing violent conflict, it encouraged the international community to maintain peace and security, including 'by giving [the UN] the resources and tools it needs for conflict prevention, peaceful resolution of disputes, peacekeeping, post-conflict peacebuilding and reconstruction' (UN, 2000). Nonetheless, the declaration carefully partitioned peace and security issues from development and, unlike the passages on development, did not impose time-bound, measurable objectives (see the sixth section, on MDGs in situations of conflict and fragility, below).

By 2011 it had once again become clear that violent conflict and fragility were major barriers in the way of attaining the MDGs: no low-income fragile or conflict-affected country has yet achieved a single MDG (World Bank, 2011, 1). More than a fifth of humanity, 1.5 billion people, live in such circumstances. Tackling poverty in these contexts is exceptionally difficult. Conflict has a severe negative impact on economic growth; in addition to the obvious hardships and human tragedies imposed on populations by violent conflict, the *2011 World Development Report* found that on average a country that experienced major violence over the period 1981 to 2005 has a poverty rate 21 percentage points higher than a country that saw no violence (World Bank, 2011, 5). Poverty is widely considered to be both the result of conflict, and a driver for future conflicts, and violent conflict has even been described as 'development in reverse'. Issues of conflict and security have come back to the centre of thinking about international development in both academic and policy circles.

There is now widespread international consensus, including across the g7+ countries, that part of the reason for the intractable nature of fragility and conflict is the existence of 'conflict traps' and vicious cycles of weak governance, poverty and violence (Collier et al, 2003). Accordingly, there is increasing focus on how such cycles can be broken, redirected, or replaced with virtuous alternatives.

A core insight here has been that making this leap from fragility and conflict to stability needs to be understood not as a single transition, but as simultaneously attempting multiple, inter-connected transitions. These multiple transitions should not be understood discretely, but as a set of reinforcing and interconnected activities that can underpin the creation of virtuous cycles. Conversely, if interventions are designed for one transition without consideration of any potential impact upon others, there is a risk of unintended consequences. Some of these transitions are described in Table 3.3.

Another significant advance in learning has been an increasing consensus that existing aid instruments are poorly fitted for work in fragile and conflict-affected environments. There is an active debate as to whether development – as pursued through the disbursement of aid – might actually exacerbate fragility and conflict. Perhaps the fundamental difficulty has been that conventional mechanisms of development partnership presuppose a functioning government with which to partner. Where state institutions are themselves in question, the mechanisms of international assistance have often undermined the key goal of consolidating legitimate and effective state institutions and legitimate market activity.

In the past ten years, a number of inter-related problems have been identified with the way that the existing aid system operates in fragile and conflict-affected settings. These features of the aid system produce unintended consequences that work to undermine the transitions

Table 3.3: Multiple transitions from conflict/fragility to stability

From	To
Conflict	Politics and security
Charisma	Management and institutional accountability
Opaqueness	Transparent management of public finances
Absence of service delivery	Nurturing human capital
Oppositional identities	Citizenship rights and formation of a civil society
Destruction	Creation of infrastructure
Subsistence and war economy	Market economy
Diversion and privatisation of state assets	Creation of public value
Marginalisation and illegitimacy	Assuming responsibilities as a member of the international community
Rule of the gun	Rule of law

Source: adapted from Ghani, Lockhart and Carnahan (2006, 108)

outlined above. Here we highlight six such problematic characteristics of the aid system: the donor rush; parallel structures; the project aid model; technical assistance; the aid footprint; and the alignment problem.

The donor rush

In many instances, a crisis or window of opportunity creates a significant degree of donor support and engagement. While welcome to some degree, it can create a flood of visitors, projects and money which can overwhelm local institutions, people and processes – as it would in any context. Overcoming this then creates its own issue of 'coordination' where it is not clear that more coordination solves the basic issue of too many projects, people and too much money – and just builds another bureaucratic layer on top of a cumbersome process. It is not coordination, but rather better design of strategy, programme and processes that are at issue.

Parallel structures

Aid actors have often responded to a perceived lack of will or capacity to deliver basic services, including health and education, by establishing their own parallel systems of provision. Perceiving a lack of state service provision, aid organisations move in to provide those services directly. While this approach is intended to address the immediate needs of citizens, or to get around the problem of working with a 'difficult' or 'unwilling' national government, the tendency of aid actors to attempt direct service provision has the consequence of establishing a 'dual state'. This approach is criticised both for its lack of sustainability and for undermining the state itself by sustaining lack of connection between the state and service delivery, and therefore the creation of bonds of citizenship. The difficulties that arise have been particularly well-documented in Haiti (for example, Buss and Gardner, 2006). While there may be a need to establish such systems in some situations, it is vital that time-bound mechanisms are established through which the state can progressively take on functions. This requires concrete, timetabled plans for co-creating the requisite human and institutional capitals.

Project aid model

Development assistance continues to be delivered predominantly through establishing thousands of discrete projects; it is estimated that in 2007 over 90,000 projects were running across the developing world (Frot and

Santiso, 2010). While projects can be an effective delivery mechanism, they suffer from a number of well-documented problems. Projects have been seen to cause fragmentation and confusion, while not necessarily representing value for money. This occurs when projects are driven by donor rather than national priorities, funded outside the national budget (raising vital planning and coordination, as well as legitimacy questions), passed through expensive layers of sub-contracting, or implemented through specially-created units outside government rules and regulations (Ghani et al, 2007). Reporting requirements impose a heavy burden upon national governments, and auditing at the project level proves extremely expensive. Once facilities such as schools are created, they need to be staffed, equipped and maintained. To be sustainable into the future, this inevitably requires the creation of the necessary national capabilities.

Technical assistance

Technical assistance has become an unregulated multibillion-dollar industry. While skilled, well-targeted technical assistance can be extremely valuable, unless balanced with systematic attention to the creation of domestic capacity and careful planning for handover, such assistance does not offer a sustainable solution.

The aid footprint

Having established a presence inside a fragile or conflict-affected country, the aid industry's economic footprint has created new economic niches existing to cater for industry needs. While the issue of limited capacity is the constant lament of international development actors in situations of fragility and conflict, the arrival of an international aid industry offering salaries that may be tens or hundreds of times what the national government can offer, works to draw what national talent exists away from essential roles within the state and into the parallel structures established by the aid industry. Further, it frequently generates resentment towards an industry that seems more oriented to enriching international staff than to devising efficient solutions to complex development needs.

Failure of security, diplomatic and developmental actors to align behind common goals and coherent sets of activities

Over the past decade, a consensus has emerged among leading donors that transitioning from violent conflict to stability requires the emergence of functioning national systems and that international assistance should work to strengthen – or, minimally, not undermine – national systems. This recognition has generated formal policy-level recognition of the need to align behind the goal of establishing functioning systems, to allow governments to articulate their own objectives and priorities, and then to act in support of those objectives. Nevertheless, coordination on the ground between multiple actors remains problematic, while there is a lag between having recognised the limitations of existing aid instruments and practices and design, and moving to implement alternative approaches.

Institutions as constraints and as foundations

The centrality of institutions as constraints to peace and prosperity

Reflecting the insights generated by scholarship within the field of New Institutional Economics, development actors have increasingly come to recognise that in understanding and addressing fragility and conflict, 'institutions matter' (North, 1990; World Bank, 2011, 76). Contrary to the connotations of chaos and collapse implied by the language of conflict and fragility, there is growing awareness that conflict-affected and fragile contexts actually constitute dynamic and remarkably durable systems of formal and informal 'rules of the game'. Within such systems, coalitions of stakeholders emerge with vested interests in perpetuating conflict and fragility (North, 1990; Ghani et al, 2006; North et al, 2009). In such settings, the formal 'rules of the game' belie a set of informal rules that interact with and subvert the formal system. Such analyses help clarify the challenge of conflict entrepreneurs and spoilers, and explain the intractability of the constraints to peace and stability. While the need for cross-contextual nuance can hardly be over-stated, nevertheless some recurrent features of fragile, conflict-affected and post-conflict environments can be identified. Three features are particularly salient: criminalisation of the economy; corruption; and exclusion from rule of law and justice. These are important features of what can be described as an institutional syndrome of 'dysfunctionality'.

Criminalisation of the economy

The nature of contemporary conflict has entailed large-scale criminality by armed actors, in part to fund conflict through high-value commodities such as drugs and diamonds. The relationships forged through such wartime activities persist into the post-conflict phase when they become a major driver of the criminalisation of the economy. The blurry nature of war to peace transitions, the presence of large numbers of people trained in violence, and the challenge of generating alternative employment opportunities all further contribute to the persistence and deepening of criminality in post-conflict settings. The criminalisation of the economy is a major challenge to stability with serious implications for politics, as powerful criminal networks reach back into the state itself, undermining much-needed confidence-building and trust between citizens and state.

Corruption

Corruption is a critical element of systemic institutional dysfunction, existing at the heart of the subversion and co-option of the formal rules of the game by informal rules. There has been some debate as to whether corruption should be treated as a 'first-tier' challenge in fragile and conflict-affected situations, where there is a need to prioritise among a seemingly endless list of pressing issues. Some argue that addressing the absence of property rights is the most critical issue for encouraging economic development, and is more urgent than addressing corruption. Others go further to posit that corruption may even enable individuals looking to circumvent bad laws and systems (O'Driscoll and Hoskins, 2003) and buying off powerful interests that could have opposed economic transformation. Thus, corruption may play a significant role in maintaining domestic peace and stability during periods of transition or reform. While more work is required to differentiate debilitating and pro-growth forms of corruption, in practice, in fragile and conflict-affected settings, where consolidating legitimate political institutions has been identified as the key challenge to breaking vicious cycles, corruption represents a formidable barrier.

Exclusion from rule of law and access to justice

The peacebuilding field recognises that one of the most common drivers of internal conflict and instability is the exclusion and disenfranchisement of groups within a society. The Commission on Legal Empowerment of the Poor estimated that at least 4 billion people are excluded from access to justice, especially fair application of the rules, and access to secure property rights (de Soto, 2001; UNDP, 2008).

Corresponding to the welcome recognition of the power of informal rules of the game, there is widespread agreement that weak state and non-state institutions explain why some countries at some times are unable to cope with the combination of stresses with which they are confronted while others manage to channel conflict through institutions (World Bank, 2011, 7).

The centrality of institutions as foundations for peace and prosperity

The goal of rupturing the syndrome of dysfunctionality requires creating an inclusive political, social and economic order embodied in the rule of law. In practice, creating such an order entails strengthening or creating requisite institutional foundations, a strategy of statebuilding. There is long-standing and widespread acceptance that statebuilding is essential to tackling conflict and fragility. As the Carnegie Commission recognised in 1998, capable states are foundational for the prevention of deadly conflict. The UN Panel on Threats, Challenges and Change recognised that 'capable and responsible states' lay at the forefront of confronting global challenges including conflict (UN, 2004, 18). The OECD Development Assistance Committee (DAC) has been instrumental in building international consensus that, in situations of conflict and fragility, national actors and international partners need to 'focus on statebuilding as the central objective' while the g7+ countries have arrived at a consensus that breaking cycles of conflict and fragility requires an agenda of peacebuilding and statebuilding to strengthen legitimate institutions and governance (OECD, 2011b, 27).

Building on these findings, it seems clear that building capable states is both an end in itself, in an international order that rests on sovereign states as its constituent units, and a means to enabling the achievement of development outcomes. In the next section we discuss in more detail the nature of the institutional foundations for peace and development.

An agenda of institution building requires a balanced approach to the roles of state, market and civil society. Conflict and fragility can be reined in by the emergence of legitimate political institutional channels for mediating sources of conflict; the provision of access to official justice mechanisms; and the extension of public goods and services. This does not by any means imply a centralised, top-down approach to statebuilding, but it does require careful attention to establishing a framework for which function should be performed at what level of governance. Successful statebuilding processes have been internally formulated and led, based on a carefully nurtured national consensus and a politics oriented towards creating stability and development.

It is by now accepted that tackling criminalisation of the economy and the emergence of the licit market is not something natural or spontaneous but something entailing dedication to the building of systems and a culture of rule of law. Finally, the role of civil society, direct citizen engagement, and the creation of civic space should not be lost or neglected as incompatible with statebuilding, but seen as an essential part of the process of fostering and widening the rights and duties of citizenship.

The citizen perspective

Citizens everywhere continue to express the same desires: freedom from want and fear, dignity and respect, and opportunity. In practice, legitimate and effective states, remain the critical mechanism for creating, enabling and realising the rights, obligations and aspirations of citizens, for creating and enhancing security, for creating the enabling environment for markets to flourish, and for mobilising citizens around collective agendas. Attention to the state as a vital unit of analysis and locus of responsibility, however, should not obscure the fact that the real test of delivery lies in whether citizens perceive that their needs and desires are being addressed. Even the most powerful and established states increasingly recognise the futility of ignoring or excluding the aspirations of their citizenry. In the period 2015–30 the degree of state responsiveness and accountability to citizen requirements is likely to become a key barometer of state fragility and effectiveness.

Advances in technology over the past decade have enabled and reinforced this trend. Post-2015, it will be much more feasible to build in social accountability monitoring for a new set of goals and targets from the beneficiaries themselves – the citizens. Transparency and accountability are emerging as a key locus of civil society activism across the national and international levels, including the work of Open Government Initiative, Transparency International, and domestic accountability movements within India. A generation of creative new approaches to empowering citizens has the potential to again reinforce the growing appreciation that stability critically depends upon establishing and maintaining the bonds of citizenship.

These trends have stark implications for international organisations seeking to partner and catalyse transitions from conflict and fragility to stability. As the state is increasingly understood as an instrument for the realisation of collective aspirations, and as pressure mounts upon national governments to strengthen the accountability loop between state and citizen, so international assistance will have to address its own accountability systems in order to remain relevant and legitimate.

One implication of the increasingly dense global webs and flows of information and connectivity has been that citizen expectations are increasingly set in terms of global standards rather than national realities. The responsibilities owed by states to their citizens are increasingly understood not as a minimal obligation of sovereignty, owed to the international system, to refrain from extreme abuse and repression, but by citizens in terms of the duty to earn legitimacy by creating predictable and inclusive order, and through delivery of rights and collective goods.

Incorporating a rights-based perspective where a core set of rights are met and the dignity of the individual respected would be highly desirable. In situations of conflict and fragility, inequality and exclusion of certain groups is often a marked feature of society, a cause of grievance and a driver of fragility and conflict. Making the transition from exclusionary state practices to creation and expansion of the rights and obligations of citizenship is a core challenge in the attempt to re-establish order and justice following conflict or in fragile contexts. At heart, the expansion of citizenship entails balancing the tension between inequality and solidarity through establishing and expanding legal status that entails both rights and obligations. Recognising the injustice of exclusion, oppression and other forms of inequality leads to pressure for change. Intransigence in the face of such pressures can force the aggrieved to seek redress outside the system, ultimately through organised violence that may ultimately overthrow the system. The ability of the social and political order to recognise injustice and address it through expansion of the rights and obligations of citizenship is an important marker of state effectiveness and resilience.

Beyond responding to pressure by acknowledging injustice, the ability to manage the pace and sequence of agreed reforms is of critical importance. Historically, societies have tackled different sets of rights – whether social, economic or political, in different sequences. In fragile states, there is an opportunity to mobilise marginalised groups such as the poor, women and the disabled, who together constitute an absolute majority of the citizenry, around agendas of rights expansion and empowerment. Where citizenship rights were traditionally located within the legal arrangements of sovereign states, the Universal Declaration of Human Rights sets out a compelling normative framework rooted in the concept of universal inalienable human rights, providing a framework for measuring states' conduct towards their citizens and to humanity more generally. This language has enduring normative appeal and practical value in providing a universal language within which citizens can articulate their claims. Finally, globalisation complicates. As the role and functions of the state are renegotiated in a number of countries, and as economy and civil society have become global, citizenship rights can no longer be conceived as relations between citizen and state but increasingly must be understood across a number of levels from global to national to local, and in relation to a range of actors including corporations, regional organisations such as the EU, and international institutions such as the World Bank (Ghani and Lockhart, 2007).

The 'what': foundations for development in countries emerging from conflict

Beyond the recognition of the foundational nature of institutions, there has been a rich debate on the nature of those institutions. The *2011 World Development Report* recognised the centrality of the provision of 'citizen security, justice and jobs' and the domestic institutions that underlie their provision (World Bank, 2011). The Carnegie Commission recognised a similar framing in 1998, of 'security, wellbeing and justice' (Carnegie Commission on Preventing Deadly Conflict, 1998, xix). The youth bulge in Africa, the Middle East and Asia (up to a million people enter the job market in South Asia each month), and the generation of 'waithood' residing in the Middle East and North Africa, have helped drive recognition of the need for a step change in attention to job creation and economic opportunity in coming years (IDPS, 2010, 1; Likhi, 2013; Dhillon and Yousef, 2009).

Recent years have seen considerable international efforts to move from the 'why' to the 'what' and 'how' of engagement in fragile and conflict-affected states. The work of the OECD DAC, including the 2005 *Paris Declaration on Aid Effectiveness* and the 2007 *Fragile States Principles*, produced consensus on the need to realign national and international efforts around common objectives, and goals, targets and indicators were widely suggested as a way to achieve this. Such goals would need to be 'achievable, holistic, focused and uniform, while also symbolising an end state towards which the international community and national governments [could] strive' (Ghani and Lockhart, 2008b, 2). In a context of rapidly proliferating indicators and objectives, there was a need to delineate and prioritise and an appropriate set of tasks and indicators that could be tailored to country context. In 2008 the Institute for State Effectiveness (ISE) suggested a list of nine indicative outcome goals for fragile states, as a basis for discussion, refinement and prioritisation through a broadly inclusive international consensus-building process (Ghani and Lockhart, 2008b).

Moving beyond a donor-driven conversation, the g7+ group of fragile states has since established itself as an influential forum representing the views of states affected by conflict and fragility. The 2011 *New Deal for Engagement in Fragile States*, signed by 15 fragile states, 20 OECD states, the African and Asian Development Banks and World Bank, the OECD, UNDG and European Union sought to create a 'broader and more inclusive' partnership by establishing 'shared principles, common goals and differential commitments' (OECD, 2011a, 1). The *New Deal* built upon a series of international fora, including the 2005 *Paris Declaration on Aid Effectiveness*, the 2007 *fragile states principles*, and the 2008 *Accra Agenda for Action*. This important work has continually restated the need for 'country leadership and ownership' of the development process, and to shift the relationship between country and international aid from donor–recipient to partnership and new forms of working. To support country leadership and ownership, the *New Deal* identified five guiding peacebuilding and statebuilding goals (PSGs), intended to lay the foundations for development in countries affected by conflict and fragility and 'enable progress towards the MDGs'. These goals were elaborated as the 2011 '*Monrovia Objectives*' (IDPS, 2011a).

The New Deal committed to developing two sets of indicators – at the country level and a set of common indicators – to enable tracking of progress in relation to each of the PSGs at the national and international levels. The working group responsible for these indicators, co-chaired by Democratic Republic of Congo and the United Nations Peacebuilding Support Office, explicitly set out to inform the discussions around the post-2015 agenda (IDPS, 2012).

The PSGs have the benefit of broad international endorsement, including by the g7+ group of fragile and conflict-affected states. By being parsimonious, they have encouraged focus around a limited number of objectives, providing a way to help orient disparate actors in prioritising between a host of pressing requirements. With full recognition that the PSGs offer simplicity and brevity, we raise five additional considerations:

1. *Politics*
   There is a need to emphasise the need for an *inclusive* political settlement, and to appreciate the profound difference between an elite pact and a genuine national dialogue/consensus-building process.

2. *Security and justice*

There is a need to ensure that security institutions are embedded within clearly delineated rules.

3. *Capacity*

While it is possible to identify a range of latent assets with fragile and conflict-affected states, the issue of capacity building cannot be put off or approached in an ad hoc way but needs to be recognised as a critical issue requiring early, urgent and systematic attention. The skills and capabilities to lead and manage the state and the market, build and nurture administrative and management capabilities over the medium and long terms, or create competitive businesses do not emerge spontaneously. Failure to address this critical issue ensures future binding constraints in the development process and helps to consign countries to ongoing dependence upon technical assistance and parallel delivery.

4. *Economic foundations*

We welcome attention to economic foundations and the stability implications of investment in job creation. However, this focus could be extended to recognise rapidly developing thinking about innovative mechanisms of partnership and additional instruments to expand the licit economy and enhance job creation.

5. *Natural disasters and environmental management*

Climate change, environmental degradation, and growing resource pressures as living standards rise and the global population continues to grow all mean that the capacity to prepare for, respond to and mitigate the effects of natural disasters and to manage the environment are now core functions and not optional extras. Whether these functions are to be performed at sub-national, national, regional or global levels, and how such functions will be built and financed now require attention.

The 'how': implementation matters

The changing global context, lessons learned about reforming the way aid organisations interact with fragile and conflict-affected countries, and recognition of the importance of institutions as constraints and as foundations have a number of implications for a policy agenda seeking to address extreme poverty in fragile and conflict-affected settings.

Harnessing globalisation

The Millennium Declaration stated that 'the central challenge we face today is to ensure that globalisation becomes a positive force for all the world's people'. In fragile and conflict-affected states, globalisation has both been a source of threats and promise. In the contemporary world, there is a need to devise mechanisms to enable people to participate in the benefits of globalisation, and to mitigate the threats that it poses. The state remains a critical building block, although the challenge of laying institutional foundations is complicated by globalisation processes.

Implementation

Implementation matters. The MDGs were blind to how implementation was organised. This allowed a plethora of activities by a range of outside actors who mobilised to meet them. While this mobilisation was welcome, there have been many questions asked as to the efficacy, cost-effectiveness and impact of expenditures, and even some questions posed as to whether the cure killed the patient. Given the weak institutional and human capital base in many contexts, a huge influx of outside resources can sometimes further damage the institutional base and set a country back on its development path by years.

It is necessary to recognise that the primary responsibility and task lies with states meeting their citizen's needs and expectations. International partners may be able to play a strong supporting role in fragile and conflict-affected countries in reaching this goal. Development goals should not lose sight of the need for effective states, or overstress the role and responsibility of the UN, aid agencies or NGOs in this regard. The goal of functioning country institutions, capable of formulating goals and policies, and of harnessing existing and latent national assets to the task of implementation, is foundational for a development process to take root. Substitution for state functions by an outside entity may be required in particular circumstances for a particular time, but in such cases the costs and benefits of that intervention must be carefully weighed, and a clear timeline and goal of restoring responsibility for the exercise of that function to domestic authorities should be set.

National reform processes

A welcome development in the discourse around conflict and fragility has been increased interest in learning from examples of successful transformation (Ghani and Lockhart, 2008a; Radelet, 2010; World Bank, 2011). Where initially much of the discussion centred on the problems with fragile and conflict-affected states, this turn has led attention to countries that have managed to generate momentum towards stability and economic growth. Countries such as Mozambique, Rwanda and Sierra Leone are increasingly investigated for lessons that might help inform efforts elsewhere. Each country faces unique possibilities and constraints, and actions taken successfully in one country, at a specific historical juncture are unlikely to prove successful if unreflectively grafted elsewhere, this trend is proving encouragingly fruitful. Nonetheless, such experiences can inform as well as inspire, provided that they are rethought in relation to current and pending opportunities and threats across the global, regional and national levels.

Some summary insights may include: the importance of national ownership of a national vision and agenda, and the recognition that no successful transformation occurred simply because of aid programmes; the importance of establishing security, rule of law and justice at an early stage; the importance of political inclusiveness and fostering of citizenship and a sense of participation; and the focus on creating capable institutions to meet citizen expectations.

International support to national reform processes

It is increasingly apparent that the system of international assistance for fragile and conflict-affected settings as currently configured is ill-suited to implementing the emerging agenda. Traditional bilateral and multilateral aid delivery, plus contractors and the many thousands of NGOs are part of this picture. However, new aid instruments, non-traditional donors, foundations, remittance flows, the international private sector and a range of other factors are all playing a significant role in a changing landscape. The challenge is to harness the vast potential of these disparate assets to an agenda of institutional regeneration, while mitigating the malign effects of lack of coordination, duplication, waste and competition. In this, the concept of the 'double compact' may provide a tool for bringing disparate actors around a shared set of a goals and a clear set of mutual rights and obligations, and 'sovereignty strategies' may provide a vehicle for organising and sequencing activities over time (Ghani and Lockhart, 2008a).

International actors cannot impose the multiple transitions and institutional foundations needed to move away from conflict and fragility until and unless a reform-minded leadership is in place. During the 1990s and 2000s a series of debates evolved around how aid actors could best operate in 'difficult partnerships'. Subsequently, evaluations of decades of engagement in countries such as Haiti found that, after billions of dollars of aid invested results fell short of expectations, lacked sustainability and had either little effect or adverse impact on governance (Buss and Gardner, 2006; Ghani and Lockhart, 2008c).

Regionalism

There has been much recent analysis on the growing importance of regionalism, and regional blocks and institutions in forming cooperative ways to address challenges and maximise opportunities, across security, economics, governance and other arena. Regional cooperation can play a particularly significant role in overcoming dynamics of conflict and promoting peaceful relations between neighbours. The formation of the European Union in the wake of the Second World War remains a seminal example, yet there are more recent examples including the Mekong, the Nile River agreement, and recent efforts including efforts in South/Central Asia along the New Silk Road/Istanbul Process and the newly formed Balkans Forum. In ongoing and future efforts to foster peace, stability and resilience, recognising how and when the region concerned can play a role will warrant careful attention.

Asset mapping

While lack of capacity is a reality for most fragile and conflict-affected countries, no country is a blank slate starting from scratch. Rather than beginning with the needs assessment model, which has tended to work from the assumption of lack of capacity to the need to import technical assistance, ISE has proposed an alternative approach which is to begin by mapping a country's existing assets, both overt and latent. The challenge is then reframed as, first, identifying and mobilising existing assets that are hidden, dispersed and fragmented, and then to find creative ways to stitch them together, while developing a reading of gaps in capabilities, prioritising between them, and finding ways to address them in the short, medium and longer terms.

Capacity building and human capital

Where technical assistance was originally conceived as a limited and targeted practice, it has burgeoned into a multibillion-dollar industry, without industry-wide standards on quality or qualifications.

To achieve the goal of exit from development assistance, partners need to arrive at a plan to move away from a long-term strategy of institutional life-support through technical assistance by joining technical assistance provision to systematic processes for equipping national actors with the skills to manage their own affairs. This requires both government and international partners to plan for their strategic human capacity requirements. In terms of technical assistance itself, the move to document recent examples of successful transition presents a welcome opportunity to identify and harness the practical knowledge and wisdom of these processes that exists in the south. In terms of the MDGs, the use of the primary education goal as a planning tool has been unfortunate in light of the desperate need to address the skills shortage in a systematic way.

Time-frames, benchmarking and the ultimate goal of exit

Exit from aid should be the shared goal of the national government and its international partners. Getting to exit requires a clearly delineated strategy for progressively reducing aid spending while systematically replacing it with domestic revenue – from customs, licenses, resource development and taxation. Here at last welcome attention is being given to the question of economic growth and how government and international partners can create the enabling and regulatory conditions for markets. A strategy for exit from aid demands the willingness to make long-term, predictable commitments, with clear accountability mechanisms and revenue generation benchmarks alongside aid reduction.

Funding mechanisms

Reflecting the need to consolidate national public financial management, the international community may be in a position to assist fragile and conflict-affected states. Currently, much assistance bypasses government channels contributing to some of the familiar problems outlined above. Budget support, and dual key multidonor trust arrangements offer options for supporting government functionality while retaining fiduciary oversight. In situations where trust in the willingness and capacity of a government to exercise acceptable stewardship of such funding streams the Governance and Economic Management Assistance Programme (GEMAP) model in Liberia may present an alternative model. In all cases, clear time-bound processes for moving towards self-sufficiency are paramount.

Sequencing

The international system of support to conflict-affected countries was designed around a mental model of war that envisaged a clear-cut phase of declared violent conflict between known actors, giving way to a formal end of hostilities (through victory of one party or negotiated settlement), followed by a recovery phase and then the resumption of 'development'. The international system assigns different roles to development, diplomatic, peacekeeping and humanitarian actors in relation to each phase. The very different nature of contemporary violent conflict, repeated and interlinked, makes these traditional assignments of responsibilities out-dated and impractical. Donors agree that while conflict-prevention, humanitarian response, stabilisation/recovery, peacebuilding and statebuilding tasks might be distinguished conceptually, the overlaps and interactions between them make it too simplistic and schematic to think about them separately (Ghani and Lockhart, 2008b; World Bank, 2011, 2).

The MDGs in situations of conflict and fragility

What did the MDGs achieve in fragile and conflict-affected situations? They undoubtedly had many strengths, providing a common set of ideals that helped orient discussions between disparate development actors and national governments. They helped concentrate attention around social development issues, and acted as a useful tool for national and international civil society and advocacy.

The effects of the MDGs in fragile and conflict-affected settings need careful reflection on at least two levels, however. At the strategic and policy level, while assisting in orienting actors around a common set of objectives, they may have provided an inappropriate framework. By dividing the development elements of the declaration from other issues that are fundamental to development, they may have led to insufficient attention being paid to security, governance and justice issues, despite their being integral to the Declaration. They gave welcome attention to social development, particularly seen from the perspective of the contemporary economic climate and the formidable challenges posed by the volumes of unemployed youth in fragile and conflict-affected states and the destabilising effects of exclusion, informality and criminal economic activity, particularly in fragile and conflict-affected states but also in generating fragility in previously stable countries. However, this could have been balanced by an emphasis on job creation and the enabling conditions for legitimate economic activity. There was no 'growth' goal. Aid was fore-grounded, but focus on economic development got lost.

The MDGs were originally conceived as global targets, based upon global trends in the 1970s and 1980s. They were not intended to be applied uniformly at the country level but were meant to set collective objectives while influencing national debates on development. In the UN Secretary General's 2001 Road Map Report, however, it was argued that the MDGs should become national goals. Subsequently, the MDGs have been widely used to judge progress at the country level, without national tailoring or regard for initial conditions. In this context, we should not be surprised that progress towards the MDGs has been most problematic in fragile states. UNDP, for example, reports that a third of the poor live in 43 fragile states, which account for half of all under-five deaths while seven of the 11 countries accounting for a third of maternal mortality are fragile (UNDP, 2010). This is not perhaps the fault of the goals, but of their application (Vandermoortele, 2011; Manning, 2009).

At the level of implementation, the MDGs may have had some undesirable effects in situations of conflict and fragility. In many cases, they resulted in a rush of international agencies clamouring to advance the MDG targets, which reinforced the well-documented and deleterious state-undermining effects of the structure and practices of the aid industry. In some cases, the MDGs were used as a planning tool. The central importance of basing activities upon national priorities and conditions, and strengthening the budget process as the locus of legitimate and accountable decisions regarding the inevitably difficult trade-offs between different priorities tended to be lost. Instead, the MDGs were used to justify decisions about what to fund, again with unintended and undesirable effects. The primary education MDG was used to concentrate education resources upon primary education, but had the unintended consequence of starving the secondary, tertiary and vocational tiers. One consequence has been to reduce the number of trained teachers, reproducing the familiar problem of capacity constraints.

The goals were not conducive to a system-wide focus on the interconnections between objectives, and the dependencies and constraints across short-, medium- and long-term horizons. The focus on primary schooling, while laudable, made it difficult to invest in an education system capable of delivering the secondary, tertiary, vocational and professional training needed to produce primary school teachers. When used in this way, progress on short-term goals may perpetuate continuing dependence. To address the needs of fragile and conflict-affected states, successor goals should be 'servants and not masters', tailored to context, and with due regard to interconnections and to the overall objective of progressively establishing effective institutions as the enablers of development.

MDG 8: The global partnership for development

MDG 8 stands apart from the other goals in addressing the international governance architecture itself. It included six targets:

- develop further an open, rule-based, predictable, non-discriminatory trading and financial system;
- address the special needs of least developed countries;
- address the special needs of landlocked developing countries and small island developing states;
- deal comprehensively with the debt problems of developing countries;
- provide access to affordable essential drugs in developing countries;
- make available the benefits of new technologies (mainly communications and information technologies).

Reform of the broader global governance arrangements, including trade and finance, is politically complex, but the indicators of making progress in accessing markets and reducing tariffs were pragmatic. Addressing the 'special needs' of the poorest countries was to be measured largely in terms of aid flows, rather than in broader terms. The Addis Agenda, as part of the post-2015 framework, re-envisioned aid to include traditional overseas development assistance, domestic resources to be mobilised by developing countries themselves, and private sector investment, including blended finance. The Jubilee Debt Campaign, meanwhile, raised global awareness and generated progress in relation to debt forgiveness. There has also been progress on affordable drugs and the diffusion of technology (which was measured primarily through the diffusion of mobile telephony and information and communication technologies (ICT)).

Viewed from the perspective of the needs of conflict-affected and fragile states and after nearly 15 years of intensive global debate about the need for far-reaching international institutional reform, MDG 8 seems to have followed an ambitious and captivating aspiration with relatively weak targets and indicators. Conceiving of the needs of the poorest in terms of aid flows and the debate on aid effectiveness looks anachronistic today in light of profound changes to the global system and as the nature of aid relationships are increasingly conceived in terms of international partnership rather than donor–recipient. International institutions increasingly recognise that their traditional business practices are not aligned to the objectives of peacebuilding and statebuilding. The goals, targets and indicators of SDG Goal 17 closely align with those of MDG 8, and enshrine measurable, time-bound progress in reforming the architecture and business practices of international governance, including aid.

Conclusion: fragile and conflict-affected settings and the post-2015 agenda

Reducing extreme poverty will require new approaches to working in fragile and conflict-affected settings. The SDGs focus on implementing a universal agenda for people, planet and prosperity, with a number of specific goals that highlight the critical importance of including governance and global partnerships across the 2030 framework. Goals 16 and 17, respectively, call for a renewed focus on the need for measurable commitments and meaningful institutional reforms. The question arises as to how fragile and conflict-affected countries in particular, will require support tailored to their individual contexts. In tackling extreme poverty in such settings, we conclude that the following key questions and challenges need to be addressed.

Understanding the security–politics–development linkages

There is a live debate as to whether establishing peace and security is a precondition for development, or whether lack of development, in particular in addressing uneven access to key rights and services, can exacerbate conflict and therefore addressing development appropriately can mitigate and contribute to resolving conflict. The multidimensionality of the challenges and solution sets requires very careful analysis as to the appropriate approach for tackling the related elements of insecurity, political instability, economic stagnation, informality and criminality, social exclusion and other challenges. The exact approach will of course be specific to each context.

Ensuring that all SDGs are given adequate attention in fragile and conflict-affected settings, not just Goal 16

One rule of thumb will be that Goal 16 cannot be addressed as a standalone goal, but progress on the other goals will all have relevance to one degree or another to establishing peace, justice and appropriate governance. While Goal 16 rightfully brings attention to governance, justice and peace, it is the inclusion of the other MDGs into a holistic implementation plan, which will ultimately drive sustainable change. In the footsteps of their MDG predecessors, the SDGs have renewed and diversified a number of goals including economic development, environmental sustainability and health, all of which are key requirements in fragile and conflict-affected contexts. Thus, cross-sectoral cooperation and the establishment of mechanisms for knowledge sharing and analysis should be incorporated as key elements in country implementation plans.

Implementation matters

The SDGs could be used to address the issues of conflict and fragility by placing special emphasis on the means and methods of their implementation, not simply the measurement of what has been achieved. Building the capability of institutions to perform key functions will be a prerequisite to meeting many of the SDGs in a sustainable manner. Many critical targets enshrined in Goals 16 and 17, including justice, accountability and transparency, require carefully nuanced implementation plans built around the aspirations of local citizens and governments. In fragile and conflict-affected settings, these plans should be carefully developed to dovetail with existing policy and planning processes and take account of existing institutional capacity and potential. They must take into account stakeholder interests and, particularly, potential winners and losers from any reform efforts, as well as to the extent to which development-related grievances are driving the conflict. The successful implementation of such plans will require considerable flexibility to allow for adaptation and adoption at the local level. We propose the use of 'double compacts' and 'sovereignty strategies' as a vehicle for organising, sequencing and aligning domestic and external policy responses.

Reform assistance instruments

Currently, many aid programmes fall short of their intended goal. The first step is to reach an honest understanding of the extent of their limitations. Understanding the appropriate design, incentives and measurements for the type of assistance that will be productive is critical.

Align strategic objectives to the goal of self-reliance

Given the centrality of building the institutions and organisations from the country themselves, and establishing not only their ability to provide the services and rule of law environment for their own people, but also raising the revenues to pay for them, there is a strong case to be made that – except in extreme cases warranting an exception – development partnerships should be harnessed to creating self-reliance in institutional capacity as well as revenue generation capability that would see countries no longer needing vast amounts – or any amounts – of aid programmes.

Catalytic mechanisms to improve policy implementation

Given the scale and changing nature of today's challenges, the need for catalytic mechanisms to improve policy are paramount. Unprecedented levels of interconnectedness afforded by globalisation may create new opportunities for collaboration and partnerships, and break down barriers to knowledge sharing that had previously hindered the spread of ideas. There is not a shortage of capital, but rather of the right risk analysis, budget systems and programmes and investments to harness that capital in private and public investment opportunities. Cultivating the right environment for creative problem solving and innovative policy development will require support for strong institutions to champion these policies, as well as for citizens and civil society who support their implementation. Implementation of the SDG objectives by a large parallel aid system working outside and around the state is no longer an option.

Time frames matter

Experience from transitions and transformations in fragile state settings demonstrate that the timelines for development occur over periods of decades rather than years. Some objectives can be met within weeks or months, others take years, still others take decades. Building appropriately sequenced roadmaps where institutional development is sequenced over time is critical. Efforts at any point in time should be selective and integrated where possible, but not necessarily comprehensive at any one point in time.

Human capital investments must be made from the start

The citizen is not only the beneficiary, but also the producer of the services and value from which they will benefit. For too long, and encouraged by the MDGs, development policy in fragile states focused on primary education often at the expense of secondary, tertiary and vocational training. Establishing an appropriate roadmap to invest in the education and training of the citizens of the country concerned so that they can lead, manage, staff and support their own development processes is paramount. It is never too soon to start this process.

Notes

[1] The so-called middle-income fragile and failed states (MIFFs).

[2] United Nations, 'World Population Prospects: The 2012 Revision', https://esa.un.org/unpd/wpp/publications/Files/WPP2012_HIGHLIGHTS.pdf.

[3] United Nations, 'World Urbanization Prospects: the 2011 Revision', www.un.org/en/development/desa/population/publications/pdf/urbanization/WUP2011_Report.pdf.

[4] United Nations, 'World Urbanization Prospects: the 2011 Revision', www.un.org/en/development/desa/population/publications/pdf/urbanization/WUP2011_Report.pdf.

[5] In this chapter 'conflict' is used as short-hand for 'violent conflict'. We recognise that there is a difference. Fragility and conflict must also be distinguished. While conflict exists in all societies, fragility is characterised by the lack of effective channels for managing conflict peacefully (Ghani and Lockhart, 2008b).

[6] This list was produced by synthesising 'drivers' identified in a survey of literature on the subject (Ghani and Lockhart, 2008b).

References

Brinkman, H-J, 2013, *Think piece on the inclusion of goals, targets and indicators for peace and security and related areas into the post-2015 development framework*, Unpublished Draft, New York: UN Peacebuilding Support Office

Buss, TF, Gardner, A, 2006, *Why foreign aid to Haiti failed*, Washington DC: National Academy of Public Administration, www.napawash.org/wp-content/uploads/2006/06-04.pdf

Carnegie Commission on Preventing Deadly Conflict, 1998, *Preventing deadly conflict: Final report*, New York: Carnegie Corporation of New York

Chandy, L, Gertz, G, 2011, *Poverty in numbers: The changing state of global poverty from 2005 to 2015*, Washington, DC: Brookings Institution, www.brookings.edu/~/media/research/files/papers/2011/1/ global%20poverty%20chandy/01_global_poverty_chandy.pdf

Cincotta, RP, Engelman, R, Anastasion, D, 2003, *The security demographic: Population and civil conflict after the cold war*, Washington, DC: Population Action International

Collier, P, Elliott, L, Hegre, H, Hoeffler, A, Reynal-Querol, M, Sambanis, N, 2003, *Breaking the conflict trap: Civil war and development policy*, Washington, DC: World Bank and Oxford University Press

De Soto, H, 2001, *The mystery of capital: Why capitalism triumphs in the west and fails everywhere else*, London: Black Swan

Dhillon, N, Yousef, TM (eds), 2009, *Generation in waiting: The unfulfilled promise of young people in the Middle East*, Washington, DC: Brookings Institution Press

ECOSOC (United Nations Department for Economic and Social Affairs), 2011a, *World urbanization prospects: The 2011 revision*, New York: Population Division, United Nations, www.un.org/ en/development/desa/population/publications/pdf/urbanization/ WUP2011_Report.pdf

ECOSOC (United Nations Department for Economic and Social Affairs), 2011b, *MDG Gap Task Force Report 2011. The Global partnership for development: Time to deliver*, New York: Development Policy and Analysis Division, United Nations, www.un.org/en/development/ desa/policy/mdg_gap/mdg_gap2011/mdg8report2011_engw.pd

ECOSOC (United Nations Department for Economic and Social Affairs), 2012a, *World population prospects: The 2012 revision*, New York: Population Division, United Nations, https://esa.un.org/unpd/ wpp/publications/Files/WPP2012_HIGHLIGHTS.pdf.

ECOSOC (United Nations Department for Economic and Social Affairs), 2012b, *MDG Gap Task Force Report 2012. The global partnership for development: Making rhetoric a reality*, New York: Development Policy and Analysis Division, United Nations, www. un.org/en/development/desa/policy/mdg_gap/mdg_gap2012/ mdg8report2012_engw.pdf

Frot, E, Santiso, J, 2010, Crushed aid: Fragmentation in sectoral aid, *OECD Development Centre Working Paper* 284, Paris: OECD, www. oecd-ilibrary.org/docserver/download/5kmn0vt7p6hl.pdf?expires= 1376384470&id=id&accname=guest&checksum=120AED274EDB 5CCF0E836C9A311B0F58

Gertz, G, Chandy, L, 2011, *Two trends in global poverty*, Washington, DC: Brookings Institution, www.brookings.edu/~/media/research/files/opinions/2011/5/17%20global%20poverty%20trends%20chandy/0517_trends_global_poverty.pdf

Ghani, A, Lockhart, C, 2007, *Citizenship*, Washington, DC: Institute for State Effectiveness, http://effectivestates.org/wp-content/uploads/2015/09/Citizenship.pdf

Ghani, A, Lockhart, C, 2008a, *Fixing failed states: A framework for rebuilding a fractured world*, Oxford: Oxford University Press

Ghani, A, Lockhart, C, 2008b, *Development effectiveness in situations of fragility and conflict*, Washington, DC: Institute for State Effectiveness (ISE), http://effectivestates.org/wp-content/uploads/2015/09/Development-Effectiveness-in-Situations-of-Fragility-and-Conflict.pdf

Ghani, A, Lockhart, C, 2008c, *Haiti: Consolidating peace, security and development*, Washington, DC: Institute for State Effectiveness, http://effectivestates.org/wp-content/uploads/2015/09/Haiti-Consolidating-Peace-Security-and-Development.pdf

Ghani, A, Lockhart, C, Carnahan, M, 2006, An agenda for state-building in the twenty-first century, *The Fletcher Forum of World Affairs* 30, 1, 101–23

Ghani, A, Lockhart, C, Nehan, N, Massoud, B, 2007, The budget as the lynchpin of the state: Lessons from Afghanistan, in JK Boyce, M O'Donnell (eds) *Peace and the public purse: Economic policies for postwar statebuilding*, Boulder, CO: Lynne Rienner

IDPS (International Dialogue on Peacebuilding and Statebuilding), 2010, *Statement of the g7+*, Dili: IDPS, www.g7plus.org/en/resources/g7-statement-dili-10-april-2010

IDPS (International Dialogue on Peacebuilding and Statebuilding), 2011a, *The Monrovia roadmap on peacebuilding and statebuilding*, Monrovia: IDPS, www.icnl.org/research/library/files/Transnational/monrovia.pdf

IDPS (International Dialogue on Peacebuilding and Statebuilding), 2011b, *A new deal for engagement in fragile states*, Busan: IDPS, www.pbsbdialogue.org/media/filer_public/07/69/07692de0-3557-494e-918e-18df00e9ef73/the_new_deal.pdf

IDPS (International Dialogue on Peacebuilding and Statebuilding), 2012, *Working group on indicators: Progress report on fragility assessments and indicators*, IDPS, www.newdeal4peace.org/wp-content/uploads/2012/12/progress-report-on-fa-and-indicators-en.pdf

Kharas, H, Rogerson, A, 2012, *Horizon 2025: Creative destruction in the aid industry*, London: Overseas Development Institute (ODI), www.odi.org.uk/publications/6687-creative-destruction-aid-industry-development-kharas-rogerson

Likhi, A, 2013, Employment and participation in South Asia: Challenges for productive absorption, *People, spaces, deliberation*, Blog, Washington, DC: World Bank, http://blogs.worldbank.org/publicsphere/employment-and-participation-south-asia-challenges-productive-absorption

Lockhart, C, 2012, *New models for engagement in fragile states*, World Economic Forum Global Agenda Council on Fragile States Report, Switzerland: World Economic Forum

Manning, R, 2009, *Using development indicators to encourage development: Lessons from the Millennium Development Goals*, Copenhagen: Danish Institute for International Studies (DIIS)

North, DC, 1990, *Institutions, institutional change and economic performance*, Cambridge: Cambridge University Press

North, D, Wallis, JJ, Weingast, BR, 2009, *Violence and social orders: A conceptual framework for interpreting recorded human history*, Cambridge: University Press

O'Driscoll Jr, GP, Hoskins, L, 2003, *Property rights: The key to economic development*, Washington, DC: CATO Institute, http://object.cato.org/sites/cato.org/files/pubs/pdf/pa482.pdf

OECD (Organisation for Economic Co-operation and Development), 2011a, *Busan partnership for effective development co-operation*, Busan: 4th High Level Forum on Aid Effectiveness, OECD, www.oecd.org/dac/effectiveness/49650173.pdf

OECD (Organisation for Economic Co-operation and Development), 2011b, *International engagement in fragile states: Can't we do better?*, Paris: OECD, www.oecd.org/countries/somalia/48697077.pdf

OECD (Organisation for Economic Co-operation and Development), 2013a, *Ensuring fragile states are not left behind: 2013 factsheet on resource flows and trends*, Paris: OECD, www.oecd.org/dac/governance-peace/conflictfragilityandresilience/docs/factsheet%202013%20resource%20flows%20final.pdf

OECD (Organisation for Economic Co-operation and Development), 2013b, *Fragile states 2013: Resource flows and trends in a shifting world*, Paris: OECD, www.oecd.org/dac/governance-peace/conflictfragilityandresilience/docs/FragileStates2013.pdf

Radelet, SC, 2010, *Emerging Africa: How 17 countries are leading the way*, Washington, DC: Center for Global Development

Sumner, A, 2012, Where do the world's poor live? A new update, *Institute for Development Studies (IDS) Working Paper* 393, Sussex: IDS, www.ids.ac.uk/files/dmfile/Wp393.pdf

UN (United Nations), 2000, *United Nations millennium declaration*, General Assembly, New York: United Nations, www.un.org/millennium/declaration/ares552e.htm

UN (United Nations), 2004, *A more secure world: Our shared responsibility. Report of the Secretary-General's High-Level Panel on Threats, Challenges and Change*, New York: United Nations, www.un.org/en/peacebuilding/pdf/historical/hlp_more_secure_world.pdf

UN (United Nations), 2012, *Realizing the future we want for all: Report to the Secretary General*, System Task Team on the Post-2015 UN Development Agenda, New York: United Nations, www.un.org/millenniumgoals/pdf/Post_2015_UNTTreport.pdf

UNDP (United Nations Development Programme), 2008, *Making the law work for everyone: Vol 1 Report of the Commission on Legal Empowerment of the Poor*, New York: UNDP, www.undp.org/content/dam/aplaws/publication/en/publications/democratic-governance/legal-empowerment/reports-of-the-commission-on-legal-empowerment-of-the-poor/making-the-law-work-for-everyone--vol-ii--english-only/making_the_law_work_II.pdf

UNDP (United Nations Development Programme), 2010, *What will it take to achieve the Millennium Development Goals? An international assessment*, New York: UNDP, www.undp.org/content/undp/en/home/librarypage/mdg/international-assessment--english-full-version/

UNDP (United Nations Development Programme), 2013a, *Human Development Report 2013. The rise of the South: Human progress in diverse world*, New York: UNDP, http://hdr.undp.org/en/media/HDR_2013_EN_complete.pdf

UNDP (United Nations Development Programme), 2013b, *Call to save lives and protect investments from war and disasters*, Press Release, Helsinki: UNDP, www.undp.org/content/undp/en/home/presscenter/pressreleases/2013/03/13/future-peace-and-growth-depends-on-systems-and-institutions-that-save-lives-and-protect-investments-from-war-and-disasters/

Vandermoortele, J, 2011, A fresh look at the MDGs, *Journal of the Asia Pacific Economy* 16, 4, 520–8

World Bank, 2011, *World Development Report 2011: Conflict, security and development*, Washington DC: World Bank, http://siteresources.worldbank.org/INTWDRS/Resources/WDR2011_Full_Text.pdf

FOUR

The impact of the global financial crisis on Millennium Development Goal attainment in Africa

Leah McMillan Polonenko

Introduction

In 2009, UNESCO wrote 'the aftershock of the global economic and financial crisis in 2008–09 risks depriving millions of children in the world's poorest countries of an education…With 72 million children still out of school, a combination of slower economic growth, rising poverty and budget pressures could erode the education gains of the past decade' (UNESCO, 2009b). Although there were significant increases in enrolment, notably throughout Africa, the global community enters 2017 with the goal of universal primary education (UPE) – the second Millennium Development Goal (MDG 2) – still not being achieved. Despite gains in primary school enrolment from the time of drafting the MDGs until its finalising, UPE was not achieved. In studying the trends and focus of education, it is clear that the momentum gained in the education sector between the time of the Education for All (EFA) policy in 2000 and 2008, declined following 2008. This coincides with the global financial crisis. Although the crisis cannot be blamed in full for declining aid and stagnating enrolment rates, the proximity of these dates is telling. In the years immediately following the financial crisis, funding to education, particularly basic education, changed, resulting in decreased availability of funds. This chapter does not argue that the economic crisis is the sole reason that MDG 2 was not achieved by the end of 2015; however, this chapter seeks to highlight the significant role financial crises can play in achieving international goals. As the world now turns to achieving the Sustainable Development Goals (SDGs), it is important to reflect on lessons learned during the MDGs to attempt to overcome mistakes of the past. As the United Nations stated in its final MDG report in 2015, 'Despite enormous progress during the past 15 years, achieving UPE will required renewed attention in the post-2015 era' (UN, 2015, 28).

The 2008 global financial crisis set us with a very important caution to consider especially when creating future global initiatives like the MDGs: global initiatives are only as good as their global conditions. The global financial crisis did create very real consequences for the education sector, particularly through the reduction of adequate funding. This chapter first sets out to demonstrate and explain these consequences to education and how the financial crisis explains in part these ramifications. Second, the cases of primary education in Ghana and Zimbabwe will be presented, highlighting the need for a strengthening of both African and global governance mechanisms in order to mitigate the effects of this crisis, and future crises, as much as possible. With the global community now focused on the SDGs, there needs to be room to allow for shifts in the global financial system. This chapter ends by suggesting some best practices for learning from the failures to education from the 2008 agenda.

There were obvious gains in primary school enrolment owing to the MDGs – from 83 per cent net enrolment in 2000 to 91 per cent in 2015 (Guardian, 2015). Nonetheless, it is important that we are still critical of the fact that 59 million children are not in school; one-fifth of whom dropped out and two-fifths of whom do not have any access to a classroom (UN, 2017). The UN Convention on the Rights of the Child stipulates in article 28 that *all* children have the right to attend primary school. At the time of writing, the world is fixated on new and real threats – global security issues on account of rising terrorism, increased migration, the question of what both Brexit and a new American administration will mean for the world, and ongoing financial and political stability throughout continents. The recent appointing of UN Secretary General António Guterres and the launch of the SDGs signify that new policies, opportunities and challenges need to be presented. How do we create a world where UPE becomes a true reality? Examining the impacts of the 2008 financial crisis on the goal of UPE in sub-Saharan Africa can help to highlight important lessons as we forge ahead to achieve SDG Goal 4 – inclusive and quality education.

Limited resources, limited opportunities

The 2008 global financial crisis has frequently been compared to the Great Depression of the 1930s. To date, ramifications from the crisis continue to be felt around the globe. For Africa, particularly troubling has been the lack of safety nets to withstand immediate financial losses. With the absence of such safety measures in place, African countries experienced a rapid and immense decline of resources as a result of governments unable to provide social resources and economic opportunities for their citizens. Without adequate resources, the effects of the financial crisis trickled down to the poorest African citizens, in some cases reversing any gains made towards the achievement of the MDGs. According to a KPMG report, 'FDI into Africa peaked during 2008, then subsequently declined as a result of the global financial crisis' (KPMG, 2012, np).

By 2015, 20 per cent of children in sub-Saharan Africa were still not attending primary school (UN, 2015, 4). Although foreign direct investment has been rising in years following the financial crisis (for example, by 17 per cent in 2010), there was 'a 12.3 percent decline in 2009' (Nova Capital, 2011, 9). Most commentators attribute this rapid decline to the financial crisis. In the world of foreign investment, instability and decline, even in one year, can have damaging effects, especially in a sector like education where continuity is essential.

The consequences to Africa as a result of the crisis were, for the most part, indirect. As western governments and financial institutions are directly affected by the economic downturn, capital flow into Africa was reduced. Africa faced most of its significant resources losses due to declining foreign direct investment, reduced remittances, decreased developmental assistance, and limited opportunities for exportation to the world market. Although other countries were definitely affected (for example, the recurring problems in Ireland, Spain and Greece), the African continent has experienced extremely high vulnerability to economic collapse on account of the financial crisis.

Foreign aid

The Millennium Declaration assumed foreign aid as a major contributor to Goal achievements. Much of the discussion regarding the MDGs revolved around issues pertaining to the effectiveness, distribution and quantity of aid. It is widely understood that donors, non-governmental and governmental agencies alike, are needed to provide funding required to global goals, including the MDGs. In fact, global policies such as the Millennium Development Goals are largely written for the donor community. They provide a blueprint upon which NGOs, IGOs and bilateral development agencies base their aid policies. The discussion surrounding foreign aid and the impact of the global financial crisis thereon is paramount to this chapter; to limit funding is to limit what is to be the very backbone of the achievement of the Goals. Indeed, foreign aid forms such an important component to these global policies that such goals and declarations mention dollar amounts needed from the foreign community in order to meet the Goals. The official website for the Millennium Development Goals, for example, includes a recurring updated pronouncement outlining an exact figure of aid money necessary to reach the Goals. The EFA policy, a declaration that augments MDG 2 – UPE and MDG 3 – equity in education, relies on the donor community for its policy input. Aid is an important piece to meeting established global targets. It is thus essential that measures are set in place to ensure that the impact of financial crises on foreign aid can be mitigated; indeed, official development assistance declines between 20 and 40 per cent with financial crises (Tomlinson, 2010). On account of the current international development system that is centred on programmes, fiscal year ends and lending cycles, most governments earmark aid dollars in three to four year increments. Due to this reality, while foreign aid allotments were drying up following the 2008 crisis, often the impacts were not felt until later. An interview with a social programming representative from ICEIDA, the Icelandic International Development Agency, in Malawi in 2010 is a clear example of this situation. Iceland suffered gravely from the global financial crisis, resulting in a near-collapse of its entire banking system. In 2010, two years after the crisis and during very volatile times in Iceland, ICEIDA was still working on education in Malawi, but major budget cuts would ensue once current programming was finished (ICEIDA author field interview, April, 2010). One will note, however, that it is usually a few years following a global downturn that Africa experiences a similar downward change in their GDP performance (IMF, 2009c, 18). When budgets tightened, it has historically been social services that governments first cut. One need only to remember the affects of Structural Adjustment Programming of the 1980s and early 1990s on health and education to note the grave impact which declines in social service spending can have (Cornia et al, 1987). According to Geo-Jaja and Magnum, 'available data suggests that they [structural adjustment programmes] have accentuated the deterioration in human conditions and further compounded the already poor economic conditions' (Geo-Jaja and Magnum, 2001). Indeed, Hutchful notes that structural adjustment reversed any gains made in African development following performance, especially in the social sector given the massive budget cuts (Hutchful, 2002).

In the education sector, limiting resources has long-term effects. A whole generation can lack appropriate literacy and numeracy skills on account of being deprived of a solid basic education in the foundational years of their study. In sub-Saharan Africa education has historically not been a sector of focus, meaning that any small change to budgets can have large consequences since the education sector is already under-funded; sub-Saharan African governments allocate a very small amount of money for education (UNESCO, 2009b, 26). In 2004, sub-Saharan Africa had a 2 per cent expenditure on public education – greater than only Central Asia (0.3 per cent).[1]

MDG 2: Universal primary education

The right to a basic education was articulated in Article 26 of the Declaration of Human Rights and reinforced in Article 28 of the 1989 Convention on the Rights of the Child.

The MDGs 2 and 3 served to ensure that more children had access to basic education. Goal 2 specifically calls for UPE as an objective, whereas Goal 3 measures the achievement of gender equality by an equal number of boys and girls in the classroom. The 2015 Global Monitoring Report from EFA articulated that gender disparity in the primary school classroom continues. The report indicates that 'there still only 92 girls per 100 boys in primary school in the region' (EFA, 2015, 1), with Chad having the lowest enrolment of girls. The 1990 World Education Forum in Dakar established global benchmarks that would signify that 'education for all' was achieved worldwide. Indeed at the beginning of the new millennium, education was deemed not only essential to development, but a basic human right that could no longer be left undelivered to millions. Yet as the aftermath of the financial crisis looms, protectionist policies and lessening donor assistance have limited the ability for EFA-abiding countries to meet their commitments. In an April 2013 press release, UNESCO admonished the international donor community for reducing their aid commitments to education, thereby threatening any opportunity for UPE to be reached by 2015. There was great momentum built for attaining UPE following the Dakar Declaration of Education for All. Following 2002, the world saw unprecedented levels of aid allocated to education. Sadly, between 2010 and 2011, aid for education declined by 7 per cent, with aid to basic education declining by 6 per cent; there was a 7 per cent decline in education aid to sub-Saharan Africa in particular. Some countries felt these decreases more than others. Tanzania's aid allotment fell by 12 per cent between 2009 and 2010, and by an entire 57 per cent in 2011. Sadly, following the historical pattern of sector loss, funding to the education sector received the greatest reductions following the global financial crisis, with allotments of aid to education declining by 'over $1.3 billion since 2010' (UNESCO, 2014, 12).

Since the origination of EFA, Africa has made considerable growth in its primary school enrolment rates. The number of children in primary school rose between 1999 and 2005 by 29 million, or 36% (UNESCO, 2008, 42). Indeed, the great strides that Africa has achieved in its enrolment cannot be overlooked (UNECA and AU, 2014). Nonetheless, MDG 2 did not call for *more* basic education enrolment, it calls for *universal* basic education enrolment. Despite the unprecedented growth across the sub-continent, rises in enrolment stagnated in 2008, and continued to stagnate through to 2012; presently we know that 20 per cent of children in SSA remain out of school and that MDG 2 and 3 were not realised. Girl child education rolls into both this MDG and gender inequality. It has been noted that girls are among the most badly affected by the global financial crisis and its aftermath. With limited funds available, opportunities for governments to devise plans to better ensure that girls can meet educational objectives are scarce. UNICEF notes that 'sub-Saharan Africa has the lowest proportion of countries with gender parity: only two out of 35 countries' (UNICEF, 2015). As mentioned in the previous section, the education of women is of extreme importance for overall development. UNICEF argues that

> educated girls are likely to marry later and have fewer children, who in turn will be more likely to survive and be better nourished and educated. Educated girls are more productive in the home and better paid in the workplace, and more able to participate in social, economic and political decision-making. (UNICEF, 2008a, n.p.)

Indeed, equality of women beginning in the education system is paramount to achieving any global development goals and thus achieving poverty reduction and overall development.

Education: a necessary link to future development

Foreshadowing the current reality, the United Nations in 2009 described sub-Saharan Africa's prospect for achieving universal primary school enrolment by 2015 as 'low' – the only region to be given such a dire descriptor; it is described with 'progress insufficient to reach the target if prevailing trends persist' (MDG, 2009).

At that time, with almost 30 per cent of the African primary school-aged population out of school, achieving UPE in six years seemed highly unlikely. The magnitude of Africa's enrolment crisis is depicted by the number of countries that are in dire need of educational improvement; the majority of African countries rest below the 80 per cent enrolment line (MDG, 2009). Although the continent did not succeed in its objective, there are important lessons to consider as primary enrolment remains important for the SDGs (in addition to secondary which is now also highlighted as a major level of focus).

The decrease in education expenditure is particularly troubling given the inevitability that the sector places on future outputs. While all eight of the MDGs worked together to ensure that future poverty reduction strategies are enabled (much like the SDGs), education delivery quickly deteriorates when funding decreases. While, for example, a country's gender inequality could be temporarily stabilised, education must be maintained if gains made previously are to continue to be effective. In the same vein, health sectors quickly relapse if not maintained. Education is thus unique in that it necessitates continual support lest it depreciates in service delivery. That is, unlike the other MDGs, education either improves or deteriorates in functionality, but it cannot remain stable. Consequently, finances and delivery are correlated, such that they will always have a negative or positive outcome – but there will always be an outcome. If national budget expenditures in either of these two sectors are forced to decrease as a result of impacts from the financial crisis, the result will be a decline in quality of these areas. This decline will not only be felt in the present environment, but will be felt as a wave, degenerating the sectors for years to come.

When first Tanzanian President Julius Nyerere stated that 'Education is not a way to escape poverty – it is a way of fighting it' (quoted in UNESCO, 2001), he was recognising the incomparable impact education has on poverty reduction and development strategies. Undoubtedly, knowledge is power. But for that power to be maintained, the knowledge must be continued. Education has been conceptualised as being not only a right in itself, but a necessary precursor to the achievement of all other rights (Gauri, 2005). As a noteworthy agent of socialisation second only to that of the family, schools empower citizens to become effective members of their community, well-suited for a life of dignity in adult life (Tomasevski, 2003). Indeed, having a primary education is the foundation upon which children can ensure that they will grow into effective citizens with a job that enables them to have a decent standard of living in adulthood. In this way in particular, education is a primary means through which one can end a familial cycle of poverty. Education capacitates, empowers and gives opportunity for life amelioration. Consequently, the education sector has the unique characteristic of either improving or decreasing the environment for long-term poverty reduction and overall national development.

The case of Ghana

Ghana is an important country to study given its reputation for maintaining a stable and progressive economic environment. Known as a 'prize pupil' in the way in which it has accepted the reforms and policies of the international community, Ghana has maintained a positive reputation in the international community (Hutchful, 2002). To illustrate, the country received the 2008 Best Investment Climate in the Commonwealth Business Council African Business Awards (Ackah et al, 2009).

Current statistics for Ghana indicate a net primary school enrolment rate of 73 per cent (UNICEF, 2016). Despite lack of UPE, the government of Ghana has long been a supporter of basic education for all children. The 1961 Education Act made basic education free and compulsory throughout the country (UNESCO, 2011, 2). 'The PNDC Law No. 42 [of 1983] declared that "without the provision of basic education for our children to meet the challenges of this environment, we would only be turning them into misfits and denying ourselves the most essential resources for national development"' (UNESCO, 2011, 2). With the aid of the IMF, Ghana implemented a Structural Adjustment Programme, beginning in 1984 with the Economic Recovery Programme I. With strategies that included reducing social sector spending and privatisation of social services, by 1992 Ghana's education enrolment had been severely diminished. Consequently, the government worked towards establishing new programmes to ensure that enrolment increased. The Ghana Poverty Reduction Strategy (GPRSP) initiated the Education Service Programme – a 2003–15 initiative providing a strategy that sought to ensure that the second MDG is achieved by 2015 (Adamu-Issah et al, 2007).

Nationally, Ghana launched the Free Compulsory Basic Education (FCUBE) programme in light of its obligations to meeting MDG 2 (and indeed the EFA policy which it signed in 1992). FCUBE worked towards better ensuring that education is adequately decentralised such that local municipalities ('District Assemblies') have the knowledge and tools necessary to provide quality education for its citizenry. Further, FCUBE worked towards implementing a cost sharing and recovery programme that would absorb the costs of fees that have hindered parents from sending their children to school in the past, including tuition, textbooks and uniforms. Ghana's good record in promoting and implementing EFA policies, in addition to its need for better funding, has resulted in the government qualifying for the EFA's Fast Track Initiative. The Fast Track Initiative was intended to increase funding to the neediest countries to better ensure that UPE would be achieved by the target year, 2015. UNESCO endorses education, acknowledging the sector as 'a development imperative', according to its Director-General, Koichiro Matsuura (Matsuura, 2009).

Over the past decade, the government of Ghana has worked diligently to improve its socio-economic status, implementing numerous policies and strategies to encourage growth. Between 2003 and 2007, Ghana's GDP grew on average 5.9 per cent per annum, demonstrating success of government strategies. Despite recent success, the financial and food crises combined to create a significant decline in Ghana's economic growth rate in future years. Inflation was 18.1 per cent in December 2008 (Ackah et al, 2009). Ghana's macro-economic stability is being eroded, with capital flows deteriorating rapidly, especially in the important timber and shea butter industries. 'Timber exports declined by 27 per cent and remittances by 16 per cent in January–February 2009, compared to the same months in 2008', according to the World Food Programme (WFP, 2009). In 2008, the exchange rate lost 23 per cent of its value against the US dollar (WFP, 2009).

Despite considerable policy efforts to boost primary school enrolment, Ghana's net primary enrolment sat at 73 per cent in 2008, a mere 2 per cent increase from 2007 levels. Previous to this, enrolment had risen from 55 per cent in 1999 to 64 per cent in 2006, indicating a substantial improvement in the education system (UNESCO, 2016). While considerable improvement over the last decade has been imminent, most troubling is the fact that these improvements have reflected substantial funding from the international community and economic growth rate within the government. The stagnation in enrolment in more recent years reflects a decline in funding to the education sector across the continent. The government of Ghana's ability to improve its education so significantly, particularly since 2006, is a result of massive financial contributions from the donor community. While Ghana has made improvements to its education system over the past decade, declining financial investment to the sector is risking a reversal of these gains. This reality increases economic shocks in

Ghana where 50 per cent of the development budget and 12 per cent of gross national income comes from official development assistance. The GPRSP estimated a US$1.79 billion funding gap necessitating external aid (IMF, 2006, 75). The government of Ghana has premised its poverty reduction strategy on the assumption that donor support will be adequate to finance the majority of these policies. Yet with funding declining, momentum has been lost.

Although the recent discovery of off-shore oil has boosted the country's economic performance, this has largely been felt in Accra and Sekondi-Takoradi, the latter being the geographical location of the oil mines. In recent years, Ghana has substantially increased its trade internationally. While these efforts have contributed to the praise the country has received for its international engagement, it is presently making the country's economic situation more volatile in light of the financial crisis. Reflecting on this, the World Bank described Ghana as being 'highly exposed' to the crisis (World Bank, 2009a).

High numbers of children involved in labour accounts for over one-third of school-aged children not entering a classroom in the northern most areas of the country (de Lange, 2007, 37). De Lange analyses that it is not ignorance that keeps parents from sending their children to school, rather economic realities (de Lange, 2007).

The most recent UNICEF statistics for Ghana indicate that the country has a 73 per cent net primary school enrolment rate (UNICEF, 2016). This fact is particularly disheartening given that the country experienced such momentum and had been making great strides toward improving its enrolment rates. The decline in funding to the education sector explains the changes to enrolment growth. Although the global financial crisis cannot be blamed entirely for a decline to Ghana's education enrolment rates, it is reasonable to conclude that the decline in funding was a direct result of economic vulnerability worldwide. The case of Ghana illustrates that future global initiatives should consider ways to account for the drying up of funding.

The case of Zimbabwe

Zimbabwe's education system was once praised as the most successful in Africa. Following independence in 1980, President Robert Mugabe made a commitment to compulsory UPE, including the complete removal of tuition fees, as outlined in the 1979 Education Act (UNICEF, 2008b). The government of Zimbabwe did not sustained the climate of optimism it once held. In the mid-1990s, under the leadership of Robert Mugabe, Zimbabwe's economy took a turn for the worse, forcing decreased budgets for social services which, in turn, deteriorated rapidly. The education system in particular has gone from a triumphed system to one described as in 'crisis'. A combination of low teacher salaries, poor attendance, school abandonment and closures, a lack of transportation and food shortages, have led to a crisis of enrolment that is worrying to the international development community and Zimbabweans alike. Moreover, the once free primary school policy has been replaced by a cost-recovery mechanism that charges tuition based on an assessment of a student's socio-economic background. The system is arbitrary and has resulted in tuition increases for all children, regardless of household income.

There was some optimism towards the end of last decade, with net enrolment reaching 91 per cent in 2009. Sadly, these rates are beginning to decline once again – by 2011, net enrolment had reduced to 87 per cent (UNZ and Government of Zimbabwe, 2012, 8). Enrolment rates are also higher in rural areas than urban areas: in 2011, NER was 84.1 per cent in rural areas, but 73.4 per cent in urban areas demonstrating a potential need for more location-specific programming. Zimbabwean girls are more likely to go to school than boys – with a 85:80 percentage ratio throughout the country (UNZ and Government of Zimbabwe, 2012, 26). The UNDP attributes this to a country-wide programme to 'sensitise parents throughout the country on the need to educate girls' (UNZ and Government of Zimbabwe, 2012, 26). Recently, the country has also been implementing programmes that specifically target vulnerable groups, particularly orphaned and vulnerable children and primary school drop-outs (UNZ and Government of Zimbabwe, 2012, 27). However, these efforts have been met with severe funding shortages, such that more than half of all children qualifying for the BEAM (Basic Education Assistance Module) programme, for example, remain unreached (UNZ and Government of Zimbabwe, 2012, 28). There is a significant lack of funding required to improve the country's education system. At present, most of the budget for education is allocated to paying teacher salaries, leaving a severely inadequate amount for learning tools and classroom facilities. The UNDP notes that 'school fees, coupled with other educational costs such as travel, exam fees and levies for various school programmes, pose challenges for many parents' (UNZ and Government of Zimbabwe, 2012, 28). Moreover, teacher salaries, the one area that *is* being paid, are still perceived as inadequate.

Zimbabwe's education crisis is influenced greatly by the declining standard of living in the country. It is understood that 'rising poverty and hunger, particularly in rural areas and disadvantaged communities, have contributed to declining school enrolment, erratic attendance, and a high dropout rate' (Moyo and Besada, 2008, 9). Health issues are included in this assessment: 1.4 million Zimbabweans, or almost 1/5 of the population, are living with HIV/AIDS, contributing to 524,000 Zimbabwean children who are orphans (Avert, 2016). These children are at a severe disadvantaged when it comes to accessing education: some need to stay home to take care of their parents and/or other siblings; many are not able to afford the direct and indirect costs of schooling. While the gravity of the food crisis can be studied on its own terms, the propelling of the food crisis by the financial crisis, the former preceding the latter, is indicative of a reinforced relationship between the two crises. For Zimbabwean society, these two crises have worked together to help spawn declining enrolment rates throughout the country. Indeed it is 'financial constraints' that remains one of the greatest barriers to the achievement of quality education in the country (UNZ and Government of Zimbabwe, 2012, 8).

Between January and April 2007, approximately 4,500 teachers resigned because of inadequate wages. Other teachers demonstrating by striking, hoping to pressure the government to give teachers a more adequate salary. During the striking period, 94 per cent of rural schools were closed, while school attendance dropped to 20 per cent of the population at the end of 2008 (whereas it rested at 80 per cent at the beginning of that same year). Passing rates for grade 7 exams has dropped to 33 per cent in 2007; almost half of primary school graduates do not proceed to secondary school (Education International, 2009).[2]

The global community has been quite vocal about its lack of support for President Mugabe. In 2000, for example, the World Bank stopped all loans going to the country as a form of sanction against the government. That said, even if the political and economic climates improve, if the education system continues to deteriorate in the process, any remedies will be lacking a new generation of educated Zimbabweans necessary for sustainability.

In many ways, Ghana and Zimbabwe are complete opposites. Ghana has maintained a positive scorecard internationally, securing a reputation as a peaceful and stable climate with a stable market. In contrast, Zimbabwe's economy has been deteriorating under the highly contested leadership of President Mugabe. Despite these large differences, both Ghanaian and Zimbabwean children have a guaranteed right to an education, as mandated within the 1989 Convention on the Rights of the Child. In both countries, declining funding has resulted in declining or stagnating enrolment rates. These declines follow the pattern of rising enrolment until the 2008 financial crisis, signalling that this event played a factor in limited opportunities for growth through limited funding.

Conclusion

Nobel Peace Prize Winner and Kenyan activist turn politician Wangari Maathai's book *The Challenge for Africa* poignantly argues that Africa must find its own solutions for its own problems. While she in no way criticises the use of aid, she suggests that the best way for Africa to emerge from her poverty trap is for the continent to look for ways out itself. At the February 2009 African Union summit, the global financial crisis served as sub-theme, acknowledging the organisation's commitment to ensuring that this crisis is resolved. At the November 2008 Conference of African Ministers of Finance and Planning and Governors of African Central Banks in Tunis, several recommendations were made to ensure that Africa emerge from the crisis with as little impact as possible. Many of these policy recommendations considered in-continental commitments of the essence. African leaders, and institutions such as the African Development Bank, were called upon for their key role in ensuring that the crisis is handled with the appropriate level of efficiency, effectiveness and African cooperation. More recently, the AU has been discussing plans for heightened integration and unification. Some argue that this plan is rehashing old arguments from the era of Nkrumah and his plans for Pan-Africanism that could potentially diminish state sovereignty. That said, in an era where global governance is becoming the norm, such regionalism might be inevitable. If not inevitable, it might prove to be the necessary element to make Africa a stronger force, better able to weather the tides of the financial storm.

Although there have been significant gains in enrolment across the continent since the Millennium Declaration, and particularly with the EFA policy aligning with the MDGs, we are still far from ensuring that all children attain a basic level of education. The global financial crisis cannot be blamed for this lack of achievement, but it certainly provides a piece to the puzzle. Funding to all sectors, particularly education, evidently declined following 2008. Donor governments needed to focus on domestic economic collapse; in a rationalist approach, governments focused inward, with developing countries losing out. But as with all problems, we have a significant opportunity to learn from the impact of the crisis on MDG 2. A major factor in the impact of the financial crisis was the heavy reliance on recurring funding. Developing governments budget for similar amounts of funding coming into their country. When ICEIDA limited its funding to Malawi, the results were more widely felt because it was assumed that certain communities would be funded by Iceland. A situation of decreased funding was never planned for. Perhaps in the post-2015 agenda this can change. Having measures where a certain amount of funding is stored in savings, for an emergency fund, could help to mitigate this problem. As always, striving for more sustainable, African-led practices will also lessen reliance on external sources. Although African solutions will not be achieved without the support of the international community, the external causes of Africa's challenges from the financial crisis signify the extent to which the continent relies on the international community for financial sustainability. Perhaps, then, this crisis is just the push necessary to allow African engagement to increase. If it is the global connectedness that has hindered African growth in this context, this might be an indication that African domestic policies need strengthening.

The climate of the recent American election and the outcome of the Brexit vote are both indicative of more protectionist ideals sweeping the globe. With the migration crisis only increasing, these sentiments will no doubt continue to flourish. However, for the new SDGs to be achieved, the global community still needs to work together to achieve their goals. Just as the goals are *written* together, they must also be *achieved* together. Historians frequently lament that we must look to the past to learn lessons for the future. The 2008 financial crisis demonstrates that international efforts must continue despite crises. Because education does not remain stagnant – it is either supported or it deteriorates. Either commitments made to achieving the SDGs are fulfilled...or we risk looking back in 2030 and questioning why another set of global development goals went yet again unrealised.

Notes

[1] That same year, North America and Western Europe were the greatest distributors at 55 per cent; Arab States were closest to SSA at 3 per cent (IMF, 2009b).

[2] See www.ei-ie.org/en/news/news_details/2420 for a similar story.

References

Ackah, CG, Bortei-Dorku Aryeetey, E, Aryeetey, E, 2009, Ghana, *Global Financial Crisis Discussion Series, Paper* 5, London: Overseas Development Institute

Adamu-Issah, M, Elden, L, Forson, M, Schrofer, T, 2007, Achieving universal primary education in Ghana by 2015: A reality or a dream?, *United Nations International Children's Emergency Fund (UNICEF) Division Policy and Planning Working Paper*, New York: UNICEF

Avert, 2016, *HIV and AIDS in Zimbabwe*, www.avert.org/professionals/hiv-around world/sub-saharan-africa/zimbabwe

Bhuiya, A, Wojtyniak, B, Rezaul, K, 1989, Malnutrition and child mortality: Are socioeconomic factors important?, *Journal of Biosocial Science* 21, 3, 357–64

Casely-Hayford, L, Lynch, P, 2003, *ICT based solutions for special education needs in Ghana*, London: Department for International Development

Cine, W, 2002, Financial crises and poverty in emerging market economies, *Working Paper* 8, June, Toronto: Centre for Global Development

Collier, P, 2008, The politics of hunger: How illusion and greed fan the food crisis. *Foreign Affairs* 87, 67–79

Cornia, AG, Jolly, R, Stewart, F, 1987, *Adjustment with a human face*, Oxford: Clarendon Press

De Lange, A, 2007, Ghana, in K Lieten, A de Groot, R van Wieren, A de Lange, and H Roschanski (eds) *Education in rural areas: Obstacles and relevance: main findings from seven country studies*, Amsterdam: International Research on Working Children, 33–42

Education International, 2009, *Zimbabwe: Teachers cancelled strike to show faith in government*, 7 May, https://www.ei-ie.org/en/news/news_details/1219

EFA (Education for All), 2015, Global Monitoring Report *No country in sub-Saharan Africa has achieved gender parity in both primary and secondary education*, Global Monitoring Report, Paris: United Nations Educational, Scientific and Cultural Organization (UNESCO) Press Releases, http://en.unesco.org/gem-report/sites/gem-report/files/SSA%20Press%20Release%20English%20Gender%20Report%202015_0.pdf

Gauri, V, 2005, Social right and economics: Claims to health care and education in developing countries, in P Alston, M Robinson (eds) *Human rights and development: Towards mutual reinforcement*, Oxford: Oxford University Press

Geo-Jaja, MA, Mangum, G, 2001, Structural adjustment as an inadvertent enemy of human development in Africa, *Journal of Black Studies* 32, 1, 30–49

Ghana NGO Coalition on the Rights of the Child, 2005, *The Ghana NGO report to the UN Committee on the Rights of the Child on implementation of the convention of the rights of the child by the Republic of Ghana*, New York: UNICEF, www.crin.org/docs/Ghana_GNCRC_ngo_report.doc

Ghazvinian, J, 2007, *Untapped: The scramble for Africa's oil*, Orlando, FL: Harcourt

Guardian, 2015, What have the millennium development goals achieved?, Datablog, *Guardian*, www.theguardian.com/global-development/datablog/2015/jul/06/what-millenniumdevelopment-goals-achieved-mdgs

Hutchful, E, 2002, *Ghana's adjustment experience: The paradox of reform*, James Curry: Oxford

ILO (International Labour Organization), 2009, *Global employment trends for women*, March, Geneva: ILO

IMF (International Monetary Fund), 2006, Ghana: Poverty reduction strategy paper, *IMF Country Report 6*, June, Washington, DC: IMF

IMF (International Monetary Fund), 2009a, Ghana: Poverty reduction strategy paper, *IMF Country Report 09/237*, Washington, DC: IMF

IMF (International Monetary Fund), 2009b, *The global financial crisis and its impact on developing countries: IMF global monitoring report*, Washington, DC: IMF

IMF (International Monetary Fund), 2009c, *The implications of the global financial crisis for low-income countries*, March, Washington, DC: IMF

Kielland, A, Tovo, M, 2006, *Children at work: Child labor practices in Africa*, Boulder, CO: Lynne Rienner

KPMG, 2012, Foreign direct investment in Africa, 1 June, http://www.blog.kpmgafrica.com/foreign-direct-investment-in-africa-2/

Lietan, K, 2007, Education in rural areas: Obstacles and relevance, *International Research on Working Children*, Amsterdam: International Research on the Exploitation of Working Children (IREWOC)

Littlefield, E, Kneiding, C, 2009, The global financial crisis and its impact on microfinance, *CGAP Focus Note 52*, February, Washington, DC: Consultative Group to Assist the Poor (CGAP)

McKinley, T, Khurasse, N, 2009, Global financial crisis and recession: What could happen to major emerging economies?, *Development Viewpoint 26*, March, London: Centre for Development Policy and Research, School of Oriental and African Studies (SOAS)

Maathai, W, 2009, *The challenge for Africa*, New York: Pantheon Books

Matsuura, K, 2009, Address by Mr Koichiro Matsuura on the occasion of the opening ceremony of the centenary celebration of King's College, 7 January, Lagos: United Nations Educational, Scientific and Cultural Organization (UNESCO)

MDG (Millennium Development Goals), 2009, *Millennium Development Goals: Progress chart*, http://mdgs.un.org/unsd/mdg/Resources/Static/Products/Progress2009/MDG_Report_2009_Progress_hart_En.pdf

Moyo, N, Besada, HG, 2008, Zimbabwe in crisis: Mugabe's policies and failures, *SSRN Electronic Journal*, www.researchgate.net/publication/228304672_Zimbabwe_in_Crisis_Mugabe's_Policies_and_Failures.zimba

Naude, W, 2009, The financial crisis of 2008 and the developing countries, *UNU-WIDER Discussion Paper* 2009/01, Helsinki: UNU-WIDER

Nova Capital, 2011, *Africa: After the global financial crisis*, New York: Nova Capital Partners, www.novacapitalpartners.com/marketcommentary/Nova%20Markets%20Commentary%20-%20Africa%202011.pdf

ODI (Overseas Development Institute), 2009, *A development charter for the G-20*, March, London: ODI

Oxfam, 2006, Causing hunger: An overview of the food crisis in Africa, *Oxfam Briefing Paper* 91, 6 July, Oxford: Oxfam International

Painceira, JP, 2008, *The role of developing-country reserve accumulation in the current financial crisis*, London: School of Oriental and African Studies (SOAS)

Ravallion, M, 2008, Bailing Out the World's Poorest, *Policy Research Working Paper* 4763, Washington, DC: Director's Office, World Bank Development Research Group

Schell, CO, Reilly, M, Rosling, H, Peterson, S, Ekstrom, AM, 2007, Socioeconomic determinants of infant mortality: A worldwide study of 152 low-, middle-, and high-income countries, *Scandinavian Journal of Public Health* 35, 3, 288–97

Tadesse, H, 2008, Food crisis in Africa: Go beyond emergency food aid and supply responses, said ECA Head Janneh, *Economic Commission for Africa Knowledge Sharing*, Addis Ababa: United Nations Economic commission for Africa (UNECA)

Tomasevski, K, 2003, *Education denied: Costs and remedies*, London: Zed Books

Tomlinson, Brian, 2010, *Crisis management: An analysis of global aid trends*, realityofaid.org, www.realityofaid.org/wp-content/uploads/2013/02/Chapter-4.pdf.

UN (United Nations), 2015, *The millennium development goals report 2015*, New York: United Nations

UN (United Nations), 2017, *Sustainable development: Knowledge platform*, https://sustainabledevelopment.un.org/sdg4

UNCTAD (United Nations Conference on Trade and Development), 2013, Foreign direct investment to Africa increases, defying global trend for 2012, United Nations Conference on Trade and Development: Press Release, 26 June, Geneva: UNCTAD

UNECA (United Nations Economic commission for Africa), 2009, *Harnessing information for development*, Addis Ababa: United Nations Economic commission for Africa (UNECA)

UNECA (United Nations Economic commission for Africa), AU (African Union), 2014, *Report on progress in achieving the Millennium Development Goals in Africa*, www.undp.org/content/dam/rba/docs/Reports/MDG_Africa_Report_2014_ENG.pdf

UNESCO (United Nations Educational, Scientific and Cultural Organization), 2001, Notes from International Workshop on Education and Poverty Eradication, Uganda, 30 July to 3 August, www.unesco.org/education/poverty/news.shtml

UNESCO (United Nations Educational, Scientific and Cultural Organization), 2008, *EFA Global Monitoring Report*, UNESCO, http://www.unesco.org/education/gmr2008/chapter2.pdf

UNESCO (United Nations Educational, Scientific and Cultural Organization), 2009a, EFA Global monitoring report. Overcoming inequality: Why governance matters, *Summary*, Paris: UNESCO Publishing

UNESCO (United Nations Educational, Scientific and Cultural Organization), 2009b, The global economic and financial crisis and its effects on education, *UNESCO Executive Board*, 181th Session, 6 April, Item 57 of provisional agenda, Paris: UNESCO.

UNESCO (United Nations Educational, Scientific and Cultural Organization), 2011, *World data on education: Ghana*, VII Ed, 2010/2011, Geneva: UNESCO, www.ibe.unesco.org/fileadmin/user_upload/Publications/WDE/2010/pdf-versions/Ghana.pdf

UNESCO (United Nations Educational, Scientific and Cultural Organization), 2014, *Education For All Global Monitoring Report – Policy Paper 13*, UNESCO, http://unesdoc.unesco.org/images/0022/002280/228057E.pdf

UNESCO (United Nations Educational, Scientific and Cultural Organization), 2016, *Ghana*, Institute for Statistics, http://en.unesco.org/countries/ghana

UNICEF (United Nations International Children's Emergency Fund), 2005, CRC Consideration of reports submitted by states parties under Article 44 of the Convention, *Ghana*, CRC/C/65/Add.34, 14 July, New York: UNICEF

UNICEF (United Nations International Children's Emergency Fund), 2008a, Millennium Development Goal 2: Achieve Universal Primary Education, www.unicef.org/mdg/education.html

UNICEF (United Nations International Children's Emergency Fund), 2008b, Zimbabwe education system in a state of emergency, Donn Bobb, United Nations Radio, www.unicef.org/media/media_45950.html

UNICEF (United Nations International Children's Emergency Fund), 2015, *Girls' education and gender equality,* www.unicef.org/education/bege_70640.html.

UNICEF (United Nations International Children's Emergency Fund), 2016, *Ghana's key development indicators,* www.unicef.org/ghana/resources_7600.html

UNZ (United Nations Zimbabwe), Government of Zimbabwe, 2012, *Zimbabwe 2012: Millennium Development Goals progress report,* Harare: Government of Zimbabwe

WFP (World Food Programme), 2009, Impact of the financial crisis on vulnerable households, *Executive brief: Ghana,* 26 May, New York: WFP Office

WHO (World Health Organization), 2009a, The financial crisis and global health: Report of a high-level consultation, *Prepared by WHO Secretariat,* 19 January, Geneva: WHO

WHO (World Health Organization), 2009b, The financial crisis and global health, *Information Note 2009/1/January 21,* Geneva: WHO

Willem te Velde, D, 2008, The global financial crisis and developing countries, *Overseas Development Institute (ODA) Background Note,* October, London: ODI

World Bank, 2007, At the crossroads: Choices for secondary education and training in sub-Saharan Africa, *Secondary Education in Africa: Synthesis,* Washington, DC: Africa Human Development Department, World Bank

World Bank, 2009a, *Ghana: Overview,* Washington, DC: World Bank Group, www.worldbank.org/en/country/ghana/overview

World Bank, 2009b, *Millennium Development Goals,* www.developmentgoals.org

World Bank, 2009c, The global economic crisis: Assessing vulnerability with a poverty lens, *World Bank vulnerable countries brief,* http://siteresources.worldbank.org/NEWS/Resources/WBGVulnerableCountriesBrief.pdf

Resource geographies in urban spaces: insights from developing countries in the post-2015 era

Cristina D'Alessandro

Introduction

The Sustainable Development Goals (SDGs) have made explicit and formal a growing trend and focus of the international community, academic scholarship and practitioners on the ground towards urban sustainability. 'Urban sustainable development' has been recognised as a complex issue with a variety of components, including: urban biodiversity and ecology; urban fresh water and food security; urban clean energy; urban climate change adaptation and resilience; and green infrastructure. Sustainable cities must be renewable, green, clean, smart and ecologically friendly, but also livable and enjoyable, esthetically and architecturally nice, socially inclusive, and so on.

Is this a realistic view? Isn't this more of a utopia, similar to what medieval writers used to do, imagining ideal and perfect cities? This idyllic scenario is impossible to achieve in a swiftly changing global system where cities are home to contradictory forces and groups that showcase diverse views on the role and goals of urban spaces, and where conflicts and terrorism may abruptly disrupt the system and its structure at any moment. This statement is even more accurate for developing and emerging countries, where a number of capacity gaps make urban sustainability a chimera on top of everyday problems and tragedies. Given these intrinsic difficulties, this chapter investigates sustainable urban resource governance in developing contexts without any regional focus or concentration on a specific resource. The chapter uses a theoretical and methodological geographical approach (meaning it focuses on spaces and spatial dynamics) to offer policy guidance on the implementation of urban sustainability within the context of the post-2015 global agenda and the SDGs.

To this extent, after this introduction, the second part is devoted to urban sustainability, explaining how the operationalisation of definitions would be difficult. The third section of the chapter gives the required definitions, focusing on the urbanisation and metropolisation processes and explaining how 'resources' are defined in this chapter. The fourth part presents theoretical and methodological approaches from resource geography, adapting them to urban environments. The fifth section presents examples and insights of cities in developing contexts to underline what is actually done and the role resources have in these processes. In the conclusion, observations and policy recommendations are proposed. If sustainability cannot be achieved, its framework can be used to foster positive and realistic change, which is exactly what the chapter wishes to explore, while focusing on metropolises and capital cities.

Investigating sustainability in urban contexts

While the implementation of the post-2015 global development agenda and the SDGs only started in January 2016, the concept of urban sustainable development goes back to the beginning of the 1990s. According to the first basic definition, a sustainable city is one 'where achievements in social, economic and physical development are made to last' (UN, 2013, 61). This definition was certainly too general and neglected the various aspects that have been pointed out since then, among which two dimensions deserve particular attention:

1. the interaction with the hinterland and with other (urban and rural) spaces, including in terms of risk transfer;
2. the crucial role of urban residents and users (tourists, migrants, workers, and so on) in support or against sustainability and the fact that sustainable cities should meet their development needs through sustainable demands on local natural resources.

Since then, the complexity of urban sustainable development has been progressively investigated, highlighting gaps, needs, additional dimensions and issues. The main characteristics of a sustainable city can be summarised as:

- attractive and livable
- climate neutral and adapted
- integrative and collaborative
- resource-saving

- eco-friendly and responsible
- clean and recycling
- resilient
- healthy
- innovative and smart

Since the 2010s, the preparatory work for the SDGs has been a major turning point, allowing the inclusion of governance, comprising peace and security issues, in the urban sustainability framework. 'Urban governance entails the fostering of urban planning and environmental management, which includes the reduction of ecological footprints, and the decentralisation of decision-making, and resource-allocation, as well as enhanced policy coordination between local and national authorities' (UN, 2013, 62). Urban governance is therefore a multi-scalar issue,[1] requiring coordination between the various levels. Fiorino (2014) also emphasises this important point, noting that his research on cities in the United States has shown that the urban level of governance is more proactive and effective when it comes to sustainability, while the national level is slower.

Sustainable cities require having already in place or creating informed networked multi-stakeholder governance structures. In order to do this, networking technologies can help to facilitate the process with big data analytical techniques, geographic information systems, and continuously updated and adjusted information, in line with rapidly changing realities and needs. This supports, at least in principle, informed decision-making and better service delivery to residents. These urban spaces using innovation to foster sustainability are called 'smart, sustainable cities'[2] in the literature (Ericsson, 2016). All the major cities implementing and testing smart cities technologies around the world are western cities, with Europe as a leading continent in this regard.

Resilience is also a fundamental trait of urban sustainability. It is not limited to the capacity to prevent and defend from natural risks and disasters, but it includes the aptitude to manage emergency situations, as normal statuses. Resilience encompasses natural events and social struggles and changes. The notion of resilience is therefore cultural and raises the question of the purposes of cities and of their inhabitants, knowing that views on these issues are contradictory and conflictual (Watson, 2014). Many initiatives have been launched by various institutions to make cities more resilient (such as the 100 Resilient Cities project, the Making Cities Resilient programme, and the World Bank resilient cities programme). Resilience is necessary for a city to be sustainable, as durability requires adaptive capacities to maintain the focus on environmental protection despite continuous and radical changes intervening over time.

In fact, the environmental dimension is key in the definition and operationalisation of sustainable cities. To emphasise this component some use the term 'eco-cities', but their definition is not unanimously accepted and varies according to the contexts and authors. In general, a reference to ecological requirements is the bottom line, mixed with socio-economic conditions, to which can be added an attention towards health concerns. An eco-city is 'a human settlement that enables its residents to live a good quality of life while using minimal natural resources' (Kheng Lian et al, 2010, 85).

Resource-efficiency is also a critical factor of urban sustainability, but it is an aspect underestimated in the literature that cannot be reduced to energy-efficiency. IN addition, resource-efficiency is often interpreted as referring to financial resources, while it is used in this chapter to include every resource (natural and more generally spatial, as defined below). In the United Nations Environment Programme (UNEP)'s report *Sustainable resource efficient cities – Making it happen!* (UNEP, 2012), infrastructure, logistics, spatial planning, design, technology and coordination across sectors are identified as key areas for making cities resource-efficient. Only global resources are considered in the publication, as their scarcity and constraints affect urban spaces, but local resources, at the urban level are not specifically considered. This is the focus that this chapter will propose.

Urban spaces and sustainability

Given the major characteristics of sustainable cities highlighted above, Allen (2009) wonders if the attention should be shifted from sustainable *cities* to sustainable *urbanisation*, explaining that: 'the apparent consensus on the urgent need to promote sustainable cities has been underlined by significant differences with regards to the questions of what sustainability means, why and how to promote it and for whose benefit' (Allen, 2009, 2). The process of setting in place measures aimed at sustainability is in fact more realistic than the expectation of a final result meeting the initial expectations. Furthermore, the quote emphasises that the situation obtained with the implementation of projects and programmes tuned to sustainability is differently interpreted and perceived, and in the end is beneficial for different stakeholders and social groups in the same city. It is therefore more effective to work at orienting urban transformation towards sustainable principles, discussed and negotiated with inhabitants and users, to set them in the most inclusive and equalitarian way possible, and done compatibly with the existing challenges and limitations.

This approach can be interpreted as a geographical approach adapted and imported from grounded theories (Kempster and Parry, 2011) and critical realism, or GeoRealism (Mäki and Oinas, 2004). A theory or an action is considered grounded and/or realistic here as they are in line with and inspired by what is observed on the ground. Local spaces, within the multiscalar and complex meaning of 'local' in a global and swiftly changing world, have to be at the origin and a proof of what is developed in theory or by methodological approaches. Local spaces are key revealing spaces for geographers willing to reconcile theory with practice (intended as policy research). To this extent, when it comes to sustainability, the concept must be grounded into the specific limitations of real spaces, as well as into the imaginaries and wishes of inhabitants and users, related to the future they want to support for a given space. 'Local' is here relative to the most appropriate scale for a given reality grounded into a definite space.

This is a way to avoid considering sustainable development as an oxymoron that may be interpreted in multiple ways, paralysing its implementation. In fact, 'there is currently no city that has been able to fully adopt the concept of sustainable development. The problematic to tackle problems from a holistic perspective is undermined by factors related to growth' (Lundqvist, 2007, 29). Other limitations must be added to urban growth and sprawl, but they are contingent and dependent on specific situations. They can include in developing contexts: leadership concerns, lack of public participation, insufficient political will, technological and capacity gaps, widespread poverty and spatial inequalities. Despite all this, using the example of Curitiba, Brazil, Lundqvist emphasises that: 'it is possible for a third world city to improve urban planning with limited means' (Lundqvist, 2007, 29). The chapter explains that, even if the city is not sustainable, it is important that the situation has been improved. This is maybe a more realistic and grounded view of sustainability: to improve a given situation with focused interventions towards sustainability standards. Projects and programmes could therefore try to make cities *more* sustainable or to build *more* sustainable urban spaces, instead of attempting to realise utopian views, even more impossible in developing contexts. The suggestion made here is also a way to link up theory and practice into real spaces in developing contexts, without trying to attain what is impossible. This attempt is in line with good fit (or good enough) governance approaches (Hanson et al, 2014; Grindle, 2007), furthermore when it comes to natural resource governance: specific contexts call for peculiar interventions and measures, adapted to the context, scale and time in which it takes place. This equally applies to urban realities.

In fact, urban spaces are becoming complex and multi-faceted, with a variety of great differences and sometimes-contradictory realities, difficult to summarise in global and unique definitions. Definitions of a city point out criteria of 'density' (including intensity of social interaction) and 'diversity', but underlining its complexity and multidimensional character (Lévy and Lussault, 2013, 1078–84); they are also critical nodes of economic, political, cultural and other networks (Massey et al, 1999). Urban flows are also related to these networks. Nevertheless, in the developing as well as in the developed world and in emerging economies, unequally dense cities are nowadays the most common scenario. The lack and loss of urban density, until recently considered as a typical characteristic of African metropolises, is currently also recognised as a feature of the western and most global cities, such as Tokyo (Smith, 2012). The *World cities report 2016* analyses the loss of density in urban areas and correlates them with urban growth and sprawl (UN-Habitat, 2016).

Urban spaces unequally dense and vertical, incontestably growing also make peri-urban areas more complex and moving. Urban–rural boundaries get blurred, especially in developing countries. All this contributes to urban problems common to most of the developing world, but also to some extent present in the rest of the world: the quality of infrastructure and service delivery, environmental and climate change concerns, social and spatial inequalities, security and safety. The widening use of the expression 'human settlements' by UN-Habitat, the OECD and others, replacing 'cities' underlines the variety and heterogeneity of urban forms (UN-Habitat, 2013). It is consequently more appropriate to refer to the 'urbanisation' and 'metropolisation' processes, emphasising the dynamics and focusing on what is changed or wants to be transformed, instead of aiming to describe and understand the numerous and different results of these urban developments. If in fact urbanisation is an ongoing process since the industrial revolution, metropolisation is a more recent phenomenon, related to globalisation and to its networked realities. It is based on connectivity (henceforth more important than proximity) and functional changes. Metropolisation recomposes urban morphology in a discontinuous way, with new and different disadvantaged spaces, as well as new centres even in peripheral locations, producing fragmented urban spaces, contesting previous distribution models of inhabitants and activities.[3] Urban spaces, independently from their size, importance and location, are undergoing processes of metropolisation.

May metropolisation be as much as possible sustainable? Is this, furthermore, possible in developing countries? In some cases, as it happens in Concepcion, Chile, within the neoliberal globalised framework, environmental discourses, mystifying sustainable development during the metropolisation process do not help in reducing risks and do not make the city more sustainable (Aliste et al, 2013).

In developed countries, as in the case of Lausanne, Switzerland, metropolisation is accompanied by urban sprawl and fragmentation, and environmental concerns related to the use of resources, especially increased use of agricultural land, more energy consumption, and air pollution. It is noted that overall, the quality of life for residents decreases (Bochet, 2005). All these problems may also be found in developing contexts, although their degree varies, being more dramatic than in the so-called developed countries. The 'new urbanism' theories suggest that metropolisation processes that produce cities with multiple and diversified centres, linked by efficient public transportation systems, are more suitable (Shearmur, 2003). This means that more sustainable cities are made through a metropolisation that conciliate in some way densification, diversity and mobility: this is more challenging in developing contexts.

Resources are key to a more sustainable metropolisation, especially in terms of avoiding an overreliance on fossil fuel. Cartwright (2015) gives interesting insights on the advantages offered by African cities in terms of setting in place urban transportation systems that do not increase greenhouse gas emissions, and that together with basic service delivery, produce poverty alleviation and early stages of green economies. This is what Cartwright calls leap-frogging by starting with efficient and affordable public transportation. It is what the city of Lagos, Nigeria, has done with the Bus Rapid Transit (BRT) system, along with a number of other African metropolises, such as Dar es Salaam, Tanzania. These solutions are economically and environmentally viable. They also confirm that low-carbon and resilient cities are more realistic in developing countries than green city projects, as attempted in western cities. Metropolisation has henceforth to target resilience, especially in terms of looking at more sustainable resource use.

For this reason, the next section offers insights on resource governance in urban contexts undergoing metropolisation processes, and to this extent it, draws inspiration from some resource geography literature.

Resource geography as an inspiring framework for resource governance in urban spaces

Human geographers have certainly been concerned by resources in various ways, but this topic has gathered limited attention over time, when compared to others. The discipline has also preferred some resources (such as land, water, environmental protected areas) over others (such as extractives, mining products), as it is more concerned by scarcity, access and governance (Bridge, 2010). The exception of 'geographical political ecology' (Peet and Watts, 1996) confirms that the reason for this limited interest is the historical marginal role of political geography within the discipline and the absence until very recently of violence (Rosière and Richard, 2011) as a relevant theme.

Geographers have explicitly pointed out that *natural* resources are *social*, as socially constructed, resource geography offers a precious opportunity to understand how resource configurations are appropriated and commodified by political and economic processes. It is what Bridge does with carbon, explaining that: '"carbon control" has become a primary objective of political and economic governance at urban, regional and international scales' (Bridge, 2010, 821). Bridge underlines three dimensions of this carbon geography, two of which are particularly relevant for us:

> a cartography of resources, reserves, fluxes, sinks and dumps that territorialises and fixes carbon in space while at the same time throwing places into new forms of relation, creating an imaginative gazetteer of enclosure and connection…[and] a biopolitics in which carbon has become the condition of possibility for the living of life and so holds the balance of life and death, whether imagined through a collapse of civilisation at the hands of peak oil or an apocalypse of climate change. (Bridge, 2010, 821)

Bridge builds on the tension between fragmentation and integration expressed by the concession with its material features; when it comes to extractive resources, enclaves, enclosures or offshore spaces (Sidaway, 2007) disconnected from the hinterland are also the norm. He also investigates the environmental and social transformation, as well as questions the 'governability' of these spaces.

How does all this relate to urban spaces? First of all, this research on extractive resources calls for a redefinition of the term of 'resource'. Resources are defined here as materials that have a crucial and high social value at a given point in time: they have a temporal and a spatial dimension. Therefore, the 'natural' dimension of a resource is relative and does not have a substantial impact on its value chain compared to its social status. The most important is its transformation process and the implications that are related to it (social, economical, environmental, political, and so on). This is in line with relational definitions of resources used in economic geography, according to which resources are services and assets for future return (Bathelt and Glückler, 2005).

Henceforth, resources can be located in the most diverse spaces and have very different geographies. Urban spaces have number of diverse resources: water, land, but also service provision, transportation, housing, employment, knowledge/education, spaces of leadership (D'Alessandro and Léautier, 2016), industrial parks, touristic areas, critical residential developments, urban parks, and so on. Being cities that are dense and at the same time fragmented, their geography could increase the fragmentation of the material shape of resources (as it is the case for land and urban agriculture). This underlines the idea that the material spatial distribution of a resource is at the attribute of focus here, instead of imaginaries and immaterial attributes. Resource geography has in fact greatly contributed to a focus on the materialities of 'concessions', meaning the spaces where resources are extracted, focusing on the mechanisms of enclosure and sequestration, as instruments of profit. Should urban governance pay attention here to prevent these modalities of isolation of resource exploitation being put in place?

The multi-scalar geographies of resources in the global and contemporary world make crucial the investigation of the scales and modes of integration of these urban spaces of resources into the other larger scales. This methodological factor also has policy implications, as experiences of successful urban resource management and governance can be scaled up and can inspire national policies. Human geography also helps to approach the relation between the material geography of resources and the social value, roles and claims on them, including when it comes to their transformation, beneficiation and environmental-related issues. Resource value chains are then social, spatial and temporal, in addition to being political and economic. 'Resource-making activities are fundamentally matters of territorialisation – the expression of social power in a geographical form' (Bridge, 2010, 825). The author specifies that for extractive carbon economies, it is a process of selective territorialisation. This chapter argues that, beyond extractive resources such as oil, resource extraction and transformation are selective processes, including some individuals, groups and spaces with adequate prerequisites, while excluding others. Larger are the profits that a resource allows and more important is the competition for the power and advantages that the resource engenders, as it is the case for key resources such as (gold, oil, diamonds, water).

The headquarters of multinational corporations and urban spaces of leadership (and henceforth of decision-making), and the spaces of extraction, transformation and facilitation are crucial nodes of hierarchical geographical networks and flows, with a specific functioning and governance, different and separate from the 'unusable useless rest'. This creates externalities, distortions and exclusions with the related social and spatial mechanisms supporting them, which is particularly critical in urban spaces. The distribution and mutual interaction of resources in urban spaces is a critical factor, with consequences on the conditions of access and exclusion, as well as on poverty: they produce or enhance social and then consequently spatial inequalities by creating competitive/comparative advantages through access. Access to resources in urban spaces is also a crucial issue for urban policies, with consequences at the national and international levels for metropolises and capital cities. Urban resources are then socially produced and related to urban transformation processes (urban growth and sprawl, construction of new infrastructure and residential areas, and so on): they change within and with the city itself.

If urban resources are fields of potential conflicts, more precisely micro-geographies of local wars, especially for crucial and highly valuable resources, the governance of urban spaces of resources is necessary, despite the challenges. Following Korf (2011), going beyond the study of the spatial configuration and dynamics of opportunity, feasibility and predation, is necessary to what she names the 'telluric geography' of these local wars. Korf explains what she means for telluric geography and how different it is from other geographical approaches of resource violence: 'we find subaltern struggles for survival and subaltern opportunisms that link local livelihood struggles with war economies, greed and grievance' (Korf, 2011, 750). Telluric is the allusion to 'his (or her) struggle over meaning and belonging, which has informed the analytics of "geography of rule, violence and affect"' (Korf, 2011, 750).

This geography of resource violence is more dramatic in urban spaces, given the spatial and social density of these spaces, as previously highlighted, and leadership concentration, explaining the reason for which protests, strikes and social exposure of claims are made in these contexts. In urban spaces, the intertwining of apparently contradictory practices of resistance or rebellion, domination, complicity, coercion, and opportunism are favoured by the urban density of people and built spaces, the concentration of emblematic spaces of decision-making, and the simultaneous presence of contradictory interests. Plus, historically, and even more in recent times for the key role of urban spaces (and especially metropolises) in politics and economic dynamics, cities are showcases of revolutions (for example, the French revolution and its spaces in Paris) and wars, including then the small-scale ones on access to local resources (such as land), and find in larger ones sounding boards for their fights.

Michael Watt's work on governable and ungovernable spaces (Watts, 2004) underlines the social and spatial disorder of resource geographies of oil, using the example of the Niger Delta, in Nigeria. He provides a detailed analysis of the dissentions, conflicts, contradictions and paradoxes between the different rationales, while making explicit the agencies of the various stakeholders involved. Contradictory interests and opposition of views and strategies explain the difficult governabilities of these spaces of oil extraction. What lessons can we take from this analysis of urban resource geographies? As for oil, urban resource conflicts are produced by the coexistence of different and certainly contradictory forms of rules. In cities, such as for extractives, resources create elites who make claims and who are supposed to defend the rights of the groups that they represent. Michael Watts refers to 'spaces of indigeneity' for these spatial dynamics, emphasising that these elites are based on ethnic criteria. At least, this is the discourse they use to legitimise their claim and status of spokesperson for a group. This is analogous to what can be found, for example, in cities where fishermen stand as a separate ethnic group, claiming legitimate and unique access rights to some traditional neighbourhoods and critical portions of the waterfront in large cities (Abidjan, Côte d'Ivoire and Dakar, Senegal stand as examples in developing countries).

Urban governance and planning has then to be mindful of urban resources, of their lack and inadequacy to social needs, of changes over time, as well as of their access, and of social (formal and informal) rules regulating their rules. Measures at the local level have to be complemented with national policies. In developing countries, generally confronted by more important and numerous challenges, this is particularly needed, especially with regards to critical issues such as the environment.

Urban spaces in developing countries: examples and insights

A large scholarship in urban geography, as well as in urban planning has shown that urban development, management and planning are generally challenging for metropolises and capital cities around the world, and even more difficult in developing countries (Pacione, 2009). Although urban development presents different scenarios, depending on national economic dynamics, on the city's location, on the urban network, and on development and urban policies at the various levels, urban planning presents similar limitations in developing contexts around the world: infrastructural gaps, inefficient or insufficient service delivery (including basic service provision), environmental deterioration and human risks, challenges of mobility and connectivity.

In Africa and in Southern Asia for instance, despite the existence of large, unplanned urban areas in the metropolises and capital cities, urban planning has proven to be a critical instrument of development, requiring a vision and commitment of the various stakeholders involved, despite being a time consuming and costly exercise. Urban planning is a value addition tool of urban resources. In fact, it produces more than mere economic return, as an efficient urban transportation system reduces congestion costs and environmental damages while increasing the quality of life for inhabitants and the attractiveness for investors, generating other and greater economic benefits. The same can be said for soft infrastructure, efficient energy production and management of urban spaces and water. In these dynamics of urban resource governance and related management and planning, three types of stakeholder are particularly crucial: the state, the private sector, and civil society. Their roles will be highlighted below.

The role of the state

The role of the state or what is called the resource–state nexus (Bridge, 2014) is visible for example in land resource management, including in urban contexts. Urban land tenure and its formalisation is a crucial issue in developing countries: the state has a central role in finding the adapted strategy and the means to implement it. This requires an articulation between national and urban policies, as demonstrated in Brazil, South Africa and India. Land administration and allocation are also important and they include the recognition of customary rights as demonstrated in Ghana, Uganda and Namibia (Durand-Lasserve and Selod, 2007).

The role of the private sector

The role of the private sector can be highlighted through the importance of public–private partnership (PPPs) for urban water utilities in developing countries. Although this trend goes back to the early 1990s, at that time most of the contracts were awarded to large multinational corporations. More recently, an interesting growth of private sector firms from developing countries has been noticed in numerous cases, including Malaysia, Philippines, Argentina, Brazil, Chile and Colombia. Beyond financing factors, the role of private sector operators is critical to improve service quality and operational efficiency, but it must be acknowledged that successful urban water PPPs are part of broader, well-designed sector reforms (as in Chile, Colombia, Ivory Coast, Morocco and Senegal), and are consequently outside the control of the operators. Urban water PPPs can also serve as an instrument of poverty/inequalities reduction, expanding the water network to poor neighbourhoods, as in Argentina, Colombia, Ivory Coast, Ecuador and Philippines, with direct impacts on social and spatial development (Marin, 2009). Developing countries can have their own private water operator, and experiences in Argentina, Ethiopia, Philippines and Senegal have shown that urban, decentralised, South–South cooperation (UDSSC) can widely contribute to bridge capacity gaps and technical know-how deficiencies of these local operators. UDSSC in fact targets not only water and sanitation, but also waste, underlining that critical urban resources are at its core and used as catalysers for urban development in developing contexts. Numerous examples of UDSSC have demonstrated that they are not only an important step to build capacities for development at various levels (public sector institutions, private sector actors, local communities, decision-makers, and so on), but that they are also useful tools to scale up local urban successes and inform national policy-making. These learning experiences are city-to-city partnerships, involving international institutions, such as UNICEF, the UNDP, the World Bank, together with NGOs and CSOs, depending on the context and projects. They are also flexible programmes through which other cities can join and where communities of practices can spread lessons far beyond the stakeholders directly involved. This is, for example, what the World Bank and Cities Alliance have supported, as part of the India, Brazil and South Africa (IBSA) Trilateral Agreement, creating the working group on Human Settlements (IBSA-HS). This initiative echoes the post–2015 efforts for urban sustainable development.

The role of civil society organisations

In a complementary way to the contribution of the private sector, as UDSSC also documents, civil society organisations (CSOs) have an important role to play in defending communities' rights in the context of resource extraction, which has been analysed through oil exploitation in Ghana (Hanson et al, 2014). Despite the fact that oil is an offshore resource in Ghana, the presence of oil blocks has consequences on the cities of Accra and Takoradi. CSOs have advocated for inhabitants' right to benefit more from this resource, while protecting them from the environmental damages incurred. Urban political–environmental issues are therefore transversal and, to be properly analysed, they need a geographical approach, taking into account not only the spaces and spatial networks involved, but also and more importantly the spatial dynamics building and transforming these environments and the role of the different stakeholders. Garth Myers (2016) has done this exercise for African cities, using some case studies such as Nairobi (Kenya), Lusaka (Zambia), Zanzibar (Tanzania), and Cape Town (South Africa) for a range of urban resources, including waste, infrastructure, water and sanitation. He also underlines the insufficient planning of African cities and the way environmental concerns are not sufficiently and properly taken into account in urban planning and policies. Resource geography and geographical approaches of political ecology have greatly emphasised the environmental dimension and its role in the conflicts engendered by resource exploitation, which has not been done as extensively in urban spaces.

Conclusions

The post-2015 development agenda and related SDGs have created a peculiar focus on urban spaces and dynamics, and on their role of increasing and enhancing social and spatial development. The SDG 11 focuses on urban planning and management, while using urban resources (transportation, housing, green and public spaces, air quality, waste and peri-urban areas) and improving their inclusive and sustainable governance. Target 11b explicitly states that the work will 'by 2020, substantially increase the number of cities and human settlements adopting and implementing integrated policies and plans towards inclusion, resource efficiency, mitigation and adaptation to climate change, resilience and disasters'.

This chapter has underlined the gap between ideals of urban sustainability and integrated urban resource management, with a variety of realities in metropolises and capital cities in developing countries, depending on a series of external and internal factors in their countries. These urban realities are not only very diversified, but also problematic, given the lack of urban planning, infrastructure and basic service provision, among other issues. Upon highlighting the discrepancy between urban academic research in social sciences, focusing on ideals of sustainable and integrated cities as often disconnected from everyday urban struggles in developing countries, this chapter emphasises the value of policy research, inspired by academic knowledge and heuristic rigour, to offer policy suggestions and advise the tackling of real problems, such as conflicts, environmental damages and risks, urban policymaking and planning. Urban policy research can draw expertise from various disciplines (urban and political geography, urban and regional planning, environmental law, political ecology, urban history, and so on) to facilitate the dialogue and collaboration among the various stakeholders for better urban resource governance in developing countries. They can contribute to better managed urban resource flows and scale them up to the national and international level. They may also use urban hubs (especially industrial hubs) to encourage transformation and value addition of urban and non-urban resources in urban spaces and for the benefit of cities, with increased returns even at the national level.

To this extent, beyond the resources *in* cities that have been at the core of this chapter, the relation between resources *and* cities still needs some specific academic investigation, in line with contemporary resource discovery and exploitation. The consequences of the discovery and exploitation of new resources (such as oil and gas, for example) on urban development, management and planning of cities in the region, and possibly in the country and beyond, in developing countries, have still to be studied. African examples such as Tanzania, Uganda, Mozambique, Senegal and Egypt make this topic of great and urgent interest.

This issue is among the critical ones supporting the thesis of academics and specialists in the field, asserting that the term 'city' (and its related expressions such as 'urban spaces') is no longer satisfactory as a way to refer to the variety of urban realities across the world, especially in developing contexts. Under the guidance of UN-Habitat the expression 'human settlements' emphasises the role of residents, users and communities – the SDG 11 refers accordingly to both 'cities and human settlements'. This new expression has the advantage, compared to 'city', to include for instance peri-urban spaces, to recognise the importance of city–hinterland relations and wider city–region relations and, in the case of border cities, the city–international relations.

All this opens a new perspective or sheds a new light on the work of Mike Hodson and Simon Marvin: *After sustainable cities* (Hodson and Marvin, 2014). The authors point out that the idealistic vision of a sustainable city was based, when it was conceived, on a double premise: a social goal (supporting the fight against poverty) and a global environmental vision. Hodson and Marvin (2014) document how with the global economic crisis, and austerity governance, to which one has to add the climate change constraint, this sustainable city has translated in the real world to darker and unfair cities. The authors also focus on the technologically and economically driven themes that have embodied sustainable city discourses, giving them a peculiar turn.

This chapter complements these views and aims to add that Hodson and Martin's eco-logics need to be grounded in real not-so-sustainable urban realities, needs and problems of developing countries, with three key realistic focuses:

1. *Environmental/ecological resource governance* has to be built by integrated management strategies and appropriate urban planning. Urban industrial hubs/parks may be among the key drivers to incorporate and disseminate environmentally friendly practices.
2. *Quality of life* for residents has to be enhanced. Sound urban resource governance can reduce poverty and inequalities, as previously shown, but it can also improve the quality of life for urban users and inhabitants. This is, in the end, the final meaning of 'development', beyond economic indicators.
3. *Capacities* have to be built at various levels: in institutions, for CSOs and communities, for private sector actors, and so on, UDSSC are effective instruments to this extent and they often focus in developing contexts on critical urban resources (such as water or waste).

Instead of sustainable cities, the SDG 11 and the post-2015 development agenda (with its other goals affecting urban spaces) could target sound urban resource governance and planning, within real spaces and constraints, especially in developing countries. After sustainable cities, the various initiatives should try to converge to improve the quality of life and spaces in human settlements, including peri-urban spaces and 'rural' spaces that have no meaning in a global world if not intrinsically connected to urban spaces.

Acknowledgement

This chapter was written as part of the Qatar Foundation's National Priorities Research Program – NPRP 6-1272-5-160.

Notes

[1] For a definition and analysis of the concept of scale, the reader may refer to the literature available in human geography (Lévy and Lussault, 2013).

[2] A *Strategic Innovation Agenda for Smart Sustainable Cities* has also been conceived by a consortium of stakeholders (www.smartsustainablecities. se/downloads/sscagenda-eng-web.pdf).

[3] Compare the *Hypergéo* website (www.hypergeo.eu/spip.php?article75).

References

Aliste, E, Di Méo, G, Guerrero, R, 2013, Idéologies du développement, enjeux socio-environnementaux et construction de l'aire métropolitaine de Concepcion (Chili), *Annales de Géographie* 694, 6, 662–88

Allen, A, 2009, Sustainable cities or sustainable urbanisation?, *Palette: UCL's Journal of Sustainable Cities*, summer, 1-3, https:// mycourses.aalto.fi/pluginfile.php/219334/mod_resource/content/1/ sustainable_urbanisation_allen.pdf

Bathelt, H, Glückler, J, 2005, Resources in economic geography: From substantive concepts towards a relational perspective, *Environment and Planning* A, 37, 1545–63

Bochet, B, 2005, Métropolisation, morphogénèse et développement durable: le cas de l'agglomération de Lausanne, *Geographica Helvetica* 60, 4, 248–59

Bridge, G, 2010, Resource geographies I: Making carbon economies, old and new, *Progress in Human Geography* 35, 6, 820–34

Bridge, G, 2014, Resource geographies II: The resource–state nexus, *Progress in Human Geography* 38, 1, 118–30

Cartwright, A, 2015, Better growth, better cities: Rethinking and redirecting urbanization in Africa, *The New Climate Economy Working Paper* www.africancentreforcities.net/wp-content/uploads/2015/09/ NCE-APP-final.pdf

D'Alessandro C, Léautier, F, 2016, *Cities and spaces of leadership. A geographical perspective*, London: Palgrave

Durand-Lasserve, A, Selod, H, 2007, The formalization of urban land tenure, http://siteresources.worldbank. org/INTURBANDEVELOPMENT/Resources/336387- 1269364687916/6892589-1269394475210/durand_lasserve.pdf

Ericsson, 2016, Laying the foundations for a smart, sustainable city, *Ericsson White Paper Uen* 284 23-3277, January, www.ericsson.com/sl/res/docs/whitepapers/wp-smart-cities.pdf

Fiorino, DJ, 2014, Sustainable cities and governance: What are the connections? in DA Mazmanian, H Blanco (eds) *Elgar companion to sustainable cities: Strategies, methods and outlook*, Cheltenham: Edward Elgar Publishing

Grindle, MS, 2007, Good enough governance revisited, *Development Policy Review* 25, 5, 553–74

Hanson, K, D'Alessandro, C, Owusu, F (eds), 2014, *Managing Africa's natural resources: Capacities for development*, London: Palgrave.

Hodson, M, Marvin, S (eds), 2014, *After sustainable cities?*, London: Routledge

Kempster, S, Parry, KW, 2011, Grounded theory and leadership research: A critical realist perspective, *The Leadership Quarterly* 22, 106–2

Kheng Lian, K, Asanga, G, Bhullar, L, 2010, Eco-cities and sustainable cities: Whither?, in *Social Space*, pp 84–92, Singapore: Lien Centre for Social Innovation

Korf, B, 2011, Resources, violence and the telluric geographies of small wars, *Progress in Human Geography* 35, 6, 733–56

Lévy, J, Lussault, M (eds), 2013, *Dictionnaire de la géographie et de l'espace des sociétés*, Paris: Belin

Lundqvist, M, 2007, *Sustainable cities in theory and practice: A comparative study of Curitiba and Portland*, Karlstad: Karlstad University, www.diva-portal.org/smash/get/diva2:4809/FULLTEXT01.pdf

Mäki, O, Oinas, P, 2004, The narrow notion of realism in geography, *Environment and Planning A* 36, 10, 1755–76

Marin, P, 2009, *Public–private partnerships for urban water utilities: A review of experiences in developing countries*, Washington, DC: World Bank

Massey, D, Allen, J, Pile, S (eds), 1999, *City worlds*, London and New York: Routledge and Open University

Myers, G, 2016, *Urban environments in Africa*, Bristol: Policy Press

Pacione, M, 2009, *Urban geography: A global perspective*, London: Routledge

Peet, R, Watts, M, 1996, *Liberation ecologies: Environment, development, social movements*, London: Routledge

Rosière, S, Richard, Y, 2011, *Géographie des conflits armés et des violences politiques*, Paris: Ellipses.

Shearmur, R, 2003, Défis de la métropolisation: gouvernance urbaine et durabilité, *Géoconfluences*, http://geoconfluences.ens-lyon.fr/doc/typespace/urb1/MetropScient.htm

Sidaway, JD, 2007, Spaces of postdevelopment, *Progress in Human Geography* 31, 3, 345–61

Smith, S, 2012, Tokyo's surprising lack of density, *Market Urbanism*, 28 June, http://marketurbanism.com/2012/06/28/tokyos-surprising-lack-of-density/

UN (United Nations), 2013, *World economic and social survey 2013: Sustainable development challenges*, New York: UN

UNEP (United Nations Environment Programme), 2012, *Sustainable, resource efficient cities – Make it happen!*, Paris: UNEP

UN-Habitat (United Nations Human Settlements Programme), 2013, *Planning and design for sustainable urban mobility: Global report on human settlements 2013*, Nairobi: UN-Habitat

UN-Habitat (United Nations Human Settlements Programme), 2016, *World cities report 2016*, Nairobi: UN-Habitat

Watson, B, 2014, What makes a city resilient?, *Guardian*, 27 January, www.theguardian.com/cities/2014/jan/27/what-makes-a-city-resilient

Watts, M, 2004, Resource curse? Governmentality, oil and power in the Niger Delta in Nigeria, *Geopolitics* 9, 1, 50–80

Part Two
Minority groups

The Millennium Development Goals, disability rights and special needs education in Ethiopia: a case study of the Oromiya region

Jeff Grischow

Introduction

The eight Millennium Development Goals (MDGs) adopted by the United Nations in 2000 cover a wide range of economic, environmental and social development priorities. In order to facilitate performance and assessment, the MDGs include 21 Targets and 60 Indicators (Higgins, 2013, iv). On education, MDG 2 calls for the achievement of universal primary education (UPE) by 2015, with Target 2A stating that 'children everywhere, boys and girls alike, will be able to complete a full course of primary schooling'. One of the most important indicators for MDG 2 is the Net Enrolment Ratio (NER), which measures the percentage of children aged 6–12 in primary school relative to the total population of that age (UNESCO, 2004, 90–1). Other indicators include the percentage of children who complete primary school after enrolling in Grade 1, and the literacy rate of men and women aged 15–24 (UNESCO, 2004, 90–1; Higgins, 2013, 1–2, 32).

Most commentators argue that it will be difficult if not impossible for Africa to meet the MDGs by 2015, including MDG 2. There is a case to be made, however, for a more positive view. For instance, in a recent North–South Institute paper, Higgins observes that Africa's progress towards the MDGs appears more promising if we consider the rate of progress (acceleration in achieving the MDGs over time) rather than the continent's achievements at a given time relative to other regions (Higgins, 2013, 5–6). This is particularly important in the case of the education MDG, which as Easterly observes, is unique because 'it is a level end-goal rather than a changes goal (that is, changes in either relative or absolute terms)' (Easterly, 2009, 29). Easterly continues:

> This creates an obvious bias against the region that starts off farthest from the absolute target of 100%, which in this case is Africa (Easterly, 2009, 29)...no matter how fast the progress of African countries or how remarkable the increases relative to Western historical norms or contemporary developing country experience, Africa will fail to meet the second MDG if it fails to pass this finish line (as it will likely fail to do because it started much further away) (Easterly, 2009, 30)...It was less likely that Africa would attain the LEVEL target of universal primary enrollment because it started with the lowest initial primary enrollment and completion. (Easterly, 2009, 32)

Beyond this, another problem with labeling Africa an 'MDG failure' is the fact that MDGs were developed as global goals based on world historical data, not as country-level or even regional goals. According to Vandermoortele, who developed the MDG framework, it is wrong to 'lament that sub-Saharan Africa will not meet the MDGs. These targets were not set specifically for that region' (Vandemoortele, 2007, 6). As such, perhaps the maximal yardstick for assessing the MDGs at the national level is to ask whether they have created an enabling policy environment for positive changes (Higgins, 2013, 7, 11). On this point, however, it is important to note that with respect to education, the MDG initiative is not the only framework for nurturing policies to increase school enrolments. In fact, the MDG organisers based MDG 2 on a programme called Education for All (EFA), which arose out of a United Nations conference on education in Jomtien, Thailand, in 1990. At the conference, representatives from 155 nations pledged to bring the benefits of education to 'every citizen in every society'. This vision was formalised at the World Education Forum held in Dakar, Senegal, in 2000, where 164 countries pledged to achieve EFA by 2015. Thus, the EFA and MDG frameworks ran in parallel and were mutually reinforcing.

Focusing on the NER, with the above discussion in mind, we find that Africa has made good progress in recent years towards UPE. After a period of expansion in the 1950s and 1960s, the continent experienced a crisis of education due to poor economic conditions in the 1980s (Kiros, 1990, Foreword). The positive trend resumed, however, in the 1990s. In fact, if we consider the *rate* of progress,

Africa has achieved more on MDG 2 than on the other MDGs. Although the continent lagged behind the 90 per cent NER of the developing world as of 2010, the African NER had grown rapidly over the previous decade (from 58 per cent in 1999 to 76 per cent in 2010). Africa also has made progress in reducing gender inequality in primary schools by encouraging the education of girls. According to a recent survey of the MDGs in Africa, most African countries made progress with regards to the 2015 MDG targets for the NER and gender parity (UNDP, 2012, 24–35; UN, 2012, 17). Progress has not been as good, however, in primary school completion rates or literacy rates for 15–24 year olds (UNDP, 2012, 28–33). Also, as of 2010 half of all 'out-of-school' children were in Africa, and all of the indicators were well below other developing regions (UN, 2012, 17–19). Still, considering the low starting point in 1999, the MDG/ EFA framework appears to have had a positive influence on primary schooling in Africa.

Turning to Ethiopia, the educational system was almost entirely in the hands of the Ethiopian church before Italy occupied the country in 1935. After Italy withdrew in 1941, Emperor Haile Selassie embarked on a ten-year period of modernisation and reform. In 1952, however, only 60,000 students were enrolled in schools from the primary to university levels. The subsequent five years witnessed little improvement, making Ethiopia an anomaly during the era of educational expansion in other African countries. In response, the Ethiopian government developed a series of five-year plans beginning in 1957. During the first Five-Year Plan school enrolments increased by 65 per cent (11 per cent per year), but still only 10 per cent of primary-age children attended school. In 1961, Ethiopia's enrolment ratio was 3.8 per cent compared to 40 per cent in Africa generally. This situation prompted the government to redouble its efforts during the second and third Five-Year Plans. As a result, between 1962 and 1973 the number of public schools increased to 1,300 and enrolments jumped to 600,000. This was a substantial increase but it still left Ethiopia with one of the lowest enrolment rates in Africa. Seeking to reverse this trend, the government sponsored an Education Sector Review in 1971 with support from the International Development Association (affiliated with the World Bank) (Wagaw, 1979, 132, 153– 4, 182–95; Ofcansky and Berry, 2002; Kebede, 2006, 10–11).

The government accepted several of the Review's recommendations in 1973, including the rapid expansion of primary education from Grades 1 to 4. However, the announcement of the new programme in early 1974 triggered a public outcry, especially from teachers who believed that the government intended to limit primary education to the first four grades. Haile Selassie promptly abandoned the reform (Wagaw, 1979, 190–5). By this time, however, a larger backlash against the imperial government had developed that culminated in a military coup and Selassie's abdication in 1974. Seeking to build legitimacy among the Ethiopian population, the new Marxist–Leninist government (known as the Derg, more of which below) sent 60,000 secondary and university students to rural areas between December, 1974 and June, 1976, to carry out a mass literacy campaign. The government claimed that this brought literacy to 160,000 peasants. Subsequently the Derg embarked on an expansion of education, in contrast to many other African countries whose programmes stagnated between the mid-1970s and the 1980s (Kiros, 1990, Foreword). In 1976, the Derg announced a broad national campaign to eradicate illiteracy among the masses. Three years later, the government launched the National Literacy Campaign (NLC), with the goal of achieving UPE by 1987 through non-formal programmes. Seventeen million people enrolled for literacy classes between 1979 and 1986, and in 1991 the Derg claimed that the NLC had achieved a national literacy rate of 76 per cent. While some authors claim that this number was inflated, it does appear that literacy improved under the NLC, although the greatest gains were in urban areas (Habtu, 1996, 116–18, 125, 130–1, 148). Meanwhile, according to World Bank data the number of students in formal primary schools also increased under the Derg, from 1.38 million in 1979 to 2.47 million in 1991 (World Bank, 2014). This increase, however, only produced an NER of 29 per cent as of 1989. The subsequent five years witnessed a coup against the Derg in 1991, the formation of a new government, and the implementation of a new constitution in 1994. These events had an impact on education, and in 1994 the NER had dropped to 19 per cent (UNESCO, 2013).

The new regime, called the Ethiopian People's Revolutionary Democratic Front (EPRDF), targeted education as a major priority, and the country made good progress towards MDG 2 between 1994 and 2010. The most recent data (2013–14) indicates an NER of 92.6 per cent (WEF, 2015, 9), which is a very impressive achievement. Ethiopia has also made good progress towards gender equality in education, reporting a rise in the Gender Parity Index in the NER for primary education from 0.87 in 2004/5 to 0.93 between 2009 and 2011, and 0.95 in 2013/14 (FDRE, 2010, 11–14; UNESCO, 2013; WEF, 2015, 15). This has happened, according to the UN's 2011 report on the MDGs in Africa, because of the 'resolute political will' of the government of Ethiopia 'to achieve universal primary education' (FDRE 2012, 25). As part of this commitment, the government of Ethiopia increased the budget allocation for education by about 3 per cent of the national budget between 2004/5 and 2009/10, which allowed it to increase the number of primary schools from 16,000 to over 25,000 in 2008/09, mostly in rural areas (FDRE, 2010, 14). These numbers point to good progress towards MDG 2.

The picture is much bleaker, however, if we consider the statistics for primary enrolments of disabled children. Although the EFA proclamation does not mention disability specifically, it does include a special emphasis on 'those in difficult circumstances,' which certainly should include the disabled (UNESCO, 2012). And yet, even though we cannot speak of EFA without including disabled children, little attention has been paid to disability in educational development until relatively recently. Indeed, it was not until 2006 that education for disabled children received international attention as part of the United Nations Convention on the Rights of the Persons with Disabilities (CRPD). After this point, governments in the South began to integrate disability into development programmes. In the same year as the CRPD, the government of Ethiopia admitted that MDG 2/EFA would not be achieved unless it could increase the NER of disabled children. This is a formidable challenge, because out of an estimated 3 million disabled Ethiopian children only 1–3 per cent have access to primary schooling (FDRE, 2006, 5–7).

In 2006, the Ministry of Education (MoE) in Ethiopia recognised this problem and affirmed its commitment to a systematic special needs education (SNE) programme (FDRE, 2006). Four years later, the Ethiopian government reaffirmed its commitment to disability programmes by ratifying the CRPD, which includes the right to free and universal primary schooling for disabled children.[1] However, the MoE lacks the financial capacity or expertise to make this commitment a reality, and it has been necessary to recruit NGOs specialising in disability and education. In the Oromiya region of Ethiopia, one of the most important organisations is Christian Horizons-Ethiopia (CH-Ethiopia), an Ethiopian–led organisation affiliated with a Canadian NGO called Christian Horizons (Ontario) and its international arm, Christian Horizons-Global (CH-Global). CH-Global has been working with the government on SNE projects since 2004, and in 2010 the organisation developed a proposal to create 50,000 primary school spaces for disabled Ethiopia children. A project of this scale would contribute greatly to universalising primary education in Ethiopia.

CH-Ethiopia has a long history of development work in Ethiopia, beginning in 1992 under the name Children's Homes International (CHI). CHI was a Canadian NGO affiliated with CH-Ontario, which had a 30-year history of providing services for developmentally disabled Canadians. In Ethiopia, CHI began with child sponsorship programmes, but its work quickly expanded to revenue-generation projects such as microcredit for women entrepreneurs. In 2007, CHI was transformed into CH-Ethiopia, a subsidiary of the newly formed CH-Global. Since then, CH-Global has provided funding and a general mandate, but CH-Ethiopia has acted largely autonomously in terms of setting local priorities, working with Ethiopian partners and implementing programmes, and it is staffed entirely by Ethiopian nationals. The organisation is based in the town of Assela in the Arsi zone of the Oromiya region.

CH-Ethiopia's work in SNE began in 2004, when (as CHI) the organisation received a request from the MoE in Assela to renovate a single school in order to increase SNE access and improve its quality. The project was a great success, and over the next four years CH-Ethiopia worked with the government to develop 67 additional SNE units across Oromiya. In 2010, CH-Ethiopia drafted a proposal to increase SNE enrolment substantially, building four new SNE units and renovating another 240, which together would provide spaces for the 50,000 children mentioned above. The remainder of this chapter will discuss the organisation's experience to date, set within the context of MDG 2, and focusing not only on the current CH-Ethiopia partnership with the Ethiopian government, but also on the historical forces since the 1970s that have come together to make that partnership possible.

CH-Ethiopia and special needs education

The current Ethiopian state (Federal Democratic Republic of Ethiopia (FDRE)) emerged out of the defeat of the Marxist–Leninist Derg regime in 1991 by a coalition of forces led by the Tigrayan People's Liberation Front (TPLF). By this time the TPLF had created an umbrella organisation, the EPRDF. The EPRDF organised the Transitional Government of Ethiopia (TGE), which drafted a new constitution in 1994. In 1995, the TGE was dissolved, elections were held, and the FDRE was born under the leadership of Meles Zenawi and the EPRDF (Marcus, 2002, 231–42). As the real power behind the EPRDF, the TPLF's strong ethno-nationalist ideology (more of which later) heavily influenced the political structure of the new state. The

FDRE constitution divided the country into 12 provinces (*kilils*) based on ethnic identities (Milkias, 2012, 72; Marcus, 2002, 233–4). The regions were divided into zones, and the zones divided into smaller units called *woredas*. These were subdivided further into very small administrative units containing as few as 50 people each. For the first ten years, the EPRDF gave most power to the zones, which oversaw *woreda* plans including educational initiatives (Markakis, 2011, 246–7).

In 2004 the MoE in Assela Zone asked CHI to improve and strengthen the Limat Behebrat Primary School, which ran the only SNE unit in Assela and Arsi (an area that included 25 *woredas*). The unit served only 22 disabled students out of a population of about one million disabled children in the region. At the time of the project's inception, the disabled students were isolated in the school, confined to a peripheral classroom near the latrine. The teachers had divided the classroom into sections for blind, deaf and physically disabled students using tarps purchased with their personal funds. The classroom was in bad repair, the teachers lacked appropriate teaching materials, and the students arrived at school hungry and without uniforms. With a budget of $35,000, CHI constructed a new 15-classroom unit, and provided furniture, teaching materials, uniforms, cookware and a breakfast programme. The NGO also provided financial assistance to children in dire poverty as an incentive to attend. While in school, the older students learned skills such as woodworking and embroidery. Teachers came on board, promoting the school in the community and connecting older students with local businesses to apprentice in skilled occupations. In 2007, Limat Behebrat School graduated eight male students in woodworking, and nine women in sewing and embroidery. The women left school to start their own cooperative (CH-Global, 2010, 17–18).

By 2008, the school's disabled population had grown to 85 students. During the same period (2004–08), CH-Global worked with Regional and Zonal Education Bureaus to increase the enrolment of children with disabilities and raise awareness of disability issues at the community level. As part of this work, the organisation sponsored conferences and training for Education Bureau supervisors, Zone Administrators and healthcare workers. They also funded and provided training for close to 200 SNE teachers. The Oromiya Education Bureau placed the graduates in schools and provided the necessary teaching materials, thereby increasing the number of spaces for disabled children. Between 2006 and 2011, CH-Ethiopia (successor to CHI) worked with the Oromiya Educational Bureau to establish 67 'newly renovated' SNE units in Arsi, West Arsi and Bale, serving 1,700 students. They also trained 198 SNE teachers, and provided capacity building workshops for existing disability associations as well as support for the creation of new disability associations. In addition, by 2010 CH-Ethiopia was providing direct support services to 600 children in Arsi zone through a sponsorship programme, and microcredit loans to 1,500 individuals, most of whom (80 per cent) were women entrepreneurs (CH-Global, 2010, 4, 9, 23; CH-Global, 2011, 1).

In 2010, CH-Ethiopia developed a proposal to complete the work on the existing SNE units and create new ones in four zones in Oromiya. In terms of bricks and mortar, the new programme would develop four new SNE units and renovate another 240 in Arsi, West Arsi, Bale and East Showa. Each of the new units would have four classrooms, and they would be built onto existing schools for non-disabled students in order to integrate the disabled students into the wider school community. The units themselves, however, would be divided according to disability so that deaf, blind and developmentally disabled children would receive specialised instruction. Students would work through the Ethiopian curriculum for Grades 1 to 8, but they also would receive 'life skills training' to prepare them for independent living. As part of the latter, students would be taught to cook light meals, which would serve not only as training but also as a daily nutritional supplement. CH-Ethiopia would provide uniforms at no cost. Integration with the non-disabled student body would occur mainly through sport and recreation on the school grounds (CH-Global, 2010, 5, 14).

In total, the project would open up new primary school spaces for 50,000 disabled Ethiopian children, out of an estimated population on 1,123,000, mainly in rural areas. There is a strong gender component to the project. In Ethiopia, far fewer girls have access to education than boys. This is especially true for disabled girls, whose parents do not send them to school, train them for employment, or allow them to marry or inherit property. As a result, existing SNE units have far more boys than girls. CH-Ethiopia has reversed this trend in its existing SNE units, which have a ratio of 54 per cent girls and 46 per cent boys. The expanded project would maintain this ratio. To support increased enrolments, the project also seeks to train 480 new SNE teachers through a 45-day training programme, and 680 teachers' assistants through a condensed, 7-day training programme. In addition, the project would create a Special Needs Resource Centre in Assela by renovating existing space at a Technical and Vocational Training Centre (TVTC) owned by CH-Ethiopia. The new centre also would develop and produce teaching materials for the SNE units, utilising its existing woodworking and metalworking workshops staffed by disabled Ethiopians. In addition, the TVTC would admit primary school graduates for skills training, and then provide microfinance loans upon graduation to support small business start-ups. This complete programme, which would support disabled Ethiopians from primary school to labour market participation, would be provided for 2,000 individuals over ten years, half of whom will be women (CH–Global, 2010, 6–15).

Beyond the classroom initiative, the programme would expand CH–Ethiopia's support for advocacy among government officials and communities in the project areas. As a central part of this initiative, the organisation promised to create disability associations and parent support groups in 48 communities. Beyond this, advocacy efforts would include 'awareness training' for individuals in government, business and religious organisations. As part of this initiative, these individuals would be invited to forums at which the disability associations and parent groups (and specific support groups for mothers) would present their issues and concerns. The forums would be preceded by advocacy training sessions for the disability and parent groups. CH–Ethiopia has held these kinds of meetings in the past, as well as 'city bazaars' showcasing products produced by disabled Ethiopians. There also is a plan to develop brochures and videos as awareness-raising tools, and to celebrate the International Day of the Disabled annually in each zone (CH–Global, 2011, 7, 11, 16).

Over the years, CH–Ethiopia has enjoyed an excellent relationship with the government of Ethiopia at all levels from the *woredas* to the MoE. This relationship deepened in 2004/5, when the government strengthened its commitment to providing places for disabled children in all government schools. In 2005, the government implemented a '*woreda* empowerment' plan that gave *woreda* officials much more power over development. These powers included the development and implementation of education programmes. However, since the establishment of the FDRE in 1995 most of the *woredas* have suffered from a lack of resources. By necessity, therefore, the *woredas* have to rely on the NGO sector with important roles played by foreign organisations (Markakis, 2011, 246–7). Since its inception, CH–Ethiopia has sought to fill this gap by enhancing the capacity of the government to expand SNE across Oromiya. To this end, CH–Global and CH–Ethiopia have developed very positive relationships with government officials. The partnership was strong enough in 2004 that the Assela branch of the MoE invited the organisation to strengthen the Limat Behebrat Primary School. This cooperative spirit continued to grow over the years. In the most important initiative, CH–Global offered to train two SNE teachers in every zone in Oromiya (72 total) at the Sebeta Teachers' College over a two-year period. In exchange, the Oromiya Education Bureau agreed to employ the teachers across the zone to create more spaces for disabled children. This plan was carried out successfully.

The 2010 proposal reinforced the need for strong ties with government officials. Most basically, it affirmed government ownership over the programme as well as 'clearly defined roles in alignment with the country's educational policies'. To sort out and manage this relationship, CH–Ethiopia appointed a Project Coordinator to work closely with the Zone Education Bureaus. The Bureaus would approve the curriculum, select, assign and pay the new teachers, while CH–Ethiopia would carry out all other responsibilities relating to the new SNE units (CH–Global, 2010, 5, 18). As noted above, CH–Global also would work with government officials to strengthen and/or create disability associations, to raise awareness about disability issues among government agencies, and to organise government–community discussion forums.

The project and human rights

Embedded within the CH–Global proposal is a strong commitment to human rights. The document sets the tone immediately by stating that in the Oromiya region, 'only 3% of the estimated one million children with disabilities have access to education. This leaves 97% (of) children with disabilities unable to exercise their basic human right to education' (CH–Global 2011, 3). The next section, which presents the proposal's objectives, refers to the 1948 Universal Declaration of Human Rights and its proclamation that education is not only a basic right in itself, but also a necessary precursor to securing other rights (CH–Global, 2011, 4). The document also quotes Kofi Annan's remark that 'education is a human right with immense powers to transform. On its foundation rest the cornerstones of freedom, democracy, and sustainable human development. At the same time, the consequences of illiteracy are profound, even potentially life threatening. They flow from the denial of a fundamental human right' (CH–Global, 2011, 8). Annan made this statement in UNICEF's 1999 *State of the World's Children* report, which focused on education and included an overview of 'the historical context in which children's right to education has been repeatedly affirmed' (UNICEF, 1999, 2). This context included the

UN's Convention on the Rights of the Child, which was ratified in 1990 and elevated education from a need to a right. The CH-Global proposal also refers to the MDGs, which established a target for the right the education by calling for universal primary schooling by 2015. While not referred to directly, the proposal's focus on gender also aligns with MDG Target 3a, which seeks to achieve women's rights through equality and empowerment (MDGs, 2000, Targets 2a and 3a). In citing the Universal Declaration, the Annan/UNICEF report and the MDGs, CH-Global draws on a long and important history of treating education as a human right. The conscious end goal of the project is to translate this right into an entitlement for disabled Ethiopians (CH-Global, 2010, 14). The proposal does not refer to disability rights explicitly, but it offers a blueprint for achieving several of those contained in the UN CRPD, including the rights to education, employment and a decent standard of living, as well as the responsibility to provide advocacy for disability issues.

CH-Ethiopia has developed its positive relationships with zone and *woreda* government officials in a political environment that can be challenging for NGOs. Some critics believe, for instance, that the EPRDF requires local NGO workers to support the government politically or even belong to EPRDF-affiliated parties (Chanie, 2007, 380). The government also controls foreign NGOs through a 2009 law that limits activities connected to certain human rights (Nega and Milofsky, 2011).[2] Yet CH-Ethiopia has been able to work with the government to deliver on the human right to education for disabled Ethiopian children. Why has the government been open to disability rights and SNE? To understand this, we have to delve into the history of the revolution and the TPLF in particular. There are two questions to be answered: how did the TPLF experience affect the political structure of Ethiopia after 1991? How did the legacy of the revolution provide an opening for disability rights and SNE? To answer these questions, we must investigate the revolutionary history of the EPRDF and its driving force, the TPLF.

The Federal Democratic Republic of Ethiopia and disability rights: historical context

> It is clear that the key policies of the Eritrean and Ethiopian Governments can only be understood in light of positions established in the course of their revolutionary struggles over the past two decades. (Young, 1996, 120)

[T]he (TPLF's) 16-year long struggle forms the background
to the present government's policies on regionalism and
continues to shape political life in Ethiopia. (Young, 1998,
193)

The TPLF fought its war against the Derg between 1975 and 1991,
but the revolutionary context stretched back to the student movement
of the 1960s. At this time, Ethiopia was an empire, ruled by the
imperial regime of Haile Selassie. At the time of Selassie's ascension
to the throne in 1916, the minority Amhara ethnic groups controlled
the imperial state, which it had created by absorbing neighbouring
ethnic groups during a period of expansion in the nineteenth century.
Until the 1960s, few of the client groups contested Amhara hegemony
on the basis of ethnic nationalism. In 1961, an ethno-nationalist
movement developed in Eritrea, which had been an Italian colony
but was now claimed by Ethiopia. The Eritreans lost the struggle and
Selassie incorporated Eritrea into the Ethiopian state in 1962. Eritrean
nationalism, however, sparked the rise of ethnic resistance against the
imperial regime. To add fuel to the fire, Ethiopia's economy stagnated
in the mid-1960s and the aging Selassie did little to reverse the decline.
Influenced by revolutions across the Third World, radicalised students
began to publicise criticisms of the empire and to call for a new,
socialist regime, one that paid attention to all of Ethiopia's ethnic
groups rather than just the Amharic-speaking core (Markakis, 2011,
162–3). One of the turning points was a 1969 article by Walleligne
Makonnen in the journal *Struggle*, published by students at the Haile
Selassie I University (HSIU). Makonnen argued that the radical
socialist students were wrong in assuming that an Ethiopian nation
existed, which could be transformed into a socialist state through
revolution. Instead, Ethiopia consisted of 12 separate nations based
on ethnicity (Tigray nation, Oromo nation, and so on), ruled by an
imperial regime (Young, 1997, 80; Makonnen, 1969, 1). Some of the
students from these 'nations' adopted Makonnen's perspective, and
by the early 1970s they had developed very strong ethno-nationalist
socialist doctrines.

The TPLF was rooted in a Tigrayan variant of this trend, growing
out of a student organisation, the Tigrayan University Students'
Association (TUSA), founded in the early 1970s. At the time, TUSA
represented the latest in a long line of Tigrayan resistance to the
imperial regime, but it was one of the first expressions of the marriage
of socialist and ethno-nationalist ideas (Berhe, 2004, 573, 576, 577).
Shortly after TUSA's formation, Tigrayan students created a more

strongly Leninist organisation called Mahber Gesgesti Behere Tigray (MAGEBT) (Progressive Tigray People's Movement). MAGEBT's members adopted Lenin's model of democratic centralism in which ideas could flow upwards but policies and power flowed downwards from the centre, and in which factionalism was strictly prohibited (Milkias, 2003, 13). During the summer vacations, students from TUSA and MAGEBT travelled to Tigray, and through underground Marxist organisations worked to politicise peasants and mobilise them against Selassie's regime (Berhe, 2004, 578).

While the radical Tigrayan students were developing these organisations, an Amharic coup erupted from within Haile Selassie's government. Coming on the heels of a major famine between 1972 and 1974, the revolution began with an army mutiny in January, 1974. This was followed by strikes by taxi drivers and teachers in February and a General Strike in March. By April, the mutineers within the army had elected a committee, the Coordinating Committee of the Armed Forces – the Derg – to lead the revolution. Pushed by radicals from the student movement, the Derg gradually took control of Selassie's institutions and resources. On 12 September 1974, the rebels arrested Selassie himself and executed him nine months later. At first, the Tigrayan activists and other radicals hoped that the Derg – as a left-leaning government – would sympathise with the cause of ethnic pluralism and perhaps even secession. However, it soon became clear that the new government espoused a strongly centralised version of Ethiopian nationalism, one which would preserve the Abyssinian/ Amharic centre that had existed for centuries (Markakis, 2011, 161–8). Shortly after the Derg took power, Tigrayan students – many with connections to TUSA – created the Tigrayan National Organization (TNO) as a foundation for military resistance against the new regime. In February, 1975, when it became clear that the Derg would attack Tigrayan 'ethno-nationalists', the TNO leadership transformed the organisation into the TPLF and prepared for a prolonged fight (Berhe, 2004, 578–82; Young, 1997, 83). By the time Major Mengistu Haile Mariam emerged as the Derg's leader in early 1977 (Markakis, 2011, 169), the TPLF was locked firmly into a struggle against the new regime.

Influenced by MAGEBT, TUSA and the TNO, the TPLF's ideology embraced ideas from Marx, Lenin, Stalin, Mao, Ho Chi Minh and Che Guevara. Mao, Ho Chi Minh and Che provided models of guerilla warfare. From Marx, Lenin and Stalin, the TPLF absorbed ideas about the 'nationalities' question. Since the late nineteenth century, Tigrayan nationalism had taken on an ethnic character, under which Tigrayans resisted Amharic domination and fought for ethnic autonomy (Berhe, 2004, 573). The TPLF thus focused on the nationalities question, rather than class. Similar to imperial Russia, the problem in Ethiopia was that the Derg represented Amhara domination of Ethiopia's nationalities – as the Czars had represented the imperialist domination of the nationalities in Russia (Young, 1998, 193). For the TPLF, therefore, the ethnic struggle was a sub-set of the class struggle, and it had to be resolved before the class struggle could be undertaken. Marx had argued this for Ireland and Lenin developed the notion further in the Russian context, where – similar to Tigray – the peasantry comprised the majority of the population. The TPLF therefore took on the Leninist model of revolution on behalf of the peasants, although like Lenin TPLF leaders developed a top-down approach in which the revolution would be fought by the elites for the peasants, not by the peasants for themselves (Berhe, 2004, 580–3; Lata, 1999, 84). From the beginning of the war in 1975, the more radical TPLF leaders embraced Lenin's political model with the goal of secession for Tigray, while the moderates envisioned ethnic autonomy within a federal Ethiopia state. Future Prime Minister Meles Zenawi, who arrived in the field in Tigray in January, 1975, took a hard line on both Tigrayan secession and Leninist political organisation. By 1978, Meles and the radicals had defeated the moderates represented by the class-based Marxist Ethiopian People's Revolutionary Party (EPRP) and the liberal–democratic Ethiopian Democratic Union (EDU) (Young, 1996, 106–7, 193; Berhe, 2004, 586–92; Milkias, 2003, 13).

In May of 1984, having secured major gains in Tigray, the TPLF decided to widen its revolution to the national level, challenging the Derg for control over the entire country. At this time, the TPLF invoked the Albanian model of self-reliance developed by Enver Hoxha. Hoxha ruled Albania from 1944 until his death in 1985, during which time he developed a unique brand of Stalinism centred on autarky and development from within. Working through the Albanian Communist Party (ACP), which he founded, Hoxha cut Albania off from the international arena and pursued self-reliant development on the basis of a highly centralised and autocratic regime. Originally a Soviet satellite and an ally of Stalin, Hoxha's government broke with the USSR in 1961 over differences with Stalin's successor Khrushchev, in favour of an alliance with China. Faced with dissent in the mid-1960s, Hoxha implemented a 'Cultural and Ideological Revolution', which purged virtually all of his opposition. Hoxha followed the purges with the collectivisation of agriculture and reforms to the education system. Albania's path to self-reliance continued after

China's rapprochement with the United States in the early 1970s, which Hoxha criticised harshly. By the time of Hoxha's death in 1985, Albania had made some notable achievements in development. The country was self-sufficient in cereals, it had developed an industrial base, and its education and health sectors had made great strides since the 1960s. This development, however, had come at the price of freedom and human rights, as Hoxha maintained a rigorously centralised Stalinist state structure well beyond Stalin's death in 1955 (Biberaj, 1990, 15–31). Influenced by this example, the TPLF under the leadership of Meles adopted Albanian Stalinist political structures and the Albanian commitment to rural and educational development.

In terms of military strategy, the TPLF pursued guerilla warfare for most of the war, on the model of Mao and his followers in the Third World. This was necessary because the Derg controlled many towns and cities in Tigray until the 1980s (Duffield and Prendergast, 1994, 26–7). Politically, the guerilla strategy meant that secrecy was very important, which made Lenin's model of political organisation attractive to the TPLF's leadership. TPLF leaders were familiar with Lenin's writings from their student days in the 1960s. Of particular importance to their political organisation was Lenin's 1902 pamphlet *What is to be Done?*, in which he argued that social revolutions had to be led by an elite vanguard party on behalf of the working class. Out of this model emerged the idea of 'democratic centralism' in which power and policies flowed from the vanguard party downwards to the masses (Lenin, 1902). Influenced by Lenin, the TPLF created a Central Committee controlled by the educated elite, who led the revolution in the name of the peasants. While Meles allowed some space for ideas to flow upwards to the Central Committee, real power flowed strictly downwards. Through a Propaganda Bureau, the Central Committee transmitted the TPLF's doctrines and policies to the peasants and reminded them that factionalism was not permitted (Lata, 1999, 87–93; Hammond, 1999, 23–4). At the grassroots level, the TPLF created elected village and regional committees for political education and development work (Duffield and Prendergast, 1994, 20). These committees were modelled on a traditional Ethiopian institution of village governance called *baito*, which under the imperial regime came to be controlled by landlords and other powerful authority figures. The TPLF transformed *baito* into a system of people's assemblies, which were incorporated into the *woreda* district administrative structure that had existed during Haile Selassie's time (Berhe, 2009, 248–53). While democratic in theory, however, in practice the TPLF controlled the electoral process very tightly and set the policies to be followed by the village and regional committees. This form of controlled democracy closely resembled Lenin's notion of democratic centralism. Under the control of the TPLF, it was hierarchical and it concentrated power in the hands of the educated inner circle (Lata, 1999, 99).

In 1983, Meles and his supporters began to develop a 'vanguard party' within the TPLF to purify the revolution and reassert its Marxist credentials. Two years later, Meles and Abbay Tsehaye created this party, which they called the Marxist–Leninist League of Tigray (MLLT) at a 13-day conference held in July, 1985. Meles had developed the Marxist–Leninist base for the MLLT beginning in 1976, while serving under Abbay (then head of the TPLF's Political Department) as the leader of the cadre school responsible for educating the Front's inner elite. Meles' position allowed him to read widely on Marxism during the war, and over time he developed an affinity for Lenin's ideas of revolutionary democracy and the vanguard party. As noted above, this model was hierarchical and power flowed strictly downwards. Meles' commitment to this Soviet model increased after he embraced the Albanian model around the time he founded the MLLT. This vision deeply influenced the TPLF after Meles captured its leadership through the MLLT soon after the conference in 1985 (Berhe, 2009, 170–6).

Below the elite, the TPLF had to gain the support of the Tigrayan peasants. This was done not only through propaganda but also by delivering public welfare, which was very important in a region prone to drought, famine and food insecurity. In the 1970s, the TPLF therefore created structures based on its Leninist ideology to bring development to peasant communities. Beyond village-level political committees, the Front developed 'civilian departments' concerned with development, including agricultural extension, health and education. As the war progressed and more peasants joined the fight, the farmers produced less and in 1978 the TPLF founded an NGO – the Relief Association of Tigray (REST) – to solicit foreign assistance for welfare and development. The earliest support for the TPLF came from a consortium of church-based NGOs, mainly from Europe, which created the Emergency Relief Desk (ERD) in early 1981 to provide support in Tigray (as well as Eritrea to the north). The ERD provided most of the support in Tigray until the famine of 1984–5, after which other foreign NGOs and governments joined the famine relief effort. Between 1984 and 1990, western organisations mounted the largest humanitarian campaign in history to that point (Duffield and Prendergast, 1994, 20–4, 47, 57, 62). As a result, 'between 1984 and 1985, scores of NGOs set up shop in Ethiopia and Sudan' to assist the famine victims in Tigray (and to a lesser extent Eritrea) (Duffield and Prendergast, 1994, 72–3). One estimate puts the amount received by the TPLF during this period at US $100 million (Berhe, 2009, 184).

In contributing massive assistance to famine-stricken Tigray, foreign NGOs played an important role in the revolution against the Derg, although opinions differ over its precise extent. In an early study, Duffield and Prendergast argued that REST used most of its foreign assistance for its intended purpose of famine relief, which indirectly helped the TPLF's military campaign by freeing up resources that had been spent on public assistance. However, this argument is not based on hard facts. Instead, Duffield and Prendergast assumed that the TPLF could not divert famine relief funds to its military wing because TPLF leaders were tied reciprocally to the peasants through kinship bonds, and because the TPLF could not risk losing political support among the peasantry (Duffield and Prendergast, 1994, 20–9). A more recent study by Aregawi Berhe paints a very different picture. Berhe claims that in July, 1985, after the formation of the MLLT, the head of REST gave its cash balance (US$100 million) to the MLLT's economic department. According to Berhe, Meles then allocated 50 per cent of the funds to the MLLT, 45 per cent to TPLF military activities, and only 5 per cent to famine victims. As with Duffield and Prendergast, however, Berhe's evidence is limited – in this case based on a single interview with a former Central Committee Member of the TPLF/ MLLT (Berhe, 2009, 184) – although Meles himself hinted at this allocation in 2001 (Milkias, 2003, 42). Regardless of which perspective is correct, however, it remains the case that the TPLF depended on foreign NGOs for its fight against the Derg during the 1980s.

As noted above, after Meles and the MLLT took over the TPLF in 1985, the Front widened its revolution to the rest of Ethiopia. In order to do so, Meles developed partnerships with other like-minded organisations to form the EPRDF (Berhe, 2009, 186–7). By this time the Derg's power had weakened considerably, and a TPLF victory was on the horizon in the late 1980s. With victory in sight, Meles visited the UK and USA in 1989–90 representing the EPRDF. The following year the Derg agreed to participate in a peace conference in London (May, 1991) brokered by the United States. As the talks descended into deadlock, Mengistu fled to Zimbabwe and EPRDF troops moved into Addis Ababa and took control of the government (Young, 1997, 167; Wossen-Taffese, 2006, 117–18). With the Derg gone, another conference was convened in Addis Ababa in July, 1991, which paved the way for the TGE. Local and regional elections were held in June,

1992, followed by elections for a Constitutional Assembly, which oversaw the drafting of the Constitution and the declaration of the FDRE in 1995 (Ottaway 1995, 70–2).

In the final phases of the revolution Meles appeared to shift away from Marxism, as he went from praising Albania in the UK in 1989 to embracing globalisation and capitalism during his visit to the United States in 1990. As most commentators have observed, however, the EPRDF's policies and practices at home continued to reflect Meles' Marxist–Leninist vision. In fact, according to Berhe the idea of revolutionary democracy became even more important to Meles after 1991, and it was regularly discussed in EPRDF circles from that time up to the present. In 1994, Meles declared that revolutionary democracy formed the basis of development in Ethiopia, and he drew a direct link between his ideas and Lenin's conception of Soviet democracy in 1919. For Lenin, parliamentary democracy was 'bourgeois democracy', which operated to the benefit of the bourgeoisie rather than the peasantry and working class. Similar to Lenin, Meles wanted to avoid bourgeois democracy by ruling on behalf of the peasants through the vanguard party established by the TPLF/MLLT during the revolution. By disseminating its ideas to the Ethiopian masses in a tightly controlled political space, the TPLF would teach the peasantry to think collectively and work toward a socialist future (Berhe, 2009, 190–1). Before this could happen, however, Ethiopia's minorities would have to be completely liberated from the cultural imperialism of the previous regimes. As such, Meles continued to be influenced after 1991 by Stalin's position on minorities, which was reflected in the FRDE's system of ethnic decentralisation (Ottaway, 1995, 73; Berhe, 2009, 190–1). At the level of the *woreda* and village committees, the FDRE's organisational structure drew on the TPLF's *baito* system in Tigray, administered through democratic centralism. After 1991, *woreda* assemblies across Ethiopia thus were expected to follow the policies set by the central government (Berhe, 2009, 248–53).

Economically, the EPRDF opened up Ethiopia's economy to foreign investment and a certain amount of private capital, although Meles did not oversee a complete conversion to capitalism (Berhe, 2004, 191). In fact, Meles equated Ethiopia's introduction of capitalism with Lenin's New Economic Policy (NEP) of 1921–24 (Milkias, 2003, 50). Developed as a response to economic stagnation and political unrest, the NEP allowed for a degree of capitalism in Russia – especially among peasant producers – while preserving communist politics and state controls over marketing and distribution (Smith, 2002, 100–1). Meles therefore had a ready model for opening Ethiopia to some capitalist forces while remaining doctrinally 'pure'. As a result, Ethiopia developed a hybrid economic system, which allowed for market forces but kept many enterprises in EPRDF hands. Perhaps what is more important is that, Meles' vision for Ethiopian development rejected large-scale urban industrialisation in favour of self-sufficient rural communities. Under this vision, most of the population would remain peasants, some would join rural agro-industries as workers, and all would be surrounded by modern towns of 5,000 to 10,000 people who would have access to the best in housing, education and health services. This vision resembled Mao's and Hoxha's projects of modernising the peasants without urbanising them (Milkias, 2003, 41–51).

After 1995, Meles faced increasing opposition from TPLF leaders within the EPRDF, especially over his 'soft' stance on Eritrean aggression in the region. During the revolution Meles had forged strong ties with the Eritrean Isaias Afeworki, the leader of the Eritrean People's Liberation Front (EPLF). Making good on his promises on secession, Meles had allowed Eritrea to secede from Ethiopia after a referendum in 1993. In 1994, Eritrea gave notice to an expansionist tendency by invading Yemen's Hanish Islands. Meles refused to condemn Eritrea's actions, despite pressure from a group within the TPLF led by Tewolde Woldemariam and Siya Abraha. In 1998, Meles ignored warnings from Siya that Eritrea was poised to invade the Ethiopian border. Three months later, Eritrea invaded and sparked the Ethiopian–Eritrean war of 1998–2000. After the war, the Tewolde–Siya group wanted to keep Eritrea high on the EPRDF's agenda. Meles refused and instead mounted a campaign in 2001 to 'reassess' the doctrines and practices of the TPLF. By this time, Meles had lost much support in Tigray as well, as his duties across the country kept him from visiting regularly. The reassessment therefore was designed to reassert his power in the face of opposition from Tewolde and Siya, and growing discontent in Tigray (Milkias, 2003, 16–22). In 2005, confident that he had regained control and had the support of most of the Ethiopian population, Meles oversaw the most open national election in Ethiopia's history. The EPRDF dominated the rural areas but the opposition ran strong campaigns in urban centres, especially Addis Ababa. In order to fend off the opposition, Meles declared a state of emergency before the election results were announced (Gill, 2010, 141–60). The EPRDF further limited political rights four years later with the 2009 law (noted above) setting limits on human rights work by foreign NGOs. The law might have reflected the fear that foreign NGOs would support the opposition against the EPRDF as they had helped the TPLF defeat the Derg during the 1980s (Nega and Milofsky, 2011, 44). Indeed, Meles referred to foreign NGOs as 'the opposition in disguise' (Gill, 2010, 182).

Unlike political rights, the EPRDF does not appear to be concerned over economic and social rights, particularly in the areas of disability and education. In fact, the government has shown a strong commitment to disabled Ethiopians since 1994, no doubt because SNE is seen as an important precursor to gainful employment and therefore an important tool in the creation of human capital and national development (FDRE, 2006, 13). Whatever the reason, the EPRDF embedded disability in the 1994 Constitution under Economic, Social and Cultural Rights, subsection 5, which states that 'the State shall, within available means, allocate resources to provide rehabilitation and assistance to the physically and mentally disabled, the aged, and to children who are left without parents or guardian' (TGE, 1994a, Article 41(5)). Other sections include disabled individuals by implication because rights are granted to 'all citizens'. The articles on education proclaim commitments to increasing resources and achieving universal education (TGE, 1994a, Article 41(4); Article 90(5)).

Ethiopia's constitution also states that the government will uphold international agreements on disability, including the Standard Rules on the Equalization of Opportunities for Persons with Disabilities (1993), and the Salamanca Statement and Framework for Action on Special Needs Education (1994) (Lewis, 2009, 21). Among other things, the Standard Rules called on states to develop SNE if needed, with the goal of equalising educational opportunities between non-disabled and disabled children, and the Salamanca Statement called on states to make SNE their highest budgetary priority (UNESCO, 2012; UNESCO, 1994). The TGE supplemented the constitution with two additional policies addressing disability. The 'Proclamation Concerning the Rights of Disabled Persons to Employment' asserted the right to employment for disabled Ethiopians, while the Policy on Education and Training promised 'special education and training' for disabled individuals, as well as SNE training for teachers and the provision of 'support input' for SNE programmes (TGE, 1994b; TGE and MoE, 1994, 4, 17, 22–9). In 2002, the MoE reviewed the education policy and reported that 'strong measures have been taken to provide Special Education to the physically disabled. Over 50 pre-primary educational units have been opened in various schools since 1994; 161 teachers of special education have been trained; and several teaching manuals have been prepared' (FDRE, 2002, 82). From this point, the government emphasised technical and vocational training, with the goal of increasing the country's human capital by placing graduates in industrial or agricultural vocations (FDRE, 2002, 90–1).

In 2006, the EPRDF issued a proclamation on SNE specifically after successfully lobbying efforts by the disabled community. In 2004, Ethiopia's Federation of People with Disabilities approached Parliament and 'demanded equal opportunities to education, training and work life'. The MOE responded by convening a 'cooperation committee', which met for the first time in 2004 to begin the deliberations that would produce the SNE two years later. The 2006 proclamation is especially notable because it accepts that 'education is a fundamental human right', well as 'one of the main factors that reduce(s) poverty and improve(s) socio-economic conditions'. This statement reflects the government's endorsement of several international instruments designed 'to honour the rights of citizens to education', including the EFA campaign and the MDGs (FDRE, 2006, 1, 11–12).

Endorsing a number of international initiatives, the EPRDF's disability proclamation set out a blueprint for increasing disabled children's access to primary education. Surveying the current state of SNE, the proclamation acknowledged that existing SNE units were confined to urban areas, had long waiting lists, were under-resourced and faced serious shortages of teachers, classrooms, materials and equipment. Teachers claimed with good evidence that *woredas* and regions omitted SNE from development plans and routinely rejected schools' budget requests for SNE funding. As a result, schools turned away disabled students – fewer than 1 per cent of disabled children had access to primary education – and the dropout rate was assumed to be very high. Regarding teacher training, the Sebeta Institute, attached to the School for the Blind in Oromiya region, was the only facility in the country. The Institute offered a 1-year course, with candidates selected by *woreda* and regional education bureaus and funding provided by the *woredas*. The programme had a capacity of 50 trainees per year, but very few applicants came forward – for example, only 16 in 2004 – due to a lack of knowledge and awareness, and the fact that SNE teachers did not receive additional remuneration for their extra training (FDRE, 2006, 7–11).

In response to this dire situation, the ERPRDF set out a strategy for SNE that promised to:

- implement the 1994 Education and Training Strategy, and the international instruments proclaiming education as a human right;

- develop and implement guidelines 'for curriculum modification and support system development in schools for learners with special needs';
- facilitate access for SN students to technical and vocational training, or higher education;
- strengthen teacher training for SNE teachers;
- improve 'the supply of trained manpower and appropriate materials to schools and other learning institutions'. (FDRE, 2006, 12)

This commitment was strengthened in 2010, when the Ethiopian government ratified the United Nations Convention on the Rights of People with Disabilities (CRPD). The UN adopted the Convention and its Optional Protocol on 13 December 2006, and opened it for signature on 30 March 2007. In ratifying the Convention, the EPRDF agreed in principle to abide by the CRPD's Articles, including the right to education as expressed in Article 24. The Article establishes the right of disabled individuals to 'an inclusive, quality and free primary education and secondary education on an equal basis with others in the communities in which they live' (UN, 2006, Article 24(2b). To this end, the CRPD calls on governments to provide support and all necessary accommodations, particularly for blind, deaf and deaf–blind students (UN, 2006, Article 24(3)). State parties are also called upon to provide training for non-disabled and disabled teachers (Article 4), and to guarantee access to tertiary education for disabled students, including vocational training (Article 5). These measures are consistent with the EPRDF's proclamation of 2006, but, as the government itself realised then, the lack of capacity in the MoE posed a formidable problem, even compared to other East African countries (FDRE, 2006, 10). As a result, the government of Ethiopia relies on NGO support in order to translate the right to education into a reality for disabled Ethiopian children. This brings us back to CH-Ethiopia, and some concluding thoughts on the reasons for the organisation's success in working with regional and *woreda* education bureaus to increase the capacity of the MoE to achieve the MDG/EFA goals.

Conclusion: CH-Ethiopia, the MDGs and Education for All

Since 2005, the EPRDF has proclaimed its commitment to disability rights in supporting international Conventions and developing its own Disability Act and SNE initiative. But why has it supported CH-Ethiopia so strongly despite the law limiting the human rights work of foreign NGOs, and what does this imply for MDG 2 in

Ethiopia? In my opinion, the history of the TPLF's revolution provides an important clue. How did the legacy of the revolution provide an opening for disability rights and SNE? As presented above, there is good evidence that Meles remained committed to his radical ideologies – revolutionary democracy, democratic centralism, ethnic self-determination, and rural socialism – from the 1970s until well into the twenty-first century, and probably up to his death in 2012. At the base of this vision stood the ideal of modernising the peasantry without allowing large-scale urbanisation. As we have seen, this vision included a patchwork of rural towns surrounded by peasant farmers. Education was not only permissible but in fact necessary to achieve this vision. It is my contention that this ideological commitment, born out of the revolution against the Derg, provided the impetus for supporting rural education, as well as the decentralisation of the delivery of educational programmes. This in turn provided an opening for Ethiopia's disability community to press for disability rights and SNE programmes.

Many observers criticise the EPRDF for exerting central control over regional and village-level organisations despite its commitment to decentralisation. Chanie, for instance, asserts that the decentralisation programme has been undermined by the practice of clientelism, under which the government, as patron, rewards loyal clients with political power at the local level. 'On the political front', writes Chanie, 'the EPRDF controls all the regional state governments in the Ethiopian federation, either directly through its member parties or indirectly through affiliate parties. The relationship between the central and regional parties is between patron and client' (Chanie, 2007, 357). As such, local officials simply do the bidding of the central government, which is dominated by the TPLF, leaving power flowing from the top downwards despite a decentralised system on paper. Chanie also argues that this political structure grew out of the TPLF revolution, specifically the doctrine of democratic centralism – a plausible idea in light of the analyses by Lata, Berhe and Milkias described above (Chanie, 2007, 362–7; Lata, 1999, Berhe, 2004; Milkias, 2003). Interestingly, however, Chanie also observes that education provides an exception to the rule in that decentralisation actually has happened effectively since 1995. Although the federal share of the education budget has risen since 1996/7, the regions still control the majority of recurrent expenditures (78 per cent) and a sizeable portion of capital expenditures (43 per cent) (Chanie, 2007, 369–70). Combined with the government's commitment to disability rights and education, the EPRDF's willingness to decentralise educational programmes means that there is good potential for regional and *woreda* educational bureaus to work with NGOs on SNE projects. In this particular case, foreign NGOs have been able to tap the Ethiopia's vibrant civil society, as described by Nega and Milofsky, to develop effective programmes based on partnerships between the central government, regional education bureaus and foreign NGOs (Nega and Milofsky, 2011, 44–6).

Within this context, CH-Ethiopia is poised to make an important contribution to the MDG/EFA campaign. The organisation draws on a wealth of experience from its Canadian counterpart, but it is entirely staffed by Ethiopians who have an intimate knowledge of the country and its challenges and opportunities. Although the organisation has not been able to secure external funding for its 2010 proposal, the current programme has been very successful. Between 2005 and 2013, when the SNE programme was handed over to the Ethiopian government, CH-Ethiopia provided new spaces for 1,900 disabled students in the Aris, Bale and West Arsi zones of Oromyia. The entire project cost $364,683 Canadian, or $192.93 per student. Most of the funding (80 per cent) came from private donations channelled through CH-Global in Canada, but CH-Ethiopia also raised 20 per cent internally. The funding covered teacher training, classroom renovations, school uniforms, educational materials and supplies, life skills training for students, summer day camps, disability awareness workshops for the public, and rehabilitation services for older students. The project focused on the first cycle of primary education (Grades 1–4), and at the time of the handover to the government in 2013, the reports from CH and the Zonal Education Office showed a completion rate of 100 per cent (CH-Ethiopia, 2014). Since 2013 the project started by CH-Ethiopia has continued to grow. As of December, 2015, 110 SNE units have been opened, 331 teachers have received training, and 2,560 disabled students have completed primary education (CH-Ethiopia, personal communication, 15 December 2015).

In addition to CH-Global/Ethiopia, the EPRDF recently listed 31 domestic and international organisations working on SNE (Lewis, 2009, 31; FDRE, 2006, 35). However, in the Arsi, Bale and West Arsi Districts of the Oromyia Region, CH-Ethiopia was the only organisation to have increased SNE enrolments between 2005 and 2013 (CH-Ethiopia, 2014). For this reason, relations with the government have been excellent at the *woreda*, regional and national levels. Indeed, CH-Ethiopia won four government awards in 2011 alone, including best performing NGO, best NGO providing children's services, best NGO in the education sector, and best entrepreneurial organisation.

This support has allowed the organisation a free hand in planning and implementing its SNE programmes, which to date have been very successful. Contributing to this success is the close attention paid to the government's priorities and its commitment to education as a human right. In fact, the 2010 proposal sits very nicely within the EPRDF's stated policies on SNE, including increased enrolment, teacher training, vocational training, employment and advocacy. And, like the government, CH-Ethiopia does not emphasise the political aspects of the right to education, nor does the organisation blame the EPRDF for the lack of access. Instead, the focus is on social inclusion, employment and health. Also, the organisation accepts the government's lead role and ownership over education programmes, including curriculum development and teacher training. The schools are government schools, and CH-Ethiopia is simply trying to increase the capacity of the regional and *woreda* educational bureaus. Most of the new SNE units are in rural areas and therefore help to reverse the urban bias of previous SNE initiatives. And the emphasis on girls' education helps to overcome the existing gender bias. But CH-Ethiopia does more than simply provide spaces for disabled boys and girls in primary schools. After graduation, the organisation vocational training for many individuals, then offers microcredit to help them integrate into the economy. The many examples of successful entrepreneurs stand as a testament to the programme's success.

To what extent can we attribute the openness of the EPRDF to SNE projects such as CH-Ethiopia's as a product of the MDGs? I would argue that certain forces were coming together anyway around the MDG education goals, connected very strongly to the TPLF's revolution against the Derg. The TPLF had been committed to rural education since the1970s in Tigray, and the Front's victory in 1991 allowed it to carry this commitment to the rest of Ethiopia. After 2000, the EFA and MDG initiatives arguably propelled those forces further and they were given another boost in 2006 with the United Nations' CRPD. The CRPD provided a platform for Ethiopian disability activists and local and foreign NGOs to take up the cause of disability rights for disabled Ethiopians, and the government responded positively in the area of disability education through SNE. In this sense, the MDGs represented one of a number of factors behind the growth of NGO-sponsored SNE initiatives in Ethiopia. Although MDG 2 has not been met in Ethiopia, the MDG framework succeeded in providing the foundation for an enabling policy environment.

What can the CH-Ethiopia case offer in terms of lessons for success? First, development practitioners need to be aware of relevant historical contexts and their relevance to development projects in the present. This is not just a question of trying to learn from past mistakes, but what is more important – in the words of Woolcock, Szreter and Rao – it involves 'exploring in detail the specific contingencies by which the dynamics of an evolving set of actors, events and institutions come to coalesce (or not) at a particular time and place, and thereby shape future action' (Woolcock et al, 2011, 80). In the Ethiopian case, the history of the TPLF/EPRDF revolution is especially important in this context. Driven to a peasant-based revolution against the Dergue, the actors behind the revolution – led by Meles Zenawi – coalesced around a philosophy or rural development in which education formed an important pillar. In my opinion this historical context helped to open the door to disability rights. Historical conditions, in other words, provided a receptive environment for the MDG policy framework relating to education and SNE. Second, in order to achieve concrete results on the ground, development projects must be locally designed, controlled and owned. In the case of CH-Ethiopia, the organisation's leaders and staff are Ethiopian nationals who are fully and intimately aware of the country's historical experiences as well as current political, economic and social conditions. Beyond this awareness, they are willing and able to partner with the country's political leaders to achieve their SNE targets. In addition, at the grassroots level CH-Ethiopia has mobilised and given a voice to disabled persons and their families, as evidenced by the creation of a network of disability associations. Taken as a whole, this case study shows that frameworks like the MDGs can establish a positive policy environment, as noted above. But the experience of CH-Ethiopia also demonstrates that success on the ground also requires knowledge of historical contexts, local ownership, and a willingness to work within specific sets of opportunities and constraints.

Notes

[1] United Nations Convention and Optional Protocol Signatures and Ratifications, www.un.org/disabilities/countries.asp?id=166.

[2] The law is called the Charities and Societies Proclamation (NGO law). It defines as 'foreign' any NGO receiving more than 10 per cent of its funding from abroad (HRW, 2009).

References

Berhe, A, 2004, The origins of the Tigray People's Liberation Front, *African Affairs*, 103, 577–92

Berhe, A, 2009, *A political history of the Tigray People's Liberation Front (1975–1991)*, Los Angeles: Tsehai

Biberaj, E, 1990, *Albania: A socialist maverick*, Boulder, CO: Westview Press

CH-Ethiopia (Christian Horizons-Ethiopia), 2014, *Report on SNE achievements, 2005–13*, unpublished manuscript, 3 February

CH-Global (Christian Horizons-Global), 2010, *Inclusive education in Oromiya region*, Kitchener: CH-Global

CH-Global (Christian Horizons-Global), 2011, *Improving access to special needs education to secure better future for children and youth with disabilities in the Oromiya region of Ethiopia*, Kitchener: CH-Global

Chanie, P, 2007, Clientelism and Ethiopia's post-1991 decentralisation, *The Journal of Modern African Studies*, 45, 3, 355–84

Duffield, M, Prendergast, J, 1994, *Without troops and tanks: The emergency relief desk and the cross border operation into Eritrea and Tigray*, Lawrenceville, NJ: Red Sea Press

Easterly, W, 2009, How the Millennium Development Goals are unfair to Africa, *World Development* 37, 1, 26–35

FDRE (Federal Democratic Republic of Ethiopia), 2002, *The education and training policy and its implementation*, Addis Ababa: Ministry of Education

FDRE (Federal Democratic Republic of Ethiopia), 2006, *Special needs program education strategy: Emphasising inclusive education to meet the UPEC and EFA goals*, Addis Ababa: Ministry of Education

FDRE (Federal Democratic Republic of Ethiopia), 2010, *Ethiopia. 2010 MDGs report: Trends and prospects for meeting the MDGs by 2015*, Addis Ababa: Federal Democratic Republic of Ethiopia

FDRE (Federal Democratic Republic of Ethiopia), 2012, *Assessing progress towards the Millennium Development Goals: Ethiopia MDGs report*, Addis Ababa: Ministry of Finance and Economic Development

Gill, P, 2010, *Famine and foreigners: Ethiopia since live aid*, Oxford: Oxford University Press

Habtu, A, 1996, *Women's education in Ethiopia in historical perspective and the (1979–91) national literacy campaign*, unpublished PhD Dissertation, New York: New School for Social Research

Hammond, J, 1999, *Fire from the ashes: A chronicle of the revolution in Tigray, Ethiopia, 1975–1991*, Lawrenceville, NJ: Red Sea Press

Higgins, K, 2013, *Reflecting on the MDGs and making sense of the Post-2015 Development Agenda*, North–South Institute Research Report, Ottawa: North–South Institute

HRW (Human Rights Watch) 2009, *Ethiopia: New law ratchets up repression*, online at www.hrw.org/news/2009/01/08/ethiopia-new-law-ratchets-repression

Kebede, M, 2006, The roots and fallouts of Haile Selassie's educational policy, *UNESCO Forum Occasional Paper Series* 10, June

Kiros, FR, 1990, *Implementing educational policies in Ethiopia*, Washington, DC: World Bank

Lata, L, 1999, *The Ethiopian state at the crossroads: Decolonization, democratization or disintegration?*, Lawrenceville, NJ: Red Sea Press

Lenin, V, 1902, *What is to be done?*, www.marxists.org/archive/lenin/works/download/what-itd.pdf

Lewis, I, 2009, Education for disabled people in Ethiopia and Rwanda, Background paper prepared for the Education for All Global Monitoring Report 2010, Reaching the marginalized, UNESCO, 2010/ED/EFA/MRT/PI/01, Paris: UNESCO

Makonnen, W, 1969, On the question of nationalities in Ethiopia, *Struggle*, 5, 2, 4–7

Marcus, HG, 2002, *A history of Ethiopia*, Berkeley, CA: University of California Press

Markakis, J, 2011, *Ethiopia: The last two frontiers*, Woodbridge: James Currey

MDG (Millennium Development Goals), 2000, *MDG 2: Achieve universal primary education*, www.mdgmonitor.org/goal2.cfm

Milkias, P, 2003, Ethiopia, the TPLF, and the roots of the 2001 political tremor, *Northeast African Studies* 10, 2, 13–66

Milkias, P, 2012, *Ethiopia*, Santa Barbara, CA: ABC-CLIO

Nega, B, 2010a, Ethiopia is headed for chaos, *Current History* 109, 727 (May),186–92

Nega, B, Milofsky, C, 2011, Ethiopia's Anti-NGO law and its consequences for economic development, *Community Development Journal* 46, Supp 2, April, 33–48

Ofcansky, TP, Berry, L (eds), 2002, *Ethiopia: A country study*, Blackmask Online, www.scribd.com/document/117028048/Ethiopia-a-country-study-Edited-by-Thomas-P-Ofcansky-and-LaVerle-Berry

Ottaway, M, 1995, The Ethiopian transition: Democratization or new authoritarianism?, *Northeast African Studies* 2, 3, 67–87

Smith, SA, 2002, *The Russian revolution: A very short introduction*, Oxford: Oxford University Press

TGE (Transitional Government of Ethiopia), 1994a, *Constitution*, Addis Ababa: TGE

TGE (Transitional Government of Ethiopia), 1994b, A Proclamation Concerning the Rights of *Disabled Persons to Employment, Transitional Government of Ethiopia, Proclamation No 101/1994 of 26 August 1994*, Addis Ababa: TGE

TGE (Transitional Government of Ethiopia), MoE (Ministry of Education), 1994, *Education and training policy*, Addis Ababa: MoE

UN (United Nations), 1993, *Standard rules on the equalization of opportunities for persons with disabilities*, www.un.org/esa/socdev/enable/dissre04.htm,

UN (United Nations), 2006, *Universal declaration on the rights of people with disabilities*, New York: UN

UN (United Nations), 2012, *The Millennium Development Goals report 2012*, New York: United Nations

UNDP (United Nations Development Programme), 2012, *Assessing progress in Africa toward the Millennium Development Goals*, MDG Report 2011, New York: United Nations Development Program

UNESCO (United Nations Educational, Scientific and Cultural Organization), 1994, *The Salamanca statement and framework for action on special needs education*, www.unesco.org/education/pdf/SALAMA_E.PDF

UNESCO (United Nations Educational, Scientific and Cultural Organization), 2004, *Education for All: The quality* imperative, Paris: UNESCO Publishing

UNESCO (United Nations Educational, Scientific and Cultural Organization), 2012, Education for All, www.unesco.org/new/en/education/themes/leading-the-international-agenda/education-for-all/

UNESCO (United Nations Educational, Scientific and Cultural Organization), 2013, UNESCO Institute for Statistics data, 2013, http://knoema.com/UNESCOISD2013Jul/unesco-institute-for-statistics-data-2013?location=1000670-ethiopia

UNICEF (United Nations International Children's Emergency Fund), 1999, *State of the world's children*, New York: UNICEF

Vandemoortele, J, 2007, The MDGs: 'M' for misunderstood?, *WIDER Angle* 1, 6–7

Wagaw, TG, 1979, *Education in Ethiopia: Prospect and retrospect*, Ann Arbor, MI: University of Michigan Press

WEF (World Education Forum), 2015, *Education for All 2015 national review report: Ethiopia*, Incheon, Republic of Korea: WEF, UNESCO

Woolcock, M, Szreter, S, Rao, V, 2011, How and why does history matter for development policy?, *Journal of Development Studies* 47, 1, 70–96

World Bank, 2014, World Development Indicators, http://databank. worldbank.org/data/views/reports/tableview.aspx#

Wossen-Taffese, M, 2006, The Contested Politics of Education in Ethiopia: Leadership Vacuity, Mass/National Alienation, Ethnic Atomization, in AA Abdi, KP Puplampu, GJ Sefa Dei (eds) *African education and globalization: Critical perspectives*, Lanham: Lexington Books, 117–34

Young, J, 1996, The Tigray and Eritrean Peoples Liberation Fronts: A history of tensions and pragmatism, *Journal of Modern African Studies* 34, 105–20

Young, J, 1997, *Peasant revolution in Ethiopia: The Tigray People's Liberation Front, 1975–1991*, Cambridge: Cambridge University Press

Young, J, 1998, Regionalism and democracy in Ethiopia, *Third World Quarterly* 19, June, 191–204

SEVEN

Facing the global challenge of youth employment

Ragui Assaad and Deborah Levison

Introduction

Social and economic challenges facing young people today must be understood in terms of complex interactions between unique demographic trends and specific economic contexts. There has been an unprecedented growth in the number of young people in the Global South in the past two decades. The regional manifestations of this growth, however, vary considerably depending on how the forces of economic globalisation have interacted with historically determined national and regional economic structures and policies. Although we will argue that unemployment is only a partial measure of employment inadequacy for youth, especially in poor countries, the ready availability of data and its widespread use make it an important starting point. Globally, the ILO estimates that the number of unemployed youth has been declining slowly since the peak of the financial crisis in 2009. The total number was projected to be 73.4 million in 2015 (ILO, 2015, 15). The global youth unemployment rate has remained fairly steady since 2010 at about 13 per cent (ILO, 2015, 15). In contrast, the global adult unemployment rate was much lower at 4.6 per cent in 2015 (ILO, 2015).

We argue in this chapter that employment inadequacy among youth is a much broader phenomenon than youth unemployment as conventionally defined. Remaining out of work to actively search for employment is often either fruitless and/or unaffordable for many youth in developing countries, if there are few wage and salary jobs to be had. Youth in these situations are forced to engage in any sort of livelihood activity they can muster, even if extremely marginal; or, if they can rely on their families for support, they may remain inactive after completing their schooling. Broader measures of employment inadequacy are needed to capture these two situations, but most of these measures will require new data collection practices.

One broader measure, called 'NEET', for 'not in education, employment or training', is increasingly being used to study youth employment challenges in OECD countries (OECD, 2012). While this measure does not take into account that many youth are engaged in unproductive or marginal employment, it does capture a broad category of youth for whom employment is either not an option or at least not one worth actively searching for. The NEET measure is not readily available for most developing countries, but we attempt to estimate it for a broad set of countries to see what it can add to the standard unemployment measure. Measuring the adequacy of employment for youth actually engaged in some sort of economic activity is even more challenging. The ILO has recently proposed a number of measures that attempt to capture the extent of labour underutilisation, including vulnerable employment, non-standard and irregular employment, but these measures have not yet received widespread acceptance and are consequently not broadly used.

While we strive to take a global perspective on youth employment challenges, our focus in this chapter is on the developing regions of Asia, Africa and Latin America. These are the regions where the great majority of youth in the world currently reside. These are also the regions where youth employment challenges are most likely to be associated with the demographic challenges posed by growing youth populations in recent decades. We focus primarily on youths aged from 15 to 24, but sometimes also consider 25- to 29-year-olds because there is growing evidence that the transition to adulthood, including the transition to work, is now more protracted and extends into these higher ages.

The demographic changes, which can be broadly characterised as the 'youth bulge' phenomenon, have been fairly similar across developing regions of the world, albeit with somewhat different timing, pace and intensity. Nearly all parts of the developing world saw unprecedented increases in both the number and proportion of youth between the ages of 15 and 24 during the past five decades, but the future trajectory of today's youth demographic will deviate substantially over the next four decades.

After attempting to characterise the dimensions of the youth employment challenge, we move to a brief review of existing attempts to address it. We focus in this discussion on education and training programmes that prepare youth for the labour market, and active labour market programmes (ALMPs) that help them transition into the world of work. We attempt to synthesise the implications and lessons learned from rigorous evaluations of such programmes. Although these programmes are fairly widespread, most of the evaluations and assessments that have been carried out so far have been done for programmes implemented in upper- and middle-income countries. The applicability to poor countries of these lessons learned is, therefore, still a work in progress.

The youth bulge phenomenon

The challenge of youth employment in the developing world is linked to a complex interaction of economic, social and demographic factors. Its recent prominence on the global agenda is clearly associated with the aforementioned explosive growth in both the number and share of youth in the population in recent decades in much of the developing world. Briefly, this youth bulge is a significant change in the age structure of the population, where the proportion of youth increases substantially compared to other age groups, both older and younger. It has emerged as a result of demographic transition: falling early childhood mortality followed, with a lag, by falling fertility. The interval of the lag results in surviving children (and, later, youth) being a larger fraction of the population than ever before, or ever after. Figure 7.1, which shows the evolution of the proportion of youth in the total population by world region, illustrates this phenomenon. The shape of the bulge depends on how fast early childhood mortality declined (which affects the steepness of the increase) and how soon fertility began to decline and the rate at which it declined (which affects the timing of the downturn and slope of the decline).

The youth bulge phenomenon does not necessarily lead to adverse outcomes for youth. A growing number of young people has undoubtedly placed considerable stress first on educational systems, as young people go through schooling ages, and then on labour markets, housing markets and health systems, as they transition to adult roles. Nevertheless, youth bulge effects relating to education, health and employment have varied considerably. The goal of this chapter is to characterise the way in which social and economic systems across the developing world have responded to the labour market challenges posed by the youth bulge. Such responses will be reflected by youth employment and unemployment rates, as well as youth earnings, about which there is much less data.[1]

As shown in Figure 7.2, the bulk of the developing world's youth population is currently in East Asia and South Asia, but also increasingly in sub-Saharan Africa.[2] Those three regions combined were estimated to have 921 million young people in 2015, 77.2 per

Figure 7.1: Youth (15–24) as a percentage of total population by region

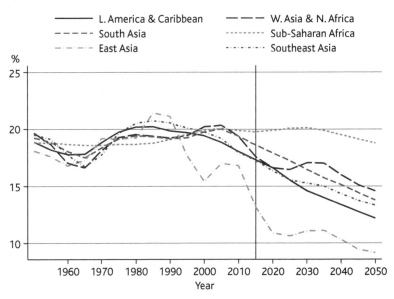

Source: Authors' calculations based on UN (2015)

Figure 7.2: Size of the youth population (15–24) by region, millions

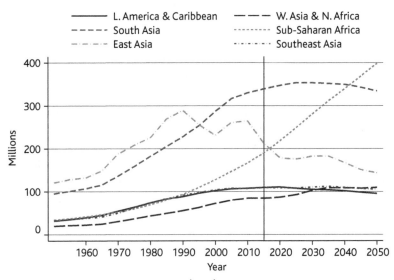

Source: Authors' calculations based on UN (2015)

cent of the world total. This number is expected to decline to 876.7 million (65.9 per cent) by 2050 (UN, 2015). The most striking aspect of Figure 7.2 is that the youth population has recently peaked or will soon peak in all developing regions except for sub-Saharan Africa, where it is expected to rise steadily to 2050. Note that while estimates past 2015 are projections, the figures are fairly certain up to about 2035 since most of these individuals have already been born (and are children), and projected early-childhood mortality has been taken into account.

The phase of the demographic transition that places the greatest demand on labour markets in terms of job creation and labour absorption is when the number of new entrants is large relative to existing workers. This is best shown by examining the percentage of youth in the working age population, which changes as countries move through the demographic transition. As shown in Figure 7.3, youth as a percentage of the working age population peaked earliest in East Asia: at about 1970 it reached approximately one-third of the working age population. By 2010, it had fallen sharply to 22.5 per cent, and it will continue to fall rapidly until about 2025, when it will reach less than half of its 1970 peak. The percentage of youth among the working age

Figure 7.3: Youth (15–24) as a percentage of working-age population (15–64) by region

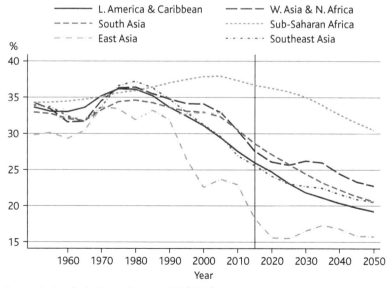

Source: Authors' calculations based on UN (2015)

population exhibits a fairly similar time trend in almost all the other developing regions. It peaked in 1980 at somewhere between 35 and 37 per cent of the working age population in Latin America and the Caribbean, West Asia and North Africa, South Asia and Southeast Asia. It fell fairly rapidly from that point on in Southeast Asia and in Latin America and the Caribbean, and somewhat more slowly in West Asia and North Africa and in South Asia until 2005. Both these regions, however, are projected to experience an accelerated rate of decline in this proportion from 2005 to 2020 (UN, 2011).

Sub-Saharan Africa is the clear outlier in this case. As shown in Figure 7.3, the percentage of youth in the working age population there peaked somewhere between 2000 and 2005 at 37.7 per cent, a level higher than in any other developing region, and it will only retreat very gradually from that peak through 2050. Based on projections of both the absolute and relative sizes of the youth population, we can expect that demographically-driven labour supply pressures will be subsiding significantly in the post-2015 developing world, except in sub-Saharan Africa.

The changing growth rate and age structure of the population that is associated with different stages of the demographic transition pose both challenges and opportunities for development. The stage of the demographic transition associated with the youth bulge is said to eventually yield a 'demographic dividend' as the economy benefits from a lower dependency ratio and a younger labour force (Bloom and Williamson, 1998; Bloom et al, 2003; Gribble and Bremner, 2012). For such a dividend to materialise, however, economic conditions must make it possible to quickly absorb the new entrants to the labour force into productive employment. In East Asia, export-led industrialisation driven by the region's rapid incorporation in the global economy combined with prior investments in education to generate a virtuous cycle of rising supply and demand for human capital. Under a different set of economic conditions, both in terms of internal policies and institutions and external factors, the demographic dividend could easily turn into a demographic burden.

Western Asia and Northern Africa provides perhaps the most pronounced instance of the 'youth demographic burden'. Authoritarian regimes used oil and oil-related revenues to create unproductive public sector employment for educated middle-class youth. As fiscal realities and demographic pressures made this policy unsustainable, educated young people were faced with either long unemployment queues or uncertain prospects in an informal economy that was unwilling to pay much of a premium for their educational credentials (Assaad,

2013). South Asia's demographic trajectory appears to be very similar to that of Western Asia and Northern Africa, but its labour market outcomes were quite different. Educated youth have done quite well, as they have integrated into the globalising service sector, although there is evidence of skill mismatches that lead to higher unemployment rates among skilled workers. Less educated youth have suffered from underemployment in the informal economy (ILO, 2013). In the future, sub-Saharan Africa is perhaps the region of the world that will face the greatest challenges with the youth bulge. Because fertility has not declined as sharply as in other regions, sub-Saharan Africa will not benefit from a demographic dividend in the coming decades. As shown in Figures 7.1 and 7.3, youth are expected to be about 20 per cent of the population there for the next couple of decades, and they will make up over 30 per cent of the working age population up until about 2045 (UN, 2011).

The challenge of youth employment

We have argued thus far that there have been varied regional outcomes in response to the youth bulge phenomenon, some positive and some negative, with the variation being primarily a function of the social and economic institutions that either allow or hinder different societies as they prepare young people for productive roles and as they deploy them in such roles. For youth bulge members to become productive labour force workers, it is essential that there is an adequately high level – and growing – demand for labour. In general, as the youth population grows into adulthood, the ratio of physical capital to labour supply falls; without demand-fed expansion, the result can include stagnating or lower wages for workers of all ages, as well as unemployment or underemployment of new entrants to the labour force. In cases of inadequate growth in labour demand to capitalise on the 'youth dividend', the forms that adverse labour market outcomes can take will depend on the structure of production, the degree of organisation or formality of labour markets, the educational composition of youth and the expectations that come along with education, and the degree of support that families can or are willing to provide as young people make their transitions to employment. In this section we discuss the challenges of measuring employment inadequacy for youth, present various measures that go beyond the standard unemployment measures, and provide recommendations for how to improve these measures.

Unemployment estimates and projections

The ILO estimates that the global youth unemployment rate rose from 11.7 per cent in 2007 to 12.8 per cent in 2009 as a result of the world financial crisis, after declining sharply from 2005 to 2007. From 2010 to 2015, the youth unemployment rate remained fairly steady at around 13 per cent. The ILO projects that the global youth unemployment rate will rise slightly to 13.2 per cent by 2018 (ILO, 2015, 80). These estimates translate into 73.4 million unemployed youth in 2015 as compared to 70.5 million in 2007. The ratio of youth to adult unemployment rates globally has hovered just under three since 1995 (ILO, 2015, 82).[3]

While youth unemployment rates in more developed economies and Central and Eastern Europe were strongly affected by the world financial crisis, peaking in either 2009 or 2010, the developing regions of the world were less affected. Still, several regions have continued to experience consistent increases in youth unemployment rates. In East Asia, the Middle East and North Africa, the ILO's projected unemployment rates for 2019 are significantly higher than rates at the peak of the crisis. In addition to these three regions, unemployment is projected to increase in Central and Southeastern Europe and CIS but to remain flat in Southeast Asia and the Pacific, South Asia, Latin American and the Caribbean, and sub-Saharan Africa (ILO, 2015, 80). However, by far the highest rates of youth unemployment will continue to be found in North Africa, where they are projected to reach 30.7 per cent, followed by the Middle East, where they are projected to reach 29.2 per cent by 2018 (ILO, 2015, 80) (see Figure 7.4).

Unemployment measures seem to show adverse outcomes for youth in some countries and not in others. Regions such as North Africa and Western Asia have experienced very high youth unemployment in the last decade, but other regions with equally pronounced youth bulges, such as sub-Saharan Africa and South Asia, experienced much lower youth unemployment, as shown in Figure 7.4.

The ratio of youth-to-adult unemployment rates is highest in Southeast Asia and the Pacific, where it was estimated by the ILO to be 5.9:1 in 2014, nearly double the world average ratio of 2.9:1. It is also quite high in South Asia and the Middle East, where it is about 4:1, suggesting that in these regions unemployment is primarily a first-time labour market insertion phenomenon (ILO, 2015).

Because of the nature of their economies and labour markets, employment challenges in some economies do not manifest themselves

Figure 7.4: Youth unemployment rates by region, ages 15–24, 2008–2019

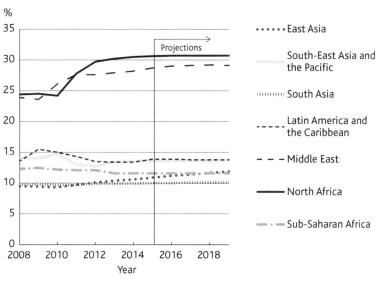

Source: ILO (2015)

as open unemployment but rather as high rates of underemployment, employment vulnerability and inadequate earnings. For open unemployment to be observed, certain conditions must be met. Open unemployment tends to be associated with queuing for formal sector jobs: where the probability of formal sector work is higher, youth and their families feel that it is reasonable for youth to remain unemployed to search for or queue for such jobs. This is the case in North Africa and the Middle East, where the dominant role of government in the economy has historically led to employment opportunities for educated workers in the bureaucracy and state sector. In recent years, however, the growth of the state-dominated formal sector has been anemic relative to the rapid growth of educated workers. Because youths' expectations have not changed, and they continue the strategy of searching and queuing, open unemployment has increased rapidly as youth bulge members enter working ages.

In other contexts, demographic pressures from the youth bulge do not manifest themselves as high youth unemployment. If formal sector jobs are scarce or are perceived to be virtually inaccessible, young job seekers will pursue any opportunities they can find on family farms or in microenterprises, petty trade or casual labour rather than remain openly unemployed. This is essentially what is happening in much of sub-Saharan Africa and South Asia, with estimated unemployment rates at 11.6 and 9.9, respectively, in 2014 (ILO, 2015, 80).

Regardless of whether adverse labour market outcomes are reflected in high youth unemployment rates or not, gendered patterns are typically observable. In the absence of adequate labour demand, girls and young women are more likely to be found doing non-labour force work, including caring labour (for young children, the ill, the disabled and the aged) and household maintenance tasks (cooking, cleaning and washing) and subsistence labour. Many will not have experienced labour force work either themselves or among their peers and therefore do not report themselves as seeking such work even if they would be able to engage in it were it available. As a result, many out-of-work young women will simply not show up among the ranks of the unemployed, especially when the 'seeking work' criterion is imposed. On the other hand, where there is a precedent for women – especially the educated ones among them – to get formal sector jobs, often in government, young women will have an incentive to queue for such jobs and therefore show up in the unemployment queue. That appears to be the case in Latin America, the Middle East and North Africa, where female unemployment rates are substantially higher than those of males (ILO, 2015, 81).

NEET: a better measure of youth employment inadequacy?

Unemployment rates are not a good measure of employment inadequacy for youth in many situations where remaining jobless while searching for work is either ineffectual or infeasible. A large number of youths may be neither in school nor employed, but may not be actively seeking employment due to discouragement or simply a lack of organised labour markets in their regions. They would not show up among the ranks of the unemployed. More important for the most rural, least-developed economies is the necessity for youth to undertake whatever livelihood activities they can find or create, even if these have extremely low levels of productivity. If they engage in any kind of economic activity for one hour or more during the reference week, they are counted as employed according to international definitions, but the quality and/or quantity of this employment is often inadequate. A measure that casts a wider net – by dropping individuals' need to report their willingness and availability for work – is the NEET measure, which refers to a population sometimes called 'idle'. This measure is particularly relevant for youth because it captures those who are not investing in their future either by acquiring human capital through education or training or by gaining experience on the job.

Gender and age patterns

Using mainly census data from the most recent decade available, Figure 7.5 shows the percentage of youth 15–24 by sex who are NEET for selected countries, by world region. That is, these youth are not going to school, and they do not admit to having labour force employment. The figures we provide might include some youth who are in training outside of formal education, as this information is not available in census data, but it is unlikely to involve a large number of youth.

Figure 7.5 shows that NEET is always higher for females than for males; usually the difference is substantial, with the female percentage who are NEET double or triple that for males. Among the 23 countries included in Figure 7.5, NEET for males ranges between 10 and 30 per cent with only four exceptions (three below 10 per cent, one above 30 per cent). NEET estimates for females, however, are almost all above 20 per cent (only two are as low as 10 per cent),

Figure 7.5: Percentage NEET by sex, youths 15–24, selected countries

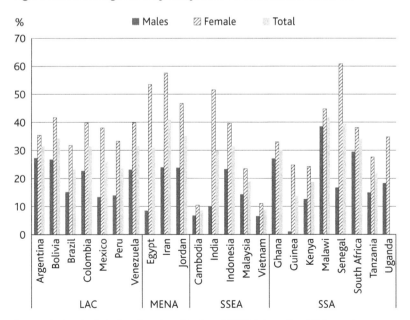

Source: Authors' calculations based on data from IPUMS-International (Minnesota Population Center, 2013)

with ten countries at or exceeding 40 per cent NEET for female youth (MPC, 2013).

While the unemployment rate is biased downward due to discouraged workers, NEET is biased upward by its inclusion of some youth who are fully occupied in non-labour market activities: parenting and doing other so-called 'reproductive' tasks that maintain the labour force. These time-consuming activities include cooking, cleaning, laundry, childcare and other caring activities for the ill and the infirm. Ideally NEET would exclude those who prefer to specialise in household work, but that information is typically not available. However, even if it were available, it would not be strictly correct to exclude them from the NEET estimate, since some of these young women and men would prefer to engage in labour market employment, if they could find jobs.

Differences in whether or not military draftees – who are mostly male – are counted among the employed reduce the comparability of the NEET estimates, in some cases biasing their levels upward. Among those countries that report draftees as not being employed, we examined the case of Egypt. We found that the NEET percentage was very high for males of age to be drafted into the military (20–24 years): almost 40 per cent (based on data from MPC, 2013). A re-estimate showed that by categorising military conscripts as employed, there was little difference between the NEET percentage and the unemployment percentage for males in Egypt.[4]

With regards to the age pattern of NEET, we note that it tends to be lower for 15–19-year-olds, some of whom are still in school.[5] This is true for both males and females. In almost every case, average percentage NEET increases between the 15–19 and 20–24 age groups. Exceptions where NEET decreases slightly going into the 20s include three countries in South East Asia (Cambodia, Indonesia and Malaysia) and three countries in sub-Saharan Africa (Malawi, Senegal and Tanzania). Overall, however, very high percentages of male and female youth are neither employed nor in school in their early 20s, the ages in which many youth complete their education and enter the labour market. Male percentages NEET are over 40 per cent in South Africa, and generally between 10 and 30 per cent. Female percentages who are NEET top out at almost 90 per cent (Malawi), but most of the examples shown range between 70 and 30 per cent. As youth move into their upper 20s, males are more likely to find labour force work, while females often show even higher levels of NEET as they marry and transition from labour force work to household and care work (based on data from MPC, 2013).

NEET and unemployment

In this section we explore the relationship between the percentage of youth who are unemployed and the percentage in the NEET category. Note that percentage of unemployed youth is not the same as the youth unemployment *rate*, which has as its denominator those employed plus those actively searching for work rather than the entire youth population. The unemployment rate answers the question: among those who want labour force work and who are actively seeking it, what fraction had not found it (at the time they were asked)? This strict concept of unemployment is more useful in some contexts than in others. Youth who have never had a job may not yet be actively searching for work, while others may have searched without success and become discouraged, and yet others may be queuing for a formal sector job without looking elsewhere. Because we are concerned with how all youth are spending their time – with unsuccessful labour market searching being one option – our denominator includes all youth, and we compute an unemployment *percentage*. This measure is sometimes called the 'unemployment ratio'.

Figure 7.6 includes only those youth found in the NEET category and shows what percentage of them meet the formal definition of unemployment (typically they must have been actively searching for work in the reference period). While in a few cases, a high percentage of NEET youth are unemployed, in most cases the opposite is true: for males, most are between about 20 and 60 per cent, while for females, most are between about 10 and 40 per cent (based on data from MPC, 2013). In other words, the majority of youth who are not employed nor in school are either truly idle, or they are engaged in non-labour force work (which, in some countries, includes the work of military conscripts).

Figure 7.7 includes a series of country-specific panels showing the percentages unemployed and NEET by single years of age, separately by sex.[6] In these panels, it becomes clear that unemployment is often a small component of NEET. For young men, the percentage who are NEET is often shaped like a small hill, rising until the late teens or early 20s, then declining slowly (see Argentina, Indonesia). In other countries, male NEET barely changes with age (see Senegal). For young women, in contrast, the percentage who are NEET often rises steeply in the mid-to-late teens, then flattens out at a very high level, or continues to grow slightly (see Iran and Indonesia).

In many countries, male and female unemployment ratios follow very similar patterns as age increases (see Argentina, Brazil), but in a few

Figure 7.6: Percentage unemployed among NEET, youths 15–24, selected countries

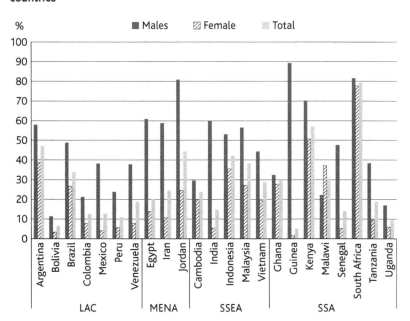

Source: Authors' calculations based on data from IPUMS-International (Minnesota Population Center, 2013)

cases they diverge substantially. Sometimes the male unemployment ratio is lower than the female ratio (see Malawi, Indonesia), but there are perhaps even more cases among our examples where the opposite is found (see Iran and Senegal). Lower female than male unemployment ratio is likely explained in some cases by young women's withdrawal from an inhospitable labour market environment – that is, they may have been discouraged from searching for jobs – rather than a higher level of effectiveness in finding jobs.

The relationship between NEET and the unemployment ratio as age increases differs systematically by gender. Consider first the case of young men. In some countries, the percentage who are NEET exceeds the percentage who are unemployed but tracks it fairly closely, with the largest gap between the two usually in the late teens or early 20s. See, for example, Argentina, Iran and Senegal (but also Cambodia, Guinea, India, Jordan, Kenya, South Africa, Tanzania and Vietnam, as shown in Assaad and Levison, 2013). In Brazil, the unemployment percentage even exceeds the NEET percentage during the teen years – because young men reported both being unemployed and being enrolled in school. (This is consistent with other evidence from Brazil suggesting

Figure 7.7: NEET and unemployment rate by single year of age and sex, selected countries, latest year

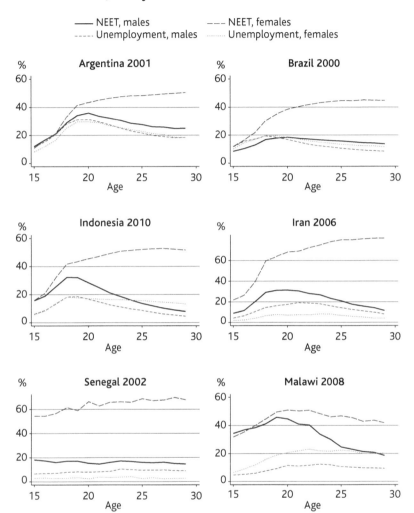

Source: Authors' calculations based on data from IPUMS-International (Minnesota Population Center, 2013)

that enrollment during the upper teens is sometimes aspirational.) In other countries, there is a large gap – 15 or more percentage points – between the male unemployment ratio and NEET at some ages. See, for example, Indonesia and Malawi (but also Bolivia, Colombia, Ghana, Uganda and Venezuela). While it is possible that this gap may be explained by military conscriptions in some of these countries, census documentation makes it clear that conscripts are counted as employed in Venezuela at least (MPC, 2013).

Next consider the relationship between NEET and the unemployment ratio by age for young women. In almost every case, there is an initially smaller but eventually very large gap between the per cent who are unemployed and the per cent who are NEET. The differences mainly lie in (i) whether there is much of a gap at age 15, and (ii) the level of the NEET line at age 25. For examples of (i), see Argentina and Brazil, where there is little or no gap at age 15, whereas in Iran, the gap is in the neighbourhood of 20 percentage points at age 15. Regarding (ii), percentages in Latin America tend to be between 40 and 60 per cent at age 25; percentages in the three Middle East and North Africa examples we considered substantially exceed 60 per cent; the sub-Saharan African countries vary substantially. Cambodia and Vietnam are unique not only among the South and Southeast Asian examples but among all the examples presented here: they have female NEET levels at age 25 below 10 per cent (based on data from MPC, 2013).

NEET and education

Are more-educated youth less likely to be out of work after they finish school, or do some find themselves with education that was not in demand in local labour markets? The panels of Figure 7.8 provide country-specific examples of NEET levels for youth who completed different levels of education, separately for males and females, by single years of age. Trends for those completing less than primary are calculated for ages 15–29, as are trends for those completing primary. Trends for those completing secondary were calculated for ages 18–29, and trends for those completing university or above were calculated for ages 22–29. Trends for females are shown in the left panels, and trends for males are in the right panels. Note that percentage scales may differ between females and males.

The notable pattern for men regarding the relationship of NEET to educational attainment is that NEET rates tend to be initially higher for educated males, but then tend to fall fairly rapidly with age. This is evidence that educated males tend to engage in longer job searches after leaving school in the hope of finding formal jobs, whereas less educated males simply transition into whatever jobs they can find. South Africa is an exception to this pattern, where, for both men and women NEET rates tend to be highest for the less educated and fall with education.[7]

For women, the pattern is more complicated. NEET rates tend to be lower for more educated females who simply have higher labour

Figure 7.8: NEET rate by single year of age, educational attainment and sex, youths 15–29, selected countries, latest year

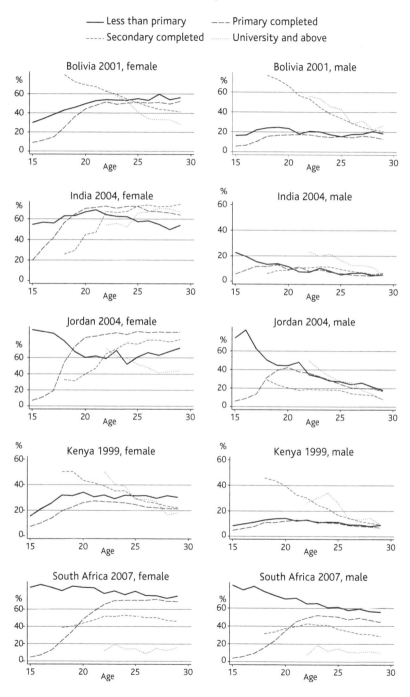

force participation rates. In most cases NEET rates increase with age as women specialise in non-labour force work, with one exception. University and in some cases secondary-educated women tend to have declining NEET rates with age, indicating that they eventually find labour force work. Thus more-educated women have patterns that are similar to those of more-educated men, where exit from school is followed by extended search and possibly queuing periods. In contrast, less-educated women tend to have short-lived employment periods after school if any, and then transition to non-labour force work and correspondingly high NEET levels. Less-educated men are mostly forced to make quick transition to the labour force.

NEET over time

Because little attention was paid to the concept of NEET in past decades, it is useful to take a look backwards to consider the percentages of youth who did not report being either employed or in school. Figure 7.9 includes a series of panels showing, for nine selected countries with data from two to four decades available via IPUMS-International, trends in NEET from age 15 to age 29. For each country included there is one figure for females and another for males.

The Mexico case is an example of one fairly typical pattern. NEET has fallen for women over time, such that each age-NEET line lies completely under the one from the previous decade. This pattern reflects the increasing labour force activity of women over time, as well as the greater number of years they are spending in the formal education system. Still, the female patterns show substantially higher levels of NEET than do those of males, reflecting women's continued responsibility for non-labour force work. Each age-NEET line rises with age from 15 to 30, since it is during these prime child-bearing years that women are most likely to leave the labour force. Except for the most recent data, from 2000, all the female age-NEET lines begin above 20 per cent. In contrast, NEET for Mexican males starts lower – under 20 per cent with one exception – and is relatively flat, although after a small rise in the late teens it trends downward slightly. Other countries with similarly shaped age-NEET time trends include Brazil, India and Senegal (based on data from MPC, 2013).

Egypt depicts a different pattern for young women, although over a shorter time period. For women, there is not a discernible shift in age-NEET patterns over time, except for a downward trend among 15–20-year-olds, who are likely to be staying longer in school. For

Figure 7.9: NEET rate by single year of age and sex over time for youth (15–29), selected countries

A. Latin America

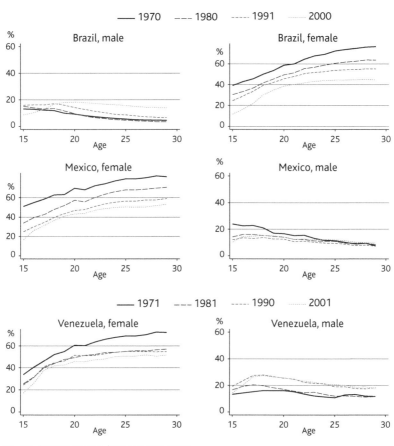

Source: Minnesota Population Center, 2015

B. Middle East and North Africa

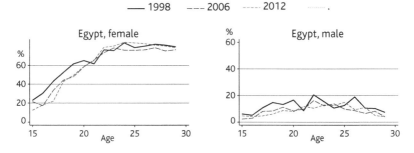

Source: ELMPS (1998, 2006, 2012)

older ages, the NEET trends for 1998, 2006 and 2012 overlie each other substantially. The sharp increase in NEET by age in Egypt reflects the gradual exit from school into non-employment rather than any substantial changes in labour force work. Similar to those for females, NEET levels among younger male youth in Egypt appear to have declined from 1998 to 2006, again probably reflecting longer schooling durations rather than increases in employment (based on data from MPC, 2013).

The pattern for Indonesia shows some similarities to Mexico as well as some differences. Female NEET rates start high, but at age 15 rates have fallen from over 50 per cent in 1971 to under 20 per cent in 2010. From age 15, in all cross-sections, NEET percentages increase with age, but the 1990 and 2010 percentages plateau below 60 per cent, compared to above 60 per cent for earlier generations. Male NEET percentages began below 20 per cent for 15-year-olds captured by the censuses of 1980, 1990 and 2010, but the 2010 trend is remarkably different to that of 20 or more years earlier. After a similar starting point at age 15, the percentage NEET rises steeply to peak at 32 per cent before starting a relatively steep decline that continues into and throughout the 20s. By about age 26 or 27, the 2010 trend line for NEET has merged with those of earlier decades. Other countries with similar patterns for recent male NEET trends include Malaysia and South Africa (based on data from MPC, 2013).

Labour underutilisation

Although NEET provides a fuller measure of employment inadequacy for many youths than does the traditional unemployment measure, it fails to capture the low quality of employment for the majority of youth in poor countries, who simply do not have the choice as to whether or not to work. This is especially true in low income economies where work often takes the form of an additional hand on a family farm or marginal activities in the urban informal economy. For males in particular, the need to earn an income to survive and support one's family means that casual or marginal employment is the only option. The situation of young women in poor countries varies a great deal more, depending on how open labour force work is to women in different cultural contexts.

To capture the inadequacy of employment for young people in developing countries, the ILO introduced the notion of labour underutilisation and applied it in a series of School-to-Work Transition Surveys (SWTS). Besides the unemployed and inactive youth who are captured in NEET, this notion includes young people in non-standard or irregular employment, which as described above, includes informal wage and salary work, casual day labour and household production activities. The latter category includes self-employed individuals with no employees and contributing family worker. Together these are referred to as 'vulnerable employment'.

Although it is currently not possible to apply this definition to a broad set of countries due to data limitations, its application to the subset of countries where SWTS surveys have been carried out shows that labour underutilisation rates for youth aged 15 to 29 are extremely high in sub-Saharan Africa, reaching 79.1 per cent in Malawi, 77.5 per cent in Liberia and 71.8 per cent in Togo (ILO, 2013, 133). The main contributors to these high labour underutilisation rates were the high rates of vulnerable employment in these countries. Among the SWTS countries in other regions, Cambodia exhibits a very similar pattern to that of the sub-Saharan African countries. Labour underutilisation is also high in other developing SWTS countries such as Egypt and Peru (67 per cent and 63 per cent, respectively) but mostly because of their high rates of irregular/temporary wage employment and relatively high NEET and relaxed unemployment rates (ILO, 2013, 133).

Faced with poor employment prospects, young men are often forced to find their way in the informal or agrarian economy in low productivity activities, where a given amount of work is subdivided over a large number of people each of whom produces very little. In some regions, such as sub-Saharan Africa or Southeast Asia, young women face a similar situation and have employment rates in the informal economy that are just as high as those of men. In other regions, less educated women find it much harder to break into the world of work and simply withdraw from labour force work. Many of these young women would undoubtedly be attracted into the workforce if employment opportunities were to materialise, as has in fact happened in Bangladesh's garment industry in recent years.

When labour markets fail youth

One of the main messages of this year's World Bank World Development Report 2013 on jobs is that jobs are essential to social cohesion. Jobs not only convey a greater sense of dignity and belonging in society but also encourage voice and participation (World Bank, 2012). The flip side is that a lack of jobs can result in reduced trust and lower levels of civic engagement, and, as recently demonstrated in the Arab Spring, can lead to social unrest and violence. In other contexts, the lack of job opportunities for youth is associated with crime and gang-related violence. The motivation to join gangs and other violent groups for unemployed and underemployed young men is not merely economic necessity, but it often stems from the need to compensate for the lack of trust, support and social ties that exclusion from productive opportunities brings about (Bell and Blanchflower, 2010).

The young men with the worst labour market options tend to be those from the most disadvantaged backgrounds, with families that are not prepared to take care of them indefinitely. Relatively more of such young men exist in countries where sex-selective abortion has resulted in substantially lop-sided sex ratios at birth. Youth bulges in those areas are also lop-sided. Such young men tend to have little education and few skills. They often cannot marry or start a family. In China such men are referred to as 'bare branches' of genealogical trees (Hudson and Den Boer, 2002, 11). It is not, perhaps, surprising that some of them turn to theft, banditry, gangs or political violence.

Consider that a youth sex ratio of 130:100 (for example) implies that out of every 100 young men, only 77 will be able to find a female partner among other youth, even if all the young women agree to marry. About one-third of men, the least marriageable, would be left without what has been called the civilising influence of marriage; this effect has more recently been attributed to a decline in serum testosterone linked to courtship and marriage (Mazur and Michalek, 1998 as cited in Hudson and Den Boer, 2002). Studies of male group behaviour have shown an increase in risky choices related to group dynamics; girls and women learn to avoid street corners where young men loiter. Similarly, the likelihood of organised aggression increases as young men with few options congregate together (Hudson and Den Boer, 2002, 15).

Hudson and Den Boer (2002) argue that the presence of 'bare branches' heightens 'the opportunity for violence to emerge and become relatively large scale' (p. 15). They and other authors (for example, Urdal, 2006) provide substantial case study and cross-national evidence of security concerns in such situations. When this tendency of unattached men for violent behaviour is combined with youth bulges, the possibilities are troubling. Some authors argue forcefully that the presence of large numbers of unemployed or underemployed, poorly educated, unmarried young men, available to be recruited into militias and guerilla groups, is a major risk factor for civil conflict. Cincotta et al (2003), for example, summarise their study based on data from 180 countries, as follows: 'the risks of civil conflict...that are generated by demographic factors may be much more significant than generally recognised, and worthy of more serious consideration by national security policymakers and researchers' (p 12). The two demographic factors they find to be most problematic are a youth bulge and a high rate of urban population growth. Other analysts suggest that population changes – including youth bulges – interact with a variety of other conditions, leading to violent conflicts (Goldstone, 2002).

The number of male youth who are NEET provides an estimate of those mostly likely to engage in violent and destabilising activities, but NEET is both an overestimate and an underestimate. It is an overestimate in that the more privileged among the non-working youth are merely biding their time, waiting for a formal sector position to open; they know they will be able to marry and may be in the process of courtship. It is an underestimate in that many employed young men are seriously under-employed, with lots of time on their hands, and possibly little hope of future options.

Disadvantaged youth

Labour markets are most likely to fail youth who fall into particular categories of disadvantage. Categories are to some extent culturally-specific, but there are some categories where disadvantage is global. In particular, youth who are physically and/or mentally disabled face substantial labour market disadvantage. If disabled youth have been unable to access education, then illiteracy may compound their other disadvantages. In many societies, female youth face many labour market disadvantages, compared to males. To the extent that sexuality is disclosed, non-heterosexual youth not only face labour market discrimination but also, sometimes, violence. Youth having darker skin tones are more greatly disadvantaged in most parts of the world. Which ethnic groups – or castes, or tribes – are disadvantaged depends on the region. In some regions, indigenous groups face substantial discrimination. Closely related to ethnicity/caste/tribe is religious affiliation, with region again determining whether Jews or Muslims, Christians or atheists (for example) are outside mainstream society and facing labour market discrimination. Migrants often fall into multiple disadvantaged groups, particularly if they are refugees from regions of war or civil conflict. Demobilised child soldiers are said to be among the worst off with respect to labour market opportunities (Freedman, 2008, 16).

Illness and chronic health problems can transform a youth with normal labour market prospects into someone with little energy or ability to find work or create work for himself or herself. Malaria alone affects millions of youth. If most youth in an area are affected, that may limit the degree to which any one youth is put at a disadvantage, but it also limits the returns that can be garnered from any productive activity. Health problems of others also affect youths' prospects. Consider, for example, that among the 33 million people estimated to be infected with HIV, 67 per cent are in sub-Saharan Africa (Oster, 2010). In many cases, youth are the designated care providers for ill parents, older siblings or other relatives. Any market work they do must mesh with their care responsibilities.

Categories of disadvantage are highly correlated with dimensions on which we have focused in this chapter: education, training and employment. But disadvantaged populations are also vulnerable to work-related problems that we have not yet discussed. These concern illicit activities: forced labour; the trafficking of youth for a particular kind of forced or coercive labour, namely prostitution or pornography; drug running and other activities related to illegal drugs; and so forth. Disabled youth may be forced to beg in order to make a living for themselves and their families. Traditional measures of employment inadequacy do not reveal many of the dimensions of employment disadvantage faced by the youth discussed in this section.

Potential solutions

There is little doubt that a necessary condition for addressing the youth employment challenge is to foster a dynamic economic environment in which economies can thrive and economic growth can lead to continuous growth in labour demand. While this depends in part on the overall health of the global economy and the external economic environment that countries are facing, it also depends on the pursuit of sound economic policies: what the World Development Report 2013 calls 'the fundamentals'. What these fundamentals consist of is fairly predictable: macroeconomic stability, good governance and the rule of law, respect for rights, a healthy investment climate and sound investments in human capital, including education and health (World Bank, 2012, Ch 9). While policies to establish such sound fundamentals are an essential component of a youth employment strategy, they are generally beyond the scope of this chapter.

Besides the fundamentals, labour market policies and institutions can potentially have important effects on youth employment and earnings. These policies include those that protect jobs or workers, set minimum levels of compensation, regulate working conditions and hours, provide social insurance and set a framework for representation and collective bargaining. Although sometimes governed by international agreements and conventions, these policies and institutions vary a great deal across countries. After a great deal of debate about the potential tradeoffs between employment protection legislation (EPL) and the rate of job creation and wage growth, a consensus appears to be emerging from a large number of empirical studies that the effects of labour regulations on the overall level of employment and wages is modest so long as the degree of protection is within a fairly broad 'plateau' (World Bank, 2012, Ch 8). There is some evidence, however, that EPL has dynamic effects on the labour markets, such as a reduction of gross labour market flows and a lengthening of the durations of both employment and unemployment (World Bank, 2012, Ch 8). These regulations may affect youth disproportionately: a study of several Latin America and OECD countries showed that the impact of EPL on young people's employment was more than twice their impact on the employment of prime age males (Heckman and Pagés, 2000).

The weak impact of EPL on employment and wages may be the result of the large role informality plays in the labour markets of most developing countries. When rules are poorly enforced or have limited coverage, the main impact is often informalisation rather than dis-employment. It does suggest, however, that the presence of strict job security rules, or other rules that increase the cost of formal hiring, will tend to relegate vulnerable groups such as women and youth to informal or more precarious forms of employment. As a result, the rules have a redistributive effect often to the detriment of youth. In any case, there is little evidence that major programmes to deregulate labour markets and weaken job security regulations and worker protections could by themselves significantly increase the level and adequacy of employment for young people, other than in a few exceptional cases where regulations are especially onerous (World Bank, 2012).

Beyond the fundamentals and traditional labour policies, an area that has attracted a great deal of attention in recent years is that of youth-targeted programmes to better prepare young people for the labour market and facilitate labour market entry. While some of these efforts take place within education systems to increase the relevance of education to the world of work, many are directed at school leavers to facilitate their transition into the labour market; these fall under the general rubric of ALMPs.

Building skills and preparing young people for the labour market

Any effort to prepare youth for productive careers must start with broad-based, high quality general education. There are frequent complaints from employers that workers with six or even nine years of education often lack the most basic literacy, numeracy and comprehension skills. The expansion of education systems around the world has often come at the expense of quality. The Education for All Global Monitoring Report of 2012 estimates that as many as 250 million children were failing to read and write by the time they reached Grade 4 (UNESCO, 2012). The report also states that the international community has failed to agree on a coherent set of internationally comparable indicators to assess equitable access to learning and life skills, which is the core of Goal 3 of the Education for All goals established in 2000 in Dakar, Senegal. When education fails to equip young people with even the most basic literacy and numeracy skills but raises their expectations with regards to the kind of job they can obtain, it simply leads to frustration and disillusionment, in addition to wasted public and private resources.

Beyond good quality basic education, education systems must provide opportunities for technical and vocational education that imparts skills that are relevant to the labour market. Technical or vocational education tracks in many contexts are often no more than inferior education tracks designed to divert students away from universities and other higher education institutions (Antoninis, 2001). Newhouse and Suryadarma (2009) examined labour market outcomes for Indonesian youth in different types of secondary education after the Indonesian government decided to dramatically expand enrollment to vocational education. Although they found that vocational school graduates fared just as well in the labour market as general school graduates despite being from more disadvantaged backgrounds, they also found that returns to vocational schooling have dropped steeply in Indonesia for the most recent cohort of men. They conclude that this raises serious questions about current efforts to expand vocational education in an increasingly service-oriented economy. Krafft (2013) also found poor returns for vocational education in Egypt and questioned continued investment in vocational education.

Dual education model

One of the ways the ILO has sought to build bridges between education and the world of work is by promoting 'dual-system education strategies', which combine school-based education with apprenticeships and on-the-job experience. This model, which has proven effective in Austria, Denmark, Germany and Switzerland, provides large numbers of young people with quality education and training in recognised qualifications demanded by firms (ILO, 2013).

In low-income countries, informal apprenticeships are often the path to job skills for some youth who drop out early from school, especially boys. While apprenticeships have served this purpose for centuries, they have disadvantages in a world where literacy is important and laws require children to attend school to a certain level or age. Combining apprenticeships with opportunities to continue education, even if it is outside formal schooling systems, could mitigate some of the disadvantages of early school leaving to become an apprentice while maintaining the important role of apprenticeships in imparting useful trade skills.

Reforming child labour policies

One policy domain where reforms can potentially ease young people's transition to employment is in the area of policies to combat child labour. As an ILO document points out, '[t]he overlap between definitions of childhood (below 18 years) and youth (ages 15–24) points to the difficulties that arise when trying to draw a distinct line between when childhood ends and when youth begins' (ILO, 2008, 16). In spite of the great concern about youth unemployment and its long-term negative effects on youth, few authors make the obvious connection to child labour policy. Although some ILO conventions aim to forbid children under 14 (or 13) access to labour force work, the 1990 UN Convention on the Rights of the Child (CRC) instead recognises 'the right of the child to be protected from economic exploitation and from performing any work that is likely to be hazardous or to interfere with the child's education, or to be harmful to the child's health or physical, mental, spiritual, moral or social development' (Article 32). In agreement with the CRC, Bourdillon et al (2010) argue that in many cases, it is better – from a child development perspective – to ameliorate hazardous conditions of employment rather than to absolutely deny children the right to work. Figuring out non-hazardous ways that children could begin to take on small amounts of work from a relatively early age could help them slowly integrate into the economic structures of their communities as they gain age, experience and skills.

Active labour market programmes (ALMPs)

ALMPs refer to a variety of strategies that may be targeted at particular groups – such as youth – to increase their employability and their likelihood of employment (or work engagement). Our discussion of

ALMPs will pay particular attention to evaluations of their employment and earnings impacts and their cost-effectiveness.

Job search assistance and job clubs are commonly used in high-income and transition economies to connect employers searching for workers with youth searching for jobs. At this point, there is limited evidence from low-income countries about the effectiveness of this kind of intervention, with most of the findings that follow coming from experience with these programmes in middle- and high-income countries (Betcherman et al, 2004). Results on how effective such programmes are in highly informal labour markets are simply not available (Martin and Grubb, 2001). The general finding from evaluations show that the two most notable impacts for participants are an increased chance of employment and a shorter average time between jobs, but there is little evidence of impact on long-term earnings (Betcherman et al, 2004; Kuddo, 2009). Job search programmes are only effective when jobs exist. They are of little use during market downturns or times of mass unemployment, when employers have their pick of many applicants (Kuddo, 2009).

Job skills training

Job skills training programmes are the most popular ALMPs in low-income countries, but they are often ill-suited for youth. For example, job skills programmes make up 93 per cent of all current ALMP programmes in the Arab-Mediterranean countries (Angel-Urdinola et al, 2010), but recent policy reviews have shown that in Latin America they have had limited to no impact on subsequent employability for youth (Card et al, 2007). The marginal skills offered by short-term training programmes are unable to compensate for years of sub-standard schooling. The ILO is adamant about the need for increased investments in quality education (ILO, 2013) and scholars have found that early and sustained investment in education will have greater impacts on first-time workers (Betcherman et al, 2004). However, there has been little communication between programme designers about best practices, leading some authors to call for urgent reforms to programme design and delivery (Angel-Urdinola et al, 2010).

Adult men and women can have positive outcomes from job skills training, and the design successes for these populations may be adaptable to youth. Small-scale and targeted programmes that coordinate closely with employers have the best outcomes (Kuddo, 2009). Similarly, on-the-job training and pathways towards employment are always more effective than classroom work (Kuddo, 2009). The success or failure of training programmes rests heavily on the existing labour market (Attanasio et al, 2011; Rodriguez-Planas, 2010). Programmes are most effective when formal jobs are available for low-skill and entry-level work. Because of this, large-scale programmes, or programmes that respond to mass layoffs or other shocks, are generally ineffective (Kuddo, 2009).

Public employment and public works projects

Expanded public employment rolls or labour-intensive public works projects are good for short-term job creation, or acting as a safety net for the most disadvantaged, but they are inappropriate for combating long-term unemployment (Kuddo, 2009; Betcherman et al, 2004; Kluve et al, 2007; Rodriguez-Planas, 2010). Jobs created by public works projects can help workers wait out the bad times, and they can even act as counter-cyclical public investments to kick-start a recovery. The most positive long-term impact of public works is the creation of a safety net for the most disadvantaged workers (Kuddo, 2009).

In low-income countries, potential benefits of public works projects may be related to 'soft' skills: timeliness, interacting with employers and co-workers, and expectations in general. To the extent that public works projects keep young men who might otherwise engage in anti-social behaviour busy, they have substantial externalities. If they target particularly disadvantaged youth, such as those with disabilities, they may help to overcome social barriers to the employability of these young people. To conclude, public works employment should be targeted only at the most disadvantaged. While these jobs offer much-needed income for some, easy-to-access but short-term employment can be counterproductive for workers with access to good job search channels (Rodriguez-Planas, 2010).

Entrepreneurship training and small business assistance

There is some evidence that entrepreneurship training and small business assistance are effective programmes for older and better educated workers, but even on that count, the evidence remains fairly weak (McKenzie and Woodruff, 2012). Older individuals are able to use their existing knowledge of local markets to plan their entrepreneurial ventures, and better-educated workers are capable of handling the accounting necessary to run a small business. The only study we found that has rigorously evaluated the effectiveness of entrepreneurship training targeted at youth was of a programme directed at undergraduate students in Tunisian universities (Premand et al, 2012). The programme was shown to increase self-employment among graduates, but only slightly, and had positive effects on job skills, business knowledge and optimism. However, the programme had no impact on overall employment. Entrepreneurship training may not be cost-effective approach to reducing overall unemployment. The new businesses are able to provide employment for graduates of training programmes but do not generate many jobs for others.

Wage subsidies

Wage subsidies or tax credits to employers are effective in increasing employment levels when specifically targeted. Target groups are slightly more likely to be hired by employers. Subsidies that are applicable to the informal sector have more of an impact for youth and women. For example, the *Proempleo* Experiment in Argentina provided a voucher to both formal and informal employers who hired within the target group. Women, youth and the better-educated gained the most from this programme, but most of the hiring was for unskilled labour in the informal sector. When skills training was coupled with the vouchers, it had no additional statistically significant effect (Galasso et al, 2004).

Wage subsidy programmes are difficult to design and implement because employers are apt to abuse the vouchers by making fake hires (Kuddo, 2009). Increased scrutiny both increases the cost of the programmes and reduces uptake (Betcherman et al, 2004). There is an additional risk of stigmatising the targeted groups (Katz, 1996).

ALMPs: a synopsis

ALMPs have proved to be moderately effective at assisting youth in obtaining first-time employment and improving the efficiency of job matching. They can sometimes overcome employers' reluctance to provide training to workers whose retention they cannot guarantee. They are also effective in reducing the adverse impact of economic downturns on vulnerable groups. Job search assistance has proven to be the most cost-effective among ALMPs for disadvantaged youth. On-going advising and job clubs are relatively low-cost interventions that can have positive effects on job matching, but they may be less effective in low-income settings where labour markets are mostly informal. Wage subsidies can be effective in bringing disadvantaged youth into waged employment, especially when such programmes target both the formal and informal segments of the economy. By reducing employers' initial hiring and training costs, wage subsidies are able to reach hard-to-employ groups.

Job skills training programmes can also be moderately effective, but only when coordinated with employers. Coordinated programmes match skills with labour market demands, easing youth's transition into work. Labour-intensive public works programmes are effective counter-cycle policies but they have little impact on long-term unemployment of youth. Lastly, entrepreneurship programmes are expensive and have little impact for disadvantaged youth. Only relatively older and better-educated youth are able to take advantage of the opportunities provided, and the businesses created by the youth do not create large numbers of jobs for others.

Conclusion

We argue in this chapter that all the developing regions of the world experienced at some point in the past two decades strong demographic pressures on their labour markets resulting from the youth bulge phenomenon. While the timing of the youth bulge differed by region, it caused rapid increases in youth populations almost everywhere in the developing world. The effect of this rapid increase in labour supply varied considerably across regions depending on each region's ability to capitalise on these human resources by investing in human capital and then putting this human capital to use in productive endeavours. East Asia, one of the earlier regions in the developing world to experience the youth bulge phenomenon, invested heavily and equitably in education and managed to sustain a virtuous cycle of rising labour demand and supply by pursuing policies of export-driven growth. Because of the one child policy in China and the very rapid fall in fertility, the share of youth in the population there fell precipitously in the 1990s, allowing for further deepening of investments in human capital. However, the interaction of the one-child policy and the strong preference of Chinese families for sons led to another worrying demographic imbalance, namely highly unbalanced sex ratios resulting from sex selective abortions. Gender imbalances will continue to rise in East Asia at least until 2025, increasing the threat of crime and civil unrest related to the unemployment and social alienation of the most disadvantaged young men.

Southeast Asia and Latin America also had a relatively early onset of the youth bulge, but a much slower deceleration of the youth population than in East Asia. The absolute size of the youth population in both these regions has already peaked and will begin to decline slowly by 2020. Despite subsiding demographic pressures, the formalising economies of these regions mean that young people have an incentive to remain unemployed while searching for suitable formal jobs and, as a result, the two regions have intermediate youth unemployment rates that the ILO projects will remain stable until 2019. A broader measure of employment inadequacy among youth, the NEET percentage, shows that youth employment rates have been rising in these two regions among young women and are fairly stable or slightly declining among young men.

South Asia is by now the world's largest region in terms of the number of youth, and the size of its youth population will keep growing, albeit fairly slowly, up to 2030. South Asia experienced a somewhat more varied demographic and economic trajectory than other world regions. India's mode of insertion into the global economy through service exports placed a high premium on education among its growing youth population. This has likely contributed to a bifurcation between the fortunes of educated youth who can participate in these globalised sectors and those with lower levels of education, who are relegated to marginal activities in India's sprawling informal economy. Bangladesh's insertion in global supply chains in the garment industry has created new opportunities for rural youth, especially young women. This has in turn increased the incentives of parents to invest in girls' education in rural areas (World Bank, 2012). Hampered by internal conflict and political instability, Pakistan and Afghanistan are well behind in terms of both their demographic transitions and their economic transformations.

The Middle East and North African region experienced a combination of a significant youth bulge coupled with rapidly rising educational attainment. However, its educational systems, accustomed to meeting the needs of oversized bureaucracies rather than globalising private sectors, are not equipping youth with the skills they need to succeed in a competitive global economy. High expectations on the part of educated youth coupled with shrinking public sector growth resulted in long periods of queuing for public sector jobs and one of the highest youth unemployment rates in the world. The frustration they experienced is undoubtedly one of the primary driving forces behind the Arab Spring, but unfortunately, the events of the Arab Spring only served to push youth unemployment rates even higher.

Sub-Saharan Africa is the only region in the world where demographic pressures on labour markets caused by the youth bulge will continue to intensify in the foreseeable future. The slow fertility decline in much of sub-Saharan Africa, and the resultant prolongation of the demographic transition, mean that the youth population in Africa will continue to grow rapidly through 2050 and beyond. Because of the agrarian and informal nature of African labour markets, these severe demographic pressures do not translate into high open unemployment rates for youth. The exception that proves the rule there is South Africa, which has a highly formalised economy, and, as a consequence high youth unemployment rates. In much of the rest of sub-Saharan Africa, employment inadequacy for youth shows up in high rates of low-productivity vulnerable employment in agriculture and in urban livelihood activities, where a given level of economic activity is subdivided across a growing number of workers. Combined with growing environmental threats, such as droughts and desertification, this dynamic, if not reversed through concerted action, is likely to result in more frequent eruptions of violence and civil conflict.

To better capture the youth employment challenges that regions like sub-Saharan Africa will be experiencing for the foreseeable future, it is necessary to develop measures of employment inadequacy that go well beyond the youth unemployment rate, which is better suited to economies with highly organised, mostly formal labour markets. The NEET percentage is a measure that moves in that direction but is still incapable of capturing the inadequacy of employment among those who have no choice but to engage in some sort of livelihood activity in order to survive. The labour underutilisation measure is another attempt in the right direction, but it, too, only crudely captures the marginality of employment and the adequacy of the earnings it generates.

Potential solutions to address the growing employment challenges faced by youth lie first and foremost in establishing the conditions for growing and dynamic economies that can compete in an increasingly globalised world economy. In the presence of adequate labour demand, the next step is to ensure that young people are equipped with the right sets of skills to participate productively in the growth process and to improve the match between their individual skills and those demanded in the labour market. The importance of high quality basic education imparting good literacy, numeracy and comprehension skills cannot be overestimated. Education and training systems need to go further and equip youth with general employability skills such analytical thinking, problem solving, creativity and communications skills. Training in specific technical skills should be planned and carried out in close collaboration with employers and trade associations, even though financing will probably need to come from public sources. The gradual integration of youth into the workforce during the education and training phase, for example through internships and apprenticeship programmes, in a much wider range of employment settings can go a long way in facilitating the transition from school to work. Active labour market policies have a role to play in helping young people transition to the labour market by improving information flows and lowering the cost of hiring and initial on-the-job training.

Acknowledgement

The authors would like to acknowledge the valuable research assistance they received from John (Jay) Bowman.

Data acknowledgements

Argentina	National Institute of Statistics and Censuses
Bolivia	National Institute of Statistics
Brazil	Institute of Geography and Statistics
Cambodia	National Institute of Statistics
Colombia	National Administrative Department of Statistics
Egypt	Central Agency for Public Mobilization and Statistics
Ghana	Ghana Statistical Services
Guinea	National Statistics Directorate
India	Ministry of Statistics and Programme Implementation
Indonesia	Statistics Indonesia
Iran	Statistical Centre of Iran
Jordan	Department of Statistics
Kenya	National Bureau of Statistics
Malawi	National Statistical Office
Malaysia	Department of Statistics
Mexico	National Institute of Statistics, Geography, and Informatics
Peru	National Institute of Statistics and Informatics
Senegal	National Agency of Statistics and Demography
South Africa	Statistics South Africa
Tanzania	National Bureau of Statistics
Uganda	Bureau of Statistics
Venezuela	National Institute of Statistics
Vietnam	General Statistics Office

Notes

[1]   The data used throughout this paper has been gathered from a variety of sources. We present data gathered from the United Nations Population Division, the International Labour Organization (ILO) and select censuses

for individual countries (see Data acknowledgements). The UN Population Division and the ILO have similar definitions for world regions, but there are some differences. We have kept the regional definitions from the original sources, which can be found on the respective organisations' websites. The reader should use caution when comparing between data sources. For example, for the UN Population Division, the Middle East falls within Western Asia (UN, 2015). Countries such as Armenia, Georgia and Cyprus as well as Arab countries are counted together. On the other hand, the ILO counts the Arab countries and Iran within the Middle East and North Africa (MENA) region. Additionally, when examining censuses from selected countries, we have generally used ILO categories but on occasion grouped regions together, such as in the case of South Asia and Southeast Asia.

2   In this section, we rely on the UN's Population Division median variant projections from the 2010 Revision of the World Population Prospects (UN, 2011).

3   The ILO's model to project youth and adult unemployment is based on Okun's Law, which relates changes in unemployment to changes in GDP. The model attempts to take into account cyclical crises and the rate at which unemployment recovers after such crises using projections on GDP growth from the IMF's World Economic Outlook. The projection model probably works well for high-income economies where unemployment tends to be cyclical, but it may not do a good job capturing trends in structural unemployment that are primarily driven by demographics and the educational composition of the labour force. See ILO (2010) and ILO (2013a) Annex E for more discussion of the ILO's projection model.

4   For our sample of countries, we were able to confirm that Argentina, Iran, Jordan, Mexico and Venezuela count all military personnel as employed. We could not confirm the employment status of draftees from census documentation in other countries.

5   See Assaad and Levison (2013) for figures showing NEET by age group.

6   We present here country-specific panels for a subset of the countries we analysed. For a complete set of figures, see Assaad and Levison (2013).

7   Several Southeast Asia countries such as Cambodia, Malaysia, Vietnam and, to a lesser extent, Indonesia, show very small differences in NEET rates by educational attainment among men.

References

Angel-Urdinola, DF, Semlali, A, Brodmann, S, 2010, *Non-public provision of active labor market programs in Arab–Mediterranean countries: an inventory of youth programs*, Washington, DC: World Bank

Antoninis, M, 2001, *The vocational school fallacy revisited: Technical secondary school[s] in Egypt*, no 2001–2022, Florence: Robert Schuman Centre, European University Institute

Assaad, R, 2013, Making sense of Arab labor markets: The enduring legacy of dualism, *IZA Discussion Paper* 7573, Bonn: Institute for the Study of Labor

Assaad, R, Levison, D, 2013, Employment for youth: A growing challenge for the global community, *Minnesota Population Center (MPC) Working Paper* 2013-07, Minneapolis, MN: MPC

Attanasio, O, Kugler, A, Meghir, C, 2011, Subsidizing vocational training for disadvantaged youth in Colombia: Evidence from a randomized trial, *American Economic Journal: Applied Economics* 3, 3, 188–220

Bell, DNF, Blanchflower, D, 2010, Youth unemployment: Déjà vu?, *Discussion Paper Series* 4705, Bonn: Institute for the Study of Labor

Betcherman, G, Olivas, K, Dar, A, 2004, *Impacts of active labor market programs: New evidence from evaluations with particular attention to developing and transition countries*, Social Protection, Washington, DC: World Bank

Bloom, DE, Williamson, JG, 1998, Demographic transitions and economic miracles in emerging Asia, *The World Bank Economic Review* 12, 3, 419–55

Bloom, DE, Canning, D, Sevilla, J, 2003, *The demographic dividend: A new perspective on the economic consequences of population change*, Santa Monica, CA: Rand Corporation

Bourdillon, M, Levison, D, Myers, W, White, B, 2010, *Rights and wrongs of children's work*, New Brunswick, NJ: Rutgers University Press

Card, D, Ibarraran, P, Regalia, F, Rosas, D, Soares, Y, 2007, The labor market impacts of youth training in the Dominican Republic: Evidence from a randomized evaluation, *National Bureau of Economic Research (NBER) Working Paper* w12883, Cambridge, MA: NBER

Cincotta, RP, Engelman, R, Anastasion, D, 2003, *The security demographic: Population and civil conflict after the cold war*, Washington, DC: Population Action International Security Demographic

ELMPS (Egypt Labor Market Survey), 1998 Version 1.0 of Licensed Data Files, Egypt: Economic Research Forum (ERF), www.erfdataportal.com

ELMPS (Egypt Labor Market Panel Survey), 2006, Version 4.1 of Licensed Data Files, Egypt: Economic Research Forum (ERF), www.erfdataportal.com

ELMPS (Egypt Labor Market Panel Survey), 2012, Version 2.1 of Licensed Data Files, Egypt: Economic Research Forum (ERF), www.erfdataportal.com

Freedman, DH, 2008, *Improving skills and productivity of disadvantaged youth*, Geneva: International Labour Organization (ILO)

Galasso, E, Ravallion, M, Salvia, A, 2004, Assisting the transition from workfare to work: A randomized experiment, *Industrial and Labor Relations Review* 128–42

Goldstone, JA, 2002, Population and security: How demographic change can lead to violent conflict, *Journal of International Affairs* 56, 1, 3–21

Gribble, J, Bremner, J, 2012, Achieving a demographic dividend, *Population Bulletin* 67, 2, 2–13

Heckman, JJ, Pagés, C, 2000, Regulation and deregulation: Lessons from Latin American labor markets, *Economía* 1, 1, 123–45

Hudson, VM, Den Boer, A, 2002, A surplus of men, a deficit of peace: Security and sex ratios in Asia's largest states, *International Security* 26, 4, 5–38

ILO (International Labour Organization), 2008, *Forging Linkages between Child Labour and Youth Employment Programmes Across Asia and the Pacific: Handbook for ILO Field Staff*, ILO, Bangkok, Thailand).

ILO (International Labour Organization), 2010, Trends econometric models: A review of the methodology, *ILO Employment Trends Unit*, www.ilo.org/empelm/pubs/WCMS_120382/lang–en/index.htm

ILO (International Labour Organization), 2013, *Global employment trends for youth: A generation at risk*, Geneva: ILO

ILO (International Labour Organization), 2015, *Global employment trends for youth 2015: Scaling up investments in decent jobs for youth*, Geneva: ILO

Katz, LF, 1996, Wage subsidies for the disadvantaged, *National Bureau of Economic Research Working Paper* w5679, Cambridge, MA: NBER

Kluve, J, Lehmann, H, Schmidt, C, 2007, Disentangling treatment effects of active labor market policies: The role of labor force status sequences, *Department of Economics Working Paper* 620, Bologna: University of Bologna

Krafft, C, 2013, Is school the best route to skills? Returns to vocational school and vocational skills in Egypt, *Minnesota Population Center (MPC) Working Paper* 2013-09, Minneapolis, MN: MPC

Kuddo, A, 2009, *Employment services and active labor market programs in Eastern European and Central Asian countries*, Washington, DC: World Bank

McKenzie, D, Woodruff, C, 2012, What are we learning from business training and entrepreneurship evaluations around the developing world?, *World Bank Policy Research Working Paper* 6202, Washington, DC: World Bank

Martin, J, Grubb, D, 2001, What works and for whom: A review of OECD countries' experiences with active labour market policies, *Swedish Economic Policy Review* 8, 2, 9–56

Mazur, A, Michalek, J, 1998, Marriage, divorce, and male testosterone, *Social Forces* 77, 1, 315–30

Minnesota Population Center, 2015, *Integrated Public Use Microdata Series, International: Version 6.4* [dataset], Minneapolis: University of Minnesota, 2015, http://doi.org/10.18128/D020.V6.4

MPC (Minnesota Population Center), 2013, *Integrated Public Use Microdata Series, International: Version 6.1* [Machine-readable database], Minneapolis, MN: University of Minnesota

Newhouse, D, Suryadarma, D, 2009, The value of vocational education: High school type and labor market outcomes in Indonesia, *World Bank Policy Research Working Paper* 5035, Washington, DC: World Bank

OECD (Organisation for Economic Co-operation and Development), 2012, *OECD Employment Outlook 2012*, OECD Publishing, http://dx.doi.org/10.1787/empl_outlook-2012-en

Oster, E, 2010, Estimating HIV prevalence and incidence in Africa from mortality, *The BE Journal of Economic Analysis and Policy* 10, 1, 1–44

Premand, P, Brodmann, S, Almeida, R, Grun, R, Barouni, M, 2012, Entrepreneurship training and self-employment among university graduates: Evidence from a randomized trial in Tunisia, *World Bank Policy Research Working Paper* 6285, Washington, DC: World Bank

Rodriguez-Planas, N, 2010, Channels through which public employment services and small business assistance programmes work, *Oxford Bulletin of Economics and Statistics* 72, 4, 458–85

Rodríguez-Planas, N, Benus, J, 2010, Evaluating active labor market programs in Romania, *Empirical Economics* 38, 1, 65–84

UN (United Nations), 2011, *World population prospects: The 2010 revision*, UN Population Division of the Department of Economic and Social Affairs of the United Nations Secretariat, New York: UN

UN (United Nations), 2015, *World population prospects: The 2015 revision*, Custom data acquired via website, United Nations Department of Economic and Social Affairs, Population Division

UNESCO (United Nations Educational, Scientific and Cultural Organization), 2012, *Youth and skills: Putting education to work. Summary of Educational for All global monitoring report 2012.* Paris: UNESCO

Urdal, H, 2006, A clash of generations? Youth bulges and political violence, *International Studies Quarterly* 50, 607–29

World Bank, 2006, *World development report 2007: Development and the next generation*, Washington, DC: World Bank

World Bank, 2012, *World development report 2013: Jobs*, Washington, DC: World Bank

EIGHT

Women's role in economic development: overcoming the constraints

Sarah Bradshaw
with Joshua Castellino and Bineta Diop

Introduction

This chapter builds on the background paper on 'women's role in economic development' produced for the High-Level Panel (HLP) on the post-2015 agenda, and also draws on the work of the Sustainable Development Solutions Network thematic group three (UNSDSN, 2013).[1] It seeks to explain why women are important for bringing about economic development and what limits their engagement in income generating activities, highlighting the key areas that must be addressed if women are to engage equally with men. It begins by providing a brief context of the evolution of thinking around women and development, describing how and why women have been integrated into processes of 'development'. It notes that to date gender equality has been understood in a relatively narrow sense and often seen as a means to achieve economic growth goals rather than as a goal in itself. It then presents the argument as to why women are key to economic development and the issues that must be addressed if they are to engage in the paid economy. It highlights that, while incorporating women into the paid economy is important for achieving economic growth, economic growth alone cannot improve the situation and position of women. To achieve gender equality demands projects and policies specifically aimed at achieving gender equality. The chapter concludes by highlighting those areas crucial for promoting gender equality that will also help bring economic growth.

The evolution of 'Women in Development' to 'Gender and Development'

The interest in including women into the development process began in the 1970s when research on African farmers noted that, far from being gender neutral, development was gender blind and could harm women (Boserup, 1970). Boserup's work highlighted that with 'modernisation' came further labour specialisation and a hierarchy of occupations emerged that favoured men. Development workers furthered this gender bias by targeting only men in agricultural extension programmes, giving them privileged access to new farming technologies. The study also demonstrated that women's contributions, both domestic and in the paid workforce, contributed to national economies, something liberal feminists developed further in arguing that the costs of modern economic development were shouldered by women. Out of this the Women in Development (WID) approach emerged. In WID, women's subordination was seen as having its roots in their exclusion from the market sphere, and limited access to and control over resources. It then constructed the problem as being women's exclusion from a benign development process, and aimed to maximise women's access to the modern sector. The key was then to effectively place women 'in' existing development by means of laws and legislation to limit the discrimination they faced, and through promoting their involvement in education and employment (see Kabeer, 1994; Moser, 1993; Ostergaard, 1992).

WID led to resources being targeted at women by development organisations and aid agencies (see Razavi and Miller, 1995). Washington-based WID activists challenged the trickle-down theories of development and lobbied for the 1973 Percy Amendment to the US Foreign Assistance Act, which required that assistance help integrate women into the national economies of foreign countries. Projects often took the form of enabling access to technology and credit and small-scale income generating activities. WID helped make women more visible within development, particularly women's significant productive or income generating contribution. Their reproductive contribution or 'carer role' was less emphasised. While WID advocated for greater gender equality, its liberal feminist roots meant little attention was given to men and to power relations between genders. For many it did not tackle the real problem – the unequal gender roles and relations that are at the basis of gender subordination and women's exclusion. It also focused on what has been termed women's 'practical gender needs' – such as providing better access to water (Molyneux,

1985; Moser, 1989). While this would reduce the amount of time women and girls must spend in domestic/reproductive activities, and through this aid their engagement in education and employment, there was no questioning as to why collecting water has been constructed as a female responsibility, or why good access to water is a 'need' of women and girls only.

In the 1980s a new approach emerged out of the critique of WID, known as Gender and Development (GAD). It sought to recognise that it is gender roles and relations that are key to improving women's lives, with the term 'gender' suggesting a focus on both women and men was needed. More recently the need to understand how gender intersects with other characteristics such as age, ethnicity and sexuality has been noted. The GAD approach recognises that it is not sufficient to add women and girls into existing processes of development but that there is a need to problematise why they are excluded, suggesting that the focus should be on addressing imbalances of power at the basis of that exclusion. GAD also questions the notion of 'development' and its benign nature, suggesting a need to shift from a narrow understanding of development as economic growth, to a more social or human centred development. It suggests the need to re-evaluate and appreciate the positive features of 'traditional' societies, and to preserve and protect the egalitarian and environmentally friendly practices that have survived (Parpart et al, 2000). GAD projects are more holistic and address women's 'strategic gender interests' through seeking the elimination of institutionalised forms of discrimination such as around land rights, or ensuring the right of women and girls to live free from violence, for example.

For the majority of large development organisations and agencies, the WID approach has now largely been replaced by GAD at least in name. GAD utilises the rhetoric of rights to promote women's 'empowerment', and this is institutionalised within the notion of 'gender mainstreaming'. Mainstreaming involves ensuring that a gender perspective is central to all activities, including planning, implementation and monitoring of all programmes, projects and legislation. While critiqued if undertaken merely as a 'tick box' exercise, gender mainstreaming offers potential for placing gender at the heart of development (see Porter and Sweetman, 2005). The 1990s also witnessed the 'rise of rights' (Eyben, 2003) as many NGOs and agencies adopted some form of 'rights based approach' to development (see Molyneux and Lazar, 2003). Such approaches have been critiqued on a number of levels, including their western-centric focus on individual rights as opposed to an approach whereby collective rights of communities and groups are addressed.

The rise of rights has also been seen as reflecting the institutionalisation and professionalisation of women's movements, a process linked to the dominance, during the 1990s, of the United Nations framework for determining women's rights. This is also seen to correspond to ongoing concerns, at least within Latin America, around the 'NGOisation' of the women's movements of the region (Alvarez, 1999). For some, far from being viewed as a force for change, the rights based approach has been seen as being depoliticising (see IDS, 2005; Molyneux and Cornwall, 2008). Yet, the potential of rights for increasing recognition of women's demands as legitimate claims has made this discourse particularly powerful.

Perhaps the most notable success for the women's movement has been the establishment of sexual and reproductive rights as 'rights' (Antrobus, 2004a). Within this has been explicit recognition of women's right to live free from violence, and a broadening of understanding of violence against women, from 'domestic' to 'gender based' (see Pickup et al, 2001). The concepts of reproductive health, reproductive rights and sexual rights became popularised during the 1980s and 1990s, especially in the United Nations conferences (for discussion, see Bradshaw et al, 2008). Reproductive health as promoted by the International Conference on Population and Development (ICPD) focuses on ensuring the 'complete physical, mental and social wellbeing' in all matters related to the reproductive system, including a satisfying and safe sex life, capacity to have children and freedom to decide if, when and how often to do so. Reproductive rights are generally discussed in relation to the ability and knowledge of couples and individuals to decide 'freely and responsibly' the number, spacing and timing of children. While there is a less universally agreed definition of 'sexual rights', this generally relates to freedom to express sexuality, enjoy sexual relations and enjoy sexual health. Those who see the purpose of sexual relations as procreation rather than pleasure may, of course, contest the idea that the ability to 'pursue a satisfying, safe and pleasurable sexual life' (WHO, 2006, 5) is a 'right'.

The achievements of these and other UN processes to expand understandings of gender, of development, and of rights were, at the start of the new millennium, to inform a new global development framework to be evaluated via the Millennium Development Goals (MDGs). These eight goals sought to improve access to education and health, improve infant and maternal mortality rates, include a focus on epidemics including HIV/AIDS, on the environment and North–South relations, and on gender. Goal 3 aimed to 'promote gender equality and empower women', yet examination of the related targets highlight that equality and empowerment was measured in terms of education, seats in parliament and women's 'non-agricultural' employment. In terms of the latter target, the focus on the non-agricultural sector was said to reflect the benefits of women's integration into the monetary economy, in terms of 'greater autonomy, control over household decision-making and personal development' (UNDP, 2010b). This focus on education, employment and formal politics suggested there was more of a WID than a GAD approach, despite, as noted above, the limitations of WID being well documented (Razavi and Miller, 1995; Parpart et al, 2000). The other goal specifically focused on women was Goal 5, which aimed to improve maternal health. While a worthy intention, rather than ensuring all women's reproductive and sexual health rights, the focus was on women as mothers. Limiting services to maternal health does not provide access to reproductive health services, and does not actively promote women's reproductive health rights to decide the timing and spacing of children or their sexual rights to enjoy a healthy sex life.

Some of the strongest critiques of the MDGs came from the women's movements (see WICEJ, 2004). Activists and analysts debated the utility of engaging with the MDGs from the beginning, and it was suggested that 'MDG' was best understood as 'most distracting gimmick' (Antrobus, 2004b). Many of the concerns rested on what was seen to have been a politicisation of the process and the involvement of fundamentalist groups – both religious (of all denominations) and economic – in ensuring the 'deliberate exclusion' of women's sexual and reproductive rights from the millennium development agenda (Antrobus, 2004b). Even the Task Force set up to review how to operationalise MDG 3 expressed serious concerns and stressed the need to include issues such as gendered rights if the goal were to succeed.

Women's 'rights', particularly sexual and reproductive rights, are, however, far from accepted as rights, and violence against women remains prevalent across the globe, so women still lack full and equal participation in economic and political life. This suggests mainstreaming has yet to succeed and that there is a need for a continued prioritisation of integrating women into development.

Evidence on the importance of women to economic development

Perhaps the most influential evidence on the importance of women for economic development has come from within the World Bank through research initiated at the end of the 1990s onwards (Dollar and Gatti, 1999; Klasen, 1999) and used to support the World Bank's 'Gender Mainstreaming Strategy' (for discussion of gender mainstreaming, see Porter and Sweetman, 2005). Launched in 2001, the strategy claims to suggest a more effective way to integrate gender-responsive actions into all the World Bank's development assistance programmes.

World Bank research highlights that societies that discriminate by gender tend to experience less rapid economic growth and poverty reduction than societies that treat women and men equally, and that social gender disparities produce economically inefficient outcomes (World Bank, 2001a). When women and girls have systematically lower access to education and health, this translates into 'less than optimal' levels of participation in economic activities. At the same time, better educated women have lower fertility rates and lowered infant and child mortality rates. Thus, equality in education can help increase a country's economic growth rates, and reduce population growth, bringing per capita growth benefits. For example, it is suggested that if the countries of Africa had closed the gender gap in schooling between 1960 and 1992 as quickly as East Asia did, this would have produced close to a doubling of per capita income growth in the region (WBGDG, 2003).

The primary pathways through which gender systems affect growth are by influencing the productivity of labour and the allocative efficiency of the economy (World Bank, 2002a). In terms of productivity, for example, it has been suggested that if the access of women farmers to productive inputs and human capital were on a par with men's access, total agricultural output could increase by an estimated 6 to 20 percent (World Bank, 2001b). This highlights the continued economic inefficiency of gender relations noted since Boserup's work in the 1970s. In terms of allocative efficiency, women's socially constructed altruistic behaviour suggests that economic resources that enter the household via women are more likely to be spent on household and children's needs. Thus, this research suggests that, while increases in household income are generally associated with reduced child mortality risks, the marginal impact is almost 20 times as large if the income is in the hands of the mother rather than the father (WBGDG, 2003).

Recognition of women as a reliable, productive and cheap labour force has seen them the preferred workforce for textiles and electronic transnational corporations since the 1980s (see Elson and Pearson, 1981). Recognition of women as 'good with money', including being better at paying back loans, has led them to be targeted in microfinance programmes (see Mayoux, 2006). Recognition of women as more efficient distributors of goods and services within the household has led to them to be targeted with resources aimed at alleviating poverty (see Molyneux, 2006). Programmes that target women with resources, such as conditional cash transfers (CCTs), were shown to be effective in Mexico (Progresa/Oportunidades) and Brazil (Bolsa Família), and are often suggested to promote 'gender equality'. Yet, the assumption that poverty reduction programmes automatically bring gender equality can be challenged. As a result, in the late 1990s, Jackson (1998) suggested the need to 'rescue gender from the poverty trap'. She highlighted that if gender equality was the goal, then gender equality programmes and projects would be the only means to achieve this goal.

The World Bank Group Gender Action Plan of 2006 committed the World Bank Group to intensify and scale up gender mainstreaming in economic sectors over four years, in partnership with client countries, donors and other development agencies. This increased the resources devoted to gender issues in operations and technical assistance, and in policy-relevant research and statistics. However, as the above highlights, the justification for including women in development in the economic growth discourse is the 'efficiency' argument, with equity concerns secondary. Indeed, the World Bank notes that 'gender sensitive' development strategies 'contribute significantly to economic growth, *as well as* equity objectives' (World Bank, 2002b, emphasis added). The Action Plan surmises that reducing gender inequalities is just 'smart economics' (World Bank, 2006). Critics suggest this 'instrumentalist' approach to engendering development, while bringing economic growth gains, will not fundamentally change the situation and position of women since the policies are not designed to explicitly address the structural causes of gender inequality (see Chant and Sweetman, 2012).

Evidence suggests that growth alone does not necessarily lead to social justice, and it is important to note that while gender equality will help bring economic growth, economic growth will not necessarily bring gender equality. Anti-poverty programmes should not be seen to be the same as gender equality programmes, and gender equality needs to be seen to be a key goal in itself, not just a means to achieve other poverty goals. Advancing gender equality requires strengthening different dimensions of women's autonomy: not just economic autonomy, but political autonomy and promoting full citizenship; promoting freedom from all forms of violence; and sexual autonomy and reproductive autonomy (Alpízar Durán, 2010).

Constraints on realising the full potential of women in the process of economic development

Investment in the human capital, health and education of women and girls is presented as a key way forward, as witnessed by the MDGs. The logic is that 'educated, healthy women are more able to engage in productive activities, find formal sector employment, earn higher incomes and enjoy greater returns to schooling than are uneducated women' (WBGDG, 2003, 6). Research suggests that educated women are more likely to invest in the education of their own children, and are more likely to have fewer children. Thus, investment in human capital has positive short- and longer-term/inter-generational outcomes and is good for both productivity gains and population decline. To date attention has focused solely on ensuring equal access of girls to primary education. Inequality of access to secondary and higher education persists, as does the limited engagement of girls in the study of science and technology, limiting the future life and employment options of adolescent girls.

Families are often unwilling to invest in the education of girls if this investment will not bring direct economic gains to them, that is, if girls continue to be valued only as wives and mothers, and/or marriage effectively transfers any potential future gains from this investment to another family. As one in seven girls marries before the age of 18 in the developing world (UNFPA, 2012), early and forced marriage remains a key issue and an important factor limiting young women's engagement in both education and economic activities. Willingness to school, feed and provide healthcare to girls is far more strongly determined by income and the costs of providing these services than is the case for boys. In 1990 Sen highlighted that there were a '100 million missing women' as testimony to how girls are discriminated against in terms of the allocation of household resources to the point that it creates a gender imbalance in some societies and countries. The numbers of 'missing women' are calculated in relation to the numbers of men and women that could be expected if both received similar care in health, medicine and nutrition. More than 100 million women are simply not there because women are neglected compared to men and, what is more important, because no one is addressing the root causes that explain why this is the case.

State institutions, including the police and the courts, continue to deny women justice. Women and girls remain unable to access justice or use existing legal standards and mechanisms to realise their rights given that in many countries there are still laws that discriminate against women in relation to family, property, citizenship and employment. Justice systems also do not address the needs of specific groups of women, with indigenous women further discriminated against, facing violence in the public and private spheres based on both gender and race (UNPFII, 2013).

Cultural factors limit women's rights and engagement in the workplace. Religion still plays a key role in determining gender norms in many cultures, and antiquated views across the spectrum of religions threaten hard won rights or deny women rights, including those related to sex and sexualities, mobility and employment. While religious fundamentalism in contemporary society is often associated with the Islamic faith, other religions also have strong views around gender roles and relations. For example, in Nicaragua a state sponsored sex education manual was withdrawn from schools after the Catholic Church objected to the use of the phrase 'sexual and reproductive rights' in the introduction, since these rights are not recognised to be rights by the Church. The political strength of the Church was further evidenced by the fact that in the run-up to the national elections, a bill promoted by the Church was passed through parliament, voted for by all the leading political parties, outlawing therapeutic abortion (Bradshaw and Linneker, 2010).

Economic 'fundamentalism' – policies and practices that privilege profits over people – further deny women rights as workers and to work. With a faith that when markets are left to operate on their own they can solve all economic and social problems, such fundamentalist views are seen in companies opposing taxes, regulations and other government measures that constrain their activities. They are also seen in the rollback of state provided social services, including affordable childcare, and removal of measures such as minimum wages based on their construction as 'distorting' the economy. Campaigns for a living wage to end in-work poverty, for example, seek to address fundamentalism one policy at a time. Yet, some suggest what is needed is not a change in policies but a change in the way that people think about the economy – so that people come to see the economy not as an impersonal mechanism that produces efficient outcomes, but as a set of institutions that can be shaped to serve their needs. That is, as much a political as an economic system.

While political culture is important for bringing change, women are often restricted or prevented from full participation in formal and informal systems and networks of power. Women continue to have a limited voice at local, community and national levels, with only one in five parliamentarians in 2014 being female (UN Women, 2015).

Women also have limited voice in the private sphere, as the home may be as much a site of oppression as solidarity for some women.

In the majority of cultures, unequal gender and generational relations exist within households, with the male 'head' having a high level of control (see Dwyer and Bruce, 1988). Women going to work is often read as meaning the man is unable to provide for his family, making men reluctant to 'allow' this to occur, limiting women's engagement in paid work through violence or the threat of violence. When women do engage in paid work it can improve their voice in the home and ability to influence household decision-making. It may also lead to conflict in the home, especially if women earn more than men, or women's employment coincides with men's underemployment or unemployment. In the last decades, a 'crisis in masculinity' has been recognised, relating to the changes in men's roles and positions through processes of globalisation, suggesting a need to focus attention on men as well if changes are to bring transformative progress towards greater equality rather than further harm women (see IDS, 2000).

Women continue to suffer from socially imposed restricted mobility and in some cultures women are unable to leave home if not accompanied by a man, effectively negating any type of paid employment. Even when women are allowed to leave, they may face verbal, sexual and physical abuse from unknown males for being 'in the street', and face gossip and stigma within their communities. The growing levels and extremes of violence against women have been captured in the notion of 'femicide' – the killing of women by men for being women (Radford and Russell, 1992). This covers such things as 'honour killings', but in Mexico, for example, it has been used to describe the large number of women being killed seemingly for going against gender norms, including engaging in paid work outside the home. Violence against women is, according to the Human Development Report for Central America 2009–10 (UNDP, 2010a), the most 'silent' crime in the region. The report talks of an 'invisible insecurity' arising from this violence noting that two out of every three women killed are killed by reason of her gender – or their death is a 'femicide'.

One in three women across the globe experience violence at some stage in her lifetime. Violence against women and girls, or the threat of violence, be it physical, sexual or emotional, both in the private and public spheres, at the hands of known and unknown men, remains a key limiting factor impeding women's mobility and engagement in processes of development.

For those women that work from home, opportunities are limited, especially for immersion within work-related and social networks. No reliable figures exist around the gendered distribution of landownership and as such caution is needed when using general statements around women's land ownership. What we do know is that globally, more men than women own land. One study of ten African nations notes that the pattern that women own less land than men, regardless of how ownership is conceptualised, was 'remarkably consistent' (Doss et al, 2013). In many cases, the gender gaps are quite large and on average only 12 per cent of women report owning land individually, while 31 per cent of men do so (Doss, 2014). The lack of rights to inherit or own land may limit women's engagement in larger-scale cash crop production, and while women are often engaged in agriculture, this often consists of cultivation of subsistence crops. Even when women can inherit land the need for male protection or male labour may mean that they will forgo this right, giving land to male relatives. Lack of land ownership may also stop them participating in schemes to improve agricultural output, while lack of wider assets disallows them from accessing loans. Given their lower asset base, women farmers may be most affected by climate change, and while having knowledge of how to adapt, they may be least able to adopt appropriate adaptation strategies.

World Bank research has highlighted how the poor are less likely to engage in higher risk–return activities and the result is that the return on their assets is 25–50 per cent lower than for wealthier households (Holzmann and Jørgensen, 2000). While not a gendered analysis, women's relative poverty, lack of assets and lack of experience might mean they are particularly 'risk adverse', keeping them from higher return economic initiatives. Against this, women have been shown to use microfinance effectively to develop small enterprises and are recognised as good at paying back loans.

During the recent financial crisis, measures to protect 'the poor' through employment programmes did not consider the gendered dimensions of crisis and of employment, making women's specific situation invisible. Yet women may have been more severely affected than men, and in more diverse ways. Economic and financial crises cannot be seen in isolation from crises in access to food, fuel and water, and to the human rights mechanims that might address these, as well as from evolving environmental and care crises (AWID, 2012). Women face particular risks during disasters and emergencies including conflict; and climate change may significantly increase the risk of both 'natural' disaster and conflict in the future. In particular the risk of physical and sexual violence may increase post-disaster. However, it is important to note that disasters, or their aftermath, may reveal existing actual levels of violence or the potential for violence rather than an increase in violence. Those who are displaced and forced to live communally may continue to carry on their private lives in public, including violence. It may be the case that the levels of violence increase due to the frustration felt by men unable to fulfil their socially constructed gendered roles of protector and provider. It may be the case that the nature of violence changes, with higher levels of violence by strangers as social systems and structures of protection break down. However, it is important to remember that women and girls suffer violence at 'normal' times, in their everyday lives, and while post-event, humanitarian actions can respond to the practical need for protection, to reduce the disaster risk of violence against women and girls needs a longer-term, strategic development focus (Bradshaw, 2013a). At present, agencies not only fail to protect women and girls, but their reproductive and particularly their productive needs are often overlooked in crisis-response and peacebuilding initiatives (see Bradshaw and Fordham, 2013).

When women are in paid employment they are more likely to be engaged in part-time rather than full-time work in the informal rather than the formal sector, and across the globe women earn less than men for comparable work. It has been suggested that the world average gender pay gap is 15.6 per cent (ITUC, 2008). However, this measure uses official data sources and is thus unable to capture female participation in the informal economy, which particularly distorts the pay gap figures in countries where such economies are large. Women's concentration in the informal sector may help to explain why they earn less than men, as may the lack of women in senior roles in the formal sector. The impact of childcare responsibilities or 'the motherhood penalty' reduces the amount women earn over their lifetimes, but a continued reason for the gender pay gap is discrimination. The gender pay gap for full-time employees cited above means that women effectively stop earning relative to men, in the UK usually on one day in November, referred to as Equal Pay Day.

Employment generation is a key component of any development model, but in order for such a model to be just, the employment on offer needs to obey minimum core labour standard thresholds, and offer fair wages and decent working conditions. Labour rights have been severely jeopardised in a globalised labour market where firms compete for cheap labour and where unions and workers' rights are considered an obstacle imposing undue cost. Women are most likely to accept low wages through lack of choice or knowledge of rights, and most likely not to belong to unions, or to work in non-unionised industries such as domestic work or the informal sector. Workers within informal sectors often lack basic labour rights and work under conditions that violate basic standards governing decent work. While the informal sector as a whole is problematic in terms of lack of safeguards, it often provides the only means of survival for many women, and some commentators argue that it is the real engine of growth that will spawn entrepreneurs of the future. The lack of rights enjoyed by many workers in the 'formal' sector also means that there has been a blurring of the distinction as the formal becomes more informalised through outsourcing. In the garment industry in Bangladesh, 90 per cent of the 1.5 million wage workers are women, often without formal contracts (Barrientos, 2010). Much of this work is undertaken by women in their homes, but young women are often a favoured workforce, especially in textiles and electronics factories where their 'natural' ability to undertake detailed, repetitive work, maintain high productivity over long hours, and command low wages make them a 'natural' choice.

The inclusion of women in the labour force, albeit in part-time, menial, poorly paid and low status jobs, contrasts with the rise in male unemployment and underemployment. The erosion of the male provider/protector role in part explains the supposed 'crisis in masculinity' documented in the academic literature (Chant and Gutmann, 2000). Young men in particular may suffer such crisis, resulting in overt displays of 'maleness', especially where unemployment is high, and male educational attainment is lower than for girls. Such crises can cause a backlash against women, as men reassert their power lost in the public sphere through violence in the private sphere, for example. While some women may wish to remain at home and care for children, and social norms construct this role for them, women increasingly have no choice other than to engage in low-paid work in poor conditions.

While increasingly engaged in remunerated work, it is important to remember that women undertake the bulk of unpaid work in the home, household plot or family business, have the primary responsibility for caring for children and older people as well responsibility for undertaking activities such as collection of water or firewood. Women play the key role in the 'care economy', which not only provides care to the young, old and sick but is vital for ensuring a productive workforce. As this work is unremunerated, it is undervalued and lies outside general conceptualisations of 'the economy'. Women engaged in paid work often face a double workday, since they may only be 'allowed' to work as long as their domestic duties are still fulfilled. This means that women are time poor and the time burden may affect their health and wellbeing. To alleviate this burden and free women to enter paid work, daughters may be taken out of school to cover domestic work, negatively affecting their education and prospects for seeking remunerated work in the future.

Women's continued inability to control their own fertility means that childbirth limits their ability to engage in productive activities. Even when reproductive health services are provided, this is not enough to ensure women's ability to access them, since men, especially when they perceive their masculinity to be threatened, may see if and when to have children to be their decision to make; with large numbers of children often read as a sign of male fertility and power. In many cultures, discussion of sexualities remains taboo, denying access and rights to those who do not conform to the heterosexual 'norm'. The sexual and reproductive rights of adolescent girls in particular may be overlooked and they may be denied access to reproductive health services if they are unmarried. Research suggests a link between education and women's ability to control their fertility, studies also suggest paid work can promote greater understanding of sexual and reproductive rights among women and a greater perception of their ability to make decisions about their own bodies (Bradshaw 2010; 2013b).

While paid work can bring benefits to women, women's economic wellbeing is not automatically or necessarily improved through this work, as women's poverty is not simply related to how much she earns. Women's poverty is caused at many different levels, sites and spaces – the community, labour market, the household (Bradshaw, 2002). Three factors contribute to women's relative poverty. Women have fewer possibilities to translate work into income, stemming from (i) their exclusive responsibility for reproductive work, (ii) the conceptualisation of their productive activities as 'helping' men, and (iii) their concentration within sectors which are either an extension of their reproductive roles (and thus lower paid) and/or within the 'informal' economy. Even when women have an income, societal/family structures and norms makes it difficult for them to transform this into decision-making capacity or to decide how it is used. This is related to perceptions around value of contribution to the household, social norms and self-esteem/relative autonomy, which influence the capacity to have a voice in decision-making processes. In addition, when women make decisions, they are less likely to take decisions that improve their personal wellbeing, and more likely to seek to improve the wellbeing of others, notably children and the elderly.

In many societies women's income is perceived as contributing to the collective finances of a family/community, while men's is often individually calibrated.

As a consequence, women's socially constructed altruistic behaviour means that economic resources that enter the household via women are more likely to be spent on household and children's needs. This means that while women who head their own households have less access to income than male headed units, since women earn less than men and do not have access to the income of a partner, they have greater control over the household income. Female headed households may not be the 'poorest of the poor' as popularly constructed since women who live with men may suffer 'secondary poverty', whereby the household overall is not poor but as the man withholds income for personal consumption, women and children within the household are poor (see Chant, 2006). When women earn, men may withhold more of their income, leaving women and children with access to the same level of economic resources (Bradshaw, 2002), however, women will have greater control over those resources.

Studies show that men may withhold up to 50 per cent of their income from the household (Bradshaw, 2002). This type of male behaviour has meant that women have been targeted within poverty reduction and social policy initiatives. Rather than tackling socially constructed behaviours and seeking greater equality within the home, such policies effectively circumvent the problem. Programmes, such as CCTs, that only target women as participants in projects or as recipients of resources may change gender roles (that is, they broaden roles considered to be part of women's mothering roles), but they do not alter gender relations. If the new role is seen to be part of a woman's mothering role or constructed as 'women's work', it does not necessarily improve the status of women. For some this type of inclusion of women in development as deliverers of services to others has meant in practice that women are assuming greater liability for dealing with poverty and ensuring wellbeing, and have progressively less choice other than to do so (Chant, 2006).

While the targeting of women with resources is welcome, the associated 'feminisation of obligation and responsibility' (Chant, 2008) for delivering policy outcomes may not only marginalise men, but add further to women's existing 'triple burdens' – of reproductive, productive and community management work (Moser, 1993). It may privilege their reproductive over their productive role, and reinforce women as mothers rather than workers. Care needs to be taken to ensure that programmes, such as CCTs, serve women's needs and women are not merely placed at the 'service of' these policy agendas (Molyneux, 2007).

Priority areas of intervention

While development is more than economic growth, economic growth remains a key driver of development and a key concern for those who developed the post-2015 agenda. The promotion of women's economic rights could act as a key driver for economic growth. Promoting women's economic rights in turn entails promoting a range of women's rights; their rights to education, mobility, voice, ownership, sexual and reproductive rights and the right to live free from violence.

Women's groups and movements across the globe continue to promote as fundamental the need to respect and defend women's sexual and reproductive rights. Women's groups and movements continue to be fundamental to promoting these rights, but many find themselves under threat for this focus on rights. While women's groups and movements are key to promote gendered rights, forging alliances with other social movements are also important to ensure widescale acceptance of these rights, as rights. In particular, there is a need to ensure acceptance of sexual and reproductive rights as rights. Sexual and reproductive rights are important for social and economic development as without such rights, women and adolescent girls cannot make decisions around fertility, with repeated childbirth preventing them from income generating activities and reducing productivity. An absence of such rights also enables early and forced marriage to continue, excluding young women from education and employment. Yet sexual and reproductive rights remain contested 'rights', with sexual rights not recognised in many cultures. There is then a need to ensure all rights for all, and to find ways to negotiate cultural differences to make sure rights are used to promote and protect society against harmful processes and practices. It is fundamental that adequate reproductive health services are provided for all, and that there is a formalisation of sexual and reproductive rights within the frameworks as 'rights' with legal protection provided for those seeking promotion of these contested rights, as well as censure where appropriate, for violation of such rights. The censure of female genital mutilation (FGM) by international organisations and national governments demonstrates how women's reproductive rights can become accepted across societal groups and can be enforced by law as well as through changes in what is seen to be as socially acceptable.

A key right for women is the right to live free from violence. Sexual, emotional and physical violence and the threat of such violence restricts women's mobility, confines women to the home, and prevents their full engagement with processes of social and economic development. As well as ensuring provision of appropriate protection to women and girls in all circumstances, including conflict and post-disaster when violence may increase, there is a need for a holistic approach if the right to live free from violence is to be realised. To escape violence, women need more than laws. Women need to be able to live independently, to earn an income, to own property, to farm land, and to have society recognise their right to live independently. Men and boys have a role to play in the prevention of gender-based violence, as well as the promotion of gender equality more generally. Changing social norms is key here and new forms of educating, including TV and radio 'edutainment' programmes that seek to educate and entertain, have been shown to be effective in bringing changes in attitudes and norms (Lacayo and Singhal, 2008; Linneker, 2006). In order to promote change there is a need to work with men and women to establish shared responsibilities and to promote women's rights in the home, as well as wider society. The achievement of gender equality demands joined up policy initiatives linking economic and sexual reproductive rights, ensuring women are able to make decisions in the economic and intimate realms.

Threats to women's rights exist on many levels, including those posed by culture, religion, and tradition but also emanating from processes of globalisation and economic change. There is need to acknowledge that a right gained is not a right maintained unless regularly monitored. As part of this, there is need to strengthen women's access to formal and informal justice systems, and ensure that these are responsive to advancing all women's equal rights, opportunity and participation. Improving women's political voice is also crucial here with international frameworks providing a key forum. For example, the Convention on the Elimination of All Forms of Discrimination against Women (CEDAW) upholds women's right to participate in public life, and the Beijing Platform for Action (BPFA) calls for removing barriers to equal participation. Similarly, the MDGs measured progress towards gender equality in part by the proportion of women in parliamentary seats. In fact, there is a history of UN commitment to women's representation. For example, UN Women back gender equality advocates in calling on political parties, governments and others to do their part, including calling for legislative and constitutional reforms to ensure women's fair access to political spheres — as voters, candidates, elected officials and civil service members (UN Women, 2015). Other initiatives encourage young men and women to engage in advocacy around making gender equality measures central to public policymaking, across the full policy spectrum, including paid and unpaid activities.

Economic policy, if it is to promote the wellbeing of women as well as the economy, not only needs to improve women's engagement in paid work by tackling structural societal and gender biases that keeps them from this, it also needs to recognise women's unpaid work as a vital part of the economy and essential for economic growth. Women's responsibility for unpaid, domestic work makes them time poor and more economically dependent on men, yet is vital for ensuring a healthy and productive workforce. While investment in infrastructure, such as water, sanitation and electricity, is important to ease the time burden associated with these tasks it does not change how unpaid work and the care economy is conceptualised and valued.

Financial, environmental and health crises intensify the need for care services with the care burden falling disproportionately on women and girls. Policies to provide affordable, quality childcare and adequate healthcare services would free women to enter paid employment and help change care work from being understood as a 'domestic' responsibility to a collective responsibility; the change in how care work is conceptualised and valued should be a longer-term goal.

In the short term, there is a need to create full productive employment opportunities for women, including young women and men. Jobs need to be decent and dignified, and reflect the fact that young (and older) women and men may need and want to dedicate time to raising a family, especially when their children are young. While national laws vary widely, the Convention on the Elimination of All Forms of Discrimination against Women suggests the need 'to introduce maternity leave with pays or with comparable social benefits without loss of former employment, seniority or social allowances' (CEDAW Article 11, 2, b). The Maternity Protection Convention C 183 adopted by the International Labour Organization in 2000 requires 14 weeks of maternity leave as a minimum condition under Article 4 (ILO, 2015). Such legislation is a starting point, but the longer-term goal should be to change how maternity and paternity is understood, and valued.

It is important to continue to provide social protection via policies that benefit women rather than just targeting them. To achieve equality in access to paid employment means changing social structures that limit some people's access to employment, and those that limit access to land and other 'productive' resources including access to finance. In particular, it means establishing social norms that promote and value women as 'good with money', to ensure not only their access to, but control over the resources they and their households generate.

In conclusion, it is important to remember that while women have a vital role to play in bringing about economic development, policies to promote economic development that seek only to include women but do not tackle the structural inequalities at the base of their exclusion, may bring growth gains, but will not achieve gender parity. Improving women's wellbeing demands explicitly addressing gender inequality and manifestations of this, such as violence against women and girls. Achieving gender equality requires specific actions to address structural gendered inequalities, which are unlikely to be achieved as convenient collateral to other policies. Policies for poverty alleviation or economic growth, even if targeted at women, do not address the structural causes of women's unequal power relations, and as such cannot transform gender inequalities. To transform gender inequalities requires far-reaching changes that go beyond simple policy prescriptions. For example, while the call in SDG 5 to 'End all forms of discrimination against all women and girls everywhere' is a worthy one, it is an overly ambitious one, making it more of an aspiration than an achievable aim. For real change to occur would require addressing the patriarchal structures – in institutions, education, the workplace and the home – that underpin gender discrimination. Similarly, while there has been some advancement in including key gender issues in the 2030 agenda, such as violence against women and girls and unpaid care work, how these goals are pursued and implemented will be key in determining the extent to which they can bring real and sustainable changes in the lives of women and girls. While the fact these issues are part of the 2030 Agenda for Sustainable Development is encouraging, important omissions from the Agenda – focused particularly on gendered and sexual identities – suggest the far-reaching changes required to end discrimination and violence are unlikely to occur. As the 59th session of CEDAW noted in an Open letter on the Post-2015 Development Agenda, 'the Post-2015 Development Agenda should have a transformative impact on the lives of women and girls. In order for that to happen it must address the legal and institutional context in which violations of sexual and reproductive health and rights arise' (CEDAW, 2015). In contrast to the HLP's illustrative goals, the SDGs do not address reproductive and sexual rights (see Bradshaw, 2015). They promote instead universal access to 'sexual and reproductive health' and only recognise 'reproductive rights' – effectively negating sexual rights, as rights. As such the extent to which the 2030 agenda can be transformative for gender equality remains open to question.

Note

[1] This chapter is based on a paper written on the request of the High-Level Panel (HLP) on the Post-2015 Development Agenda, to provide background information on the role women have, and can play in economic development (see Bradshaw et al, 2013). The request focused on women and on economic development, rather than on the wider issue of gender and development. The HLP asked that the paper address three questions: What is the evidence base to support investing in women? What are the current constraints on realising the full potential of women in the process of economic development? What are the priority areas of intervention necessary to unblock these constraints? This chapter also draws on the work of the Sustainable Development Solutions Network (SDSN) Thematic Group 3 on Gender, Inequalities, and Human Rights (see UNSDSN, 2013) and we would like to thank the members of TG3 for their comments and contributions.

References

Alpízar Durán, L, 2010, Key note speech at High-Level Roundtable: 'The implementation of the Beijing Declaration and Platform for Action, the outcomes of the twenty-third special session of the General Assembly and its contribution to shaping a gender perspective towards the full realization of the Millennium Development Goals', *54th session of the UN Commission on the Status of Women (CSW)*, New York: United Nations Headquarters, 1–12 March

Alvarez, SE, 1999, Advocating feminism: The Latin American feminist NGO 'Boom', *International Feminist Journal of Politics* 1, 2, 181–209

Antrobus, P, 2004a, *The global women's movement: Origins, issues and strategies*, London: Zed Books

Antrobus, P, 2004b, MDGs: The most distracting gimmick, in C Barton and L Prendergast (eds) *Seeking accountability on women's human rights: Women debate the Millennium Development Goals*, pp 14–16, www.banulacht.ie/onlinedocs/WICEJ_Seeking_Accountability_on_Womens_Human_Rights_UN_MDGs_(2004).pdf

AWID (Association for Women's Rights in Development), 2012, Getting at the roots: Re-integrating human rights and gender equality in the Post-2015 Development Agenda, *Association for Women's Rights in Development*, October, www.awid.org/Library/Getting-at-the-roots-Reintegrating-human-rights-gender-equality-in-post-2015-development-agenda

Barrientos, S, 2010, Gender and ethical trade: Can vulnerable women workers benefit?, in S Chant (ed) *The international handbook of gender and poverty: Concepts, research, policy*, Cheltenham: Edward Elgar

Boserup, E, 1970, *Woman's role in economic development*, New York: St Martin's Press

Bradshaw, S, 2002, *Gendered poverties and power relations: Looking inside communities and households* [*La pobreza no es la misma ni es igual: Relaciones de poder dentro y fuera del hogar*], Managua: Puntos de Encuentro

Bradshaw, S, 2010, *Decisiones Económicas e Intimas de las Mujeres.* Nicaragua: Puntos de Encuentro, http://sidoc.puntos.org.ni/isis_sidoc/documentos/13137/13137_00.pdf

Bradshaw, S, 2013a, *Gender, development and disasters*, Northampton: Edward Elgar

Bradshaw, S, 2013b, Women's decision-making in rural and urban households in Nicaragua: The influence of income and ideology, *Environment and Urbanisation* 25, 1, 81–94

Bradshaw, S, 2015, Gendered rights in the post-2015 development and disasters agendas, *Institute of Development Studies (IDS) Bulletin*, 59–65

Bradshaw, S, Linneker, B, 2010, Poverty alleviation in a changing policy and political context: The case of PRSPs in Latin America, in S Chant (ed) *International handbook on gender and poverty*, Cheltenham: Edward Elgar, 516–21

Bradshaw, S, Fordham, M, 2013, *Women and Girls in Disasters.* Report produced for the Department for International Development, UK http://gcrsp.eu/assets/uploads/women-girls-disasters.pdf

Bradshaw, S with Castellino, J, Diop, B, 2013, Women's role in economic development: Overcoming the constraints, *Background paper prepared for the High-Level Panel on the post-2015 agenda*, UN Sustainable Development Solutions Network, May, www.post2015hlp.org/the-report/

Bradshaw, S, Castillo, V, Criquillion, A, Wilson, G, 2008, Women mobilising to defend abortion rights in Nicaragua: Is therapeutic abortion the wrong right to promote?, in M Mukhopadhya (ed) *Gender, rights and development*, Gender, Society and Development series, Amsterdam: Royal Tropical Institute (KIT) and London: Oxfam

CEDAW (Convention on the Elimination of All Forms of Discrimination against Women), 2015, Open letter on the inadequate recognition of sexual and reproductive health and rights in the Post-2015 Development Agenda, *The Convention on the Elimination of All Forms of Discrimination against Women (CEDAW)*, 59th session, Geneva, 20 October, 7 November 2014

Chant, S, 2006, Re-thinking the 'feminization of poverty' in relation to aggregate gender indices, *Journal of Human Development* 7, 2, 201–20

Chant, S, 2008, The 'feminisation of poverty' and the 'feminisation' of anti-poverty programmes: Room for revision?, *Journal of Development Studies* 44, 2, 165–97

Chant, S, Gutmann, M, 2000, Mainstreaming men into gender and development: Debates, reflections and experiences, *Oxfam working papers*, Oxford: Oxfam Publishing

Chant, S, Sweetman, C, 2012, Fixing women or fixing the world? 'Smart economics', efficiency approaches, and gender equality in development, *Gender and Development* 20, 3, 517–29

Dollar, D, Gatti, R, 1999, Gender inequality, income, and growth: Are good times good for women?, *Gender and Development Working Papers* 1, May, Washington, DC: World Bank, http://siteresources. worldbank.org/INTGENDER/Resources/wp1.pdf

Doss, C, 2014, Killer fact check: 'Women own 2% of land' = not true. What do we really know about women and land?, *Oxfam Blog*, 21 March, https://oxfamblogs.org/fp2p/killer-factcheck-women-own-2-of-land-not-true-what-do-we-really-know-about-women-and-land/

Doss, C, Kovarik, C, Peterman, A, Quisumbing, A, van den Bold, M, 2013, Gender inequalities in ownership and control of land in Africa myths versus reality, *International Food Policy Research Institute (IFPRI) Discussion Paper* 01308, December, Washington, DC: IFPRI

Dwyer, D, Bruce, J, (eds), 1988, *A home divided: Women and income in the Third World*, Stanford, CA: Stanford University Press

Elson, D, Pearson, R, 1981, 'Nimble fingers make cheap workers': An analysis of women's employment in Third World export manufacturing, *Feminist Review* 7, 87–107

Eyben, R, 2003, The rise of rights: Rights-based approaches to international development, *Institute of Development Studies (IDS) Policy Briefing* 17, Brighton: IDS

GTZ (Deutsche Gesellschaft für Technische Zusammenarbeit), 1999, *Gender responsive land tenure development*, Sector-Project Land Tenure in Development Cooperation, GTZ, December, www.bridge.ids. ac.uk/sites/bridge.ids.ac.uk/files/docs_genie/gtz/Land_Tenure.pdf

Holzmann, R, Jørgensen, S, 2000, Social risk management: A new conceptual framework for social protection and beyond, *Social Protection Discussion Paper Series* 0006, February, Washington, DC: Social Protection Unit, Human Development Network, World Bank

IDS (Institute of Development Studies), 2000, *IDS Bulletin* special edition on Men, masculinities and development, 31, 2

IDS (Institute of Development Studies), 2005, *IDS Bulletin* special edition on Developing rights, 36, 1

ILO (International Labour Organization), 2015, *The Maternity Protection Convention*, C 183, 2000, www.ilo.org/dyn/normlex/en/f?p=NOR MLEXPUB:12100:0::NO::P12100_ILO_CODE:C183

ITUC (International Trade Union Confederation), 2008, *The global gender pay*, Brussels: ITUC

Jackson, C, 1998, Rescuing gender from the poverty trap, in R Pearson, C Jackson (eds) *Feminist visions of development: Gender analysis and policy*, pp 39–64, London: Routledge

Kabeer, N, 1994, *Reversed realities: Gender hierarchies in development thought*, London: Verso

Klasen, S, 1999, Does gender inequality reduce growth and development? Evidence from cross-country regressions, *Gender and Development Working Papers* 7, November, Washington, DC, World Bank, http://siteresources.worldbank.org/INTGENDER/Resources/wp7.pdf

Lacayo, V, Singhal, A, 2008, *Pop culture with a purpose! Using edutainment media for social change: Puntos de Encuentro, Soul City and Breakthrough share experiences from Nicaragua, South Africa, India and the US*, Hague: Oxfam Novib – Knowledge Infrastructure for and between Counterparts portal

Linneker, B, 2006, Sexto Sentido TV and progressive opinion formation among young people in Nicaragua 2001–2005, *Working Paper, International Cooperation for Development (ICD)*, September, Managua: ICD and Puntos de Encuentro, www.linneker.pwp.blueyonder.co.uk/docs/Brian_SSTV_Informe_2006.doc

Mayoux, L, 2006, Women's empowerment through sustainable micro-finance: Rethinking 'best practice', *Discussion paper, Gender and micro-finance*, www.genfinance.net

Molyneux, M, 1985, Mobilization without emancipation? Women's interests, the state, and revolution in Nicaragua, *Feminist Studies* 11, 2, 227–54

Molyneux, M, 2006, Mothers at the service of the new poverty agenda: PROGRESA/Oportunidades, Mexico's Conditional Transfer Programme, *Journal of Social Policy and Administration* 40, 4, 425–49

Molyneux, M, 2007, Two cheers for conditional cash transfers, *Institute of Development Studies (IDS) Bulletin* 38, 3, 69–75

Molyneux, M, Cornwall, A (eds), 2008, *The politics of rights: Dilemmas for feminist praxis*, Routledge: London

Molyneux, M, Lazar, S, 2003, *Doing the rights thing: Rights-based development and Latin American NGOs*, London: Intermediate Technology Development Group Publishing

Moser, C, 1989, Gender planning in the Third World: Meeting practical and strategic gender needs, *World Development* 17, 11, 1799–825

Moser, C, 1993, *Gender and development planning*, London: Routledge

Ostergaard, L (ed), 1992, *Gender and development*, London: Routledge

Parpart, J, Commelly, P, Barriteau, E (eds), 2000, *Theoretical perspectives on gender and development*, Ottawa, ON: Commonwealth of Learning, International Development Research Centre

Pickup, F with Williams, S, Sweetman, C, 2001, *Ending violence against women: A challenge for development and humanitarian work*, Oxford: Oxfam

Porter, F, Sweetman, C, 2005, *Mainstreaming gender in development: A critical review. Has gender mainstreaming made a difference after 10 years?*, Oxford: Oxfam

Radford, J, Russell, D, 1992, *Femicide: The politics of woman killing*, Buckingham: Open University Press

Razavi, S, Miller, C, 1995, From WID to GAD: Conceptual shifts in the women and development discourse, *Occasional Paper* 1, February, New York: United Nations Research Institute for Social Development, United Nations Development Programme

Sen, A, 1990, More than 100 million women are missing, *New York Review of Books* 37, 20

UN Women, 2015, *Facts and figures: Leadership and political participation*, www.unwomen.org/en/what-we-do/leadership-and-political-participation/facts-and-figures#sthash.V3m1zrkL.dpufhttp://www.unwomen.org/en/what-we-do/leadership-and-political-participation/facts-and-figures

UNDP (United Nations Development Programme), 2010a, *Human development report for Central America 2009-2010. Opening spaces to citizen security and human development*, United Nations Development Programme, http://www.latinamerica.undp.org/content/rblac/en/home/library/human_development/informe-sobre-desarrollo-humano-para-america-central-2009-2010.html

UNDP (United Nations Development Programme), 2010b, MDG 3: Promote gender equality and empower women, *Thematic Paper*, March, New York: UNDP, www.oecd.org/social/gender-development/45341361.pdf

UNFPA (United Nations Population Fund), 2012, From childhood to womanhood: Meeting the sexual and reproductive health needs of adolescent girls, *Fact Sheet: Adolescent Girls' Sexual and Reproductive Health Needs*, New York: UNFPA

UNPFII (United Nations Permanent Forum on Indigenous Issues), 2013, *Study on the extent of violence against women and girls in terms of article 22(2) of the United Nations Declaration on the Rights of Indigenous Issues* E/C19/2013/9, New York: UNPFII

UNSDSN (United Nations Sustainable Development Solutions Network), 2013, *Report of Thematic Group 3: Gender, human rights and social inclusion*, September, New York: UNSDSN

WBGDG (World Bank Gender and Development Group), 2003, *Gender equality and the Millennium Development Goals*, Washington, DC: WBGDG

WHO (World Health Organization), 2006, *Defining sexual health. Report of a technical consultation on sexual health 28–31 January 2002*, Geneva: World Health Organisation, http://www.who.int/reproductivehealth/topics/gender_rights/defining_sexual_health/en/

WICEJ (Women's International Coalition for Economic Justice) (eds), 2004, *Seeking accountability on women's human rights: Women debate the millennium*, New York: WICEJ

World Bank, 2001a, *Social protection strategy: From safety net to springboard*, Washington DC: World Bank

World Bank, 2001b, *Engendering development through gender equality in rights, resources, and voice*, New York: Oxford University Press

World Bank, 2002a, *Integrating gender into the World Bank's work: A strategy for action*, Washington, DC: World Bank

World Bank, 2002b, *Integrating Gender into the PRS Monitoring and Evaluation*, World Bank Poverty Reduction Strategy Papers (PRSP) Source Book, Washington DC: World Bank

World Bank, 2006, *Gender equality as smart economics: A World Bank Group Gender Action Plan* (Fiscal years 2007–10), Washington DC: World Bank

NINE

Marginalised minorities in conflict: women and Millennium Development Goals

Sarah Hoesch and Alireza Saniei-Pour

Introduction

Increasing violence in volatile corners of the world has had a dramatic impact on human populations, especially on women. Unrest has extended social inequalities, which has further marginalised women both at micro and macro levels. In a report on 'Gender, conflict and the MDGs' Ngozi Eze (2011, 2) revealed that as of 2011, '70% of the 1.3 billion people living in extreme poverty are women, who perform 66% of the world's work and produce half its food while earning only 10% of the world's income and owning less than 1% of its property.' The majority of these women reside in turbulent regions of the world where the pace of developing adequate governance mechanisms and delivering adequate economic development has been less than desirable.

This disparity was internationally acknowledged for the first time in 1945 when the UN Commission on the Status of Women established a set of standards regarding Women's Rights to promote gender equality and motivate governments to change or establish laws to reflect the international conventions on women's rights (Cockerton, 1999). In 1948, the Universal Declaration of Human Rights was adopted as the first international document manifesting the Universality of human rights (Papoutsi, 2014). Social stratifications, such as race or gender, were not emphasised in separate, independent charters. It was through gradual adaptations of other charters in the following years, such as the Convention on the Elimination of all forms of Discrimination Against Women (CEDAW) in 1979, or the Declaration on the Elimination of Violence against Women in Vienna in 1993 that recognised women's struggle for just rights and their fight for gender equality (Sen and Mukherjee, 2013).

It was only in 2008 that the UN Security Council, through Resolution 1820 stressed that systematic sexual violence during conflict can constitute a war crime, crime against humanity, and/or act of genocide (United Nations Security Council, 2008). The same Resolution demands protection and prevention measures from parties in armed conflict; protection from violence in refugee and displaced person camps; and affirms the need for women's full participation in the peace-building process (UNDP, 2008).

The third of the eight Millennium Development Goals (MDGs) acknowledges the necessity of fighting discrimination against women and seeks to promote gender equality. Until 2015 progress had been made, especially in terms of women and girls education: two thirds of developing countries achieved gender parity at the primary level and 41 per cent of paid workers outside of agriculture were women (UN, 2015). Yet, these numbers were misrepresentative of the situation in conflict countries as a UNESCO Policy Paper revealed in 2013. It is estimated that of the 69 million children not attending lower secondary school, 20 million or approximately 30% live in conflict-affected countries. Amongst these 20 million, 11 million were female (UNESCO, 2013). Gender disparities and inequalities, especially in wages and the availability of equal opportunities, prevail. Critical voices proclaim that the goal of gender equality is anything but achieved, indicating that 'the achievements have been far from transformative for women' (Ford, 2015). Important areas such as violence against women, access to assets and other resources of physical capitals such as land, sexual and reproductive rights have remained unchanged (Sen and Mukherjee, 2013).

It is important to highlight that success or the claims of 'achievements' should not only be seen as states' ability to pass appropriate legislations but also as their ability to enforce and implement them. In many developing states, laws might exist but gaps within the legislation, a lack of enforcement mechanisms and the chaos induced by conflict prevents actual progress. For example, despite appropriate laws in Tanzania that prohibit marriage below the age of 18, child marriages are still a common phenomenon, particularly in rural areas. Only 16 per cent of children below the age of 5 have been registered with the civil authorities (Human Rights Watch, 2015). This raises the question of whether any actual impact has been made.

The MDGs put significant emphasis on reducing inequalities by promoting gender equality, empowering women and expanding the role of women in society. Though the Goals intended to set a precedent in tackling these problems and issues, women's universal rights have not yet fully been achieved. In fact, in conflict and post conflict states their standings have deteriorated. For instance, the rise of radical Islam in the Levant as the result of civil war in Syria and political instability in Iraq have led to the complete collapse of women's economic role, as well as their freedoms and rights. The alleged sexual harassment of women in Central African Republic by United Nation's peacekeeping corps highlights the institutional failure of the same body whose mandate is to protect and enforce rights.

The post-2015 framework needs to set a stronger tone in enforcing the targets. This chapter will reflect on certain legal, political, economic and ideological problems standing in the way of women's empowerment and gender equality. It will reflect on the sociological and legal conception of women as minorities and the term minority itself. It will further elaborate on women's position in conflict, focusing on sexual violence as a tool of terror and analysing the current situation with regards to political representation and representation in peace negotiations. It will briefly touch on legal discrimination, which is aggravating conflict and post-conflict situations, and then return to the minority problematic. Finally, it will recommend a way forward with the post-2015 framework based on the limitations and problems that the MDGs faced.

Women as a minority

It is often hard to achieve justice during periods of conflicts due to lack of access to judiciaries, the lack of preventive mechanisms and general chaos. In order to ensure that justice can be restored after conflict, accessible tools are needed to gain legal compensation. One aspect of international law that might hinder this compensation with regards to women, especially women in conflict, is the terminology of women as a minority.

Women are not a statistical minority as they consist of roughly half of the world's population, therefore to regard them as a minority might seem bizarre to some. One of the most influential definitions of the term 'minority' until 1945 was provided by sociologist Robert Wirth (Meintel, 1993, 1): 'We may define a minority as a group of people who, because of their physical or cultural characteristics, are singled out from the others in the society in which they live for differential and unequal treatment and who therefore regard themselves as objects of collective discrimination'.

It was only in 1951 that sociologist Helen Mayer Hacker (1951) analysed why women should fall under this definition due to their ascribed status in society and the everyday discrimination they faced. Distinguishing her interpretation of 'minority' from Wirth's, she also provided reasons why members of a minority group do not necessarily have to regard themselves as objects of discrimination. This analysis began to gain importance when the status of women was seen separately from its male counterparts in the 1970s. Since then anthropologists and sociologists have acknowledged the unequal treatment of women, which results in and originates from sexism (discrimination based on sex). As a result, the accepted definition of minority widened to include a focus on power relations and status disadvantages. Differences in access to wealth, prestige, healthcare and in some societies food played a major role in allowing for women to be defined as a minority status group (Meintel, 1993). Consequently, the widespread sociologist definition of a social minority group now refers to groups with less power or fewer resources.

There has been a movement to improve women's rights since their recognition in 1945, especially through legal instruments. Laws act as 'management agents for suppressing, confining, limiting, guiding, directing, standardizing, integrating, adapting and changing behaviour' (Papoutis, 2014, 309) and are therefore useful tools to fight the gender gap. Yet, in the legal sphere women rights are different from minority rights. Although, there is no general definition of 'minorities' in terms of law, the United Nations Minorities Declaration refers to national, ethnic, religious and linguistic minorities. As a result, women do not specifically fall under the legal definition of a minority and are protected underneath an umbrella of other rights instead.

Although the absence of women in the UN definition of minority diverges from their inclusion in the sociological definition, it is not necessarily problematic. Indeed, it is extremely important to protect women's rights, along with different ethnic, religious or linguistic groups; however, the concept of intersectionality is important. Intersectionality refers to a differing intensity of discrimination with regards to interrelated intersectional systems of society. As an example, these systems include gender, class, race, ethnicity and ability (Crenshaw, 1993). A conflict related to gender inequality will very rarely be as simple as women versus men. Our society is structured into different classes, ethnicities, races and nationalities and some women can maintain a more privileged status than a man of another race or ethnicity depending on the society in which they live (Boundless, 2015). To disregard connections between gender and other societal status characteristics hinders a successful elimination of gender inequalities. As Camilla Ida Ravnbøl (2010) points out in her essay on *The Human Rights of Minority Women*, the separation between categories of gender and race/ethnicity within the international community and legal system can become a gap that excludes minority women, such as Romanian women, which Camilla explores in her essay. The essay describes how Romanian women face challenges of discrimination from society at large, but also within their own communities because of strict patriarchal traditions constraining their access to education and engagement in the workforce. It furthermore emphasises common racial stereotyping, prejudice and ethnic discrimination in the justice system, leading to ineffective remedies and lack of procedural guarantees for Romanian women. The essay cites women activists who point out anti-Romanian attitudes in state-backed health institutions where Romani women are often refused help, even in urgent circumstances such as child delivery. Furthermore, the essay highlights the increased verbal or physical abuse of Romanian women who wear traditional clothes in the public sphere. She criticises the disregard of the connection between 'minority' characteristics and women. Furthermore, the essay refers to rape with racial dimensions as another form of discrimination affecting minority women.

The problem in terms of international human rights law is that – as described above – there are now two separate protection umbrellas referring to minority women. There is legislation referring to them as a minority, such as the Committee on the Elimination of Racial Discrimination (CERD), which typically refers to characteristics shared by all members of the group. For example, minority-focused legislation typically focuses on the protection of language, the right to exist and the right to traditional economic activities. It does not, however, typically focus on women or include any gendered aspects in its content. Of course, minority-focused legislation still benefits minority women indirectly, for example in terms of educational quotas. However, as described in the introduction, there is a need for legislation that benefits minority women directly by recognising discrimination challenges faced by this particular group. While CEDAW seeks to eliminate all forms of discrimination against women, it makes no reference to minority groups. It focuses on women as a whole, with a paragraph about the particular plight of rural women being the only exception. Consequently, should a minority woman seek protection under this legislation, it can only address the discrimination she faces as a woman, not as a woman of a minority group. Consequently, to gain full protection women must seek protection under both legal frameworks separately. This means that the discriminatory action is viewed as either minority-related or women-related, rather than interrelated. Furthermore, seeking protection under two frameworks doubles the work, creating particular challenges for minority women who are already disadvantaged in their access to education, information, legal assistance and wealth (Ravnbøl, 2010).

As was presented, the term 'minority' is used differently in international law compared to the sociologist definition. This disparity, and the resulting separation of women's versus minority rights in international law can lead to lack of social justice for minority women and other socially disadvantaged groups. One way forward could therefore be to redefine the term 'minority' in international law to the more modern explanation of the power statuses of different groups within a society. Since this approach would be quite drastic, another possibility would be to note the interrelations between different social aspects (that is, gender and race) to ensure one avenue for discrimination compensation.

Balancing out the injustice done to certain groups within our society is not privileging this group; it is an act of working towards equal diversity. As will be pointed out later, intersectionality plays an important role in conflict. It is therefore essential to point to this legal problematic, in terms of achieving post-conflict justice and even preventing atrocities being committed during conflict.

Women in conflict

To understand the struggle of women in conflict states, it is essential to first deconstruct and unbundle the socio-economic fabric of the respective societies prior to the start of the conflict. Recognising the existing obstacles limiting women from having access to equal socio-economic entitlements and opportunities, which qualifies them as a minority group requires the full understanding of the legacy of oppression and injustice endured by women. This legacy is heavily affected and complicated by conflict, which leads to a deviation from the natural state due to an external shock that often preys upon the existing vulnerabilities of minority groups.

The nature and scope of conflicts has drastically changed in the last two decades with the ease of tensions after the reintegration of the former socialist countries in Eastern Europe into the global liberal economy. Today's major wars are characterised as domestic incursions and intra-state violence as opposed to total war between countries. However, the central themes that most conflict states have with one other are that most of them were former colonies and that the basis of their governance mechanisms and rule of law on democratic tenants were less evident. For many conflict states, the culture of oppression inherited from the colonial era was carried into the post-independence era and caused a vicious cycle. For example, the Central African Republic, the Democratic Republic of Congo, Burundi and Syria are considered some of the most volatile regions of the world today, and happen to be former French and Belgian colonies. During the colonial era, colonisers in central Africa such as Leopold II, disrupted existing tribal dynamics for self-enriching purposes, which ultimately hindered the foundation of stable governance mechanisms in the post-independence era. In turn, this has limited women's rights and inclusion in the social and economic fabric of these states.

According to the International Labour Organisation (ILO, 2013a), women in sub-Saharan Africa (SSA) have a higher rate of participation in the informal sector than men. For example, the patterns in informal sector employment show that up to 82 per cent of informal, non-agricultural activities in Mali are performed by women. The majority of SSA states demonstrate the same trend (ILO, 2013a). In contrast, men dominate the formal sector, which enjoys greater stability. By nature, the informal market yields lower wages than the organised formal sector. Consequently, while women are fairly active in the informal sector, their dedication and participation does not result in high paying incomes nor equal wages compared to their male counterparts. Looking towards the Middle East and North Africa (MENA) region, the role and participation rate of women in economic activities are much lower compared to those of their male counterparts. According to the World Bank (2013), labour market participation by women in the MENA region is half that at the global level. Women face constraints in obtaining adequate skills, decision-making powers, and adequate private sector prospects. The conservative and male dominated hierarchical control of social dominance is perhaps among the largest contributors to women's inability to access the workforce. Both the sub-Saharan and MENA situations highlight the economic vulnerability of women and their continued dependency as a result. Vulnerability is defined as the perceived and existing risk of individuals and households falling into poverty in the future if either economic or social situations deteriorate (Mannila, 2015).

The existing insecurities that form vulnerability can be categorised as:

- *Labour market insecurity*
  Not all those employed in the labour market enjoy employment stability as the quality and term of the job is not guaranteed. This

lack of guarantee reinforces economic vulnerabilities associated with the sourcing a livelihood.

- *Employment insecurity*
A lack of protection against discriminatory and unjust practices can result in arbitrary dismissals. The lack of appropriate regulations to uphold labour laws can influence hiring and retention procedures.

- *Job insecurity*
This occurs when a lack of potential future opportunities for building a stable career or engage in a meaningful way.

- *Work insecurity*
This happens when there is a lack of insurance for occupational hazards and or work security in case of accident or illness.

- *Skill reproduction insecurity*
This entails a lack of opportunities to fully engage in training, skills and competency building and the absence of an environment where the appropriate skills are utilised. Sadly, in the informal market rarely does equilibrium between skills and the quality of the job exist.

- *Income insecurity*
This happens when there is a lack of predictability with regards to earned income in the future given the unstable nature of jobs.

- *Representation insecurity*
In the informal market, the engaged workforce does not enjoy collective bargaining and thus cannot substantially raise demands or have their complaints examined and addressed. To a large degree, they lack representation in comparison to the formal sector.

(Mannila, 2015 and ILO, 2015)

Correspondingly, given the larger representation of women in the informal market or a lack of their large presence in economic activities, as in case of the MENA region, these insecurities lead to vulnerability, and vulnerability to marginalisation. Ultimately, the disproportionate market power conferred on men makes women economically underprivileged and thus a 'minority' in terms of their economic subjugation.

If in normal circumstances the deterioration of living standards and increased poverty are the likely outcomes of the economic marginalisation of women, their vulnerability and its consequences are even more severe in the event of a conflict. Accordingly, this chapter will explore this topic by focusing on *sexual exploitation*, *social consequences* (for example, child or forced marriage), and further *social isolation* – all from an economic and legal perspective. It is of interest to note that the economic susceptibility of both women and their families is a primary factor behind the unfortunate appearance of such situations, as well as the deterioration of the rule of law.

Sexual exploitation from a socio-economic perspective

Trafficking, sexual exploitation and violence against women are some of the consequences of wars. The gender based violence, degradation of women's status and their vulnerability to exploitation are prevailing problems occurring in most conflict regions across the globe. It is important to recognise that even though the sexual objectification of women as a commodity leads to the same unfortunate end, the motives behind the exploitation differ. In one case, mistreatment and abuse are forced upon women through coercion and violence while in the other case women reluctantly engage in the activity as a last resort for survival. For example, in the eastern regions of the Democratic Republic of Congo where many people have been displaced due to the ongoing civil conflicts, as with many other conflict regions, women sell themselves for money, protection and basic human needs such as food (UNIFEM, 2002).

As one of the victims said:

> 'I am only thankful that my mother and father cannot see the way I am living now because they did not raise me to do these things. But what else can I do? There is no one to help. I must take care of my children.' (UNIFEM, 2002)

The sex trade has become an important industry in the absence of an adequate support system and jobs for some of the most vulnerable members of the society. As a socio-economic minority, many women do not have a say over their own sexual health and are subjugated to their male 'partners'' demands. As a result, many women in the sex trade are at risk of contracting sexually transmitted diseases such as HIV/AIDS (UNIFEM, 2002). This in turn creates a vicious cycle where women and their families are placed in a poverty trap even in post-conflict periods.

In addition to the economic connotation behind sexual exploitation as a survival measure, the trafficking and abuse of women is associated with racketeering and for profit exploitation as well. In essence, it is a form of sexual slavery where women are forced to perform labour and forced sex work (UNIFEM, 2002). In recent years, there is an increasing awareness about the atrocities that occur in illegal and conflict mines through the use of forced labour. Both the forced imposition of labour by warring factions, as well as multinational corporations' increasing demands for mineral resources are linked to continuing labour exploitation (ILO, 2013b). In the conflict ridden East Kivu region of the Democratic Republic of Congo, for instance, it is estimated that up to 30 per cent of the labour force in Coltan mines is made up of forced labour. Furthermore, there is documented evidence that even the elderly women in these conflict regions are abducted to perform domestic work (ILO, 2013b). This means that the perpetrators of violence wield their monopoly over the use of power in conflict regions to exploit minorities for financial gain, and they may go beyond these acts into even more sinister ways. In the ongoing Syrian–Iraqi crisis, within the territories held by the Islamic State of Iraq and Syria (ISIS), according to Crawford (2015, 2):

> [There are] slave markets, [where] women are sold into sexual slavery in exchange for a pack of cigarettes. The trafficking of women in armed conflict and their use as sex slaves and camp followers – to the financial and military profit of the violent extremists and armed groups who force them into it – is being documented daily. The violent commodification of women and girls is an essential element to the business of extremist groups in the Middle East and Africa.

The International labour Organization (ILO) has estimated that forced labour and modern-day slavery globally generate around US$150 billion annually, with more than half arising through exploitation of women and children. Sexual exploitation alone makes up US$99 billion (Leubsdorf, 2014).

Under normal socio-political conditions, the marginalisation of women as the result of poverty and lack of equal access to socio-economic opportunities, such as education or labour force participation, makes women susceptible to human trafficking and economic exploitation. In conflict states, as argued above, in addition to economic vulnerability, through absence of rule of law, women, as minorities, are forced to act as 'economic agents' for the imposing groups to earn additional profits.

Sexual violence as a tool of terror: a framework regarding conflict solution

'Rape is probably history's oldest and least condemned crime' (Mukwege, 2013). Still, before the late twentieth century there has been little focus on sexual violence, especially sexual violence during wartime and therefore there remains a lack of documentation of these crimes (Bourke, 2014). The newly gained recognition through the United Nations through the UN Council Resolutions 1820 (2008), 1888 (2009), 1960 (2010) and 2106 (2013) on women, peace and security, along with other worldwide institutions, is a response to feminist thinking in the late 1960s 'which insisted that attention be paid to female sexual autonomy, power and pleasure' (Bourke, 2014, 19). Even in more recent conflicts, such as in Bangladesh in 1971 and Guatemala between 1960 and 1996, mass rape and general eruption of sexual violence has still been mainly ignored by the media in the west, whereas the atrocities committed in Yugoslavia in the 1990s and in Rwanda in 1994 gained worldwide attention. The most likely reasons for this increased attention was the demand for greater focus on women as their own individuals, on bodily autonomy and on sexual violence by activists around the globe. There was also a strengthening of international legislation and an increase in research and resources regarding sexual violence and gender-related discrimination. Where rape used to be seen as an unavoidable collateral in war before – for example during both world wars after which multiple countries stood accused of mass rapes, none of them were recognised as crimes in court – after the immense number of rapes of women in former Yugoslavia (up to 60,000 women between 1992 and 1995) came to light, the UN Security Council acted and declared rape an international crime that needed to be addressed. The International Criminal Tribunal for Rwanda set up in 1994 followed this declaration and found the first person guilty of rape as a crime of genocide (United Nations Prevent Genocide Rwanda, 2014).[1] The implementation of these ad hoc tribunals by the United Nations for the first time recognised sexual violence and systematic rape as tools of war for the purposes of ethnic cleansing and genocide (Leatherman, 2007). These tribunals led to the inclusion of rape as a war crime and crime against humanity in the Statute of the 2000 Rome treaty regarding the International Criminal Court (Leatherman, 2007). These changes in international law allow prosecution for sexual crimes and to bring justice to the assaulted women and girls (just as it does for men and boys).

In reality, multiple problems stand in the way of implementing these laws. Reasons for the use of rape and sexual violence as a systemic and tactical strategy of war by conflict groups needs looking into. One of the problems may lay in the structure of the 'new wars' that are often centred on ethnicity, religion or race and have replaced confrontation over political positions. They are often fragmented into multiple warring parties that have spread-out small arms and light weapons (as seen in the Eastern Democratic Republic of Congo). The funding of these new wars is often conducted through shadow economies linked to general global systems of profit-seeking (Leatherman, 2007). Therefore, a big part of the 'new wars' is linked to economic gains and resources. One way to gain these resources is to terrorise local communities, which can be ensured by sexual violence. Sexual violence serves as humiliation for enemy communities that are no longer able to 'protect' their women; it serves to spread fear, to quell resistance and to consolidate power (Leatherman, 2007). In former Yugoslavia, for example, rape by Bosnian-Serb forces was explicitly accepted or even commanded by military personnel and it was aimed at particular ethnic groups. The raping – often conducted in public – forced families to flee their villages and therefore worked towards the goal of 'ethnic cleansing' (Swiss and Giller, 1993). There have also been reports of women being solely reduced to their reproductive function. Governor Kashim Shettime was quoted in the Nigerian Newspaper, *The Punch*, stating that Boko Haram was intentionally 'getting their captives pregnant' (Iaccino, 2015) and keeping them under observation until the fourth to fifth month to make an abortion harder or impossible. The quote went on to explain that Boko Haram believes that the children will be born with the group's inherited spiritual conviction (Iaccino, 2015). Furthermore, sexual violence is used as an instrument to build up group solidarity by rewarding participation and fragmenting opponent communities (Leatherman, 2007). In a lot of conflict countries, such as the Congo, victims of sexual violence, especially rape, are often not allowed or are too ashamed to return to their communities, which leaves them displaced and the fabric of the community destroyed, which significantly affects the country's economy (Mukwege, 2013).

As shown above, rape is used very tactically and intentionally to achieve certain goals. But there is another side to it. Even when military authorities officially disapprove of rape, raping is often not penalised or simply seen as an unavoidable collateral of war (Bourke, 2014, 19). This was the case for the Second World War in which basically all parties have been accused of mass rapes but no investigation was conducted – partly because one party could not charge another for doing something they had done as well – and women's statements about their sexual assaults were rejected by police and military institutions (Women2000, 1998). In Korea, an estimate of between 100,000 and 200,000 Asian women, mostly Korean, were sent into sexual slavery and acted as so-called 'comfort women' (Swiss and Giller, 1993). In Vietnam in 1968 during the My Lai massacre, about 20 women and girls were raped by members of the US army while the commanders had substantial knowledge about the happenings (Wood, 2010). There were no convictions regarding the rape and only one conviction of the commanding officer for the killings of around 500 civilians (BBC News, 1998). Throughout the conflict in the Democratic Republic of Congo, from 1997 to 2003 (conflicts in the Eastern region of DRC persist until today), all armed parties have been accused of sexual assaults and mass rapes, including very systematic rapes to intimidate other forces, but also individual soldiers who raped women without a specific 'purpose' (Human Rights Watch, 2002). Furthermore, so-called runaway norms are established during conflict to reinforce solidarity and justify dominance over opponent groups. These norms allow members of the group to commit atrocities, such as rape, to the opponents group members by placing group traditions on top of the property of individuals. They also create a form of social pressure to participate in them, since those challenging these norms will get punished and those who doubt them remain silent out of fear. These runaway norms erase safe spaces and serve as justification of extreme violence, such as systemic rape in war (Leatherman, 2007). The question that emerges here is that what can be done to combat the economics behind the sexual exploitation?

In terms of conflict resolution, the theory of 'balance of power' is the most popular and has shaped a lot of political thinking. It is based on minimising the negative effect of conflicts with the ultimate aim being peace through implementation of conflict management resolutions by all committed stakeholders. This approach often proved successful in short-term. This theory fails to adopt a transformative strategy however, and therefore enhances male-dominated approaches to peace-making in patriarchal society. Another theoretical approach emphasises that all factors relating to structural violence must be transformed in order to achieve long-term peace (Leatherman, 2007). Therefore, we have to understand why mostly women fall victims to these violent tactics.

Even though the short-term objectives are clear, they say more about the way women and girls are seen in general. While sexual violence is not a part of every conflict, and not inevitable since rapists are not born, they become (Bourke, 2014), the continued patriarchal system in almost all these societies makes room for sexual violence as a tool of war. It constructs violence against women as permissible and makes the female body a 'territory' – something that can be owned. This way of thinking precedes conflict situations and is not created during them. It is not necessarily meant negatively, since it often uses benevolent forms of sexism, such as the perception of women's bodies as symbols of 'purity' (Leatherman, 2007). These constraints reflect a denied access to basic human rights and cultural norms regarding rape, forced marriages, and codes regarding family honour (Leatherman, 2007). As seen above, once the remaining security measures, such as the community, break down during conflict, these prevailing or underlying attitudes towards women's bodies, as a form of property and a means of reproduction, escalate, leading to more sexual violence and more displacement. This escalation reaches into post-conflict, not only leading to physical and emotional trauma, but also stigmatisation and diseases. For example, 67 per cent of rape survivors from the 1994 genocide in Rwanda are HIV positive (Nagarajan, 2012).

According to Nowrojee (1996, 1), providing an analysis on the Rwandan Genocide and its aftermath:

> Although the exact number of women raped will never be known, testimonies from survivors confirm that rape was extremely widespread and that thousands of women were individually raped, gang-raped, raped with objects such as sharpened sticks or gun barrels, held in sexual slavery (either collectively or through forced 'marriage') or sexually mutilated...According to witnesses, many women were killed immediately after being raped. Other women managed to survive, only to be told that they were being allowed to live so that they would 'die of sadness'.

Outcomes and representation: from a socio-political perspective

An unfortunate consequence of conflicts is the constraints, whether economic or social, that they impose on families and individuals. It forces them to resort to actions that otherwise would not have had happened. The exploitation of women and girls goes beyond sexual misuse as it can have social consequences as well. For instance, forced or underage marriage, emigration and unwanted pregnancy are the social consequences of conflict on women. From an economic perspective, the underlying economic hardship is identified both as the underlying cause behind such actions as well as its outcome. In other words, it can generate a vicious cycle that ultimately destroys the social fabric of communities and its associated members.

As a consequence of the Syrian war, similar to other conflicts, there was a large exodus of Syrians both to neighbouring countries, such as Turkey, as well as far away regions, such as Northern Europe. Such displacement has socio-economic impacts on the people who are fleeing; among one, the forced marriage of women with the locals. Particularly in Turkey, the notion of 'co-wives' (polygamy) is on the rise. According to Mehves Evin (2014), the issue of co-wives is not innocent at all. Most Syrian women are forced into getting married because they are desperate. The financial situation of families who fled the war is often very bad, and they have neither a house nor a job. Thus, many families prefer to say yes to any 'groom candidate', which in turn makes the brides vulnerable to exploitation and abuse. In a sense, it is an economic transaction with the provision of 'safety' as the objective. In many incidences, forced marriage is agreed upon in exchange for rent, demanded by the destitute families. These relationships based on exploitation rather than mutual emotional consent and many of the women are being taken as second or third wives (Mehves Evin, 2014). Similar trends have also been observed in Jordan and other neighbouring countries hosting a large number of Syrians. Child marriage has become a major concern in refugee camps where girls as young as 12 are being forced to marry (Save the Children, 2014). In addition to using marriage to alleviate poverty, buy protection and decrease the number of economically dependent family members, many families wrongfully assume that early marriage can bring stability for their daughters. However, the reality represents itself differently where the social consequences of such actions not only do not help women but furthers their economic dependence. Early pregnancy, the increase of vulnerability to abuse, and early marriage as a barrier to further education, prevents women's economic independency and empowerment in the long term, and ensures the creation and continuation of a vicious cycle (Save the Children, 2014). Forced marriages also distort the social development in post conflict states. To combat this, ensuring girls' and women's continued education, providing economic support for families, empowering girls and their respective families with relevant information and skills, and establishing and executing relevant laws are essential to combat such phenomena (Save the Children, 2014).

Representation: political representation and peace keeping operations

The third MDG specifically mentions the proportion of seats held by women in national parliaments. At first glance, this part of the MDGs seems to have been addressed extensively. After all, the number of women in parliament doubled from 1995 to 2015. The average of women parliamentarians lies at 22 per cent now (UN, 2015). Statistics show that 37 states have less than 10 per cent women in parliament, including six with no women at all. Nordic countries on average have the highest number of women representatives with 41.1 per cent; the Americas follow with an average of 25.5 per cent, Europe with 24.4 per cent, sub-Saharan Africa 23.0 per cent, Asia 18.4 per cent, Middle East and North Africa 17.1 per cent and the Pacific 15.1 per cent. As of August 2015, 17 per cent of government ministers were women with the majority overseeing social sectors (Inter-Parliamentary Union, 2015). In Rwanda, a post conflict country, tables have turned. As of 2017, women constitute 61.3% of the parliament, the highest percentage in the world (Inter-Parliamentary Union, 2017).

The goal of an average of 30 per cent of women in parliament has not been achieved. This not only refers to countries in conflict – which on average have a lower percentage of women in parliament than the global average of 22 per cent, and in which women occupy only 14.8 per cent of ministerial positions (UN Security Council, 2015) – but also stable countries within Europe and the Americas. Even in cases of women ministers, the majority are responsible for traditionally 'women' bound sectors such as family (Inter-Parliamentary Union, 2015). In terms of foreign affairs representation, in the US only two members out of 18 in the US Senate Foreign Relations Committee are women (Foreign Senate, 2015), while in the House of Representatives there were six out of 46 (House of Representatives, 2015) in 2015. Meanwhile the UN Security Council only in 2014 'achieved' women's representation to be at an unprecedented 40 per cent with six women ambassadors out of 15 (UN Security Council, 2014). The percentage of UN field missions headed by women has fluctuated between 15 and 25 per cent since 2011, with five of 15 operations being headed by women in 2013 (Secretary-General Ban-Ki-Moon and United Nations, 2013).

While women's representation in conflict countries is generally lower, it is highly concerning to see that even in organisations committed to gender equality, women are only represented in certain areas and left out of peacekeeping operations. This also shows in a statistic revealing that between 1992 and 2011, less than 4 per cent of signatories to peace agreements and less than 10 per cent of negotiators at peace tables were women (UN Women, 2012). According to a UN Women survey, little progress has been achieved since 2000, with some of the most 'note-worthy' participations of women in peace negotiations taking place before the resolution. For example, in El Salvador in the 1990s women were present at almost every negotiations table, and in Burundi prior to the resolution in 2000 where an All-Party-Women's Peace Conference was held by UNIFEM after which a list of recommendations was handed to the facilitators of the peace negotiations (UN Women, 2012). It is not surprising that only few peace keeping operations target or even mention gender-related issues and that only 2 per cent of aid to fragile states and economies in 2012 and 2013 targeted gender equality as a principal objective (Coomaraswamy, 2015). Only US$130 million out of almost US$32 billion of total aid went to women's equality organisations and institutions (Coomaraswamy, 2015), although these exact organisations have had serious impacts on peace-keeping efforts in conflict countries such as Liberia (Bekoe and Parajon, 2007).

Given the fact that half of the world's population consists of women, it seems obvious that half of the voices heard during any form of crucial political debate should be women (Nakaya, 2003). Surveys indicate that women's participation increases the probability of peace agreements to last longer (up to 15 years or by 35 per cent) (Coomaraswamy, 2015), which is most probably a result of the inclusion of a broader variety of perspectives. While it has been proven that educational improvements alone cannot transform unequal power relations and that other areas such as political representation and bodily autonomy need to be fulfilled as well (Sen and Mukherjee, 2013), there seems to be a lack of will to fulfil this transformation with regards to foreign policy representatives, peace keeping negotiations and the funding of women's equality organisations and institutions aiming to establish peace in their communities. Excluding women from transforming conflict countries means missing out on the perspectives of a group of people representing half of the world's population. As was elaborated, the 'new wars' are transformations from state-centralised military into more extensive threats that touch on poverty-related issues and environmental challenges. Given the historically traditional role that makes women so vulnerable to poverty, their perspectives are crucial.

Legal discrimination aggravating women's situation in conflict

There are hundreds of different cultures and communities in this world following different legal systems and varying ideologies and values.

Therefore, it is impossible to refer to every cultural background of groups in conflict in one chapter. The following paragraph provides a brief overview.

It is extremely important as far as legal discrimination against women, peace keeping and transformative work is concerned, to learn and know about the specific cultural and societal background of a country or community. As already shown, for various economic reasons the feminisation of poverty is a reality. The harsh economic situation of women in conflict countries partly comes from pre-conflict existing legal norms that disadvantage women. In many countries, especially in those struggling with patriarchal traditions, there are often legal constructions, including systems of magistrate courts and traditional leaders, that discriminate against women (Ovis, 2005). In non-conflict countries, such as Namibia and Zambia, customary law applies under certain circumstances. When customary law applies, it can often – not always and once again depending on the culture of the specific country – negatively target or restrict women (Mungwini, 2007). In Namibia for example, inheritance laws can be highly damaging for widowed women, as in-laws can deprive the widow from her property – even against a contradicting will of the former husband – for not being from the town and therefore being a 'foreigner'. In these situations, seeking help from a magistrate can invoke further discrimination, as a traditional leader might blame the women for not keeping up good relations with her parents (Ovis, 2005). In Zambia, although men and women are equal before the law and legally have an equal right to access land, in reality a married woman will often only have access to the land through her husband. For a local chief, it would be 'unthinkable to allocate a plot to a married woman in her own right' (Machina, 2002, 10). Other legal disadvantages include the limitations on entering into contracts without approval of the husband, forced marriage and laws that allow violence towards women.

During conflict, and especially when women become widows or displaced and communities are being shattered, the few existing security mechanisms dissolve, leaving women in greater socio-economic danger. Conflict at the same time offers possibilities of gender-role changes. The absence of men in communities may result in new roles of women leadership, new women-run businesses and new political representation by women (USAID, 2007, 1). One of the best modern examples for this is Rwanda. During the Rwandan genocide in 1994, between 500,000 and 1,000,000 people had been killed, which equalled roughly 70 per cent of the Tutsi population within the country and about 20 per cent of the total population within the country. Some of the main consequences of the conflict period were the economic destruction of the country and the destruction of the social fabric of many communities. Rape during the war resulted in unwanted pregnancies (the estimate is about 2,000 to 5,000), victims' exclusion from their community and sexually transmitted diseases. After that the country had to rebuild. As mentioned earlier, Rwanda is world-leading in its proportion of women parliamentarians, but much more has been achieved. Above 40 per cent of Supreme Court Judges and Ministry Permanent Secretaries are women (Republic of Rwanda, 2011). Furthermore, passed legislation has led to guarantees for equal rights regarding succession and inheritance, which has led to a decrease in the economic dependency of women. The government has also introduced a 'zero-tolerance' towards gender based violence by introducing an 'anti-gender-based violence law' and the institution of so-called Isange One Stop Centres, which provide support to gender-based violence victims in order to prevent re-victimisation, delayed justice and spoiled evidence. Further, newly-implemented legislation also requires that women make up at least 30 per cent of the posts in decision-making organs (Kamatali, 2016).

Intersectionality: socio-economic isolations and setbacks

The emergence of conflict distorts established empowerment and equality mechanisms and undermines achievements. It enhances both social and economic dependency and isolates women from their long due aspirations. This is the result of a mixture of different factors including exploitation and loss of rights. It is an intersectionality of pre-conflict realities with the consequences of conflict that shapes the future for women and their rights. Perhaps Afghanistan and its tumultuous past best reflect the severity of effects of conflict on women. According to Amnesty International, women were among the major victims of the war; not only in terms of their subjection to discriminatory laws and exploitation, but also in terms of losing what they had achieved in the years following the Afghan civil war, and ultimately the Taliban takeover.

> Until the conflict of the 1970s, [Afghanistan in] the twentieth century had seen relatively steady progression for women's rights in the country. Afghan women were first eligible to vote in 1919 – only a year after women in the UK were given voting rights, and a year before the women in the United States were allowed to vote. In the 1950s, purdah (gendered

separation) was abolished; in the 1960s a new constitution brought equality to many areas of life, including political participation. (Amnesty International, 2013)

Yet, with the start of civil war and the Taliban's takeover, women's role increasingly rolled back to the point where they were not allowed to work, hold offices, study, speak in public and even be present outside without the presence of a male family member (Amnesty International, 2013). The social subjection of women meant their complete isolation and their increasing dependency on the opposite sex for economic protection. Despite increasing gender rights with the ousting of the Taliban, the discrimination, abuse and dependency of women continues. Thus, the conflict deflected the progressive trend into a vicious cycle of isolation.

The partition of Yugoslavia and the ensuing violence showcased a similar picture. The new constitution in the Socialist Federal Republic of Yugoslavia after the Second World War promised women equal rights in all fields including economic and political life and state engagements. They were openly encouraged to participate in public arenas (Bonfiglioli, 2012). Yet, similar to Afghanistan, the war inflicted unspeakable atrocities on women. The 1990s marked a period of sexual violence for women of all ages as a political tool to cause terror (Hirsch, 2012).

This is regrettably a trend observed in many conflict-ridden states. As a result, in the post conflict era, it is essential to revise and bring back the progressive values and halt the continuation of a vicious cycle.

Intersectionality: women and gender

While it is important that gender based violence in general is eradicated, one particular problem is that gendered violence and discrimination is often not as simple as men versus women. It includes all constellations – including men on men violence and violence by women, although numerically less – but it tends to address groups with multiple minority-characteristics the most (Nowrojee, 1996). Sexual violence escalates in times of conflict, just as legal discrimination aggravates women's socio-economical situations in conflict. Most often in conflict (just as in situations of peace) these aggressions target certain groups more depending on, for example, their racial, ethnic, religious and nationalist background (Leatherman, 2007). The disadvantaged positions of these minorities are often further aggravated. Therefore, the recognition of the problematic of intersectionality becomes even more important during conflict (UNPO, 2011).

One group in particular seems to be forgotten too often when it comes to gender-related violence. During conflict, security mechanisms fall apart, chaos erupts and safe spaces disappear. For LGBTI (lesbian, gay, bisexual, transgender and intersex) people this falling apart of safety nets can have deadly results. Not only are there still countries actively punishing homosexuality, and states that do not recognise varying sexualities, gender identities and sexes as anything but a choice, during conflict the result of revealing one's gender as an LGBTI person can be worse than it would have been pre-conflict. In conflict countries, such as Iraq, it has been reported that even random exterior factors such as one's choice of clothing, or the length of one's hair can connotate not being 'manly' enough, and lead to prosecution for the crime of homosexuality (Human Rights Watch, 2009). This not only contradicts the UN declaration on gay rights as a part of the international Free and Equal campaign in 2012, it also wrongly reinforces gender stereotypes by drawing a distinct line between masculinity and femininity. It is important to include LGBTI people when talking about gender-based violence and to empower all women, including, for example, transgender women. So far, there has been a lack of civil society organisations, states and peace operations working towards women's empowerment and gender equality that document, report and end violence and discrimination towards members of the LGBTI community (Human Rights Council, 2011). The UN's Women, Peace, and Security framework does not specifically include or report on LGBTI people, which is partly because of the objections of countries such as Egypt, Kenya, Uganda, Zimbabwe, Bangladesh and Tanzania where identifying as homosexual can lead to 'lifetime imprisonment, forced labour, public whippings and other corporal punishment' (Samelius and Wägberg, 2005, 20).

Therefore, LGBTI women are only protected through international rights on the protection of women, which is not sufficient when it comes to discrimination specifically directed at transgender women, homosexual women or queer women.

While homophobic violence is reported in all regions, it takes on more extreme forms during conflict. In addition to general harassment, LGBTI people may become targets of religious extremists, paramilitary groups and extreme nationalists. Lesbians and transgender women are especially at risk, given gender inequality and power relations within communities and families (Human Rights Council, 2011). The NGO, Colombia Diversa, for example, warns that armed actors in Colombia, which has been rattled by guerrilla fights since 1964, tried to seek control of territory through 'social cleansing' proclamations. 'Social cleansings' are meant to eliminate all individuals who do not conform with the traditional standards of a group, and therefore threaten to strengthen community beliefs against the guerrillas (Colombia Diversa, 2015). According to USAID (2014), Colombia reported the fourth highest rate of murder of transgender people in the world between 2008 and 2013. One of the biggest problems is the lack of information on this issue due to the fear of documentation, meaning statistics are difficult to gather and protection mechanisms are difficult to tailor as a result (Colombia Diversa, 2015).

> 'They hunt us down for fun. They don't want me to dress like a woman so I don't. I wear a dishdasha (traditional Kuwaiti male garment) now. I cut my hair short. After all that I was still arrested, beaten, and raped for having a smooth, feminine face. What can I do about my face?' (Amani, 2011, as cited in Moumneh et al, 2012, 1)

A way forward: conclusion

Picking up on the introduction, the attention on gender-related topics and the acceptance of a need for change regarding gender equality has (very) slowly started to progress. With the adoption of CEDAW in 1979; the Vienna Conference in 1993 acknowledging the right to self-determination; the UN International Conference on Population and Development in Cairo in 1994 which committed to sexual and reproductive health and rights, women's empowerment and male responsibility; and the Fourth World Conference on Women in Beijing in 1995, steps have been taken towards women's equality (unfortunately, not necessarily gender equality). While civil societies and governments worldwide participated in this process, the MDGs were 'formulated by a small group of rich countries and not by the global community; and there was no place given to civil society organisations' (Sen and Mukherjee, 2013, 7). MDG 3 proclaimed to 'promote gender equality and women's empowerment' but it used education, wage employment in the non-agricultural sector and the proportion of seats held by women in national parliament as the only indicators. This seems to have resulted in a large focus on education, but leaves out too many other important factors. The Sustainable Development Goals (SDGs) for post-2015 seem to pick up on that mistake and explicitly target all forms of discrimination against women and girls.

While it is agreed, that education plays a fundamental role in the empowerment of women and girls, it cannot be the only goal. 'How women empower themselves varies in different contexts and cultures, but certain elements are common and central. Empowered women are not only able to access resources, or participate in politics and public life, but also enjoy bodily autonomy and integrity, freedom from violence' (Sen and Mukherjee, 2013, 7). Therefore, we need to not only address the immediate inequalities but also change consciousness and challenge existing patriarchal structures in all countries (Sen and Mukherjee, 2013).

Furthermore, colonialism and imperialism play a distinctive role in the fight for women's rights. As was shown, communities have different perceptions, laws and economic systems. The question remains: 'How does one fight for women's rights without being complicit in the racism and prejudice that characterises Northern attitudes toward Southern countries or the majority–minority dynamics within particular societies?' (Coomaraswamy, 2002).

Committing to human rights should not re-step into colonialist behaviour and therefore inherently into ways of supremacy. One important task in this regard will be self-reflection. As reflected in various studies, many western and non-conflict countries do not live up to the standards set by the United Nations, including the MDG goals; this has to change, especially in areas relating to foreign affairs and international relations. The countries of the United Nations committed to women's empowerment need to start actually empowering their women and establishing equality.

In terms of women in conflict, there seem to be short- and long-term goals. In the short term and in order to combat the sexual exploitation of women in conflict states, a broad political, legal and operational response is necessary. The political response can broadly be defined as both domestic and international efforts to stabilise the situations and create pathways for the return to stability. In essence, existing hostilities between opposing factions that have created the ongoing volatilities in the first place have to be addressed. The objectives behind reaching peace accords and the preparation for post-conflict periods are key to ensuring the minority groups' protection in the intermediate and long term.

> Global efforts to eliminate sexual violence in conflict must also be conscious of the broader political, economic, and social environment…[the] international efforts aimed at combating sexual violence should account for how women

and men make sense of their own political and social identities and the degree to which these understandings may inhibit or promote this particular form of violence. (Crawford, 2015, 3)

In cases of dealing with extremist groups, such as ISIS, where direct negotiations with these types of groups are not realistic, the materialisation of an international political arrangement and reaching a unified political solution with other actors (for example, the Assad regime and other opposition groups in the Syrian case) is required. For example, it was through political and diplomatic manoeuvring that the recent truce between Syrian government forces and rebel opposition groups over the city of Homs was reached. As the main benefactors of the deal, women, children and the severely injured were given priority to leave the city first (Perry and Heneghan, 2015). The legal response is necessary to establish a coherent mechanism to bring violators to justice and to send a strong message that such actions will not be tolerated either through local and national level judicial systems or through international law with the involvement of the International Criminal Court if necessary. This response includes the stronger enforcement of the recently established legal language around sexual violence; it also includes training of legal representatives and prosecuting cases. Moreover, it requires oversight of the actions of police or state sanctioned militias in order to ensure the legality of their activities and to ensure an equal representation of women within the law enforcement and legal hierarchy. Lastly, the operation must convey the importance of capability building among first responders to be adequately qualified to address sexual related violence (Crawford, 2015). Gender awareness, especially in environments where local culture is substantially different, play a crucial role in establishing a trust network between local populations and the responders. For example, the recent emerging allegations over the UN peacekeepers' abuses in the Central African Republic highlight the importance of the legal framework to prosecute the individuals if found guilty.

Furthermore, with regards to sexual violence as a tool of terror, the support of local women's organisations is essential. Additionally, the implementation of laws and the transformation of institutions should be promoted and healthcare support is a necessity. In terms of political representation, as said, there need to be more women on all sides. In terms of peace keeping or peace directed negotiations, some form of women's participation should be ensured while trying to respect cultural ideas and working closely with community members.

In regards to intersectionality, international human rights need to be more inclusive of all women and need to acknowledge that gender equality does not equal women, but includes all gender-related disadvantaged people. There needs to be an instrument that ensures that justice can be provided when multiple offences towards different minority-characteristics are committed. This could be an international declaration acknowledging intersectionality and offering legal access on this basis, or it could mean redefining the term minority to make it more inclusive or avoiding the term altogether.

In the long term though, the only way of ensuring women's empowerment in its entirety, would be an ideological approach, namely to reflect on the way in which women are seen in our society, to build consciousness and to transform institutions to be more equal. Gender equality cannot be achieved without taking into account colonial heritage and imperialism, without tackling globally-spread sexism and our idea of society.

Note

[1] Within the three months of genocide in 1994 between 100,000 and 250,000 women were raped in Rwanda.

References

Amnesty International, 2013, *Women in Afghanistan: The back story*, www.amnesty. org.uk/womens-rights-afghanistan-history#. VnK1Or8XUeN

BBC News, 1998, *Murder in the name of war – My Lai*, London: BBC, http://news.bbc.co.uk/2/hi/special_report/1998/03/98/mylai/64344.stm

Bekoe, D, Parajon, C, 2007, *Women's role in Liberia's reconstruction*, Washington, DC: United States Institute of Peace, www.usip.org/publications/women-s-role-in-liberia-s-reconstruction

Bonfiglioli, C, 2012, *Becoming citizens: The politics of women's emancipation in socialist Yugoslavia*, www.citsee.eu/citsee-story/becoming-citizens-politics-women%E2%80%99s-emancipation-socialist-yugoslavia

Boundless, 2015, Women as a minority, *Boundless Sociology*, Boundless, www.boundless.com/sociology/textbooks/boundless-sociology-textbook/gender-stratification-and-inequality-11/women-as-a-minority-88/women-as-a-minority-507-10466/

Bourke, J, 2014, Rape as a weapon of war, *The Lancet*, www.thelancet.com/journals/lancet/article/PIIS0140-6736%2814%2960971-5/abstract

Cockerton, CM, 1999, The United Nations and the Advancement of Women, 1945-1996, Book Review, *International Journal of African Historical Studies*, 32, 2–3, 588

Colombia Diversa, 2015, *Human rights situation for lesbian, gay, bisexual and transgender persons in Colombia: 2015 Report*, https://duckduckgo.com/?q=social+cleansing+colombia+site%3Acolombiadiversa.org

Coomaraswamy, R, 2002, Identity within: Cultural relativism, minority rights and the empowerment of women, *The George Washington International Law Review* 34, 3, www.questia.com/read/1P3-238358541/identity-within-cultural-relativism-minority-rights

Coomaraswamy, R, 2015, *Preventing conflict, transforming justice, securing the peace: A guide study on the implementation of United Nations Security Council Resolution 1325*, New York: UN Women

Crawford, K, 2015, Conflict and extremist-related sexual violence, *United States Institute of Peace Working Paper* 187, www.usip.org/sites/default/files/PB187-Conflict-and-Extremist-Related-Sexual-Violence.pdf

Crenshaw, K, 1993, Mapping the margins: Intersectionality, identity politics, and violence against women of color, *Stanford Law Review*, http://socialdifference.columbia.edu/files/socialdiff/projects/Article__Mapping_the_Margins_by_Kimblere_Crenshaw.pdf

Deen, T, 2013, United Nations: Urged to practice what they preach, *Inter Press Service News Agency*, www.ipsnews.net/2013/11/u-n-urged-to-practice-what-it-preaches-on-gender/

Evin, M, 2014, Syrian refugees sold as 'co-wives' in Turkey, www.contributoria.com/issue/2014-05/531b15dbd63a707e78000177/

Eze, N, 2011, Gender, Conflict, and the Millennium Development Goals, *Women for Women International*, www.insightonconflict.org/media/wp-content/uploads/2010/11/MDG_Briefing_final.pdf

Ford, L, 2015, What is the Millennium Development Goal on gender equality all about?, *Guardian*, www.theguardian.com/global-development/2015/mar/26/millennium-development-goal-three-gender-equality-explainer

Foreign Senate, 2015, *United States Senate Committee on Foreign Relations: Membership*, www.foreign.senate.gov/about/committee-membership

Hacker, HM, 1951, Women as a Minority Group, *Social Forces* 30, 1, 60

Hayes, C, 2011, Gender, conflict and the MDGs, *Women for Women International*, www.womenforwomen.org.uk

Hirsch, ML, 2012, *Women under siege: Bosnia*, www.womenundersiegeproject.Org/conflicts/profile/bosnia

House of Representatives, 2015, *Membership*, House Committee on Foreign Affairs, http://foreignaffairs.house.gov/about/membership

Human Rights Council, 2011, *Discriminatory laws and practices and acts of violence against individuals based on their sexual orientation and gender identity*, United Nations General Assembly, www2.ohchr.org/english/bodies/hrcouncil/docs/19session/a.hrc.19.41_english.pdf

Human Rights Watch, 2002, *The war within the war: Sexual violence against women and girls in Eastern Congo*, New York: Human Rights Watch

Human Rights Watch, 2009, *Iraq: Stop killings for homosexual conduct*, New York: Human Rights Watch, www.hrw.org/news/2009/08/17/iraq-stop-killings-homosexual-conduct

Human Rights Watch, 2015, *Ending child marriage in Africa: Opening the door for girls' education, health, and freedom from violence*, New York: Human Rights Watch, www.hrw.org/news/2015/12/09/ending-child-marriage-africa

Iaccino, L, 2015, Nigeria: Boko Haram impregnated girls 'to guarantee new generation of fighters', *International Business Time*, www.ibtimes.co.uk/nigeria-boko-haram-impregnated-girls-guarantee-new-generation-fighters-1500022

ILO (International Labour Organization), 2013a, *Women and men in the informal economy: A statistical picture*, www.ilo.org/wcmsp5/groups/public/−-dgreports/−-stat/documents/publication/wcms_234413.pdf

ILO (International Labour Organization), 2013b, Combating forced labour and trafficking in Africa: Current responses and a way forward, *Background paper*, Lusaka.www.ilo.org/wcmsp5/groups/public/−-africa/documents/meetingdocument/wcms_229620.pdf

ILO (International Labour Organization), 2015, *Representation Security Index*, www.ilo.org /dyn/sesame/SESHELP.NoteRSI

Inter-Parliamentary Union, 2015, *Sluggish progress on women in politics will hamper development*, Press release, www.ipu.org/press-e/pressrelease201503101.htm

Inter-Parliamentary Union, 2017, *Women in national parliaments*, www.ipu.org/wmn-e/classif.htm

Kamatali, JM, 2016, Rwanda: Balancing Gender Quotas and an Independent Judiciary, in G Bauer and J Dawuni (eds) *Gender and the judiciary in Africa: From obscurity to parity?*, New York: Routledge

Leatherman, J, 2007, Sexual violence and armed conflict: Complex dynamics of re-victimization, *International Journal of Peace Studies*, www.questia.com/read/1G1-178359709/sexual-violence-and-armed-conflict-complex-dynamics

Leubsdorf, B, 2014, Modern forms of slavery generate $150 billion a year in profits for exploiters, *The Wall Street Journal*, 19 May http://blogs.wsj.com/economics/2014/05/19/modern-forms-of-slavery-generate-150-billion-a-year-in-profits-for-exploiters/

Machina, H, 2002, *Women's land rights in Zambia: Policy provisions, legal framework and constraints*, http://citeseerx.ist.psu.edu/viewdoc/download?doi=10.1.1.439.9143&rep=rep1&type=pdf

Mannila, S, 2015, Informal employment and vulnerability in less developed markets, in J Vuori, R Blonk, RH Price (eds) *Sustainable working lives*, Netherlands: Springer, 17–33

Meintel, D, 1993, What is a minority?, *UNESCO Courier*, June, www.questia.com/read/1G1-14156366/what-is-a-minority

Modupe, AN, 2013, *Rights of women in the pre-colonial and post-colonial era prospects and challenges*, https://unilorin.edu.ng/publications/abdulraheemnm/RIGHTS_OF_ WOMEN_IN_THE_PRE_COLONIAL_AND_POST_COLONIAL_ERA.pdf

Moumneh, R, Reid, G, Stork, J, Whitson, S, 2012, *They hunt us down for fun: discrimination and police violence against transgender women in Kuwait*, New York: Human Rights Watch

Mukwege, D, 2013, Congo: No peace without women. An interview with Denis Mukwege, *Journal of International Affairs* 67, 1, www.questia.com/read/1G1-353517751/congo-no-peace-without-women-an-interview-with-denis

Mungwini, P, 2007, 'Forward to the past': Dilemmas of rural women's empowerment in Zimbabwe, *African Sociological Review*, www.codesria.org/IMG/pdf/09_Debates.pdf

Nagarajan, C, 2012, An appraisal of Rwanda's response to survivors who experienced sexual violence in 1994, *Wagadu: a Journal of Transnational Women's and Gender Studies*, 10, 108–131

Nakaya, S, 2003, Women and gender equality in peace processes: From women at the negotiating table to postwar structural reforms in Guatemala and Somalia, *Global Governance* 9, 4, www.questia.com/read/1G1-111201939/women-and-gender-equality-in-peace-processes-from

Nowrojee, B, 1996, *Shattered lives: Sexual violence during the Rwandan genocide and its aftermath*, Human Rights Watch/Africa, Human Rights Watch Women's Rights Project, Fédération Internationale des Ligues des Droits de l'Homme, Human Rights Watch, New York: Human Rights Watch, www.hrw.org/reports/1996/Rwanda.htm

Ovis, M, 2005, 'No peace in the marriage' inheritance disputes and law reform possibilities: when Essa Zumbuku married her husband, a teacher, in 1993, she did not foresee that her husband's untimely death would cause a rift between her and her in-laws, *Sister Namibia*, 17, 4, 8–11

Papoutsi, E, 2014, Minorities under international law: How protected are they?, *Journal of Social Welfare and Human Rights*, http://jswhr. com/vol-2-no-1-march-2014-jswhr

Perry, T, Heneghan, T, 2015, Syrians leave rebel-held Homs area in truce deal, *Reuters*, 9 December, www.reuters.com/article/us-mideast-crisis-syria-idUSKBN0TS

Ravnbøl, CI, 2010, The human rights of minority women: Romani women's rights from a perspective on international human rights law and politics, *International Journal on Minority and Group Rights*, 17, 1, 1-45

Republic of Rwanda, 2011, *Gender statistics: Achieving MDG: 3*, http:// statistics.gov.rw/publications/article/rwanda-continues-achieve-mdgs

Samelius, L, Wagberg, E, 2005, *Sexual orientation and gender identity issues in development: A study of Swedish policy and administration of lesbian, gay, bisexual and transgender issues in international development cooperation*, Swedish International Development Cooperation Agency (Sida) Health Division

Save the Children, 2014, *Too young to wed: The growing problem of child marriage among Syrian girls in Jordan*, www.savethechildren.org.uk/ sites/ default/files/images /Too_ Young_to _Wed.pdf0H420151209

Secretary-General Ban-Ki-Moon, United Nations, 2013, *Secretary-General, at International Forum, says women now head five of fifteen United Nations Peacekeeping Operations*, www.un.org/press/en/2013/ sgsm15276.doc.htm

Sen, G, Mukherjee, A, 2013, *No empowerment without rights, no rights without politics: Gender-equality, MDGs and the Post-2015 Development Agenda*, www.dawnnet.org/feminist-resources/sites/default/files/ articles/no_empowerment_without_rights_no_rights_without_ politics_gender_equality_mdgs_and_the_post_2015_development_ agenda.pdf

Swiss, S, Giller, JE, 1993, Rape as a crime of war: A medical perspective, *The Journal of the American Medical Association* 270, 5, 612–15

UNDP (United Nations Development Programme), 2008, Sexual violence against women, men and children in armed conflict, *Background Note*, Parliamentary Hearing, United Nations, Bureau for Crisis Prevention and Recovery, New York: UNDP, www.ipu. org/splz-e/unga08/s2.pdf

UNESCO (United Nations Educational, Scientific and Cultural Organization), 2013, *Children still battling to go to school*, www.unesco. org/new/en/media-services/single-view/news/children_still_ battling_to_go_to_school/

UNIFEM (United Nations Development Fund for Women), 2002, The independent expert assessment: On the impact of armed conflict on women and the role of women in peace building, *Progress of World's Women*, 1, www.unwomen.org/~/media/headquarters/media/ publications/unifem/mediakit_eng.pdf

United Nations, 2015, *The Millennium Development Goals Report*, www.un.org/millenniumgoals/2015_MDG_Report/pdf/MDG%20 2015%20rev%20(July%201).pdf

United Nations Prevent Genocide Rwanda, 2014, The justice and reconciliation process in Rwanda, *Background Note*, www.un.org/ en/preventgenocide/rwanda/about/bgsexualviolence.shtml

United Nations Security Council, 2008, *Resolution 1820*, www. securitycouncilreport.org/atf/cf/%7B65BFCF9B-6D27-4E9C-8CD3-CF6E4FF96FF9%7D/CAC%20S%20RES%201820.pdf

United Nations Security Council, 2014, *Report of the Secretary General on women and peace and security*, www.un.org/ga/search/view_doc. asp?symbol=S/2014/693

United Nations Security Council, 2015, *Report of the Secretary General on women and peace and security*, www.un.org/en/sc/documents/ sgreports/2015.shtml

UNPO (Unrepresented Nations and People Organization), 2011, *Intersectional discrimination, multifaceted problems: Minority women, violence and peace-building*, http://unpo.org/downloads/359.pdf

UN Women, 2012, *Sourcebook on women, peace and security: Overview of contents*, www.unwomen.org/en/digital-library/ publications/2012/10/un-women-sourcebook-on-women-peace-and-security.#sthash.vEOvMlhN.dpuf

USAID, 2007, *Women & Conflict*, www.usaid.gov/sites/default/files/ documents/1865/toolkit_women_and_conflict_an_introductory_ guide_for_programming.pdf

Women2000, 1998, *Sexual violence and armed conflict: United Nations response: United Nations Division for the Advancement of Women*, www. un.org/womenwatch/daw/public/w2apr98.htm#21

Wood, EJ, 2010, *Rape is not inevitable in war*, yalejournal.org/wp-content/uploads/2010/09/105217wood.pdf

World Bank, 2013, *Women in MENA enter labor markets at half global rate says World Bank Report*, www.worldbank.org/en/news/press-release/2013/03/15/women-in-mena-enter-labor-markets-half-global-rate-says-world-bank-report

Part Three
Micro challenges

Ideas from early childhood development approaches to contribute to Millennium Development Goals' achievements in Latin America[1]

Laura Agosta

Introduction

The following article focuses on the analysis of the trends that Latin America is following in terms of early childhood development programmes (ECD) and how some innovations are shaping the debate. The relevance of this topic in terms of the Millennium Development Goals (MDGs) and their successor, the Sustainable Development Goals (SDGs), is that some key ECD programmes adopt a multi-sectorial and comprehensive approach to human development that relate to many of the development goals. They focus on child development while also aiming at achieving results that will improve the children's lives and opportunities in adulthood.

   The article will start with a conceptualisation of ECD and an analysis of the importance and characteristics of these programmes and their characteristics in the region. There is evidence that suggests that intervening with social policies at early ages are among the most important public policies in terms of achieving equality. It has been proven that investing in the early stages of life, yields better and more equal outcomes in development for the society as a whole. Even if social protection policies in the region have been around for a long time, the integral approach to early childhood presents innovative ways to deliver greater impact and achieve different aspects of the region's SDG objectives.

   Much of the debate on ECD and international development policy is currently focused on how to expand the services to extend the coverage. This debate was also promoted by the MDG philosophy of increasing coverage of basic services and this is certainly a challenge in Latin America where income inequality has also created inequalities at birth. Nevertheless, it is also important to reflect on the quality of the services in ECD and what works and what does not.

Unfortunately, impact studies that analyse the improvements of children's condition as solely the consequence of ECD programmes are not widely available. Many programmes have been studied in terms of the impact of certain components, such as the conditional cash transfers impact on poverty alleviation in Mexico or Colombia, or the impact of dietary supplement for children in Jamaica. Araujo et al refer to a recent study that performs a meta-analysis of evaluations on the impact of changes in delivery of childcare services. This study found that there were no more than six evaluations in the region which revealed positive effects in the measurement of some child development indicators, which does not allow for broader conclusions on the impact of these programmes in terms of health and nutrition (Araujo et al, 2013).

Nevertheless, in terms of social policy management, the region is looking at some concrete examples that appear to have been successful and that are shaping the discussion. Identifying some of these key approaches to ECD programme management and implementation can lead to some conclusions on programmes that could be effective for SDG achievement.

Some theory behind early childhood development policies

There are different policies that address childhood development and ECD is a subset of these policies. *Early childhood* policies by definition are policies that target children in their first years, but are mostly sectorial. This means that there are early childhood policies in education, health, social protection, to name some; but what they have in common is that they target children usually younger than 5 or 6 years old. These types of policies have been among the first ones that modern states have implemented as public policies in Latin America, especially in the area of health. These policies tend to be universal through the public system of hospitals or schools.

Child protection policies refer to policies that aim at protecting a particular subset of children: those that face current or potential problems related to abuse or neglect. The situation of children who are beneficiaries of these programmes varies in accordance to the type of policy. In other words, preventive and awareness raising policies usually target larger groups of the population (as for example public campaigns against sexual exploitation) whereas first response and referral activities focus specifically on children who have been victims or who are extremely likely to be victims of abuse and neglect and are usually institutionalised.

ECD programmes usually refer to policies that address health, education and social behaviour for children (in an integral way) from the moment they are conceived to when they enter primary school. These policies are targeted not only to the child, but also to his or her family, and there is a community component as well. Adding the word 'development' implies that these policies have as an ultimate goal to foster achievement in development goals in a more holistic way. The idea behind the justification of ECD is that early childhood development outcomes (such as cognitive development, socio-emotional development and physical wellbeing and growth) have a significant impact on life outcomes (such as schooling, health, fertility, earnings and risky behaviours) (Vegas and Santibáñez, 2010, 5). This approach is closely related to the goals that were promoted by the UN through the MDGs. More often than not, these goals show improvements in an interrelated way and that is the way they should also be analysed.

In other words, in general, ECD policies are courses of action that focus on improving the living conditions of pregnant women and of their children until they are 5 or 6 years old with the goal of 1) improving cognitive development of children, 2) improving their physical wellbeing and ensuring their growth, 3) increasing their ability to socialise with others (Vegas and Santibáñez, 2010), and 4) serving as equalisers for children in a society (Irwin et al, 2007).

In the cycle of public policies for ECD, there are some important concepts that are critical to their formulation and later implementation.

The 'ecological' approach

Early childhood development programmes tend to have an 'ecological' conception of the development of human beings, which is critical during our first years. The idea behind this concept is that policies take into consideration the dynamic interaction between the individual and his or her surroundings. These policies usually include activities to strengthen the different circles where children grow: their families, their community and, lastly, the state. In other words, the dimensions of early childhood development 'are affected by individual neurobiology, relationships with caregivers and physical and psychosocial exposures in caregiving environments' (Anderson et al, 2003). For this reason, many ECD policies have components that support women integrating into the labour force, and improve their educational situation or access to healthcare.

Through the lens of an ecological perspective, ECD programmes not only target beneficiaries themselves (children and, often, their pregnant mothers, mostly through the health and educational systems), but they also have strategies to work within the institutional context that interacts with the child, by increasing services, interconnecting them and improving their quality. A good environment for child development has proved to be key for our brain and social skills.

In terms of implications for public policies, ECD programmes tend to have two types of protective measures: internal (related to the evolution of the child to develop personal tools for their psychological and social wellbeing), and external (that allow the optimisation of the environmental influences to reach better levels of development).

A chance to break the poverty cycle

ECD programmes are based on the belief that investing in early childhood has important benefits when it comes to breaking the intergenerational cycle of poverty in a society and that investing in the first years has high returns. In other words, not only 'what happens to the child in the early years is critical for the child's development trajectory and life course' (Irwin et al, 2007, 7), but also studies show that many of these strategies have higher returns than doing so at later stages in life. According to Heckman, 'early interventions promote economic efficiency and reduce lifetime inequality. Remedial interventions for disadvantaged adolescents who do not receive a strong initial foundation of skills face an equity–efficiency trade off. They are difficult to justify on the grounds of economic efficiency and generally have low rates of return' (Heckman, 2008, 52).

This often leads to an approach to public policy from a 'human rights' perspective in which some universal services are provided to all children to ensure equality. The ECD programme starting point is that addressing the threats to child development early on can really make a difference in these future adults' economic and social opportunities, as well as their human development.

An emphasis on the 'vital cycle' approach

Following this idea, professionals involved in these programmes set milestones that are important for human development through the study of the evolution of human beings, their relationship with their family and other biological critical periods. This approach allows programmes to develop interconnected services and track information on how children are reaching these milestones. Failure to do so sets an alert in the system and creates opportunities for referrals, further visitations, and the development of new services to attend to these specific needs.

Most of the times, ECD programmes identify a promotion, a prevention and rehabilitation strategy, corresponding to different segments of the population in terms of their needs. Almost all of the children benefit from services that promote healthcare whereas a reduced number usually need services that deal with prevention strategies. An even smaller number of children require rehabilitation processes (Gobierno de Chile, 2008).

A systematic approach and coordination among agencies

One of the main characteristics of ECD is the necessary interconnectivity between agencies that provide different services for early childhood. This is definitely a challenge for programme budgeting, implementation and further evaluation. Using the categories developed by the World Bank (Vegas and Silva, 2011), ECD programmes have some components of sectorial programmes (specific services to some or all children), as well as multi-sectoral ones (children receive or should receive other programmes that offer equality in opportunities for them to reach the maximum capacity in their life).

The justification for implementing coordinated programmes in child development is twofold. On the one hand, as stated above, psychological considerations of the biological and social evolution of children demand an integral approach to child development. The progressive focus on systems approach to child development has been a shift from previous approaches that used to focus on single childhood problems. This new paradigm includes different legal and policy frameworks, as well as the joint work of different stakeholders (both public and private) involved in the different stages of children's development. It is also a shift from a 'treating' perspective to a 'preventative' one in which the state has a proactive role detecting, assessing and addressing potential and real risks early in the life of children, instead of adopting a merely reactive position. Coordination between agencies and public and private sectors is therefore another key element to these policies.

On the other hand, ECD programmes accompany another broader tendency in public policy. These are the new public management tools that understand public governance as: (i) a continuous changing context, (ii) the perspective of population diversity, (iii) strategies shaped by civil society, and (iv) governance through networks and partnerships (Snape and Taylor, 2004). The role of the government is to provide the framework in which the different agencies and stakeholders coordinate their work to improve the development outcomes of children.

Some conditioning factors for child development

Families' socio-economic and educational conditions are key when it comes to child development. Duncan et al show in their study on economic deprivation and child development published in the early 1990s, that family income and poverty status have a significant impact on children's cognitive behaviour (Duncan et al, 1994). Moreover, other studies also show a correlation between this outcome and the influence of parents' educational attainment and economic opportunities.

One of the most important challenges for child development is the vulnerability to which women are exposed in the labour market: employment vulnerability, lower levels of social protection and income instability. Not being able to develop a professional career fully because of the previous points, renders women more vulnerable to being in poverty as they grow older (Vegas and Santibáñez, 2010). Moreover, women tend to be more vulnerable in terms of job stability when important economic crises arise.

It is often the case that women are not able to fully participate in the labour force not because of their levels of education, but because they simply do not have a social safety network that promotes quality services for daycare and early education for children. Some studies show that the elasticity of the supply of women in the labour force with respect to the price of childcare in some countries varies from −0.13 to −0.2 (Elborgh-Woytek et al, 2013). Providing families with the possibility of sending their children to childcare is clearly a key component of ECD. The necessity of women being able to fully integrate into the labour force is also one of the main drivers for the implementation of ECD policies.

Being a child in Latin America

Of the total population in Latin America and the Caribbean, 26 per cent are between 0 and 14 years old (World Bank, 2012b), a proportion that has been declining for the past 50 years.

As the proportion of children over the total population shrinks in Latin America, that of people over 65 years old increases, as population growth reduces. Latin America is experiencing similar dependency ratios to those seen in Europe.

Latin America has improved its economic condition in recent decades which has made it possible to adopt some ambitious public policies for long-term development in many areas (OECD, 2012). Moreover, the World Bank explains that the middle class has increased by 50 per cent in the region, representing now 30 per cent of the overall population (World Bank, 2012a). It is, however, still the case that the poverty headcount ratio at $1.90 a day in 2013 for Latin America and the Caribbean is around 5% (World Bank, 2012b).

Even if economic conditions overall have improved and inequality decreased, this does not mean that these conditions are reflected in the lives of children. The World Bank highlights that 'many countries in Latin America and the Caribbean have relatively low poverty rates among the population as a whole, but much higher poverty rates among children aged 0 to 6 years' (Vegas and Santibáñez, 2010, 18). Moreover, in most countries of the region 'nearly half of all children aged 0 and 6 years are concentrated in the bottom three deciles of the national income distribution' (Vegas and Santibáñez, 2010, 20). Poverty rates among young people have increased in Latin America in the last decades. According to the UN, 40.5 per cent of children and adolescents in the region are poor. This means that 70.5 million people under the age of 18 are currently poor, and that 16.3 per cent of children live in extreme poverty (CEPAL, 2013).

Despite the fact that poverty rates among children is high, the region has made impressive strides when it comes to the infant mortality rate. By 1970, 118 children of 1,000 born would die before reaching the age 5, whereas in 2010 that number averaged 23 for the entire region (UNICEF, 2012). This number is well below the world's mean (57) and the levels of Africa (111) and East Asia (67) (UNICEF, 2012, 83). This impressive decrease in mortality rates is associated with the region's investment in health programmes that target women and children and general primary care, as well as better coverage of universal services such as access to clean water.

Nonetheless, children still face some dramatic health problems. Being underweight when they are born is still one of the main challenges that children face in the region. As an average between 2006 and 2010, 8 per cent of children were born with this problem (UNICEF, 2012, 95) and this varies in the region in terms of the different countries. Achieving better standards in child nutrition was intrinsically related to achieving better results in almost all of the SDGs. These problems are very much linked with the economic situation of the countries. In this sense, in the poorest countries of the region like Honduras, Haiti or Nicaragua, a higher proportion of children are underweight, suffer from nutrient deficiencies as there is also a higher percentage of people living in extreme poverty. These countries also face higher infant and child mortality rates than the rest of the region.

Enrollment in early childhood care education services does not show alarming figures in the region. As a matter of fact, preprimary gross enrollment rates in the region are above 60 per cent (Vegas and Santibáñez, 2010, 36). This figure is very close to the ones that are found in North America and Europe. This is mostly because preschool is commonly mandatory and public and also in alignment with the efforts of the countries of the region to universalise primary education.

As children go through the education system, it is evident that they face other problems such as drop out and repetition. The region as a whole had a primary school dropout rate close to 20 per cent, which is lower than what it was in 2000 (Vegas and Santibáñez, 2010, 36). In general, there has been a positive trend in the region in terms of public expenditure in the education system. As an average, countries went from investing approximately 4.5 per cent of their GDP in education to investing 5.2 per cent (Bellei, 2013).

It is important to remember that informality in the labour market in Latin America is about 47.7 per cent among employed people who do not work in the agriculture sector (ILO, 2012). Due to the traditional role of women in terms of being more dependent on the husband in the household, women in Latin America tend to work more in the informal sector than men. This is especially the case in countries such as Bolivia, Paraguay, Peru and Guatemala where more than half of employed women are working in the informal sector. Part-time paid employment is also much more common among women than men.

The picture depicted above calls for critical and practical solutions in terms of public finances as the countries of the region will have to progressively use more public funds to support an ageing population as the younger generations decrease in number. Economic growth has made it possible to achieve better conditions for children in the region but there are still elements to improve. Fiscal support efforts will then be required to support not only the elderly, but also the younger generations who are facing concrete and lasting development challenges. Even if the region presents differences between countries, the vulnerability of children in Latin America makes it necessary to create special programmes to attend to their needs. Addressing the needs of children at an early age, is key to sustaining socio-economic improvements.

ECD in Latin America

Latin American countries have a history of different actors, private and public, providing social services. In the majority of the countries of the region, the first social protection services were delivered on the basis of social assistance and it was usually provided by the Catholic church. Later on, other civil society organisations took over some of these activities and then the state started having a more proactive role developing more complex systems by the beginning of the twentieth century. Countries in the south cone, such as Argentina, Brazil, Chile and Uruguay were the first to develop these types of systems in the region, whereas Caribbean countries developed them later, after 1950 (Ferreira and Robalino, 2010). These first social assistance government services were destined primarily to people in a working relationship, therefore coverage was limited to the urban working class. These programmes were funded by the contributions of employees and employers. In the late 1980s, countries started to implement more complex social protection programmes that functioned like safety nets. In addition to those original programmes, there were several new ones targeting vulnerable populations in order to alleviate poverty. As Robalino and Ferreira explain, many of these programmes were funded by social investment funds, which is budget put to one side in a discretionary way to deal with different government priorities.

Within decades, it became obvious that governments could not expect everybody to be employed in the formal sector, therefore it was imperative to develop social programmes especially tailored to address the problems of the unemployed and those who worked in the informal sector. Of course, as seen before, because family socio-economic conditions are very intimately related to child development, this change was also important for how child development policies were shaped. Another paradigm was developed (associated also with the return to democratic government regimes): the notion that people have a 'right' to access these services, that goes beyond their employment status. Among the types of social assistance programmes that were a product of this new approach, were conditional cash transfers (CCT). These programmes 'offer cash assistance to poor families, provided that members, usually children, meet certain conditions on school attendance and healthcare use' (Ferreira and Robalino, 2010, 11).

ECD programmes in Latin America usually combine elements from social insurance, social protection and transfers. They respond to the need of the state to address some of the inequality of opportunities at birth suffered by the population. There are different types of ECD programmes in the region, but the common denominator is that they usually target not only aspects that have to do with children's wellbeing during their early years, but also with providing their parents or caregivers with opportunities for better parenting and participating fully in the labour force (Vegas and Santibáñez, 2010).

It is possible to distinguish different strategies in ECD in the region (see Table 10.1).

One of the strengths of the Latin American region that enabled the creation of ECD has been the important health system developed at the beginning of the twentieth century. Some countries developed very strong networks and systems, even if access to it has not been very equal, as in the case of Chile. It was on this system that the ECD system was able to develop so strongly, as will be seen below. Moreover, Latin America as a region has been able to implement many ECD different schemes in recent decades, especially in those countries that have enjoyed good fiscal balances, booms in commodity prices and a general reduction of poverty levels due to economic growth. These characteristics helped the creation of funds more or less systematised to address the problems that children were facing.

Table 10.1: Different strategies in ECD in Latin America

Type of programme	Example of countries that implemented them
Conditional cash transfers	Mexico, Chile, Nicaragua
Parenting	Jamaica, Bolivia, Honduras
Nutrition and supplementation	Mexico, Colombia
Child care	Colombia, Guatemala, Mexico
Unconditional cash transfers	Ecuador
Intersectoral coordination	Chile, Colombia

Source: Compiled by author, based on Vegas, E, Santibáñez, L, (2010)

The challenge remains, will these services be as strong in moments of crisis? Luckily, many countries such as Chile, Mexico and Colombia have made these programmes permanent government policies, with the creation of laws or other institutional mechanisms to avoid these programmes being easily suppressed.

Some innovations of early childhood development programmes that can be lessons for the SDGs

The cases of the ECD systems in Chile and Jamaica have been identified by the World Bank as 'perhaps the ones with stronger political support for ECD' (Vegas and Santibáñez, 2010) in the region.

ECD programmes in these countries have been the result of a strong political decision at the presidential level, followed by a coordinated effort between agencies and the active participation of key ministries such as the Ministry of Finance. In Chile, a special commission was organised to understand the reasons behind the fact that women were not joining the labour force and they understood that delays in children's development were some of the causes behind the fact that women were not working. There are of course, differences in the population composition and social challenges in each of these countries.

As seen before, Chile has always been among the countries with more developed social protection systems in the region, and among the first ones to do so. Moreover, compared to the region as a whole, Chile has fewer children living in poverty than the region's mean.

Jamaica, in the Caribbean, represents not only the area of the region that developed social protection systems in a later stage, but is also characterised by the fact that the role of the state and civil society was very different during colonial times compared to the Spanish tradition. As a result, for example, the delivery of publicly-funded services is performed by private organisations (Araujo et al, 2013).

The monitoring and tracking system of Chile Crece Contigo (ChCC)

ChCC is the early childhood development programme that has been in place in Chile since 2007. The programme is part of the inter-sectoral system of social protection (Law 20379) and is an integral protection programme for childhood that aims at guiding, protecting and supporting children and their families through universal actions and services, as well as focusing on the protection of children in vulnerable situations.

The programme's objective is to make a personalised history of the trajectory of a child's development from the moment he or she is conceived to when he or she enters the educational system at 4 or 5 years old. The programme has a multidimensional focus in the sense that it works with biological, physical, psychical and social components of children's evolution. The programme combines some awareness raising initiatives to promote children's schooling at early ages, practical and education activities for pregnant and new mothers as well as a support for children's health through the health system. It also offers a component that entails a subsidy for families and mothers in their fifth month of pregnancy until the child is 18 years old (as long as the father and/or the mother does not have any social insurance and are part of the 40 per cent of lower income families in the country). ChCC leverages the already wide primary healthcare system across the country, as well as the network for childcare (access to which is very unequal among the population). Moreover, the programme used many of the successful examples on childcare and development that municipal government and civil society organisations had already been putting in place before the system was created. In this sense, it is possible to view ChCC as a programme that glued together many of the already available resources for early child development, but that, by putting them under the same system and making it universally available with a special tracking system, now offers all Chilean children the possibility of reaching better developmental standards.

Perhaps one of the most innovative parts of ChCC was the introduction of the tracking system of the development trajectory of children cared for in the public health system. This system allows professionals in the health system to track the information on the beneficiaries of the programme. Every child who is born in a public hospital or attends a public hospital for treatment is entered into this system, and physicians need to update those records as the child develops. This system also allows doctors to make referrals to other professionals if children present certain delays in their development.

This tracking system differs from regular health checks for children in the health system as it also includes the monitoring and tracking of psychosocial risks that children are exposed to during the years covered by the programme. In this way, the interconnected network of professionals and agencies that form ChCC can detect and refer cases that need further assistance.

The tracking system begins when the pregnant woman goes to the hospital for the first checkup. Then, as in any other checkup during pregnancy or of the child, the risk assessment process is meant to determine if the woman or the child are vulnerable from a health or social perspective. If the child's health is vulnerable, he or she is then referred to other health professionals as needed. If there is a condition of social vulnerability, the municipal government receives the case and measures are taken, as for example improving housing conditions for that particular family. Moreover, referrals to the education system are also crucial for children's future development (Gobierno de Chile, 2012).

To render the tracking system possible, professionals from various disciplines are trained on not only how to complete the important information about the child's progress but also on how to make a good referral when the child presents any type of delay in his or her development.

ChCC has developed a training system for nurses, doctors and other professionals with a handbook of procedures that is key to understanding not only the services that are important for a child and the expectations on his or her evolution but also what to do, and how to make a referral within the system.

This system also allows the detection of families that need to receive special economic help like cash transfers. The possibility of having the information consolidated in one place, reduces the risks of duplication of programmes.

One of the biggest contributions to ECD programmes from ChCC is this tracking system that accounts for the programme's results and achievements. As a matter of fact, the complexity of the interagency interaction and the ecological conception of public policy in ECD makes it difficult not only to account for successes at the agency level but also at the beneficiary one. Indeed, the success of the programme is seen many years later, in many different spheres of human wellbeing, and as a result of a coordinated effort between different agencies. Hopefully, this tracking system will allow experts to follow many cohorts of children in the system and assess the improvements in their wellbeing.

Unfortunately, the baseline data for this type of intervention it is hard to get. The results on the improvement in child development indicators may also be harder to identify and attribute solely to this particular programme.

Parenting stimulation as a component of ECD programmes in Jamaica

As mentioned before, stunting is a problem for children in Latin America. Jamaica has implemented several programmes to address this issue that are based on nutritional components, as well as a parenting curriculum to provide parents with tools to improve their children's development. As in Chile, the ECD programme in Jamaica has been built on the existing structure of the health system. As early as the beginning of the twentieth century the country developed health centres for children situated all over the country. By the beginning of the current century, the government created the basis of an integrated and multi-sectorial programme to address early childhood development, which was coordinated by the Commission for Early Childhood. This commission is composed of representatives of several ministries and agencies that coordinate their work towards early childhood development: health, education, social services, finance and planning. Representatives from academia and the private sector also participate in this commission. The strategy that this commission created aims to provide children from 0 to 8 years old with services for their early development, involving parents in the process.

The impact of the Jamaica case has been well studied. The programmes that addressed these issues were mostly focusing on supplemental nutrition as well as parenting guidance.

Parenting guidance in the Jamaican early childhood development context consists of different elements such as: weekly half-hour visits by community health agents over a period of one year, demonstration by health agents of play activities involving the mother and the child and specially trained community health aides who implement the intervention. These types of interventions are among the ones that have been more studied in the region showing positive results. A study that followed the development of children at age 17–18 years old (after a first study when they were 11–12 years old) shows that 'stunted children who received home-based stimulation in early childhood showed sustained cognitive and educational benefits at age 17–18 years' whereas there were 'no sustained benefits from supplementation' (Walker et al, 2005, 6). The authors also showed that 'there are sustained cognitive benefits and positive impacts on programme participants' school achievement and dropout rates' (Vegas and Santibáñez, 2010, 64). This was a study where the intention to treat was analysed using two cohorts: stunted and non-stunted children aged 17–18. These same children were previously randomly assigned at age 9–24 months to supplementation (1kg milk-based formula per week), stimulation (weekly play session), both types of intervention or no intervention at all. Moreover, these interventions have proved to be effective not only for the child but also for the mother and the family context (Vegas and Santibáñez, 2010).

These studies showed that what was important in these interventions, besides extra doses of supplementation for nutrients, is the bond that these parenting stimulation processes create between children and their mothers or caregivers. As a consequence of the success demonstrated by the implementation of stimulation and parental guidance, the Roving Caregivers programme was created in 1992. Through this initiative, caregivers provide direct support to children and their families who would otherwise lack access to formal early childhood development services. These caregivers are specially trained to visit homes in need to introduce families to developmentally appropriate childcare practices. They particularly work on engaging children in stimulation activities, teaching parents to replicate them and discussing with them child-related matters. A cost–benefit analysis of the Roving Caregivers programme in the Caribbean shows that this programme is substantially cheaper than alternative ECD interventions.

Positive conclusions for ECD management

Chile Crece Contigo is an example of an integrated intervention towards the promotion of child development that is consistent from the implementation and the tracking point of view. The system of services in place to assist pregnant women and children in order to assess their social and health vulnerabilities has a tracking system attached that allows these services to effectively reach the most vulnerable. At the local level, this informational system requires training and a good flow of information between the different agencies involved in the process. At the national level, a structure that oversees and highlights the importance of a tracking system is as important as the system itself. Of course, not every early childhood development system is prepared to develop such complex and integrated services and a tracking system. The starting point for a strong one is always a good health system for primary care. That is the structure upon which a good early childhood development policy can grow.

A sound tracking system allows professionals in the system to understand children's delays and problems earlier on in their lives and act accordingly. ChCC builds on the successful achievements of the health and education system in the country, but the programme adds the component of being able to deliver quality services tailored to a child's specific needs. Even if there are not yet many comprehensive impact studies of the results of the programme as a whole, if interpreted correctly this tracking system could lead to improvements in the services provided by the health and education system.

The success of the interventions in Jamaica and other countries of the region reinforce the idea that improving the way parents and caregivers relate to their child development needs, as well as how children are being stimulated, are at the base and are necessary conditions to achieve these basic goals. ECD interventions that address child development needs and enhance the family context can lead to more effective results.

Evidence of studies in this field suggests that nutritional supplementation has a higher impact in reducing the consequences of stunting among children when it is implemented with a parenting component. The experience of the Roving Caregivers programme shows that economic condition should not be an obstacle for families to receive parental guidance and children the proper stimulation. In fact, these initiatives can be replicated and are relatively lower cost interventions, as it relies on training families about how to be better equipped to deliver child development activities.

The Roving Caregivers programme can also be an asset in those countries where ECD programmes are not as developed or where social safety nets are not as strong in terms of institutions. This is the reason why this programme is quickly expanding to other countries in the Caribbean. Another benefit of the programme is that it employs people who have just graduated from high school, creating not only job opportunities but also a space where they can remain engaged with healthy social practices. But perhaps one of the most important contributions of this programme is that it restores 'the central role of the home and family in the early stage of child development and changing the paradigm by restoring balance between home and familial stimulation and institutional intervention' (Jules, 2010, 6).

Even if the idea of coordinated policies is theoretically sound, empirically there is a general lack of evidence to make a strong case for coordinated activities. The lack of indicators that comprehensively look at the outcomes on children's wellbeing and inter-agency coordination indicators are key to producing this evidence.

Inter-agency coordination in ECD systems must happen at three levels. At the 'policy level' interagency practice, different national and local agencies as well as non-governmental stakeholders define the general objectives for child development. At the 'programme level', governmental agencies need to work together for an integrated and coordinated service response and at the 'direct service level', agencies should work together to address the needs of each child in a coordinated way with other agencies (New South Wales Government, 2006). As said before, little evidence on the effectiveness of inter-agency cooperation in the ECD system is available. Nevertheless, important lessons can be learnt from studies that focus on some of the many aspects of ECD.

Political and legal mandate

The rationale behind the need for inter-agency coordination to achieve a common outcome in terms of early child development should be expressed in a specific law or mandate. This legislative mandate needs to be accompanied by a strong political will with regards to the relevant governmental agency or the highest political representative to effectively implement what the law stipulates.

General institutional framework

Main traditional frameworks of governance within partnerships claim that there are three types of models: market model, hierarchies and networks (Thompson, 1991). A network strategy entails a form of coordination that is achieved by less formal and more egalitarian means (Ranade and Hudson, 2003) and that involves the participation of both governmental and non-governmental stakeholders.

When assessing the possibilities of coordination among agencies it is imperative to take into consideration the historical trajectories of the different agencies and their institutional linkages. The trajectory of decentralisation policies is also key in this analysis, as is the record of partnership between the public and private sectors in the system.

Often, cooperation strategies emerge as a consequence of a process of decentralisation within the government structure, which encourages the different agencies to seek a partnership with others to achieve a common goal.

Benefits and stakes for each of the actors involved

The different agencies should see in the cooperation strategy a gain in terms of their own activities. In this sense, it is possible to identify some key decision criteria that govern these inter-agency relations such as: (i) the fulfilment of programme requirements, (ii) the maintenance of a clear domain of high social importance (in terms of exclusiveness, autonomy or dominance), (iii) the maintenance of orderly, reliable patterns of resource flow and (iv) the extended application and defence of the agency paradigm (Ranade and Hudson, 2003). A long and complicated negotiation may be required to guarantee these for the different organisations involved in the strategy; but, if done correctly, it is likely to provide successful solutions to the coordination strategy.

Particularly important is the selection of the stakeholder that will participate in this partnership. The possibility of leaving aside important stakeholders just because of weaker negotiation power or including stakeholders who are not as relevant or representative simply due to inter-personal relations between the different authorities may undermine the effectiveness of the policy.

Compatibilities in the administrative structure

Coordination is more likely to work when agencies have similarities in the funding structure, planning cycle and decision-making process. Identifying a common framework in these aspects is crucial to achieve more sustainable ways of coordinated efforts among agencies. This is particularly difficult when the system includes non-governmental actors as part of the strategic partnerships for the child development system.

Conclusion

Latin American countries have a long history of social assistance and social protection policies, as well as institution development. Successful ECD programmes in the region have drawn upon these strengths and, combining this with political will and available funding, the region has the chance to experiment in enhancing the already available health and education structure by providing services and coordination of different policies and programmes that are assumed to be key for child development. Even if there are not yet many impact studies of integral approaches to ECD in the region, evidence highlighted before shows that it is likely that ECD programmes could have a larger impact on child development as opposed to isolated child development programmes.

Besides the impact of particular child development interventions, what is especially alluring about the way the region is conceptualising ECD is the holistic approach to it and the notion that public services have to focus on what the person needs at each development stage, more than a particular service from a particular ministry or agency. It shifts the analysis to assess programme effectiveness from a mere institutional one assessing programme achievements in health, education and so on, to really look at the impact in people's quality of life. And some programmes, such as ChCC, are starting to develop a tool to do that.

As seen before, ECD programmes are based on the premise that child development does not happen in a vacuum, but that the family and community context is crucial. Moreover, strengthening traditional education and health institutions is key to implement effective early childhood care. Conceptualising the achievements of MDGs and SDGs through this lens, could be an important contribution to the movement as we tend to analyse the achievements towards each of the goals separately from the others and there is usually little discussion about the 'institutional framework' that would render possible a coordination of efforts.

Note
[1]   The first edition of this article was written between 2012 and 2013.

References

Anderson, LM, Shinn, C, Fullilove, MT, Scrimshaw, SC, Fielding, JE, Normand, J et al, Task Force on Community Preventive Services, 2003, The effectiveness of early childhood development programs: A systematic review, *American Journal of Preventive Medicine* 24, 3, 32–46

Araujo, MC, López Bóo, F, Puyana, JM, 2013, *Overview of early childhood development services in Latin America and the Caribbean*, https://publications.iadb.org/bitstream/handle/11319/3617/BID_Panorama_ENG%20%28Web%29.pdf?sequence=2

Bellei, C, 2013, Situación Educativa de América Latina y el Caribe: Hacia la educación de calidad para todos al 2015, UNESCO Santiago de Chile: Imbunche Ltda

CEPAL (Economic Commission for Latin America and the Caribbean), 2013, *Social Panorama of Latin America 2013*, http://repositorio.cepal.org/bitstream/handle/11362/36736/S2013869_en.pdf

Duncan, GJ, Brooks-Gunn, J, Klebanov, PK, 1994, Economic deprivation and early childhood development, *Child Development* 65, 2 (Children and Poverty), 296–318

Elborgh-Woytek, K, Newiak, M, Kochhar, K, Fabrizio, S, Kpodar, K, Wingender, P, Clements, B, Schwartz, G, 2013, *Las mujeres, el trabajo y la economía: Beneficios macroeconómicos de la equidad de género. Documento de análisis del personal técnico del FMI*, www.imf.org/external/spanish/pubs/ft/sdn/2013/sdn1310s.pdf

Ferreira, FH, Robalino, DA, 2010, *Social protection in Latin America: Achievements and limitations*, The World Bank, Working paper, http://documents.worldbank.org/curated/en/226681468053951908/pdf/WPS5305.pdf

Gobierno de Chile, 2008, *Ministerio de Salud, Manual para el apoyo y seguimiento del desarrollo psicosocial de los niños y niñas de 0 a 6 años*, http://web.minsal.cl/sites/default/files/files/2008_Manual-para-el-Apoyo-y-Seguimiento-del-Desarrollo-Psicosocial-de-los-Ninos-y-Ninas-de-0-a-6-Anos.pdf

Gobierno de Chile, 2012, *Comprehensive protection system for early childhood 'Chile Crece Contigo' (Chile Grows with you)*, www.odi.org.uk/sites/odi.org.uk/files/odi-assets/events-presentations/1296.pdf

Heckman, JJ, 2008, The case for investing in disadvantaged young children, *Big ideas for children: Investing in our nation's future*, pp 49–58, https://heckmanequation.org/resource/the-case-for-investing-in-disadvantaged-young-children/

ILO (International Labour Organization), 2012, *Panorama Laboral 2012: América Latina y el Caribe*, http://www.ilo.org/wcmsp5/groups/public/---americas/---ro-lima/documents/publication/wcms_195884.pdf

Irwin, LG, Siddiqi, A, Hertzman, C, 2007, *Early child development: A powerful equalizer*, Final report to the World Health Organization (WHO) Commission on social determinants of health, Geneva: WHO

Jules, D, 2010, *Positioning the Roving Caregivers programme as a Caribbean model*, Barbados: Caribbean Child Support Initiative (CCSI), www.globalchilddevelopment.org/sites/default/files/documents/RCP%20Position%20Paper%20REPORT.pdf

New South Wales Government, 2006, *New South Wales interagency guidelines for child protection intervention*, www.victimsservices.justice.nsw.gov.au/sexualassault/Documents/Child-Protection-Interagency-Guidelines.pdf

OECD (Organisation for Economic Co-operation and Development), 2012, *Eclac Latinamerica Economic Outlook*, Paris: OECD

Ranade, W, Hudson, B, 2003, Conceptual issues in inter-agency collaboration, *Local Government Studies* 29, 3, 32–50

Snape, S, Taylor, P, 2004, *Partnerships between health and local government*, Abingdon: Routledge

Thompson, G (ed), 1991, *Markets, hierarchies and networks: The coordination of social life*, Thousand Oaks, CA: Sage

UNICEF (United Nations International Children's Emergency Fund), 2012, *Estado Mundial de la infancia 2012*, New York: UNICEF

Vegas, E, Santibáñez, L, 2010, *The promise of early childhood development in Latin America and the Caribbean issues and policy options to realize it*, Washington, DC: World Bank, http://siteresources.worldbank.org/EDUCATION/Resources/278200-1099079877269/547664-1099079922573/ECD_LAC.pdf

Vegas, E, Silva, V, 2011, *Fortalecimiento de políticas públicas y programas de Desarrollo Infantil Temprano en America Latina y el Caribe*, Washington, DC: World Bank

Walker, SP, Chang, SM, Powell, CA, Grantham-McGregor, SM, 2005, Effects of early childhood psychosocial stimulation and nutritional supplementation on cognition and education in growth-stunted Jamaican children: Prospective cohort study, *The Lancet*, 366, 9499, 1804–7

World Bank, 2012a, *América Latina: clase media crece a niveles históricos*, World Bank, www.bancomundial.org/es/news/feature/2012/11/13/crecimiento-clase-media-america-latina

World Bank, 2012b, World Bank DataBank, http://databank.worldbank.org/data

Exploring the National Economic Empowerment and Development Strategy (NEEDS) as a micro-Millennium Development Goals' framework in Nigeria

Adebusuyi Isaac Adeniran

Background to the study

Conceptually, as a socio-economic framework for enabling sustainable human development in Nigeria, the National Economic Empowerment and Development Strategy (NEEDS) had focused on introducing the basic targets of the Millennium Development Goals (MDGs) into government policy, at both national and grassroots' levels. Although the NEEDS has been projected as a medium-term strategy (2003–07), it has derived significant impetus from Nigeria's long-term goal of eradicating poverty by means of a participatory approach (NPC, 2005). NEEDS is a nationally coordinated framework of action in close partnership with the state and local government authorities (through their respective State Economic Empowerment and Development Strategy (SEEDS) and Local Economic Empowerment and Development Strategy (LEEDS) platforms). Besides the federal government's NEEDS, each state and local government prepares its respective SEEDS and LEEDS in line with set NEEDS targets, which identifies priority programmes for key aspects of human development.

Operationally, NEEDS focuses on four key strategies: reorienting national values, reducing poverty, creating wealth and generating employment. In order to bring related targets of the NEEDS plan into timely fruition, the welfare of the people, their health, education, physical security and political and socio-economic empowerment would be prioritised in the implementation process. In this light, the NEEDS plan proposes to reduce poverty and inequality among Nigerians by adopting the following strategies:

1. to improve irrigation systems and the entire agricultural architecture since half of the Nigerian populace (that is, approximate 85 million people) subsists on agriculture and lives in rural areas. Also, the NEEDS sought to enable an integrated rural development programme in order to stem the tide of rural–urban migration in Nigeria;

2. to improve and make education accessible to all categories of the Nigerian populace, especially children (individuals who are up to 12 years of age) who constitute half of the entire population;

3. to improve the state of healthcare delivery and accessibility with specific emphasis on HIV/AIDS and other preventable diseases, such as malaria, tuberculosis and reproductive health-related diseases;

4. to enable special empowerment programmes (such as provisioning of safety nets, mass housing and pension reforms) for people who are vulnerable to the ravages of poverty, such as women, children, the disabled and the elderly; and

5. to invest in and so improve infrastructural facilities, with specific emphasis on electricity and roads.

Ostensibly, such policy advancements as presented above are not new to development policy in Nigeria. For instance, there has been the Directorate for Food, Road and Rural Infrastructure (DFRRI) policy and the Better Life (BL) policy. However, NEEDS did present a seemingly people-oriented framework for addressing the scourge of poverty in the country. This builds on an earlier effort to produce the Interim Poverty Reduction Strategy (IPRS) and the detailed consultative processes related to it. NEEDS observed that aside from empowering Nigerians in meeting basic existential needs, such effort should be made enduring. Against this background, the plan has recognised the need for governments at all levels to not only improve individual incomes, but also address an array of other social and economic factors that reinforce poverty and social exclusion. It was hoped that this plan would help 'create a Nigeria that Nigerians can be proud to belong to and grateful to inhabit; a Nigeria that rewards hard work, protects its people and their property, and offers its children better prospects than those they may be tempted to seek elsewhere' (FGN, 2001).

NEEDS recognised the importance of avoiding the mistakes of past development plans and strategies in Nigeria. For instance, it projected a government–citizens' partnership in its advancement, and proposed a coordination of action at the federal, state and local levels – attributes that were conspicuously absent from related development plans in the country thus far. Despite these initiatives, the NEEDS policy equally became part of the usual trend of policy misadventure in the country. Within the timeframe for its implementation, the plan could not attain a significant proportion of its target before it was jettisoned by succeeding Nigerian governments. Upon assumption of office in 2007, the late Nigerian President Umar Yar'Adua replaced the NEEDS plan with his 'Seven Point Agenda' plan, which emphasises: power and energy, food security and agriculture, wealth creation and employment, land reforms, mass transportation, security and education.

Statement of research gap

Despite immense human and natural wealth and the periodic commissioning of cogent poverty reduction plans, such as the NEEDS, a considerable percentage of the Nigerian populace has remained poor, and socio-economic development has been inhibited over time and space. As observed in the 2013 *Human Development Report* (HDR), Nigeria is rated a 'low human development' country with a Human Development Index (HDI) rank of 153 out of the 186 countries considered (UNDP, 2013). This current rating shows no progress from the 2009 HDR ranking of 158 for Nigeria out of the 182 countries that were considered (UNDP, 2009). Indeed, 64.4 per cent (106.3 million) and 83.9 per cent (138.4 million) of Nigerians were reported as subsisting on less than US$1.25 and US$2 per day from 2000 to 2007 respectively (UNDP, 2009).

Poverty as a dynamic phenomenon has been adjudged as having many causes in Nigeria, all of which intersect with one another. However, as noted in the NEEDS framework (FGN, 2001), a paramount source of 'absolute' poverty in the country has been a

> gross lack of basic services, such as, potable water, accessible education and health care. Another has been lack of assets, such as land, tools, credit and supportive networks of friends and family. A third has been lack of income, including food, shelter, clothing, and empowerment (that is, political power, confidence and dignity).

Why, however, has NEEDS failed to grant all Nigerians equal access to societal resources? Why have various governments in Nigeria often been keen on assuming control of major sources of national income instead of focusing on delivering essential social services to the people? What have been the contributions of a seemingly stifling bureaucratic structure in Nigeria to the failures of such socio-economic development policies as the NEEDS? This study explores the specific impacts of the NEEDS policy in the process of improving the condition of existence in Nigeria by means of engendering socio-economic inclusivity. What achievements has it been able to make? What impediments have constrained its functioning? What lessons have been, or could be learnt from related achievements and failures of past development policies in Nigeria, for instance the DFRRI and BL failures? These and associated inquiries are addressed in the study.

Objectives of study

The fundamental focus of this study is to explain the impact of the NEEDS, as a domestic MDG framework, on the drive towards enhancing the state of existence of Nigerians. Other specific objectives include:

1. to analyse the functionality of NEEDS as a socio-economic development policy;
2. to examine the intersections of bureaucracy, implementation mechanisms and failures of the NEEDS plan; and
3. to extract and present probable lessons from the NEEDS experience.

Theoretical and methodological framework for the study

The study's specificities are situated within a hybrid of 'comparative' and 'crisis' perspectives of development policy. Comparative orientation focuses on affirming from the developmental experiences of other societies or countries in the process of effecting sustainable changes within the socio-economic, and sometimes, political structures of a specific society. Related perspectives, however, are typically concerned with specific policies rather than with the entire policy system (Kohli et al, 1991; Moran and Wood 1993; Evers et al, 1994). Some comparative intents might be motivated by such inquiries as 'Have we got our policies right?', or 'Are there better ways of doing this?' Such approaches rely on the conviction that there are alternatives from which the preferred choice is selected. Meanwhile, it is imperative to view 'policy borrowing' in the context of structural impacts on the choice that is made.

Against this background, an output variant of the comparative analysis has opined that a comparison of outcomes and achievements rather than a comparison of spending or institutional arrangements should be the focus (Smeeding et al, 1990). They focus on explaining how achievements arise and are motivated by both pragmatic concerns and by wider theoretical objectives. Differences between nations in terms of poverty, inequality, health or literacy are given attention; yet such variances serve as platforms for raising questions about the context relationship between policy inputs and actual outcomes. A key theme in such a situation has been the need to pay attention to the broad context within which any apparent policy 'effort' occurs. For example, any measure to reduce inequalities, as presented by the NEEDS plan in its initial proposition, needs to be analysed with the size of the initial 'problem' and the effects of other policies in mind. Comparativism, thus, plays a significant role in disentangling interactions of this kind, which cannot be easily identified in a case of one country.

Utilising the word 'crisis' to simply describe some dilemmatic stagnation in prioritising social or development policy may be inappropriate; however, when used to refer to a combination of events that are likely to produce a radical transformation of social institutions, it is more tenable (Dye, 1998). In Marxist summation, 'crisis' postulates the evolution of capitalist institutions to a point at which the polarisation of society is so absolute and the conflict between classes so intense that revolution will occur. Marxist analyses of the development of the welfare state have, indeed, seen it as playing a role in postponing the arrival of the crisis within capitalism, but then facing tensions, which undermine its ameliorative effect. Over time and space, the price to be paid for the achievement of social and industrial peace through social/development policy expenditure tends to rise. This follows logically from the fact that such measures postpone rather than abolish the realisation of the capitalist crisis (Offe, 1984). In particular, the role of social/development policy in 'legitimising' an unequal and exploitative society; dealing with victims of the capitalist system and offering 'social benefits to buy off proletariat discontent becomes increasingly expensive' (Offe, 1984). As a consequence, a conflagration that transcends the enclosure of capitalism emanates. 'If political decisions are not made to cut costs, they intensify discontent, yet if cuts are not made, increasing public sector costs undermine enterprise' (Offe, 1984; Marx and Engel, 1848).

While Nigeria's NEEDS plan has been apt in adapting the frameworks of the MDGs in driving its objectives; in implementation however, a clear departure has been noted. Basic factors in this regard have been the inability to put into relevance the subsisting institutional peculiarities of the country in adapting the MDGs' framework, such as a lack of political will to drive the plan and ingrained corruptive tendency among the supposed drivers of the policy's objectives.

Theoretical synthesis

Although this study affirms that a policy framework already utilised successfully elsewhere could be relevant in any adaptive context, such policy design should address the societal peculiarities of the adapting societies in order to avert probable crisis within the socio-economic functioning of the receiving society. While the 'crisis' view of functional 'market involvement by all' seems to be relevant to the framework of the NEEDS plan, its stance on an outright ideological shift seems to be incompatible within the subsisting context of the Nigerian mixed-economic system. Specifically, since the envisaged exchange of means of production between the 'bourgeoisie' (that is, the political and business elites) and the 'proletariat' (that is, the working class) has continued to be illogical, over time and space, the Nigerian case cannot in any way be an exception. This study, therefore, adopts a mixed-economic approach, in which capitalism will still accommodate productive welfarist elements in seeking the enhancement of the condition of existence of a given people – in this case, the Nigerian populace.

The study employs exploratory research design, which combines both in-depth interviewing (primary source) and evaluative research (secondary source) that probes into existing governmental data. The method of content analysis is engaged in interpreting relevant information.

Conceptual interpretation of the NEEDS plan

A human development approach to social regeneration would depict the role of the state (and other non-state actors) vis-à-vis the welfare of its citizens. Dye (1998, 3) affirms it as the authoritative allocation of values for the totality of a society. This affirmation gives immediate attention to two probable inquisitions. First, since the livelihood of humans is routinely affected by their individual actions and by the actions of others, what is then the specific expectation of the state in relation to service or welfare provisioning? Second, what are the variants of actions, which usually have implications for welfare provisioning? Table 11.1 establishes useful associative interpositions between these inquiries.

While the state could intervene directly in enabling human development, through social security payments for instance, to

Table 11.1: State, society and human development

Facilitator	Source of income	Indicator
Individuals	Work, skills and so on	Contract/reciprocity
Families	Sharing, kinship	Network
Communities	Charity and communality	Culture and norms
State/government	Interventions and benefits	Rules and laws

Source: Authors' conception, 2013

influence the pattern of income and original distribution of incomes, it could also provide services and regulate activities to influence what individuals or organisations do to provide income or services.

The NEEDS plan had specifically projected wealth creation, employment generation, poverty alleviation and value re-orientation as its cardinal goals, for instance, by means of provisioning of safety nets to the vulnerable class, mass housing, pension reforms, and changing of unhealthy perception of the country by its citizens. These targets ought to have provided an imperative macroeconomic framework for operationalising the plan by means of 'empowering people', 'promoting private enterprise' and 'changing the way the government does its work' (FGN, 2001).

'Empowering people' under the NEEDS should have entailed provisioning of the needed environment for the private sector to thrive. As such, sustainable opportunities for employment generation and wealth creation would have been provided. A system of incentives that rewards creativity and reprimands corruptive tendencies would have also been enabled (FGN, 2001).

'Promoting private enterprise' under the NEEDS had focused on making the private sector the fulcrum of economic growth, thereby making a clear departure from subsisting and the inefficient pattern of direct government involvement in service provisioning. The role of the government at all levels (local, state and federal) was projected to be limited to that of 'enabler, facilitator and regulator'. Against this background, deregulation and privatisation would be promoted (FGN, 2001).

'Changing the way the government does its work' under the NEEDS aimed at restructuring governance. For instance, the over-bloated civil service had to be cut in order to encourage engagement of individuals in other much more productive activities in the private sector. The process of governance was projected to transmute from corruption-inclined to the one that facilitates development. Essentially, governmental budgeting was expected to be an offshoot of a process that connects policy with government income and its expenditure (FGN, 2001).

Meanwhile, inadequate monitoring and evaluation (M&E) procedures coupled with weakened civil society organisations (CSOs) due to the non-participatory disposition of the Nigerian ruling class, caused more of the Nigerian citizenry to become disempowered compared to before the NEEDS. Thus, the NEEDS became a victim of the incongruence it sought to address. The NEEDS was able to facilitate better private sector participation in the economy by liberalising key sectors in Nigeria, such as the telecommunication sector. Various foreign service providers are therefore active players in the economy now. Nigerians are better off now in comparison to before the NEEDs since only the state could offer such services previously, usually in a rather epileptic pattern. When the moribund Nigerian Telecommunication Limited (NITEL) was the monopolistic service provider, less than 10 per cent of the Nigerian populace could access telephone services. However, within the liberalised era, 75 per cent to 80 per cent of the Nigerian populace now have access to telephone services. Either in the city or in the village, an average Nigerian can presently afford a telephone. However, extant corruption in the public sector still hampers the growth of the private sector functionaries in the country. This gives immediate attestation to the fact that 'the way the government does its work' in Nigeria has refused to give way to improved measures of transparency, accountability and prevalence of rule of law.

It is worth noting that unlike the stateless 'economic man' society, the modern state demands the grounding of socio-economic services in various kinds of governmental structures (Kamerman, 1983). That is, a societal response to an individual need may come from 'a variety of institutions ranging from the family up to (and perhaps beyond) the nation-state' (Kamerman, 1983). These institutions, however, cannot be analysed in isolation. They interact with each other, they collaborate with each other, they have expectations of each other and they may be able to control or regulate each other (Kamerman, 1983).

Evaluating the functionality of the NEEDS plan

While the primary focus of the NEEDS has been poverty reduction in Nigeria through the empowerment of the citizens by means of productive re-distribution of wealth; establishing an association between aggregate macro-economic determinants and the micro-level distribution of income and incidence of poverty under the framework of the plan has tended to be cumbersome. Notably, it has been impossible to reconcile encouraging economic indices with the state of the human condition under the NEEDS. Meanwhile, various platforms exist in attempting related measurement. An approach focuses on assessing the specific percentage of households that have been taken out of poverty within the framework of the NEEDS plan by means of enhancement of their income level. For instance, NEEDS had projected to attain 4.8 per cent growth in real private consumption and 2.0 per cent growth in real private consumption per capita by 2007. However, subsisting pre-NEEDS' rates have continued to drop unabated.

Another method is by measuring the standard of living through the establishment of a poverty line that delineates the poor from the non-poor. For instance, the United Nations (UN)'s Human Development Index (HDI) model, for which less than US$1 per day is the threshold for poverty, has been engaged by the NEEDS in its projection from 2003 to 2007. 'The absolute poverty definition is, therefore, premised on some minimum nutritional standard that is converted into minimum food expenses to which is added certain expenditures for clothing and shelter' (FGN, 2001). A household is thus adjudged poor if its income or consumption level is below this minimum.

For the NEEDS, the MDG targets have been engaged as its benchmarks, including the targets to eradicate extreme poverty, achieve universal basic education, promote gender equality, reduce child mortality, improve maternal health, combat HIV/AIDS, malaria and other diseases, ensure environmental sustainability and develop a global partnership for development.

Related projections of the NEEDS were configured under selected socio-economic targets as presented in Table 11.2.

From all indications, NEEDS as a poverty alleviation plan in Nigeria could not achieve a significant proportion of its targets until its replacement by the 'seven-point agenda' programme, which was put in place by the succeeding government of late President Umar Musa Yar'adua in 2007. Just like similar policies before it, NEEDS largely failed in helping poor Nigerians to escape the poverty entanglement due to the stifling bureaucracy that has given birth to wrong and ineffective implementation procedures. As surmised by this in-depth interview (IDI) respondent:

> 'the problem has not been with the NEEDS policy, but the inability of those who are responsible for its implementation to employ the indices advanced by the MDGs' framework from which the policy has derived its impetus.' (IDI, Male, Researcher, 47 years, Ile-Ife, Nigeria, 10 May 2013)

Table 11.2: Selected socio-economic targets under NEEDS, 2003–07

Targets	2003	2004	2005	2006	2007
Education					
Adult literacy (%)	57.0	–	–	–	65.0
Health					
HIV/AIDS prevalence rate (%)	6.1	–	–	–	5.0
Immunisation coverage (%)	39.0	–	–	–	60.0
Access to safe water (%)	64.1	–	–	–	70.0
Access to adequate sanitation (%)	53.0	–	–	–	65.0
Infrastructure					
Power generation	–	4,000	5,000	7,000	10,000
Roads (rehabilitation/maintenance and construction of new roads, km)	3,000	3,500	3,500	4,000	4,000
Macro-economic					
Growth in real GDP (%)	10.2	5.0	6.0	6.0	7.0
Growth in oil sector (%)	23.0	0.0	0.0	0.0	0.0
Growth in non-oil sector (%)	3.3	7.3	8.5	8.3	9.5
Reduction in poverty incidence (%)	5.0	5.0	5.0	5.0	5.0
Minimum number of new jobs (millions)	–	1.0	2.0	2.0	2.0
Growth in real private consumption (%)	–	4.8	4.8	4.8	4.8
Growth in real private consumption, per capital (%)	–	2.0	2.0	2.0	2.0
Inflation rate (%)	15.0	10.0	9.5	9.5	9.5

Source: National Planning Commission, Abuja, Nigeria, 2005

Contrary to the envisaged 60 per cent, 70 per cent and 65 per cent targets for immunisation coverage, access to safe water and access to adequate sanitation respectively by 2007, the NEEDS plan could not achieve more than the initial 2003 estimates of 39 per cent, 64.1 per cent and 53 per cent respectively. The state of child and maternal mortality has worsened. For instance, with its approximate population of 165 million inhabitants (2012 estimate) accounting for about 2 per cent of the world's total, Nigeria is presently responsible for nearly 10 per cent of the total global estimate for maternal death (Adeniran, 2013). Besides poor infrastructure, a significant factor in this respect has been the soaring rate of midwives' attrition due to the poor conditions of service.

Before the arrival of the NEEDS in 2003, Nigeria was able to generate 4,000 megawatts of electricity for its 165 million inhabitants – a comparatively paltry amount in comparison to the 10,000 megawatts that the plan projected would be generated by 2007. Not only could the plan not achieve this target, production capacity dropped during the period of NEEDS. By the end of 2007, half of Nigeria's total population (that is, 71.1 million) were living without access to electricity (UNDP, 2007). The submission of this IDI respondent presents the situation clearly:

> 'in areas of electricity, roads upgrading and construction, the plan has failed. Prevalent corruption of government officials and politicians has remained at the foundation of these problems.' (IDI, Male, Lecturer, 40 years, Ile-Ife, Nigeria, May 12, 2013)

While NEEDS was able to record significant progress in its target on adult literacy (its target of 65 per cent coverage by 2007 was successfully met) and gender equality (the National Gender Policy was successfully approved and implemented), the policy generally left poor Nigerians worse off than before. Meanwhile, a significant factor in this regard has been the plan's inability to near any of the expected sectoral targets within its framework of operation.

NEEDS' dysfunctionality: interposing bureaucracy and policy outcomes

Why it is that poverty pervades a nation of such vast wealth as Nigeria? Why is it that Nigerians are getting poorer and socio-economic development has been largely inhibited? Why is it that no development plan or poverty alleviation strategy (for instance the NEEDS plan), has ever worked in Nigeria? Adeniran (2007) affirms that:

> unlike their counterparts in Malaysia and other South Asian nations in the 1960s and 1970s, Nigerian political leaders have often found it difficult to ensure the sustainability of a reform agenda once adopted…Often time, they are routinely keen on engaging development policy as a mere political tool for self-aggrandisement rather than as means for emancipating their people.

While the Nigerian political class has not been particularly forthcoming in moving the society forward in terms of transformative policy implementation and sustainability, on the part of the citizenry, questions have not been forthcoming. Engaging an applied functionalist perspective, Gans (1995) argued that certain groups in the society benefit from the existence of the poor and poverty. Specifically, the existence of poverty seems to be functional to the non-poor groups, which the political elites formidably represent in Nigeria. Often such elitist classes are at the root of poverty since they engage in various corruptive practices, such as bribery and embezzlement of public funds. Socio-economic growth is therefore inhibited since political survival is more appealing than devoting energy to human development.

At another level, social inequality, being a reflection of the extent of prevalent unfairness in the distribution and access to societal resources by the people, is lacking among Nigerians and has been worsening over time and space. Using the food energy intake (FEI) approach, Aigbokhan (2000) in his study observes that an increasing number of Nigerians were living in absolute poverty over the study periods – that is, 38 per cent in 1985, 43 per cent in 1992 and 47 per cent in 1996. Meanwhile poverty was higher in rural areas than in urban areas in Nigeria – that is, 38 per cent, 35 per cent and 37 per cent in urban areas, and 41 per cent, 49 per cent and 51 per cent in rural areas within the same study period. A significant factor in this respect has been gross neglect of the rural areas relative to the urban centres in measures of basic service provisioning.

While revenues from crude oil have been increasing over the years, most Nigerians have been falling deeper into poverty (Soludo, 2005). In 1980, an estimated 28 per cent of Nigerians lived in poverty. Indeed, this relatively tenable standard of living was seen as the impetus for the attractiveness of migrants, especially from the West African sub-region, to Nigeria. By 1996, about 66 per cent of the population had income of less than US$1 per day, and in 2011 it had risen to 70.8 per cent (UNDP, 2013). The extent of political instability and policy inconsistency, largely facilitated by a long period of military interregnum in the national politics, have been observed as the greatest contributors to such a retrogressive descent in the process of human emancipation.

Ostensibly, poverty reduction has been the most difficult developmental challenge for the Nigerian government, especially since the introduction of the *structural adjustment programmes* in mid-1980s. Of course, it has been the greatest obstacle to the pursuit of sustainable socio-economic growth in the country. While the NPC (2005) put the life expectancy at birth in Nigeria at 54 years, the HDR (UNDP, 2009, 173) pegged it at 47.7 years with the probability of an individual not surviving up to the age of 40 years or more at 37.4 per cent (2005–10). In addition, 53 per cent of the entire population did not have access to an improved water source. It was equally noted that while the GDP per capita for the fellow African oil-producing nation of Libya was $14,364 in 2007, Nigeria had an abysmal GDP per capita of $1,969 during the same period (UNDP, 2009, 171–3). Other social indicators, especially from the beginning of the NEEDS era, have been getting weaker. The argument here is that more than any other cause, the political leadership in Nigeria has been more culpable in the country's descent into poverty.

This argument has become more tenable in light of the fact that varying manifestations of poverty in the country, like gross unemployment, lack of access to land and credit facilities and inability to save and own assets, could have been nipped in the bud through an effective implementation of a re-distributive development plan. This was addressed by the NEEDS in its initial propositions; however, a lack of political will on the part of the political actors has made this lofty intent elusive. In planning, the NEEDS was more all-encompassing when compared to previous development plans in the country. It adopted a structural approach towards poverty alleviation, whereby all concerned (policy planners at all levels and the beneficiaries) would be procedurally involved in the implementation process. It had planned to attack poverty by empowering individuals and also by restructuring the system from an autocratic one to a participatory one. It seemed to be more concise and collaborative, involving the federal, state and local governments in the proposed implementation. However, its failure had been largely enabled by dysfunctional implementation and a lack of formidable M&E mechanism. As a matter of routine, the same bureaucracy that stifled previous development plans in the country was engaged in the M&E process. As such, this important component of the policy implementation had not reflected any meaningful break from the hitherto lacklustre trend. The text of the following IDI submission succinctly presents this stance:

> 'unlike other poverty alleviation programmes before it, NEEDS had laid more emphasis on human development in its initial proposition, however, it has unceremoniously gone the wrong way of all previous development policies in the country due to the usual weak bureaucratic structure involved in its M&E procedure.' (IDI, Female, Trader, 58 years, Ile-Ife, Nigeria, 13 May 2013)

Ostensibly, the NEEDS plan had been adjudged to be different from all previous plans ever targeted at poverty alleviation in the country. Such difference has been mainly noted at the level of policy advancement and not in its implementation process.

Specific findings of the study

1. While the NEEDS plan had presented a commendable platform for policy projections in Nigeria, its implementation frameworks have been largely dysfunctional. As such, it has been unable to contribute significantly to the process of poverty alleviation in the country since most of its set goals have remained unmet.
2. Aside from an apparent lack of political will on the part of the political class, extant bureaucratic structures in Nigeria have stifled the NEEDS in attaining any meaningful goals.
3. A clear departure from the conceptual goals of the NEEDS (as enabled by the MDG targets) has been noticed in the process of implementing policy goals related to the NEEDS.
4. The NEEDS plan was not an outright failure since it was able to achieve limited progress, notably in adult literacy and women empowerment. However, such achievements have been overshadowed by subsisting failure of significant targets of the plan.
5. Weakened CSOs have made a critical evaluation of the functionality of development frameworks like the NEEDS infeasible in Nigeria. An important factor in this regard has been the unwillingness of governments at all levels in the country to see the CSOs as partners in progress, rather than avoidable antagonists.

Recommendations

1. Independent and functional M&E mechanisms should be institutionalised vis-à-vis the process of policy implementation in Nigeria so that policy projection is no longer a problem for the country. Rather than utilising the same set of bureaucratic apparatuses that have inhibited related goals of previous development plans in the country, an objective M&E framework should be institutionalised.
2. Relevant reforms and regulations should be enabled in order to facilitate greater transparency and accountability in conducting government business in Nigeria. The secrecy that rules the business of governance has continued to present an antithesis to socio-economic progress in the country.
3. In post-2015 development planning and implementation Nigeria should not deviate from conceptual frameworks for policy implementation. The NEEDS has been routinely predicated upon a formidable framework; however, the process of implementing its goals has been in outright variance of such conceptual framework. Hence, the failure of the plan.

4. In subsequent policy implementation process in Nigeria, relative achievements of the NEEDS, for instance the success it has recorded in the aspects of adult literacy and women empowerment should be consolidated.

5. In order serve as imperative watchdogs for development policy projection and implementation in Nigeria, various international funding organisations should intervene to strengthen CSOs working in related areas in Nigeria. This has become necessary in view of the lack of readiness demonstrated by governments at various levels (local, state and federal) to partner with the CSOs in order to drive the society forward.

Concluding comments

While the need for such a policy framework for the NEEDS to address the challenges and threats posed by poverty and other social incongruence in Nigeria cannot be over-emphasised, there is an extant need for adequate and productive implementation of such within a tenable evaluative framework. This has become more imperative in light of the failure of related policy frameworks, such as the NEEDS plan. Against this affirmation, the role of a functional M&E mechanism has been emphasised. Various CSOs that work in related areas in Nigeria should be encouraged in terms of capacity building and financing, especially by notable international funding organisations.

In a nutshell, this chapter has presented various factors that have contributed to the inefficiency of the NEEDS (as a socio-economic development policy in Nigeria) in bringing a much-touted respite to suffering Nigerians. For instance, prevalent corruption of the political class, stifling bureaucracy, inactive CSOs and an uninformed citizenry have all been implicated.

Nevertheless, for subsequent policy projections in Nigeria to achieve related targets, such pitfalls as already espoused in the implementation of the NEEDS should be avoided while associated modest achievements as recorded by the policy should be explored productively.

References

Adeniran, AI, 2007, Africa and the evolving modernity, in O Akinwumi, OO Okpeh, CBN Ogbogbo, A Onoja (eds) *African indigenous science and knowledge system*, Abuja: Roots Books and Journal

Adeniran, AI, 2013, Gender ascriptions and morbid maternal mortality in Nigeria, Paper delivered at the *National Workshop on Meeting the Challenges of Implementing the National Reproductive Health Policy in*

Nigeria: The Role of Civil Society Organizations, 4–5 February, Benin City: Centre for Population and Development

Aigbokhan, BE, 2000, *Poverty, growth and inequality in Nigeria: A case study*, Kenya: African Economic Research Consortium

Brady, D, 2003, Rethinking the sociological measurement of poverty, *Social Forces*, March, 715–52

Dye, TR, 1998, *Understanding public policy*, Hillsdale, NJ: Prentice Hall

Evers, A, Pijl, M, Ungerson, C, 1994, *Payments for care: A comparative overview*, Aldershot: Avebury

FGN (Federal Government of Nigeria), 2001, *National Economic Empowerment and Development Strategy (NEEDS)*, Abuja: Federal Government of Nigeria

FOS (Federal Office of Statistics), 2000, *Incidence of poverty in Nigeria, 1980–1996*, Abuja: Federal Office of Statistics

Gans, HJ, 1995, *The war against the poor: The underclass and anti-poverty policy*, New York: Basic Books

Hill, M, 1996, *Social policy*, Upper Saddle River, NJ: Prentice Hall

Kamerman, SB, 1983, The mixed economy of welfare, *Social Work* 28, 5–11

Kohli, M, Rein, M, Guillemard, AM, Gunsteren, H, 1991, *Time for retirement: Comparative studies of early exit from the labour force*, Cambridge: Cambridge University Press

Marx, K, Engels F, 1848, *The Communist Manifesto*, Marx/Engels Selected Works, Vol 1, pp 98–137, Moscow: Progress Publishers, 1969

Mitchell, D, 1990, *Income transfers in ten welfare states*, Aldershot: Avebury

Moran, M, Wood, B, 1993, *State, regulation and the medical profession*, Milton Keynes: Open University Press

NPC (National Planning Commission), 2005, *National Economic and Empowerment Development Strategy*, Abuja: National Planning Commission

Offe, C, 1984, *Contradictions of the welfare state*, London: Hutchinson

Schaffer, RT, 2005, *Sociology* (9th edn), New York: Mc-Graw Hill

Smeeding, TM, O'Higgins, M, Rainwater, L, 1990, *Poverty, inequality and income distribution in comparative perspectives*, Hemel Hempstead; Harvester Wheatsheaf

Soludo, C, 2005, *NEEDS Report*, Abuja: Central Bank of Nigeria

UNDP (United Nations Development Programme), 2007, *Human Development Report*, New York: UNDP

UNDP (United Nations Development Programme), 2009, *Human Development Report*, New York: UNDP

UNDP (United Nations Development Programme), 2013, *Human Development Report*, New York: UNDP

Developmental crises affecting the United Nations' Millennium Development Goal achievements in Bangladesh: a critical perspective

Saleh Ahmed

Introduction

Bangladesh is one of the major developing countries in the Global South. In recent years, the country has played an important role in the changing pattern of regional peace, development and politics. The country has shown demonstrable progress based on different development indicators, such as reducing extreme poverty rates and hunger, ensuring universal primary education and decreasing the gender gap in education and the workforce.

Major development challenges, however, continue to affect the country's growth and development performance. Despite being culturally and racially homogenous in comparison to most of its neighbouring countries, a large portion of Bangladesh's population is still deprived of development efforts initiated by the government, non-governmental organisations and international agencies. In response to this issue, the government of Bangladesh and its agencies were actively involved from the beginning in framing, planning and implementing the Millennium Development Goals (MDGs) with the United Nations agencies in the local context.

The deadline for achieving the MDGs was 2015, and many countries and regions, including Bangladesh, fell short. What are the factors or crises that played a detrimental role in preventing MDG progress? In Bangladesh, the contributing factors were likely to have been its large poverty-stricken population, climate change, different types of natural disasters, confrontation politics, a negative financial and institutional capacity, heavy dependence on foreign aid, greater urban centralisation, weak civil society and global issues such as oil and food price increases. Economic recession in the west also had a tremendous impact on Bangladesh's chances of achieving the MDGs.

The findings of this chapter aim to contribute to public policy discourse on why not only Bangladesh, but also other countries with similar socio-economic and cultural contexts, did not achieve the MDG targets by the given deadline. Thus far, the development discourse has been muted on the importance of considering uncertainty factors that were likely to have jeopardised the pace of MDG progress. This chapter therefore provides a critical perspective on a country-specific development challenges and helps to refine our development thoughts and strategies for the future through the consideration of all possible challenges and uncertainties.

Background

For more than a decade, the MDGs were the major framework for international aid, cooperation and development initiatives at the local, national and international level. These goals were time-bound, aiming to reduce some of the world's major human development challenges by 2015. The goals were analytically grounded in the human development paradigm, and represented global commitments and compacts (Jahan, 2009). A number of contemporary global challenges, such as economic recession, commodity price increases and environmental degradation, made it difficult for some countries to achieve the MDGs by 2015. This was particularly true for the poor and marginalised populations in the Global South (Majid, 2009; Islam and Buckley, 2009; Sachs and McArthur, 2005; Chibba, 2011). Moving forward, these challenges have made it hard to predict the success of the post-2015 development framework (Fukuda-Parr, 2012).

This chapter focuses on development challenges in a low-income, developing country, specifically Bangladesh. The challenges faced within this country are likely to be similar to those in other geographical regions with comparable social, economic and political contexts. The chapter is structured as follows: first, the next section outlines the history, achievements and challenges of the MDGs; second, it analyses the challenges within the Bangladesh context; and finally, the chapter discusses the potential success of the post-2015 development framework considering all future challenges.

Facts of Millennium Development Goals

Theoretical background

To many, 'development' is raising peoples' living standards, along with industrialisation and/or scientific progress (Pieterse, 2009). Scholars have experienced a number of ideological transitions within the core arguments of 'development'. Today 'development' is very much synonymous with how we survive in the future, rather than emphasising how we improve on the past (McMichael, 2004). The notion of development has its origins from the colonial era, when Europeans began to develop systems of government and concentrated on the emerging national states, which were virtually industrial systems primarily driven by the products of colonial labour regimes (McMichael, 2004).

Modern development thinking has largely focused on economic growth. Industrialisation became the core component of development as illustrated by Rostow's *Stages of Economic Growth* in the 1960s. Later, the concept of development included modernisation, and development thinking encompassed economic growth with political modernisation, such as nation building (Pieterse, 2009). In the 1970s, new alternative development theories were introduced with a focus on social and community development, or what Friedmann (1992) identified as 'human flourishing'. The human dimension of development received further attention and focus, when Amartya Sen mentioned development as human capabilities, entitlements and freedoms (Sen, 1999). In subsequent years, Sen's work on capabilities, entitlements and freedoms became the foundation for the United Nations Development Programme's (UNDP) yearly flagship Human Development Report, where the 'enlargement of people's choices' became the central focus of the developmental approach (Pieterse, 2009). The concepts of development have revolved around human progress over time as illustrated in Table 12.1.

Development policy, however, is criticised for its excessive orientation towards 'a mainstream economics-based agenda' rather than towards 'the importance of social and political process and patterns of poverty' (Apthorpe, 1999). Development is an endless process, not the end (McMichael, 2004), and that implies that the MDGs are not static innovations. The concepts and the practices of development have gone through and will continue to go through a continuous process of metamorphosis in addressing contemporary global human and environmental challenges. The MDGs were the outcomes of decades' long international negotiations and initiatives of

Table 12.1: Meanings of development over time

Period	Perspective	Meaning of development
1800s	Classical political economy	Remedy for progress
1850>	Colonial economies	Resource management, trusteeship
1940>	Development economics	Economic growth – industrialisation
1950>	Modernisation theory	Growth, political and social modernisation
1960>	Dependency theory	Accumulation – national, autocentric
1970>	Alternative development	Human flourishing
1980>	Human development	Capacitation, enlargement of people's choices
1980>	Neoliberalism	Economic growth – structural reform, deregulation, liberalisation, privatisation
1990>	Post-development	Authoritarian engineering, disaster
2000	MDGs	Structural reforms

Source: Pieterse, 2009

global development frameworks, which were mostly initiated in the early 1970s (Nayyar, 2012).

The targets of the MDGs were focused on some of the major development challenges in the Global South, such as (i) eradicating extreme poverty and hunger; (ii) achieving universal primary education; (iii) promoting gender equality and empowering women; (iv) reducing child mortality; (v) improving maternal health; (vi) combating HIV/ AIDS, malaria and other diseases; (vii) ensuring environmental sustainability; and (viii) developing a global partnership for development (UN, 2012d). In total, the MDGs consisted of eight goals and 21 targets (UN, 2012d), and by signing them, world leaders promised to do everything possible to alleviate these human development challenges.

In some regions (or countries), the targets of the MDGs were achieved ahead of the deadline (UN, 2012e,h). Worldwide positive changes became visible in poverty reduction, universal primary schooling, gender equality, access to safe drinking water and upgrading the lives of slum dwellers in urban areas (UN, 2012b,g). On the global scale, declining trends in terms of child mortality, tuberculosis and deaths by malaria, as well as considerable developments in treatments for HIV victims were very much visible; however, these trends did not apply in every region (UN, 2012h).

The overall picture was disjointed with large variances across regions (Manning, 2009; UN, 2010b; UN, 2012b). Substantial progress was evident in many parts of the Global South, while a large portion of people in sub-Saharan Africa and South Asia were facing different developmental challenges (UN, 2012c; Hogan et al, 2010).

Achievements

The MDGs were a strong multi-lateral commitment to make meaningful change through concerted global efforts, mostly in the Global South. UN Secretary-General Ban Ki-moon described the progress achieved by highlighting the 20 per cent decrease in deaths related to malaria worldwide between 2000 and 2009; the 35 per cent drop in child mortality under the age of five years between 1990 and 2009; and the 21 per cent decrease in infections related to HIV/AIDS between 1997 and 2009 (Women Deliver, 2011). The World Bank (2016) added to these numbers by highlighting that the percentage of the world's population living on less than $1.90 a day was 10.7 per cent in 2013 compared to 12.4 per cent in 2012 and 35 per cent in 1990. Additionally, as of 2013, 767 million people were living on less than $1.90 a day, down from 881 million in 2012 and 1.85 billion in 1990.

Apart from this, the 35 least developed countries (LDCs), particularly the heavily indebted poor countries (HIPCs), received debt cancelations (Tribe and Lafon, 2009). Debt relief aided poor countries in addressing the spiral of debt, poverty and/or political and economic instability (Gautam, 2005). Evidence shows that the burden of debt can cause socio-political chaos and violence (Kaufman and Stallings, 1991). As a result, debt relief can aid countries in enhancing public spending on social sectors, such as education, maternal health, healthcare for HIV/AIDS victims, and to control diseases such as tuberculosis (Tribe and Lafon, 2009). The MDGs played an instrumental role in building regional financial and administrative capacities. This enhanced states' capability to manage different development projects, as well as build and/or reinforce the state's resiliency capacity in response to man-made or natural disasters.

Overall challenges

The core problem with the MDGs was the 58 countries, which according to Collier, were 'falling behind and often falling apart' (Collier, 2007, 3). He argued that the focus of the MDGs was misleading because 80 per cent of the world's poor were in the countries which were making progress, and not receiving MDG benefits as a result. According to Collier, the world should have focused on the bottom billion who live in those 58 countries (Collier, 2007).

Apart from this, there were a number of issues, which adversely affected the MDG targets. For example, most of the world's poor people in the Global South are marginalised farmers (Dixon and

Gulliver, 2001; IFAD, 2003). Without explicitly highlighting these people in the MDG framework, it was difficult for developing nations to accomplish the targets set by the MDGs. Therefore, smallholder farmers in the Global South should be at the core of the post-2015 implementation framework. Their livelihoods are heavily dependent on the production and distribution of agro-products (Bresnyan and Werbrouck, 2008). Access to fertilisers or the information relating to agro-markets was absent in MDG 1: End Poverty and Hunger. To end poverty and hunger worldwide, agricultural targets for poor farmers should be a critical component of the post-2015 implementation framework.

There was also a policy mismatch in MDG 2, where primary education and school enrollment were prioritised over other important education targets. As a result, issues such as learning outcomes, secondary and post-secondary education, or the quality of education were inadequately addressed. Primary education contributes to the basis for economic growth and societal progress, but secondary and post-secondary education contribute to sustaining growth and progress (Krueger and Lindahl, 2001). MDG 3 was also criticised due to its limited scope in addressing several gender specific issues, such as freedom from violence and adult literacy among women, particularly in the unprivileged poor rural communities.

Additionally, one of the most pressing challenges of contemporary human history, namely climate change, received an underwhelming level of attention within the MDG framework (Urban and Sumner, 2009). For the Pacific island small states, such as Samoa and Kiribati and other countries with low lying, long coastal regions such as the Maldives or Bangladesh, rising sea levels and/or extreme climate events can pose severe human risks (Adger et al, 2005; Barnett and Adger, 2003; UN, 2010a).

Often the positive outcomes due to poverty reduction in rate and in number in the aggregate level are criticised for actually being due to rapid economic growth in the Chinese Peninsula and India, where the world's largest share of poor populations reside (Curtis and Poon, 2009). Indeed, inadequate attention was paid in the MDGs to local and regional poverty dynamics. The MDGs also didn't properly address what makes some people and/or regions poorer than the other people or neighbouring regions and what factors contribute to poverty.

The MDGs were also criticised for being generic and, in many cases, for the targets being overly simplistic. They did not accommodate regional and local level dynamics or variations (Collier, 2007). For example, the UN wants to significantly decrease the global rate of child mortality, but the reality is that every area has different starting points. In sub-Saharan Africa child mortality is higher than in any part of the world (UN, 2012a,f). On the other hand, the rates of child mortality are far less in Latin America than any other region in the Global South (UN, 2012g). The same is true for aggregate poverty information. In recent decades, there has been a dramatic decrease in poverty rates in Southeast Asia (UNESCAP, 2007). This was mostly possible due to rapid economic growth on the Chinese Peninsula, which helped to lift 475 million people out of extreme poverty (UN, 2009). This success obscures a lack of progress elsewhere when analysed on an aggregate level.

Regional risks and vulnerabilities (for example, terrorist threats) always have tremendous influence on shaping the development landscape. Additionally, how a country is governed can play a vital role (Earle and Scott, 2010). At the national level, if the government and/or governance system are weak or if the state capacity to deliver services to its citizens is limited, then there is a higher chance of political instability that could block development efforts at the local or national level (Fosu, 1992). The socio-political chaos in Haiti illustrates the potential impacts of such a risk. Additionally, the MDGs failed to address uncertainties like sudden commodity price increases. Commodities and oil price increases push millions of people in low-income countries to further impoverishment and extreme poverty. These crises have tremendous implications, particularly for the eradication of poverty and hunger, maternal health and infant mortality (Islam and Buckley, 2009). Past research has also shown that food price increases can even cause political turmoil (Lagi et al, 2011).

In addition to food crises, the world also experienced a global financial crisis. This crisis not only affected aid flow from developed to low income developing and/or under-developed countries, but it also had an impact on remittance flows to the LDCs, which is one of the biggest sources of national income in places like Bangladesh, Haiti and India (Cali and Dell' Erba, 2009). Lower remittance flows had a negative impact on national and individual level spending on social services, such as health and education.

In the context of all these inter-connected issues and realities, it was a challenging task to achieve the MDG targets. However, if world leaders and the policy makers work to overcome the above challenges, it will aid in ensuring everyone has the ability to frame their own futures with honour and dignity.

The MDGs challenges in Bangladesh

Bangladesh's population is predominantly Muslim and its geography is largely low-lying riparian areas (Vaughn, 2010). Almost 98 per cent of the population are Bengali and the remaining 2 per cent comprises tribal populations and non–Bengali Muslims (CIA, 2016).

A large population, massive poverty, weak governance, poor infrastructure and different types of natural disasters, such as floods, cyclones and droughts, are among the major development challenges in Bangladesh (Streatfield and Karar, 2008; Kaufmann et al, 2000; Sobhan, 1998; World Bank, 2004). These undermined the country's ability to achieve the MDGs by the 2015 deadline. Since the very beginning of the MDGs, the government of Bangladesh was committed to this global effort to confront contemporary human challenges. It is important to mention that the major developmental challenges of Bangladesh are not unique to this country. Similar types of challenges abound in many parts of the Global South with similar social, political, economic and environmental conditions. Some of the major developmental challenges, which undermined Bangladesh's success with regards to the MDGs, are discussed below.

Population

According to the CIA Country Factbook, the current estimation (July, 2016) of Bangladesh's population is 156,186,882 (CIA, 2016). The majority of them are poor and not engaged in mainstream economic activities. To some extent they are dependent on government subsidies and are a burden on available, but extremely scarce public resources.

Often the state needs to subsidise food and energy along with many subsistence items to these large, poverty stricken populations. Public resources are often directed to support livelihood opportunities instead of investments in more productive sectors, such as infrastructure, industry, education and research. This undermines the country's potential for further growth and development, and contributed to Bangladesh's inability to achieve the targets of the MDGs. National policies and initiatives failed to engage these large populations in the mainstream workforce by providing different types of skill development training. In the end, these populations became a burden on the national economy. Thus, population size and growth in Bangladesh played an important role in shaping Bangladesh's MDG performance.

Poverty, inequality, hunger, poor health and education enrollments

Approximately 80 per cent of Bangladesh's population lives on less than $2 a day (Vaughn, 2010). This poverty contributes to hunger and hunger contributes to poor health. This, in turn, causes poor engagement with workforce services and poor production outcomes.

In Bangladesh, poverty levels differ between urban and rural areas, causing spatial poverty traps (Ahmed, 2008). For example, in southwest Bangladesh, different environmental impacts, such as rising sea levels, increased salinity in water and farmlands and seasonal cyclones, contribute to higher regional poverty levels.

The issue of developmental challenge can be discussed from another perspective. Poverty and education are very much intertwined. Low enrolment in primary schools and subsequent completion are concentrated not only in certain regions but also among certain segments of the population (for example, minority or ethnic groups) (Ahmed and Ypanaque, 2010). For traditionally culture rich countries such as Bangladesh, prejudices create unequal opportunities based on gender, ethnicity, income, language or disabilities (Ahmed and Ypanaque, 2010). These unequal opportunities become quite visible and create obstacles for the completion of MDGs, more so with regards to MDG 2 (Ahmed and Ypanaque, 2010). The global target for universal primary education (MDG 2), remains off-track. The critical challenge is readjusting their goals to target the bottom 10 per cent (Rahman and Islam, 2009). In Bangladesh, more than half of the children from the bottom two income quintiles never even enrolled in primary schools and students from lower unprivileged clusters of society are more unlikely to complete their schooling (Ahmed and Ypanaque, 2010). In the 1990s, demographic and health surveys showed that the improvements for access to basic education benefited mostly children from privileged families, while children from poor families experienced little or no improvement (Filmer and Pritchett, 1999).

The country moved forward to ensure universal primary education, but what about education opportunities among the ethnic minorities. Should the ethnic minorities need to study in their own languages or should they study in the official national language, Bangla? This is a big debate and the country needs to address this challenge.

Not only education, but differential health impacts are also visible among the rural and urban people. Medical facilities are more available in urban areas, but in the rural areas the availability of skilled physicians is rare, and that is true for other associated medical facilities. Infant mortality and maternal mortality is higher therefore in rural areas than urban areas (Ronsmans and Graham, 2006).

The impacts and benefits of UNMDGs should be equally distributed among all classes of people irrespective of their beliefs, ethnicity, location, social and economic status and so on. Otherwise development and developmental opportunities among specific classes or groups not only contribute to intergenerational inequality, but can also even generate further socio-political tensions in the community and at the national level.

Global environmental change

Bangladesh is one of the countries in the Global South, which is extensively and consistently suffers from global environmental change, more particularly from the adverse impacts of climate change. Right now with a population of more than 160 million in an area the size of Wisconsin, the country experiences sea-level rises and increasing tropical cyclones and floods. Nature, unfortunately, is not very friendly towards Bangladesh. Bangladesh's former Country Representative for the International Union for Conservation of Nature (IUCN), Dr Ainun Nishat once stated that 'We are nature's laboratory on disasters. We don't have volcanoes. But any other natural disasters you think of, we have it' (Inman, 2009). Climate change exacerbates these preexisting issues. It follows that climate change will contribute to the reversal of Bangladesh's social and economic growth. 'All of that [climate change impacts] combines to [make] a recipe for pretty horrific disaster,' was a point made by Dr A Atiq Rahman, Executive Director of the Bangladesh Centre for Advanced Studies and one of the lead authors on the recent report of the Intergovernmental Panel on Climate Change (Inman, 2009).

Natural disasters are common phenomena in Bangladesh. These disasters make poor people vulnerable to different structural risks. People become even poorer by extensive exposure to these natural disasters. Bangladesh is already a disaster-prone country and every year the country is exposed to floods, torrential rains, erosions and cyclones (Government of Bangladesh, 2008). Currently, due to the impacts from a changing global environment, the country is experiencing increasing trends in terms of tropical cyclones and other natural disasters.

On 15 November 2007, Cyclone Sidr struck the coastal region of Bangladesh before moving to inland areas. From human deaths to disrupting local, regional and national economics and affected social conditions, Sidr caused considerable destruction (Government of Bangladesh, 2008). Poor, marginalised people were the major victims of this cyclone (see Table 12.2).

These impacts were visible in a large area, not only in the coastal region, but also the inland of Bangladesh. Joint damage, loss and needs assessment by different national and international aid agencies estimated that there were also some spatial variances of the disaster impacts. The coastal regions were affected more severely than the inland communities.

Whatever the spatial variances of this natural disaster, it is important to note that for a low-income developing country like Bangladesh, tropical cyclones such as Sidr can have an adversely impact on the national economy. For rehabilitation and reconstruction, the government must re-focus their investments in the cyclone affected regions. Redirecting investments for rehabilitation and reconstruction can deflect attention away from development programmes such as the MDGs.

Table 12.2: Overall summary of damages and losses from Cyclone Sidr

Sector	Sub-sector	Disaster effects		
		Damage	Losses	Total
Social sectors		65.0	21.1	86.0
	Health and nutrition	2.4	15.0	17.5
	Education	62.5	6.0	68.5
Infrastructure		1,029.9	30.9	1,060.8
	Housing	839.3	–	839.3
	Transport	116.0	25.0	141.0
	Electricity	8.3	5.2	13.6
	Water and sanitation	2.3	0.7	2.9
	Urban and municipal	24.6	–	24.6
	Water resource control	71.3	–	71.3
Productive sector		25.1	465.0	490.1
	Agriculture	21.3	416.3	437.6
	Industry	3.8	29.5	33.3
	Commerce	–	18.2	18.2
	Tourism	–	0.9	0.9
Cross-cutting issues		6.1	0.0	6.1
	Environment	6.1	–	6.1
Total		1,158.0	516.9	1,674.9

Source: Government of Bangladesh, 2008

Poor governance and confrontational politics

The political landscape is fairly complex in Bangladesh and intertwined with many social, economic and environmental determinants. The country suffers due to its poor governance and lack of institutional capacity. The present governance structure is heavily influenced by the country's colonial heritage. The purpose of colonial administration was its own preservation, and the preservation of its status of distinctness and detachment from the people whom they ruled (Mehrotra, 2008). The postcolonial state was superimposed on the structure of the colonial state (Mehrotra, 2008), and was born through the euphoric enthusiasm of developmentalism (Heller, 2001). However, in the post-colonial era, many of the countries in the Global South failed to accomplish the goals of human development. Bangladesh is one of those countries, where still the trajectory of development is in flux, mostly due to the absence of good governance and the presence of confrontational politics (see Figure 12.1).

Bangladesh's weak political culture is often criticised for its high levels of corruption. Weak democratic practices have been always subject to pressure from the military (Vaughn, 2010). An absence of good governance and democratic practice undermine the country's development potential (Davis and McGregor, 2000; Karim and Fair, 2007).

Politically motivated communal and ethnic violence

Politically motivated communal and ethnic violence are common in Bangladesh. These types of violence can create further development obstacles in particular communities or ethnic groups. It is particularly true for the religious minorities in remote rural areas (for example, Hindus in the local context) and in the hill regions among the ethnic minorities. It is therefore very important to observe how one particular community or ethnic group is performing compared to others with regards to the development targets. Aggregate information on a particular region is misleading in terms of assessing MDG success for any specific community or ethnic minority group.

Weak civil society

In every country, civil society plays an important role and contributes to the country's governance, development and enlightenment. However, as democracy is weak in Bangladesh, its civil society faces

Figure 12.1: Governance indicators in Bangladesh

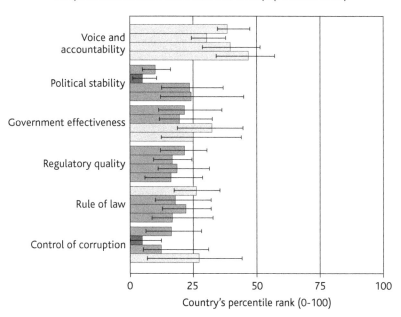

BANGLADESH
Comparison between 2010, 2005, 2000, 1996 (top-bottom order)

Country's percentile rank (0-100)

Note: The governance indicators presented here aggregate the views on the quality of governance provided by a large number of enterprise, citizen and expert survey respondents in industrial and developing countries. These data are gathered from a number of survey institutes, think tanks, non-governmental organisations and international organisations.

Source: Author's online calculation from World Governance Index

various challenges. The government sees the civil society as a threat to them, causing civil society to exist in a submissive environment. Due to the absence of strong civil society, the ruling party and political opponents are rarely questioned by civil society for their activities and responsibilities to Bangladeshi citizens. It might be difficult to link the relationship between strong civil society and MDG performance, yet it is important to note that without a strong civil society, it is more difficult for countries to achieve higher levels of accountability, transparency and pro-poor outcomes with any development agenda.

Cross-border water issues

Cross-border water issues are another important developmental challenge for the country. Bangladesh usually experiences water shortages during the summer season as most of the water flows come from upstream countries. In recent years, water shortages have generated political tensions among the countries in the region.

It is important to remember that Bangladesh is a densely-populated country. The majority of the population live in rural areas and are dependent on agriculture. In most cases, they use traditional agriculture practices and depend heavily on the weather.

Shortages of water can contribute to decreases in agriculture production, which can contribute to regional food insecurity, hunger and poor health, as well as contribute to increased levels of poverty. Therefore, low water flow from upstream countries can directly contribute to Bangladesh's achievements with regards to development targets.

Unstable economy

Bangladesh's economy is closely linked with the global economy. If there is economic recession in the Global North, then the national economy is also affected. A large number of Bangladeshi citizens live abroad and send remittances, making it a major share of country's income. This can be severely affected by the economic recession, particularly in the western developed nations. Global economic recession can also contribute to lower aid flows, fewer foreign direct investments and fewer exports to developed nations. Together, these global impacts can adversely affect national spending on social sectors, such as education, health and national safety nets. Therefore, an unstable international economy can have a significant impact on development progress.

Apart from the above-mentioned issues, aid dependency, lack of decentralisation, development inequality among ethnic minorities, and oil and food price increases can adversely affect development progress. Many of us can recall the oil and food price increase in 2007–08. This affected a large portion of the world's population in many regions of the Global South by aggravating poverty, hunger, malnutrition and political turmoil in many developing nations. Bangladesh is one of the countries that faced challenges due to the oil and food price increase.

Conclusion

While creating development policy and frameworks, policy makers often pay little attention to uncertainty factors and their ability to affect desired outcomes. These uncertainty factors are becoming more significant than ever for many of the countries in the Global South.

In the media or in the academic literature, the tendency is to focus on MDG success stories. However, many of these success stories do not necessarily address the failed attempts, challenges or difficulties of achieving these goals. It is therefore important to address those challenges. If policy makers at both the national and international level can learn from these challenges, the future of development policy will be less susceptible to future developmental risks and vulnerabilities.

Right now, countries such as Bangladesh are confronting different types of uncertainties, which jeopardised the country's efforts to achieve the MDG targets. However, at the same time, these 'country-level' challenges offer us renewed perspectives on why some countries or regions failed to achieve their MDG targets. They highlight what needs to be done by the global society, government and the local community to avoid similar challenges or uncertainties to achieve future development goals and targets.

References

Adger, WN, Hughes, TP, Folke, C, Carpenter, SR, Rockstrom, J, 2005, Social-ecological resilience to coastal disasters, *Science* 309, 1036–9

Ahmed, S, 2008, *Impacts of rural road infrastructure among most disadvantaged groups: An explorative scenario analysis from southwestern Bangladesh*, Unpublished Masters' Thesis, Stockholm: The Royal Institute of Technology

Ahmed, S, Ypanaque, PJM, 2010, Achieving United Nations Millennium Development Goals by 2015: A comparative performance assessment of Bangladesh and Peru, *Journal of Bangladesh Institute of Planners* 3, 77–88

Apthorpe, R, 1999, Development Studies and Policy Studies: In the short run we are all dead, *Journal of International Development* 11, 535–46

Barnett, J, Adger, WN, 2003, Climate dangers and Atoll countries, *Climate Change* 61, 321–37

Bresnyan, E, Werbrouck, P, 2008, Value chains and small farmer integration, *World Development Report Agriculture for Development, Latin America and the Caribbean Region (LCR) series*, Washington, DC: World Bank, www-wds.worldbank.org/external/default/WDSContentServer/WDSP/IB/2012/06/07/000333037_20120607010752/Rendered/PDF/693840BRI0P1100sed06060201200Agri05.pdf

Cali, M, Dell'Erba, S, 2009, The global financial crisis and remittances: What past evidence suggests, *Overseas Development Institute (ODI) Working Paper* 303, London: Overseas Development Institute, www.odi.org.uk/sites/odi.org.uk/files/odi-assets/publications-opinion-files/4408.pdf

Chibba, M, 2011, The Millennium Development Goals: Key current issues and challenges, *Development Policy Review* 29, 1, 75–90

CIA (Central Intelligence Agency), 2016, *The World Factbook: Bangladesh*, www.cia.gov/library/publications/the-world-factbook/geos/bg.html

Collier, P, 2007, *The bottom billion: Why the poorest countries are failing and what can be done about it*, Oxford: Oxford University Press

Curtis, D, Poon, Y, 2009, Why a managerialist pursuit will not necessarily lead to achievement of MDGs, *Development in Practice* 19, 7, 837–48

Davis, PR, McGregor, J, 2000, Civil society, international donors and poverty in Bangladesh, *Commonwealth and Comparative Politics* 38, 1, 47–64

Dixon, J, Gulliver, A, 2001, *Farming systems and poverty: Improving farmers' livelihoods in a changing world*, Rome: Food and Agriculture Organization (FAO) and World Bank, ftp://ftp.fao.org/docrep/fao/003/y1860e/y1860e.pdf

Droege, S, 2010, *International climate policy: Priorities of key negotiating parties*, Berlin: Stiftung Wissenschaft und Politik

Earle, L, Scott, Z, 2010, *Assessing the evidence of the impact of governance on development outcomes and poverty reduction*, www.gsdrc.org/docs/open/EIRS9.pdf

Filmer, D, Pritchett, L, 1999, The effect of household wealth on educational attainment: evidence from 35 countries, *Population and Development Review* 25, 1, 85–120

Fosu, AK, 1992, Political instability and economic growth: Evidence from sub-Saharan Africa, *Economic Development and Cultural Change* 40, 4, 829–41

Friedmann, J, 1992, *Empowerment: The politics of alternative development*, Oxford: Blackwell Publishers

Fukuda-Parr, S, 2012, Should global goal setting continue, and how, in the post-2015 era?, *United Nations Department of Economic and Social Affairs (UN DESA) Working Paper* 117, ST/ESA/2012/DWP/117, New York: UN, www.un.org/esa/desa/papers/2012/wp117_2012.pdf

Gautam, M, 2005, *Debt relief for the poorest: An OED review of the HIPC initiative*, Washington, DC: The International Bank for Reconstruction and Development and World Bank, http://siteresources.worldbank.org/IDA/Resources/HIPC_OED_review.pdf

Government of Bangladesh, 2008, *Cyclone Sidr in Bangladesh: Damage, loss and needs assessment for disaster recovery and reconstruction*, Dhaka: Government of Bangladesh

Heller, P, 2001, Moving the state: The politics of democratic decentralization in Kerala, South Africa, and Porto Alegre, *Politics and Society* 29, 1, 131–63

Hogan, M, Foreman, KJ, Naghavi, M, Ahn, SY, Wang, M, Makela, SM, Lopez, AD, Lozano, R, Murray, CJL, 2010, Maternal mortality for 181 countries, 1980–2008: A systematic analysis of progress towards Millennium Development Goal 5, *The Lancet* 375, 9726, 1609–23

IFAD (International Fund for Agriculture Development), 2003, *Achieving the Millennium Development Goals by enabling the rural poor to overcome their poverty*. Rome: IFAD, www.ifad.org/gbdocs/gc/26/e/panel.pdf

Inman, M, 2009, Where warming hits hard, *Nature Reports Climate Change* 15 January, www.nature.com/climate/2009/0902/full/climate.2009.3.html

Islam, AS, 2006, The predicament of democratic consolidation in Bangladesh, *Bangladesh e-journal of sociology* 3, 2, www.bangladeshsociology.org/BEJS%203.2%20Sardar.pdf

Islam, R, Buckley, G, 2009, Rising food prices and their implications for employment, decent work and poverty reduction, *International Labour Office (ILO) Employment Working Paper* 30, www.ilo.org/wcmsp5/groups/public/–-ed_emp/documents/publication/wcms_108535.pdf

Jahan, S, 2009, The Millennium Development Goals beyond 2015, *IDS Bulletin* 41, 1, 51–9

Karim, TA, Fair, CC, 2007, *Bangladesh at the crossroads*, www.usip.org/sites/default/files/resources/sr181.pdf

Kaufmann, D, Kraay, A, Mastruzzi, M, 2010, *The Worldwide Governance Indicators: Methodology and analytical Issues*, The Worldwide Governance Indicators (WGI) project, Washington, DC: World Bank, http://info.worldbank.org/governance/wgi/

Kaufmann, D, Kraay, A, Zoido-Lobaton, P, 2000, Governance matters: From measurement to action, *Finance and Development: A Quarterly Magazine of the IMF* 32, 2, www.imf.org/external/pubs/ft/fandd/2000/06/kauf.htm

Kaufman, RR, Stallings, B, 1991, The political economy of Latin American populism, in R Dornbusch, S Edwards (eds) *The Macroeconomics of Populism in Latin America*, pp 15–43, Chicago, IL: University of Chicago Press

Khan, MM, 1997, Urban local governance in Bangladesh, in N Islam, MM Khan (eds) *Urban Governance in Bangladesh and Pakistan*, Dhaka: Centre for Urban Studies

Krueger, AB, Lindahl, M, 2001, Education for Growth: Why and for whom?, *Journal of Economic Literature* XXXIX: 1101–36

Lagi, M, Bertrand, KZ, Bar-Yam, Y, 2011, The food crises and political instability in North Africa and the Middle East, *Physics and Society*, arXiv:1108.2455v1

McMichael, P, 2004, *Development and social change: A global perspective*, Thousand Oaks, CA, London and New Delhi: Pine Forge Press

Majid, N, 2009, The global recession and developing countries, *Employment Working Paper* N 40, International Labour Organization (ILO) Employment Sector, Geneva: ILO, www.ilo.org/wcmsp5/groups/public/–-ed_emp/–-emp_elm/–-analysis/documents/publication/wcm_041819.pdf

Manning, R, 2009, *Using indicators to encourage development: Lessons from the Millennium Development Goals*, Copenhagen: Danish Institute for International Studies

Mehrotra, S, 2008, Democracy, decentralization and access to basic services: An elaboration of Sen's capability approach, in F Comim, M Qizilbash, S Alkire (eds) *The capability approach: Concepts, measures and applications*, pp 385–420, Cambridge: Cambridge University Press

Najam, A, Huq, S, Sokona, Y, 2003, Climate negotiations beyond Kyoto: Developing countries concerns and interests, *Climate Policy* 3, 221–31

Nayyar, D, 2012, *The MDGs after 2015: Some reflections on the possibilities*, www.un.org/millenniumgoals/pdf/deepak_nayyar_Aug.pdf

Pieterse, JN, 2009, *Development theory: Deconstructions/reconstructions*, London: Sage

Rahman, MdO, Islam, MT, 2009, Universal Primary Education for All towards Millennium Development Goal 2: Bangladesh perspective, *Journal of Health Management* 11, 2, 405–18

Rahaman, MR, 2007, Origins and pitfalls of confrontational politics in Bangladesh, *South Asian Survey* 14, 101–15

Ronsmans, C, Graham, WJ, 2006, Maternal mortality: Who, when, where and why?, *Lancet* 368, 1189–200

Sachs, J, McArthur, JW, 2005, The Millennium Project: A plan for meeting the Millennium Development Goals, *Lancet* 365, 347–53

Sen, AK, 1999, *Development as Freedoms*, Oxford: Oxford University Press

Sobhan, R, 1998, How bad governance impedes poverty alleviation in Bangladesh, *OECD Development Centre*, www.oecd-ilibrary.org/development/how-bad-governance-impedes-poverty-alleviation-in-bangladesh_466441620275

Streatfield, PK, Karar, ZA, 2008, Population challenges for Bangladesh in the coming decades, *Journal of Health, Population and Nutrition* 26, 3, 261–72

Sumner, A, Tiwari, M, 2009, After 2015: What are the ingredients of an 'MDG-Plus' agenda for poverty reduction?, *Journal of International Development* 21, 834–43

Tribe, M, Lafon, A, 2009, After 2015: Promoting pro-poor policy after the MDGs: The Plenary Presentations and Discussion, *After 2015: Promoting Pro-Poor Policy after the MDGS, Report on the EADI–DSA–IDS–ActionAid–DIFID High Level Policy Forum*, June 2009, www.researchgate.net/publication/237540076_After_2015_Promoting_Pro-Poor_Policy_after_the_MDGS_-_The_Plenary_Presentations_and_Discussion

UN (United Nations), 2009, *The Millennium Development Goals Report 2009*, New York: UN, www.un.org/millenniumgoals/pdf/MDG_Report_2009_ENG.pdf,

UN (United Nations), 2010a, *The Millennium Development Goals Report 2010*, New York: UN, www.un.org/millenniumgoals/pdf/MDG%20Report%202010%20En%20r15%20-low%20res%2020100615%20-.pdf

UN (United Nations), 2010b, *Keeping the Promise: United to achieve the Millennium Development Goals*, New York: United Nations, www.un.org/en/mdg/summit2010/pdf/mdg%20outcome%20document.pdf

UN (United Nations), 2012a, Ban names high-level panel to map out 'bold' vision for future global development efforts, *UN News Centre*, www.un.org/apps/news/story.asp?NewsID=42597&Cr=mdgs&Cr1#.UkzTS4ashcY

UN (United Nations), 2012b, *Realizing the future we want for all: Report to the Secretary-General, UN system Task Team on the Post-2015 UN Development Agenda*, www.un.org/millenniumgoals/pdf/Post_2015_UNTTreport.pdf

UN (United Nations), 2012c, Targeting efforts to meet MDGs expectations, *DESA News*, www.un.org/en/development/desa/docs/newsletter/desa-news/DESANewsJuly2012.pdf

UN (United Nations), 2012d, *The official United Nations site for the MDG Indicators*, http://mdgs.un.org/unsd/mdg/

UN (United Nations), 2012e, *The Millennium Development Goals Report 2012*, New York: United Nations, www.un.org/millenniumgoals/pdf/MDG%20Report%202012.pdf

UN (United Nations), 2012f, Rio+20: Ban urges world leaders to build on sustainable development commitments, *UN News Centre*, www.un.org/apps/news/story.asp?NewsID=42315#.UkzWTYashcY

UN (United Nations), 2012g, *World economic situation and prospects 2012: Global economic outlook*, www.un.org/en/development/desa/policy/wesp/wesp_current/2012wesp_prerel.pdf

UN (United Nations), 2012h, *The Millennium Development Goals: 2012 Progress Chart*, http://mdgs.un.org/unsd/mdg/Resources/Static/Products/Progress2012/Progress_E.pdf

UNCSD (UN Conference on Sustainable Development), 2012, Current ideas on Sustainable Development Goals and Indicators, *UNCSD Briefs* 6, https://sustainabledevelopment.un.org/index.php?page=view&type=400&nr=327&menu=35

UNESCAP (UN Economic and Social Commission for Asia and the Pacific), 2007, *Persistent and emerging issues in rural poverty reduction*, Bangkok: UNESCAP

Urban, F, Sumner, A, 2009, After 2015: Pro-poor low carbon development, *IDS in Focus Policy Briefing* 9, 4, http://opendocs.ids.ac.uk/opendocs/bitstream/handle/123456789/2527/After%202015%20-%20IDS%20in%20Focus%2009.pdf?sequence=1

Vaughn, B, 2010, *Bangladesh: Political and strategic developments and US interests*, Washington, DC: Congressional Research Service (CRS) Report for Congress, www.fas.org/sgp/crs/row/R41194.pdf

Women Deliver, 2011, 2015+: What happens to the Millennium Development Goals when they expire?, http://archive.womendeliver.org/updates/entry/2015-what-happens-to-the-millennium-development-goals-when-they-expire

World Bank, 2004, *Understanding the economic and financial impacts of natural disasters*, Washington, DC: World Bank, https://openknowledge.worldbank.org/handle/10986/15025

World Bank, 2013, *Bangladesh reduced number of poor by 16 million in a decade*, www.worldbank.org/en/news/press-release/2013/06/20/bangladesh-reduced-number-of-poor-by-16-million-in-a-decade

World Bank, 2016, *Poverty: Overview*, Washington, DC: World Bank, www.worldbank.org/en/topic/poverty/overview

Between progress, stasis and reversals: an analysis of the Millennium Development Goals in Nigeria

Olabanji Akinola

Introduction

The turn of the twenty-first century witnessed a renewed attempt by world leaders to significantly reduce global poverty by 2015. This renewed attempt came in the form of the Millennium Development Goals (MDGs) with the view to halting the global rise of hunger, illiteracy and diseases. However, while the MDGs have succeeded in serving as the reference point in the fight against global poverty, various stakeholders in developing and developed countries replaced the MDGs with the newly launched Sustainable Development Goals (SDGs) in 2015. The reformulation of the MDGs into the SDGs is partly a reflection of the reality that some of the MDG targets, and in some countries most of the targets, were, unfortunately, unmet by the 2015 MDGs deadline. Among other issues, problems associated with the global food, fuel and financial crises of 2007/2008 as well as domestic insecurity and instability in some countries affected the outcomes of the MDGs. Nonetheless, when put together, these factors, in combination with a number of other political, economic and social issues, explain the failures of meeting the MDG targets in Nigeria.

To this end, this chapter analyses Nigeria's efforts and failures to achieve the MDGs by 2015. The chapter mainly argues that the journey of the MDGs in Nigeria was a chequered one characterised by little progress, considerable stasis and undeniable reversals in some parts of the country. It maintains that when examined synoptically, Nigeria's experience with the MDGs reveals important issues that need to be addressed in order for the country to achieve the SDGs by 2030.

As the chapter explains, issues relating to ineffective implementation strategies, poor state capacity and corruption, all contributed to the poor performance recorded in achieving the MDGs in Nigeria. Consequently, the chapter maintains it is imperative for governments at all levels in Nigeria (federal, states and local), the private sector and civil society, to address some of these problems. What is more important, and within the context of moving towards achieving the SDGs, the chapter situates Nigeria's experience with the MDGs within the broader context of the country's political, socio-economic and developmental challenges. These include, but are not limited to, the prevalence of bad governance and economic mismanagement. Overcoming these challenges will be necessary for Nigeria's poverty reduction and sustainable development efforts in the coming years.

The chapter proceeds in three sections. The first section provides a synoptic overview of the journey of the MDGs in Nigeria. The section highlights some of the efforts made by Nigerian governments at different levels to achieve the MDGs amid many socio-economic and political challenges. The second section discusses the challenges associated with achieving the MDGs in Nigeria as defined by (i) ineffective and incoherent implementation framework and strategies and (ii) pervasive corruption in the country. The third section examines some recommendations for overcoming the current challenges in relation to future poverty reduction and development strategies in Nigeria. These recommendations address the role of state and non-state actors in repositioning Nigeria for sustainable progress on poverty reduction and development. The chapter then concludes that, although Nigeria's performance with the MDGs has been woeful, given the right policies and programmes, as well as improved state capacity, the country can rise above the current challenges and achieve better outcomes with the SDGs. The analysis provided in this chapter is supported by research findings obtained during six months of fieldwork conducted in Nigeria between May and October 2013. Some of the information provided were obtained through one-on-one interviews and archival research on issues relating to poverty reduction among vulnerable people in the country.

Nigeria and the MDGs: a synoptic overview

The MDGs were created in recognition of the need to ensure socio-economic development and reduce the spread of poverty. Thus, Hulme (2007, 2) notes, the MDGs were 'the world's biggest promise – a global agreement to reduce poverty at historically unprecedented rates through collaborative global action' around results-based management and human development ideas. The eight MDGs were announced in 2000 at the Millennium Declaration during a meeting of various heads of states and governments at the United Nations headquarters in New York. They included the following: (i) eradicate extreme poverty and hunger; (ii) achieve universal primary education; (iii) promote gender equality and empower women; (iv) reduce child mortality; (v) improve maternal health; (vi) combat HIV/AIDS, malaria and other diseases; (vii) ensure environmental sustainability; and (viii) develop a global partnership for development. Coincidentally, the announcement of the MDGs happened just over a year after Nigeria returned to democratic rule in 1999. The window of political opportunity offered by the return to democratic rule was, therefore, critical to Nigeria's engagement in the world.

Having been made a pariah state by the international community due to its suspension during military rule from organisations such as the Commonwealth, Nigeria's crisis of poverty and underdevelopment at the turn of the century caused many citizens to live below the poverty line. Despite the country's enormous human, natural and material resources, the country's social indicators, especially those relating to life expectancy at birth, literacy rates and per capita income had fallen by 1999 due to poor economic management and political leadership. Thus, the timing of the MDGs was an opportunity for Nigeria to reverse its fortunes as a country and the newly elected civilian President Olusegun Obasanjo expressed his readiness to lead the country to prosperity. During his inaugural speech on 29 May 1999, President Olusegun Obasanjo noted that,

> Nigeria is wonderfully endowed by the Almighty with human and other resources. It does no credit either to us or the entire black race if we fail in managing our resources for quick improvement in the quality of life of our people. Instead of progress and development, which we are entitled to expect from those who governed us, we experienced in the last decade and a half, a[nd] particularly in the last regime but one, persistent deterioration in the quality of governance, leading to instability and the weakening of all public institutions.[1]

Unsurprisingly, in his bid to reintegrate Nigeria back into the comity of nations, President Olusegun Obasanjo was one of the heads of states and governments who signed the Millennium Declaration that ushered in the MDGs in 2000. To be sure, the living conditions in Nigeria in 1999 were very bad. The United Nations Human Development Report of 1999 ranked Nigeria among countries with low human development. Ranked 146th out of 174 countries, the country's per capita income was US $920, the adult literacy rate was 59.5 per cent, and the life expectancy for women and men was 51.5 and 48.7 years respectively (UNDP, 1999, 136). Moreover, according to the World Bank's 2000/2001 World Development Report, the percentage of Nigerians living below $1 per day was estimated to be 70.2 per cent (World Bank, 2001, 281). The latter figure, when compared to a poverty rate of approximately 28 per cent in 1980 (NPC, 2004; Olaniyan and Bankole, 2005; British Council Nigeria, 2012), suggests Nigeria's development had greatly worsened within two decades. The country's ranking as the most corrupt country in the world in 1997 and 2000 by Transparency International (TI) on its annual Corruption Perception Index reports (TI, 1997; 2000) provides part of the explanation for Nigeria's reversal of fortunes.

During his first tenure as President (1999–2003), President Obasanjo embarked on a series of international trips to lobby the international community for debt relief of Nigeria's approximately $30 billion external debt as at 2000 (Okonjo-Iweala, 2012, 5). In order to effectively tackle the issues of poverty and underdevelopment, especially in relation to critical sectors such as education, health, agriculture and public infrastructure, the Nigerian government at the federal level pursued the debt relief agenda vigorously until it secured some debt relief from leading debtors such as the Paris club in 2005. More so, in its efforts to pursue a neoliberal economic agenda, the federal government adopted the World Bank's Poverty Reduction Strategy Paper (PRSP) for Nigeria and subsequently developed a version of the PRSP for its own development programme, the National Economic Empowerment and Development Strategy (NEEDS) in 2004.[2] This was launched a year after the President secured a second term in office in 2003. Being a federation with 36 sub-national states and 774 local governments, the individual states and local governments were encouraged by the federal government to develop their own state and local government versions of NEEDS. Hence, various states and local governments launched the State Economic Empowerment and Development Strategies (SEEDS) and Local Economic Empowerment and Development Strategies (LEEDS) across the federation.

Following the NEEDS model, the SEEDS and LEEDS were designed to develop the economies of states and local governments by encouraging private sector involvement and developing programmes that contribute to the four goals of NEEDS which were wealth creation, employment generation, poverty reduction and value reorientation (NPC, 2004). Other than the overall attempt to develop Nigeria through NEEDS and limited MDGs related interventions across the country, it is important to note that there was no specific national implementation framework in Nigeria until 2005 when the Office of the Senior Special Assistant to the President on the MDGs (OSSAP-MDGs) was created.[3] This perhaps was partially due to the belief that NEEDS would be enough to overcome the development challenges of the country and the fact that the government at that time required some debt relief in order to leverage resources to finance the MDGs. Essentially, NEEDS was designed to improve the macroeconomic environment in Nigeria with the hope that this would generate economic growth and the benefits would 'trickle down' to the population.

As part of the efforts to improve the macroeconomic framework of the country, the government sought to encourage more private sector involvement in the management of the economy based on free market principles and policies such as privatisation, deregulation and liberalisation. But these policies did not depart from some of those implemented during the Structural Adjustment Programmes (SAPs) in the 1980s and 1990s under the direction of the International Monetary Fund (IMF) and World Bank. Nigeria commenced the implementation of SAP in 1986 under the regime of General Ibrahim Babangida who was Nigeria's military head of state and president between 1985 and 1993. Among the major elements of the SAPs in Nigeria were the privatisation of formerly owned state enterprises, deregulation and trade liberalisation. Unfortunately, Nigeria's experience in implementing its SAP in the 1980s was riddled with corruption and mismanagement leading to unsuccessful programmes and policies which were designed to produce economic and social development for Nigerian citizens.

Furthermore, although the federal government did launch interventionists' programmes, such as the Universal Basic Education (UBE) programme in 1999 and created the National Poverty Eradication Programme (NAPEP) in 2001 for the purposes of improving literacy and reducing poverty respectively, these interventions were not significant departures from the past. Like the various interventions under the military, these new interventions have had limited effects. Notably, the military governments of Generals Ibrahim Babangida (1985–93) and Sani Abacha (1993–98) introduced various poverty alleviation programmes such as the Better Life Programme and Family

Economic and Advancement Programme. More so, the Babangida regime created the Directorate of Food, Roads and Rural Infrastructure (DFRRI) to focus on poverty reduction and rural development. But in light of their inability to raise the living standards of many Nigerians, the failures of these intervention programmes, as well as those of the agencies created by different governments to tackle poverty in Nigeria, have contributed to the high rates of poverty in the country. More so, considering governments at different levels in Nigeria do not have adequate capacity to implement programmes, implementing these interventions in a three-tiered federal state not only affected the pre-MDGs interventions but significantly affected the progress of the country after the MDGs were introduced.

There was nonetheless a boost for the achievement of MDGs in Nigeria when the country secured debt relief of $18 billion in 2005 from the Paris Club as it encouraged the federal government to create the OSSAP-MDGs in 2005 to oversee Nigeria's strategy for achieving the MDGs (SPARC, 2013). As mentioned earlier, the main attempt to achieve the MDGs before the creation of OSSAP-MDGs was the NEEDS initiative. Thus, the creation of the OSSAP-MDGs within the Presidency was a major step to directly address the coordination and organisational problems related to achieving the MDGs. The office was established to serve as a secretariat to the Presidential Committee on the Assessment and Monitoring of the MDGs, and a Senior Special Assistant, appointed directly by the President of Nigeria, heads the office. The debt relief of 2005 freed some $1 billion that would have been used to service Nigeria's debt annually (SPARC, 2013). The $1 billion saving, known as the debt relief gain (DRG), was preconditioned by the creditors to be put towards supporting poverty eradication and other pro-poor programmes in the country (SPARC, 2013).

Having realised the immense difficulties of attempting to implement federal government projects all over the country without the involvement of states and local governments, the OSSAP-MDGs established a Conditional Grant Scheme (CGS) in 2007 for states and local governments to provide matching grants for shared projects (SPARC, 2013). The CGS operates based on the 'buy in' of states and local governments who submit proposals for projects that they intend to implement in relation to the MDGs every year. But this is premised on the condition that the OSSAP-MDGs only provides additional matching grants for states and local governments that already have 50 per cent of the estimated funds in place for the proposed project, programme or policy.[4] The CGS was adopted in order to ensure that the states and local governments utilise their local expertise to determine priority areas for intervention. In addition, it was determined that to better develop and implement programmes, states and local governments are more likely to have a sense of ownership over the programmes if they invest some of their own financial resources. Programmes and projects that are MDG-related, like the construction of schools, hospitals and boreholes or other social amenities in communities, could qualify for counterpart funding arrangements between the OSSAP-MDGs and state and local governments.

The OSSAP-MDGs funds other programmes through national and state agencies such as NAPEP's conditional cash transfer (CCT) programme called 'In Care of the People' (COPE) in states and local governments as well. The first phase of COPE implementation involved 12 states in the federation (NAPEP, 2007). Subsequent phases have since been implemented in different states. Also, the OSSAP-MDGs in 2008 introduced a 'Quick Wins' initiative defined as special intervention projects in various parts of the country identified by national parliamentarians in their local constituencies for urgent intervention. Essentially, with the Quick Wins initiative, every Senator and Member of the House of Representatives is responsible for identifying projects in their constituencies eligible for funding (Jones, 2012, 5).

Based on the various strategies highlighted above, the OSSAP-MDGs also commenced work on implementing and monitoring MDG-related progress in Nigeria. In November 2008, the OSSAP-MDGs produced a *Mid-point assessment of the Millennium Development Goals in Nigeria 2000–2007*. This was followed in 2010 by the *Nigeria Millennium Development Goals report 2010*. The publication of these reports provided insights into what had been done in Nigeria's attempt to achieve the MDGs. While both reports note that progress had been made in certain areas like child mortality rates, they also state clearly that the progress has been slow due to factors relating to poor public infrastructure among other domestic and global issues such as the financial and food inflation crises. According to the Mid-Point Assessment of 2008, 'the nation has made appreciable progress on Goals 2 and 8, as well as some partial progress on Goals 3 and 6, but faces serious challenges on Goals 4, 5 and 7 and some indicators of Goal 6' (OSSAP-MDGs, 2008, 122). By 2010, the OSSAP-MDGs notes in its conclusion that,

> The trends in progress towards the MDGs are mixed, just as the prospects of meeting the respective MDG 2015 targets are variable. Some MDG indicators (such as universal primary education, prevalence of HIV/AIDS and ratio

of girls to boys in primary education) show encouraging trends and prospects...Given the shortfalls in achievements, and looking towards the targets, Nigeria needs a big push forward. (OSSAP-MDGs, 2010, 57-8)

If the various reports by local and international agencies on Nigeria's successes on the MDGs are anything to go by, however, the 'big push forward' that relates to financial and political commitments recommended in the 2010 report cited above was not big enough to push the country towards achieving any of the goals (NBS, 2011; 2012; British Council Nigeria, 2012). Even though the 2010 report indicates that progress has been made on goals relating to achieving universal education, Nigeria faced serious challenges with respect to not only achieving this specific goal but all the other goals as well. For example, Nigeria still has one of the highest numbers of out of school children in the world (10.5 million) and gender disparities still exist in the enrolment of school children (British Council Nigeria, 2012).

More so, there is an obvious rural–urban differential bias against girls and the dropout rates for girls and boys are high as well. Child and maternal mortality rates also remain considerably high and access to retroviral drugs for people living with HIV/AIDS are still low (British council 2012). With the poor performance on the MDGs, Nigeria's 152rd position on the United Nations Development Programme Human Development Report of 2015 appears self-explanatory. The condition is especially sobering considering the country was ranked 151 on the UNDP HDR in 2000 when the MDGs were launched (UNDP, 2000). Some reasons Nigeria failed to achieve significant progress on the MDGs are analysed in the next section.

Challenges to the progress of MDGs in Nigeria

Many factors explain the slow and almost complete lack of performance on some of the MDGs in Nigeria, but these can be broadly summarised under two major factors: the (i) problem of implementation which is partly due to poor state capacity, and (ii) corruption. Although these problems are interrelated, they do constitute fundamental challenges in their own rights within the Nigerian context.

Problem of implementation

In a country where public institutions have consistently suffered neglect from successive governments at all levels, the absence of any attempt to have a coherent, consistent and focused implementation strategy created enormous bottlenecks for achieving the MDGs in the early years of its introduction in Nigeria. The logic of having to first generate growth and expect the population to gain from such growth was flawed considering that previous similar programmes under the SAPs failed to achieve any meaningful progress on the human development front. In this regard, the neglect of public institutions in the health and education sectors that could have aided the social development of the country was detrimental in the overall development of the country. Moreover, the re-enactment of 'trickle-down' neoliberal economics in the name of economic reforms deemed necessary to create a macroeconomic environment has been criticised worldwide owing to its failures in many countries.

Specifically, the implementation of economic policies by government institutions displayed a lack of understanding about the main objectives of policies imported from outside the country, such as SAPs. The Nigerian experience with its SAPs, as many have observed, was a tragic one for the country's development. The debt crisis of the 1980s and the introduction of the SAPs to solve it only prolonged the problem into the 1990s with Nigeria's debt load increasing (Lewis, 1996). Yet, at the return of democracy in 1999, the adopted development trajectory rehashed the experience of the previous two decades. As before, the expectations of the trickle-down approach did not materialise due to improper diagnoses of the problems and the inappropriate policies proffered to solve them. As a result, the MDGs had virtually no coherent or focused attention from governments at all levels in the first six years of the new millennium. Related to the problem of attempting to achieve the MDGs through trickle-down economics were the political problems associated with intergovernmental relations in the country. Nigeria is a federation with sub-national governments who share jurisdictions over issues such as health and education with the federal government.

Over the years, the federal government has centralised powers, making it very strong in relation to the states and local governments. But even though it is shared, the responsibilities for providing public primary education and healthcare services fall mainly to fiscally weak states and local governments. The overbearing attitude of the federal government in seeking to implement plans such as the UBE, whereby it did not effectively engage the states and local governments, did not take long to unravel and undermine the success of the programme. For instance, since the states and local governments depended mainly on federal allocations for their operations, the irregularity of such allocations affected the budget implementation processes in many states and local governments of the federation. By virtue of its improper implementation strategy, the federal government which is based in Abuja could not effectively reach out to the local communities where actual development and the MDGs needed to be achieved. The result was stasis in many aspects.

Moreover, the commitment of many states and local governments to the federal government led initiatives on the MDGs was low given their own focus on pursuing various poverty reduction and development programmes through the SEEDS or LEEDS. While some states prioritised education related goals, others moved on health and agriculture. When put together, however, the increasing level of poverty in the country reflects limited successes. Additionally, when MDG outcomes are disaggregated by states, the outcomes are worse off for the northern states in comparison to their southern counterparts (NBS, 2011). Although this may not be unconnected to the overall poorer socio-economic circumstances of most northern states in Nigeria, the protracted conflicts caused by the activities of the Islamic terrorist organisation known as Boko Haram has immensely retarded development in the region (Akinola, 2015). Moreover, the motives of some political actors at the state and local government levels were sometimes unclear and only served to consolidate their political bases, whether in line with the parties in power at the state or in connection with the political powers and actors seeking to undermine progress within the states for their own selfish political reasons (Akinola, 2015).

Furthermore, while the creation of OSSAP-MDGs was a clear recognition of Nigeria's implementation problems within the first six years of the launch of the MDGs in 2000, problems associated with poor intergovernmental relations affected the MDGs outcomes. Principal among these was the lack of implementation structures which resulted in the creation of inconsistent structures on an ad hoc basis with respect to some programmes and projects. Since the OSSAP-MDGs was responsible for coordinating and monitoring projects all over the country, the inadequacy of trained personnel on monitoring and evaluation created a huge gap in proper implementation. To fill this gap, consultants were hired mainly from the private sector and civil society organisations in Nigeria to supervise some of the projects across the six geopolitical zones in the country and submit reports to the OSSAP-MDGs.

As one consultant explained, however, there were no serious checks and balances in place to supervise and effectively monitor the implementation of projects.[5] When reports identifying certain gaps in the implementation of programmes and projects at the state and local government levels are actually submitted, no action is taken most of the time.[6] This could be due to lack of proper coordination, outright inability to investigate such reports or simply collusion between project contractors and programme supervisors working for OSSAP-MDGs. Consequently, despite the creation of the OSSAP-MDGs, serious gaps remained in the attainment of the MDGs. Although the ineffective coordination between the federal, state and local governments improved with the establishment of the OSSAP-MDGs, it was far from resolved.

Put together, without adequate coordination among various ministries, departments and agencies of the governments at all levels, implementation of MDG programmes and policies was difficult in many respects, not least due to poor state capacity at various levels of government. Several scholars have contributed to the discourse on state capacity and the literature on the subject is quite extensive. Generally used to refer to the ability of states to respond effectively to demands of society through the exercise of state power politically, economically, technically, administratively and so on, 'state capacity' is often considered a yardstick to determine how strong or weak states are (Onyeoziri, 2005). In relation to socio-economic development, Pritchett et al argue that 'successful implementation of most governmental endeavours requires capable organizations that induce and support productive day-to-day practices by large numbers of individuals: teachers must teach, policemen must police, engineers must engineer, regulators must regulate, tax collectors must collect taxes' (Pritchett et al, 2012, 1).

To be sure, the MDGs constitute mainly a set of goals intended to alleviate the living conditions of poor people all over the world. However, the responses of states such as Nigeria at best can be regarded as a travesty of state capacity to deliver the basic public services required to meet the most rudimentary demands from citizens in several local communities. For instance, in a study conducted to ascertain the levels of public service delivery in six Nigerian states in the areas of socio-economic amenities provisioning, budget, governance and effectiveness of public complaint processes, the average scores for all the states in each area was below 50 per cent (CPPC, 2013). The performance ratings were based on citizens' perception of states' provision of services such as primary healthcare, schools, water supply, roads, electricity, waste disposal management, market, drainage system, skill acquisition and empowerment centres and agricultural support facilities. Putting the low-performance ratings into perspective, it is important to emphasise that although some states perform better than others, the overall performance in areas such as education and health is poor. In addition, the lack of effective provision of electricity remains the bane of development in Nigeria as the country remains energy poor despite being a major oil and gas producer.

While a lack of adequate power supply and public infrastructure continue to hamper socio-economic progress generally (NAPC, 2009; Okafor, 2008), this affected the general performance of efforts put towards achieving MDGs specifically. What is more, part of the major challenges encountered in the implementation of the MDGs in Nigeria is the glaring case of poor technical and administrative capacity from the federal to the local levels. The problem has existed since the colonial days when many Nigerians could not acquire the requisite skills to work in the colonial administration owing to lack of access to education, among several other problems. The first university in Nigeria was only created in 1948, 12 years before independence and almost 90 years after the colonial conquest by the British. The initial efforts to educate Nigerians and employ competent staff in public services at all levels was done in the early days of independence until the 1980s when the SAPs were introduced. One direct consequence of SAP and policies was the evisceration of quality service in public institutions. There has been a gradual fall in the technical and administrative capacity of public staff since the SAPs were introduced. At the end of military rule in 1999, public institutions in Nigeria had become derelict.

Today, and in line with Pritchett et al's (2012) observation about state capabilities, Nigeria has teachers that cannot teach, regulators that cannot regulate, and tax collectors that cannot collect taxes due to lack of technical and administrative capacities. Poignantly, the implication for the MDGs is not difficult to recognise as the quality of education and health in the country continue to fall, even as the poor and vulnerable increasingly rely on public institutions. The constant strike actions embarked upon by unions in all the sectors further illustrate the Nigerian predicament. The stasis in achieving the MDGs cannot be overemphasised. Strike actions have become a mainstay of Nigeria's public life since the days of SAPs, and the education and health sectors have been the worse for it. For instance, following a protracted strike action over the non-payment of teachers' salaries in 1992, some Lagos state primary school pupils were promoted to the next class without any examination. Then in 1993, only students in eight out of the 15 local governments that existed in Lagos state at that time enrolled for the First School

Leaving Certificate Examination due to strike actions as well (Eminue, 1995, 43). Within the past decade alone, various unions representing critical sectors of public life, from education to health and power supply, have embarked on numerous strikes to press home demands for better conditions of service and/or more resources to carry out their individual and institutional responsibilities.

Furthermore, the state capacity problem manifests itself in the political and economic aspects of daily life in Nigeria. The federal, states and local governments have constitutionally assigned responsibilities that they are expected to perform sometimes in partnership with one another. To be sure, the 1999 constitution of Nigeria assigns 68 items on the exclusive legislative list to the federal government and 30 items on the concurrent legislative list for both the federal and state governments with some residual delegated powers to the states and local governments (FGN, 1999). But despite its enormous powers, the federal government is incapable of delivering the much-needed effectiveness in managing the country (Aiyede, 2005). This is despite the fact that the federal government also takes the largest share in national revenues when compared to the states and local governments: the federal government gets 56 per cent of the revenues while states and local governments share 24 and 20 per cent respectively (Egwaikhide, 2004). Considering that most of the public services are located at the state and local government levels, many observers have advocated a review of the revenue formula in favour of the states and local governments (Egwaikhide et al, 2004).

The relative strength of the federal government vis-a-vis the states and local governments has not positively translated into meaningful development for the majority of Nigerians whose demands for basic improvements in their living conditions such as those captured by the MDGs remain largely unattended to. Given that Nigeria has continued to grow in population and the necessary public institutions have not responded accordingly to the demands of the population, it is imperative that various state and local governments improve their revenue base and rebuild their public institutions for effective service delivery. As it stands, the federal government's inability to effectively engage the state and local government exacerbates the implementation problem even as the ability to keep up with basic service provisions such as healthcare, electricity and pipe-borne water continues to fall. However, corruption at all levels, especially within the federal government given the resources available therein, has been a major challenge for achieving any meaningful progress as discussed in the next section.

Corruption and the MDGs in Nigeria: one challenge too many

Corruption is arguably the most common factor in all other problems in Nigeria. As mentioned earlier, Nigeria was ranked by Transparency International as the most corrupt country in the world in 1997 and 2000. Currently, Nigeria ranks 138 on a scale of 168 on the 2015 corruption perception index (TI, 2015). Corruption is systemic in Nigeria, and the systemic nature of the malaise makes it even more detrimental to socio-economic development in the country. Corruption exists in both the public and private sectors in Nigeria and corrupt practices, ranging from open bribery to extortion and looting of funds by officials, are prevalent. In particular, corruption within public institutions continues to affect development in the country and if there were to be a contest for the most corrupt public institution in the country, the front runners might be so many that a clear winner may not emerge. Cases of stolen funds meant for education, health, security, pensions and so on, abound in Nigeria, that any discerning observer will conclude that no progress can be made unless a decisive step is taken to fight the scourge.

As the events of the last five decades of independence in Nigeria show, corruption has developed its own personality and network with which it metaphorically fights back. Public officials and politicians are capable of stealing from state accounts and then use their ill-gotten wealth to bribe other state officials who are supposed to prevent such theft in the first place. The judiciary, unfortunately, has also been caught up in the corruption ring, even though some judges have continued to maintain fairness in the discharge of their duties. Given the prevalence of corruption in Nigeria, efforts to achieve the MDGs were massively dominated by allegations of corruption with the explicit participation of government officials. A striking example is the withdrawal of HIV/AIDS funding in 2011 by the Global Funds to Fight AIDs, Tuberculosis and Malaria. The Global Fund's intervention in Nigeria was suspended owing to allegations of mismanaged and stolen funds by some Nigerian state and non-state organisations amounting to a fraud of over $474.4 million.[7] The Global Fund had earlier in 2006 discontinued some of its grants to Nigeria citing the non-fulfilment of programme objectives (Salaam-Blythe, 2008). Given that MDG 8 revolved around global partnership for development, such monumental fraud and mismanagement constituted a setback for the implementation of MDGs in Nigeria. Moreover, the paucity of funds for effective implementation and monitoring meant that the loss of such a source of funding further placed people in dire need of assistance in precarious conditions.

Furthermore, the activities of OSSAP-MDGs have not gone without corruption allegations amounting to how programmes are implemented. Apart from the fact that reports of corruption to the Office are often not attended to as mentioned above, the operation of the Quick Wins initiative mentioned in the first section is considered by some observers as a means of political corruption involving parliamentarians seeking to use the MDGs constituency projects for electoral purposes. Following its creation in 2008, many politicians sought to influence how the Quick Wins initiative projects were implemented. The pressures on the OSSAP-MDGs increased as the Nigeria 2011 general elections approached and the OSSAP-MDGs became engrossed in debates over the non-implementation of some projects in the constituencies. Although some had alleged in the first instance that the whole idea of Quick Wins was an attempt by the executive arm of government to placate members of the legislature, the controversies surrounding the Quick Wins as the 2011 elections approached illustrated the electoral motives of some parliamentarians.[8]

The latter view was because of the desire by some politicians to score cheap points with constituents/voters rather than genuine interests in contributing towards the achievement of the MDGs.[9] The weak accountability structures in the country made it possible for parliamentarians to not answer questions about the projects, not even from their own constituency members.[10] In the end, the Quick Wins initiative had very little impact on the lives of many Nigerians and the commitment level of OSSAP-MDGs to advancing the course of achieving the MDGs in Nigeria was questioned by many observers. As some stakeholders who worked with the OSSAP-MDGs in the early days of its establishment mentioned during interviews, the commitment of the OSSAP-MDGs as an institution set up for advancing the MDGs in Nigeria waned over time due to political interference in its activities.[11] One civil society activist maintained political interference and the politicisation of some of the activities of the OSSAP-MDGs, particularly with reference to issues surrounding the Quick Wins initiative, was a major setback to Nigeria's MDG efforts.[12]

What comes out from the above is that Nigeria's progress on the MDGs was stalled in some areas and progress in some other areas was reversed as some of the MDG gains were lost due to corruption, poor state capacity and improper implementation strategies. Coupled with the fact that the terrorist activities of Boko Haram in the northern parts of Nigeria – where poverty rates are a lot higher compared to the south – increased tremendously between 2009 and 2015, the failure to achieve the MDGs in Nigeria increased the poverty of many people in the affected areas. In light of the devastation and destruction caused by the activities of Boko Haram, the current state of poverty and development in Nigeria raises concerns about how the country will reposition itself to achieve any of the SDGs by 2030. Moreover, considering the group targets state and non-state targets, including school children, teachers and local health workers as it protests against western education and seeks to Islamise Nigeria, achieving the SDGs will be a herculean task for the Nigerian government as it battles against the group. Nevertheless, in order to achieve the SDGs, governments at all levels in Nigeria would have to renew their strategies and sustain their efforts. Taking into consideration the recent efforts of the new government in Nigeria to promote socio-economic development, fight corruption and end the Boko Haram insurgency, some suggestions about how to make this possible are discussed below in the final section of this chapter.

Nigeria and the Sustainable Development Goals

As argued in the preceding sections, Nigeria needs to overcome certain challenges in order to achieve the SDGs. The new 17 SDGs build on the eight MDGs and have a timeline of 2030. But to ensure the SDGs would be achieved at the set date, more equitable and sustainable development frameworks at the international and domestic levels will be necessary. As the report of the United Nations Secretary-General's High-Level Panel of Eminent Persons on the Post-2015 Development Agenda that preceded the launching of the SDGs maintains, the Post-2015 Development Agenda needs to make 'five big, transformative shifts'. These include leaving no one behind in the development process, putting sustainable development at the centre of development plans, transforming economies for job creation and inclusive growth, building peaceful and effective, open and accountable institutions for everyone, and forging a new global partnership for development (UN, 2013). When combined, these shifts are expected to deliver the gains of development to many citizens around the world. Nevertheless, if the lessons learnt from the MDGs are things to go by, countries such as Nigeria need to first get right their own internal political economies and state capacities for development. The prognosis for Nigeria can include three major imperatives to achieve the SDGs by 2030.

First, unlike what the leaders of Nigeria have tried to do in the past three decades to develop the country using neoliberal economic policies that only increase poverty and inequalities in the country, the time is ripe for the country to consider reinventing itself as a developmental state, albeit a socially democratic one. That is, a state where governmental apparatus is proactively used to support both public and private institutions for the overall benefit of the citizens through policies and programmes that foster socio-economic development and reduce poverty and inequality. The arguments for developmental states in Africa is not new as many authors and organisations such as the United Nations Economic Commission for Africa have added their views and support for establishing such states in Africa (see Mkandawire, 2001; Gana et al, 2003; Edigheji, 2005; 2010; Amuwo, 2008; Aiyede, 2009; UNECA, 2011; Akinola, 2013).

However, while many observers support developmental states, it must be added that each African state has to craft its own developmental features in line with its political, economic, social and environmental structures, taking into consideration past mistakes in designing such states in the early days of independence. For a state such as Nigeria, a socially democratic and developmental state will be helpful in advancing an equitable and just federal system. This kind of developmental state would also support development at all levels through a better understanding of intergovernmental relations in a three-tier federal system. The calls for the restructuring of the Nigerian federation in a way that devolves greater powers to the sub-national units must, therefore, be taken seriously (Amuwo et al, 1998). A more focused socially democratic and developmental state in Nigeria will likely be able to tackle the problems of underdevelopment in the country. Focusing on the critical sectors, in particular, will be crucial.

The education, health, agriculture and public infrastructure sectors are the sectors which the various governments in Nigeria should make considerable investments to address years of neglect and halt the negative effects the failures in these sectors continue to have on the populace. The governance of these sectors must be inclusive of non-state actors such as citizens and civil society organisations and corruption should be fought effectively. Essentially, well thought out development plans that are similar to the national development plans of the 1960s and 1970s must be developed for the country. The new development plans should be socially inclusive of all segments of society and should contain coherent and consistent policies and programmes. This would help avoid the crises of policy inconsistencies that Nigeria experienced during the MDGs period.

It is noteworthy that although the People's Democratic Party (PDP) ruled Nigeria for 16 years from 1999 to 2015, the level of policy inconsistency was quite high and this affected the development of Nigeria as a whole.

Tellingly, despite being from the same political party, President Obasanjo's administration (1999–2007), which designed NEEDS, was succeeded by President Umaru Yaradua's administration (2007–10) which discontinued NEEDS and replaced it with the 'seven-point agenda'. The seven-point agenda revolved around plans to improve the energy supply, security, wealth creation, education, land reforms, transportation and Niger Delta development (Dode, 2010). After the death of President Yaradua in 2010 and the subsequent election of his former vice president, Goodluck Jonathan, as President in 2011, the latter replaced the seven-point agenda with the 'Transformation Agenda'. This is despite the fact that President Jonathan was the vice president in President Yaradua's administration. Maintaining policy consistency in government was, therefore, difficult at the national level, even though the economic thrust was largely neoliberal in nature. The developmental policy and programme inconsistencies have partly been responsible for Nigeria's apparent crisis of (under)development. As such, a more focused socially democratic and developmental state should also ensure that consistent policy trajectories with measurable targets and indicators are established and supported by necessary legislation at the national level. This should also include a clear plan for industrial development to generate employment for many Nigerians, especially the youths.

Although the new government of President Muhammadu Buhari has not radically departed from Nigeria's neoliberal development trajectory since taking over in May 2015, the government's renewed efforts at social investment indicates that it is more sensitive to the plight of the poor. Specifically, if implemented properly, the proposed 500 billion Nigerian Naira (N) social investments expenditure – out of the total N6.06 trillion 2016 national budget – may have a positive effect on the lives of some people and unemployed youths. The social investment expenditure as proposed by the government will be used to employ more primary and secondary teachers, expand the coverage of conditional cash transfers to 1 million poor and vulnerable Nigerians and provide skills acquisition and training to some unemployed youths. Yet, if the necessary social and economic policies are not put in place and/or more detrimental neoliberal policies are pursued, the effects may end up being negative and the poor will be poorer as the experience of the recent past illustrates. Nonetheless, it would be important to explicitly design a transparent and accountable implementation strategy to ensure the social investments get to the right people at the right time.

A second major imperative for Nigeria in the post-2015 SDGs period is a sustained war against corruption and indiscipline. Here, 'securitising' corruption for development in Nigeria is a sine qua non for development, that is, the state should conceptualise corruption as a problem that poses essential threats to Nigerians and then utilise all available resources at its disposal to fight it. A securitisation approach to development in Nigeria will entail that the federal government of Nigeria declares a state of emergency on corruption and subsequently utilises available legal means and enabling laws to fight it. Corruption should be framed as a crime against humanity and seen as posing an existential threat to the lives of citizens in the country. This will create the ambience for framing and re-strategising to fight the malaise. It is nevertheless important to add that although fighting corruption will not be easy, it remains necessary to fight it if Nigeria aspires to create a viable, vibrant and disciplined socially democratic and developmental state.

Despite current efforts to fight corruption in Nigeria, the main anticorruption agencies in Nigeria – the Independent Corrupt Practices Commission (ICPC) and the Economic and Financial Crimes Commission (EFCC) – lack the necessary human and material resources to effectively wage the war on corruption in the country. More so, the existing laws for fighting the war on corruption are weak, making it easy for corruption to easily fight back as corrupt elites manipulate the judicial system to their own favour. Considering the anticorruption agencies rely on the federal government for their funding and the appointments of their chairpersons, Nigeria's political elites have also found it easy to manipulate the activities of the agencies through inadequate funding and political interference. If Nigeria is to achieve meaningful socio-economic development, winning the war on corruption is a prerequisite. Getting the government to declare a state of emergency on corruption would not be easy, but if local and international organisations, civil society and respected individuals join forces to maintain pressure on the government to fight corruption vigorously, some efforts may be put to the demand. Indeed, as the ongoing trials of persons accused of stealing funds meant to buy arms for the military to fight Boko Haram in the past decade illustrate, corruption features prominently as an explanatory factor in Nigeria's failures to curtail the activities of the terrorist group. But without adequate human and material resources and sustained public support for the war on corruption, not only winning the war on terrorism but achieving the SDGs will be nearly impossible.

Third and finally, there is an urgent need for effective leadership at the individual and institutional levels in Nigeria. Many Nigerian leaders have failed to emancipate the rest of society in ways that encourage the younger generation to contribute their own quota to the system. Worse still, the selfish disdain for the populace has created a country where many young people are increasingly becoming despondent as opportunities to eke out a living continue to be elusive. The high remuneration of politicians holding public offices at all levels has been a drain on the resources of the country, especially as many citizens live below $1 a day. Leaders need to understand that the prosperity of the country as a whole is key to promoting national unity and integration. Arguably, the current problems regarding Boko Haram's terrorism are partly as a result of failures of visionary leadership to anticipate the problems. The high level of youth unemployment in the country created a steady pool of youths who were easily recruited by the fundamentalists to unleash terror on the country and its innocent citizens. More than 10,000 Nigerians have died since 2009 when the Boko Haram leader Mohammed Yusuf was killed by security forces while millions have been maimed, internally displaced, and/or forced to become refugees in neighbouring countries (Akinola, 2015). The terrorist attacks have affected the whole country and there seems to be no end in sight despite the efforts of the government. Development cannot take place in an atmosphere of conflict and insecurity.

Conclusion

Achieving the MDGs in many African countries has proved a herculean task. This is due to a range of internal and external factors. Internal factors such as conflicts, bad governance and corruption proved to be very detrimental to the achievement of the MDGs. External factors such as the food, fuel and financial crises of the last decade also took a toll on the MDGs being achieved by 2015. The sections above have tried to situate the Nigerian experience with the MDGs while envisaging possible solutions that can help the country achieve the SDGs by 2030. Notably, the return of democracy to Nigeria in 1999 has so far not been met with commensurate progress in overcoming the key challenges of poor public services and infrastructure. On the contrary, the decay in public infrastructures such as roads, schools and healthcare centres, relied upon by many poor people, remains. Thus, progress on the MDGs was stalled as a result of the absence of the enabling environment within which the goals could be pursued and attained.

In addition, the initial lack of efforts on the MDGs in Nigeria because of inadequate funds affected the attainment of the goals. The absence of any coherent strategy until 2006 when the OSSAP-MDGs was created also prevented any major effort being taken. Moreover, the problem of poor implementation strategies emerged as a major obstacle to achieving the MDGs as none of the federal, state and local governments possessed the necessary administrative and technical skills to effectively implement the programmes designed for achieving the MDGs. Poor state capacity at all levels shows that the journey of the MDGs in Nigeria was chequered and necessary changes would be important for achieving the SDGs. Adding the corruption debacle to this mix appears to have further worsened the plight of the poor people in Nigeria as some of the necessary funds for implementing the MDG-related programmes were pilfered by officials responsible for handling them. The lack of transparent and accountable mechanisms in Nigeria has also made it possible for many accused persons to walk free without facing justice or prosecution over embezzled funds. When combined, the problems associated with achieving the MDGs highlight the need for drastic changes that would enable Nigeria to achieve the SDGs.

Consequently, moving beyond the MDGs, Nigerian governments at all levels must take proactive steps in correcting some of the problems identified in this chapter. Fighting corruption would be very important in any effort to achieve progress in the country. Moreover, it would be imperative for the government to develop a socially democratic and developmental state approach to intervening in key sectors such as education, health, infrastructure development and agriculture. This chapter thus argues that in order for Nigeria to achieve the SDGs, the following recommendations should be taken into account: (i) the country should effectively fight corruption; (ii) redesign its development agenda and improve the quality of leadership at institutional and individual levels for better accountability; and, (iii) develop a clear monitoring and evaluation strategy to oversee the implementation of the SDGs.

Finally, it is important to reiterate that this chapter has been a modest attempt to provide insights into Nigeria's efforts at achieving the MDGs. The challenges encountered in the process of implementing the MDGs were spelt out and the imperative of moving forward within the context of a post-2015 SDGs international and domestic development agenda mentioned. The suggestions on the way forward presented in this chapter are by no means exhaustive in terms of the steps Nigeria needs to take in order to achieve sustainable development. But when viewed as building on the lessons learnt about the MDGs in Nigeria, they constitute some necessary imperatives. In concluding this chapter, therefore, it is important to note that while the room for improvement is still wide, engaging Nigerians in the development of the country remains a crucial, yet fully untapped, asset the country can benefit from for its development as the increasing levels of citizen activism in the country indicate. Perhaps it is necessary to close with the words of a civil society organisation representative interviewed in Nigeria in June 2013 about the fight against corruption and underdevelopment in the country, 'We will come to a time when the forces against will not be able to resist the forces for.'[13]

Notes

[1] Inaugural speech by President Olusegun Obasanjo at his swearing-in ceremony as President and Commander-in-Chief of the Federal Republic of Nigeria on 29 May 1999, www.dawodu.com/obas1.htm.

[2] NEEDS was launched in 2004 by President Olusegun Obasanjo. It was considered the blueprint for taking Nigeria's development challenges. The four main goals of NEEDS were: wealth creation; employment generation: poverty reduction: and value reorientation. According to the NEEDS document, one of the major thrusts for development was to encourage the share of the private sector in the management of the Nigerian economy. This explains much of the Federal government's efforts at promoting privatisation, deregulation and liberalisation of formerly publicly controlled enterprises. For details about NEEDS, see National Planning Commission (2004), *National Economic Empowerment and Development Strategies (NEEDS)*, Abuja: Federal Republic of Nigeria.

[3] See http://sdgs.gov.ng/about-sdgs/

[4] Interview with OSSAP-MDGs staff, 24 June 2013.

[5] Interview with CSO activist, 4 June 2013.

[6] Interview with CSO activist, 4 June 2013.

[7] See www.businessdayonline.com/NG/index.php/news/76-hot-topic/23724-global-fund-may-suspend-nigeria-over-4746m-fraud

[8] See www.nigerianbestforum.com/blog/mdgs-quick-win-as-campaign-tools-for-2011-election/

[9] See www.nigerianbestforum.com/blog/mdgs-quick-win-as-campaign-tools-for-2011-election/

[10] Interview with CSO activist, 4 June 2013.

[11] Interviews with staff of organisations working with OSSAP-MDGs, May to June 2013.

[12] Interview with CSO activist, 4 June 2013.

[13] Interview with CSO representative, 13 June 2013.

References

Aiyede, ER, 2005, Intergovernmental relations and the strengthening of the Nigerian Federation, in E Onwudiwe, RT Suberu (eds) *Nigerian federalism in crisis: Critical perspective and political options*, pp 220–30, Ibadan: Programme on Federalism and Ethnic Studies (PEFS)

Aiyede, ER, 2009, The political economy of fiscal federalism and dilemma of constructing a developmental state in Nigeria, *International Political Science Review* 30, 3, 249–69

Akinola, O, 2013, Africa's third independence: A sine qua non for development, in N Andrew, NE Khalema, T Oriola, I Odoom (eds) *Africa yesterday, today, and tomorrow: Exploring the multi-dimensional discourses on development*, pp 60–77, Newcastle upon Tyne: Cambridge Scholars Publishing

Akinola, O, 2015, Boko Haram insurgency in Nigeria: Between Islamic fundamentalism, politics and poverty, *African Security* 8, 1, 1–29

Amuwo, A, 2008, Constructing the democratic developmental state in Africa: A case study of Nigeria, 1960–2007, *Occasional Paper* 59, Johannesburg: Institute for Global Dialogue

Amuwo, A, Agbaje, AAB, Suberu, RT, Herault, G (eds), 1998, *Federalism and political restructuring in Nigeria*, Ibadan: Spectrum Books

British Council Nigeria, 2012, *Gender in Nigeria report 2012: Improving the lives of girls and women in Nigeria: Issues, policies and actions* (2nd edn), Nigeria: British Council Nigeria

CPPC (Centre for Public Policy Cooperation), 2013, *Policy brief: Government's Service Delivery Scorecard*, Ibadan: CPPC

Dode, RO, 2010, Yar'adua 7-Point Agenda, MDGs and Sustainable Development in Nigerian, *Global Journal of Human Social Science* 10, 4, 2–8

Edigheji, O, 2005, *A democratic developmental state in Africa?*, Research Report, Johannesburg: Centre for Policy Studies

Edigheji, O (ed), 2010, *Constructing a democratic developmental state in South Africa: Potentials and challenges*, Cape Town: HSRC Press

Egwaikhide, F, 2004, Intergovernmental fiscal relations in Nigeria, in FO Egwaikhide, ER Aiyede, SA Benjamin, HD Dlakwa, and A Ikelegbe (eds) *Intergovernmental relations in Nigeria*, pp 1–24, Ibadan: PEFS

Egwaikhide, FO, Aiyede, ER, Benjamin, SA, Dlakwa, HD, Ikelegbe, A (eds), 2004, *Intergovernmental relations in Nigeria*, Ibadan: PEFS

Eminue, O, 1995, The myth of local government autonomy in Nigeria, *Ibadan Journal of the Social Sciences* 1, 1, 27–47

FGN (Federal Republic of Nigeria), 1999, *The Constitution of the Federal Republic of Nigeria 1999*. Abuja: FGN

Gana, AT, Egwu, SG, African Centre for Democratic Governance (eds), 2003, *Federalism in Africa: The imperative of democratic development*, Vol II, Trenton, NJ: Africa World Press

Hulme, D, 2007, The making of the Millennium Development Goals: Human development meets results-based management in an imperfect world, *Brooks World Poverty Institute (BWPI) Working Paper* 16, Manchester: BWPI

Jones, D, 2012, Review of the institutional structures and processes related to the MDGS in the Parliament of Nigeria, Geneva: Inter-parliamentary Union, www.ipu.org/splz-e/unga13/nigeria.pdf

Lewis, P, 1996, From prebendalism to predation: The political economy of decline in Nigeria, *Journal of Modern African Studies* 34, 1, 79–103

Mkandawire, T, 2001, Thinking about developmental states in Africa, *Cambridge Journal of Economics* 25, 289–313

NAPC (National Productivity Centre), 2009, *Effect of power supply on the productivity of micro, small and medium scale enterprises (MSMES) in Nigeria*, Abuja: NAPC

NAPEP (National Poverty Eradication Programme), 2007, *In care of the people*, Abuja: Federal Government of Nigeria

NBS (National Bureau of Statistics), 2011, *Nigeria Multiple Indicator Cluster Survey main report*, Abuja: Federal Republic of Nigeria

NBS (National Bureau of Statistics), 2012, *Nigeria poverty profile 2010*, Abuja: Federal Republic of Nigeria

NPC (Nigerian National Planning Commission), 2004, *Meeting everyone's needs: National Economic Empowerment and Development Strategy*, Abuja: NPC

Okafor, EE, 2008, Development crisis of power supply and implications for industrial development in Nigeria, *Studies of Tribes and Tribals* 6, 2, 83–92

Okonjo-Iweala, N, 2012, *Reforming the unreformable: Lessons from Nigeria*, Cambridge, MA and London, England: MIT Press

Olaniyan, O, Bankole, AS, 2005, Human capital, capabilities, and poverty in rural Nigeria, *Ibadan Journal of the Social Sciences* 3, 2, 13–27

Onyeoziri, F, 2005, Federalism and state capacity in Nigeria, *Ibadan Journal of the Social Sciences* 3, 2, 1–12

OSSAP-MDGs (Office of the Senior Special Assistant to the President on the MDGs), 2008, *Mid-point assessment of the Millennium Development Goals in Nigeria 2000–2007*, Abuja: OSSAP-MDGs

OSSAP-MDGs (Office of the Senior Special Assistant to the President on the MDGs), 2010, *Nigeria Millennium Development Goals report 2010*, Abuja: OSSAP-MDGs

Pritchett, L, Woolcock, M, Andrews, M, 2012, Looking like a state: Techniques of persistent failure in state capability for implementation, *United Nations University World Institute for Development Economics Research (UNU-WIDER) Working Paper* 2012/63, Helsinki: UNU-WIDER

Salaam-Blythe, T, 2008, The global fund to fight AIDS, tuberculosis, and malaria: Progress report and issues for congress, *Congressional Research Service (CRS) Report for Congress*, Washington, DC: CRS, Library of Congress

SPARC (State Partnership for Accountability and Capability), 2013, *Delivering debt relief locally: The Conditional Grants Scheme,* Abuja: SPARC

TI (Transparency International), 1997, *Corruption perception index*, Berlin: TI

TI (Transparency International), 2000, *Corruption perception index*, Berlin: TI

TI (Transparency International), 2015, *Corruption perception index*, Berlin: TI

UN (United Nations), 2013, *A new global partnership: Eradicate poverty and transform economies through sustainable development*, New York: United Nations

UN (United Nations), 2015, *A new global partnership: Eradicate poverty and transform economies through sustainable development*, Report of the High-Level Panel of Eminent Persons on the Post-2015 Development Agenda, New York: United Nations

UNDP (United Nations Development Programme), 1999, *Human Development Report*, New York: United Nations

UNDP (United Nations Development Programme), 2000, *Human Development Report*, New York: United Nation

UNDP (United Nations Development Programme), 2015, *Human Development Report*, New York: United Nations

UNECA (United Nations Economic Commission for Africa), 2011, *Economic report for Africa*, Addis Ababa: United Nations

World Bank, 2001, *World Development Report 2000/2001: Attacking poverty*, Washington: The World Bank

FOURTEEN

North Africa and Middle East: economic performance and social progress

Manmohan Agarwal and Badye Essid

Introduction

The North Africa and Middle East (NAME) region has been witnessing considerable political change since early 2011. Revolutionary movements in Tunisia and Egypt rapidly drove leaders out of power. In Libya, Kaddafi's loyalists have also come to power. In Syria, Bahrain and Yemen, there is great ferment and governments are trying to maintain control of the country. Other countries such as Morocco, Algeria and Jordan are implementing new social and constitutional rules to preempt possible uprisings. Many experts argue that the Arab Spring is caused by non-democratic regimes that have not responded to popular aspirations. Specifically, social inequalities could be the basis for the population's uprising. In this chapter, we explore the economic and social performance of the NAME countries in order to examine the validity of the analysis that links inequalities to the uprisings.

The debt crisis affected developing countries throughout the 1980s and resulted in a considerable slowdown in the rate of economic growth in the countries in Latin America and sub-Saharan Africa (SSA). Economists and policymakers concluded that macroeconomic stability is a necessary condition for recovery. Macroeconomic stability was part of the reform package that came to be called the Washington consensus (Williamson, 1989). The policies embedded in this consensus were implemented in part as conditions attached to loans granted by the International Monetary Fund and the World Bank. Meanwhile, during the 1990s, developing countries particularly in Latin America and SSA were still facing economic stagnation. These developing countries were facing a deterioration of public services and serious damage to their education and health services (Cornia et al, 1988). These results led economists and policymakers to shift their attention to policies that could improve, simultaneously, human conditions and macroeconomic stability (Desai, 2007).

During the 1990s there was increasing attention to the level of social development in developing countries. Hulme (2009) surveys developments that resulted in the crystallisation of ideas regarding the importance of social progress in developing countries. These ideas regarding social development were the result of an extensive range of studies. As an illustration, the Human Development Reports ranks countries according to their level of social development. The World Development Report for 1990 also concentrated on the theme of poverty. Meanwhile, the UN, during the 1990s, organised a number of international conferences to analyse various aspects of social achievements.[1] These conferences resulted in attempts at the Development Assistance Committee (DAC) of the OECD to rethink the goals of development and what should be the role of the international community in achieving these goals. These discussions at the DAC resulted in the enunciation of the International Development Goals (IDGs).[2] The IDGs were further revised into the Millennium Development Goal (MDG) declaration at the UN in 2001, with participation of countries from the entire world, including donors and aid recipients (Hulme and Fukuda-Parr, 2009).

The region of NAME has been a laggard among developing country regions in both economic performance as well as social progress. We examine in this chapter both the economic performance as well as the social achievements in the region. We first compare the NAME region to other developing regions.[3] Then we compare the performance of the countries in the region among each other. We argue in this chapter that the economic performance in this region was not strong enough by itself to influence decisions by households that would have resulted in better social progress. In addition, governments in the region did not undertake the necessary programmes that would have made more of an impact on the social scene, and some possible reasons for this non-action are discussed below. We show that the necessary expenditures were within the fiscal capacity of the governments. Lack of such expenditures could be the result of a weak civil society which could not push governments to undertake social expenditures. Alternatively, it could be due to governance that was not strong enough to better deliver services to the poor within the expenditures that were undertaken in the NAME countries. The political regimes that were usually non-democratic made the situation even worse in most of the countries, and the lack of good governance has definitely persisted (Loewe, 2006). In addition, there were in most of the countries no organised parties, whether political or trade unions that speak for the poor. In some cases, there had been strong public demand, but governments had been able to contain these demands usually by becoming progressively more repressive.[4] We also argue that civil society organisations that could have pressured governments to pay more attention to the social needs have been lacking.

The rest of the chapter is organised as follows. We discuss the economic performance of NAME countries in the second section in terms of their growth performance and factors such as investment rates and export performance, which influence the rate of growth. We present social progress made in the NAME region in the third section in terms of progress in achieving the MDG goals. We present some concluding observations in the fourth section.

Economic performance in the NAME region

The regional economy

The NAME region been the second slowest growing region since the oil price increases of 1973–74. This result is based on calculating the compound average annual growth between 1974 and 2010 for every region. The NAME region is growing faster than only SSA, and even this tendency is not true for recent years (Table 14.1). Per capita incomes in NAME did not decline in 2009 unlike in Latin America (LAC) and SSA. However, correspondingly, the recovery in 2010 has been weaker. The region has lagged particularly behind Asia, including South Asia (SA) and East Asia and Pacific (EAP). Since 1974 per capita incomes in EAP have grown 5 times that in NAME and in SA about two and a half times that in NAME. Despite this slow growth, the

Table 14.1: Growth of per capita income (% per year)

	1965-73	1974-82	1983-90	1991-2000	2000-05	2006	2007	2008	2009	2010
World	3.3	0.8	1.8	1.2	1.6	2.6	2.3	0.1	−3.6	2.5
High income	4.3	1.6	3	1.7	1.5	2.3	1.9	−0.5	−4.1	2.1
LAC	3.6	1.5	−0.2	1.7	0.9	4.2	4.4	2.7	−3.4	4.4
SSA	2.3	0.1	−1.1	−0.4	2	3.3	4.1	3.1	−0.3	2.7
NAME	1.3	−0.5	1.1	2.2	3.6	4.1	2.4	1.4	1.6	3.6
SA	0.2	2	3.5	3.2	4.8	7.3	6.7	3.4	5.6	7.3
EAP	4.5	4.5	6.3	6	7.5	8.9	11.4	7.6	6.5	8.5

Source: World Development reports, various issues, World Bank, Washington DC and World Development Indicators, World Bank, Washington DC

NAME region is relatively rich, having a higher per capita GDP than all other regions except LAC (Table 14.2). The poor performance of the region has a mixture of causes, such as low rates of investment, investment patterns and a heavy reliance on natural products which has limited growth in other sectors, particularly manufacturing. Investment as a percentage of GDP has been stagnant in the region and is much lower than in Asia, though comparable to that of LAC and SSA (Table 14.3). When we take a look at the investment pattern we can argue that the industrial structure in many of the countries of the region is biased towards petrochemical industries which have a high capital output ratio rather than towards labour intensive industries such as textiles. This means that for the same amount of investment the increase in output is less.

Many resource-rich countries have a comfortable balance of payments position. For instance, oil-exporting countries such as Saudi Arabia, Russia and the UK or a gas exporting country such as Norway run current account surpluses. This means that their exchange rate is

Table 14.2: Per capita income, 2009

	Purchasing power parity	Atlas method*
Developing countries	5,599	2,968
LAC	10,286	7,007
SSA	2,051	1,125
NAME	7,911	3,597
SA	2,972	1,107
EAP	6,026	3,163

Note: See World Development Indicators (2011) for a discussion of the Atlas and of the Purchasing Power Parity Methods.

Source: World Bank (2011) World Development Indicators, World Bank, Washington DC

Table 14.3: Gross fixed capital formation (% of GDP)

	1965-73	1974-82	1983-90	1991-2000	2000-05	2006	2007	2008	2009
World	23.6	23.9	22.5	22	20.6	22	22	21	20
High income	24.4	23.8	22.3	21.4	20.4	21	21	20	18
LAC	20.1	22.7	19.2	19.3	17.8	20	20	21	20
SSA	21.8	24	18.5	17.2	17.4	19	20	22	22
MNA		26.5	23.3	21.7	20.6	21	23	23	
SA	14.8	17.8	20	21.4	25	29	31	31	32
EAP		28.4	28.5	32.6	25.6	26	26	26	26

Source: World Development reports, various issues, World Bank, Washington DC and World Development Indicators, World Bank, Washington DC

more appreciated than other countries with a similar level of income. The appreciated exchange rate means that the agricultural and other industrial goods cannot compete in the international market and so the shares of these sectors in GDP is lower than for other countries. This phenomenon is called the 'Dutch disease' (Corden and Neary, 1982). The share of manufacturing is much lower in the NAME region than in other regions (Table 14.4) and this could be a reflection of the Dutch disease. Also the share has halved in the last two decades showing its relative stagnation. Many of the countries that do not depend on oil rely on other natural resources, such as phosphates in the case of Tunisia and Morocco. Tourism earnings, but more importantly the earnings from the Suez Canal, have a similar effect in Egypt.

Investment rates in all the developing country regions except EAP have been increasing this century, with those in LAC and SSA from the very low levels they had reached in the 1980s and 1990s (Table 14.3). Investment rates fell in NAME between 1974–82 and 2000–05.[5] However, the two years before the financial crisis saw an increase in the investment–GDP ratio in NAME and this increase seems to have been maintained since the crisis. The higher investment rates in these recent years may be because off the higher demand arising from the relatively rapid growth in the world economy particularly the developing economies.

Investment rates in NAME have been generally higher than in LAC or SSA. But growth rates of GDP have been lower. This implies that the capital–output ratio has been high, of the order of 6 (Agarwal, 2008). The higher capital–output ratio might reflect either a lower efficiency of industries that have been established or that capital intensive industries have been set up. The latter may, in turn, reflect

Table 14.4: Sector composition of GDP (%)

	Agriculture			Manufacturing			Services, etc.		
	1980-2000	2001-05	2006-09	1980-2000	2001-05	2006-09	1980-2000	2001-05	2006-09
LAC	8.5	6.4	6.0	23.3	18.5	17.2	56.4	61.9	61.9
SSA	18.2	17.7	14.3	16.5	13.8	13.1	50.0	52.0	54.4
NAME	10.4	8.7	7.6	10.5	7.0	5.4	38.3	34.3	31.3
SA	29.3	21.0	18.4	16.1	15.5	16.1	45.1	52.4	53.6
EAP	7.5	4.3	3.6	26.7	22.6	22.5	54.3	62.8	63.9

Note: See World Development Indicators (2011) for a discussion of the Atlas and of the Purchasing Power Parity Methods.

Source: World Bank (2011) World Development Indicators, World Bank, Washington DC

the attempt by these countries to establish downstream oil-based industries, which typically have higher capital–output ratios.

The lower rates of investment–GDP ratios may also reflect lower absorptive capacity as investment opportunities may be limited because of the small size of the domestic markets and the inability to export because of lack of competitiveness due to the Dutch disease. Investment rates have usually been lower than savings rates, particularly in recent years because of lack of absorptive capacity and this has meant that these economies have had large current account surpluses (Table 14.5). These economies have a high share of exports of goods and services in GDP. But there are three aspects to this which distinguish these economies from other developing countries. First, the share tends to fluctuate considerably depending on the price of oil. Second, the share of manufactures in exports is only about 16 per cent: much lower than for other developing countries and has been declining (Table 14.6). Furthermore, the share of agricultural products is also much lower than in other regions and has also been declining. This poor performance in exports of agricultural and manufactured products reflects perhaps the Dutch disease. Third, the region has a negligible export of IT (information technology) related services (World Bank, 2011).

The performance of the countries of NAME

Though population is almost equally divided between North Africa and the Middle East, the latter is much richer as per capita income is over three times that in North Africa (Table 14.7). Only Libya in North Africa has a comparable per capita income. To ensure that our study takes into account the large gap between countries in the NAME region we decided for the purposes of our analysis to divide

Table 14.5: Current account balance on goods and services (% of GDP)

	1965-73	1974-82	1983-90	1991-2000	2001-05	2006-08
World	0.2	0.3	0.4	0.4	0.4	0.8
High income	0.4	0.2	0.2	0.6	0.6	0
LAC	−0.5	−1.5	3.3	−1.1	3	0.5
SSA	−1.1	−1.5	1.2	−1.3	1.5	0.5
NAME	8.7	−5.5	0.6	5.8	9.4	
SA	−1.7	−3.8	−4.4	−3.5	−0.8	−2.2
EAP	−1.9	−1.2	0.4	1.8	0.2	9.4

Source: World Development reports, various issues, World Bank, Washington DC and World Development Indicators, World Bank, Washington DC

Table 14.6: Merchandise exports (%)

	1991-2000	2001-05	2006-09	1991-2000	2001-05	2006-09
	Agricultural raw materials exports + food exports			Fuel exports		
LAC	24.3	18.3	17.8	27.3	17.9	20.0
SSA	7.3	12.1	16.1	37.8	36.0	35.9
NAME	4.1	3.1	2.6	63.2	70.6	69.6
SA	24.1	13.0	13.1	3.5	5.0	11.8
EAP	10.6	5.5	5.5	6.9	4.8	6.8
	Ores and metals exports			Manufacturing exports		
LAC	8.1	6.3	8.4	39.8	56.2	52.3
SSA	7.0	9.8	15.7	23.8	33.5	31.6
MNA	8.6	1.4	1.3	23.9	21.7	19.5
SA	3.4	3.4	5.2	68.0	77.4	68.3
EAP	2.6	2.3	3.8	77.5	85.3	81.4

Source: World Development reports, various issues, World Bank, Washington DC and World Development Indicators, World Bank, Washington DC

Table 14.7: Size of the economies of NAME and their incomes, 2009

	Population (millions)	GNI ($b)	GNI per capita ($b)	GDP growth rate 1990-2000	GDP growth rate 2000-05	GDP growth rate 2005-09
World	6,775	59,133	8,728	2.9	3.0	2.2
NAME	377	2,151	5,819	4.4	4.3	4.9
NAME1	70	787	19,518	4	5	5
NAME2	157	409	3,835	5	4	5
Algeria	35	154	4,420	1.6	4.4	2.9
Egypt	83	172	2,070	4.4	3.8	6.0
Libya	6	77	12,020	3.7	4.2	5.5
Morocco	32	90	2,770	2.7	4.4	4.8
Tunisia	10	39	3,720	5.0	4.5	4.7
Jordan	6	24	3,980	4.8	6.0	6.9
Kuwait	3	117	43,930	7.1	7.8	6.7
Lebanon	4	34	8,060	8.9	3.4	5.5
S. Arabia	25	439	17,700	3.3	4.0	3.0
Syria	21	51	2,410	5.4	4.0	4.6

Source: World Development reports, various issues, World Bank, Washington DC and World Development Indicators, World Bank, Washington DC

the region into two sub-groups. First is called NAME 1 and consists of the oil and natural gas exporting countries: Libya, Algeria, Saudi Arabia and Kuwait. The second group is called NAME 2 and consists of the other NAME countries. Not all the countries are included in the analysis because of lack of information about these countries in the World Bank's data set. The countries that are included are mentioned in the tables.

Growth of GDP accelerated in the region in the second half of the first decade of the twenty-first century (Table 14.7). However, growth rates in the countries of the region are quite volatile over the past two decades. Few countries have done consistently well over the two decades. We do not perceive a difference in growth rates between NAME 1 and 2 countries. For instance, the Spearman rank correlation[6] between growth in the decade of the 1990s and that in the first half of the 2000s and the second half of the 2000s is essentially zero. Neither are the poorer countries growing faster and catching up or the richer countries growing slower. This is also borne out by the rank correlation between per capita income in 1990 and per capita income in 2009 which is 1 for the 10 countries of the region that we examined. However, Kuwait has done well through the last two decades being the second fastest growing economy in the 1990s and the second half of the 2000s and the fastest growing in the first half of the 2000s. Jordan has steadily improved its performance from being the fifth fastest growing country in the region in the 1990s to second in the first half of the 2000s and the fastest in the second half of the 2000s. Egypt, the poorest country in our sample, performed very poorly until 2005, but improved its performance subsequently (Table 14.7).

Investment rates for the majority of the countries of the region declined during this period (Table 14.8). This was true for both NAME 1 and NAME 2 countries. Investment ratios declined between 1990–2000 and 2001–05 for eight countries in the region and increased for only two, namely Libya and Morocco. Between 2001–05 and 2006–09, investment ratios declined for four countries and increased for four countries. But for only one country, Morocco, was the investment ratio during 2006–09 higher than in the period from 1990 to 2000. Furthermore, the richer countries, NAME 1, have a lower investment ratio than the poorer countries. This is not because the richer countries lack savings; in fact, they run a large current account surplus (Table 14.9). In contrast, NAME 2 countries run large deficits; they are larger than the deficits run by many other developing countries. This suggests that there is a lack of investment

Table 14.8: Investment to GDP ratio

	1990-2000	2001-05	2006-09
NAME	22.8	22.6	
NAME1	18.7	17.9	17.0
NAME2	24.1	21.8	21.8
Algeria	25.7	23.8	
Egypt	20.2	17.2	18.7
Libya	12.7	13.1	
Morocco	22.6	26.1	28.7
Tunisia	25.4	24.0	23.2
Jordan	26.8	21.6	26.8
Kuwait	17.2	17.1	
Lebanon	27.4	19.4	12.2
Saudi Arabia	19.3	17.6	17.0
Syria	22.2	22.3	21.4

Source: World Development reports, various issues, World Bank, Washington DC and World Development Indicators, World bank, Washington DC

opportunities in the richer countries a reflection perhaps of the Dutch disease syndrome. The low and stagnant investment ratios in the region are in sharp contrast to the situation in the other regions. The low and in many cases falling investment ratios suggest that there is only a limited prospect for any significant acceleration in growth. The incremental capital–output ratio is at best about 4 (Agarwal, 2008) so

Table 14.9: Current account balance on goods and services (% of GDP)

	1991-2000	2001-05	2006-09
NAME	0.6	5.8	9.4
NAME1	−1.4	18.6	26.9
NAME2	−1.5	−2.3	−4.2
Algeria	5.2	20.7	16.9
Egypt	1.5	2.4	0.0
Libya	4.0	15.4	33.1
Morocco	−1.3	2.9	−2.1
Tunisia	−4.2	−2.4	−2.7
Jordan	−4.4	−0.2	−10.2
Kuwait	−8.8	23.6	36.2
Lebanon	−20.5	−11.1	
Saudi Arabia	−5.9	14.8	21.4
Syria	0.9	3.9	0.7

Source: World Development reports, various issues, World Bank, Washington DC and World Development Indicators, World Bank, Washington DC

that the current investment rates can only generate a growth rate of about 5 per cent per year and faster growth would require a step up in investment rates.

The share of exports of goods and services in GDP has been increasing for the countries of the region (Table 14.10) as is the case for other developing country regions. This is true for both NAME 1 and NAME 2 countries though the ratio is much higher for the richer energy exporting countries and the gap has increased over the past two decades. The NAME 1 countries have a negligible share of agricultural exports (Table 14.11). Despite the importance of exports for these economies the share of manufactures (Table 14.12) and of information and communication technologies (ICT) related exports is relatively low for the region. The small share of exports of manufactures reflects the generally unimpressive performance of the sector. The share of manufacturing in GDP has been declining in all the countries except Egypt (Table 14.13).

In brief, economic growth has been relatively poor in NAME compared to other developing country regions. Investment rates have been low and the agricultural and manufacturing sectors play a limited role, presumably because of the Dutch disease. The economic performance of the energy exporting countries (NAME 1) and the others (NAME 2) are broadly similar.

We now discuss the performance of our set of countries in the region in terms of progress towards achieving the MDGs.

Table 14.10: Export of goods and services (% of GDP)

	1991-2000	2001-05	2006-09
NAME	36.1	44.0	52.9
NAME1	34.8	48.9	55.6
NAME2	30.0	33.2	37.0
Algeria	27.6	39.5	45.5
Egypt	21.4	23.2	29.5
Libya	28.3	54.0	51.6
Morocco	26.1	30.0	34.0
Tunisia	40.7	42.0	49.4
Jordan	49.2	48.4	50.6
Kuwait	46.0	53.8	62.9
Lebanon	12.2	18.0	22.3
Saudi Arabia	37.2	48.1	62.5
Syria	30.5	37.5	36.0

Source: World Development reports. Various issues. World Bank. Washington DC and World Development Indicators. World Bank. Washington DC

Table 14.11: Percentage of merchandise exports: agricultural raw materials exports, food exports and fuel exports

	Agricultural raw materials exports + food exports			Fuel exports		
	1991-2000	2001-05	2006-09	1991-2000	2001-05	2006-09
NAME	4.1	3.1	2.6	63.2	70.6	69.6
NAME1	5.6	5.4	7.3	86.5	87.2	77.8
NAME2	19.7	16.4	15.7	20.3	21.2	18.2
Algeria	0.6	0.2	0.2	95.7	97.1	97.7
Egypt	14.3	15.1	10.0	42.3	42.5	51.0
Jordan	20.3	15.2	15.3	0.0	0.3	0.6
Kuwait	0.4	0.2	0.2	89.1	93.4	95.6
Lebanon	22.3	20.6	16.1	0.1	0.3	0.4
Libya	0.6	–	–	94.3	–	–
Morocco	29.4	22.5	20.9	2.4	2.5	2.1
Saudi Arabia	0.9	0.8	0.6	90.3	89.1	90.0
Syria	20.8	15.8	21.5	66.8	71.2	40.0
Tunisia	11.3	9.3	10.4	10.4	10.2	15.0

Source: World Development reports, various issues, World Bank, Washington DC and World Development Indicators, World Bank, Washington DC

Table 14.12: Percentage of merchandise exports: ores, metals and manufacturing exports

	Ores and metals exports			Manufacturing exports		
	1991-2000	2001-05	2006-09	1991-2000	2001-05	2006-09
NAME	8.6	1.4	1.3	23.9	21.7	19.5
NAME1	0.4	0.2	0.3	6.8	5.6	4.4
NAME2	9.1	6.6	6.8	50.4	53.9	56.9
Algeria	0.5	0.4	0.6	3.2	2.3	1.5
Egypt	5.3	3.8	3.9	37	30.7	25.5
Libya	0	–	–	5.1	–	–
Morocco	11.6	8.1	11	56.6	66.8	66
Tunisia	1.4	1.3	1.4	76.9	79.1	72.5
Jordan	27.1	16.6	10	52.6	67.9	74
Kuwait	0.3	0.1	0.2	10.1	4.9	4
Lebanon	8.3	9.1	12.2	69.3	69.6	70
Saudi Arabia	0.4	0.2	0.2	8.6	9.5	7.7
Syria	1.1	0.8	2.1	10	9.1	33.3

Source: World Development reports, various issues, World Bank, Washington DC and World Development Indicators, World Bank, Washington DC

Table 14.13: Value added (% of GDP)

	Agriculture			Manufacturing			Services, and so on		
	1980-2000	2001-05	2006-09	1980-2000	2001-05	2006-09	1980-2000	2001-05	2006-09
NAME	10.4	8.7	7.6	10.5	7.0	5.4	38.3	34.3	31.3
NAME1	5.7	4.6	4.5	16.3	14.0	13.2	53.5	54.6	56.4
NAME2	12.7	11.0	9.7	9.5	8.8	10.1	44.3	40.4	36.4
Algeria	11	9.9	8.7	17.7	18.1	16	50.8	49	48.8
Egypt	17	15.9	13.8	14.7	17.3	19.7	68.4	69.8	66.7
Jordan	4.7	2.7	2.8	5.4	2.6	–	50.1	48.1	–
Libya	–	3.7	2	18	16.7	15.2	51	55.8	56.3
Morocco	17.4	16.3	15.4	9.6	10.1	9.4	45.2	40	34.5
Tunisia	13.6	11.6	9.6	23	20.4	18.6	52.5	60.1	63.4
Kuwait	0.4	0.5	–	13.8	12.6	10.1	68	71.4	73.6
Lebanon	7.2	6.4	6.5	–	4.8	4.5	–	25	20.3
Saudi Arabia	5.7	4.4	2.7	15.7	8.6	11.3	44	42	46.7
Syria	29.9	24.4	19.4	18	18	17	57.7	59.7	60.3

Source: World Development reports, various issues, World Bank, Washington DC and World Development Indicators, World Bank, Washington DC

Progress towards achieving the MDGs

We now discuss how far these countries have progressed in meeting the MDGs before analysing the relation between the performances in the economic area and in achieving MDGs. The socials goals embedded in the MDGs reflect the idea that poverty is a multi-dimensional concept and does not merely reflect a lack of income and food. This multi-dimensionality is reflected in the construction of the human development index of the UNDP. It is believed that a higher score on the index enables an individual to better realise his/her potential. So a society with a high score enables its citizens to pursue a more meaningful life. This concept of welfare is in contrast to the material concept underlying the usual specification of the utility function where utility or wellbeing depends only on the goods consumed and reflects the broader concept of welfare as developed largely by Sen (1980; 1985; 1989).

Poverty and malnourishment

The goal under this MDG is to halve, between 1990 and 2015, the proportion of people who are below the poverty line and halve the proportion of the hungry. The malnourishment is of children under the age of 5 and is measured by their weight for their age and they are considered to be malnourished if they are two standard deviations less than the mean for that age.

Poverty levels in NAME are considerably lower than in the other regions (Table 14.14). But there has been very slow decline in the poverty rate. Large reduction in poverty requires rapid economic growth if there are no special social programmes. For instance, the largest reduction in poverty has been in EAP and to a lesser extent in SA which has also grown very rapidly.

Tackling these residual low levels of poverty would require special programmes as the poor are likely to be special groups not normally reached by normal economic activity. To reach the requisite target specified by the MDG would have required the countries in the region to reach 1.5 per cent of the population, which is about 5.6 million people. Even if we assume that these people had no income so that the state had to give each of them $1.25 per day (the threshold for poverty) throughout the year, the sum required would be just over 0.1 per cent of GDP. (The UN estimates the poverty gap to be about 1 per cent of GDP which is much more than the sum required to enable the poverty target to be met.) This sum of just above 0.1 per cent of GDP compares to the 20–25 per cent that is raised in taxes. We, therefore, conclude that it was well within the fiscal capacity of the governments to reach the poverty target. Similarly, the ratio of malnourished children is very low in the region (Table 14.14). The low levels of hunger and malnourishment reflect in part the subsidised food programmes in many of the countries of the region, for example, Egypt. Again, resources do not seem to be the main problem. The fundamental problem is one of having programmes that reach the vulnerable groups.

Programmes such as school feeding by World Food Programme (WFP) provide incentives to education and at the same time combat

Table 14.14: Poverty and malnourishment

	Poverty		Malnourishment	
	1990	2005	2000	2008
LAC	11.3	8.2	34.2	31.7
SSA	57.6	50.9	28.3	25.2
NAME	4.3	3.6	12.2	
SA	51.7	40.3	43	41
EAP	54.7	16.8	12.4	11.9

Source: World Development reports, various issues, World Bank, Washington DC and World Development Indicators, World Bank, Washington DC

malnourishment (Pereznieto et al, 2010). Programmes promoting health for pregnant women and children under 5 also exist. Therefore, all the individual countries have very low levels of poverty and malnourishment.

Mortality

The goals for reducing mortality rates are to reduce child mortality by two-thirds and reduce maternal mortality by three-quarters. The region was in the middle in comparison to other regions with mortality rates better than SA and SSA but worse than EAP and LAC (Table 14.15). It has, however, done very well in reducing mortality rates. It has the best performance in reducing maternal mortality and the second best in reducing infant and child mortality rates. As mentioned above most of the countries have programmes for pregnant women and children under 5. It should be able to meet its target for reductions in both child and maternal mortality rates. Countries have usually found it easier to reduce child mortality than maternal mortality (UN, 2005). This is because child mortality can often be reduced by acting against specific causes of death by providing vaccinations and inoculations. Reducing maternal mortality is more complex as such deaths can occur through a multiplicity of causes and the entire system needs to be improved to reduce such deaths.

Most of the countries have made significant progress. The richer countries unsurprisingly have lower mortality rates (Table 14.16), but the gap has been shrinking as the poorer countries have had a faster rate of decline. Countries significantly lagging behind are Libya and Jordan. Kuwait also seems to be lagging as it shows little progress; but this is because it started with very good values for the indicators.

Table 14.15: Mortality rates – differences between developing regions

	Infant			Child			Maternal		
	1990	2005	% reduction	1990	2005	% reduction	1990	2005	% reduction
LAC	41.9	22.3	46.8	52.5	26.8	49	140	91	35
SSA	109.5	88.3	19.4	180.8	143	20.9	870	710	18.4
NAME	57.2	32.3	43.5	75.6	39.8	47.3	210	98	53.3
SA	89.1	61.1	31.4	124.9	81.3	34.9	610	330	35.9
EAP	41.3	25.6	38	54.7	31.7	42	200	100	50

Source: World Development reports, various issues, World Bank, Washington DC and World Development Indicators, World Bank, Washington DC

Table 14.16: Mortality rates – differences among countries in NAME

	Infant mortality			Child mortality			Maternal mortality		
	1990	2005	% reduc- tion	1990	2005	% reduc- tion	1990	2005	% reduc- tion
NAME	57.2	32.4	43.4	75.6	39.8	47.4	210.0	98.0	53.3
NAME1	33.0	20.1	39.1	39.1	23.0	41.2	100.3	55.5	44.6
NAME2	44.8	22.9	48.9	57.3	26.7	53.5	167.0	72.0	56.9
Algeria	51.0	33.0	35.3	61.0	38.0	37.7	250.0	120.0	52.0
Egypt	65.5	25.2	61.5	89.5	30.0	66.5	220.0	90.0	59.1
Libya	31.8	19.3	39.3	35.7	21.2	40.6	100.0	68.0	32.0
Morocco	68.9	38.6	44.0	88.8	44.5	49.9	370.0	130.0	64.9
Tunisia	39.0	20.0	48.7	49.7	23.3	53.1	130.0	67.0	48.5
Jordan	32.2	22.9	28.9	39.3	27.1	31.0	110.0	66.0	40.0
Kuwait	13.9	9.1	34.5	16.7	11.0	34.1	10.0	9.0	10.0
Lebanon	32.9	14.6	55.6	40.2	16.6	58.7	52.0	29.0	44.2
Saudi Arabia	35.1	18.9	46.2	43.1	21.9	49.2	41.0	25.0	39.0
Syria	30.1	16.0	46.8	36.4	18.4	49.5	120.0	50.0	58.3

Source: World Development reports, various issues, World Bank, Washington DC and World Development Indicators, World Bank, Washington DC

Saudi Arabia is showing very limited progress in the area of maternal mortality.[7]

Education

All the regions made progress with regards to education. Primary education is almost universal (Table 14.17). Public free education has been at the core of social services in NAME region (Lockheed et al, 1999). Also, all the regions are close to achieving gender parity or near gender parity in primary education. Again, religious factors do not seem to have been a barrier to achieving such parity. While parity in secondary and tertiary education has not been reached, there has been considerable progress.

The regional achievements in the area of education are mirrored in that of the countries in that there is no country in the region which is lagging significantly in educational achievements (Table 14.18). Surprisingly, however, the richer countries are lagging behind in enrolment rates, although they have narrowed the gap and have even gone ahead as far as gender equality is concerned. For instance, the lowest sex ratio in primary education is 90 for Morocco. For most of the others it is at least in the mid-90s. Similarly, for primary enrolment

Table 14.17: Education

	Pr. enrolment		Male/female ratio	
	1990	2005	1990	2005
LAC		98.3		97
SSA		69.8		88.3
NAME		89.2		95.2
SA		84.8		93.3

Note: Data for 1990 for the regions is not available; data for EAP is also not available for 2005.

Source: World Development reports, various issues, World Bank, Washington DC and World Development Indicators, World Bank, Washington DC

Table 14.18: Primary school enrolment

	Enrolment		Female–male ratio	
	1990	2005	1990	2005
NAME		89.2		95.2
NAME1	72.5	88.8	84.8	96.8
NAME2	84.2	92.9	87.7	95.6
Algeria	87	97	84	93
Egypt		89.6	84	94
Libya				98
Morocco	56.2	87.5	67.5	89.3
Tunisia	92.6	98.1	88.3	97.1
Jordan	97.6	96.2	99.4	100.6
Kuwait		86.5	95.4	105.3
Lebanon			96.7	97.2
Saudi Arabia	58.5	83	75.2	91.2
Syria	90.4	93.1	90.4	95.3

Note: Numbers presented in this table represent the number of girls enrolled at school for 100 boys.

Source: World Development reports, various issues, World Bank, Washington DC and World Development Indicators, World Bank, Washington DC

the lowest ratio is 83 for Saudi Arabia, which is a huge improvement over the figure of 59 in 1990. Furthermore, only three other countries have a ratio fewer than 90, and for one of them, Morocco, this is again a vast improvement over the 1990 number.

In brief, the countries of the region generally have high levels of social achievement with either very low levels of poverty and hunger or rapid progress as in education and mortality rates. Also, the gap between the richer and poorer countries is narrowing as far as achievements in the areas of education and mortality rates are concerned.

A major problem with special programmes targeted to the poor is often their inability to reach the poor because of corruption, as the poor may be unaware of the programmes or their entitlements. As Indian Prime Minister Rajiv Gandhi had once declared at a news conference in the 1980s, only 15 per cent of the funds allocated by the government reach the intended beneficiaries.

High levels of social consciousness and an active civil society can help in ensuring that the poor access the programmes. This is illustrated by the Brazilian experience. The basic social welfare programme implemented by the government of President Lula in Brazil is Zero Hunger (Agarwal et al, 2010). The centerpiece of this programme is that it provides a family allowance, Bolsa Familia, on condition that the children attend school. It is a broad set of about 30 programmes that seeks to improve the conditions of the poor, by tackling hunger, education, health and empowerment. It includes provision of food, water, helping to build infrastructure and so on. The innovative feature of the programme is that identification of the poor and the delivery of the services is decentralised and involves civil society. Most evaluations deem the programme to be a success.

Similarly, civil society has played a significant role in the promulgation of many of India's social programmes. Persons who were prominent in organising civil society groups to work with the poor had a significant representation on the National Advisory Council (NAC) which was chaired by Mrs Gandhi, the President of the ruling party. She pushed the government to implement the recommendations of the NAC. India's rural employment scheme, National Rural Employment Guarantee Act (NREGA), which has been successful in providing income to the poor, was enacted and implemented under pressure from the NAC. The social activists have continued to monitor the implementation of the scheme and pointed various lacunae which were then corrected. Another measure, the Right to Information Act, also pushed by the NAC, has helped to uncover improprieties in the implementation of the NREGA and other social schemes, as well as administrative procedures and so has improved delivery of services to the poor.[8] Civil society was also instrumental in getting the government to amend the constitution to have education until the age of 14 declared a fundamental right. These groups are now pushing for food security and asking the government to make the right to food another a fundamental right.

Conclusion

The NAME region is relatively rich compared to the other developing countries regions. Correspondingly, it has relatively good social indicators with low levels of poverty, hunger and mortality rates. These are much better in NAME than the really poor regions of SA and SSA, but not as good as EAP and LAC. The problem in the NAME region has been a lack of dynamism. GDP in the region has grown slowly despite the resources. Moreover, the improvement in the social indicators has been limited.

The usually low levels of poverty and better social indicators reflect in part higher wages. This, together with the Dutch disease phenomenon that afflicts a number of countries in the region, suggests that a growth strategy relying on development of labour intensive manufacturing or services is unlikely to succeed. These countries will have to move up the value chain. This, however, requires the labour force to be better educated.

As far as social progress is concerned, the countries had the resources to reach the targets in poverty and reduction of malnourishment, but governments need to put in place appropriate programmes to reach the poor. Experience in other countries, such as Brazil and India, suggest that a strong civil society is helpful in the proper design and delivery of services to the poor (Agarwal et al, 2010). Civil society seems to be weak in these countries. But the issue of governance is complex and needs to be further analysed. Countries with poor governance are usually not able to reduce maternal mortality. These countries, however, have been able to do so.

We now make some tentative recommendations on how social progress can be sped up, which would be necessary to meet the new development goals accepted by the international community: the sustainable development goals (SDGs). Two channels can help a country achieve more rapid social progress. One is a higher rate of growth, the other is special programmes aimed at the disadvantaged. The countries in East Asia have made tremendous progress in improving the living standards of their people and achieved almost all the MDGs. But the countries of the region do not have very many social programmes (Agarwal, 2017). Their success has been based on the unprecedented rates of growth in the countries of the region. On the other hand, social progress in Latin America has occurred despite slow growth because of the contingent benefit programmes. This difference can be noted when the improvement in a social indicator relative to the growth in per capita income is calculated. This relation is much higher in Latin America and NAME than in East and South Asia.

The approach to be adopted by the countries of NAME would depend on the constraints facing each individual country. Managing social programmes needs an efficient and low corruption administrative system. This is more easily achieved if there is very active involvement of civil society organisations in the design and monitoring of the programmes. This is what the experience of other countries suggests.

A higher growth rate would require higher investment rates. Given that the countries of the NAME region receive limited economic aid and the international aid environment is becoming more restrictive, higher investment would require a higher rate of domestic savings and the ability to convert savings into investment. This in its turn requires institutions to intermediate between savers and investors. Countries in Asia have used different institutions to perform this task than countries in Latin America. Again, the approach adopted would depend on a country's particular situation. International experience would point out the prerequisites for the different methods that could be used for successful intermediation.

Acknowledgements

We want to thank Professor Mongi Boughzala for his valuable comments. We also thank Sean Walsh and Zachary Osborn for their help. The views expressed in this chapter are those of the authors. No responsibility for them should be attributed to any organisation with which they have been or are associated.

Notes

[1] Some of these conferences are identified in the introduction. For a more detailed description see (Agarwal, 2011).

[2] We do not discuss these IDGs here as many of them were incorporated in the MDGs. See (Hulme and Fukuda-Parr, 2009) for a discussion of these IDGs and their subsequent conversion into MDGs.

[3] These other regions are East Asia and Pacific (EAP), Latin America and Caribbean (LAC), South Asia (SA) and sub-Saharan Africa (SSA).

[4] The political evolution and the ebb and flow of popular movements in Egypt provide a very good example of this.

[5] Causes for generally low investment rates in NAME are discussed below.

[6] The Spearman rank correlation calculates the correlation between the ranks of the objects according to two different criteria.

7 Since all the countries on the region are Islamic it is unlikely that religious factors explain the difference in performance.

8 For instance, because of the right to information (RTI) a contractor on a project under the NREGA scheme must provide a list of the people hired by him and what he is paying them. Since this information is public it is not easy for him to misrepresent the number of people he has hired or what he is paying them.

References

Agarwal, M, 2008, Changing economic power, *Discussion Paper* 143, New Delhi: Research and Information Systems

Agarwal, M, 2011, Reshaping international organizations to achieve the MDGs, paper presented at a conference on Multilateral Development Cooperation in a Changing Global Order at the North–South Institute, Ottawa, June

Agarwal, M, 2017, BRICS and MDGs, in M Agarwal, Jing Wang, J Whalley (eds) *China and India: The International Context and Economic Growth, Manufacturing Performance and Rural Development*, Singapore: World Scientific, 325–41

Agarwal, M, Besada, H, White, L, 2010, Social challenges and progress in IBSA, *South African Journal of International Affairs* 17, 3, 333–60

Corden, WM, Neary, JP, 1982, Booming sector and de-industrialization in a small open economy, *Economic Journal* 92, 4, 825–48

Cornia, GA, Jolly, R, Stewart, F, 1988, *Adjustment with a human face: Protecting the vulnerable and promoting growth*, Oxford: Clarendon Press

Desai, M, 2007, Introductory remarks: Why India will to meet the Millennium Development Goals, in M Agarwal, AS Ray (eds) *Globalization and the Millennium Development Goals*, Delhi: Social Science Press

Hulme, D, 2009, *The making of the Millennium Development Goals: Human development meets results based management in an imperfect world*, Manchester: Brooks World Poverty Institute, Manchester University

Hulme, D, Fukuda-Parr, S, 2009, *International norm dynamics and 'the end of poverty': Understanding the Millennium Development Goals (MDGs)*, Manchester: Brooks World Poverty Institute, Manchester University

Lockheed, M, Avins, J, Chang, MC, Darnell, B, Demetriou, V, Ezzine, M, Maughan, P, Millot, B, Mulatu, M, Parker, M, Pham, DK, Steier, F, Yuki, T, Schubert, J, Van Eeghen, W, 1999, *Education in the Middle East and North Africa: a strategy towards learning for development*, Washington, DC: World Bank

Loewe, M, 2006, *Middle East/North Africa and the Millennium Development Goals: Implications for German development cooperation*, Studies 19, Bonn: German Development Institute

Pereznieto, P, Marcus, R, Cullen, E, 2011, Children and social protection in the Middle East and North Africa, *Overseas Development Institute (ODI) Project Briefing* 64, London: ODI

Sen, A, 1980, Equality of what, in M McMurrin (ed) *The Tanner Lectures on Human Values*, Salt Lake City (UT): University of Utah Press

Sen, A, 1985, *Commodities and capabilities*, Oxford: Elsevier Science

Sen, A, 1989, Development as capability expansion, *Journal of Development Planning* 19, 41–58, reprinted in S Fukuda-Parr and AK Shiva Kumar (eds) *Readings in human development*, New York: Oxford University Press, 2003, 3–16

UN (United Nations), 2005, Who's got the power: Transforming health systems for women and children, coordinated by A Mushtaque, R Chowdhury, A Rosenfield, *UN Millennium Project, Task Force Reports*, New York: UN

Williamson, J (ed), 1989, *Latin American adjustment: How much has happened?*, Washington, DC: Institute for International Economics

World Bank, 2011, *World Development Indicators, 2011*, Washington, DC: World Bank

Part Four
Looking forward

United Nations Millennium Development Goals (UN MDGs) and the Arab Spring: shedding light on the preludes?

M Evren Tok, Nancy Elbassiouny, Sofia Samper and Mohammed Sayeed Showkath

Introduction

Most western social scientists, Arab academics and secular intellectuals alike utterly failed to predict the powerful social and political explosion that led to a change of regime in several Arab countries, including Egypt, Tunisia and Yemen. Among Arab Nations, this phenomenon has been referred to as an 'Arab Awakening', while in the west it has been called an 'Arab Spring'. Tariq Ramadan explains that there is a lack of consensus on how to refer to this historical turning point for the Arab world; 'some call it the "Arab Spring", others, the "Arab Revolutions"; still others more cautious, use the neutral term "Arab uprisings". It remains difficult to ascertain, and to assess, what has happened, and what is happening, in the Middle East'. He goes on to say, 'An irreversible shift is clearly underway but no one is able to pinpoint exactly what is going on in these mass protests or to predict their ultimate outcome' (Ramadan, 2011). No matter what name we give it, the phenomenon was a result of a combination of both socioeconomic and political grievances. Amid this complexity, our aim is to understand if the Millennium Development Goals (MDGs) provided a concrete background to illuminate the preludes to the Arab Spring.

The countries used for this study include Tunisia, Egypt, Syria and Yemen, and they were chosen based on their ability to illustrate the wide range of outcomes for the MDGs, as well as the broad range of processes in the dynamics of the Arab Spring. Additionally, these represent various states according to Arab regional groupings: Egypt and Syria form part of the Mashreq countries, Tunisia represents the Maghreb states, while Yemen is part of the Arab least developed countries (LDCs) grouping. The only group not represented here is the core Gulf Cooperation Council States, several of which have indirectly experienced the Arab Spring. Although they have a role to play in outcomes and international civil society engagement in the MDG process regionally, they are more or less 'on-track' to achieve the MDGs compared to the other state groups (UN, 2010).

On 14 January 2011, Tunisia's president, Zine El-Abidine Ben Ali fled to Saudi Arabia, and as of mid-March 2013, Tunisia's new Islamist-led broadened government had set a timeframe for the completion of a draft constitution by April of 2013, with elections expected to take place by December 2013 at the latest. The situation in Syria, which began with a civil uprising, has evolved into a severe humanitarian disaster and, to date, there are over 1 million Syrian refugees living in neighbouring countries. In Egypt, Tahrir square has become a global icon and 11 February 2011 has become a very important day as it was the day that Egyptian president Hosni Mubarak resigned after 30 years in power. That being said, general political dissatisfaction and protest in Egypt is ongoing. Finally, despite the replacement of the Yemeni president Ali Abdullah Saleh on 27 February 2012 by his successor Abd al-Rab Mansur al-Hadi as a result of presidential elections, Yemen remains largely off-track for improvements in quality of life due to ongoing instability.

Before we discuss the effects of the Arab Spring on the achievement of the MDGs and on Arab civil society, it is important to identify the common features of the national uprisings in the countries included. One significant feature that is common to the five countries studied is the fact that the demonstrations were primarily youth-driven. This element is very important, because as Adeel Malik has pointed out, '[t]he real struggle for change in the Arab world will only begin when the dust from its youth revolutions has finally settled down' (Malik and Awadallah, 2013, 12–13). According to Omani professor Zidjaly, the phenomena that hit the Arab world could best be described as a 'youthquake' initiated by internet-savvy Arab youth (Zidjaly, 2011). Other common features include the fact that there were rising aspirations among people in the region due to increasing literacy rates and better access to higher education, a lack of economic opportunities, and a lack of concrete government reforms. Further, the use of modern technology, such as mobile phones, the internet and social networking technologies, including Facebook and Twitter, was also a common denominator. Most of the movements organised, communicated, raised awareness and were mobilised by harnessing the potential of these modern technologies. In all of the countries studied except Syria, sustained campaigns of civil resistance, such as rallies, strikes and protests, helped bring about the fall of despotic regimes. Another significant point to mention is that in all the countries studied, the various national uprisings came out of grassroots movements and in none of these countries was there any visible leadership behind the movements.

These revolutions shared similar slogans and tactics and seemed to find inspiration from each other. A good example is the Tunisian revolution. It inspired the events that led up to the popular protests in Egypt that ultimately led to the collapse of Mubarak's regime. An increase in human rights violations, political corruption, unemployment, underemployment, poverty, despotism and more importantly an unequal distribution of wealth that seemed to be concentrated in the hands of a few elites, were significant preludes to the Arab Spring that led to the fall of several authoritarian regimes. Although there are many similarities in these countries' experiences, there is also one significant difference – the role of the military in the uprisings. In the case of Syria and Yemen, the military stayed loyal to the regime, while Egypt and Tunisia had a completely different experience.

There are several factors that are responsible for weak development. Slow economic growth, resource constraints, the slow pace of institutional reforms, inadequate capacity and skill shortages, uneven income distribution, lack of enabling environment to attract investment, poor social inclusion and lack of political will. In addition to this, political instability, conflict and economic sanctions also cripple development. Depending on the economic and social conditions, some factors play a more significant role than others. It is difficult to give a standardised weightage to the factors (Salamey, 2015). The Arab World's pre-Arab-Spring progress in achieving the MDGs differed from country to country. The latest reports on the MDGs in the Arab region prior to the Arab Spring were prepared in 2010 when major concerns included food security and food prices, as well as the ramifications of the global financial crisis (UN, 2010). Yet, according to the 2012 MDG Report, there have been pervasive positive worldwide trends that could be valid for the Arab world as well. For instance, both the number of people living in extreme poverty and poverty rates fell in every developing region. While reporting on indicators for achievement of the MDGs varied greatly between states in 2010 with some countries close to attaining their goals, in many instances movement toward achieving the MDGs had encountered severe obstacles (UN, 2010). The accuracy and reliability of official statistics is a further challenge to assessing MDG achievement. Another crucial challenge, as presented by Dani Rodrik, is the claim that there is little evidence to suggest that those successes were the result of the MDGs themselves. China implemented policies that engineered history's greatest poverty eradication programme prior to, and independently from, the Millennium Declaration and the MDGs.[1]

While some scholars argue that the Arab Spring was a promising movement for enduring improvements in quality of life led by civil society mobilisation, the immediate result in terms of MDG achievement is a regression due to the instability created through popular protests, which are ongoing. The protests that took place after the fall of the previous regimes have claimed even more lives in some of these countries than during the initial revolutions. This section will review the progress of the selected states as indicated by 2010 reporting, and consider the effects of the Arab Spring on the achievement of the MDGs. While the Arab Spring appears to have caused a set-back in the MDGs, this chapter suggests that the MDGs were not designed to be flexible or account for more complex political processes that, over the longer term, increase wellbeing and quality of life through civil society organising.

Analysis of MDG implementation

Even though the MDGs were mainly developed with the LDCs' specific needs in mind, they were also meant to serve two other very important purposes. One purpose of the MDGs was to serve as criteria for donor countries in their decision to allocate international aid to developing countries and the other was to enable developing countries and the international community to monitor donors' commitment and fulfilment of the aid. The MDGs became fully operational, and were implemented through all the UN agencies and various stakeholders through a variety of funding mechanisms. Insufficient financing of the MDGs emerged as a significant threat to their achievement following the global financial crisis in 2008. Due to funding shortfalls, significant efforts have been made since 2000 to address funding needs and provide innovative funding mechanisms, yet by the 2008 global financial crisis, significant financial obstacles were indicated as a hurdle to achieving the MDGs (Reisen, 2004). The Arab Spring is also a reaction to the reverberations of the global financial crisis, and it is largely recognised that the food price riots and unemployment, paired with repressive political regimes, are the most salient issues that led to the Arab Spring. In addition, disenfranchised youth, who felt a lack of opportunities and economic exclusion, contributed significantly to the popular protests and uprising. After all, it was one young Tunisian man, who set himself aflame to protest against this lack of economic opportunity, his inability to support his family through his small business, and the overall injustice and oppression propagated by the authorities.

The MDGs were a state-led process, with national policy frameworks, whereby government representatives participated in formulating national strategies, policies and reporting on MDG achievement over the past 15 years. This factor is significant to keep in mind when considering the Arab Spring, in that civil society movements were directly oriented towards ousting their political leaders and the establishments that had signed up to the MDG process. This does not mean that the goals themselves became suspect or the object of protest, but that the political leadership that had instated the MDGs either disappeared, or acted against the principles of the MDGs. Despite this fact, the 2012 United Nations Report on Global MDGs mentions the Arab Spring only in passing in a few instances, as a challenge to the achievement of specific MDGs due to conflict situations and political transitions (UN, 2012). This limited analysis of the link between the MDGs and the regional uprisings may be due to the fact that there has been an attempt to de-politicise MDG finance mechanisms.

The efforts to increase funding in order to propel MDG achievement often de-politicises the 'development' process. Before the Arab Spring, concerns for achievement lay mainly in resource mobilisation. This approach may have ignored the power dynamics and structures that maintained repressive regimes. The MDG focus on results through indicators and country-ownership may have sidelined a deeper understanding of the process and the complexities of social change. Although the MDGs can serve as possible indicators of quality of life, as well as give us some insight into the conditions of various populations, in the Arab region, as Table 15.1 illustrates, relying on them exclusively posed problems due of the complexity of the region.

Country Profiles: MDG Progress for Tunisia, Egypt, Syria and Yemen

The summary of the MDG Progress Reports for Arab States published online on 23 September 2013 by UNDP suggests that, '[t]he Arab region has made impressive progress towards some MDGs. But achievements are uneven' (UN, 2013, 97–100). The report further

Table 15.1: MDG progress (achievement of MDGs prior to the Arab Spring)

MDGs		Yemen	Syria	Egypt	Tunisia
1	Eradicate extreme poverty and hunger	Unlikely	Unlikely	Unlikely	Fair
2	Achieve universal primary education	Likely	Fair	Fair	Likely
3	Promote general equality and empower women	Unlikely	Unlikely	Unlikely	Unlikely
4	Reduce child mortality	Likely	Fair	Fair	Fair
5	Improve maternal health	Unlikely	Fair	Strong	Unlikely
6	Combat HIV/AIDS, malaria and other diseases	Unlikely	Fair	Unlikely	Unlikely
7	Ensure environmental sustainability	Unlikely	Fair	Fair	Fair
8	Develop global partnership for development	Likely	Fair	Fair	Fair

Source: UN, 2010, 45

explains that the region also 'lags behind' on several of the important targets, including addressing and resolving the issue of hunger. Many of the MDG gains in several of the countries in the Arab region have either ceased or regressed. This is as a result of the 'political, social, and economic transitions' that have taken place since 2010, shortly after most of the MDG Progress Reports for the Arab States were written. The region's least developed country, Yemen, has also fallen short of any major achievement in the MDGs, especially on issues related to 'nutrition, food security, access to water and sanitation, and child and maternal mortality' (UN, 2013, 97–100). Prior to the Arab Spring, the region had experienced some progress in the achievement of some of the MDGs, including primary school enrollment, which rose from 85 per cent in 1999 to 92 per cent in 2011, and reducing infant mortality by two thirds (UN, 2013). The region continues to lag on the goal of empowering women (Table 15.2).

Tunisia

Despite a successful revolution and being one of the most resilient states in the region in terms of regaining stability, the Tunisian economy is still weak, and despite the emergence of a democratic regime, political instability is still an issue with recent political upheaval. Despite these ongoing obstacles, it is very likely that the political shift in Tunisia has ushered in a positive turn for the wellbeing of Tunisian people through the emergence of a strong civil society. Tunisia offers hope for a relatively smooth democratic transition compared to other countries in the region.

Table 15.2: Pre- and Post-Arab Spring unemployment rates: Tunisia, Egypt, Syria and Yemen

Country		Year	Unemployment rates					
			Male		Female		Total	
			Youth	Total	Youth	Total	Youth	Total
Tunisia	Pre-Arab Spring	2008	–	–	–	–	–	12.4
		2009	–	11.3	–	18.8	–	13.3
		2010	27.8	10.9	32.7	18.9	29.4	13
	Post Arab Spring	2011	40.8	15	45.5	27.4	24.3	18.3
		2012	35.7	14.6	41.8	25.6	37.6	18.1
		2013	–	–	–	–	–	17.5
Egypt	Pre-Arab Spring	2008	–	–	–	–	–	8.7
		2009	15.7	5.2	56.2	23	25.6	9.4
		2010	14.7	4.9	54.1	22.6	24.8	9
	Post Arab Spring	2011	22.5	8.9	53.2	22.7	29.7	12
		2012	28.1	9.3	57.1	24.1	34.6	12.7
		2013	–	–	–	–	–	12.7
Syria	Pre-Arab Spring	2008	–	–	–	–	–	10.9
		2009	12.1	5.7	43	22.3	16.7	8.1
		2010	16.4	6.2	43.5	22	20.4	8.4
	Post Arab Spring	2011	–	–	–	–	–	8.4
		2012	–	–	–	–	–	8.4
		2013	–	–	–	–	–	8.4
Yemen	Pre-Arab Spring	2008	–	–	–	–	–	15
		2009	–	11.3	–	40.2	–	14.6
		2010	26	12.4	43.8	74	33.7	17.8
	Post Arab Spring	2011	–	–	–	–	–	17.9
		2012	–	–	–	–	–	17.8
		2013	–	–	–	–	–	17.2

Source: International Labour Organization (ILO) Global Employment Trends, 2014

The economic impact of the unrest and political upheaval was high in Tunisia. Various factors contributed to the decline in economic growth. The Libyan crisis had enormous influence on Tunisian economy, reducing growth by 36 per cent; the European economic crisis caused the tourism and export industry to dwindle. The former reduced by 37 per cent during the first ten months of 2011 (AfDB, 2012). Despite modest political success, the government faces urgent challenges to address the weak economy, steady decline in tourism revenues, persistent youth unemployment and inadequate service delivery. From 2010 to 2011, there was a 5.3 per cent increase in the unemployment rate and the male youth unemployment rate increased by 13 per cent from 27.8 to 40.8 per cent. The female youth unemployment went up by more than 12 per cent from 32.7 per cent in 2010 to a staggering 45.5 per cent.

After the onset of the Arab Spring and ousting of long-term president Ben Ali, the political elites were mired in conflict with different parties vying for control, most notably the Islamist and secular party. Tunisia's first free elections were held in October 2011 and the Islamist Ennaahda party came into power with 41 per cent of the votes. This surprise election victory upsetted the securlar liberals who continue to downplay the policy reforms proposed by the government. The interim government was tasked with reforming Tunisia's constitution. After several consultations with technocrats, political parties and civil society, a new constitution was adopted in January 2014. New elections were then held between October and December 2014, and the ongoing onslaught against the Islamist party led to the defeat of the Ennahda party. However, the Ennahada party managed to secure the second-largest bloc of seats. Nidaa Tounes won the election and formed a coalition with other secular parties and Ennahada party. The political crisis in the country was overcome by informal negotiations, but the resilience of these partnerships has yet to be tested. The transitional government's objective was to ensure political stability, macroeconomic stabilisation, job creation, confidence building in the market for investors and security for tourists (Arieff and Humud, 2015; Natter, 2015; El-Issawi, 2012).

Tunisia has been one of the fastest growing countries in the region since the 1990s, reaching per capita income of $4,070 in 2010. Economic and social indicators show great progress as a result of economic growth. Two decades of accelerated growth has increased social spending and financing of pro-poor projects. In 2005, only 3.8 per cent of the population lived below the national poverty line. As a result, Tunisia managed to make substantial progress in the achievement of the MDGs, including extreme poverty reduction (MDG 1), universal primary education (MDG 2), reduction of child mortatility (MDG 4), and access to drinking water and basic sanitation (MDG 7a–b). Less progress has been made when it comes to maternal mortality (MDG 5), although the government had planned to increase the budget for paternal care before the revolution. Even before the onset of MDGs, Tunisian government was actively spending on various sectors to improve the social condition of the population; although, the funding has not been constant. The public spending in this regard was 27.3 per cent in the early 1990s, and it declined to 21.2 per cent in 2000 before increasing to 29.7 per cent in 2008. Public spending for education sector on all levels was very high, reaching 20.7 per cent in 1990, and then 25 per cent between 2006 and 2008 (on average). Unfortunately, the public spending for the health sector declined significantly from over 10 per cent during the 1970s and 1980s to 5.7 per cent in 2008. This is because of the growth of the private healthcare system. In the post-revolution period, the public expenditures for social sectors diminished and hindered progress in achieving all the targets by 2015 (Mohamed and Sanchez, 2011; AfDB, 2012). Mohamed and Sanchez (2011) observed that the government required 5.7 to 7.1 per cent of GDP per year to meet the MDG goals in primary education, child and maternal mortality, water and sanitation by 2015. Because of the political transition, it was politically and economicaly infeasible to scale up the funding, which resulted in a further decline of national savings.

Despite some achievements, what led to the political upheaval in 2010 is not that surprising. Unequal distribution of wealth, lack of employment opportunities for young people, a stifled private sector, dysfunctional institutions, corruption and poor governance were the major contributors of frustration and resentment against the government. Compared to 2000, governance had worsened by 2010 with most of the indicators showing a declining trend. Voice and accountability, government effectiveness and control of corruption were weaker in 2010, while there was a modest increase in the rule of law. The growing youth unemployment rate worsened because of the 2007–08 financial crisies, reaching up to 25 per cent by the end of 2010 and 32 per cent in 2013–14. The market was not creating enough jobs for the ever-rising number of graduates, and the challenges to migrate from Tunisia to Europe continued to increase, contributing to a lost generation and sense of deprivation and hopelessness (AfDB, 2012).

The future of development depends on political progress. The last four years of political reconstruction remained resilient and relatively peaceful in terms of resolving the political differences. Nevertheless, the situation is fragile. The ongoing political democratisation process provides an opportunity to address some of the key structural challenges that have hindered development and compounded inequality. Besides making radical political reforms and boosting the security apparatus, the government must invest in rebuilding the economy, and creating jobs for educated youth, as well as building institutions to provide necessary skillsets for youth to transition from university to companies. To ensure stability, growth and economic prosperity, the government should continue to deepen democracy at all levels, increase transparency and accountability, and create new mechanisms to stem corruption. There should be a major shift in bargaining terms between the government and citizens: from obligatory loyalty to active engagement, mutual respect, and trust. See Table 15.3.

Egypt

An important factor that led to Egypt's revolution was the country's high unemployment rate, especially among youth. Unemployment continues to be a major challenge to Egypt's economic recovery and ultimate transition to Democracy. According to the International Labor Organization (ILO) (2012), the global youth unemployment rate was 13 per cent in 2012, Egypt's central statistical bureau, the Central Agency for Public Mobilization and Statistics (CAPMAS), also reported a 39 per cent unemployment rate among Egyptians aged 20 to 24 in December 2012.

Egypt has a new set of challenges to manage, including harassment of women, an increase in crime, the successive food and fuel inflation, and the severe security issues raised by confronting terrorists in Sinai, which is considered by some as lawless. In a statement published 10 August 2014, on the Republic of Egypt's State Information Service (SIS) website, Interior Minister Mohamed Ibrahim said, 'Egypt has the upper hand in its fight against terror' and 'the security forces would spare no effort to uproot terrorism from Egypt'.

Egypt's experience with the Arab Spring quickly transformed from a large-scale uprising against a dictator who had reigned for over 30 years, to free and democratic elections that brought Mohamed Morsi, a member of the Islamist Muslim Brotherhood's Freedom and Justice Party (FJP), to power. His power was short lived as a more massive revolt was staged and with the military's intervention, once again Egypt's ruler was deposed. It is important to understand the key actors in Egypt's recent transition to have a better understanding of the dynamics that either hinder or foster Egypt's achievement of the MDGs. Some of the key actors include Egypt's military, the Muslim Brotherhood, liberals, secularists and Salafis or ultra-conservatives.

The Egyptian military enjoys considerable power, prestige and independence within the state. According to Article 200 of the Egyptian constitution, '[t]he armed forces belong to the people, and their duty is to protect the country, and preserve its security and the integrity of its territories'. Public perception of the military shifted from resentment towards an accomplice of the old regime to calling upon them to rescue Egypt from Morsi, who was considered an 'inept and autocratic' ruler (Tabaar, 2013). Egypt's military was established

Table 15.3: MDG progress: country analysis for Tunisia

Goals	Pre-Arab Spring Source: National Report on Millennium Development Goals, May 2004 Findings and challenges	Post Arab Spring Source: Assessing Development Strategies to Achieve the MDGs in The Republic of Tunisia UN Department for Social and Economic Affairs October 2011 Findings and challenges
1: Eradicate Extreme Poverty • Reduce poverty by half • Achieve full/productive employment for all • Reduce hunger by half	• Poverty reduced from 22% in 1975 to 4.2% in 2000 • The percentage of people living on less than a 1$ a day declined from 1.5% in 1990 to 0.5% in 2000 • 50% of population was poor and food insecure • The poor were concentrated in rural areas (62.3% of population) • Food insecurity regressed	• In 2005, 3.8% of the population was in extreme poverty and 81% was middle class • Economic growth declined to 4.6% in 2008 from 6.3% in 2007 • GNI in 2010 was 3 times higher than in 2007 • Unemployment was on the rise • Was one of the fastest growing economies in North Africa and MENA region before revolution
2: Achieve Universal Primary Education • Universal enrolment in basic education	• Public education was free • Primary education was compulsory • Regional disparities	• In 2005, government spending on education was 7.3% of GDP and 20.8% of total government expenditures • The enrolment rate for both boys and girls aged 6 went up from 96.3% in 1990-91 and then to 99.2% in 2008-09 • Decline in quality of education • 22.9% of the population aged 10 and above were illiterate compared to 46.2% in 1984 and 31.7% in 1994

(continued)

Table 15.3: MDG progress: country analysis for Tunisia (continued)

Goals	Pre-Arab Spring Source: National Report on Millennium Development Goals, May 2004 Findings and challenges	Post Arab Spring Source: Assessing Development Strategies to Achieve the MDGs in The Republic of Tunisia UN Department for Social and Economic Affairs October 2011 Findings and challenges
3: Promote Gender Equity • Enrolment in basic education • Share in paid jobs • Representation in parliament	• 99% enrolment of both girls and boys in primary school • Legislation enacted to promote gender equity • Ministry of Women's Affairs, the Family and Children established • High illiteracy rate for girls • 1 of 3 women enter the labour market • Regional disparities	• One of the most advanced countries on the issue of gender equality in the MENA region • Women only make up 26% of working population
4: Reduce Child Mortality • Reduce by two-thirds • Measles immunisations	• Child mortality declined to 22.1 in 2002 from 51.4 per thousand in 1985 • Increase in vaccination coverage with 83.6% of infants immunised • Regional disparities	• Child mortality rate declined from 37.3 per 1,000 live births in 1990 to 18.4 per 1,000 in 2007 • Rural child mortality double that of urban areas
5: Improve Maternal Health • Reduce mortality rate by two-thirds • Access to reproductive health services	• Reproductive health integrated into basic healthcare services • Regional disparities	• Maternal mortality rate reduced from 74.8 per 100,000 live births in 1990 to 54.8 per in 2,000 • Lack of referral and transport
6: Combat HIV, AIDS, malaria, and so on	• National programme launched to ensure medical care is free for HIV/AIDS patients • Lack of awareness of HIV/AIDS	• Social stigma of HIV/AIDS • More education is needed

(continued)

Table 15.3: MDG progress: country analysis for Tunisia (continued)

Goals	Pre-Arab Spring Source: National Report on Millennium Development Goals, May 2004 Findings and challenges	Post Arab Spring Source: Assessing Development Strategies to Achieve the MDGs in The Republic of Tunisia UN Department for Social and Economic Affairs October 2011 Findings and challenges
7: Ensure Environmental Sustainability • Recovering Deforestation • Half no. of people without access to improved sanitation services • Improve living conditions of poor neighbourhoods	• Water and soil conservation policies implemented costing about 135 million Tunisian dinar • Drinking water accessible to 93.6% of population in 2002 – 82.6% in rural areas • 59.9% of the population had access to improved sanitation services in 1994 and 70% in 2002 • Climate change • Fragile ecosystem, salinisation • Limited resources • Regional disparities in sanitation	• 98% of the population has access to safe drinking water as compared to 75% in 1990 • Regional disparities
8: Global Partnership for Development	• Bilateral partnership agreements for free trade with Morocco, Egypt and Jordan • Member of WTO since 1995 • First country to sign a partnership agreement with EU which led to a free trade area in 2008 • Tunisia's World Solidarity Fund unanimously adopted by the UN in 2002 • Initiator country of the World Summit on the Information Society since 1998 • Efforts made to gradually open the economy to outside world	

371

in 1922 and its structure hasn't changed significantly since 1952. It is the largest and strongest military in the Middle East and Africa and is ranked the thirteenth largest and most powerful military in the world (GFP, 2016). Egypt's armed forces are made up of four branches: the army, navy, air force and air defence forces.

The military is led by a supreme council (SCAF) made up of 21 military officers for all four branches. Egypt's president is also the head of the armed forces and holds the title, 'Supreme Leader of the Egyptian Armed Forces'. According to the CIA World Factbook, in 2012, 1.72 per cent of Egypt's GDP went towards the military's budget and in 2014 the military budget was $4,400,000,000 (GFP, 2016). The military engages in road and property construction and has its own business assets, including its own hospitals, clubs, factories, gas stations and other real estate. In addition to its many commercial and business interests in Egypt, it is estimated that the military controls anywhere from 5 to 40 per cent of the economy. Prior to the Arab Spring, President Abdel Fattah el-Sisi served as the head of Egypt's military intelligence until he was appointed by former President Morsi to be Egypt's Minister of Defence. See Table 15.4.

Syria

Over 100,000 Syrian refugees have fled to nearby Iraq, which is struggling with its own stabilisation (UNHCR, 2013). António Guterres, the UN High Commissioner for Refugees, explains that, '[w]ith a million people in flight, millions more displaced internally, and thousands of people continuing to cross the border every day, Syria is spiraling toward full-scale disaster' (5–7). Guterres has also stated that the UN is 'doing everything we can to help, but the international humanitarian response capacity is dangerously stretched. This tragedy has to be stopped' (UNHCR, 2013, 5–7).

Syria is the starkest example of the unravelling of MDG progress and ongoing strife. The Syrian Arab Spring began in March 2011 and has continued to the present with increasing violence, destruction of infrastructure, and massive displacement. Despite the continued assault by 'rebels' against the ruling Baath party led by President Assad, Assad has not capitulated. It is certain that the ongoing conflict will severely undermine any potential progress on the MDGs that may have been achieved. Although massive humanitarian efforts are essential, political stability will be key to ensuring a smooth transition for Syria after the fall of President Assad's regime.

Table 15.4: MDG progress: country analysis for Egypt

Goals	Pre–Arab Spring Source: UNDP Egypt Millennium Development Goals Report 2010 Findings and challenges	Post Arab Spring Source: UNDP Human Development Report 2013 and other various reports Findings and challenges
1: Eradicate Extreme Poverty • Reduce poverty by half • Achieve full/productive employment for all • Reduce hunger by half	• 3.4% extreme poverty in 2008, down from 8.2% in 1990 • Permanent jobs decreased from 89% in 2005 to 82% in 2008. • Almost 50% of the population is poor and food insecure. • Regional disparities • Rapid population growth • Women and youth are majority of unemployed	• Rise in unemployment rate • Larger percentage of population poor • Escalating inequalities • Food inflation
2: Achieve Universal Primary Education • Universal enrolment in basic education	• Net enrolment ratio increased from 65% in 1990 to 96% in 2008/09 • Regional disparities	• Adult literacy rate is 72%
3: Promote Gender Equity • Enrolment in basic education • Share in paid jobs • Representation in parliament	• Significant sexual harassment • Minimal female participation in political and government sector • Rural women most vulnerable	• Sexual harassment legislation enacted and enforced for the first time in Egypt's history • No significant participation in political life for women • Unemployment rate for women very high
6: Combat HIV, AIDS, malaria, and so on	• Inadequate data on HIV/AIDS • Hepatitis B and C are a major issue	• Insufficient data

(continued)

373

Table 15.4: MDG progress: country analysis for Egypt (continued)

Goals	Pre–Arab Spring Source: UNDP Egypt Millennium Development Goals Report 2010 Findings and challenges	Post Arab Spring Source: UNDP Human Development Report 2013 and other various reports Findings and challenges
7: Ensure Environmental Sustainability • Recovering Deforestation • Half no. of people without access to improved sanitation services • Improve living conditions of poor neighbourhoods	• Efforts to activate the National Environmental Action Plan • Increased access to safe potable water and sanitation services • Climate Change • Depleting natural resources • Pollution • Energy shortages	• Only 4% of rural population has adequate sanitation • Loss of biodiversity • Depleting water, oil and gas resources • Climate change • Energy shortages • Water shortages • Air pollution
8: Global Partnership for Development	• Debt percentage of GDP fell from above 100% in 1990/91 to 16.7% in 2008/09 • Exports increased from $10,452.50 million in 2003/04 to $25,168.90 in 2008/09 (increase of 140%)	• 26.7% of population are internet users

Several years into the Syrian Crisis, the number of Syrian refugees who have fled to nearby countries has far surpassed the million mark. Since January 2014 alone, over 400,000 refugees have sought safety in neighbouring host countries including Turkey, Lebanon and Jordan. The majority of those refugees are children under the age of 11. The refugee crisis has also had a major impact on the host countries. Since the onset of the Syrian Crisis, Lebanon's population has increased by 10 per cent, Turkey has spent over $600 million to set up 17 refugee camps and is currently in the process of setting up more camps to accommodate the need. Jordan's energy, water, health and education sectors are extremely strained.

According to the UNHCR, more than half of the million Syrian refugees are children and for most of these children, schooling has been inaccessible. Throughout the region, the Arab Spring has had a significantly negative effect on education, but it has had an especially detrimental effect in Syria. Prior to the Arab Spring, the region was making the most progress compared to all other regions in ensuring that education was accessible to most of its citizens. Education for Syrian children, both for those internally displaced and refugees living outside of Syria, is lacking. The UN and other humanitarian organisations have dedicated resources and programmes to help manage the crisis. Yet while they have launched specific programmes to ensure accessibility to primary education for Syrian refugees, nothing effective has been done to address the issue for internally displaced Syrians living within Syria's borders.

Regarding the promotion of gender equality and closing the gender gap, Syria had begun to demonstrate slight progress prior to the Arab Spring, yet currently the condition of Syrian women is deteriorating. In a speech before the UN Human Rights Council in Geneva on 26 February 2013, regarding the dire humanitarian situation in Syria, UNHCR Assistant High Commissioner, Erika Feller, explained that many displaced civilians were subject to gender-based violence and that, 'this displacement is not only about loss of homes and economic security. It is also, for many, accompanied by gender-based crimes, deliberate victimisation of women and children and a frightening array of assaults on human dignity'. In addition to a lack of access to education, for most Syrians living within Syria or in host countries, access to adequate healthcare and housing is also a major issue. See Table 15.5.

Table 15.5: MDG progress: country analysis for Syria

Goals	Pre-Arab Spring Source: Syrian Arab Republic Third National MDGs Progress Report 2010 Findings and challenges	Post Arab Spring Source: UNDP Human Development Report 2013 and other various reports Findings and challenges
1: Eradicate Extreme Poverty • Reduce poverty by half • Achieve full/productive employment for all • Reduce hunger by half	• Rate of those employed to population ration reduced from 46.6% in 2001 to 44.8% in 2008 • National poverty rate decreased from 12.6% in (1996/1997) to 9.9% in (2006/2007) • 2.4% decline in people below food poverty line from 1996 (3.6%) to 2007 (1.2%) • Regional poverty disparities	• Devastating humanitarian crisis
2: Achieve Universal Primary Education • Universal enrolment in basic education	• Net primary school enrolment (ages 6-11) rose from 95.4% in 1990 to 99% in 2008 • Low quality of education	• Internally displaced children out of school
3: Promote Gender Equity • Enrolment in basic education • Share in paid jobs • Representation in parliament	• Gender disparities reduced on all educational levels (primary to university) • The percentage of women in wage employment in service sector rose from 21% in 1991 to 29% in 2007 • Women's participation in parliament increased from 2% 1971 to 12.4% 2011 • 7% of ministers and ambassadors were women and women and held 20% of the professional positions in government • Educational ratio improvements did not lead to sufficient improvements in women's participation in the economic and political life	• Over 145,000 Syrian refugee women head the family as single mothers • Many refugee women and children are exploited and subject to abuse • Many girls are forced into marriage as child brides

(continued)

Goals	Pre-Arab Spring Source: Syrian Arab Republic Third National MDGs Progress Report 2010 Findings and challenges	Post Arab Spring Source: UNDP Human Development Report 2013 and other various reports Findings and challenges
4: Reduce Child Mortality • Reduce by two-thirds • Measles immunisations	• Under 5 mortality fell significantly from 41.7% in 1993 to 18.9% in 2008 • Increase in immunisation from 73.3% in 1993 to 87.8% in 2006 • Measles immunisation 92.4% in 2006, up from 83.5% in 1993	• Access to adequate health services limited • Over 5.5 million children have been affected by the civil war • Immunisation rate decreased due to civil war
5: Improve Maternal Health • Reduce mortality rate by two-thirds • Access to reproductive health services	• National maternity mortality ratio fell from 107 deaths per 100,000 live births in 1993 to 56 in 2008. • Disparities exist between governorates • The Eastern region is the most vulnerable due to lower educational and economic levels. Most births in this region are also at home and attended by traditional midwives • Inadequate maternal care in rural areas • There is a higher need for awareness in the rural areas	• The civil war has affected women's access to adequate healthcare and especially maternal healthcare • More women are giving birth at home as a result of the war • Less women have access to reproductive health services and education • According to Save the Children, more than 60% of Syrian hospitals and 38% of primary healthcare facilities have been damaged or destroyed • Production of pharmaceutical drugs has fallen by 70% • Midwives have run out of the medicines and equipment required for deliveries • Amount of Caesarean section deliveries has more than doubled due to women opting 'to schedule their deliveries rather than risk going into labour in an insecure context'

(continued)

Table 15.5: MDG progress: country analysis for Syria (continued)

Goals	Pre-Arab Spring Source: Syrian Arab Republic Third National MDGs Progress Report 2010 Findings and challenges	Post Arab Spring Source: UNDP Human Development Report 2013 and other various reports Findings and challenges
6: Combat HIV, AIDS, malaria, and so on	• 22% of population is aged 15-24 and make up 34% of registered HIV/AIDS cases • Stigma against HIV positive individuals • Lack of awareness	• Insufficient data
7: Ensure Environmental Sustainability • Recovering Deforestation • Half no. of people without access to improved sanitation services • Improve living conditions of poor neighbourhoods	• Proportion of land covered by forest declined from 15% in the first half of the century to 3% in 2007 • The percentage of people using improved drinking-water sources rose from 65.6% in 1990 to 92% in 2007 • The percentage of people using improved sanitation increased from 55% in 1990 to 82.4% in 2009 • Excessive deforestation • Urban–rural disparities	• Climate change and severe drought • The civil war has had devastating effects on the environment and access to sanitation
8: Global Partnership for Development	• Syria is working on achieving membership in the WTO • Lowest recipient of ODA in the region • 90% of ODA channelled to social infrastructure and only 10% towards economic sector	• Syrian ties with its allies (Russia, China and Iran) • Government sanctions and embargoes from several countries, including the EU

Yemen

Yemen is one of the poorest countries in the Arab world. Even before the Arab Spring, there were several incidents of conflicts between different tribal groups struggling to control Yemen's scarce natural resources. As the Arab Spring was unfolding, the primary focus of the government was to curb violence and conflicts between warring tribal groups, and mitigate the possibility of Al-Qaeda taking over during the country's power vacuum. In the meantime, Yemeni citizens were demanding speedy economic and social reforms that would enable positive economic growth, including increased expenditures for social services, such as education, healthcare and the creation of decent jobs for youth and adults alike. The government had difficulty addressing these issues simultaneously, which caused protests in 2012 and 2013. The political crisis continued until a full-blown conflict erupted in late 2014 (Kronefeld and Guzansky, 2014; Rózsa, 2012). The fragile situation turned into complete chaos, resulting in the total breakdown of Yemeni society. General living conditions deteriorated further, increasing malnutrition, food insecurity and inadequate access to water, social welfare and health care. This had far-reaching impacts on vulnerable segments of the population, such as women, youth and children. In addition to growing social tension and political conflict, in March 2015, a Saudi-led coalition intervened in the country, causing widespread damage that exacerbated the socio-political situation. After nine months of intervention, over 2.5 million people became internally displaced, 1.8 million children were out of school, 6,000 people died, 28,000 were injured and 600 health facilities were shut down (UNHCR, 2016). According to a 2016 UNICEF assessment of Yemen, over 20 million people were in need of urgent humanitarian assistance, of which 9.9 million were children. In addition, 320,000 children under 5 were at risk of severe malnutrition and 15.2 million people were in need of immediate health assistance (UNICEF, 2016).

In the last decade, Yemen's oil revenues declined steadily due to the sabotage of oil infrastructure and political instability. Declining revenues from the mining sector and lack of investment in the private sector for almost two decades, as well as unequal distribution of wealth and resources, including public sector employment opportunities, were some of the major causes of poor levels of development throughout Yemen. Between 1990 and 2010, the economic situation in Yemen was turbulent. Early in the 1990s, the remittances of Yemenis living in Kuwait dropped substantially because of the Iraqi invasion of Kuwait, causing a huge inflow of Yemenis back to their country. Despite the unification of South and North Yemen (and its associated increase in wage bills) and civil war of 1994, the growth was surprisingly higher, reaching an average of 5.5 per cent between 1990 and 1999, declining since then to an average of 4 per cent. The per capita growth rates were, however, not high enough to reduce poverty on a larger scale. Between 1990 and 2014, oil exports accounted for 90 per cent of total exports and 75 per cent of government revenue (Al-Batuly et al, 2011). The boost in oil revenues facilitated several reforms such as civil service and public financial management, the introduction of general sales tax, an anticorruption drive, improved social safety nets and adjustments in fuel subsidies. Unfortunately, most of these reforms were partially implemented with significant delays because of growing opposition from different interest groups. Like other Gulf Cooperation Council (GCC) countries, Yemen is a rentier state that extracts the rents from strategic economic sectors, such as oil and gas, agriculture, water and telecommunications. The oil revenues or rents are used for political purposes in that they are distributed among political, tribal and military elites, and used to pay the rising wages of public sector employees and subsidies. The network of political, tribal and military elites block much-needed economic, social and institutional reforms. Very limited progress was therefore observed in the field of education and health. In later years, oil revenues continued to decline, resulting in reduced spending on basic social services such as education and health (World Bank, 2015; Al-Batuly et al, 2011).

In a recent household survey, 59 per cent of Yemeni households had access to improved drinking-water sources. The 40 per cent with non-improved access to drinking water sources relied heavily on wells, springs and tanker trucks. For over 85 per cent of the population, drinking water is available on their premises. Overall the inequality between the urban (76 per cent) and rural (50 per cent) population in terms of access to improved drinking water is high. The same survey indicates that nearly 83 per cent of the urban population has access to improved sanitation, whereas, the rural population has only 30.5 per cent. One half of the rural female and one-quarter of the rural male population in Yemen has no formal education. In the past few years, however, education attainment has improved in urban and rural areas (NHDS, 2015). After the unification of North and South Yemen, the government made concerted efforts to equalise the wellbeing of both regions. Following several fiscal and budgetary reforms, the government adopted a structural adjustment programme in 1995 and Poverty Reduction Strategy Papers (PRSP). Since 1991, social spending for education and health increased significantly, however, it also fell short of the PRSP target. In 1991, the GDP shares for health and education were 1.1 and 4.4 per cent. The GDP share of education increased two percentage points, while for health, despite the growing population, the GDP share remained constant. In 2006, social spending for education, health, and social protection was 6.1, 1.7 and 0.1 per cent of GDP respectively. Even the modest growth achieved over the last two decades regressed because of increasing conflict. Recent statistics show the grave concern for the collapsing healthcare system in Yemen. Nearly 600 health facilities shut down because of lack of basic supplies.

Yemen receives less than $13 per capita per annum of foreign aid compared to other LDCs. Between 1990 and 2014, the total Overseas Development Assistance (ODA) received was $10.3 billion, in current prices. The ODA increased from $0.45 billion to $1.16 billion between 1990 and 2014 (OECD, 2016). Another dataset indicates that the total committed ODA for four major MDG goals between 1990 and 2010 was $1.98 billion, of which 62 per cent of the budget went to water supply and sanitation, 32 per cent to primary education, and 6 per cent to nutrition (AidData, 2016). From 2000, donors increasingly focused on MDGs, despite recurring humanitarian and security needs. ODA was thus ineffective; unable to make any substantial changes in improving the economic situation and reducing poverty. Abo al-Asrar (2013) argues the aid committed by donors was not disbursed because of the poor absorptive capacities of Yemen's government institutions, a lack of government cohensiveness, and a lack of clear project plans for the requested aid. Other factors contributing to this were the 'perception of a corrupt network of patronage, a weak administrative system, and a precarious situation'. As a result of declining oil and gas revenues, public investment declined sharply from 9.2 per cent of GDP in 2003 to 4.6 per cent of GDP in 2010. Foreign direct investment (FDI) was also limited to the oil and gas sector, accounting for 88 per cent of total FDI (Abo al-Asrar, 2013).

Recent bombings by Saudi Arabia left Yemen's general infrastructure, such as roads, power generation, drainage and water distribution networks, in rubble (Kouddous, 2016). In the past, the oil pipelines were sabotaged by terrorist groups, leading to declines in oil production (Wilson, 2014). There is no end in sight to the ongoing conflict between the Houti rebels and the Saudi government. Should the conflict end, however, the government will have the enormous burden of rebuilding the state, as most of the social and physical infrastructure are damaged. The post-conflict recovery and reconstruction effort should include robust plans, policies and development finance to ensure sound development and restore long-term security and stability in the country. One of the ways to avoid future conflict and political-economic obstacles is to ensure power is shared between different political and tribal groups. While it would take a considerable amoung of time to heal political divisions and build mutual trust between government, opposition groups, tribal members and citizens, these stakeholders should work together in making economic and institutional reforms. It is very difficult for Yemen to focus on development goals set by international institutions. The country should therefore set its own national goals, addressing key concerns, such as peace, security, stability and rehabilitation of basic infrastructure with a focus on education and health care. Additionally, the government must speed up its reforms to ensure the civil service is inclusive and that there is an equitable provision of public sector jobs. Once the national goals are on-track, the Yemeni government needs to consider mainstreaming the UN's Sustainable Development Goals (SDGs) and creating necessary policy packages. This is an opportunity for the postwar government to address structural problems, such as cronyism, corruption and poor distrubution of economic wealth and natural resources. Having said that, it is also a very delicate issue, as any of these reforms could bring unease among the opposition or other tribal groups, resulting in another wave of violence and conflict. People-centred development should be at the heart of the agenda for any political party. The resilience of state–society relations depends on genuine inclusive growth, wealth creation, adequate service delivery, creation of decent jobs in all sectors and effective management of natural resources. Regarding the local institutions, multilateral and bilateral donors have a major role to play in building a peaceful and vibrant society and rebuilding Yemen's infrastruture. The previous aid experience in Yemen indicates that there was a lack of disbursement of fully committed ODA because of dysfunctional instituions. The new government should therefore build a strong administrative system and transparent and accountable institutions to disburse aid and develop focused project plans. Additionally, the government must coordinate with all a variety of stakeholders in adminstering development finance. It would be unfair to expect that Yemen will achieve the SDG goals by 2030, even if there is sufficient funding. Instead, the government should set up feasible national goals given the country's political and social realities. See Table 15.6.

Table 15.6: MDG progress: country analysis for Yemen

Goals	Pre-Arab Spring Source: UNDP Yemen Millennium Development Goals Report 2010 Findings and challenges	Post Arab Spring Source: UNDP, 'Will Yemen be able to achieve the MDGS by 2015? Status at a glance' and The National Social Protection Monitoring Survey, 2012 Findings and challenges
1: Eradicate Extreme Poverty • Reduce poverty by half • Achieve full/productive employment for all • Reduce hunger by half	• In 2009, 42.8% of the population lived below the national poverty level • Food insecurity as a result of low agricultural productivity, limited financing options and access to credit by farmers/fishermen. • Regional disparities	• Deteriorating humanitarian situation • Almost 50% of the population is poor and food insecure. • Security threats continue to stall economic and political progress • Increased unemployment • Poverty rates have increased
2: Achieve Universal Primary Education • Universal enrolment in basic education	• The net enrolment rate increased from 52.7% in 1990 to 69.8% in 2008 • Lack of resources to improve education	• Low attendance • Severe regional and wealth disparities
3: Promote Gender Equity • Enrolment in basic education • Share in paid jobs • Representation in parliament	• Women occupied 1 of 301 seats in parliament and 2 of 38 seats in the Shoura Council • Regional disparities • Cultural and economic obstacles to equity	• Women's' political participation has been brought up to 35% • Deteriorating progress in most areas

(continued)

Table 15.6: MDG progress: country analysis for Yemen (continued)

Goals	Pre-Arab Spring Source: UNDP Yemen Millennium Development Goals Report 2010 Findings and challenges	Post Arab Spring Source: UNDP, 'Will Yemen be able to achieve the MDGS by 2015? Status at a glance' and The National Social Protection Monitoring Survey, 2012 Findings and challenges
4: Reduce Child Mortality • Reduce by two-thirds • Measles immunisations	• By 2009, Yemen became a polio free country according to WHO standards • Child Mortality rates amongst children under 5 decreased from 122 cases per 1,000 live births in 1992 to 78.2 in 2006 • Measles and tetanus were still prevalent • Insufficient financial resources allocated to health sector	• Successful measles immunisation programme • Insignificant reduction in child mortality rate • Even though 75% of population live in rural areas, public health facilities in those areas are still inadequate
5: Improve Maternal Health • Reduce mortality rate by two-thirds • Access to reproductive health services	• Maternal mortality rates increased from 351 cases per 100,000 live births in 1997 to 365 cases in 2003 • 77.2% of deliveries took place at home by traditional methods and 84.3% of maternal mortalities were from home based deliveries • One third of total maternal mortalities were women under 20 years of age • Limited healthcare services for mothers and children, especially in rural areas • Women are not able to make decisions related to reproductive health • Limited resources allocated towards family planning and reproductive health	• Maternal mortality rates have increased • Lack of adequately trained staff, properly equipped health facilities, or the spread of information on health matters, especially in rural areas

(continued)

Table 15.6: MDG progress: country analysis for Yemen (continued)

Goals	Pre-Arab Spring Source: UNDP Yemen Millennium Development Goals Report 2010 Findings and challenges	Post Arab Spring Source: UNDP, 'Will Yemen be able to achieve the MDGS by 2015? Status at a glance' and The National Social Protection Monitoring Survey, 2012 Findings and challenges
6: Combat HIV, AIDS, malaria, and so on	• Number of registered cases of HIV/AIDS has increased from 1 in 1990 to 2,882 in 2009 • Incidence of malaria declined from 1263 cases per 100,000 people in 1990 to 600 in 2009. • Malaria spread rates decreased from 48% in 1998 to 8% in 2008 • Insufficient awareness of HIV/AIDS • Malaria is still a critical and serious health issue	• Insufficient data
7: Ensure Environmental Sustainability • Recovering Deforestation • Half no. of people without access to improved sanitation services • Improve living conditions of poor neighbourhoods	• Erosion, desertification and soil salinisation reduced arable land by 1.8% annually between 1999 and 2006 • 53% of rural and 43% of urban populations cannot access safe drinking water • 77% of the population were not using improved sanitation services in 2008 • Water scarcity • Climate change • Limited stable arable lands	• Access to clean drinking and renewable water sources are still very scarce • Inadequate sanitation • Inadequate housing • Water scarcity, climate change, global warming

(continued)

Table 15.6: MDG progress: country analysis for Yemen (continued)

Goals	Pre-Arab Spring Source: UNDP Yemen Millennium Development Goals Report 2010 Findings and challenges	Post Arab Spring Source: UNDP, 'Will Yemen be able to achieve the MDGS by 2015? Status at a glance' and The National Social Protection Monitoring Survey, 2012 Findings and challenges
8: Global Partnership for Development	• Yemen obtained observer status in the WTO in 1999 and is working its way to full membership • Ranking in Global Doing Business Report in 2009 improved to 98th out of 181 countries compared to 123rd in the 2008 report • Yemen integrated in several GCC organisations • Trade partnership with GCC countries has grown from $3.5 billion to $5.1 billion (48% increase between 2005-2008) • Civil society organisations increased to 4,369 in 2008 • Yemen is the least developed country seeking WTO membership • Low per capita income and weak IT awareness • Limited financial and absorption capacities of national economy and weak investment attraction	• Limited energy resources, limited access to internet. • Foreigners can now do business in Yemen without a local partner. • Due to weak financial sustainability in Yemen as a result of the ongoing decline in oil production and oil revenues, the World Bank transferred its loans portfolio for Yemen to grants.

Prospects for the region in the post-2015 era

The authors of the Arab Development Challenges Report published by UNDP in 2011 assert that 'the Arab world is richer than it is developed' (23) and as such it will be necessary to rethink a 'new Arab development model, where issues of stability are not addressed solely from a security standpoint and above all where progress is not simply viewed in terms of utility of goods and services (such as a growth in per capita income), but rather in terms of substantive capabilities to choose a life one has reason to value' (UNDP, 2011, 1).

Although, there have been ongoing negotiations to put an end to this conflict, the reality on the ground is different. Nevertheless, one should create strategies for future development and peace in the country. In the post-settlement plan, the aim of the government and the international donors should not be limited to rebuilding the shattered infrastructure, but should include 'strengthen[ing] and solidify[ing] peace in order to avoid relapse in the conflict' and addressing the structural causes of the conflict, recognising equity at political and economic issues (Boutros-Ghali, 1992, 21).

For the war-torn countries, the SDGs are more a luxury than a necessity. In the initial years, it would be challenging to integrate SDGs in their development policies because public safety, security, repatriation and resettlement will dominate the agenda. Intergovernmental organisations, international NGOs, foreign donors and local civil society have a major role to play in building a coherent policy of economic and social development, as well as mechanisms to address the immediate concerns of citizens. International donors should increase humanitarian aid for short-term relief and development assistance for long-term sustainable development. A fast-track development process is possible with the support of all local stakeholders for a swift economic recovery and social rehabilitation process. The government's effort towards political resettlement should go hand-in-hand with a coherent and comprehensive policy framework that integrates economic, social and environmental issues. It is difficult to offer a single policy for all countries in this region as they have different starting points and require different interventions and strategies to yield a positive outcome. Tunisia and Egypt are politically and economically unstable, but are relatively peaceful with sporadic, low-intensity conflicts. The immediate focus for these countries is to stabilise the economy, build confidence for tourists and investors, and create jobs, primarily for youth. In contrast, Syria and Yemen will require that security and political stability take centre stage. Alongside political resettlement, these countries must engage in other key elements like public safety, infrastructure recovery, food security, agricultural rehabilitaiton, health, education and social welfare needs. It is challenging to consider all the above-mentioned elements in the post-conflict or resettlment period. They are needed, however, otherwise the inclusive development process will be seriously undermined. Currently, it is very difficult to predict whether the new governments will promote the democratic process in all institutions or consolidate power and maintain authoritarianism in the name of security and conflict prevention. The transition process offers an opportunity to address the systemic crises that plagued these countries for several decades. It would be unwise to expect the changes to happen quickly; building transparent and democratic institutions take times and requires strong political will.

The transformation during the course of the Arab Spring was extraordinary in terms of the variation in its nature and intensity. While many highly-entrenched dictatorships have come to an end, the future of political liberalisation in the region is uncertain, with many commentators pointing toward the 'possibility of authoritarian reversals and even an Arab "Winter" replacing the Arab Spring' (Onis, 2012, 48). This chapter illustrated that SDG progress in the post-Arab-Spring period could be reached if the implementation of the post-2015 agenda is more attuned to the social and economic realities of these crisis-prone countries. An integral requirement of this process is to rethink and re-evaluate the power, dynamism, and essential role of civil society in the Middle East.

According to Van Der Hoeven (2012), Tunisia, Egypt and Jordan were among the eight best performing countries with respect to progress in the MDGs during 2010. Despite this glowing performance on MDG progress, however, youth unemployment was and remained significantly high in these countries. Therefore, progress in achieving the SDGs is not a guarantee for socially inclusive and economically sustainable growth.

Across the four countries reviewed, in 2010 many were already predicting significant limitations to total achievement of the MDGs. Challenges of instability were identified in the 2009/10 reports, prior to the political upheavals of 2011, as a potential obstacle to MDG achievement. Despite these challenges, the dissolution of despotic power and the rise of civil society to claim its rights are outcomes that may lead to increased capabilities for transformative social change outside the realm of MDG indicators. In Egypt and Tunisia, the initial revolutions resulted in new political leadership. These revolutions, led by civil society, were political processes that enabled populations to pursue regime change and, eventually, meaningful reforms. In Syria, however, the regime has not been changed and a massive humanitarian emergency has resulted.

The political process of the Arab Spring has slowed economic growth in the Arab region, yet it is likely that, despite the continued crisis, the SDG process and attainment of indicators will be bolstered by populations cognisant of their rights and of the possibility of successfully claiming them. Furthermore, theories of change that take into account more complex contexts and contingencies may be developed to allow space for consideration of political processes and permit more flexibility in calculating their general impact (Vogel, 2012). At present, it is important to remember that long-term forecasting for the region will be difficult because as British politician and Member of Parliament, George Galloway, explained, a revolution is a process and not an event. As a result, it is far too early to predict the final outcome (Salman, 2013).

Note

[1] www.project-syndicate.org/commentary/after-the-millennium-development-goals-by-dani-rodrik#cXlmEw3viuui6WIk.99

References

Abdelbaki, HH, 2013, The Arab Spring: Do we need a new theory?, *Modern Economy* 4, 3, 187–96

Abo al-Asrar, F, 2013, Myopic solutions to chronic problems: The need for aid effectivess in Yemen, *Center on Democracy, Development, and the Rule of Law (CDDRL) Working paper* 141, Standford, CA: CDDRL

Abootalebi, AR, 2013, Democracy's fourth wave? Digital media and the Arab Spring, *Choice* 51, 4, 720

AfDB (African Development Bank), 2012, *Tunisia: Economic and social challenges beyond the revolution*, Abidjan: African Development Bank

AidData, 2016, *Country-level research datasets*, http://aiddata.org/country-level-research-datasets

Al-Batuly, A, Al-Hawri, M, Cicowiez, M, Lofgren, H, Pournik, M, 2011, *Assessing development strategies to the MDGs in the Republic of Yemen*, New York: United Nations Department of Economic and Social Affairs (UN DESA)

Al Jazeera, 2013, Tunisia set to unveil coalition government, *Al Jazeera*, www.aljazeera.com/news/africa/2013/03/20133875839472262.html

Amnesty International, 2012, *Year of rebellion: The state of human rights in the Middle East and North Africa*, London: Amnesty International

Arieff, A, Humud, CE, 2015, *Political transition in Tunisia*, Washington, DC: Congressional Research Service

Asia News Monitor, 2013, Egypt: Analyst says Egyptian events not a military coup, *Asia News Monitor*, 5 July

BBC, 2013, Former Egyptian Deputy PM Al-Salmi refutes claims of military coup d'Etat, *BBC Monitoring Middle East*, 5 July, London: BBC

Behr, T, Siitonen, A, 2013, Building bridges or digging trenches? Civil Society engagement after the Arab Spring, *Finnish Institute of International Affairs (FIIA) Working Papers* 77, 4–25

Berti, B, 2013, *Strategic nonviolent struggle in the Middle East before the 'Arab Spring'*, Video webcast, www.youtube.com/watch?v=b30OrMA4KTY

Boose, J, 2012, Democratization and Civil society: Libya, Tunisia and the Arab Spring, *International Journal of Social Sciences and Humanity* 2, 4, 310–15, www.ijssh.org/papers/116-CH317.pdf

Boutros-Ghali, B, 1992, *An agenda for peace*, New York: United Nations Department of Public Information, www.un-documents.net/a47-277.htm

Brister, M, 2013, Economic inclusion, democracy, and the Arab Spring, *Center for International Private Enterprise (CIPE) Development Blog*, CIPE, www.cipe.org/blog/2013/02/11/economic-inclusion-democracy-and-the-arab-spring/#.UTOJV6XI2Sq

Chant, S, 2008, The feminization of poverty and the feminization of anti-poverty programmes: Room for revision?, *Journal of Development Studies* 44, 2, 165–97

Chemingui, MA, Sanchez, MV, 2010, *Realizing the Millennium Development Goals through socially inclusive macroeconomic policies. Country Study: Assessing development strategies to achieve the MDGs in the Republic of Tunisia*, New York: United Nations

Chicago Tribune, 2013, After the Arab Spring, *Chicago Tribune*, 30 January, http://search.proquest.com/docview/1282506782?accountid=49936

Clark, H, 2013, Helen Clark: Opportunities for economic and political inclusion in the Arab Spring, *Huffington Post*, www.huffingtonpost.com/helen-clark/opportunities-for-economi_b_870955.html

Cornell University, 2013, *Arab Spring: A research and study guide*, Ithaca, NY: Cornell University, http://guides.library.cornell.edu/arab_spring

Daily Post, 2013, Egyptian coup leaves only violence for Islam, *Daily Post*, 1 August

Economist, The, 2013, After Egypt's double spring: Keep going, *The Economist*, Special report: The Arab Spring, 13 July, 408, 16–S.16, http://search.proquest.com/docview/1399960299?accountid=49936

El-Issawi, F, 2012, The Tunisian transition: What would be the face of the second republic?, *Strategic Update report*, May, London: Centre for the Study of International Affairs, Diplomacy and Grand Strategy (IDEAS), London School of Economics

Fleishman, J, 2011, Libya's revolt may reroute 'Arab Spring'; unlike in Tunisia and Egypt, force is what tipped the balance. Uprisings in Syria and Yemen could change. *Los Angeles Times*, 28 August, http://search.proquest.com/docview/885505869?accountid=49936

Freeman, C, 2013, Coup chief accused of stirring up Egyptian Civil War, Edition 3, *Irish Independent*, 23, 25 July

GFP (Global Firepower), 2016, Countries ranked by military strength (2016): The complete Global Firepower list puts the military powers of the world into full perspective, *Global Firepower*, www.globalfirepower.com/countries-listing.asp

Hulme, D, 2003, Chronic poverty and development policy: An introduction, *World Development* 31, 3, 399–402

Hulme, D, 2009, *The Millennium Development Goals (MDGs): A short history of the world's biggest promise*, Manchester: Brooks World Poverty Institute, University of Manchester

ILO (International Labour Office), 2012, *Global employment trends for youth 2012*, ILO, www.ilo.org/global/research/global-reports/youth/2012/lang--en/index.htm

ILO (International Labour Office), 2014, *Global employment trends 2014: The risk of a jobless recovery*, ILO, http://ilo.org/global/research/global-reports/global-employment-trends/2014/lang--en/index.htm

Jackson, D, 2013, White House to decide if Egyptian act was a 'coup', *Gannett News Service*, 8 July

Jones, N, Presler-Marshall, E, 2012, Governance and poverty eradication: Applying a gender and social institutions perspective, *Public Administration and Development* 32, 4–5, 371–84

Kalpakian, J, 2013, Between reform and reaction: The Syrian and Moroccan Responses to the Arab Spring, *The Innovation Journal* 18, 1, 1–20

Kershaw, I, 20080, How democracy produced a monster, *The New York Times*, The Opinion Pages, www.nytimes.com/2008/02/03/opinion/03iht-edkershaw.1.9700744.html?_r=0

Kouddous, SA, 2016, *In Yemen, civilians suffer relentless bombing by Saudi-led coalition*, https://theintercept.com/2016/01/11/in-yemen-civilians-suffer-relentless-bombing-by-saudi-led-coalition/

Kronefeld, S, Guzansky, Y, 2014, Yemen: A mirror to the future of the Arab Spring, *Military and Strategic Affairs* 6, 3, 79–99

Madichie, N, 2011, IRENA – Masdar City (UAE) – exemplars of innovation into emerging markets, *Foresight* 13, 6, 34–47, www.emeraldinsight.com/doi/abs/10.1108/14636681111179582

Makiya, K, 2013, The Arab Spring started in Iraq, *International Herald Tribune*, 6, 8 April

Malik, A, Awadallah, B, 2013, The economics of the Arab Spring, *World Development* 45, 296–313, http://dx.doi.org/10.1016/j.worlddev.2012.12.015

Maskery, S, 2014, After Arab Spring peace reigns again on the River Nile, *Western Daily Press* 2, 29 April

Mohamed, C, Sanchez, M, 2011, *Assessing development strategies to the MDGs in the Republic of Tunisia*, New York: United Nations Department of Economic and Social Affairs (UN DESA), July

Natter, K, 2015, *Revolution and political transition in Tunisia: A migration game changer?*, Washington, DC: Migration Policy Institute

Newswire, 2013, It's Not a Coup: The American Egyptian Strategic Alliance's letter to President Obama on Egypt, *US Newswire*, 15 July

NHDS (National Heath and Demographic Survey), 2015, *Yemen: National Heath and Demographic Survey 2013*, Sana'a: Ministry of Public Health and Population

Noueihed, L, Warren, A, 2012, *The battle for the Arab Spring: Revolution, counter-revolution and the making of a new era*, New Haven, CT: Yale University Press

OECD (Organisation for Economic Co-operation and Development), 2016, The Global Picture of Oversees Development Assistance, Paris: OECD, www.oecd.org/dac/stats/data.htm

Onis, Z, 2012, Turkey and the Arab Spring: Between ethics and self-interest, *Insight Turkey* 14, 3, 45–63

Panayiotides, N, 2012, The regional implications of the Arab uprising, *Palestine–Israel Journal of Politics, Economics, and Culture* 18, 1, 71–7

Ramadan, T, 2011, *Middle East: Independence and dependency*, http://tariqramadan.com/english/middle-east-independence-and-dependency/

Reisen, H, 2004, Innovative approaches to funding the Millennium Development Goals, *Organisation for Economic Co-operation and Development (OECD) Development Centre Policy Brief* 24, Paris: OECD

Rózsa, E, 2012, The Arab Spring: Its impact on the region and on the Middle East conference, *Policy Brief, Academic Peace Orchestra Middle East*, 9/10, August, Frankfurt am Main: Academic Peace Orchestra Middle East, Peace Research Institute Frankfurt (PRIF)

Rush, M, 2012, Give Arab Spring time to bloom, *Gannett News Service*, 5 February

Salamey, I, 2015, Post-Arab Spring: Changes and challenges, *Third World Quarterly* 36, 1, 111–29

Salman, P, 2013, 'Arab Spring: Revolution is a process', *Dawn* (Karachi), 17 February, www.dawn.com/2013/02/17/arab-spring-revolution-is-a-process/

Sprusansky, D, 2013, Anti-Egyptian coup protests, *Washington Report on Middle East Affairs* 32, 8, 53–4

Tabaar, MA, 2013, Assessing (In)security after the Arab Spring: The case of Egypt, *PS: Political Science & Politics* 46, 4, 727–35, http://dx.doi.org/10.1017/S1049096513001261

Times, The, 2013, Egyptian coup doesn't mean end of the Arab Spring, *The Times*, 13 July

UN (United Nations), 2010, *The Third Arab Report on the Millennium Development Goals 2010 and the impact of the global financial crisis*, New York: United Nations and the League of Arab States

UN (United Nations), 2012, Review of the contributions of the MDG Agenda to foster development: Lessons for the post-2015 UN development agenda, *Discussion Note*, New York: System Task Team of the Post-2015 UN Development Agenda

UN (United Nations), 2013, *Human Development Report 2013. The Rise of the South: Human Development in a Diverse World*, New York: UNDP, http://hdr.undp.org/sites/default/files/reports/14/hdr2013_en_complete.pdf

UNDP (United Nations Development Programme), 2009, *MDG attainment in the Palestinian context*, New York: UNDP, www.undp.ps/en/mdgs/mdgopt.html

UNDP (United Nations Development Programme), 2010, *Syrian Arab Republic third national MDGs progress report*, New York: UNDP, www.undp.org/content/dam/rbas/report/MDGR-2010-En.pdf

UNDP (United Nations Development Programme) and the Egyptian Ministry of Economic Development, 2010, *Egypt's progress toward achieving the Millennium Development Goals 2010*, New York and Cairo: UNDP and the Egyptian Ministry of Economic Development

UNDP (United Nations Development Programme), 2011, *Arab Development Challenges Report 2011: Towards the Developmental State in the Arab Region*, UNDP, www.undp.org/content/undp/en/home/librarypage/hdr/arab-development-challenges-report-2011.html

UNESCO (United Nations Educational, Scientific and Cultural Organization), 2013, *Summary of progress toward Education for All*, Paris: UNESCO, www.unesco.org/new/fileadmin/MULTIMEDIA/ HQ/ED/ED_new/pdf/Summary%20of%20progress%20towards%20 EFA-colors.pdf

UNHCR (United Nations High Commissioner for Refugees), 2013, *Number of Syrian refugees reaches 1 million mark*, Geneva: UNHCR, www.unhcr.org/513625ed6.html

UNHCR (United Nations High Commissioner for Refugees), 2016, *Yemen: Monthly factsheet*, December, Geneva: UNHCR

UNICEF (United Nations International Children's Emergency Fund), 2016, *Yemen: Humanitarian situation report*, January, Geneva: UNICEF, http://reliefweb.int/sites/reliefweb.int/files/resources/UNICEF%20 Yemen%20Humanitarian%20SitRep%2030%20Dec%202015%20 -%2012%20Jan%202016.pdf

Van Der Hoeven, R, 2012, *MDGs Post 2015: Beacons in turbulent times or false lights?* New York: UN System Task Team on the Post 2015 UN Development Agenda

Vogel, I, 2012, *Review of the use of 'Theory of Change' in international development*, Review Report, London: Department of International Development

Wilson, N, 2014, Yemen's main oil pipeline bombed by tribesmen, *International Business Times*, www.ibtimes.co.uk/yemens-main-oil-pipeline-bombed-by-tribesmen-1464455

World Bank, 2015, *The Republic of Yemen: Unlocking the potential for economic growth*, Washington, DC: World Bank

Zartman, IW, 2014, Waiting for the Arab Spring, *Middle East Journal* 68, 3, 465–8

Zidjaly, NA, 2011, From Oman, with love, *The New York Times*, 7 March, www.nytimes.com/2011/03/08/opinion/08al-zidjaly. html?_r=0&pagewanted=print

Food security, inclusive growth, sustainability and the sustainable development agenda[1]

Craig Hanson
with contributions from Tim Searchinger,
Richard Waite, Betsy Otto,
Brian Lipinski and Kelly Levin

Introduction

Over the next several decades, the world faces an historic challenge and opportunity at the nexus of food security, economic development and the environment. The world needs to be food secure. The world needs agriculture to contribute to inclusive economic development, and the world needs to reduce agriculture's impact on the environment.

This nexus has several implications for policymakers as they outline and implement the 2030 Agenda for Sustainable Development, adopted by the United Nations in September 2015. Critically, this agenda has an explicit goal on food security. However, it is also important that the food security goal includes some sustainability targets and indicators.

This chapter examines the food security challenge to 2050, and lays out six core propositions related to food security and sustainability. With an eye to implications of the food security challenge for the sustainable development agenda, it then details three proposed food security targets that integrate sustainability. These targets include reducing the rate of food loss and waste, and achieving low–carbon agriculture and water–efficient food production (Table 16.1). Finally, the chapter offers some reflections on how these targets would help the world feed a growing population in a manner that alleviates poverty and advances economic development while reducing pressure on its natural resources.

Table 16.1: Proposed food security targets that integrate sustainability

Target relative to 2015	Indicator	Metric	Means of implementation (not exhaustive)
By 2030, reduce the rate of food loss and waste by 50%	Share of food produced or harvested that is lost or wasted between the farm and fork	Percentage of food loss and waste	Improve harvesting and storage techniques Conduct consumer education campaigns to reduce waste
By 2030, reduce the greenhouse gas emissions from food production by 25%	Total greenhouse gas emissions from food production, including both crops and livestock	Tons of carbon dioxide equivalent	Reduce emissions from direct production (eg, cattle, fertiliser, rice) Increase cropland and pastureland productivity
By 2030, reduce the water-intensity of agricultural production by 30%	Cubic metre of irrigation water consumed per ton of food produced	Tons per cubic metre of water	Improve productivity of rain-fed agriculture Increase irrigation efficiency

The food security challenge

Over the next several decades, the world faces a grand challenge – and opportunity – at the nexus of food security, economic development and the environment.

First, the world needs to be food secure

The United Nations Population Division projects the global human population to grow from 7 billion in 2012 to 9.7 billion by 2050 (UN DESA, 2015).[2] Half of the population growth will be in sub-Saharan Africa (UN DESA, 2015), where agricultural productivity and soil quality is exceptionally low and where reliance on imports of basic staples is already high. Moreover, at least 3 billion people are likely to enter the global middle class by 2030,[3] and they will almost certainly demand more resource-intensive foods such as meats and vegetable oils (Foresight, 2011). At the same time, approximately 795 million of the world's poorest people remain undernourished even today (FAO, IFAD and WFP, 2015). Many poor households are already close to the margins, as shown when food riots in 2008 broke out in more than 25 countries in response to spikes in food prices, which had left many people unable to afford basic food staples (Bush, 2010). To sufficiently feed all people by 2050, without measures to restrain food demand growth by the world's more affluent or to reduce waste, worldwide food annual crop production (Searchinger et al, 2013) (in caloric content) will need to increase by roughly 70 per cent from 2006 levels (Searchinger et al, 2013).[4] Since the majority of the world's farms are operated by smallholders,[5] and it is generally on their farms that the larger productivity gaps exist (FAO and OECD, 2012), a large part of any supply increase will need to come from them.

Second, the world needs agriculture to contribute to inclusive economic development

Seventy-five per cent of the developing world's poor live in rural areas, and many depend on agriculture for their principal livelihood (Ravallion et al, 2007). Although agriculture directly accounts for approximately 3 per cent of global gross domestic product (GDP), it employs more than 2 billion people around the world at least part-time (World Bank, nd). Many of the world's poorest people are themselves farmers and, according to the World Bank, GDP growth originating in agriculture can be more effective at reducing poverty than growth arising from other economic sectors (World Bank, 2008). Women make up 41 per cent of the agricultural workforce worldwide and the majority of agricultural workers in South Asia and sub-Saharan Africa (FAO, 2007; World Bank et al, 2009). Because increasing income to women has disproportionate benefits for alleviating hunger (FAO, 2011), assisting women farmers is a particularly effective way to reduce poverty and enhance food security.

Third, the world needs to reduce agriculture's impact on the environment and natural resources

Agriculture is a major contributor of greenhouse gas emissions, the largest consumer of fresh water among economic sectors, and the largest cause of conversion of natural ecosystems. In the future, agriculture will need to adapt to a changing climate in order to ensure adequate food production. At the same time, when done right, agriculture can provide numerous benefits beyond food production and jobs including building material and soil fertility.

The convergence of these three needs poses one of the paramount challenges of the next several decades: how can the world adequately and fairly feed a growing population in a manner that alleviates poverty and advances economic development while reducing pressure on natural resources? This chapter provides several perspectives on answering this question. Through a number of core propositions, it makes the case that integrating sustainability considerations into the goals and targets relevant to food security and nutrition in the 2030 Agenda for Sustainable Development will be critical. It continues by recommending several targets – along with their associated indicators and means of implementation – that would incorporate sustainability considerations.

This chapter focuses on the sustainability dimensions of food given their significant importance in underpinning long-term food security. It does not focus on other dimensions of food security such as access or utilisation. Although we recognise these are critically important aspects of food security, they are beyond the scope of our analysis.

Meeting the food security challenge: six core propositions

1. Food security is multi-dimensional

According to the United Nations Food and Agriculture Organisation (FAO), 'food security exists when all people, at all times, have physical and economic access to sufficient, safe and nutritious food to meet their dietary needs and food preferences for an active and healthy life' (FAO, 2006). Implicit in this definition is the recognition that food security is multi-dimensional. There have been many formulations of what the components of food security are. For instance, the Committee on World Food Security identified four main dimensions or 'pillars':[6]

- *availability* is ensured if adequate amounts of food are produced and are at people's disposal;
- *access* is ensured when all households and all individuals within those households have sufficient resources to obtain appropriate foods for a nutritious diet (through production, purchase, or donation);
- *utilisation* is ensured when the human body is able to ingest and metabolise food because of proper healthcare, nutritious and safe diets, and an adequate biological and social environment;
- *stability* is ensured when the three other pillars are maintained over time.

Several experts have argued for a pillar on environmental sustainability, which is ensured only if food production and consumption patterns do not deplete natural resources or the ability of the agricultural system to provide sufficient food for future generations (Richardson, 2010; Daily et al, 1998). Therefore, for the purposes of this chapter, we identify five pillars of food security (Figure 16.1).[7]

Figure 16.1: Pillars of food security

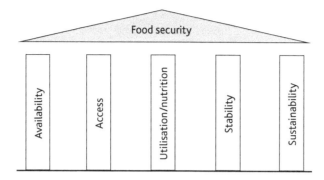

Sources: Gross et al, 2000; Richardson, 2010; Daily et al, 1998

2. Achieving food security will require increasing not only food access but also food supply

Given the unequal distribution of food today around the planet, one might think that food security could be achieved by only improving food access and ensuring that the food already generated is distributed more equally among the world's population. Yet, even if all the food calories consumed in the world in 2009 were equally distributed across the projected population in the year 2050, and no food calories were lost between farm and fork, those calories would still fall short of the FAO's 'average daily energy requirement' by about 100 kilocalories (kcal) per person per day. The shortfall would be roughly 650 kcal per person per day if the current rate of food loss and waste – 24 per cent of all produced calories per year – were to remain unchanged in 2050.[8] The world will need to increase food supply as part of the solution to food security – and in an increasingly resource-constrained world, this implies increasing productivity.[9]

3. Food supply is dependent on environmental sustainability

The sustainability dimension is an often overlooked but important pillar, particularly since it underpins many of the others (Figure 16.2). For instance, food availability is dependent on the state of the environment and the natural resource base. The current global food production system – what is grown where, how and when – has evolved within a climate that has been relatively stable over the past 8,000–10,000 years. Production of rain-fed and irrigated crops is dependent on supplies of freshwater at appropriate levels at the

Figure 16.2: Links between selected pillars of food security

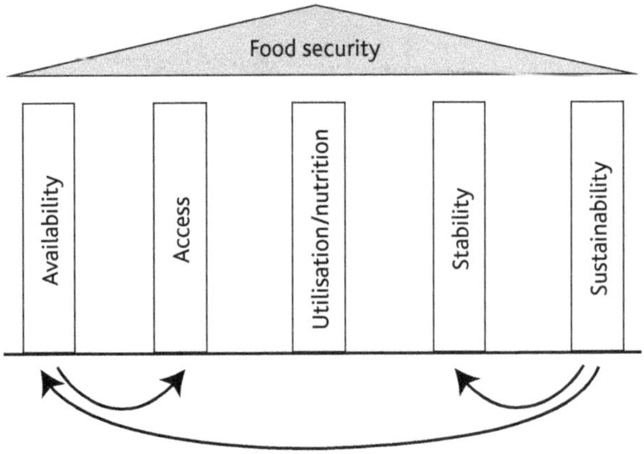

Sources: Gross et al, 2000; Richardson, 2010; Daily et al, 1998

appropriate times during the growing season. Natural ecosystems located in or around farmland underpin agricultural productivity by providing soil formation, erosion control, nutrient cycling, pollination, wild foods, genetic material, regulation of the timing and flow of water and more (MEA, 2005). Furthermore, oceans and inland water bodies currently contribute 16 per cent of global animal-based protein supply, and fish are the primary source of such protein for nearly 1.3 billion people.[10]

In turn, access is partly dependent on availability. For example, food supplies in a region can become constrained when crop yields decline due to extended heat waves or lack of sufficient water to irrigate crops. As a result, the price of food can increase or access to locally produced food can become constrained, thereby increasing dependence of local populations on food imports. And when this occurs in regions where people do not have sufficient income, economic access becomes an acute food security issue. Likewise, sustainability by definition underpins long-term stability. If food production is not sustainable from an environmental perspective, then it is not stable over time.[11]

4. But many of the environmental underpinnings of food supply are being degraded or are facing limits, making attaining food security more difficult

Many of the environmental foundations of food supply currently face challenges of resource scarcity and degradation:

- *Climate change*

  The global average surface temperature increased by 0.85°C from 1880 to 2012 and is projected to increase another 0.3°C to 4.8°C by the end of the twenty-first century.[12] Climate change is projected to have large adverse effects on agricultural yields due to higher temperatures, extended heat waves, flooding and shifting precipitation patterns. Rising sea levels from climate change will also reduce cropland productivity and viable cropland area in some coastal regions (IPCC, 2014).

- *Terrestrial ecosystems*

  The conversion of natural ecosystems has led to a decline over the past half century in the quantity and quality of 60 per cent of ecosystem services analysed by the UN Millennium Ecosystem Assessment (MEA, 2005). Many of the ecosystem services, such as soil formation, aquifer recharge and flood control are important for farmland productivity. Furthermore, land degradation affects approximately 20 per cent of the world's cultivated areas (Bai, 2008).

- *Water*

  Many crop-generating regions currently face significant water stress, where near-term demand outstrips supply. The recent droughts and associated declines in crop production in parts of Australia, East Africa, Russia and the United States are cases in point. Over the coming decades, water stress is projected to increase due to growing demand for water and poor water management, coupled with the impacts of climate change (Figure 16.3) (WRI and Coca Cola Company, 2011).[13]

- *Oceans*

  Wild fish landings from marine water bodies have stagnated over the past 20 years, gradually declining from a peak of 88 million tons in the mid-1990s to 82 million tons by 2013 (FAO, 2016).

Failure to address these environmental and natural resource impacts will likely hamper food supply and therefore food security. For instance, crop productivity can suffer when soil organic matter, erosion control and pollination decline as natural ecosystems are converted or degraded (MEA, 2005). Depleting freshwater aquifers poses a threat to food production in several major breadbaskets (MEA, 2005). Wild fish catch is projected to decline in coming decades if more fish stocks become overexploited.

Figure 16.3: Change in water stress by 2025 in agricultural areas (based on IPCC scenario A1B)

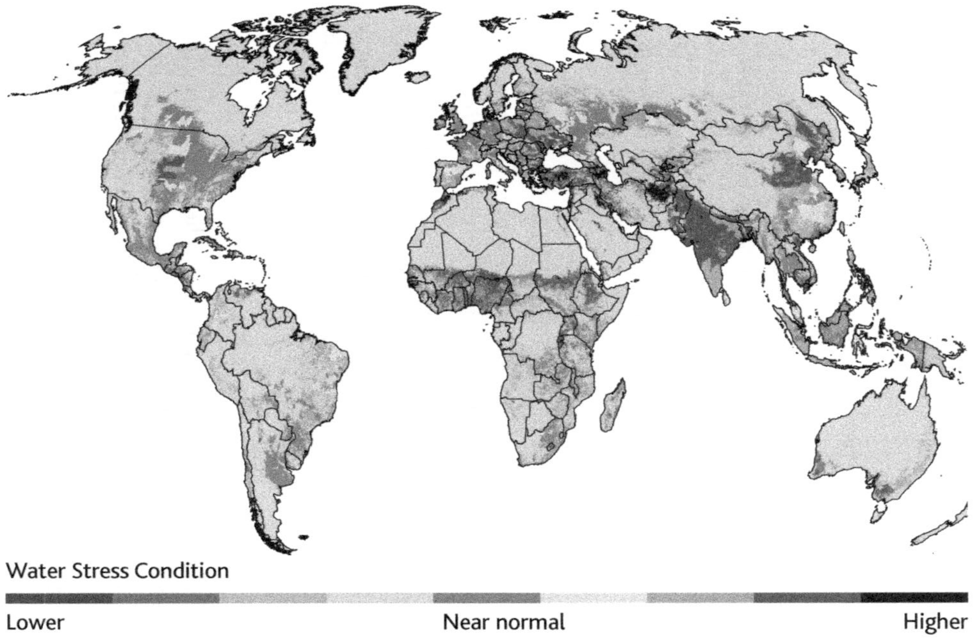

Water Stress Condition

Lower   Near normal   Higher

Note: Areas in the palest grey contain no croplands.
Sources: WRI and Coca-Cola Company, 2011; cropped areas from Ramankutty et al, 2008

Climate change, in particular, threatens to have major impacts. For example, the latest science indicates that climate change will have net adverse consequences for global crop yields due to higher temperatures, extended heat waves and shifting precipitation patterns (Figure 16.4) (IPCC, 2014). By mid-century, yields of wheat, maize and soybean could decline by 14–25 per cent, 19–34 per cent and 15–30 per cent, respectively, with a warming of 2.2–3.2°C compared with pre-industrial temperatures and no carbon dioxide fertilisation (World Bank, 2012). With a one metre rise in sea levels, almost 11 per cent of South Asia's agricultural land is projected to be vulnerable to flooding (World Bank, 2012). By the end of the century, the planet's 'drought disaster affected area' is projected to grow from 15 per cent to approximately 44 per cent, with regions facing the greatest increases being southern Africa, the United States, southern Europe, Brazil and Southeast Asia (World Bank, 2012).

5. The food production system itself is contributing to this degradation

The global food production system itself contributes to this environmental degradation in several ways (Figure 16.5):

- *Climate change*
  Agriculture accounts for approximately 24 per cent of global greenhouse gas emissions as of 2010. This figure includes 13 per cent from agricultural production, namely methane from livestock, nitrous oxide from fertiliser use, and carbon dioxide from tractors and fertiliser production. Land use change, which is primarily driven by agriculture, contributed about another 11 per cent (Searchinger et al, 2013).[14]

- *Terrestrial ecosystems*
  Since the invention of agriculture 8,000–10,000 years ago, growing crops and raising livestock have been the primary cause of ecosystem loss and degradation of natural ecosystems (MEA, 2005). Today, 37 per cent of the planet's landmass outside of Antarctica is used to grow food – 12 per cent as croplands and 25 per cent as grazing lands.[15] When deserts, permanent ice and lakes and rivers are excluded, the figure rises to nearly 50 per cent. Yet agriculture continues to expand and is the dominant driver of tropical deforestation (Kissinger, 2012), the conversion of carbon-rich peatlands and associated impacts on biodiversity (MEA, 2005).

Figure 16.4: Projected climate change impact on crop yields (3°C warmer world)

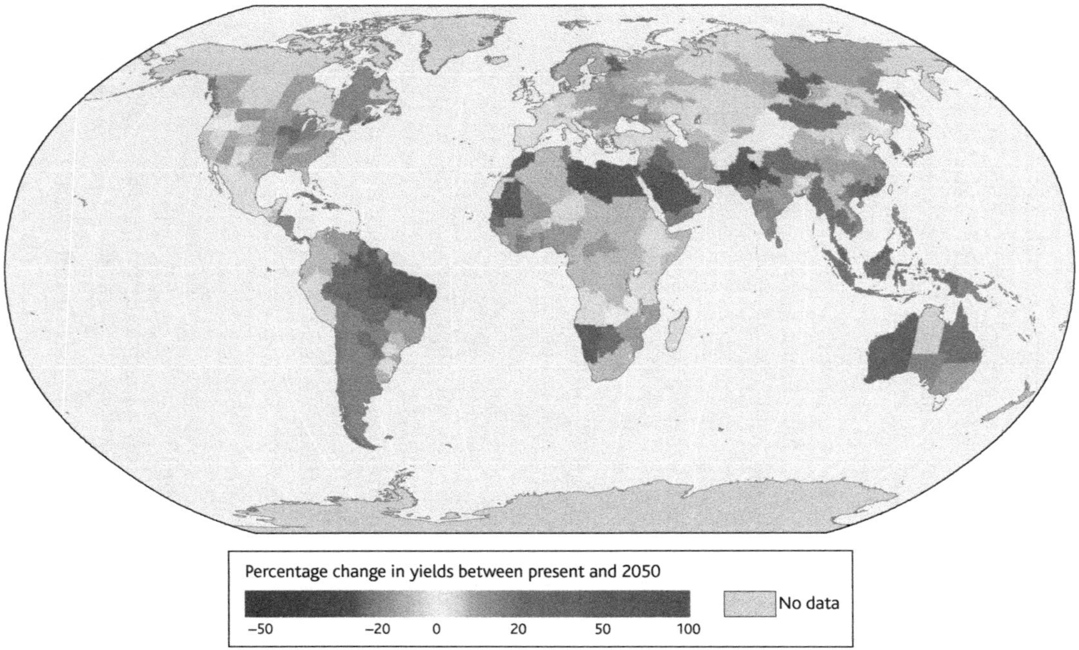

Percentage change in yields between present and 2050

−50 −20 0 20 50 100 No data

Source: World Bank, 2010

Figure 16.5: Food production system's share of global impact (%) (~2010)

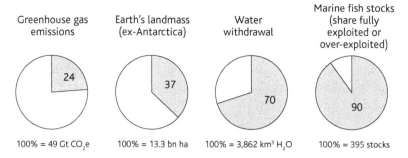

Source: WRI analysis based on IEA, 2012; EIA, 2012; Houghton, 2008; FAO, 2011c; FAO, 2012a; Foley et al, 2005; FAO, 2014

- *Water*
  Agriculture is responsible for approximately 70 per cent of all freshwater withdrawn from rivers, lakes and aquifers, and for 80 to 90 per cent of such water that is actually consumed and not returned (Foley, 2005). Agriculture also has a major impact on water quality; it is the primary source of nutrient runoff from farm fields, which creates 'dead zones' and toxic algal blooms in coastal waters and aquatic ecosystems (Selman and Greenhalgh, 2009).

- *Oceans*
  While the global wild fish catch has stagnated over the past 20 years, the percentage of stocks that are overfished continues to rise. In 2011, for instance, 29 per cent of marine fish stocks were classified as overexploited and another 61 per cent were fully exploited, while only 10 per cent were exploited at less than their full potential (FAO, 2014). Fishing now occurs across one-third of the world's ocean surface, leaving only the most inaccessible waters at the two poles and the unproductive waters of the high seas unexploited (Swartz et al, 2010).

6. Food consumption patterns also are impacting the sustainability of food security

How food is produced is not the only facet of the food production system having an impact on the sustainability and equity of food security. How food is consumed has implications as well. Three consumption-side issues of particular relevance are food loss and waste, overconsumption and competing uses of food.

- *Food loss and waste*
  Measured in caloric content, 24 per cent of all food produced is lost or wasted between the farm and the fork (Searchinger et al, 2013).[16] By commodity type, cereals are the largest source of food loss and waste, at slightly more than half, followed by roots and tubers (Figure 16.6). Food loss and waste equates to food-insecure people and communities having to grow or pay for even more food to meet their energy and nutritional needs. Economically, it equates to wasted financial and labour investments that reduce the income of actors in the food value chain. Environmentally, it equates to wasted water, land and energy, and unnecessary greenhouse gas emissions – especially for resource-intensive foods such as meat and milk (Rejinders and Soret, 2003).

- *Overconsumption*
  More people in the world today consume too much food than consume too little. In 2013, an estimated 2.1 billion people were overweight or obese – more than two and a half times the number of chronically undernourished people in the world (Ng et al, 2014; FAO et al, 2015). Besides affecting resource consumption, obesity has human health and financial costs. For instance, according to an OECD study, obese people on average incur 25 per cent higher healthcare costs than people of normal weight (OECD, 2010).

Figure 16.6: Sources of food loss and waste (2009)

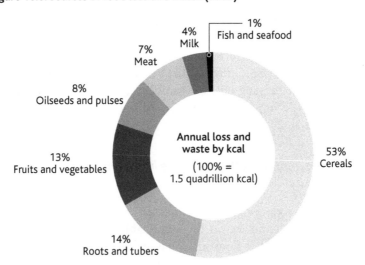

Source: WRI analysis based on FAO, 2011b

- *Competing uses of food crops*

  Take biofuels, for example. Producing 10 per cent of the world's liquid transportation fuel by 2050 would require 29 per cent of all the world's crops produced in 2010, as measured by their energy content (Searchinger and Heimlich, 2015).[17] Indeed, all of the chemical energy contained in 100 per cent of all the world's crops in 2011 equalled just 14 per cent of the world's primary energy consumption.[18] Such additional demands would make achieving food security even more difficult (Searchinger et al, 2013).[19]

Implications for the 2030 Agenda for Sustainable Development

A number of implications for the sustainable development agenda follow from the food security challenge and these six propositions. First, it is commendable that the 2030 Agenda has an explicit goal to 'End hunger, achieve food security and improved nutrition and promote sustainable agriculture'. Producing and distributing food is a hallmark foundation of human civilisation (Diamond, 1997) and is a prerequisite for political stability, sustainable development and inclusive economic growth (World Bank, 2008). At the same time, demand for food is projected to dramatically increase over coming decades.

Second, it is important that any goals and targets relevant to food security include some sustainability considerations. The Millennium Development Goals (MDGs) had only one target and two indicators relating to food security (Box 16.1). This target and its indicators may have served well the 2000–15 period, but the sustainability challenges and opportunities facing the global food system over coming decades suggest that merely replicating these targets and indicators in the Sustainable Development Goals (SDGs) would have been insufficient for achieving food security.

Box 16.1: Food security in the 2000–15 MDGs

Food security was reflected by one target and two indicators in the MDGs
- *Target 1.C*: halve, between 1990 and 2015, the proportion of people who suffer from hunger;
- *Indicator 1.8*: prevalence of underweight children under five years of age;
- *Indicator 1.9*: proportion of population below minimum level of dietary energy consumption.

Third, suitable candidate sustainability targets include a target on the rate of food loss and waste, low-carbon agriculture and water efficient food production. That said, not every target and indicator associated with a food security goal needs to be sustainability-oriented. For example, targets relating to prevalence of undernourishment, stunting or malnutrition continue to be relevant and worthy of inclusion in the 2030 Agenda's goal on food security.

Finally, any target should align with the core principles for the sustainable development agenda, including (Hazlewood, 2012):

- *Poverty and wellbeing*
  Eradicating multi-dimensional poverty and improving the wellbeing and security of people and the planet sustainably should be the overriding objective of the sustainable development agenda.

- *Sustainability*
  Global goals, targets and indicators for poverty eradication and improved wellbeing must integrate economic, social and environmental dimensions of sustainability and their inter-linkages, with equity and resilience as cross-cutting priorities.

- *Universality*
  An agenda to eradicate poverty and achieve sustainable and equitable development must be a shared agenda, whereby goals are applicable to all countries but reflect diverse development pathways and implementation capacities.

- *Multiple tiers of action*
  Achieving the goals and targets should be amenable to individual and household actions, national development frameworks and global collective action.

The following elaborates on three candidate sustainable food security targets.

Food loss and waste: context

'Food loss and waste' refers to the edible parts of plants and animals produced or harvested for human consumption but not ultimately consumed by people.[20] In particular, 'food loss' refers to food that spills, spoils, incurs an abnormal reduction in quality such as bruising or wilting, or otherwise gets lost before it reaches the consumer. 'Food waste' refers to food that is of good quality and fit for consumption, but is not consumed because it is discarded after it reaches consumers – either before or after it spoils (FAO, 2011b). Food loss and waste occurs along the food value chain, including:

- *production* or harvest in the form of grain left behind by poor harvesting equipment, discarded fish, and fruit not harvested or discarded because it fails to meet quality standards;
- *handling and storage* in the form of food degraded by pests, fungus and disease;
- *processing and packaging* in the form of spilled milk, livestock trimmings, damaged fish and fruit unsuitable for processing;
- *distribution and market* in the form food discarded due to bruises or 'sell-by date' expiry;
- *consumption* in the form of food bought by consumers, restaurants and caterers but not eaten (FAO, 2011b, cited in Lipinski et al, 2013).

FAO estimates that 32 per cent of all food produced in the world, in terms of weight, was lost or wasted in 2009 (FAO, 2011b). However, food types vary widely in terms of their water and caloric content per kilogram. Measured in terms of caloric content, global food loss and waste equated to approximately 24 per cent of all food produced (Searchinger et al, 2013).[21] One out of every four calories produced is not ultimately consumed.

The distribution of this food loss and waste varies significantly between developed and developing regions (Figure 16.7). More than half of food loss and waste in the developed world occurs at the point of consumption, or 'close to the fork'. In contrast, two-thirds to three-quarters of food loss and waste in the developing world occurs during the production and storage stages, or 'close to the farm' (Searchinger et al, 2013).[22]

Food loss and waste: candidate target

Such big inefficiencies suggest big opportunities for economic, social and environmental improvement – and thus a worthy target for the sustainable development agenda. We propose the following target and its associated indicator and metric:

- *Target:* by 2030, reduce the rate of food loss and waste by 50 per cent;
- *Indicator:* share of food produced/harvested that is lost or wasted between the farm and fork;
- *Metric:* per cent of food loss and waste.

Figure 16.7: Distribution of food loss and waste across the value chain by region (% of kcal lost or wasted)

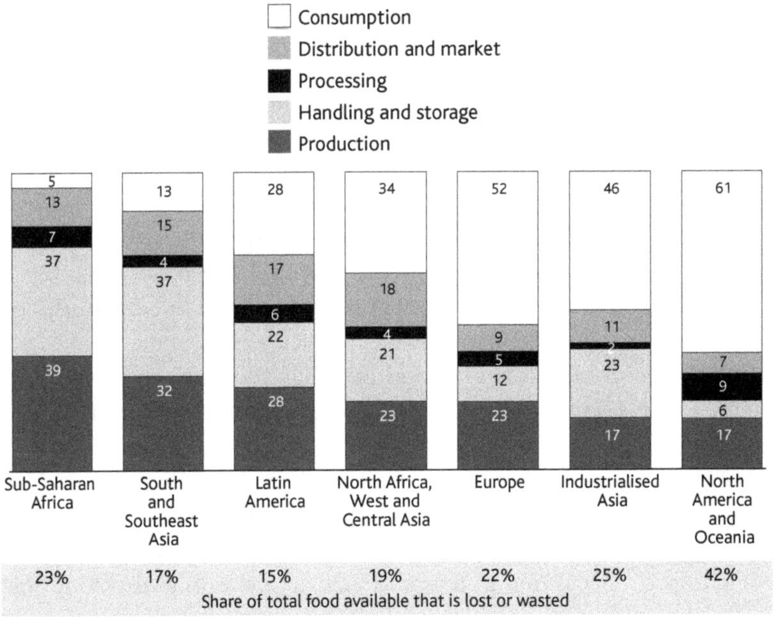

Legend:
- Consumption
- Distribution and market
- Processing
- Handling and storage
- Production

	Sub-Saharan Africa	South and Southeast Asia	Latin America	North Africa, West and Central Asia	Europe	Industrialised Asia	North America and Oceania
Consumption	5	13	28	34	52	46	61
Distribution and market	13	15	17	18	9	11	7
Processing	7	4	6	4	2	2	9
Handling and storage	37	37	22	21	5	23	6
					12		
Production	39	32	28	23	23	17	17
Share of total food available that is lost or wasted	23%	17%	15%	19%	22%	25%	42%

Note: Numbers may not sum to 100 due to rounding.
Source: WRI analysis based on FAO, 2011b

Such a target is ambitious. It implies that the rate of food loss and waste in 2030 would decline from its current level of 24 per cent to 12 per cent (on a caloric basis) or from 32 per cent to 16 per cent (on a weight basis). Yet some are already making similarly ambitious goals. In 2012, for example, the European Commission set a target of reducing food waste by 50 per cent by 2020 throughout Europe.[23]

There is precedent for progress. For instance, the Waste and Resource Action Programme (WRAP) in the United Kingdom has achieved a 13 per cent reduction in household food waste nationwide from 2007 to 2010 (WRAP-UK, 2011). Pilot efforts in Benin, Cape Verde, India and Rwanda have reduced food loss for a number of commodities by more than 60 per cent through a variety of low-cost storage and handling practices (WFLO, 2010).

The target is measurable. The methods from FAO's *Global Food Losses and Food Waste: Extent, Causes, and Prevention* (2011) could be replicated to create a baseline and measure progress. Setting a target would also serve to increase the quality and periodicity of data collection.

Furthermore, the target performs well against the core principles (Table 16.2).[24]

Table 16.2: Performance against core principles: reducing food loss and waste

Principle	Reducing food loss and waste could …
Poverty and wellbeing	• Increase the share of food grown by smallholder farmers that is available for their own consumption and/or for sale to the market. • Reduce the likelihood that smallholders become net food buyers.
Sustainability	• Lower demands on water, land, and energy, and lower greenhouse gas emissions (environmental). • Reduce the likelihood of social disruption due to acute food scarcity (social). • Curtail wasted financial and labour investments (economic).
Universality	• Involve all countries. For instance, developing countries have much to do to reduce losses at the production and storage stages while developed countries have much to do to reduce waste at the consumption stage.
Tiers of action	• Involve all actors. For instance, households can take steps to reduce waste at home, food retailers can improve food screening and inventory handling procedures, and countries and international institutions can introduce initiatives and policies that improve food storage and handling.

Food loss and waste: means of implementation

Fortunately, a number of strategies for reducing food loss and waste along the value chain are already known (Figure 16.8) and, if implemented at scale, could go a long way toward achieving the proposed target (Lipinski et al, 2013). For example:

- for the production step, principle opportunities involve improving harvesting techniques and altering strict aesthetic standards that can encourage farmers to leave tubers and vegetables with surface blemishes in the field;

- for the handling and storage step, one solution is to improve access to simple, low-cost food storage systems for low-income farmers. Another is to improve roads, storage facilities, electricity, refrigeration and improved food processing in general;

- ways to reduce loss and waste during the processing and packaging step include increasing secondary uses of trimmings and re-engineering food manufacturing processes;

- strategies for reducing loss and waste in the distribution and market step include reducing blemish waste at the store, facilitating donation of unsold goods, and improving inventory systems to better match food demand and supply and thus reduce shelf losses;

Figure 16.8: Potential solutions to reduce food loss and waste (not exhaustive)

Production	Handling and storage	Processing and packaging	Distribution and market	Consumption
Facilitate donation of unmarketable crops	Improve access to low-cost handling and storage technologies (eg, evaporative coolers, storage bags, metal silos, crates)	Re-engineer manufacturing processes	Facilitate increased donation of unsold goods	Facilitate increased donation of unsold goods from restaurants and caterers
Improve availability of agricultural extension services	Improve ethylene and microbial management of food in storage	Improve supply chain management	Change food date labelling practices	Conduct consumer education campaigns
Improve market access	Introduce low-carbon refrigeration	Improve packaging to keep food fresher for longer	Change in-store promotions	Reduce portion sizes
Improve harvesting techniques	Improve infrastructure (eg, roads)		Provide guidance on food storage and preparation to consumers Improve inventory systems	Ensure home economics taught in schools, colleges and communities

Source: WRI analysis based on FAO, 2011b

- for the consumption step, WRAP has launched consumer education campaigns with major retailers, such as the 'Love Food, Hate Waste' programme that provides practical tips on food storage, how to avoid confusing 'sell by' and 'use by' dates, and so forth. (WRAP-UK, 2011)

Climate and agriculture: context

Agriculture is a major contributor of anthropogenic greenhouse gas emissions that are contributing to climate change. As of 2010, agriculture in some form accounted for approximately 24 per cent of global greenhouse gas emissions (Figure 16.9) (Searchinger et al, 2013).[25] About 13 per cent of emissions came from the food production process, most notably:

- methane emissions generated through enteric fermentation in the stomachs of ruminants – cattle, goats and sheep;
- methane and nitrous oxide emissions from ruminant wastes decomposing on pastures;
- nitrous oxide emissions from croplands and grasslands, derived particularly from fertilisers;
- carbon dioxide emissions from on-farm energy consumption as well as from the manufacture of farm tractors, irrigation pumps, other machinery and key inputs such as fertiliser;
- methane and nitrous oxide emissions from rice paddies;
- methane emissions from the manure managed in storage facilities and barns, primarily from pigs and cattle feedlots.

Approximately 11 per cent of global greenhouse gas emissions came from land use, land-use change and forestry (LULUCF) (Houghton, 2008). The majority of land-use change in the world results from agriculture, in the form of the conversion of forests, wetlands and grasslands into farms and grazing pastures. For instance, agriculture was responsible for roughly 80 per cent of tropical deforestation between 2000 and 2010 (Kissinger et al, 2012).

Climate and agriculture: candidate target

Such a large share of greenhouse gas emissions from agriculture suggests a large opportunity for improvement – and thus a worthy target for the sustainable development agenda. We propose the following target and its associated indicator and metric:

Figure 16.9: Estimated global greenhouse gas emissions by source (2010)

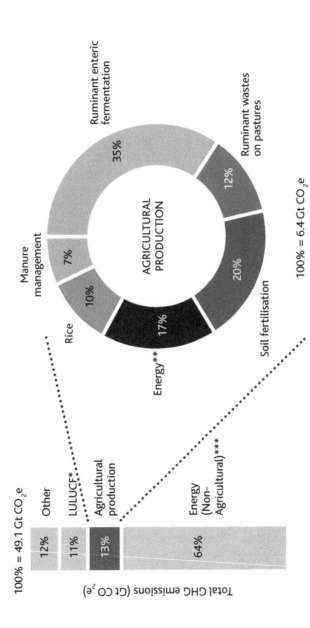

Notes: Numbers may not sum to 100 due to rounding. * LULUCF = Land Use, Land Use Change, and Forestry. ** Includes emissions from on-farm energy consumption as well as from manufacturing of farm tractors, irrigation pumps, other machinery, and key inputs such as fertiliser. It excludes emissions from the transport of food. *** Excludes emissions from agricultural energy sources described above.

Source: WRI analysis based on UNEP, 2012; FAO, 2012a; EIA, 2012; IEA, 2012; and Houghton, 2008 with adjustments

- *Target:* by 2030, reduce the greenhouse gas emissions from food production by 25 per cent;
- *Indicator:* total greenhouse gas emissions from food production, both crops and livestock;
- *Metric:* tons of carbon dioxide equivalent (CO_2e).

Such a target is ambitious yet roughly aligned with an emissions reduction trajectory to limit global warming to 2°C by mid-century (UNEP, 2012).[26] It implies that the global greenhouse gas emissions from food production would decline from its 2010 level of roughly 6.5 gigatons of CO_2e to 4.9 gigatons of CO_2e in 2030, even as total food production increases.

Data sources for this target already exist. At a minimum, the greenhouse gas emissions to be included in the indicator are those from direct agricultural production, including emissions from livestock and crop production. To the degree that emissions from land conversion to agriculture can be confidently estimated, they should also be included. In that case, the current emissions levels and the 2030 target amount on an absolute basis would need to be revised to include land use change emissions.

The target performs well against the core principles (Table 16.3).[27]

Table 16.3: Performance against core principles: reducing the greenhouse gas intensity of agriculture

Principle	Reducing the greenhouse gas intensity of agriculture could ...
Poverty and wellbeing	• Increase the productivity of smallholder farmers and reduce excess application of expensive inputs.
Sustainability	• Cut global emissions and lower demand for land (environmental). • Generate new jobs and sustain rural livelihoods (social). • Increase productivity of agriculture, stimulate new technologies and agricultural practices, and create new market opportunities (economic).
Universality	• Involve all countries. Every agricultural producing country can do something to make its agriculture more climate-friendly. For instance, some developing countries can increase use of no-till practices and on-farm agroforestry. Some countries with advanced agricultural systems can take steps to improve fertiliser use efficiencies and lower livestock emissions. Flexibility can be provided to accommodate national circumstances and allow countries that can go further the possibility to do so.
Tiers of action	• Involve all actors. For instance, farming households can implement on-farm climate-smart agricultural practices. Countries can introduce policies and incentives to stimulate low-carbon agriculture. International institutions can facilitate financial investment and technology transfer to encourage adoption of these practices.

Climate and agriculture: means of implementation

A number of strategies exist for reducing the greenhouse gas intensity of food production. For example, to reduce the direct emissions from agricultural production, farmers can (see Searchinger et al, 2013):[28]

- improve livestock feed efficiency and quality;
- improve efficiency of fertiliser application, most notably less in regions that apply too much, more in regions that apply too little, and with greater precision just about everywhere;
- use zero-till or reduced-till soil management practices;
- implement alternative wetting and drying rice paddy management practices.

To reduce pressure to convert natural ecosystems to cropland, farmers can:

- boost yields through improved soil and water management practices, including integration of nitrogen-fixing trees and plants in and around farmland;
- improve yields through more precise management of inputs and careful seed selection;
- close the 'yield gap' among smallholders.

To reduce pressure to convert natural ecosystems to grazing land, farmers can improve pastureland productivity by:

- selectively using more grains and high protein oilseed meals as a grass supplement, particularly during the dry or cold seasons when grass production drops off;
- improving healthcare for livestock animals and the types of animal breeds so that the animals produce more meat and milk from the same amount of forage and feed;
- planting pastures with grasses and legumes to produce more digestible forage;
- grazing animals more efficiently by rotating them among parts of a field;
- adding shade trees to reduce animal stress and maintain moisture levels, particularly in tropical areas.

These are only a sample of the wide range of strategies available to achieve this target.

Water and agriculture: context

Water is essential for world agricultural output. Water enters the agricultural system in two primary ways – rain-fed agriculture and irrigated agriculture. Rain-fed systems account for 80 per cent of cultivated land across the globe and 60 per cent of total crop production (FAO, 2011c). Irrigated agriculture accounts for about 20 per cent of cultivated land and 40 per cent of global food production. Irrigated crop yields are more than two-and-a-half times greater than those of rain-fed agriculture globally (WWAP, 2012).

Much irrigation comes from surface water sources – namely lakes, streams and rivers. Where these are less available for irrigation, groundwater is tapped. Globally, two-thirds of groundwater use is for irrigation, and the rate of groundwater abstraction has at least tripled over the past 50 years and continues to increase (WWAP, 2012).

Irrigation accounts for 70 per cent of total water withdrawals from rivers, lakes and aquifers globally. In OECD countries, agricultural water withdrawals account for less than half of total withdrawals. But in Brazil, the Russian Federation, India and China, they account for more than 60 per cent, with India's irrigation accounting for as much as 87 per cent of its total water withdrawals (WWAP, 2012).

Increased demand for food over coming decades will coincide with increased demand for water for domestic and industrial uses and climate change. Future global agricultural water consumption, including both rain-fed and irrigated agriculture, is estimated to grow by 19 per cent globally by 2050 (WWAP, 2012).

Water and agriculture: candidate target

The water stress that many watersheds may face over coming decades could pose a threat to food security. Having a target aimed at reducing the water-intensity of agricultural production could spur innovation, investment and adoption of practices that mitigate and adapt to this threat. We propose the following target and its associated indicator and metric:

- *Target:* by 2030, reduce the water intensity of crop production by 30 per cent;
- *Indicator:* cubic metre of irrigation water consumed per ton of food produced;
- *Metric:* tons per cubic metre of water.

Such a target is ambitious and, of course, the relative importance of 'cubic metres of water consumed per ton of food produced' will vary by location; it is more important in water-stressed regions than in those that are water abundant. Data for this target could come from FAO and FAO's Aquastat database, presuming data on water withdrawal can be feasibly converted into water consumption. Furthermore, the target performs well against the core principles (Table 16.4).[29]

Table 16.4: Performance against core principles: reducing the water intensity of agriculture

Principle	Reducing the water intensity of agriculture could ...
Poverty and wellbeing	• Reduce smallhold farmer and poor community vulnerability to food shortages or price spikes due to droughts. • Protect smallholder yields against competition for available surface water from upstream water users.
Sustainability	• Reduce strain on local water resources, aquatic ecosystems, and water-dependent biodiversity (environmental). • Improve local access to food and sustain rural livelihoods (social). • Increase agricultural productivity, boost farmer incomes, and improve local economies generally (economic).
Universality	• Involve all countries. Every agricultural producing country has opportunities to improve its water-use efficiency rates in agriculture.
Tiers of action	• Involve all actors. Every actor from individual smallhold farms to very large farming operations, nations, and multinational corporations with large supply chains can take appropriate steps to reduce agriculture-related water use. For example, smallholders can make adjustments in cropping, tillage, and watering techniques. Nations can reform policies to remove incentives for over-irrigation. The private sector can implement standards to improve performance in global supply chains. International institutions can invest in efficient irrigation systems and facilitate technology transfer to encourage adoption of water efficiency practices.

Water and agriculture: means of implementation

Many strategies exist to reduce the water intensity of food production. For example, to improve the productivity of rain-fed agriculture, farmers can:

- implement conservation tillage practices such as zero tillage and reduced tillage to maximise rainfall infiltration into soils and reduce run off;
- use rainwater harvesting techniques such as contour bunds to maximise water retention in the field.

To reduce overall agricultural water consumption, farmers can:

- select crops whose water requirements match the water availability of where they are grown;
- select crops that have lower evapotranspiration-to-productivity ratios or that are adapted to low-water environments;
- utilise more effective and precision crop, soil and nutrient management strategies to ensure higher yields for every litre of water.

To reduce evaporative and leakage losses from irrigation, farmers can:

- line irrigation canals;
- ensure the timing and amount of irrigation are tailored to crop requirements;
- select efficient irrigation methods, such as micro-drip and subsurface systems, that have low evaporation losses and that are well suited to the location and crop.

These are only a sample of the wide range of strategies available to achieve this target.

Concluding reflections

These proposed targets for the sustainable development agenda on food security are important in a number of ways. They re-affirm that food security is worthy of a dedicated SDG. They recognise that food security is dependent, at least in part, on the sustainability of food supply. They ensure that the means of implementation associated with any suite of food security-related targets would avoid practices that exacerbate any negative impacts of food production or consumption on climate, water and ecosystems. They satisfy core principles of poverty alleviation, human wellbeing, sustainability, universality and multiple tiers of action. And they encourage government policy coherence. We expand on each of these points below.

1. *Food security is worthy of a dedicated SDG.* Demand for food is projected to increase 70 per cent between 2006 and 2050, due to population growth and growing per capita consumption of meat and other resource-intensive foods. Nearly a billion people remain undernourished even today. Food security is a prerequisite for political stability, sustainable development and inclusive economic

growth. The quantity of food produced in 2009 will be insufficient to adequately feed the projected population in 2050. Closing this 'food gap' will most likely be met through an increase in production of food calories and a reduction of overconsumption (such as by reducing food loss and waste). Of course, these measures will only guarantee sufficient *availability* of food, which is necessary but not sufficient for food security. Other SDGs – especially those dedicated to poverty alleviation and health – should complement this goal to ensure that all people have sufficient *access* to and *utilisation* of food.

2. *Food security is dependent, at least in part, on the sustainability of food supply.* Many of the environmental underpinnings of food supply are being degraded or are facing limits, making attaining food security more difficult. Climate change, water scarcity and degradation of terrestrial and marine ecosystems threaten to reduce future yields and thereby compromise the world's food supply.

3. *The means of implementation associated with any suite of food security-related targets should avoid practices that exacerbate the negative impacts of food production or consumption* on climate, water, terrestrial ecosystems and oceans. A food loss and waste reduction target would help the world increase the global food supply without having to increase water, land, energy, greenhouse gas emissions associated with food production. The climate and water targets would help the world increase the global food supply while reducing agricultural greenhouse gas emissions and reducing water use per ton of food produced.

4. *Food security targets must satisfy core principles* of poverty alleviation, human wellbeing, sustainability, universality and multiple tiers of action. These targets all contribute to eradicating multi-dimensional poverty and improving the wellbeing and security of people and the planet sustainably – the overriding objective of the sustainable development agenda. Furthermore, these targets are applicable to all countries but flexible enough to reflect diverse development pathways and implementation capacities. These targets are amenable to individual and household actions, national development frameworks and global collective action.

5. *Food security targets must encourage government policy coherence.* For example, there are a number of ways to increase food supplies or otherwise achieve food security that are not aligned with meeting

other national or international policy goals and conventions. To illustrate, converting remaining natural forests into grazing land or cropland may increase food production but would at the same time undermine efforts to address climate change (the United Nations Framework Convention on Climate Change) and protect biodiversity (the United Nations Convention on Biological Diversity). Likewise, such conversion might run counter to indigenous rights, efforts to build a robust forest products industry, water supply protection policies, or other national goals. If faithfully pursued, the proposed targets would ensure policy alignment between sectors and global issues.

If the sustainable development agenda were to adopt the proposed food security targets, the world will take a measurable step toward adequately and fairly feeding a growing world population in a manner that alleviates poverty and advances economic development while reducing pressure on its natural resources.

Notes

[1] The views expressed herein are those of the authors and do not necessarily reflect those of the World Resources Institute.

[2] An estimated 9.7 billion people in 2050 reflects the medium fertility scenario.

[3] 'Middle class' is defined by OECD as having per capita income of US$3,650–US$36,500 per year or US$10–US$100 per day in purchasing power parity terms. 'Middle class' data from Kharas (2010).

[4] WRI calculations from datasheets provided by Alexandratos and Bruinsma, 2012.

[5] Of the world's farms 85 per cent are 2 ha or less (von Braun, 2008); calculated from data in FAO (2010).

[6] The following definitions are paraphrased from Gross et al (2000).

[7] These five pillars are from the following papers: Gross et al (2000); Richardson (2010); Daily et al (1998).

[8] Authors' calculations, updated from Searchinger et al (2013), based on the FAO Food Balance Sheets (FAO, 2012). Daily calorie availability from both plant- and animal-based foods in 2009 was 2,831 kcal/person. However, 'available food' includes food that people waste in their homes or dining out, and ultimately do not consume. To estimate consumption, WRI adjusted

'availability' figures downward using regional estimates of food loss and waste given in FAO (2011b). This adjustment led to an estimate of daily calorie consumption of 2,433 kcal/person. As a comparison, the FAO suggested average daily energy requirement (ADER) – the recommended amount of caloric consumption for a healthy person – for the world in 2009–14 was 2,353 kcal/person/day, suggesting that in 2009, enough food was available to feed the global population.

Looking forward to 2050, however, more food will be necessary to feed a growing population. Multiplying the 2009 daily per capita food consumption figure of 2,433 kcal/person by the 2009 global population of 6,811,453,000 yields a total daily global calorie consumption of 16,572,265,149,000 kcal. Spreading this number of calories evenly among the projected 2050 global population of 9,725,148,000 people results in a daily calorie consumption of only 1,704 kcal/person, or roughly 650 kcal/person/day short of the ADER. Even if food loss and waste were completely eliminated by 2050 – from its current global average rate of 24 per cent down to zero – daily calorie consumption would still only be $(1,704)/(0.76) = 2,242$ kcal/person/day, still roughly 100 kcal/person/day short of the ADER.

[9] In order to increase food production without increasing use of scarce natural resources – such as land and freshwater – agriculture will need to increase *productivity*, that is, produce higher levels of food per unit of land, water and other scarce resources.

[10] Authors' calculations from FAO (2012b). Nearly 1.3 billion people live in countries where the level of animal protein consumption from fish exceeds 25 per cent.

[11] See Richardson (2010). This author further discusses the interplay between the four 'traditional' pillars of food security and environmental sustainability.

[12] Relative to 1986–2005 levels (IPCC, 2014).

[13] Cropped areas from Ramankutty et al (2008).

[14] WRI analysis based on the following sources with adjustments: UNEP (2012); FAO (2012a); IEA (2012); EIA (2012); Houghton (2008). These figures exclude downstream emissions from the entire food system in processing, retailing and cooking, which are overwhelmingly from energy use, and which must be addressed primarily by the broader transformation of the energy sector.

[15] Figures exclude Antarctica (FAO, 2011c) as cited in Searchinger et al (2013).

[16] WRI analysis based on FAO (2011b). 'Food loss and waste' refers to the edible parts of plants and animals that are produced for human consumption but that are not ultimately consumed by people.

[17] Calculation presented in Searchinger and Heimlich (2015). The calculation relies on energy projections from the US Energy Information Agency, FAO data for crop production and a variety of sources to estimate 2010 biofuel production and feedstocks. The calculation represents the energy in crops measured by their higher heating value as a percentage of that total world energy.

[18] Calculations by authors using: crop data from FAO (2012b); energy and water contents of crops from Wirsenius et al (2010); and comparing to global energy consumption estimates by the US Energy Information Agency. Primary energy consumption is the energy contained in the fuels used for energy purposes.

[19] These authors estimate that meeting a target of 10 per cent of global transportation fuel from biofuels would increase the 2050 crop calorie gap from 69 per cent to roughly 100 per cent.

[20] In this chapter, 'food loss and waste' does not include by-products that could be edible – such as bones, organs, skins, seeds, peels, hulls, bran – but that in specific supply chains are not intended for human consumption and are discarded or used as non-food; food discarded but that is redirected to food banks and eaten by people; food grown intentionally for feed, seed or industrial use; animal death or sickness during the production stage; and overconsumption beyond recommended caloric needs.

[21] Calculations based on FAO (2011b).

[22] Calculations based on FAO (2011b).

[23] 'Avoiding food wastage' www.europarl.europa.eu/sides/getDoc.do?type =TA&language=EN&reference=P7-TA-2012-14.

[24] See above discussion on core principles for the sustainable development agenda. Principles are laid out in Hazlewood (2012).

[25] See discussion in note 14.

[26] UNEP estimates that stabilising emissions at 21 gigatons by 2050 is necessary to meet the 2°C climate target agreed upon at the fifteenth session of the Conference of Parties (COP 15) of the UN Framework Convention on Climate Change in Copenhagen in 2009. The 2°C scenario roughly corresponds with the Representative Concentration Pathway (RCP) 2.6 scenario, which is the lowest climate change scenario analysed by global

modelling teams for the new assessment by the Intergovernmental Panel on Climate Change. (Authors' calculations from data presented in Figure 6 of van Vuuren et al (2011).)

[27] See above discussion on core principles for the sustainable development agenda. Principles are laid out in Hazlewood (2012).

[28] This report includes a more in-depth discussion of these different options.

[29] See above discussion on core principles for the sustainable development agenda. Principles are laid out in Hazlewood (2012).

References

Alexandratos, N, Bruinsma, J, 2012, SUA-BF calculation of production increases, Unpublished data, Rome: Food and Agriculture Organization of the United Nations (FAO)

Bai, ZG, Dent, DL, Olsson, L, Schaepman, ME, 2008, *Global assessment of land degradation and improvement*, Washington, DC: ISRIC (International Soil Reference and Information Centre) (World Soil Information)

Bush, R, 2010, Food riots: Poverty, power and protest, *Journal of Agrarian Change* 10, 119–29

Daily, G, Dasgupta, P, Bolin, B, Crosson, P, du Guerny, J, Ehrlich, P, Folke, C, Jansson, AM, Jansson, BO, Kautsky, N, Kinzig, A, Levin, S, Mäler, KG, Pinstrup-Andersen, P, Siniscalco, D, Walker, B, 1998, Food production, population growth, and the environment, *Science*, 281, 5381, 1291–2

Diamond, J, 1997, *Guns, germs and steel*, New York: WW Norton

EIA (US Energy Information Administration), 2012, *Annual energy outlook 2012: With projections to 2035*, Washington, DC: EIA

European Union Parliament, 2012, *European Parliament resolution of 19 January 2012 on how to avoid food wastage: Strategies for a more efficient food chain in the EU*, Brussels: European Commission, www.europarl.europa.eu/sides/getDoc.do?type=TA&language=EN&reference=P7-TA-2012-14

FAO (Food and Agriculture Organization of the United Nations), 2006, Food security, *Policy Brief*, FAO Agricultural and Development Economics Division with support from FAO Netherland Partnership Programme and the EC-FAO Food Security Programme, Rome: FAO

FAO (Food and Agriculture Organization of the United Nations), 2007, *Gender equality: Ensuring rural women's and men's equal participation in development*, Rome: FAO

FAO (Food and Agriculture Organization of the United Nations), 2010, *2000 world census of agriculture*, Rome: FAO

FAO (Food and Agriculture Organization of the United Nations), 2011a, *The state of food and agriculture. Women in agriculture: Closing the gender gap for development*, Rome: FAO

FAO (Food and Agriculture Organization of the United Nations), 2011b, *Global food losses and food waste: Extent, causes, and prevention*, Rome: FAO

FAO (Food and Agriculture Organization of the United Nations), 2011c, *The state of the world's land and water resources for food and agriculture*, FAOSTAT, Rome: FAO

FAO (Food and Agriculture Organization of the United Nations), 2012a, *Global forest land-use change 1990–2005*, Rome: FAO

FAO (Food and Agriculture Organization of the United Nations), 2012b, Food balance sheets, *FAOSTAT*, Rome: FAO

FAO (Food and Agriculture Organization of the United Nations), 2014, *The state of world fisheries and aquaculture*, Rome: FAO

FAO (Food and Agriculture Organization of the United Nations), 2016, *Global capture production 1950–2013*, Rome: FAO

FAO (Food and Agriculture Organization of the United Nations), IFAD (International Fund for Agricultural Development), WFP (World Food Programme), 2015, *The state of food insecurity in the World 2015. Meeting the 2015 international hunger targets: Taking stock of uneven progress*, Rome: FAO

FAO (Food and Agriculture Organization of the United Nations), OECD (Organisation for Economic Co-operation and Development), 2012, *Sustainable agricultural productivity growth and bridging the gap for small-family farms*, Interagency Report to the Mexican G20 Presidency, with contributions by Bioversity, CGIAR Consortium, FAO, IFAD, IFPRI, IICA, OECD, UNCTAD, Coordination team of UN High Level Task Force on the Food Security Crisis, WFP, World Bank and WTO, Rome: FAO

Foley, J, DeFries, R, Asner, GP, Barford, C, Bonan, G, Carpenter, SR, Chapin, FS, Coe, MT, Daily, G, Gibbs, H, Helkowski, J, Holloway, T, Howard, E, Kucharik, C, Monfreda, C, Patz, J, Prentice, IC, Ramankutty, N, Snyder, P, 2005, Global consequences of land use, *Science*, 309, 5734, 570–4

Foresight, 2011, *The future of food and farming: Final project report*, London: The Government Office for Science

Gross, R, Schoeneberger, H, Pfeifer, H, Preuss, HJA, 2000, *The four dimensions of food security: Definitions and concepts*, Brussels: European Union, Internationale Weiterbildung und Entwicklung gGmbH (InWEnt) and FAO

Hazlewood, P, 2012, A framework for integrating sustainability and equity into a Post-2015 Development Agenda, *PowerPoint presentation* at the Regional Meeting and Stakeholder Consultation on the Post-2015 Development Agenda, Bali, 13–14 December 2012, Washington, DC: World Resources Institute

Houghton, RA, 2008, Carbon flux to the atmosphere from land-use changes: 1850–2005, in *TRENDS: A compendium of data on global change*, Oak Ridge, TN: Carbon Dioxide Information Analysis Center, Oak Ridge National Laboratory, US Department of Energy

IEA (International Energy Agency), 2012, *World energy outlook 2012*, Paris: IEA Publications

IPCC (Intergovernmental Panel on Climate Change), 2014, Summary for policymakers, in CB Field, VR Barros, MD Mastrandrea, KJ Mach, MAK Abdrabo, N Adger, YA Anokhin, OA Anisimov, DJ Arent, J Barnett, V Burkett, R Cai, M Chatterjee, S Cohen, W Cramer, P Dasgupta, DJ Davidson, F Denton, P Döll, K Dow, Y Hijioka, Hoegh-O Guldberg, RG Jones, RN Joner, RL Kitching, RS Kovats, JN Larsen, E Lin, DB Lobell, IJ Losada, GO Magrin, JA Marengo, A Markandya, BA McCarl, RF McLean, LO Mearns, GF Midgley, N Mimura, JF Morton, I Niang, IR Noble, LA Nurse, K O'Brien, T Oki, L Olsson, M Oppenheimer, JT Overpeck, JJ Pereira, ES Poloczanska, JR Porter, HO Pörtner, MJ Prather, R Pulwarty, A Reisinger, A Revi, P Romero-Lankao, OC Ruppel, DE Satterthwaite, DN Schmidt, J Settele, KR Smith, DA Stone, AG Suarez, P Tschakert, R Valentini, A Villamizar, R Warren, TJ Wilbanks, PP Wong, A Woodward, and GW Yohe (eds) *Climate change 2014: Impacts, adaptation, and vulnerability. Part A: Global and sectoral aspects. Contribution of Working Group II to the Fifth Assessment Report of the Intergovernmental Panel on Climate Change*, Cambridge, UK: Cambridge University Press

Kharas, H, 2010, *The emerging middle class in developing countries*, Paris: OECD

Kissinger, G, Herold, M, de Sy, V, 2012, *Drivers of deforestation and forest degradation: A synthesis report for REDD+ policymakers*, Vancouver, Canada: Lexeme Consulting

Lipinski, B, Hanson, C, Lomax, J, Kitinoja, L, Waite, R, Searchinger, T, 2013, Reducing food loss and waste, *Working Paper, Installment 2 of Creating a Sustainable Food Future*, Washington, DC: World Resources Institute

MEA (Millennium Ecosystem Assessment), 2005, *Ecosystems and human well-being: Synthesis*, Washington, DC: Island Press

Ng, M, Fleming, T, Robinson, M, Thomson, B, Graetz, N, Margono, C, Mullany, EC, Biryukov, S, Abbafati, C, Abera, SF, and Abraham, JP, 2014, Global, regional, and national prevalence of overweight and obesity in children and adults during 1980–2013: a systematic analysis for the Global Burden of Disease Study 2013, *The Lancet* 384, 9945, 766–81

OECD (Organisation for Economic Co-operation and Development), 2010, *Healthy choices*, Paris: OECD

Ramankutty, N, Evan, A, Monfreda, C, Foley, J, 2008, Farming the planet: 1. Geographic distribution of global agricultural lands in the year 2000, *Global Biogeochemical, Cycles* 22, GB1003, doi:1010.1029/2007GB002952

Ravallion, M, Chen, S, Sangraula, P, 2007, New evidence on the urbanization of global poverty, *World Bank Policy Research Working Paper* 4199, Washington, DC: World Bank

Rejinders, L, Soret, S, 2003, Quantification of the environmental impact of different dietary protein choices, *American Journal of Clinical Nutrition* 78 (suppl), 664S–8S

Richardson, RB, 2010, Ecosystem services and food security: Economic perspectives on environmental sustainability, *Sustainability* 2, 3250–548

Searchinger, T, Heimlich, R, 2015, Avoiding bioenergy competition for food crops and land, *Working Paper, Installment 9 of Creating a Sustainable Food Future*, Washington, DC: World Resources Institute

Searchinger, T, Hanson, C, Ranganathan, J, Lipinski, B, Waite, R, Winterbottom, R, Dinshaw, A, Heimlich, R, 2013, *Creating a sustainable food future: Interim findings*, Washington, DC: World Resources Institute

Selman, M, Greenhalgh, S, 2009, Eutrophication: Sources and drivers of nutrient pollution, *World Resources Institute (WRI) Policy Note*, Washington, DC: WRI

Swartz, W, Sala, E, Tracey, S, Watson, R, and Pauly, D, 2010, The spatial expansion and ecological footprint of fisheries (1950 to present), *PLoS ONE*, 5 (e15143)

UN DESA (United Nations, Department of Economic and Social Affairs), 2015, *World population prospects: The 2015 revision*, New York: Population Division, UN DESA

UNEP (United Nations Environment Programme), 2012, *The emissions gap report 2012*, Nairobi: UNEP

Van Vuuren, D, Edmonds, J, Kainuma, M, Riahi, K, Thomson, A, Hibbard, K, Hurtt, G, Kram, T, Krey, V, Lamarque, JF, Masui, T, Meinshausen, M, Nakicenovic, N, Smith, S, Rose, S, 2011, The representative common pathways: An overview, *Climatic Change* 209, 5–31

von Braun, J, 2008, *Poverty, climate change, rising food prices, and the small farmers*, Washington, DC: International Food Policy Research Institute

WFLO (World Food Logistics Organization), 2010, Identification of appropriate postharvest technologies for improving market access and incomes for small horticultural farmers in sub-Saharan Africa and South Asia, *WFLO Grant Final Report*, Alexandria, VA: WFLO

Wirsenius, S, Azar, C, Berndes, G, 2010, How much land is needed for global food production under scenarios of dietary changes and livestock productivity increases in 2030?, *Agricultural Systems* 103, 621–38

World Bank, 2008, *World development report 2008: Agriculture for development*, Washington, DC: World Bank

World Bank, 2010, *World development report 2010: Development and climate change*, Washington, DC: World Bank

World Bank, 2012, *Turn down the heat: Why a 4°C warmer world must be avoided*, Washington, DC: World Bank Group

World Bank, FAO (Food and Agriculture Organization of the United Nations), IFAD (International Fund for Agriculture Development), 2009, *Gender in agriculture sourcebook*, Washington, DC: World Bank

World Bank, nd, World Development Indicators, http://databank. worldbank.org/Data/Home.aspx.

WRAP-UK (Waste and Resources Action Programme), 2011, *New estimates for household food and drink waste in the UK*, Banbury: WRAP-UK

WRI (World Resources Institute), Coca-Cola Company, 2011, Aqueduct water risk atlas global maps 1.0, Washington, DC: World Resources Institute, http://wri.org/aqueduct

WWAP (World Water Assessment Programme), 2012, *The United Nations World Water Development Report 4: Managing water under uncertainty and risk*, Paris: United Nations Educational, Scientific and Cultural Organization (UNESCO)

SEVENTEEN

Outlook for global development finance: excess or shortage?

Andrew Sheng

Introduction

The global financial community is still struggling with what the future of finance should look like since emerging from the Great Recession at the turn of this decade. Three immediate trends are discernible:

1. First, as excessive leverage and the shadow banking system have been identified as the major causes of instability in the financial system, policy makers and regulators are preoccupied with putting in place stringent standards and regulations to prevent another financial crisis.

2. Second, massive quantitative easing programmes by the central banks in the four reserve currency zones (G4 or US, Eurozone, United Kingdom and Japan) to restore financial stability and stimulate economic growth are flooding world capital markets with liquidity, thus keeping interest rates at historic lows and placing in jeopardy the viability of pension funds and individual savings because of a prolonged period of negative returns.

3. Third, the emerging markets are struggling with high capital inflows, rising asset prices, as well as declining commodity prices and export-led growth even as the advanced economies slow.

In the wake of deleveraging of the global banking system through new regulatory rules on banking and shadow banking (which is still evolving among the international financial community), there is a risk that the world may enter a period of synchronised recession. Developing countries will be trapped in a situation where the lending capacity of the Bretton Woods institutions is constrained due to reluctance of the advanced countries to allow the growing role of emerging markets in the world economy to be reflected in their voting power. At the same time, the advanced countries are unwilling to extend more aid due to their ongoing financial crisis and large debt overhang.

To sum up, the emerging markets have considerable room to deepen their financial systems to mobilise resources for development, although there is sufficient evidence from the experience of advanced economies that beyond a certain point, financialisation can be counterproductive. This chapter takes the position that financing development needs a 'whole-of-system' approach to development, and examines alternative sources of financing in the context of cultural and regional variances, including Islamic banking, and future sources of development finance.

Financing development

Globally, there is unlikely to be any shortage of savings to fund investment. The real bottleneck or constraint in development financing is the *quality* of intermediation, at both the domestic and international levels, rather than the *quantity*. Indeed, one of the problems of modern finance is that if the spread (between the lending rate and the cost of funds) declines due to competition and the lowering of transaction costs through technology, the financial business needs to expand transaction volume and book size in order to maintain the same level of profit. Hence, in the face of increasing competition and decline in spreads, the volume of transactions has gone up, the size of the largest players rises with scale expansion and concentration, and risks intensify as leverage increases. In other words, speed and scale plus complexity added to system fragility.

There is awareness that system stability and resilience depends on the *quality* of financial intermediation. If the quality of intermediation suffers from the three mismatches – liquidity, foreign exchange and structural – and there is insufficient exercise of credit discipline and hard budget constraint (the exit of insolvent and inefficient institutions), then the financial sector will embark on 'financialisation of credit for its own profit', thus creating unsustainable bubbles and ultimately financial crash.

This was the fundamental flaw of the current banking and shadow-banking model, whereby the banking industry created credit (and shadow credit) through moving leverage off-balance sheet and off-shore to escape the regulatory net and increasing transaction volume through proprietary trading. As advanced country regulators did not pay sufficient attention to this leverage, the financial system as a whole became skewed by leverage and the chase for yield. This has contributed to widening inequality, since there was less attention paid to inadequate financial access by under-privileged groups, lending to SMEs and lending to finance infrastructure and other development projects with long gestation, namely lack of financial inclusion.

This calls for an examination of the current and future sources of development finance, focusing on both products and institutions, particularly long-term institutions capable of funding development. There are, of course, other sources of funding from the foreign sector, through capital flows and sources of domestic funding.

Future sources of development finance

Financial depth in the emerging market economies (EMEs) is still low, as out of total financial assets–GDP ratio of 195 per cent of GDP, the banking sector accounted for 113 per cent of GDP or roughly 58 per cent of total financial assets (IMF, 2014). This dichotomy is evident in China, for example, where banking assets accounted for 241.6 per cent of GDP (Poon, 2014), whereas pension, insurance and mutual funds accounted for 19.6 per cent of GDP (OECD, 2011, 8; Poon, 2014, 11; TheCityUK, 2011a, 6; World Bank, 2014; author's calculations). In contrast, banking system assets accounted for only 21.1 per cent of total financial assets in the United States (IMF, 2011b, 11; Federal Reserve System, 2013b, 113; author's calculations). In particular, there is significant room for further deepening of EME capital (stock and debt) markets, which currently represent only 82 per cent of GDP (IMF, 2014). Capital market development, especially of the equity market – as opposed to the debt market – will have the added advantage of helping to deleverage the real sector and promote more sustainable growth.

Foreign sector

As indicated above, foreign capital in the form of foreign direct investments (FDI), foreign portfolio investments and foreign aid are traditionally important sources of development funding for EMEs. There are, however, limits to foreign borrowing because excessive reliance on foreign funding makes an economy vulnerable to foreign exchange liquidity risks when there is a sudden exodus of funds. Studies of the Asian financial crisis indicated that Asian crisis economies became vulnerable when their net foreign exchange liabilities exceeded 50 per cent of GDP (Sheng 2009, 69, Table 2.1). Another indicator of foreign exchange vulnerability is embedded in the Maastricht criteria, which specifies that the current account deficit must not exceed 3 per cent of GDP since current account deficits require foreign exchange funding.

In 2012, the US had a current account deficit of −3.0 per cent of GDP (Bureau of Economic Analysis, 2013a), and a net international investment position (net foreign exchange) deficit of 27.3 per cent of GDP (US Bureau of Economic Analysis, 2013b; World Bank, 2014; author's calculations).

The recent McKinsey Global Institute (MGI) study on financial globalisation (2013) suggests that while EMEs have received a larger share (32 per cent) of global capital flows in 2012, compared with 5 per cent in 2000, these sources of saving may be declining as the advanced markets begin to age. Global current account imbalances have begun to narrow, as there was a 30 per cent reduction in current account deficits in terms of GDP. One compensating factor is that intra-EME savings are beginning to flow, as South–South portfolio and direct investments are rising.

The good news is that 40 per cent of cross border flows are in the form of FDI, the more stable form of capital flows. However, because advanced market interest rates are near zero, leveraged carry trades take advantage of interest rate arbitrage and generate large amounts of hot money flows that can be destabilising.

The MGI study observed that capital flows to and from developing countries have actually rebounded since the sharp decline in 2008–09. In 2012, an estimated $1.5 trillion in foreign capital in the form of South–South and North–South loans, FDI, equity and bonds flowed into emerging markets. Reflecting the surpluses of capital-exporting EME countries, capital flows out of developing countries rose to $1.8 trillion in 2012. Central bank foreign reserves accounted for roughly 45 per cent of the total stock of foreign assets. Another $1.9 trillion of these foreign assets are in other emerging markets or what is referred to as South–South investment.

These trends indicate that at the global level, the EMEs are not short of funds for foreign development, but since they are themselves surplus economies, substantial development finance can be obtained by increasing the efficiency of domestic intermediation and paying attention to the macro-prudential aspects of financing so that the whole economy will be more stable, with greater efficiency as well as financial inclusivity.

Data from TheCityUK show that while emerging economies still lack a presence in global financial market activity (holding only 19 per cent of world financial assets in 2011), their combined share in all the financial markets has been rising in recent years, particularly in equity markets, derivatives exchange trading, banking and insurance (2012a; 2012b; 2013b; author's calculations).

Emerging economies' share of global financial assets in 2011 comprise:

- equity markets capitalisation (22 per cent);
- new equity issues (43 per cent);
- derivatives exchange trading (30 per cent);
- global banking assets (24 per cent);
- life and non–life insurance (14 per cent);
- domestic bond markets (11 per cent);
- value of international portfolio investments in EMEs is increasing (7.6 per cent).

Because savings remain high in EMEs, financial asset growth has been fast relative to GDP growth, with the single exception of pension assets. Between 2005 and 2011, nominal GDP in EMEs rose by 131 per cent, and other than slower pension asset growth, the rate of growth in mutual funds doubled. Growth in domestic bonds, insurance premiums and equity market capitalisation increased by between two and a half and three times. Bank assets increased more than four times and contracts traded on derivatives exchanges grew by more than six-fold between 2005 and 2011.

Domestic sector development

Another recent study by TheCityUK showed that conventional assets under management (AUM) of the global fund management industry have increased to a record $80 trillion in 2011 (2012b). In relative terms, the total fund management industry managed roughly 31 per cent of total global financial assets of $24.6 trillion at the end of 2011 (TheCityUK, 2012b; author's calculations). TheCityUK estimates that funds increased by a further 5 per cent in the first three quarters of 2012 to $84 trillion and likely grew to around $85 trillion by the end of 2012.

Pension assets account for nearly 40 per cent of total funds with the remainder split almost equally between mutual funds and insurance funds. Together with alternative assets (sovereign wealth funds (SWFs), hedge funds, private equity funds and exchange traded funds) and funds of wealthy individuals, assets of the global fund management industry amount to around $120 trillion. These figures again support this chapter's assessment that there are sufficient long-term sources of funds to finance future development, including the 2030 Agenda for Sustainable Development.

According to TheCityUK estimates, total AUM as of end of 2011 amounted to $79.8 trillion. The advanced economies accounted for the bulk (95.6 per cent) of the total AUM, whereas the EMEs accounted for $6.4 trillion or 8.0 per cent only (TheCityUK, 2012a; 2012b; author's calculations). In terms of AUM to GDP, the advanced economies were much more sophisticated, accounting for 181.2 per cent of GDP, whereas EMEs had a comparable ratio of only 30.5 per cent of GDP (TheCityUK, 2012a; UN data; author's calculations).

This analysis indicated two trends. The first is that the advanced economies have superior asset management skills, since they also manage much of the savings of the EMEs. The second is that there is considerable potential for the asset management industry in the EMEs to grow.

The corollary of this observation is that EMEs must put priority to develop the asset management industry in order to beef up the available resources for development finance.

The future of development finance, however, can only be sustainable within the following four parameters:

1. Finance must serve the real sector, with surplus savings being used to finance consumption and investment that meet the needs of the community in an inclusive way.
2. Finance should have lower leverage and must assist the real economy in achieving high net worth and solvency. The financial system must have the ability to absorb the risks and uncertainties from external shocks and from the internal dynamics that create fragility.
3. Finance must have channels to help engineer financial inclusivity and green growth.
4. Finance is responsive to the adoption of innovation and technology to improve access by the under-served sectors of the economy.

The future of development finance

Essentially, the future of development finance must embark on three paths:

- first, deepen capital markets to reduce the current overdependence on banks for short-term financing and deepen equity markets to reduce the leverage of creditors;

- second, develop long-term institutional investors such as pension funds and insurance companies that invest long-term funds to finance long-term projects such as infrastructure and conservation of natural resources (for example, rainforests and marine resources);
- third, harness the growing resources that are being built up in SWFs, private equity and venture capital to absorb higher risks and support innovative investments that promote long-term growth.

Path 1: Deepening capital markets in EMEs

As the banking sector continues to dominate the financial system in many EMEs and developing countries, a key area of reform is to reduce the double mismatch problem (maturity and currency mismatch) that arises from using short-term domestic bank deposits and short-term foreign currency loans to finance long-term local currency investments.

In the absence of effective domestic capital markets in the past, excess savings from current account surpluses in EMEs were parked as foreign exchange reserves in the G4 countries. By advancing the pace of capital market development, EMEs can rechannel some of the surpluses toward development finance in the developing world. It will also provide a conduit for long-term financing that meets the needs of institutional investors, such as insurance, pension funds, asset management and equity funds and SWFs. The development of asset securitisation markets would also be important, including secondary mortgage corporations to create secondary mortgage markets for promoting more affordable home ownership.

It is understood that developing long-term institutional investors will be a long-term effort, requiring not just expertise and skills (such as actuaries and asset managers), but also major reforms in licensing, portfolio requirements and changes to labour and social security laws.

Path 2: Meeting the strategic objectives of institutional investors

In order to develop long-term institutional investors such as pension funds and insurance companies to better intermediate EME savings to fund long-term development finance, there is a need for a multi-prong approach to address existing barriers to long-term financing. The Group of Thirty (G30) Working Group on Long-term Finance (G30, 2013) cited four principles to support the growing need for long-term finance and address regulatory changes, market developments, issues of international coordination and the creation of new institutions:

- The financial system should channel long-term savings to meet the growing investment needs of the real economy.
- Long-term finance should be supplied by entities with committed long-term horizons.
- A broad spectrum of financial instruments should be available to support long- term investment.
- An efficient global financial system should promote economic growth through stable cross-border flows of long-term finance, supported by appropriate global regulations.

As noted in the G30 report, ensuring an adequate supply of long-term finance to match the needs of the global economy as it emerges post-crisis is a major challenge. In particular, there is an urgent need for sufficient long-term finance. The solutions are not simple: they are complex, multifaceted and multidimensional. No single authority can drive change in this arena. But the findings of the G30 report make clear that strengthening the provision of financing for long-term investment will be critical to the building of a solid foundation for economic growth and job creation and the achievement of the 2030 Agenda for Sustainable Development in the years to come.

Institutional investors or non-bank financial intermediaries (led by pension funds, insurance companies, mutual funds, SWFs, hedge funds and private equity funds) represent a segment of the financial system that is rapidly catching up with the banking system. Assets of the global fund management industry have accelerated from $13.8 trillion in 1990 (IMF, 2005, 67) to $60.3 trillion in 2009 (IMF, 2011a), with estimates from TheCityUK placing the figure at $80 trillion in 2011. Including alternative assets, which would include investments in commodities and real estate, the crude estimate is that global AUM amounted to roughly $120 trillion in 2011. In comparison, global banking assets amounted to $113.8 trillion in 2011.[1]

In other words, the asset management business is becoming more important than banking business, especially if such asset managers are able to improve on the risk–reward tradeoff of providing higher returns relative to risks than short-term bank deposits. Given the aging profile of both advanced economies and parts of the EMEs, higher returns to savers would help alleviate poverty and address social inequalities.

Given the low yields arising from quantitative easing and low interest rate policies in the advanced markets, the asset allocation strategies of private and official institutional investors have changed since the global financial crisis. They have become more risk conscious, especially with respect to liquidity and sovereign credit risks, but at the same time, amid a low interest rate environment, they are seeking new asset classes that have positive long-term growth prospects and yield positive returns. In fact, institutional investors' allocations to emerging markets are already on a rising trend. EMEs should therefore position themselves to capture the rise in investment capital to emerging markets by developing their domestic capital markets based on the eight cornerstones of efficient markets, namely:

1. common values, beliefs and ownership;
2. defined property rights, resources and low transaction costs;
3. information, knowledge, technology, wisdom/experience;
4. common standards;
5. codes, rules and laws;
6. processes and procedures;
7. structure, architecture, hierarchy;
8. incentives and governance.

The remainder of this section examines the institutions that EMEs should foster in order to deepen their financial systems.

Pension funds

Pension funds are among the largest institutional investors in both advanced and developing countries with global AUM estimated at $31.4 trillion in 2011 or 40 per cent share of global AUM (TheCityUK, 2013b, estimates). Pension funds have traditionally invested significantly in equities (average of 50 per cent according to IMF data) and bonds (32 per cent in 2003). Other assets include real estate, private equity, commodities and hedge fund products.

   In 2012, TheCityUK estimated global pension assets to have grown to $33.9 trillion (2013b). In 2008, the industry suffered a 16 per cent drop in pension assets. The largest pension markets in the world are in the US (56 per cent of assets), the UK (10 per cent), Canada (7 per cent), Japan (4.7 per cent) and Australia and the Netherlands with 4 per cent each. These countries have pension assets in excess of $1 trillion each.

   Pension assets of $30.5 trillion in 34 OECD (advanced) countries accounted for 97 per cent of the end-2011 global total (TheCityUK, 2013b, calculation from datafile). The OECD weighted average asset–GDP ratio for pension funds increased from 67.3 per cent of GDP in 2001 to 72.4 per cent of GDP in 2011 (OECD, 2012). EMEs accounted for less than 3 per cent of total global pension assets, therefore suggesting that they have significant potential to grow, given their faster GDP and saving rates. The larger EME pension markets include Brazil ($308 billion); South Africa, South Korea, Mexico and Chile with between $100–200 billion each. By comparison, the weighted average pension asset–GDP ratio for selected non-OECD markets was only 15.1 per cent.

Policy makers engaged in the reform of financial systems in EMEs also recognise the prudence of mobilising long-term pension funds for long -term investments in emerging markets, such as in infrastructure financing (Asia alone will need a total of $8 trillion over the period 2010–20) (ADBI, 2009). Pension funds are also active investors in domestic bond markets and investors in alternative investments that take long-term risks within an economy.

In the advanced economies, the onset of a prolonged period of monetary easing, low interest rates and consequent fall in government bond yields, have diluted the returns on pension fund portfolios, leaving them with growing financing gaps, especially in Europe. An anticipated trend among pension fund managers is to seek new models to address their funding gaps that will not preclude investing in emerging markets if there are opportunities for higher returns.

In contrast, the current state of development of EME pension funds still lags that of the advanced economies. Given their nascent stage of development, EME pension funds have a huge potential for future growth that will help to open up an untapped source of development finance. The potential is especially significant amid the rapidly expanding EME economies, young demographic profile and growing labour force. In the case of China, for example, AUM by pension funds have increased five-fold from US$8 billion in 2005 to US$41 billion in 2010 (TheCityUK, 2013b). They represent only 0.7 per cent of GDP (OECD, 2011), however, compared with the global average of 46 per cent of GDP (World Bank, 2014; TheCityUK, 2013b).

Even a small increase of Chinese pension funds to, say, 10 per cent of GDP would add significantly to social security and provide an additional source of long-term funding for developing the domestic debt and equity markets (author's own estimates).

The Central Provident Fund in Singapore and the Employees Provident Fund in Malaysia are models of how employee savings have been successfully recycled to finance home ownership and funding of government expenditure on social infrastructure.

The above discussion suggests that the sizeable reserves of EME pension funds can help meet the much-needed financing for development. Development of long-term pension funds will also address the maturity, foreign exchange and structural mismatches of the banking system, and hence promote financial stability. By participating in long-term finance, pension funds and insurance funds will also be able to preserve and enhance their fund position and reserves. This will contribute to promoting inter-generational equity, and provide a relatively more stable rate of return.

The potential for EME pension funds to provide long-term funds for development will, however, require policy action to create an enabling environment for their growth. In particular, institutional reforms and an appropriate governance structure are important to facilitate the growth of EME pension funds.

Insurance companies

The insurance industry is both an important risk intermediary as well as an important source of long-term funds and an active institutional investor in capital markets. According to the IMF (2011a) and TheCityUK (2010) estimates, insurance companies had asset holdings of $20 trillion or 28.6 per cent of total global AUM in 2009. TheCityUK (2012b) data estimated that insurance assets have increased further to $24 trillion by the end of 2011. Insurance companies hold the highest proportion of their assets in fixed-income instruments (about 50 per cent in domestic bonds and another 10 per cent in foreign bonds), and the balance mainly in domestic and foreign equities. As a result, the returns on insurers' investment portfolios have suffered because of persistent low bond yields. In this low interest rate environment, life insurance companies are badly affected because they typically cannot reprice their policies, which could involve tenures of 30 years or more. In framing the future of finance in EMEs, insurance companies could invest more in long-term development finance projects, such as in infrastructure, in order to match their long-term liability profile. Given their long-term liability profile, insurance companies are also important investors in alternative investments, including taking equity in projects with social impact.

TheCityUK estimated that global insurance premiums amounted to $4.6 trillion (2013a). Premiums dropped by 1.1 per cent in advanced countries and increased by 1.3 per cent in emerging markets.

Advanced economies account for the bulk of global insurance premiums. The top four groups account for over half of total premium income, with Europe being the most important region, followed by North America and Asia, of which Japan was the most important. The US and the UK account for only 7 per cent of the world's population, but take up over a third of the world's insurance premiums. Emerging markets accounted for over 85 per cent of the world's population but generated only around 10 per cent of premium revenue.

As in the case of pension funds, the EME insurance industry is also less developed compared with the advanced economies, but constitutes one of the fastest growing segments of the financial system. Reflecting a combination of low penetration rates, strong fundamentals and rapid economic growth, the insurance industry in China, for example, expanded by four times from US$171 billion in 2005 to US$720 billion in 2010 (Trusted Sources, 2011). But this only accounted for 11.6 per cent of GDP in 2010 (Trusted Sources, 2011), compared with a global average of 38 per cent of GDP (World Bank, 2014; TheCityUK, 2011b). Similar patterns of under-insurance occur in other EMEs.

Efforts to encourage EME insurance companies to assume a greater role in providing long-term development finance will not only address the industry's search for long-term assets to match their long-term liabilities, they will also promote greater liquidity in the capital market and reduce overreliance on the banking sector for long-term finance, thereby facilitating greater financial stability.

Sovereign wealth funds (SWFs)

SWFs, which are special purpose investment vehicles that are owned by governments to increase the yields on their surplus investments have the potential to become a major source of long-term development finance in EMEs. SWFs were commonly established out of balance of payments surpluses, official foreign currency operations, privatisation proceeds, fiscal surpluses and revenues from the wealth of oil exporting countries. SWFs have the mandate to employ a wide range of investment strategies with a medium- to long-term timeframe. Large surplus economies such as Norway and oil-exporting economies such as Abu Dhabi and Qatar have SWFs that invest in both advanced and emerging markets. The Singapore, Chinese and Malaysian SWFs have also become major investors in emerging markets, taking long-term equity positions and investing in infrastructure projects in Asia and Africa.

SWFs are the fastest growing new financial institutions with long-term strategic aims. In 2003, their total size was estimated at only $500 billion (Truman, 2010). By 2012, TheCityUK estimated that SWFs increased to a record $5.2 trillion, including an additional $7.7 trillion held in other sovereign investment vehicles, such as pension reserve funds, development funds and state-owned corporations' funds, and $8.4 trillion in other official foreign exchange reserves. The CityUK projections suggest that governments of SWFs, largely those in emerging economies, have access to pools of funds exceeding $20 trillion (2013c).

Generally, SWFs have three main dimensions in their objectives, namely stabilisation, development and intergenerational equity.

- Stabilisation funds smooth out the effects of the key national income generators (for example, oil or copper) on the national economy and budget, focusing less on getting superior returns. These funds may not participate in long-term investing as they need to provide large capital funding, particularly in times of stress. Hence, their assets are mainly cash and high-grade fixed income.
- Developmental funds channel economic surpluses into the long-term promotion of the national economy, making long-term investments.
- Multigenerational funds provide financial support for future generations and have a long-term investing mandate. These funds aim to improve intergenerational equity, smoothing revenues generated and improving welfare for the next generations. Their assets are more diversified with greater exposure to risky assets.

SWFs represent potential long-term investors and they will likely become the largest contributor of long-term capital in the future. The world needs patient capital for stable, long-term economic growth. Their investment, if properly made, will help fund future social obligations of ageing populations. They need to transform their resources into sustainable and stable future income, creating broader social benefits.

Considering their size, SWFs have the ability to protect the economy from destabilising fluctuations and boom/bust cycles if the funds are well managed. They can also take on the shock-absorbing role in global financial markets, at least in terms of reducing short-term market volatility. When the global financial crisis unfolded, SWFs provided the crucial capital to economies in urgent need of new funding. Since they are often the only part of the government bureaucracy that understands markets, they play an important educational role in the formulation of public policy. Even though they can be a source of stability, it should be noted that they also represent a possible conflict of interest since SWFs compete with the private sector in market activities. At the same time, they can enter into public–private partnerships to invest in projects that have large social impact and benefits, while reducing commercial risks for the private sector.

The EMEs are likely to increase their investments in SWFs with their surplus savings in order to obtain higher returns and deploy such investments more efficiently. Given their long-term resources and their stable capital base, SWFs have natural first mover advantage to take on the role to support these imperatives. Operating within an appropriate governance framework and good institutions, SWFs can play their role to contribute to the global public good through 'real' money contracts and non-casino-based capitalism.

Other institutional investors

According to TheCityUK (2012b), total funds under management other than pension and insurance funds, comprise mutual funds ($23.8 trillion), hedge funds ($1.9 trillion), private equity funds ($2.2 trillion) and exchange traded funds (ETF or $1.4 trillion). These represent a substantial pool of funds of another $30 trillion that are in search of investment in quality assets that generate good returns.

This chapter has excluded discussion over money market funds ($23.8 trillion AUM) and Exchange Traded Funds ($1.4 trillion AUM) because they are essentially short-term instruments that contribute more towards liquidity and management of portfolio but less towards long-term development finance.

In addition, private wealth alone accounted for an estimated $42 trillion or 59.8 per cent of global GDP in 2011. For example, the World Economic Forum (WEF) and Oliver Wyman (WEF and Wyman, 2011) report estimated that in 2009, the family offices (private management of family wealth) managed $1.2 trillion and foundations/endowment funds managed another $1.3 trillion. As EMEs move into the middle-income stage, the size of such funds is likely to grow significantly, relative to their counterpart funds in the advanced markets. This private wealth is beginning to become more active in social impact investment, driving finance back towards social responsibility and tackling areas of risk that traditional finance has avoided.

The academic literature on development finance has tended to pay less attention to the evolution of new, long-term investors that are increasingly playing a major role in the development of financial markets. Although there has been considerable attention on the speculative role of hedge funds, in recent years different long-term investors have emerged with the capacity to hold illiquid assets for a long time, and the capability to get themselves involved in the management of such assets, including in the governance framework.

As discussed above, in the case of SWFs, other funds, such as private equity, venture capital, family offices, endowment funds, social impact funds and the like have long-term horizons, and are able to withstand short-term illiquidity and asset price volatility in order to realise long-term value.

These funds very quickly build up specific expertise, such as infrastructure funds or real estate investment trusts, that have the capacity to identify, implement, manage and realise value through traditional markets. They arose because the traditional or conventional investment products, such as bank deposits, mutual funds, fixed income debt and listed equity are by nature short-term and do not provide sufficient yield. At the same time, the traditional institutions, such as the banking industry, are heavily regulated and are not able to take long-term investor risks.

The combination of huge demand for infrastructure investments in both the advanced and emerging economies mean that this trend of alternative investment vehicles can only grow relative to the traditional financial institutions, such as banks. McKinsey has argued that part of the reason for the recent high level of saving relative to investment is that there was under-investment in the advanced economies to the tune of $20 trillion (MGI, 2013).

Islamic finance

Islamic finance is an example of equity-based financing that has been neglected for a long time, because the savings of the Muslim community (where there is a prohibition on usury or payment of interest) was not tapped. In recent years, pioneered by Malaysia and the Gulf economies, Islamic finance has grown in size to roughly $1.6 trillion, mostly through the development of Islamic banking (80 per cent) and the issuance of sukuk or Islamic bond products (14.6 per cent) (Kuwait Finance House Research Ltd, 2013). Between 2007 and 2011, Islamic banking assets grew at a compound annual growth rate of 21.1 per cent.

With the creation of the Islamic Financial Services Board, the Accounting and Auditing Organization for Islamic Financial Institutions (AAOIFI) and the multilateral central banking facility for Islamic finance, the framework for Islamic finance is ready to take off, as the global Islamic population amounted to 1.6 billion, residing in economies that are naturally resource rich, stretching from parts of Africa, Middle East, Central and South Asia to Indonesia.

Since Islamic finance encourages financing for the real sector using real commodities, the scope for Islamic insurance projects (Takaful) as risk-sharing instruments carries great promise. As these long-term institutions begin to grow, alternative sources of development finance are being cultivated to suit specific needs.

Financial inclusion and green growth

'Financial inclusion' is defined as the delivery of financial services, at affordable costs, to the disadvantaged and low-income groups – segments with little access to financial services. Financial inclusion became important as policy makers became aware that tackling poverty requires the poor to learn how to help themselves, which is facilitated by equal access to funding and financial services.

In many EMEs, such as India, financial inclusion and financial literacy go hand in hand, because the poor must be educated to learn how to do business and how to use modern financial services. The policy action is to reduce transaction costs for the poor or under-privileged, and empower them through technology, better bank branch networks and provision of services that are more user-friendly. These include no-frills accounts, relaxation on know-your-customer (KYC) norms, including unique identification (UI) numbers for the poor, using agent banking to reach the poor, adoption of mobile technology to increase coverage, adoption of simple electronic banking, credit cards for small trade payments, and encouragement of new bank branches in unbanked rural areas.

In Indonesia, for example, wet-market banking through mobile bank units has been particularly successful in providing instant credit to small farmers and traders in wet markets. While these forms of micro-credit, often provided jointly through non-governmental organisations (NGOs), may have been successful in providing short-term credit, they have not been able to increase the capital base of SMEs to allow them to invest for the future.

The rise of charitable foundations and family offices has given rise to a new form of development funding, especially in green growth and anti-poverty programmes. The foundations have the resources to provide seed capital for farmers to deal with environmental problems, such as forest conservation, marine stock replenishment, and so on, whereas long-term institutions, such as policy banks, can help supplement resources by funding the infrastructure for such green growth projects to be implemented.

The area of 'impact investing', in which endowment foundations and family offices attempt to incubate social entrepreneurs to engage in development is still very new. They align investments or projects that make social change, with funding from sources that feel that returns on investment should not be just financial but social as a whole. This area of funding is growing fast and could be another source of development funding that warrants closer attention.

Path 3: Innovating the financing of investment

There is increasing awareness that development is not just about finance, but about governance, institutional incentives, developing property rights infrastructure and the international environment. Increasingly, EMEs must be able to innovate in order to generate growth within resource constraints. This means investments in hard and soft infrastructure, specifically in the property rights infrastructure that protect property rights for markets to function more effectively.

Education and knowledge skills can be imported, but mistakes can be made in adopting policies that do not fit local conditions or distort incentives that worsen system efficiency, social equality or environmental sustainability. For example, the import-substituting policies that were fashionable in the 1950s proved to be protective of inefficient industries and encouraged rent-seeking that was ultimately corrosive on development.

The following section examines the specific issues related to funding for investment in infrastructure and small and medium enterprises (SMEs). Investments that contribute to social inclusiveness would include the financing of housing for the low- and middle-income groups. Investing in a green infrastructure is for the future welfare of the next generation.

Investment in infrastructure

In the early 1990s, 70 per cent of total infrastructure investments in EMEs were publicly financed, 22 per cent were privately funded and the balance of 8 per cent was funded by ODA (Do, 2012). Given the constraints on public funding and ODA from the advanced markets, the composition of infrastructure funding is likely to change, with greater private sector financing of infrastructure and this implies a bigger role for deep and liquid capital markets in EMEs to provide long-term financing, preferably with back-end loaded amortisation schedules.

Although long-term infrastructure has been traditionally implemented and funded through the public budget, the capacity of many EME bureaucracies to design, implement and fund such complex projects is increasingly constrained by a lack of professional talent, bureaucratic red-tape and institutional and political complexities. Many of the problems in implementing cross-jurisdictional projects involve the complex coordination of different bureaucratic interests across different ministries, agencies and different levels of government, such as centre–local or municipal authorities. Because these interests are not aligned and coordinated, many projects faced insuperable delays or major policy changes, such as changes in tax or tariff rates, that make such projects non-viable.

In recent years, based on the UK experience, large-scale infrastructure projects have moved toward adopting a public–private partnership (PPP) approach. The PPP basically involves a contract between a public-sector authority and a private-sector party to invest in developing a public good, typically in transportation, water, health and education, with risks and funding shared between the public and private sectors.

PPPs have been tested in Europe and the advanced countries and over the past two decades, nearly 1,400 PPP deals were signed in the European Union, involving a capital value of €260 billion (Kappeler and Nemoz, 2010, 7). Investment through PPPs has slowed down due to the global financial crisis, while in some EMEs, PPPs have been subject to public criticism due to allegations of corruption, lack of effective supervision and uneven implementation. The lesson here is not to reject PPPs wholesale, but to learn from recent experience how to overcome the implementation gaps in the different approaches of PPP, improve transparency, such as in the bidding and enforcement, that will improve not only the policy design but also the PPP governance and management.

Investment in SMEs (mezzanine capital)

Mezzanine capital is rapidly emerging as an innovative source of financing for SMEs. Originally from Europe, it has now spread to Asia. Mezzanine capital is a broad term covering hybrid, flexible financing instruments that lie in-between (mezzanine) pure equity and pure debt financing. It is attractive to SMEs because no collateral is needed and investors provide part-equity and part long-term financing with repayment upon maturity. Mezzanine capital investments are typically for improvement of balance sheet structure/equity ratio, or to help the SMEs to grow by injecting capital to expand the business or to fund buy-outs. Mezzanine capital can help SMEs to compete more effectively and graduate to become the next generation of companies with the track record and scale to be publicly listed. The current model of financing investment through IPOs (initial public offerings) is more suited to local corporate champions and global multinationals.

As indicated above, newer and long-term institutional investors like private equity (PE) firms are proliferating due to opportunities in nurturing promising and innovative SMEs in emerging markets. But PE and venture capital firms also need exit mechanisms, so that they can cash in on their mezzanine investments and re-invest the proceeds in newer ventures.

There is greater awareness that there is an intermediary step between formal stock markets, which are favourable for capital raising for larger enterprises, and the market for capital by SMEs. In China, for example, there are now informal property rights exchange markets at the local (city) level, which started off as information exchange platforms for trading in illiquid shares in SMEs or state-owned enterprises (SOEs) that are not listed.

Increasingly, these property exchanges are becoming mezzanine trading platforms for the exchange of equity in SMEs, the regulation of which has not been formalised. These exchanges are still nascent and their future is as yet uncertain, but they illustrate an example of where institutional innovation can evolve to meet market needs.

Investment in rental housing

Investment in low cost housing is typically undertaken by the public sector. Countries that have established secondary mortgage corporations are seeking to make home-ownership more affordable for the lower and middle-income groups. There is now new thinking that another niche to meet the ever-rising demand for housing among the low and middle income groups because of urbanisation pressures is for institutional investors to invest in large-scale rental housing.

To the individual, renting with an option to buy at the end of a period is more affordable than the substantial capital outlay required in the conventional approach to house ownership via a bank loan. The Australian Housing and Urban Research Institute (AHURI) (2013) concluded that institutional investment was 'the most desirable source of finance to achieve long-term growth in supply of rental housing'

(AHURI, 2013, 34). The main barrier to this scheme is that rental housing is an unknown asset class with no track record of performance. However, if institutional investors in current times are including low-risk investments in their portfolio, those investors that have socially responsible investment programmes would see rental housing as 'a stable low-risk, low-return asset that adds an "infrastructure flavour" to investors' portfolio'.

The G20 development strategy

The strategy of fostering a conducive environment for financing of investment and identifying new sources for long-term investment in the current global economic landscape already has been adopted by the G20 (2012). The key issues raised by the Russian presidency in 2013 and the stance of this chapter on the policy and implementation issues are summarised in Table 17.1.

The impact of technology on development finance

No study on the future of development finance can ignore the impact of technology because it offers new channels, products, services and modes of thinking and behaviour for the web-empowered consumer/ investor. Traditional analysis of financing development has not taken into consideration, for example, the massive impact that mobile phone technology alone can have on the financial intermediation and credit provision process.

Technology will influence finance in the following areas:

- *Technology is able to disintermediate the traditional channels in banking and the capital markets by reaching out directly to the stakeholders*
  China has demonstrated that it is not necessary for emerging markets to go through the sequential order of financial deepening in order to grow, previously understood to mean moving upwards from less complex money markets to foreign exchange markets, treasury bills and bond markets, towards more complex markets for corporate bonds and equity and ultimately, asset-backed securities and financial derivatives. Technology will enable emerging markets to leap-frog and develop different financial markets in parallel or in reverse order. For example, the Taobao e-commerce and payments platform in China allows consumers to be sellers, buyers and investors at the same time.

Table 17.1: The key issues raised by the Russian presidency in 2013 and this author's stance on the policy and implementation issues

G-20 'Wish list'	Policy objectives	Policy implementation suggestions
1. Strengthening public policy and improving public–private partnership (PPP) in terms of promoting financing for investment	Quality of development finance in infrastructure	The reality on the ground is that the problem with PPP is the governance, transparency and contractual enforcement. Too often, opaqueness of PPP contracts and execution results in corruption, contract dispute, changes in terms mid-stream and delays in project implementation that result in acrimony and frustration. Major barriers to PPP execution are land acquisition and state-centred relations in revenue and burden sharing in project implementation.
2. Addressing governance issues in financing and development	Overarching pre-condition for financial institutions, markets and governments	Good corporate governance begins with good credit culture, regulatory discipline, monetary discipline and fiscal discipline. These are key functions of the state.
3. Elaborated measures to support investments in small-and medium-sized enterprises and start-up businesses	Improve financial access by SMEs to generate employment and innovation	Improving access by SMEs requires regulatory flexibility to allow banks to innovate in credit schemes, and to leverage on technology to reduce transaction costs, improve monitoring of credit quality and enable borrowers to have access to sound financial and business advice.
4. Public policy on inclusivity and access	Social equity and inclusivity for the under-privileged	Technology can broaden access and deepen financial services through mobile technology and smartphones. The state can help improve physical and property rights infrastructure that would reduce transaction costs for those without access, improve their knowledge and skills and reduce regulatory barriers to business and social services.
5. Measures to meet capitalisation needs of global banks	Global financial stability	The priority is to implement macro-prudential measures at the national level, through strong cooperation with foreign regulators and standard settings to improve monitoring capital, liquidity and other risks of domestic and foreign banks.

(continued)

Table 17.1: The key issues raised by the Russian presidency in 2013 and this author's stance on the policy and implementation issues (contd.)

G-20 'Wish list'	Policy objectives	Policy implementation suggestions
6. Macro-prudential measures for financial stability	National financial stability	The priority must be to identify what are the vulnerable points in the domestic financial system – where the mismatches and weak links in financial network exist. There is no one-size-fits-all solution, but a multi-prong systemic approach for system stability.
7. Recommendations on regulatory changes that would bring about change in banking business models towards funding the real economy	Alignment of incentives between domestic banks and national interests	Priority should be to have tripartite discussions between regulators, the financial sector and stakeholders (investors, borrowers, customers) to identify where and what are the issues that create barriers to systemic stability and the need for trade-off between efficiency, fairness and system-wide stability.
8. Analysis of the role of possible sources of financing for investment (institutional investors, equity markets, government guarantees)	Deepening of capital markets to ameliorate liquidity, foreign exchange and structural mismatches, including overall leverage	There must be balance between the development of the banking system and the capital markets, with balance between serving the needs of large enterprises and SMEs. Institutional and product innovation is often blocked by excessive licensing constraints, turf conflicts and the inability to tap informal sources of savings. As indicated in this study, the quantity of savings for development may be available, but not at the quality and accessibility desired.
9. Public policy on institutional setup and incentives for long-term funding	Improving pension and insurance funds for long-term social security objectives	These two sectors have been grossly underdeveloped in EMEs due to obsolete portfolio restrictions and insufficient policy attention to the long-term benefits of social security from both sectors. These sectors deserve policy priority for development.
10. Analysis of FDI trends, patterns and impact to maximise their growth enhancing capacity	Importing foreign capital, long-term stable funding and access to foreign technology, markets and skills	FDI clearly has priority over short-term portfolio flows. Within the fund managers, SWF, infrastructure funds and those who have long-term horizon should be welcome

(continued)

Table 17.1: The key issues raised by the Russian presidency in 2013 and this author's stance on the policy and implementation issues (contd.)

G-20 'Wish list'	Policy objectives	Policy implementation suggestions
11. Policy to attract equity funding and push for long-term projects	Encouragement of long-term institutional investors as a source of development finance	Tax incentives should be considered for such investors.
12. Recommendations on how to increase multilateral development banks' (MDBs) lending capacity. Institutional setup on strengthening MDB lending	MDBs help to strengthen project financing with advisory skills	Since MDBs are constrained by their capital, employ co-financing project financing and design with local financial institutions.
13. Expansion of Sovereign Wealth Funds (SWFs)	Improving long-term funding in domestic infrastructure projects	SWFs and state-owned policy banks have become important providers of long-term capital and credit. Currently, the China Development Bank (CDB) lends annually more than the World Bank. The rules regarding investments by SWFs should be transparent and subject to Santiago Principles.
14. Mobilise long-term equity funds from relevant sources, for example Islamic finance	Provide for sector needs, for example Islamic finance as a potential source of development finance	May need specific legislation for development of such finance.

- *Technology lowers transaction costs*
  Technology has enabled the creation of alternative trading systems (ATSs) to bypass stock exchanges to avoid unnecessary friction costs and other barriers to the free flow of capital. Technology has also enabled e-commerce, e-payment and e-banking to flourish through the use of mobile phones and tablets. In e-commerce, SMEs can actually raise capital directly from small investors provided the trust factor can be resolved.

- *The 'clicks' have an edge over the 'bricks'*
  The borderless clicks (e-banking) have lower transactions cost and high information content that reach out to a massive network of users not limited by geography; the location-bound bricks (bank branches) are weighed down by high overheads, staff, rules, regulations and traditional mindsets. Examples where mobile phone operators have successfully by-passed banks by providing new forms of mobile banking are in Kenya, India, China and Pakistan. In Kenya, small payments in rural areas are made through mobile phone transfers, rather than cash, thereby enhancing financial inclusion. In Pakistan, the number of people who have mobile phones make up 85 per cent of the population as against only 12 per cent of the population who have bank accounts. These numbers on the predominance of mobile phone users in a community, combined with the rapid upgrading of mobile technology to smartphones and smart applications can only mean a continuous innovation in the delivery of financial services and products that will change the entire financial intermediation game.

What is clear is there will be creative destruction because traditional banks will lose customers to new lifestyle platforms that provide e-commerce, e-payment and e-banking such as Taobao, Paypal and Tencent.

In summary, technology brings about both opportunities and challenges to development finance. On the one hand, it can provide alternative sources of liquidity and channels for financial inclusion. On the other hand, it creates its own governance issues. By moving payments systems into non-banks, which are thriving because they are customer-centric, the biggest challenge faced by the regulator is how to bring the 'shadow banking' in both informal markets and cyberspace into a framework where systemic risks can be monitored, how to prevent fraud, manipulation and abuse of the law and how to ensure trust. There should be new levels of regulation to ensure a level playing field.

Strengthening South–South investment

As of 2008, developing countries accounted for around 37 per cent of global trade and nearly three-quarters of global growth, with South–South flows contributing to half of the total (OECD, 2010). By 2030, these South–South interactions are expected to be one of the main engines of growth, accounting for 57 per cent of global GDP (OECD, 2010).

Since the global crisis, developing countries have increasingly attracted private investment and capital. Net private capital flows increased from $110 billion in 2008 to about $386 billion in 2009 and further to an estimated $659 billion in 2010 (UN, 2011), thus surpassing ODA levels of about $67 billion in 2008 (DFID, 2014). This is an encouraging trend as global factors such as climate change, food security and health issues among others indicate an increasing need for South–South and triangular efforts. Institutional building has become another focus of South–South initiatives that have the support of the G20. In support of the private sector role in South–South investment, the UN report called upon governments to step up efforts to create an enabling environment, both national and cross border, that includes the provision of effective physical regulatory and legal infrastructure.

The potential for development finance has been enhanced due to the growing resources available to EME policy-based banks, such as policy-based banks in China (China Development Bank), Brazil, South Africa, as well as regional banks, such as the announced BRICS (Brazil, Russia, India, China and South Africa) development bank. The China Development Bank alone has a balance sheet three times larger than the World Bank and lends more than the World Bank's annual credit disbursements globally. A BRICS Bank is already under serious consideration.

Consequently, there are alternative development resources available, some of them tied to projects or suppliers, which can enhance the capacity of EMEs to accelerate their development and achieve the 2030 Agenda for Sustainable Development.

Implementation issues on financing of climate change

Finance has a critical role to play in achieving climate change goals. During the UN Conference on Climate Change in Copenhagen in 2009, the international community committed to mobilise US$100 billion per year in climate financing for developing countries by 2020 (Bhattacharya et al, 2015). The United Nations April 2015 report (UN, 2015c) calls for an additional US$3 trillion per year in new financing by 2030. On 12 December 2015, 196 Parties to the UN Framework Convention on Climate Change (UNFCCC) adopted a new legally-binding framework to tackle climate change, with rich nations to maintain a commitment to provide US$100 billion per year to 2025 and beyond 2025 with US$100 billion as a floor. Developing countries are expected to provide voluntary support (Climate Focus, 2015).

While there is broad agreement that developed countries need to provide financial support to developing countries, in order to achieve their respective climate change targets, the COP21 negotiations in Paris will be long on promises and expectations, but are likely to be short on hard funding from governments that have become cash-strapped because of the global financial crises. Key challenges remain, such as how to apportion the US$100 billion pledge in climate finance in an equitable manner. At the same time, much work will need to be done after Paris to get the world under 2°C or 1.5°C of warming.

The United Nations' April 2015 report listed a total of 17 Sustainable Development Goals (SDGs), of which there are five implementation agenda relating to finance:

1. strengthening domestic resource mobilisation, including through international support to developing countries, to improve domestic capacity for tax and other revenue collection;
2. full implementation of official development assistance commitments by developed countries, including the commitment to achieve the target of 0.7 per cent of gross national income for official development assistance (ODA/GNI) to developing countries and 0.15 to 0.20 per cent of ODA/GNI to least developed countries; ODA providers are encouraged to consider setting a target to provide at least 0.20 per cent of ODA/GNI to least developed countries;
3. mobilising additional financial resources for developing countries from multiple sources;
4. assisting developing countries in attaining long-term debt sustainability through coordinated policies aimed at fostering debt financing, debt relief and debt restructuring, as appropriate, and addressing the external debt burden of highly-indebted poor countries to reduce debt distress;
5. adopting and implementing various investment promotion regimes for least developed countries.

Further, the 21st Conference of the Parties to the United Nations Framework Convention on Climate Change (COP21/CMP11), held in Paris, France during 30 November–11 December 2015, produced a new agreement, but the United States unilaterally withdrew from the agreement in June 2017.

The aim of COP21 is to build a 'Paris Climate Alliance', with the goal of keeping the average global temperature rise below 2°C compared to pre-industrial levels and adapt societies to existing disruption. The COP21 agreement is also expected to include the role of finance in supporting climate change goals for a more sustainable environment.

The Paris Climate Alliance comprised four major components as follows (UN, 2015b):

1. the negotiation of a universal agreement in accordance with the Durban mandate, establishing rules and mechanisms capable of gradually increasing its ambition in order to keep within the 2°C limit;
2. presentation by all countries of their national contributions prior to COP21, in order to generate forward momentum, based on national realities of implementation;
3. the financial aspect, which should enable support for developing countries and financing of the transition towards low-carbon, resilient economies before and after 2020;
4. strengthening of the commitments of civil society and non-governmental stakeholders and the multi-partner initiatives of the Agenda of Solutions or Lima–Paris Action Agenda, in order to involve all stakeholders and begin concrete actions prior to the entry into force of the future agreement in 2020.

In addition, the final international agreement on climate change has to meet five conditions (UN, 2015b).

1. universal, concluded by all and applicable to all countries;
2. ambitious, to enable us to stay below 2°C and thus send the economic players the necessary signals to launch the transition to a low-carbon economy;
3. balanced, between mitigation and adaptation, and providing for adequate implementation resources as regards financing, access to technologies and capacity building;
4. flexible, taking into account the situations, specificities, needs and capabilities of each country, including the least developed countries and Small Island States;

5. sustainable and dynamic, with a long-term goal in line with the 2°C limit, to guide and strengthen action to combat climate change, with a periodic review to increase the level of ambition.

Notwithstanding the many challenges ahead, there are encouraging signs of progress since Copenhagen (Lilleholt, 2015). The international community appears to be on track to reach the goal agreed to in Copenhagen of mobilising US$100 billion a year in climate financing for developing countries by 2020. Funding is expected to come from both the public and private sectors, including new innovative mechanisms to catalyse public and private sector capital and scale up outcomes. Half of the US$3 trillion of new funding will need to come from the private sector, with the balance sourced from governments, development agencies, multilateral, regional and national development banks (Meltzer, 2015).

In this regard, an encouraging development is the increasing role of green business leaders in climate finance. For example, Goldman Sachs announced in November that it would invest US$150 billion in green energy by 2025 (SolarServer, 2015). Significantly, an agreement at COP21 in Paris would establish a much-needed global framework to reduce total greenhouse-gas emissions, which is a strong foundation for the global transition to a green economy.

Conclusion: a holistic 'back to basics' approach to development finance

This background chapter proposes a more systemic and holistic approach to understanding and charting the direction for achieving the new SDGs in the context of recent trends in development finance. By considering the micro, macro, meso (institutional) and meta (values) aspects that cut across the rapidly changing real sector and financial system, this chapter has looked into the diverse and complex mega-trends that drive the policy options on how development finance may evolve.

At the macro level, the chapter reviewed the current state of global financial markets and the impact which stringent financial regulations and quantitative easing programmes have on savings and capital inflows in emerging markets. At the macro-level, there should be sufficient savings to fund development from various sources.

At the micro-level, much depends on how finance will continue to serve the real sector based on how incentives are shaped through regulation, enforcement and corporate governance. Advances in technology, in particular mobile phone technology, are already transforming the intermediation of development finance.

At the institutional (meso) level, which links the macro-trends with the micro-behaviour, the chapter examines the substantial resources that institutional investors (led by pension funds, insurance companies, SWFs and private wealth) can bring to bear on long-term financing of infrastructure, health, housing, education and other socially inclusive development projects. They are different from conventional sources in that they also bring direct management expertise into the funding and management of projects.

Finally, the chapter advocates a return to the fundamental principles, values and assumptions (the meta) that underlie the effective operations of the financial system and this is about the restoration of fiduciary principles, good corporate governance, trust and credit culture. A mindset shift is necessary to move out of short-term financialisation for short-term profits towards long-term sustainability and system resilience. Finance must serve the real sector and therefore the state has an important role to prevent the financial sector 'financialising' its own interests through increasing leverage without limits. This has created an imbalance of over-reliance on short-term banking, and an under-emphasis of long-term institutional investors such as pension, insurance and alternative investment funds that can help fund long-term development.

The answer to the question: are there enough savings to finance development, must be yes. There are enough resources, globally, regionally and domestically for long-term investment in development, including financing for climate change. Globally, institutional investors have AUM amounting to $120 trillion in 2011, larger than global banking assets, and still growing.

Although the global financial crisis has led many long-term investors to reassess their liability profile, investment beliefs and risk appetite, the 2011 study by Oliver Wyman in collaboration with the WEF (WEF and Wyman, 2011) indicated that certain 'asset classes have gained increased attention post-crises along a spectrum from generating returns in growth markets to protecting core capital from downside risks'. More than 40 per cent of defined pension funds anticipate increasing their allocations to emerging markets equity (Pyramis Global Advisors, 2010) and there is also an emerging trend for long-term investors (such as large SWFs and pension funds) to co-invest together. By keeping investment horizons too short (as in bank deposits), the financial sector has not yielded positive real returns for savers and investors to protect their interests. Hence, the financial sector can serve the real sector best by taking a long-term sustainable approach that delivers higher real returns commensurate with the risks. This calls for higher quality of financial intermediation, especially in AUM.

The second message is that there must be good corporate governance and appropriate regulation that aligns the investment framework and governance processes with their obligations and their long-term investing mandates from stakeholders. To restore balance between banking and capital markets, the financial policy-makers would have to use a combination of structural reforms (such as encouraging long-term institutional investors through tax and licensing incentives), institutional reforms (such as creation of asset securitisation markets, strengthening clearing and settlement platforms and enhancing exit mechanisms) and appropriate portfolio restriction rules that enable better alignment of interests between investment judgement and returns to investors.

The third message is about technology changing the delivery and access processes in development finance. By broadening the base for access to finance, through new technology that lowers transaction costs and enables trade and investments in real-time, EMEs can leap-frog financial development through technological and institutional innovation. To further this objective, all stakeholders, including regulators, should be open to new forms of financial intermediation.

Acknowledgements

The author is grateful to his colleagues at the Fung Global Institute and his associates in Kuala Lumpur, in particular, Mrs Tan Wai Kuen, Professor Kwek Kian Teng, Dr. Cho Cho Wai, Mr Ng Chow Soon, Ms Theresa Chan, Ms Jodie Hu, Ms Ma Jing and Ms Eva Yi for their research, data analysis and inputs for this chapter. Ms Xu Jiajun and Dr Homi Kharas were most helpful in providing guidance, references and comments. All errors, omissions and opinions are those of the author alone.

Note

1   Sources of data: IFS, OECD and IMF staff estimates.

References

ADB (Asian Development Bank), 2011, *Asia 2050: Realizing the Asian century*, Mandaluyong: ADB

ADBI (Asian Development Bank Institute), 2009, *Infrastructure for a Seamless Asia,* Tokyo: ADBI

AHURI (Australian Housing and Urban Research Institute), 2013, *Financing rental housing through institutional investment, Volume 1: Outcomes from an Investigative Panel*, Melbourne, VI: AHURI

Bhattacharya, A, Ebinger, CK, Frank, C, Kharas, H, Weifeng Liu, McArthur, JW et al, 2015, *COP21 at Paris: What to expect*, Washington, DC: Brookings, www.brookings.edu/wp-content/uploads/2015/11/COP21atParis.pdf

Cihak, M, Demirguc-Kunt, A, Feyen, E, Levine, R, 2013, Financial development in 205 economies, 1960 to 2010, National Bureau of Economic Research (*NBER*) *Working Paper* 18946 (April), Cambridge, MA: NBER

Climate Focus, 2015, *The Paris Agreement Summary*, www.climatefocus.com/sites/default/files/20151228%20COP%2021%20briefing%20FIN.pdf

DFID (Department for International Development), 2014, Table 9: Net ODA from DAC donors to developing countries 2008–2012, *National Statistics*, www.gov.uk/government/uploads/system/uploads/attachment_data/file/367730/Table9.csv/preview

Do, Duc Minh, 2012, Seminar 1: Urban infrastructure development and financing, *Financing policies for urban infrastructure development in Vietnam*, 23 October, Hanoi: Asia-Pacific Finance and Development Center, www.jointokyo.org/files/cms/news/pdf/Presentation_Prof_Do_Duc_Minh.pdf

Economist, 2011, The emerging world begins to seize the lion's share of global markets, *Economist*, 4 August, www.economist.com/blogs/dailychart/2011/08/emerging-vs-developed-economies

Federal Reserve System, 2013a, Flow of funds accounts of the United States: Flows and outstandings, Third Quarter 2011, *Federal Reserve Statistical Release* (March), Washington, DC: Federal Reserve System

Federal Reserve System, 2013b, Flow of funds accounts of the United States: Flows and outstandings, Third Quarter 2013, *Federal Reserve Statistical Release* (December), Washington, DC: Federal Reserve System, www.federalreserve.gov/releases/z1/20131209/z1.pdf

G20 (Group of Twenty), 2012, *G20 Russian Presidency report*, St. Petersburg: Russia in G20, http://en.g20russia.ru/docs/g20_russia/outline

G30 (Group of Thirty), 2013, *Long-term finance and economic growth*, Washington, DC: Group of Thirty

IMF (International Monetary Fund), 2005, Aspects of global asset allocation, in *Global financial stability report: Market developments and issues*, pp 65–102, Washington, DC: IMF, www.imf.org/external/pubs/ft/gfsr/2005/02/pdf/chp3.pdf

IMF (International Monetary Fund), 2011a, Long-term investors and their asset allocation: Where are they now?, in *Global financial stability report: Grappling with crisis legacies*, Chapter 2, Washington, DC: IMF, www.imf.org/External/Pubs/FT/GFSR/2011/02/pdf/ch2.pdf

IMF (International Monetary Fund), 2011b, Statistical appendix in *Global financial stability report: Grappling with crisis legacies*, Washington, DC: IMF, www.imf.org/External/Pubs/FT/GFSR/2011/02/pdf/statappx.pdf

IMF (International Monetary Fund), 2013, *Global financial stability report: Old risks, new challenges*, Washington, DC: IMF

IMF (International Monetary Fund), 2014, Statistical appendix, in *Global financial stability report: Moving from liquidity to growth-driven markets*, April, Table 1, Washington, DC: IMF, www.imf.org/external/pubs/FT/GFSR/2014/01/pdf/text.pdf

Jorda, O, Schularick, M, Taylor, A, 2011, Financial crisis, credit booms and external imbalances: 140 years of history, *International Monetary Fund (IMF) Economic Review*, Washington, DC: IMF

Kappeler, A, Nemoz, M, 2010, *Public–private partnerships in Europe: Before and during the recent financial crisis*, Economic and Financial Report 2010/04, Luxembourg: European Investment Bank, www.bei.europa.eu/attachments/efs/efr_2010_v04_en.pdf

Kuwait Finance House Research Ltd, 2013, *Global Islamic banking 2013*, Kuala Lumpur: Kuwait Finance House Research Ltd

Levine, R, 2005, Finance and growth: Theory and evidence, in P Aghion, S Durlauf (eds) *Handbook of economic growth*, Vol 1, 865–934, Philadelphia, PA: Elsevier

Lilleholt, LC, 2015, Project syndicate, *The Copenhagen-Paris Express*, 2 December, www.project-syndicate.org/commentary/un-climate-change-paris-copenhagen-by-lars-christian-lilleholt-2015-12

Meltzer, JP, 2015, Financing sustainable infrastructure, *Brookings Brief*, 17 November, Washington, DC: Brookings, www.brookings.edu/~/media/Research/Files/Reports/2015/11/16-paris-climate-talks/financing-sustainable-infrastructure-meltzer.pdf?la=en

MGI (McKinsey Global Institute), 2013, *Financial globalization: Retreat or reset?*, New York: McKinsey & Company

North, DC, 2005, *Understanding the process of economic change*, Princeton, NJ: Princeton University Press

OECD (Organisation for Economic Co-operation and Development), 2010, Perspectives on global development 2010: Shifting wealth, *OECD Multilingual Summaries*, Paris: OECD, www.oecd.org/development/pgd/45451514.pdf

OECD (Organisation for Economic Co-operation and Development), 2011, *Pension Markets in Focus* 8, Paris: OECD, www.oecd.org/finance/private-pensions/48438405.pdf

OECD (Organisation for Economic Co-operation and Development), 2012, *Pension Markets in Focus* 16, Paris: OECD, www.oecd.org/daf/fin/private-pensions/PensionMarketsInFocus2012.pdf.

Poon, D, 2014, China's development trajectory: A strategic opening for industrial policy in the South, *United Nations Conference on Trade and Development (UNCTAD) Discussion Paper* 218, Paris, UNCTAD, http://unctad.org/en/PublicationsLibrary/osgdp20144_en.pdf

Pyramis Global Advisors, 2010, *Global Defined Benefit Survey*, London: Pyramis Global Advisors

Rodrik, D (ed), 2003, *In search of prosperity: Analytic narratives on economic growth*, Princeton, NJ: Princeton University Press

Sheng, A, 2009, *From Asian to global financial crisis*, New York: Cambridge University Press

Smith, A, 1776, *The wealth of nations*, London: W Strahan and T Cadell.

SolarServer, 2015, *Goldman Sachs announces USD150 billion clean energy target by 2025*, www.solarserver.com/solar-magazine/solar-news/current/2015/kw45/goldman-sachs-announces-usd-150-million-clean-energy-target-by-2015.html

Summers, L, 2003, *Godkin lectures*, Cambridge, MA: Kennedy School of Government, Harvard University

TheCityUK, 2010, *Fund management report 2010*, London: TheCityUK, www.thecityuk.com/research/our-work/reports-list/uk-fund-management-2014/

TheCityUK, 2011a, Financial services in emerging economies, *Economic Trend Series* (June), www.thecityuk.com/research/our-work/reports-list/financial-services-in-emerging-economies-2012/

TheCityUK, 2011b, *Fund management report*, www.thecityuk.com/research/our-work/reports-list/fund-management-2012/

TheCityUK, 2012a, Financial services in emerging economies, *Economic Trend Series* (July), www.thecityuk.com/research/our-work/reports-list/financial-services-in-emerging-economies-2012/

TheCityUK, 2012b, *Fund management report 2012*, London, UK: TheCityUK, www.thecityuk.com/research/our-work/reports-list/fund-management-2012/

TheCityUK, 2013a, *Insurance 2013*, London, UK: TheCityUK, www.thecityuk.com/research/our-work/reports-list/insurance-2013/

TheCityUK, 2013b, *Pension markets 2013*, London, UK: TheCityUK, www.thecityuk.com/research/our-work/reports-list/pension-markets-2013/

TheCityUK, 2013c, *Sovereign wealth funds 2013*, London, UK: TheCityUK, www.thecityuk.com/research/our-work/reports-list/sovereign-wealth-funds-2013/

Truman, EM, 2010, *Sovereign wealth funds: Threat or salvation*, Washington, DC: Peterson Institute of International Economics

Trusted Sources, 2011, *Insurance companies and pension funds as institutional investors: Global investment patterns*, Report prepared for the City of London Corporation, London: City of London Economic Development, www.cityoflondon.gov.uk/business/support-promotion-and-advice/promoting-the-city-internationally/china/Documents/Insurance%20companies%20and%20pension%20funds%20report.pdf

UN (United Nations), 2009, *Report of the Commission of Experts of the President of the UN General Assembly on reforms of the international monetary and financial system*, New York: UN

UN (United Nations), 2011, Financial flows to developing countries, in *World economic situation and prospects 2011*, Chapter 3, New York: UN, www.un.org/en/development/desa/policy/wesp/wesp_archive/2011wesp.pdf

UN (United Nations), 2015a, *What is COP21?*, Conference on climate change, COP21/CMP11, Paris, France, 30 November–11 December 2015

UN (United Nations), 2015b, *COP21: The stakes*, United Nations conference on climate change, COP21/CMP11, Paris, France, 30 November–11 December 2015

UN (United Nations), 2015c, *Transforming our world: The 2030 Agenda for Sustainable Development*, New York: UN, https://sustainabledevelopment.un.org/content/documents/21252030%20Agenda%20for%20Sustainable%20Development%20web.pdf

UNDP (United Nations Development Programme), 2010, *What will it take to achieve the Millennium Development Goals? An international assessment*, New York: UNDP

UNDP (United Nations Development Programme), 2011, *The state of South–South cooperation, Report of the Secretary-General*, New York: UNDP

US Bureau of Economic Analysis, 2013a, *US current-account deficit increases in 2012*, http://blog.bea.gov/2013/03/15/us-current-account-deficit-annual/

US Bureau of Economic Analysis, 2013b, *US net international investment position: end of the fourth quarter and year 2012* (Fourth Quarter), www.bea.gov/newsreleases/international/intinv/2013/pdf/intinv412.pdf

World Bank, 2012, *Global financial development report 2013: Rethinking the role of the State in finance*, Washington, DC: International Bank for Reconstruction and Development and World Bank

World Bank, 2013a, *Global development horizons, capital for the future: Saving and investment in an interdependent world*, Washington, DC: International Bank for Reconstruction and Development and World Bank

World Bank, 2013b, *The little data book on financial development 2013*, Washington, DC: International Bank for Reconstruction and Development and World Bank.

World Bank, 2014, Data: GDP (current US$), http://data.worldbank.org/indicator/NY.GDP.MKTP.CD

World Economic Forum, Wyman, O, 2011, *The future of long-term investing*, New York: World Economic Forum USA Inc

EIGHTEEN

Conclusion

Jason McFarlane, Hany Besada, Kathryn Anne Brunton and Alireza Saniei-Pour

The twenty-first century has been a remarkable era for emerging nations. It is bound with success stories: the rise of China, sociopolitical upheavals in North Africa and the Middle East, and the resiliency of integrated economies – such as South Africa and Brazil – when faced with the shocks of the 2008 financial crisis. The Millennium Development Goals (MDGs), in their own respect, were not spared from the ups and downs of the previous years. While some achievements have been a success – such as a decrease in the number of people living in extreme poverty as highlighted in Chapter Three – other areas have been less successful. For that reason, a post-2015 extension of the program was required.

The 2030 Agenda for Sustainable Development and resulting Sustainable Development Goals (SDGs) were adopted at the United Nations Sustainable Development Summit on 25 September 2016. These seventeen ambitious SDGs support the elimination of poverty and address the underlying and interrelated issues that have an impact on global development efforts.

This book has argued that the Post-2015 Development Agenda must focus more attention on the role of women and gender rights if the targets outlined in MDG 3 are to be achieved. In addition, it must take a new and more complex set of challenges into account that, if not addressed properly, can undermine the objectives of the programme. The 2030 Agenda for Sustainable Development has incorporated a strategy for the various challenges and competing interests that have hindered development efforts previously. The SDG of achieving gender equality and empowering all women and girls is one example (UN, 2015).

Interestingly, many of those affected by extreme poverty will soon be found in war-torn and fragile states as demonstrated in Chapter Three – sub-Saharan Africa in particular. Addressing poverty in environments where good governance and commitment from international institutions and foreign donors have declined will be a question of interest that needs to be tackled. In these situations, international financial assistance and reform of the financial system will not be adequate on their own. Preconditions and special requirements need to be established before traditional financial approaches – such as revitalisation of the rule of law, good governance and an end to conflict. How can Central African Republic or South Sudan implement poverty reduction policies when government is losing its control over these countries and their governmental institutions are deteriorating? Ultimately, good governance and institution-building is highly relevant for the Post-2015 Development Agenda.

In addition, although the data indicates a decreasing trend in aggregate poverty, the livelihood of millions of people in the developing world is not as encouraging as the data suggests. For example, the emergence of China and other East Asian states has contributed to the downward trend (Kaplinsky, 2005). This has construed the perception of those living in other regions – sub-Saharan Africa in particular – where more needs to be done. The Post-2015 Development Agenda must include a strategy suitable for both emerging countries and developing states.

In conjunction with poverty reduction, the Post-2015 Development Agenda needs to address the growing problem of youth unemployment. In the long run, economic development is not possible without facilitating greater productive capacity and aiming to provide more jobs. Labour is fundamental to production in developing countries – particularly sub-Saharan Africa – and its scarcity can obstruct development efforts. Many states – such as South Africa – are already facing a youth unemployment 'crisis'. Given the slow decline in fertility rates, youth unemployment is expected to create even more challenges for national and local governments, which can jeopardise the stability of affected countries. Notably, the 2030 Agenda for Sustainable Development identifies youth unemployment as a major concern (UN, 2015). This position is welcomed, but the development and implementation of projects and programmes that result from the Agenda must incorporate objectives that address this issue.

In terms of international finance and the recipient–donor relationship, implementation of the Post-2015 Development Agenda will require certain adjustments. Even though literature supports the adequacy of available funds for development in the long run, as demonstrated in Chapter Seventeen, that might not be the case. The impact of the 2008 recession and quantitative easing in recent years has distorted the macroeconomic policies of emerging countries. The massive quantitative easing implemented by the major reserve currency zones – such as United States, Eurozone, United Kingdom and Japan

– has made foreign investments in emerging countries less attractive. This was notably evident in the sudden shock of the Turkish lira, South African rand and Brazilian real in 2013 (The Economist, 2013).

The South to North trend in asset allocation is expected to continue in the coming years as interest rates are expected to increase in the developed world. The Post-2015 Development Agenda must take into account the macroeconomic vulnerabilities of the developing world. Ultimately, these types of exogenous shocks can create challenges for financial and fiscal stability of the affected states, which can adversely affect the desire of states to participate in the programme and its development objectives. Further, the role of technology in intermediating development finance in the post-2015 context will be inevitable. Mobile phone technology – such as of M-Pesa in Africa – will provide an improved structure for how funds can be distributed at the micro level.

The Post-2015 Development Agenda must reflect a concerted effort to draw lessons from the positive and negative experiences of the Millennium Development Goals (MDG) and apply them to challenges that endure. These challenges are vast, varied and their prioritisation differ from country to country – highlighting the importance of treating the Post-2015 Development Agenda as a dynamic framework that can adapt to local issues.

Adaptation will be a major test for the effectiveness of the Post-2015 Development Agenda and its implementation over the next 15 years. Experiences from the MDGs have taught that uniform and static implementation of set goals is an undesirable and ineffective means of achieving meaningful progress globally. That is not to say the MDGs did not achieve meaningful progress. They have produced significant results on a global scale; however, policymakers must continually search for methods of improvement, and adaptation to changing environment is one such method that experience has taught.

For example, MDG 2, which was to achieve universal primary education by 2015, generated soaring primary school enrolment globally. Nevertheless, it soon became evident that having children physically in a classroom was not enough in itself to support quality education. The national implementation of MDG 2 led to countries ensuring primary school enrolment in schools with insufficient resources; many schools continue to be understaffed, teachers do not have proper training, and pertinent books are outdated or inexistent. Evidently, preoccupation with meeting MDG, Post-2015 Development Agenda, and other development requirements can lead to neglect of emerging issues. Adaptation will be a consideration for policymakers at the outset of the Post-2015 Development Agenda and continually throughout its implementation.

The legacy and success of the Post-2015 Development Agenda will depend on the successful pursuit, implementation and realisation of these goals; however, policymakers need to prioritise addressing predicaments – such as the ongoing financial and Eurozone crisis – and identifying trends that indicate imminent emergencies. Adaptation and simulation will be the key to success for this programme – as will the commitment of those responsible with reinforcing its goals.

Moreover, to implement a comprehensive framework for achieving development goals, policymakers must be cognisant of overlap between them. Ultimately, this allows policymakers to bridge their efforts in generating development outcomes, which will produce viable, long-term solutions for the challenges they face. For example, addressing nutrition in youth will have trickle-down effects for their education. A proper, nutritional diet will have a positive impact on a child's health; however, it will also facilitate the child's learning and overall improvement in education. Root causes of development challenges will remain an obstacle to goals and targets until policymakers develop a comprehensive framework that addresses these types of bridging relationships. The focus on interrelated and underlying issues in the 2030 Agenda for Sustainable Development is a positive development in this regard.

Further, reducing or eliminating the disadvantages individuals and families in poverty endure will contribute to sustainable development outcomes, poverty reduction trends and socioeconomic parity within societies. Chapter Two explains that an individual or family's exit from poverty can only be sustainable with inclusive social and political policies that reach those in poverty and extreme poverty – such as 'employment, fiscal redistribution, and preferential access to basic services' (p 20).

The Post-2015 Development Agenda must avoid the perpetual overreliance on donor aid to achieve local development objectives. National development programmes and objectives may require foreign aid and technical assistance for their establishment and early stages; however, every effort must be made to transition towards local ownership. Ultimately, national governments must be involved in the design stages of their programmes, and implementation must be compatible with national policy processes. A cohesive national development strategy and the appropriate governance frameworks will provide the foundation needed for eventual graduation of developing countries from foreign aid programmes. Notably, the implementation strategy of the Agenda underscores the importance of the national ownership principle and the mobilisation and effective use of domestic resources (UN, 2015). This is a movement in the right direction.

When appropriate and effective, efforts must be made to integrate new technology into implementation policies, processes and practices. What is important is that this must be done in an inclusive manner. Any exclusive access to technological innovation may perpetuate the disadvantages those in poverty often encounter. For example, with the expansion of mobile phones and internet access in developing societies, farmers have gained access to market information which they may not have been able to acquire otherwise. When one farmer or a group of farmers have exclusive access to a mobile phone with internet and, consequently, market information, the others are faced with a striking disadvantage. While the development of mobile phones into personal computers may not have been considered when the MDGs were agreed upon, their importance and prevalence in the developing world today is undeniable. Ultimately, the ability of policymakers to ensure equitable and inclusive access to technological innovations will have an important impact on sustainable development and the success of the Post-2015 Development Agenda.

The importance of deliberations and decisions made during the implementation of the Post-2015 Development Agenda cannot be understated. The outcome of careful considerations, studies, negotiations, arguments and agreements will have serious implications for remote individuals and families in poverty. This book assembles a collection of chapters with various cases and topics that support sustainable development by analysing failures and successes throughout the implementation of the MDGs. Nevertheless, a great lesson for all readers to take is that the Post-2015 Development Agenda must be a means to an end rather than an end in itself. The MDGs have taught that goals must be continually monitored, measured and evaluated. Policies must reflect what will work regardless of the Post-2015 Development Agenda. These chapters will act as recommendations on what hasn't worked in the past and what can work in the future – a relevant resource for as long as post-2015 development decisions are being made.

References

Economist, The, 2013, The end of the affair, *The Economist*, www.economist.com/news/finance-and-economics/21579461-prospect-less-quantitative-easing-america-has-rocked-currency-and-bond

Kaplinsky, R, 2005, *Globalization, poverty and inequality: Between a rock and a hard place*, Cambridge: Polity Press

UN (United Nations), 2015, *Transforming our world: The 2030 Agenda for Sustainable Development*, 12 August, www.un.org/pga/wp-content/uploads/sites/3/2015/08/120815_outcome-document-of-Summit-for-adoption-of-the-post-2015-development-agenda.pdf

Index

Note: Page numbers in *italics* indicate figures, tables and boxes. Page numbers followed by the letter 'n' refer to end of chapter notes.